RESEARCH COMPANION TO THE DYSFUNCTIONAL WORKPLACE

NEW HORIZONS IN MANAGEMENT

Series Editor: Cary L. Cooper, CBE, *Professor of Organizational Psychology and Health, Lancaster University Management School, Lancaster University, UK*

This important series makes a significant contribution to the development of management thought. This field has expanded dramatically in recent years and the series provides an invaluable forum for the publication of high quality work in management science, human resource management, organizational behaviour, marketing, management information systems, operations management, business ethics, strategic management and international management.

The main emphasis of the series is on the development and application of new original ideas. International in its approach, it will include some of the best theoretical and empirical work from both well-established researchers and the new generation of scholars.

Titles in the series include:

Research Companion to the Dysfunctional Workplace

Management Challenges and Symptoms

Edited by

Janice Langan-Fox

Professor of Management, Swinburne University of Technology, Australia

Cary L. Cooper CBE

Professor of Organizational Psychology and Health, Lancaster University Management School, UK

Richard J. Klimoski

Professor of Psychology and Management and Dean, School of Management, George Mason University, USA

Edward Elgar
Cheltenham, UK • Northampton, MA, USA

Published by
Edward Elgar Publishing Limited
The Lypiatts
15 Lansdown Road
Cheltenham
Glos GL50 2JA
UK

Edward Elgar Publishing, Inc.
William Pratt House
9 Dewey Court
Northampton
Massachusetts 01060
USA

Paperback edition 2008

A catalogue record for this book
is available from the British Library

Library of Congress Cataloguing in Publication Data

Research companion to the dysfunctional workplace : management challenges and symptoms /
edited by Janice Langan-Fox, Cary L. Cooper, Richard J. Klimoski
     p.   cm.—(New horizons in management series) (Elgar original reference)
   Includes bibliographical references and index.
   1. Organizational behavior. 2. Conflict management. 3. Organizational effectiveness.
   4. Corporate culture. I. Langan-Fox, Janice, 1946– II. Cooper, Cary L. III. Klimoski,
   Richard J.

   HD58.7.R47 2007
   658.3'045—dc22

                                                  2007002142

ISBN 978 1 84542 932 4 (cased)
ISBN 978 1 84844 252 8 (paperback)

Printed and bound in Great Britain by MPG Books Ltd, Bodmin, Cornwall

Contents

Contributors

Vikas Anand, Sam M. Walton College of Business, University of Arkansas, USA

Anjana Anandakumar, University of Technology, Sydney, Australia

Neil Anderson, University of Amsterdam Business School, The Netherlands

Julian Barling, School of Business, Queens University, Kingston, Ontario, Canada

Thomas E. Becker, Department of Business Admininstration, University of Delaware, Newark, DE, USA

Nadin Beckmann, Australian Graduate School of Management, Sydney, Australia

Rebecca J. Bennett, Department of Management and Information Systems, College of Administration and Business, Louisiana Tech University, USA

Graham Brown, Lee Kong Chian School of Business, Singapore Management University

Ronald J. Burke, Schulich School of Business, York University, Toronto, Canada

Stewart R. Clegg, University of Technology, Sydney, Australia

Jeanette N. Cleveland, Department of Psychology, The Pennsylvania State University, USA

Cary L. Cooper, Lancaster University Management School, UK

Erin Coyne, Fisher College of Business, Department of Management and Human Resources, Ohio State University, USA

Guy Doron, Department of Psychology, University of Melbourne, Australia

Iva Embley Smit, Faculty of Social and Behavioural Sciences, Work and Organizational Psychology, University of Amsterdam, The Netherlands

Adrian Furnham, Department of Psychology, University College, London, UK

Rosina M. Gasteiger, University of Amsterdam Business School, The Netherlands

Sharon L. Grant, Faculty of Business and Enterprise, Swinburne University of Technology, Melbourne, Australia

Jerald Greenberg, Department of Management and Organization, National University of Singapore Business School, Singapore

David Greenberger, Fisher College of Business, Department of Management and Human Resources, Ohio State University, USA

Kevin Henderson, Sam M. Walton College of Business, University of Arkansas, USA

M. Sandy Hershcovis, I.H. Asper School of Business, University of Manitoba, Canada

Robert D. Hisrich, Thunderbird, The Garvin School of International Management, Arizona, USA

John R. Hollenbeck, Department of Management, Michigan State University, USA

Timothy A. Judge, Warrington College of Business, Department of Management, University of Florida, USA

Michael D. Johnson, Department of Management, Michigan State University, USA

Mahendra Joshi, Sam M. Walton College of Business, University of Arkansas, USA

Glen E. Kreiner, Smeal College of Business, The Pennsylvania State University, USA

Michael Kyrios, Department of Psychology, Swinburne University of Technology, Melbourne, Australia

Janice Langan-Fox, Faculty of Business and Enterprise, Swinburne University of Technology, Melbourne, Australia

Jeffery A. LePine, Warrington College of Business, Department of Management, University of Florida, USA

Roy J. Lewicki, Fisher College of Business, Department of Management and Human Resources, Ohio State University, USA

Audrey S. Lim, Department of Psychology, The Pennsylvania State University, USA

Julie Lutz, Thunderbird, The Garvin School of International Management, Arizona, USA

Teal McAteer, DeGroote School of Business, McMaster University, Canada

Kim Mather, University of Wolverhampton Business School, Compton Campus, Wolverhampton, UK

Roger C. Mayer, Department of Management, College of Business Administration, University of Akron, Ohio, USA

Richard Moulding, Department of General Practice, University of Melbourne, Australia

Kevin R. Murphy, Department of Psychology, The Pennsylvania State University, USA

Maja Nedeljkovic, Department of Psychology, Swinburne University of Technology, Melbourne, Australia

Fiona Pavlakis, Australian Graduate School of Management, Sydney, Australia

Tyrone S. Pitsis, University of Technology, Sydney, Australia

Christopher R. Rate, Department of Psychology, Yale University, Connecticut, USA

Sandra L. Robinson, Sauder School of Business, University of British Columbia, Vancouver, Canada

Eduardo Salas, Department of Psychology and Institute for Simulation and Training, University of Central Florida, USA

Michael Sankey, Faculty of Commerce, University of Melbourne, Australia

Marc J. Schabracq, Faculty of Social and Behavioural Sciences, Work and Organizational Psychology, University of Amsterdam, The Netherlands

Debra L. Shapiro, Robert H. Smith School of Business, University of Maryland, MD, USA

Dana E. Sims, Department of Psychology and Institute for Simulation and Training, University of Central Florida, USA

Robert J. Sternberg, School of Arts and Sciences, Tufts University, Massachusetts, USA

Edward C. Tomlinson, Boler School of Business, John Carroll University, Ohio, USA

Mary Ann Von Glinow, Dept. of Management and International Business, College of Business Administration, Florida International University, USA

Robert E. Wood, Australian Graduate School of Management, Sydney, Australia

Les Worrall, University of Wolverhampton Business School, Compton Campus, Wolverhampton, UK

Preface

I once interviewed a man called 'Tony' about how he did his job. He worked in a national communications organization and had recently taken up a position as a liaison officer after his previous job as a truck driver. The job required him to liaise between the shopfloor, of which he was a member, and management. His story (later indirectly corroborated by executives) told of secret meetings with management, staged performances at union meetings (throwing chairs etc.), and other extraordinary actions and hidden communications with either the manager or union leaders. His phone bill, which covered long late-night conversations with troubled shopfloor workers about family or work, was astronomical. Tony controlled and managed everything. However, he was paid only for his shopfloor liaison officer job despite having informal responsibility for the efficient running of his unit, the pastoral care of the workers, and the propping up of management. Tony contrived to appear on the side of the union and the shopfloor, and although never appearing to support management (at meetings, he made the manager the butt of jokes), secretly colluded with management in order to bring about productive organizational outcomes. Both sides knew he was a power broker, but it was never spoken about. Tony was an altruist at heart. He saw that someone had to step in and take charge of things and, with little education (he hadn't even finished high school) and no management experience, he did a terrific job. This was the way things got done in the organization – to avoid strikes, to compensate for an inexperienced and incompetent manager in charge of 120 staff, and to help workers who lived in constant fear of losing their jobs because of it. Furthermore, according to executives, this case was repeated across at least six other units in this national organization.

This is just one example of organizational dysfunction and the coping that took place to keep things going. There are surely a myriad of other cases like this that we all can bring out, stemming from our own work experiences.

Tony taught me a lot. I also began to realize that other people must also know of organizational dysfunction, perhaps derived from a more systematic perspective. As a consequence, the idea for this book emerged.

Organizational dysfunction, then, characterizes a facet of today's workplace that is often hidden or ignored. While this aspect of organizational life may be evident to insiders, there are few systematic treatments of the dynamics of such dysfunction that capture the complexity of both its insidious nature and its powerful consequences – for employees, families, customers or for the firm as a whole. Our book offers such an examination and more. That is, in a modest way, it is also a testimony to the life of many unsung workplace heroes or heroines who, on a daily basis, must cope with such challenges as inefficiency and incompetence; people suffering from a disorder or a disposition, or the effects of these on people around them; people doing things they have to do and don't want to do; organizational systems that don't work well, make work and must be circumvented, and who make it all appear . . . normal!

When approached, authors of international repute enthusiastically embraced the idea of the book. Hardly anyone turned down the opportunity to write a chapter on their dysfunction topic of choice. These outstanding authors come from diverse backgrounds including clinical psychology, organizational psychology, management and business, entrepreneurship and from consulting. We, as editors, are very grateful for their enthusiasm, generosity and wonderfully interesting and well-written chapters.

Consequently, we believe that the resulting collection of chapters brought together for this volume will be invaluable for a wide variety of readers: researchers from different disciplines – workplace health, psychology, commerce, management. Although we already know a great deal, as is made clear throughout the volume, there are still many issues or applied problems that need further investigation. Similarly, consultants and professionals-in-training will be better prepared to offer high-quality service delivery if they take to heart the many lessons already learned as presented throughout our text. And of course, those responsible for ensuring the effectiveness of work organizations, including managers, supervisors and HR professionals, should gain useful insights on how to improve the design of human resource policy and practices as well as how best to create the kind of progressive workplace culture that most of us desire.

We are grateful to Jo Betteridge of Edward Elgar, our publishers, and to Edward Elgar himself, who loved the idea of the book because of his own experiences! Cary, Richard and I wish to thank them for their assistance. Without it, this book would never have been published.

Janice Langan-Fox
November 2006

Introduction

This book delves into the 'underbelly' of organizations. It's about subversiveness, counterproductive behaviour, psychological disorders, and nearly every other aspect of an organization that could become dysfunctional. To be sure, organizational dysfunction has always existed in one form or another. Moreover, it is often at the heart of works of fiction or tabloid exposés. However it has only recently become a focus for systematic investigation and a field of research. Thus you, the reader, should find the content of this volume novel, exciting and, we predict, useful. Our treatment of dysfunction is extensive and detailed. The authors of the volume discuss the features of dysfunction – what they are, what they do to an organization, what research has been conducted and what was found. They also describe what happens when 'toxic issues' become comfortably bedded down and institutionalized. But then they go on to make recommendations for interventions and improvements. They give us hope for the future.

The book is organized around two themes: 'Barriers to productive work' and 'Managing organizational mayhem'. The first theme explores organizational dysfunction as it concerns individuals, and the second examines broader issues of dysfunction and the effects involving teams, managers and organization-wide systems.

Contributors responded to a broad class of variables related to the 'dysfunctional organization'. Rate and Sternberg (Chapter 1) address what they see as a crisis of courage in corporate boardrooms. They state that up to two-thirds of people currently in management positions fail and that groups of people collude to overlook the negative actions of colleagues, resulting in a failure of *courage*. Focusing on behaviours such as intentionality, deliberation, risk, good purpose and personal fear, the authors show that organizations can develop programmes to enhance courageous behaviour.

Adrian Furnham (Chapter 2) examines the pathology of senior managers 'who create and maintain a toxic culture epitomized by mistrust, dishonesty and lack of equity'. Adrian pursues the idea that many 'successful' bosses may have psychopathic, narcissistic and histrionic personality disorders which, although they may sometimes help them in business settings, will eventually result in a dysfunctional workplace for others.

Kyrios, Nedeljkovic, Moulding and Doron (Chapter 3) focus on one disorder, obsessive-compulsive personality disorder (OCPD), which represents a common problem affecting workplace performance. By examining the aetiology, assessment and workplace effects of individuals with OCPD, engagement in work tasks, and their workplace relations, Kyrios et al. reveal that the negative aspects of the disorder can be controlled and managed.

Workplace bullying is one aspect of organizations that is difficult to control and manage. Langan-Fox and Sankey (Chapter 4) explain how the problem emerges, develops and eventually 'grips' the life of the victim. The chapter reviews the literature to date, reporting both empirical and theoretical work, and details crucial elements of the organization that facilitate bullying, as well as strategies that can be taken to prevent recurrence.

Glen Kreiner (Chapter 5) depicts how the 'struggle for self' emerges in dysfunctional ways in the workplace by examining eight dysfunctions that stem from imbalanced identity boundaries and suboptimal identification states, and concludes by suggesting ways that can reduce the impact of these dysfunctions.

Shapiro and Von Glinow (Chapter 6) ask the question – what happens when leaders are in fact the disruptive force in their organization? In developing a new theoretical framework that helps illuminate 'bad leadership', they convey the dynamics associated with employees' hierarchical status and how stature is associated with sources of power that enable senior employees to remain in post long past it is appropriate to remove them.

Schabracq and Smit (Chapter 7) ask what good leadership is, and how it relates to ethics and integrity. The authors scrutinize the influence of values in acting as a guideline and control for behaviour at work.

Loss of employee trust in management (Chapter 8) has many negative outcomes for a business. Roger Mayer discusses how multiple workplace dimensions from referents of trust, sources of risk, and past behavioral performance affect employees' trust in management. Based on classical conditioning, he argues that in severe situations replacing the leader may be the only practical option to restore trust.

Workplace deviance, the subject of Becker and Bennett's chapter (Chapter 9) is highly costly and unfortunately not much is known about how misbehaviour might be reduced. Various antecedents have been suggested, but the authors believe that one promising route to understanding employees' social contexts lies in the phenomenon of employee attachment.

Chapter 10 (Burke and McAteer) reports on research into workaholism and long work hours, and found that the old saying, 'hard work never killed anybody', was supported. But theirs is not just good news, as they go on to show that it is not 'how hard you work, but why, and how you work hard that matters', when it comes to negative consequences.

Cleveland, Lim and Murphy (Chapter 11) identify the characteristics of individuals, organizations and situations that can lead to the success or failure of performance appraisal and feedback systems. In summarizing their review, they conclude that rather than relying on formal systems of appraisal, self-evaluations can prove highly useful, and attempts should be made to improve relationships between supervisors and subordinates.

Anandakumar, Pitsis and Clegg (Chapter 12) illustrate how dysfunctional workplaces are typified by divergence in emotions towards one's workplace, co-workers and management. Their work in a neo-natal intensive care unit illuminated the importance of managing emotions at work, and the need for management training in people management skills.

Wood, Beckmann and Pavlakis (Chapter 13) discuss the negative side of humour as a manifestation of dysfunctional behaviour. They then go on to relate such forms of humour to such things as failure-producing team cultures and individual censure, including the exclusion of individuals from groups (sometimes referred to as being 'sent to Coventry'). The authors are concerned that research to date has concentrated all too much on humour as a positive force to the neglect of its potentially dark side, which is more common in organizations.

Joshi, Anand and Henderson (Chapter 14) spotlight four practices: organizational compensation and rewards; organizational structure; ethical codes of conduct; and systems and procedures for handling the discovery of corrupt acts. They explain how these practices can either help induce, or be used to prevent, what they term the 'normalization' of corruption.

Brown and Robinson (Chapter 15) believe that eliminating territories at work would not be possible, and even if it were, it would only undermine commitment to the organization.

But protecting territory has certain costs. The authors provide insights on how to harvest the benefits of territoriality without incurring its dysfunction.

Hershcovis and Barling (Chapter 16) review workplace aggression and stress the value of focusing on the relationship between the perpetrator and victim. This is because in their research they have found that the nature of the relationship affects such things as the onset of aggression by perpetrators and how aggression is experienced by victims. Their research also identifies predictors and consequences of aggression, and the constraints that have to be overcome for a thorough examination of the perpetrator/victim relationship.

Managers who are thinking of suing or sacking their employees for theft need first to read Chapter 17 by Tomlinson and Greenberg! They argue that there are many cases where employees guilty of theft are merely 'righting a wrong' and that where a more constructive approach to obtain justice is not available, theft provides an alternative route. The authors elaborate how a key to preventing theft is for managers to understand how employees form perceptions of fairness and then go on to create a workplace culture that people see as just.

Team-based organizational structures are becoming a common feature of the contemporary workplace. The next three chapters clearly demonstrate that this nominally progressive development also can have a dark side. The difficulty of working together as a team is addressed by Sims and Salas (Chapter 18), who argue that it is all too common to undermine team performance through failing to effectively manage a set of key factors, for example team leadership. These authors also outline the characteristics of effective teams.

Johnson and Hollenbeck (Chapter 19) believe it is easier for individuals to learn from their experience than it is for work teams. Consequently teams suffer from motivation and coordination losses that are unique and related conditions that they characterize as involving interpersonal, 'between-minds' information processing. On a more affirmative side, they give us insights into how organizations need to address such challenges if team learning is going to occur.

Judge and LePine (Chapter 20) reflect on the 'downsides' of traits generally deemed positive, especially in a team setting. Even a quality thought to be attractive in a person, such as extraversion, has a negative side. For example, extraverts are predisposed to accidents. They also discuss ways in which generally desirable personality traits of team members will have negative effects on team functioning. They conclude with advice on improving our personnel selection systems as a way to address some of these issues.

Grant (Chapter 21) argues that the personality characteristics of managers help determine the development of managerial styles. The author considers 'adaptive' and 'maladaptive' behavioural styles for their impact on the manager, on other employees and on the organization, and presents various interventions that could be considered.

Hisrich and Lutz (Chapter 22) outline how small entrepreneurial firms must tackle the problem of employing good staff in order to succeed, and how this needs to be done in a timely fashion. More importantly, they illustrate how appropriate motivation and compensation systems need to be in place so that mistakes can be avoided.

At a more macro level Worrall, Cooper and Mather (Chapter 23) set out to construct a multidisciplinary, multi-level understanding of workplace stress and organizational dysfunction and to dissect how organizational contexts are changing and filter through to

xvi *Research companion to the dysfunctional workplace*

affect workers' perceptions and experiences. The authors use a large time-series data set developed out of the Quality of Working Life project, to explore a 'best of times–worst of times' theme. Their goal is to help the reader to better understand and manage changes in the workplace so as to reduce the negative consequences that are often observed otherwise.

Anderson and Gasteiger (Chapter 24) write about the pressures promoting innovation in organizations. They point out that what has typically been thought of as a positive set of forces in organizations can also become problematic, and document their disruptive effects on individual creativity and work group innovation. In illuminating such problems, the authors review the empirical and theoretical literature that relates to the 'dark side' of innovation.

In the final chapter of this volume Lewicki, Greenberger and Coyne (Chapter 25) explore why subcultures develop and how these subcultures come to fit into the context of the larger organization. They ask whether some organizational cultures are more fertile in cultivating subcultures, and when and where these subcultures come to be labelled as dysfunctional. The authors debate whether it's actually possible for organizations to use subcultures to enhance themselves and increase adaptability, engagement and trust among organizational members.

Collectively, the 25 chapters touch on critical themes that we think will be highly useful in stimulating ideas for future research in this unusual area of the dysfunctional organization. Happy reading!

PART I

BARRIERS TO PRODUCTIVE WORK

1 When good people do nothing: a failure of courage

Christopher R. Rate and Robert J. Sternberg

A stark reality haunts the halls of business management – American corporations, among others worldwide, are shaking and suffering from crises of courage. Abraham Maslow (1954), one of the founders of Humanistic Psychology, once spoke of the consequences of people frozen in fear, and of the blunders that follow in fear's wake: 'it seems that the necessary thing to do is not to fear mistakes, to plunge in, to do the best that one can, hoping to learn enough from blunders to correct them eventually'. All too often, however, people fail to 'plunge in' and 'learn'. All that remains are the blunders.

A growing body of research indicates that up to two-thirds of people currently in management positions fail (Dotlich and Cairo, 2003; Hughes et al., 2002). Blunders abound. Managers find themselves fired, demoted, or moved to less influential and visible positions, or, in extreme cases, imprisoned (Charan and Colvin, 1999; Hughes et al., 2002; Lomardo et al., 1988). For example, one of the largest business scandals (Enron Corp.) in US history came to a close as former CEOs Kenneth Lay and Jeffrey Skilling were convicted on 25 counts of conspiracy and fraud. Their convictions carry sentences of up to 45 years and 185 years in prison, respectively ('Enron's Lay and Skilling Found Guilty', 2006).

How does derailment of this magnitude happen? Individuals in these management positions (such as Lay and Skilling) are almost always highly intelligent, well-educated, savvy and highly experienced business people with proven, successful track records. It is paradoxical that leaders like these orchestrated spectacular blunders and scandals – fiascos that led to several major US corporate collapses – Adelphia, Arthur Andersen, Global Crossing, HealthSouth, Tyco, WorldCom and others (Sternberg, 2005). Spectators of corporate mayhem find CEOs such as Lay and Skilling convenient scapegoats for business failures and for the vast devastation left in the wake of their actions. What is going on?

Management derailers

Conceptualizing a failure of courage

Despite recent headlines detailing corporate malfeasance and governmental corruption, many of us still expect, albeit naively, that our leaders will do the right thing; we expect them to act honorably, and to act in accordance with organizational and institutional values and ethics. In a word, when bad things happen, we expect these leaders to act with courage. But when our leaders fail us, we are often left wondering who should be held accountable. Does the blame for dysfunctional management reside solely with senior management, or does accountability more appropriately belong to the entire organization? If, in fact, the entire organization is culpable, then who will stand up to the leaders when they do not perform as expected? Who will assume the risk of challenging inappropriate organizational behaviors? Who will make the 'right' choice, particularly when that might mean losing one's livelihood? Who will act with courage?

One might posit that to ask 'who' will act is not quite the appropriate question. Rather, one should consider 'why' and 'how' someone acts or fails to act. Or, perhaps, all these questions need to be asked. For the purpose of our current discussion, an investigation of 'why' and 'how' one fails to act *courageously* within an organizational context is required. Unfortunately, the investigation of courage is noticeably absent in the management literature (Beyer and Nino, 1998; Cavanagh and Moberg, 1999; Harris, 2000).

When good people do nothing, institutions (government, private, non-profit) experience serious consequences. When *entire* groups of good people collude to overlook, deny, or manage around the negative actions of their fellow employees, senior executives and others, they demonstrate a *failure of courage*. Dotlich and Cairo (2003: 149) underscore this phenomenon: 'We have witnessed the demise of once great companies such as Enron, Kmart, Global Crossing, Tyco, and others – realizing far too late that one factor in their failure was the fact that no one could tell the emperor the truth'. *Why?* Simply stated, those around the 'emperor' lacked courage.

When good people do nothing (i.e. when they fail to act when the situation necessitates an *appropriate* action), there is a failure of courage. This failure is not necessarily the same as *cowardice*, or in today's vernacular, *spinelessness*, *gutlessness*, or other words of similar meaning. The bottom line, though, is that failure to act courageously, especially during a time of organizational change or crisis, can have catastrophic effects on the entire organization. Not only is it the responsibility of organizational leaders to step up and behave in a courageous manner when the situation necessitates such action, but it is also the responsibility of all individuals within an organization to do the same.

Although a failure of courage has its price, acting courageously can also be costly. When individuals choose to behave courageously by addressing failure or corruption within an organization, these individuals are often socially and organizationally ostracized, and they may experience long-term economic harm and psychological injury (Rothschild and Miethe, 1999). Avoiding such negative consequences can be a compelling basis for failing to act courageously and, instead, for 'minding one's own business' and for being a proponent of the *status quo*. It is the responsibility of the collective organization to create and sustain an atmosphere and culture where courageous behavior can be developed and exercised, thereby reducing retributive sanctions on the part of the organization.

Other conceptualizations of dysfunctional management

Other constructs might also be considered in understanding the issue of dysfunctional management and management failure (McCauley, 2004). Management failure is arguably a function of individual behavior and a culture that tolerates it. It is not happenstance, nor is it solely the result of a declining economy, natural disaster, or other event over which we have little or no control. For this reason, researchers of 'dark side' management typically focus on individuals' characteristics, traits or behaviors (Dotlich and Cairo, 2003). Managers fail because of how they act in certain situations. They tend to rely on specific ways of thinking, speaking and acting that ultimately cause them to fail.

The phenomena of managerial derailment and dysfunctional management have been described and conceptualized in a variety of ways. Van Velsor and Leslie (1995), focusing on managerial skills and abilities, identified four categories of deficiencies that consistently predict derailment: (1) problems with interpersonal relationships; (2) failure to build and lead teams; (3) inability to change or adapt during a transition; and (4) failure to meet business objectives. Following this line of inquiry, Mumford et al. (2000) highlight problem-solving capabilities needed by organizational leaders that enable them to successfully engage in the complex issues they face (e.g. creative problem solving, social judgment skills and organizational knowledge). Focusing on the personality of the manager, Conger (1999) and Hogan and Hogan (2001) identify personality components and undesirable characteristics that correlated with managerial success or failure. Dotlich and Cairo (2003), in their interesting book, *Why CEOs Fail*, expand upon the Hogan and Hogan (2001) discussion of 11 undesirable behaviors and add pragmatic advice to help managers recognize and positively address these behaviors.

Finkelstein (2003), in his book, *Why Smart Executives Fail*, addresses the personal characteristics that have the potential to create catastrophic corporate collapse. For example, Finkelstein asserts that managers fail when they choose not to cope with innovation and organizational change; misread the competition; or cling to inaccurate forms of reality. Sternberg (2005) suggests that some smart people (i.e. CEOs, senior executives and leaders in general) simply act foolishly. Foolish behavior is due, in part, to fallacies in smart people's thinking processes. The preceding sample of studies is not exhaustive, but is illustrative of research in this business domain. However, once again, the construct of courage is not considered.

Courage is an understudied phenomenon, yet critical in a world with continued failures of it. It allows us to function as individuals and as a group in the face of moral, psychological, social and physical obstacles. Despite its importance, we do not have a clear understanding of the concept. Therefore this chapter seeks, first, to address three issues in order to establish a framework or foundation for pursuing a fourth issue, which is critical to addressing one ongoing problem of dysfunctional management.

1. Propose a common framework for understanding just what, in fact, courage is.
2. Describe the current status of courage-related research.
3. Illustrate how courage works as a process.
4. Suggest ways in which organizations can develop individuals and create environments to assure courageous behavior will be employed when necessary.

What is courage?
In efforts to understand better and to establish exactly what courage is, the origins of courage, its definitions and its components are addressed.

Caveats of courageous behaviors
Given the history of fragmented conceptualizations of courage, the following four points might be helpful in establishing a more precise understanding of courage:

1. Courage is a complex, multidimensional construct composed of 'necessary, but insufficient' dimensions. Several definitions and descriptions of courage point to at least four apparent components – intentionality, risk, noble aim, fear.
2. Courageous behavior is rare. The thresholds of risk, nobility and fear must be sufficiently high in order for this construct to exemplify behavioral excellence. This supererogatory standard is above and beyond what many of us do, that is, how we behave on a daily basis. In this case, courage seems to be a *phasic* phenomenon,

emerging when needed, rather than a *tonic* phenomenon, demonstrating a trait-like quality of the individual (Lopez, et al., 2003; Peterson and Seligman, 2004).

3.   Courage is more appropriately expressed in terms of the 'act' rather than the 'actor' (i.e. defining courage in terms of behavior rather than in terms of personality or character traits). Saying an 'actor' has a courage trait based on a single 'act', or has a courageous personality independent of the context of his or her behavior is somewhat questionable and suspect (Beyer and Nino, 1998; Rate et al., in press; Walton, 1986). The 'actor' does not equal the 'act'. In fact, studies have indicated no significant personality differences between people purported to act courageously and those who do not (Near and Miceli, 1996; Rothschild and Miethe, 1999). And while Rachman (1990) found subtle physiological differences between 'courageous' and 'noncourageous' actors (e.g. decorated versus non-decorated bomb disposal operators) in their ability to suppress fear, this difference did not translate into behavioral differences.

4.   Although *courage* is often used interchangeably with *bravery, boldness, fearlessness* or *intrepidness*, they are not synonymous. Indeed, courage connotes a level of nobility and worthiness in purpose not necessarily present in these other constructs (Walton, 1986).

Courage: the beginnings

Throughout recorded history, the question of 'what courage is' has piqued the interest of philosophers, research scientists and laypeople, spurring the continuing debate over the concept of courage and its meaning for human behavior, virtue and morals. Notwithstanding centuries of philosophical musings, psychological inquiries and discussions by laypeople, there remains no universally accepted definition of courage. In many ways, we are no closer than we were when the character Socrates conceded this point near the end of the Platonic dialogue, *Laches*, with the words, 'then . . . we have not discovered what courage is'.

In modern times, 'courage' and 'courageous' behavior are often reserved for exemplary acts. For example, the actions of Frank Serpico remain a commonly cited exemplar of courageous behavior. Serpico, a New York City police officer, exposed corruption at the highest levels within the New York City Police Department. Even though he stood for what he believed was morally right, he was ostracized by his own department and eventually lost his life in the line of duty – some suspect as a direct result of his fellow officers' failure to provide appropriate backup in a hostile situation (Beyer and Nino, 1998; Glazer and Glazer, 1989; Walton, 1986).

Today, 'courage' is used to depict and describe a disposition underlying individuals' behavior across myriad kinds of situations and everyday acts (Evans and White, 1981; Putman, 1997, 2001; Woodard, 2004). This view diminishes the standing of courage as a basis for morally exemplary behavior. In fact, some believe that American culture over the last 30 years or so has 'defined down' courage. That is, courage has been 'attributed to all manner of actions that may indeed be admirable but hardly compare to the conscious self-sacrifice on behalf of something greater than self-interest' (McCain and Salter, 2004: 13).

A cursory review of headlines and recent publications reveals several contexts for the discussion and description of courage. One can find numerous publications addressing 'courage' in the scholarly domains of patient–physician relationships (Bunkers, 2004; Clancy, 2003; Finfgeld, 1995, 1998; Shelp, 1984), military leadership (Cox et al., 1983; Gole, 1997; Miller, 2000), politics (Kennedy, 1956), business/management (*Fast Company*, 2004; Klein and Napier, 2003; Meisinger, 2005) and organizations (Cavanagh and Moberg, 1999; Kilmann et al., 2005), to name just a few. Although this literature is growing at an accelerated rate, it actually says little about the nature or form of courage or about its development (Harris, 2000; Srivastva and Cooperrider, 1998; Walton, 1986).

Philosophers, empirical researchers and laypeople have all found the endeavor of researching and defining courage quite challenging. To describe someone or someone's actions as courageous is to suggest a construct that is, at the same time, both descriptive and evaluative. To reach a definition that everyone will agree upon or even subscribe to, therefore, is not a simple undertaking. In an effort to appreciate this subject matter, we need to see where we have been to get a sense of where we are going. We will begin by investigating the origins of the word and concept, 'courage'. This discussion will be followed by a brief look at a select number of definitions of courage.

Origin/etymology of 'courage'
The word *courage* is grounded in Western and Eastern ancient philosophical traditions. The ancient Greeks, namely Socrates, Plato and Aristotle, called it *andreia*, meaning 'manliness', typically found in the overt actions of the soldier on the battlefield (Aristotle, 1987). Saint Thomas Aquinas (1922) also identified courage with masculine strength, *fortitudo*, yet broadened the application of courage to include overt actions and inaction or instances of endurance (Shelp, 1984). Departing from 'manly' courage, the fourth-century BC Confucian thinker Mengzi (Mencius) called courage, *da yong*, a category of 'great courage'. *Da yong* is directed toward morally praiseworthy ends, and is the result of a continuing process of self-cultivation (Ivanhoe, 2002).

Today, *andreia*, *fortitude* and *da yong* are translated as 'courage', but over the last 700 years the word 'courage' itself has taken on several different meanings. 'Courage', first adapted from the Old French word *corage* or *curag* (the root, *cor*, is Latin for 'heart'), denoted the idea that courage comes from 'the heart as the seat of feeling, thought, spirit, mind, disposition, and nature' (*Oxford English Dictionary*, 1989). The earliest appearances of *corage* were found in literary works *circa* 1300. The next few hundred years witnessed numerous variations on the spelling of courage, with the emergence of its present-day spelling, *courage*, by the sixteenth century (*Oxford English Dictionary*, 1989).

Although courage is usually used in our modern lexicons to describe people who have a quality of mind that allows them to face danger without fear, it has also been referred to as bravery or boldness. In today's vernacular, dozens of words are used synonymously with courage: audacity, fearlessness, heroism, valor, fortitude, bravery, resolution, spirit and boldness. Although there are similarities and overlapping dimensions between courage and these other words, they are not, for our purposes, conceptually synonymous.

Through its evolution, many definitions of courage have now become outdated. For example, meanings implied by the definition of courage as 'spirit, liveliness, lustiness, vigour, vital force or energy', that is, anger, pride, confidence, boldness, sexual vigour and inclination, are all now obsolete. These meanings were typically found in literary texts (e.g. Chaucer, Shakespeare) dating between the mid-sixteenth and seventeenth centuries (*Oxford English Dictionary*, 1989).

Although the word *courage* conjures up countless images of boldness, bravery, valor and heroism, it is possible for this word to have a more concise, focused meaning. Efforts toward this end have been made in modern lexicons such as the *Oxford English Dictionary* (1989), which defines courage as 'the quality of mind which shows itself in facing danger without fear or shrinking'. Variations on this definition comprise today's assorted definitions of courage.

Recent definitions of courage
Table 1.1 lists a number of select definitions and descriptions of courage. The entries range from Rachman's (1990: 12) description of courage as the ability 'to approach a fearful situation despite the presence of subjective fear and psychophysiological disturbances' to Shelp's (1984: 354) complex, multidimensional definition of courage as 'the disposition to voluntarily act, perhaps fearfully, in a dangerous circumstance, where the relevant risks are reasonably appraised, in an effort to obtain or preserve some perceived good for oneself or others recognizing that the desired perceived good may not be realized'.

The evolving and domain-specific meanings of courage speak volumes as to why we still stumble toward a consensus definition. Arguably, intelligent minds across the centuries have failed in their attempts to garner broad support for their definitions. We have yet to advance the domain to a more broadly accepted conceptual definition of courage. Lopez et al. (2003) succinctly summarize the issue we will address: 'Though we have been able to parse out the different types of courage by establishing between-brand differences, we have been less successful at determining the elements or components of courage. Thus, what is common to all brands remains unclear' (189). Whether we refer to brands, types or definitions of courage, Table 1.1 contains enough information to gray the beards of the wisest of the ancient Greek philosophers and Chinese sages.

Perhaps the charge that we have failed to understand courage is somewhat overstated. A careful examination of current definitions of courage reveals that we may be closer to a consensus definition than we previously had thought. An extensive and comprehensive review of the literature on courage reveals that there is considerable overlap of definitional components and dimensions.

Based on this fact, we would propose a multidimensional definition of courage that could be used as a conceptual benchmark to evaluate the presence of courageous behavior across domains and populations. It also provides a solid foundation for highlighting significant areas essential for developing individual courage, or at a minimum, its components, within an organization. We describe courage as (a) an **intentional** act executed after willful **deliberation**, (b) involving the acknowledgment and endurance of **substantial risk** to the actor, (c) attempting to bring about a **noble good** or worthy purpose, (d) persisting, perhaps, despite the presence of **personal fear** (Rate et al., in press). Each of these dimensions is now briefly described below.

The core components of courage

Intentionality/deliberation   In order for an act to be considered courageous, it must be performed with a level of intentionality or deliberation – it is a choice. In the field of social cognition, observers consider a behavior *intentional* when it appears purposeful or done intentionally – that is, based on reasons (beliefs, desires) and performed with

Table 1.1   Selected definitions and descriptions of courage

Source	Definitions and descriptions
Cavanagh and Moberg	'Courage, also called fortitude or bravery, is the ability to endure what is necessary to achieve a good end, even in the face of great obstacles' (1999: 2).
Evans and White	'An empirical definition of courage probably involves three important attributional dimensions: (a) the fear level of the person making the attribution; (b) the perceived fear level of the attributee; and (c) salient features of the situation e.g., objective risk involved and so on' (1981: 420).
Gould	Courage is revealed in three dimensions: (1) fear; (2) appropriate action; and (3) a higher purpose (2005).
Kilmann et al.	A courageous act in an organization includes five essential properties: (1) member has free choice to act; (2) member experiences significant risk; (3) member assesses the risk as reasonable; (4) member's contemplated act pursues excellence or other worthy aims and (5) member proceeds despite fear with mindful action (2005).
Klein and Napier	Courage involves five factors: candor (speak and hear the truth), purpose (pursue lofty and audacious goals), rigor (invent disciplines and make them stick), risk (empower, trust, and invest in relationships), and will (inspire optimism, spirit, and promise) (2003).
Rachman	'Willing and able to approach a fearful situation despite the presence of subjective fear and psychophysiological disturbances' (1990: 12).
Peterson and Seligman	Emotional character strengths (bravery, persistence, integrity and vitality) 'that involve the exercise of will to accomplish goals in the face of opposition, external or internal' (2004: 29).
Shelp	'The disposition to voluntarily act, perhaps fearfully, in a dangerous circumstance, where the relevant risks are reasonably appraised, in an effort to obtain or preserve some perceived good for oneself or others recognizing that the desired perceived good may not be realized' (1984: 354).
Shepela et al.	Courageous resistance: 'selfless behavior in which there is high risk/cost to the actor, and possibly the actor's family and associates, where the behavior must be sustained over time, is most often deliberative, and often where the actor is responding to a moral call' (1999: 789).
Walton	Courage consists of three characteristics: '1) careful presence of mind and deliberate action, 2) difficult, dangerous, and painful circumstances, and 3) a morally worthy intention . . . at the agent's personal risk and suffering' (1986: 3).
Woodard	Courage is defined as the 'ability to act for a meaningful (noble, good, or practical) cause, despite experiencing the fear associated with perceived threat exceeding the available resources' (2004: 174).
Worline et al.	Courage (in organizational settings) 'involves risk, has been freely chosen, demonstrates considered assessment of consequences, and pursues excellence within the circumstances where it occurs' (2002: 299).

awareness. In many contexts, people read the intentions underlying others' behavior effortlessly; in other contexts, however, we can only reasonably assume to know a target actor's intentions.

In our view, an act of courage is not forced or coerced. Consider the whistleblower who has blown the whistle only under threat of criminal indictment. In this instance, the behavior of the whistleblower should not be considered courageous despite risk, fear or noble ends, because the behavior was coerced. This points to a dysfunctional atmosphere and culture where an individual must be faced with an external threat before he or she is willing to stand up for what is 'right'.

Known substantial risk   During deliberations, the actor must assess the risk involved in one's potential actions. Wallace (1978: 78) wrote: 'Someone who sees no peril [risk] in what he does is not acting courageously'. How does one, therefore, calculate risk? Risk contains both an objective, but probabilistic, component, and a subjective component. Expressions of risk are usually described in terms of the probability of harm and its severity. The acceptability of risk is a matter of personal and social-value judgment. Often one assesses risk as unacceptable. The severity of risk underlies why Rothschild and Miethe (1999) report that over half of US employees who observe conduct they consider to be unethical or illegal in the workplace remain silent. While understandable, the silence at times can be deafening.

Additionally, Walton (1986) noted that there are many risks, difficulties and dangers we take that should not properly be called courageous. Daring for daring's sake is thrill-seeking, rashness and recklessness. However, substantial known risk in conjunction with the dimension noble/good purpose, allows us appropriately to frame the risk of our actions. Two views provide perspective on this notion; 'the greater the sacrifice, risk, and danger of carrying out a good objective, the more meritorious is the course of action directed to that end' (Walton, 1986: 191), and 'the more valued and worthy the goal, the greater the willingness to incur risk to bring it about' (Miller, 2000: 153).

Noble good   A courageous action must be directed toward a valued and worthy goal – one having merit. We would argue that any definition of courage that excludes this 'noble' dimension is insufficient to capture the essence and nature of courage. Some have argued that this ethical dimension is what separates the concept of courage from other concepts and behaviors, such as bravery and intrepidity (Walton, 1986) and thrill-seeking (Gould, 2005). Furthermore, Woodard (2004: 174) asserts that 'courage includes a quality of grace, nobility, credibility . . . Without these qualities, an act that would other-wise be courageous would simply be reckless'. One could argue that the more noble the cause or purpose of the action, all else being equal, the more courageous the act. Rothschild and Miethe (1999) point out that the majority of the whistleblowers they interviewed acted from the position of personally held values. It was their belief that the behavior they reported was wrong, illegal, unethical and harmful. Yet a substantial minority of whistleblowers acted out of self-interest, that is, to avoid being cast as a scapegoat, to receive a promotion or a raise, or simply to punish management. The intents of these actions are clearly not worthy causes and are not appropriately labeled as courageous, but the issue becomes more complex. Noble good might be judged through the eyes of the beholder.

Actions despite personal fear 'You can't be courageous without fear . . . How can you have courage if you have no fear?' (Philips, 2004: 229). Fear has many names and many faces, but essentially it is an emotion or feeling of agitation or anxiety caused by the presence or imminence of danger. We can generate many stories, or movies we have seen, of individuals acting despite fear, and the many unnamed individuals who have failed to act as personal fear has overcome them. There is continued debate over the role of fear defining courage. For some, fear is a prerequisite for courage (Evans and White, 1981; Gould, 2005; Putnam, 1997; Woodard, 2004). Many implicit-theoretical studies have shown that people consider the ability to act despite fear, or overcoming fear, to be central to courageous acts. For others, the emotion of fear is less central or peripheral to describing courageous behavior. It is just one obstacle an individual may overcome when acting in a courageous manner (O'Byrne et al., 2003; Rate et al., 2005; Shelp, 1984; Shepela et al., 1999; Walton, 1986).

Summary
Why are we interested in courage? Courage is critical to ethical organizational effectiveness and efficiency. The meaning of courage has evolved since the ancients first pondered its value to society. Even though the most recent definitions seem variable on the surface, there may be more consensus than first thought. The components of intentionality, risk, noble good and fear emerge from these definitions. A clear understanding of what courage is helps us to investigate this construct through continued empirical work and to identify why or where failures of courage occur (as far as an organization is concerned).

Empirical studies of courage

Implicit-theory studies of courage
The vast majority of studies are implicit studies investigating people's implicit notions of courage. According to Sternberg (1985) and Sternberg et al. (1981), implicit theories are people's own cognitive constructions. Such theories reside in people's heads, and need to be discovered rather than invented because they already exist. Implicit theories tell us about individuals' views of what courage, or anything else, is. Wegner and Vallacher (1977: 21) echo this point: 'the layman . . . lives by his theory . . . The systems we call "implicit theories" are the individual's reality'. Generally speaking, implicit theories are theories of word usage, and in this case, the word 'courage' is of extreme interest to a vast number and variety of people, from academic scholars, to military members, to the ordinary citizen.

O'Byrne et al. (2000) questioned 97 people and found that their views of courage varied considerably. Participants in their study described courage as 'taking action', 'standing up for what one believes in', 'sacrificing' and 'facing threats/fears/challenges and overcoming obstacles'. Courage was perceived as having characteristics of an attribute, behavior and attitude, incorporating both mental and physical strength as components.

Philips (2004) conducted a multicultural study of people's notions about courage. His participants included 20 individuals from Montclair, New Jersey; 16 Native American seniors in a western US high school; 19 fifth-grade students in Japan; and 10 residents of a facility for the mentally ill in the USA. His quest focused on questions Socrates would have asked the ancient Greeks. The particular question of interest here was: what is courage? The dialogue in New Jersey took place three months after September 11th, 2001. One of the comments in reference to courage included, 'Anyone who tries to rescue someone, in a situation where he could die . . .' (208). One Native American senior commented, 'Our values are to endure, to persevere, to overcome, if the goals are worth fighting for' (222). This group agreed that courage was shown by actions. The group of Japanese students described courage in someone as being 'willing to risk his life against impossible odds to help out others' (226) and that 'you can't be courageous without fear . . . How can you have courage if you have no fear?' (229). Philips's final group, mentally ill individuals, suggested that 'courage has to begin with saving yourself, so you can reach out to others' (236). Several elements of courage surfaced through this study: courage required sacrifice – putting oneself at risk for another. More specifically, to have courage is to endure, persevere and overcome. Courage involves challenging the status quo through dissent and fighting for social justice. Finally, courage required overcoming fear for a good purpose.

Another study recently applied an implicit-theories approach to the study of attributes associated with bravery. In their implicit-theory approach, Walker and Hennig (2004) investigated people's conceptions of different types of moral exemplars (just, brave and caring) to determine if they could be construed as prototypic person concepts. Participants in their three-study investigation were predominantly Canadian-born undergraduate university students. In Phase I, participants were asked to write down the characteristics, attributes or traits of a 'highly' brave person. Nearly 3000 responses were compiled from 268 participants. The attributes were deemed accessible and salient in people's everyday experiences. These responses were distilled to a list of 120 items. In Phase II, participants rated these items on how accurately each word described a highly brave person. The free-listing data in Phase I and the prototypicality-rating data of Phase II provide evidence that the moral exemplars are organized as prototypes in people's understanding, with some attributes regarded as more central and others as more peripheral. Multidimensional scaling of the *brave* exemplar following the third phase similarity-sorting task of 60 prototypic attributes suggested two dimensions labeled *selfless* and *agentic*. The selfless dimension was anchored at the positive pole by attributes such as *fearless, risk-taking, faces danger* and *adventurous* – the other pole was anchored by attributes such as *goal-oriented, focused, determined* and *motivated*. The agentic dimension was anchored on the positive pole by attributes such as *fearless, daring* and *faces danger*, and on the negative pole by *respectful, honorable, noble* and *loyal* attributes. The understanding of the *brave* exemplar was additionally rounded out by themes of *dedication* and *self-sacrifice*. Their results showed conceptions that are consistent with the 'highly' brave person and consistent with the personality attributions made by participants in their second phase, which emphasized dominance/extroversion.

Woodard (2004) used an implicit-theories approach in an effort to develop a measure of courage. Ten experts with varied areas of specialty in the field of psychology generated statements considered representative of assessing the construct of courage, defined as 'the ability to act for a meaningful (noble, good, or practical) cause, despite experiencing the fear associated with perceived threat exceeding the available resources' (174). Two hundred laypeople then rated the items on a five-point scale in terms of their agreement with the statements. Each item was also accompanied by a fear-rating question to establish the level of fear that the respondent might associate with the situation, and a third question asking the respondents whether or not they had experienced the situation posed in the item. Factor analysis revealed four dimensions labeled: (a) *Endurance for positive outcomes* – including behaviors such as 'acts despite bullying as a minority'; (b) *Dealing with groups* – including behaviors such as 'help grieving family', and 'rejection by others for goals'; (c) *Acting alone* – including behaviors such as 'accept job despite criticism', and 'avoid confronting my own pain'; and (d) *Physical pain/breaking social norms* – including behaviors such as 'intervene in domestic dispute' and 'endure pain for political secrets'. The factors were found to have a strong correlation with each other, suggesting a relationship among the ideas that contributed to deciding whether or not to act in a courageous manner. The concepts represented by the factors have further illuminated the basic manner in which people conceive of the construct of courage. Their results, supported by results from the previously mentioned studies, indicate that people view the nature of courage as multidimensional.

In a series of interview-based studies in the nursing domain, chronically ill adolescents (Haase, 1987), middle-aged adults (Finfgeld, 1998) and older adults (Finfgeld, 1995) were asked to describe a situation in which they thought they were courageous. They were instructed to describe their thoughts, feelings and perceptions as they remembered experiencing them. Collectively, their findings regarding courage pointed to the development of attitudes and coping methods, highlighting the process of becoming and being courageous in the face of chronic illness. As with other domains, there remains little understanding of how courage fits into the larger framework of psychological strength and health processes.

Evans and White (1981) conducted an experimental manipulation study of people's implicit theories of bravery (used synonymously with courage). In their study, 124 adolescents viewed video tapes of a young adult actor seen to approach a vivarium, remove the lid, pick up a large harmless but exotic snake, handle it for some moments, put it down, and finally replace the lid. Participants were then asked to rate three questions on a scale from 1 'Not at all frightened (brave)' to 5 'Very frightened (brave)'. Two questions focused on how frightened or brave the actor was, respectively, while the third question asked how the observer would have felt about picking up the snake. Their analysis revealed that the underlying tendencies were that participants responding with higher personal fear attributed more bravery (courage) to the actor. Overall, it appeared that their participants attributed bravery to the target actor if the actor was doing something that would have frightened them. Evans and White (1981) concluded that courage probably involved, in part, not only the perceived fear of the target actor, but also the fear level of the person making the evaluation.

Szagun (1992) conducted an age-related study of German children's understanding of courage. Ninety children participated in three age groups (5–6, 8–9 and 11–12). In a structured interview, the children were asked a series of three questions that addressed: (a) risk taking; (b) overcoming fear; and (c) awareness of risk. As an example of 'risk taking', the children were presented the following scenario and questions: 'Two children are climbing a tree. One of them has climbed trees before, and the other one is climbing a tree for the first time. Is one of the children courageous, or are both? If both, is one child more courageous than the other, or are both equally courageous?' (409). Two other scenarios addressed the latter two questions. Results of this study revealed that the criteria for courage differed for the younger and older children. The youngest group regarded having no fear and performing risky action as typical of courage, whereas the older two groups thought that overcoming fear and taking a subjective risk were characteristic of courage. In addition, the 11- to 12-year-old group noted that there must be some reflection in risk taking if the risk were to be considered courageous. In other words, the action must be a result of deliberate or intentional cognitive processes.

In a second study, Szagun (1992) had the same groups of children rate the degree of courage for 12 different risks on a five-point scale, from 1 ('not courageous') to 5 ('very courageous'). Six items involved physical risks (e.g. climbing a tree; diving off a 3-meter board) and six involved psychological/social risks (e.g. sticking to one's beliefs, even though one is laughed at; standing up for something good and just, even if one may be taken to prison). Again, there were disparate results between the youngest and two older groups. The youngest group regarded physical risks as being typically courageous, whereas the older groups regarded both high physical risks and morally good psychological risks as being typically courageous. Szagun argued that this study provided evidence that, as children grow older, they understand courage increasingly psychologically and non-physically. A longitudinal study of children's understanding of courage would further substantiate this developmental claim.

Recently, Rate et al. (2005) set out to discover the nature and use of people's implicit theories of courage. They conducted four studies in order to accomplish these particular goals. Responses collected from the US Air Force Academy and Yale University participants revealed no differences between genders or academic institutions across the four studies.

In their first study, they compiled a master list of behaviors people regarded as descriptive of an ideally courageous individual. One hundred seventy-five individuals recorded over 1000 behaviors that were subsequently distilled to a list of 639 items. It was clear from this expansive list that there was significant variance in people's views of courageous behavior; however, core themes emerged and were exemplified by actions involving *risk*, *sacrifice*, *doing the right thing* and *acting despite fear*.

In their second study, they sought to discover people's conceptions of courage through the dimensions they used to evaluate and judge other people. One hundred twenty-six participants rated 639 behavioral items generated from the previous study. Participants rated the items on a nine-point scale as to how 'distinctively characteristic' the items were of an ideally courageous individual. Results indicated that people seem to have prototypes corresponding to the concept of courage. Furthermore, the factor analyses revealed that the prototypical behaviors were also organized into sensible factors. These five factors that one uses to judge or evaluate others – thus, differentiating among people in terms of courage and courageous behavior – were labeled: (a) *deliberation and intentionality* (e.g. knows one's limitations, considers risks, plans, forms goals); (b) *substantial personal risk-taking* (e.g. participates in extreme activities, acts with a flavor of recklessness); (c) *persistence despite fear* (e.g. follows through even if scared, does not give in to fear); (d) *noble physical self-sacrifice for others* (risks one's life to save others, sacrifices self to save another); and (e) *stalwart of noble moral principles* (e.g. does what is right even if unpopular, stands up for the rights of others).

Through a third study, they continued to uncover the organization underlying the individual's conception of courage itself. Participants sorted 60 prototypic behaviors (generated in the second study) into as many or as few groups as the participants deemed appropriate based on which behaviors were 'likely to be found together' in a person. Cluster analysis revealed a three-cluster solution. The clusters were labeled: (a) *self-sacrifice/risk for others*; (b) *non-physical/social-oriented acts for noble ends*; and (c) *self-focused perseverance despite fear*. The results from this study nicely illustrated what is meant when someone is characterized as being 'courageous' or as having 'courage'.

The previous studies elucidated the nature of courage and the dimensions people use to evaluate levels of courage in others. Behaviors including risk, sacrifice, perseverance despite fear, intentional or deliberate action and noble purpose continued to emerge throughout the three previous studies. These factors seem to form, or at least to be at, the core of the concept of courage. Knowing these factors existed was on its own remarkable, but revealing whether or not people actually use them when evaluating others' levels of courage remained a point of interest and required further investigation. As such, the authors conducted a fourth and final study to examine this very issue.

Through this fourth study, they sought to discover the extent to which people actually used behaviors associated with courage in their evaluations of other people's courage. One hundred sixty-nine participants rated 33 vignettes. The vignettes described scenarios of varied situations and contained manipulated levels of individual behaviors on four dimensions (i.e. *intentionality/deliberation*; *presence of personal fear*; *noble/good act*; and *known substantial personal risk*). In an effort to assure independence of dimension and courage ratings, one half of the participants were asked to evaluate the presence of four dimensions in the vignettes. The other half of the participants evaluated the vignette protagonist's level of courage. Regression analysis revealed courage could be predicted at a high level by knowing people's ratings of the four dimensions.

Summary
Implicit-theory studies provide an understanding of people's notions of the psychological construct of 'courage' in everyday terms, while serving as a launching point to further investigate the implicit organization of 'courageous' behavior. The collective efforts of these researchers have provided a firm foundation upon which to build and investigate the psychology of courage. These studies have provided at least a glimpse into what people think courage is, including its nature, its components, and a step closer to an agreed upon definition.

We should note some areas of investigation that perhaps would advance this domain. Further research into the structure of courage is required to determine if the structure is multidimensional, one-dimensional with 'necessary' but 'insufficient' levels, or some combination of the two. Also, questions of social comparison, motivated cognition and the role of emotion as they apply to assessing courage in others should be investigated, to name but a few. However, before we can propagate the study of courage, the field must reach a consensus as to what is meant by 'courage' and 'courageous' behavior, for, without consensus, we will continue to re-create the wheel, watch it spin, but never allow it to roll down the path of scientific advancement.

Courage as a process
Evaluating an act of courage requires us to make reasonable presumptions on the basis of what is known. This understanding is based on both objective and evaluative dimensions of a particular act. Our presumptions may be correct or incorrect, but in the absence

of evidence to the contrary, they are reasonable. As observers of a courageous act, we base our understanding and evaluation on a reconstruction of the target actor's understanding of his or her own actions. Walton (1987: 598) refers to this as a 'teleological framework of narrative discourse – a kind of story that exhibits a sequence of actions carried out in a particular situation to aim at a goal beyond that situation'.

Figure 1.1 illustrates this evaluative process. In optics, the dispersion of light through a prism is a phenomenon that causes the separation of white light into its color spectral components. These spectral components can then be recombined to once again produce white light. While perhaps simplistic, a similar process is followed in evaluating an individual's behavior as *courageous*. An individual's behavior is perceived by an observer. The observer disperses the behavior into its components, attending to behaviors deemed prototypical of courageous behavior (e.g. intentionality, noble good, known risk and personal fear). Components of the behavior not associated with or peripheral to the evaluation of courage are either ignored or inhibited. In order to be recombined during the evaluation process, each of the 'courage' components must exceed an undetermined threshold. The recombined components define the individual's action in the eyes of the observer. The observer then assesses the level of the individual's courage.

To illustrate this conceptualized evaluation process, we use the salient example of a failure of courage depicted by the actions of the administrators and engineers leading up to the Space Shuttle *Challenger* disaster just 72 seconds after liftoff on 28 January 1986. Up until the launch, engineers expressed concern over damage to the shuttle's O-rings in previous launches and the unusually cold temperatures at launch time. Under extreme political and economic pressure and the possibility of serious scheduling backlogs, NASA managers dismissed this information and decided to proceed with the launch. This decision resulted in the deaths of seven brave people, and had serious repercussions for NASA. The space administration's reputation has never been completely restored (Beyer and Nino, 1998; Maier, 1992).

From the previous discussions in this chapter, the behaviors considered central to courageous actions were determined to include intentionality and deliberation, substantial known risk, noble/good purpose and, perhaps, personal fear. The evaluation model depicted in Figure 1.1 helps determine where a failure of courage occurred in the previous case study. The four components were present before the decision to launch, but a breakdown in courageous behavior occurred. NASA managers succumbed to external political and economic pressures to launch. The launch could no longer be appropriately considered as serving a noble purpose, rather an act of self-interest to relieve these pressures. In fact, the chief engineer, who knew of the substantial risks the O-rings presented to flight safety, and whose job it was to approve the launch, was asked to 'take off his engineering hat and put on his managerial hat'. This simple act allowed him to go along with the launch. In this decision, he chose to act for expedience over what he knew was 'right'. These actions may be more appropriately labeled as reckless.

In evaluating one's level of courage, we attend to its component behaviors (i.e. intentionality, known personal risk, noble/good purpose and personal fear) while those behavioral components deemed more peripheral are suppressed, inhibited or ignored. When the behaviors relevant to courage reach or exceed some undefined threshold, we then recombine them into what we would appropriately call *courage* or *courageous* behavior. If, however, a required component of our concept fails to reach this threshold (as in the

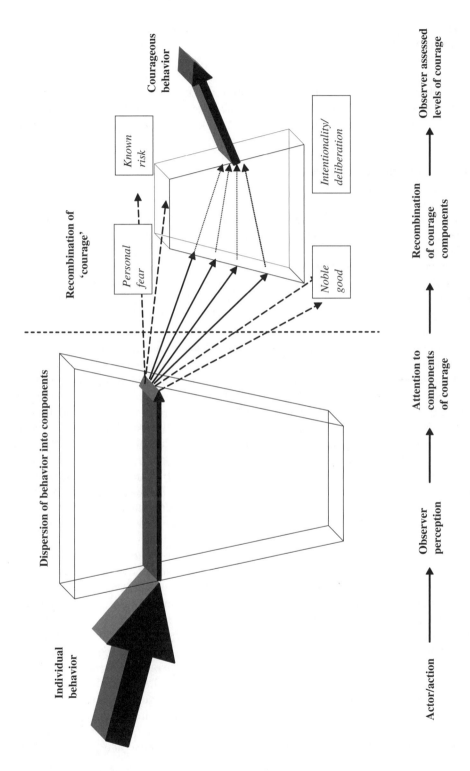

Figure 1.1   *Courage as a process: depiction of the evaluation of individual behavior as courageous*

Challenger disaster), then our evaluation of the behavior would have been appropriately labeled as something other than *courage*.

Summary
Understanding what courage *is* and *is not* and how one evaluates the levels of courage in others provides a firm foundation upon which the development of courage can begin to be conceptualized and constructed. In order to develop courage, one must first know what it is that one is attempting to develop.

Developing organizational courage
A goal of any healthy organization is to operate effectively and efficiently. The ability of people within an organization to act courageously is essential to this goal. In efforts to reach this goal, two questions must be addressed: (1) is it possible to develop courage and courageous behavior in the individual? and (2) what can organizations do to promote courageous actions?

Some would argue that courage cannot be directly developed in an individual. Rather, the focus is appropriately placed on the development of the components of courage in the hope that the components will be synthesized to enable courageous behavior as a situation requires. Managers can, however, overcome and prevent failures of courage by implementing suggestions from transformational and charismatic leadership theories (Conger, 1999). For example, in efforts to develop decision-making skills (described as the intentional/deliberation component of courage), employees should be included in efforts to address and solve group and organizational problems. Appropriate responses to risk and fear can be directly addressed when organizations intellectually stimulate their employees by encouraging them to question assumptions, reframe problems, and look for creative and innovative approaches to business. By focusing on the intrinsic rewards of work – emphasizing the heroic, moral and meaningful aspects of work – and de-emphasizing the extrinsic side, while at the same time creating rewards for groups rather than individuals, employees will become aware of noble and worthy ends rather than self-interested outcomes (Gergen and Gergen, 1998). The likelihood of observing courageous or courageous-like behavior increases with the enactment of comprehensive plans to develop its components. An organizational culture and atmosphere must also exist that can sustain their development.

It is incumbent upon organizations to create a culture in which courageous behavior can be sustained. Through the explicit statement of an organization's vision of ethics and morals, employee's behaviors are positively affected (Cavanagh and Moberg, 1999). Developing programs and opportunities for a free flow of information and communication (Gergen and Gergen, 1998) reduces levels of fear in the organization. Essentially, creating a supportive climate for learning that uses stories that exemplify courageous behavior and express ideas and lessons learned from experience helps employees behave in a more courageous manner (Beyer and Nino, 1998; Cavanagh and Moberg, 1999).

However, an organization's ultimate goal is to strive to create an environment where individual courage is not needed (Kilmann et al., 2005). That is, there is no risk of reprisal, ostracism or loss of job, and any fear of retribution or public humiliation have been eliminated. A failure of courage is no longer an issue. Kilmann et al. (2005) refer to this type of organization as a quantum organization. It promotes effective action without fear.

Until an organization transcends to this level, the development of courage, its components and a sustaining culture must continue.

Conclusion

Business blunders and catastrophes . . . When good people do nothing, there is a failure of courage. But a crisis of courage does not need to exemplify today's corporations. When good people do act, courageous behavior increases the effectiveness and efficiency of the organization, saving jobs, pensions, reputations and lives.

Understanding courage – its meaning and use – is essential to propagating courageous behavior throughout an organization. The meaning of courage has evolved since the Ancients and even recently is defined in various ways. Although the definitions vary, courage research has contributed to the emergence of several core components of courage (i.e. intentionality/deliberation, known risk, personal fear and noble/good purpose). Focusing on these components, then, organizations can begin to develop programs to enhance courageous behavior and create an atmosphere and culture to sustain these efforts.

Maslow (1954) was rightfully optimistic that we could 'learn enough from blunders to correct them eventually'. It is too late for Lay and Skilling, but managers of other organizations can learn from their blunders. When good people do something, they can prevent failures of courage.

Acknowledgments

The authors would like to thank Dr Frank Seitz for his comments and feedback on previous revisions of this chapter.

References

Aquinas, T. (1922), *The Summa Theologica.* Translated by the Fathers of the English Dominican Province, London: Burns, Oates, & Washbourne.

Aristotle (1987), *The Nicomachean Ethics* (J.E.C. Welldon, trans.), Amherst, NY: Prometheus Books.

Beyer, J.M. and D. Nino (1998), 'Facing the future: backing courage with wisdom', in S. Srivastva and D.L. Cooperrider (eds), *Organizational Wisdom and Executive Courage*, San Francisco, CA: New Lexington Press, pp. 65–97.

Bunkers, S.S. (2004), 'Socrates' questions: a focus for nursing', *Nursing Science Quarterly*, **17**, 212–18.

Cavanagh, G.F. and D.J. Moberg (1999), 'The virtue of courage within the organization', in M.L. Pava and P. Primeaux (eds), *Research in Ethical Issues in Organizations*, Stamford, CT: JAI Press, pp. 1–25.

Charan, R. and G. Colvin (1999), 'Why CEOs fail', *Fortune*, **139**(12), 68–75.

Clancy, T.R. (2003), 'Courage and today's nurse leader', *Nursing Administration Quarterly*, **27**, 128–32.

Conger, J.A. (1999), 'Charismatic and transformational leadership in organizations: an insider's perspective on these developing streams of research', *Leadership Quarterly*, **10**, 145–80.

Cox, D., R. Hallam, K. O'Conner and S. Rachman (1983), 'An experimental analysis of fearlessness and courage', *British Journal of Psychology*, **74**, 107–17.

Dotlich, D.L. and P.C. Cairo (2003), *Why CEOs Fail*, San Francisco, CA: Jossey-Bass.

'Enron's Lay and Skilling found guilty' (2006), *Fox News*, retrieved 25 May 2006, from www.foxnews.com.

Evans, P.D. and D.G. White (1981), 'Towards an empirical definition of courage', *Behavioral Research and Therapy*, **19**, 419–24.

Fast Company (2004), 'The courage issue', September.

Finfgeld, D.L. (1995), 'Becoming and being courageous in the chronically ill elderly', *Issues in Mental Health Nursing*, **16**, 1–11.

Finfgeld, D.L. (1998), 'Courage in middle-aged adults with long-term health concerns', *Canadian Journal of Nursing Research*, **30**, 153–69.

Finkelstein, S. (2003), *Why Smart Executives Fail*, New York: Penguin Group.

Gergen, M.M. and K.J. Gergen (1998), 'The relational rebirthing of wisdom and courage', in S. Srivastva and D.L. Cooperrider (eds), *Organizational Wisdom and Executive Courage*, San Francisco, CA: New Lexington Press, pp. 134–53.

Glazer, M.P. and P.M. Glazer (1989), *The Whistleblowers: Exposing corruption in government and industry*, New York: Basic Books.

Gole, H.G. (1997, Winter), 'Reflections on courage', *Parameters: US Army War College Quarterly*, 147–57.

Gould, N.H. (2005), 'Courage: its nature and development', *Journal of Humanistic Counseling, Education and Development*, **33**, 102–16.

Haase, J.E. (1987), 'Components of courage in chronically ill adolescents: a phenomenological study', *Advances in Nursing Science*, **9**, 64–80.

Harris, H. (2000), 'Courage as a management virtue', paper presented at the Ninth Annual Meeting of the Association for Practical and Professional Ethics, Arlington, VA.

Hogan, R. and J. Hogan (2001), 'Assessing leadership: a view from the dark side', *International Journal of Assessment and Selection*, **9**, 40–51.

Hughes, R.L., R.C. Ginnett and G.J. Curphy (2002), *Leadership: Enhancing the Lessons of Experience*, New York: McGraw-Hill.

Ivanhoe, P.J. (2002), 'The virtue of courage in the Mencius', in B. Darling-Smith (ed.), *Courage*, Notre Dame, IN: University of Notre Dame Press, pp. 65–79.

Kennedy, J.R. (1956), *Profiles in Courage*, New York: Harper & Brothers.

Kilmann, R.H., L.A. O'Hara and J.P. Strauss (2005), 'Developing and validating a quantitative measure of organizational courage', manuscript submitted for publication.

Klein, M. and R. Napier (2003), *The Courage to Act: 5 Factors of Courage to Transform Business*, Palo Alto, CA: Davies–Black Publishing.

Lomardo, M.M., M.N. Ruderman and C.D. McCauley (1988), 'Explanations of success and derailment in upper-level management positions', *Journal of Business and Psychology*, **2**, 199–216.

Lopez, S.J., K.K. O'Byrne and S. Peterson (2003), 'Profiling courage', in S.J. Lopez and C.R. Snyder (eds), *Positive Psychological Assessment: A Handbook of Models and Measures*, Washington, DC: American Psychological Association, pp. 185–97.

Maier, M. (1992), *Red Flags, Smart People, Flawed Decisions: Morton Thiokol and the NASA Space Shuttle Challenger Disaster*, Binghamton, NY: State University of New York.

Maslow, A. (1954), *Motivation and Personality*, New York: Harper.

McCain, J. and M. Salter (2004), *Why Courage Matters: The Way to a Braver Life*, New York: Random House.

McCauley, C.D. (2004), 'Successful and unsuccessful leadership', in J. Antonakis, A.T. Cianciolo and R.J. Sternberg (eds), *The Nature of Leadership*, Thousand Oaks, CA: Sage, pp. 199–221.

Meisinger, S.R. (2005), 'The four Cs of the HR profession: being competent, curious, courageous, and caring about people', *Human Resource Management*, **44**, 189–94.

Miller, W.I. (2000), *The Mystery of Courage*, Cambridge, MA: Harvard University Press.

Mumford, M.D., S.J. Zaccaro, F.D. Harding, T.O. Jacobs and E.A. Fleishman, (2000), 'Leadership skills for a changing world: solving complex social problems', *Leadership Quarterly*, **11**, 11–35.

Near, J.P. and M.P. Miceli (1996), 'Whistle-blowing: myth and reality', *Journal of Management*, **22**, 507–26.

O'Byrne, K.K., S.J. Lopez and S. Peterson (2000), 'Building a theory of courage: a precursor to change?', paper presented at the 108th Annual Convention of the American Psychological Association, Washington, DC.

O'Connor, K., R. Hallam and S. Rachman (1985), 'Fearlessness and courage: a replication experiment', *British Journal of Psychology*, **76**, 187–97.

Peterson, C. and M.E.P. Seligman (2004), *Character Strengths and Virtues: A Handbook and Classification*, Washington, DC/New York: American Psychological Association/Oxford University Press.

Philips, C. (2004), *Six Questions of Socrates*, New York: W.W. Norton & Company.

Plato (1987), *Laches* (J.H. Nichols, Jr trans.), in T.L. Pangle (ed.), *The Roots of Political Philosophy: Ten Forgotten Socratic Dialogues*, Ithaca, NY: Cornell University Press.

Putman, D. (1997), 'Psychological courage', *Philosophy, Psychiatry and Psychology*, **4**(1), 1–11.

Putman, D. (2001), 'The emotions of courage', *Journal of Social Philosophy*, **32**(4), 463–70.

Rachman, S.J. (1990), *Fear and Courage*, 2nd edn, New York: W.H. Freeman and Company.

Rate, C.R., J.A. Clarke, D.R. Lindsay and R.J. Sternberg, in press, 'Implicit theories of courage', *Journal of Positive Psychology*.

Rothschild, J. and T.D. Miethe (1999), 'Whistle-blower disclosures and management retaliation: the battle to control information about organization corruption', *Work and Occupations*, **26**, 107–28.

Shelp, E.E. (1984), 'Courage: a neglected virtue in the patient–physician relationship', *Social Science and Medicine*, **18**(4), 351–60.

Shepela, S.T., J. Cook, E. Horlitz, R. Leal, S. Luciano, E. Lutfy, C. Miller, G. Mitchell and E. Worden (1999), 'Courageous resistance: a special case of altruism', *Theory and Psychology*, **9**, 787–805.

Srivastva, S. and D. Cooperrider (eds) (1998), *Organizational Wisdom and Executive Courage*, San Francisco, CA: New Lexington Press.

Sternberg, R.J. (1985), 'Implicit theories of intelligence, creativity, and wisdom', *Journal of Personality and Social Psychology*, **49**(3), 607–27.

Sternberg, R.J. (2005), 'Foolishness', in R.J. Sternberg and J. Jordan (eds), *A Handbook of Wisdom: Psychological perspectives*, New York: Cambridge University Press, pp. 84–109.

Sternberg, R.J., B.E. Conway, J.L. Ketron and M. Bernstein (1981), 'People's conceptions of intelligence', *Journal of Personality and Social Psychology*, **41**(1), 37–55.

Szagun, G. (1992), 'Age-related changes in children's understanding of courage', *Journal of Genetic Psychology*, **153**(4), 405–20.

The Oxford English Dictionary (1989), 2nd edn, Oxford: Oxford University Press.

Van Velsor, E. and J.B. Leslie (1995), 'Why executives derail: perspectives across time and cultures', *Academy of Management Executive*, **9**, 62–72.

Walker, L.J. and K.H. Hennig (2004), 'Differing conceptions of moral exemplarity: just, brave and caring', *Journal of Personality and Social Psychology*, **86**(4), 629–47.

Wallace, J.D. (1978), *Virtues and Vice*, New York: Cornell University Press.

Walton, D.N. (1986), *Courage: A Philosophical Investigation*, Los Angeles, CA: University of California Press.

Walton, D.N. (1987), 'The virtue of courage', *The World and I*, **12**, 595–609.

Wegner, D.M. and R.R. Vallacher (1977), *Implicit Psychology: An Introduction to Social Cognition*, New York: Oxford University Press.

Woodard, C.R. (2004), 'Hardiness and the concept of courage', *Consulting Psychology Journal: Practice and Research*, **56**(3), 173–85.

Worline, M.C., A. Wrzesniewski and A. Rafaeli (2002), 'Courage and work: breaking routines to improve performance', in R. Lord, R. Klimoski and R. Kanfer (eds), *Emotions at Work*, San Francisco, CA: Jossey-Bass, pp. 295–330.

2 Personality disorders and derailment at work: the paradoxical positive influence of pathology in the workplace

Adrian Furnham

1. Introduction

There are many reasons why workplaces are dysfunctional (Farson, 1997; Finkelstein, 2003). One lies in the pathology of senior managers who create and maintain a toxic culture epitomized by mistrust, dishonesty and lack of equity (Furnham, 2004; Kets de Vries, 1999). The label 'pathology' refers to something more than incompetence, being a bully, inefficient or corrupt. It is to assert that some bosses may have personality disorders, and that it is these disorders that account for behaviour which results in a dysfunctional workplace for others. In this chapter I shall concentrate on an intra- and interpersonal psychological perspective while acknowledging that inevitably situational and organizational factors nearly always play a role in precipitating derailment. Thus whilst a manager may be perfectly effective and competent under certain conditions his or her 'pathology' may cause specific problems when work pressures rise or unusual conditions occur.

Although laypeople (and psychiatrists) think in *categorical* terms (i.e. 'he is or is not a psychopath'), psychologists think in *dimensional* terms. Thus there are degrees to which one can be accurately described as an extravert, a neurotic and indeed a psychopath. In this chapter I shall talk about those with personality disorders in type-terminology. This is partly because most people talk and think in typological rather than dimensional terms (she is tall, he is extraverted, they are neurotic). Further, the way psychiatrists think about, and measure, disorders is essentially in typological terminology where, if individuals manifest a certain number of behaviours associated with a disorder (say eight out of 12), they fulfil the criteria of caseness or labelling. However, these cut-off points are always fairly arbitrary, and an individual who has 12 out of 12 critical behaviours is a rather different person from one who manifests the required eight alone. There appears to be no research on this topic, although the criteria behaviour are given equal weight, it is likely that some are much more deleterious to psychological functioning at work than others. This will be discussed later in the chapter.

Most psychological researchers try to be parsimonious in their trait descriptions. Thus all individuals can be 'profiled' on a set number of dimensions. These profiles may then be used to identify individuals who are particularly prone to derailment, failure or dysfunctional management techniques. That is, there is often evidence of co-morbidity with specific personality disorders. It is not unusual for a person to be a 'case' on more than one dimension at the same time. Thus one could be labelled simultaneously as a narcissistic *and* histrionic personality. This is not unusual, and indeed may be expected from the fact that these disorders lie on different axes. The central point, however, is that everyone has a unique psychopathology profile and it is important to attempt to describe and explain an individual's psychological function and dysfunctioning in terms of the total profile.

Three categories or types are most commonly implicated in management derailment. They are, in order of frequency: antisocial (psychopath), narcissistic and histrionic. Machiavellianism (which is not strictly a personality disorder) has been considered as another dimension (Jakobwitz and Egan, 2006). The first three have been described as the 'dark triad' of personality (Paulus and Williams, 2006), although there is some disagreement about all dimensions. In lay terms, psychopaths are selfish, callous, superficially charming, lacking in empathy and remorseless; narcissists are attention seeking, vain, self-focused and exploitative, while Machiavellians are deceptive, manipulative and deeply self-interested.

Paradoxically, these disorders often prove to be an asset in acquiring and temporarily holding down senior management positions. The charm of the psychopath, the self-confidence of the narcissist, the clever deceptiveness of the Machiavellian and the emotional openness of the histrionic may be, in many instances, useful business traits. When candidates are physically attractive, well educated and intelligent, *and* have a 'dark triad' profile, it is not difficult to see why they are selected for senior management positions. In this sense assessors and selectors must bear part of the blame for not selecting out those who often so spectacularly derail. They do not recognize in the biography of the individual all the crucial indicators of the disorder. Alternatively the biography as portrayed in the CV may easily be a work of fiction.

This chapter asserts that it is ironic that personality disorders may serve certain individuals well in particular businesses in climbing the ladder of success. If they are bright and intelligent, their disorder profile may initially seem beneficial, even attractive, in the business environment. However, it is likely to be discovered over time and to lead to manifold types of business failure (McCall, 1998).

When thinking of a psychopath, the lay person often conceives of a dangerous mass murderer or perhaps the amazingly successful confidence trickster. Similarly, many would admire the self-confidence of the person with a narcissistic personality disorder. Further, the emotionality and showiness of the histrionic personality-disordered manager in a creative job may lead others to rate them as creative rather than disturbed. The clever deviousness of the Machiavellian may also be admired as an indication of toughness. In this sense, 'mild' forms of these pathologies could appear generally, or at specific times, which could be very advantageous.

Two recent developments in the research on personality disorders have alerted psychiatrists and psychologists to the real possibility of some senior (and junior) managers having such disorders. The first is the increasing literature on what is called the 'successful psychopath' (Hall and Benning, 2005). Indeed, their abnormal behaviours appear to be advantageous in certain settings; hence the emergence of the classification, almost oxymoronic, of the successful psychopath. Studies have been made of successful businesses and groups of individuals who have not been incarcerated or had many problems with the law despite their amoral and immoral behaviour.

The second development comes more from psychology than psychiatry, and has involved the development of measures of the personality disorder (Furnham and Crump, 2005). As noted earlier, whereas psychiatrists often favour typological classifications (one is, or is not, a . . . . according to a 'cut-off' score), psychologists prefer the dimensional approach. Thus there are degrees of disorders, which are logically related to 'normal' traits. Indeed, the *spectrum hypothesis* suggests that many personality disorders simply occur in those individuals with very high or very low particular personality-trait scores. The very 'conscientious' may manifest symptoms of obsessionality or the 'neurotic' forms of hysteria. It is understandable that an individual with a particular profile might be able to function very successfully in the business environment. Indeed, in particular environments (business sectors) at certain times (bull/bear markets) it may be particularly advantageous to have an inclination towards some personality disorder.

It is possible to conceive of unusual working environments that may almost require some of the beliefs and behaviours associated with certain of the disorders. Thus military special forces may find the callousness associated with a psychopath advantageous. Equally those in quality control or health and safety may find various obsessional checking behaviours beneficial to the job. However, it should be pointed out that these are more likely to be an exception rather than the rule.

Trait psychologists have also tried to examine the links between traits and disorders to develop a more parsimonious description of individuals (De Clercq and De Fruyt, 2003; Durrett and Trull, 2005; Hogan and Hogan, 1997; Millon, 1981; Rolland and De Fruyt, 2003; Saulsman and Page, 2004; Widiger et al., 2001, 2002). This also helps to give some psychosocial and biological explanations, as the theorizing on the origins, mechanisms and processes associated with traits probably exceeds that of the personality disorders. A great deal of the psychiatric work on disorders is about classification. There is considerably less research on both the aetiology (and prognosis) of these disorders and the behavioural mechanisms and processes that describe and explain how they function. The rapprochement between (clinical and personality) psychology and psychiatry is to be welcomed.

This chapter will first examine three personality disorders often implicated in dysfunctional workplaces. It will then examine the 'overlap' between disorders and traits. Third, it will consider how and why personality-disordered individuals come to do as well as they do at work, and how they can be both recognized (diagnosed) and helped.

2.   Personality disorders

Psychiatrists and psychologists share various assumptions with respect to personality. Both argue for the stability of personality over time. The *Diagnostic and Statistical Manual of Mental Disorders* (DSM) criteria talk of 'enduring pattern', 'inflexible and pervasive', 'stable and of long duration'. The pattern of behaviour is not a function of drug use or some other temporary medical condition. Furthermore, the personality pattern is not a manifestation or consequence of another mental disorder. Personality traits and personality disorders are stable over time and consistent across situations. Thus there should be obvious biographical clues to an individual's make-up. This perhaps explains the popularity of biodata in selection (Gunter et al., 1993).

Both psychologists and psychiatrists believe that personality factors relate to cognitive, affective and social aspects of functioning. Both disorders and traits affect how people think, feel and act. It is where a person's behaviour 'deviates, markedly' from the expectations of that individual's culture that personality disorders are manifest. 'Odd behaviour' is not simply an expression of habits, customs, or religious or political values professed or shown by people of particular cultural origin. In other words it is odd to all people within a cultural context, and that includes the curious and often bizarre world of business!

The DSMs note that personality disorders all have a long history and have an onset no later than early adulthood. There are some gender differences: thus the antisocial disorder is more likely to be diagnosed in men, whereas the borderline, histrionic and dependent personality is more likely to be found in women. Some personality disorders have symptoms similar to other disorders – anxiety, mood, psychotic, substance-related and so on – but they have unique features. The essence of the difference between normal traits and disorders is as follows: 'Personality Disorders must be distinguished from personality traits that do not reach the threshold for a Personality Disorder. Personality traits are diagnosed as a Personality Disorder only when they are inflexible, maladaptive and persisting and cause significant functional impairment or subjective distress' (American Psychiatric Association, 1994: 633). In this sense disorders can partly be seen as extreme traits. Indeed, the *spectrum* hypothesis posits that disorders are extreme traits, between one and two standard deviations from the norm (Furnham, 2006). Thus psychopaths/ antisocial individuals are extremely low on 'agreeableness' (or 'psychoticism', in Eysenck's terminology), while 'histrionic' types are extremely 'neurotic' and 'obsessive-compulsive', extremely 'conscientious'. The question, of course, is where to draw the line to distinguish an 'extreme' trait from a personality disorder. Furthermore, the range of personality disorders seems wider than that of traits, and it is clear that some disorders do not appear to be clearly related to personality trait, at least as defined by the five-factor model (Furnham and Crump, 2005).

The DSM-IV provides a clear summary:

General diagnostic criteria for a Personality Disorder
A. An enduring pattern of inner experience and behaviour that deviates markedly from the expectations of the individual's culture. This pattern is manifested in two (or more) of the following areas:
    (1) cognition (i.e. ways of perceiving and interpreting self, other people, and events)
    (2) affectivity (i.e. the range, intensity, liability, and appropriateness of emotional response)
    (3) interpersonal functioning
    (4) impulse control
B. The enduring pattern is inflexible and pervasive across a broad range of personal and social situations.
C. The enduring pattern leads to clinically significant distress or impairment in social, occupational or other important areas of functioning.
D. The pattern is stable and of long duration and its onset can be traced back at least to adolescence or early childhood.
E. The enduring pattern is not better accounted for as a manifestation or consequence of another mental disorder.
F. The enduring pattern is not due to the direct physiological effects of a substance (e.g. a drug of abuse, a medication) or a general medical condition (e.g. head trauma). (1994: 633)

There are ten or more defined and distinguishable personality disorders, some of which will be considered in due course: 'Paranoid personality disorder' is a pattern of distrust and suspiciousness such that others' motives are interpreted as malevolent. 'Schizoid personality disorder' is a pattern of detachment from social relationships and a restricted range of emotional expression. 'Schizotypal personality disorder' is a pattern of acute discomfort in close relationships, cognitive or perceptual distortions, and eccentricities of behaviour. 'Antisocial personality disorder' is a pattern of disregard for, and violation of, the rights of others. 'Borderline personality disorder' is a pattern of instability in inter-personal relationships, self-image, and affects and marked impulsivity. 'Histrionic person-ality disorder' is a pattern of excessive emotionality and attention seeking. 'Narcissistic personality disorder' is a pattern of grandiosity, need for admiration, and lack of empathy. 'Avoidant personality disorder' is a pattern of social inhibition, feelings of inadequacy, and hypersensitivity to negative evaluation. 'Dependent personality disorder' is a pattern of submissive and clinging behaviour related to an excessive need to be taken care of. 'Obsessive-compulsive personality disorder' is a pattern of preoccupation with orderliness, perfectionism and control. 'Personality disorder not otherwise specified' is a category pro-vided for two situations: (1) the individual's personality pattern meets the general criteria for personality disorder and traits of several different such disorders are present, but the criteria for any specific disorder are not met; or (2) the individual's personality pattern meets the general criteria for a personality disorder, but the individual is considered to have a disorder that is not included in the classification (e.g. passive aggressive personality dis-order). (1994: 629)

It should be noted that these personality disorders are grouped along different axes or different clusters. Three groups are usually distinguished: A (paranoid, schizoid, schizo-typal); B (antisocial, borderline, histrionic, narcissistic) and C (avoidant, dependent and obsessive-compulsive). It is those disorders in Cluster B associated with low conscien-tiousness and agreeableness that are considered in this chapter. These appear to be those most related to management dysfunction.

It should also be noted that with each different edition of the manual (DSM) there are noticeable changes. Some disorders get dropped and others emerge. This is of interest and concern to all taxonomic specialists, but need not concern us unduly here.

One of the most important ways to differentiate a particular personal *style* from per-sonality *disorder* is flexibility. There are plenty of difficult people at work but relatively few whose rigid, maladaptive behaviours mean they continually have disruptive, troubled lives. It is their inflexible, repetitive, poor stress-coping responses that are the mark of many disorders (Furnham, 2004).

Personality disorders influence the sense of self – they way people think and feel about themselves and how other people see them. The disorders often powerfully influ-ence interpersonal relations at work. They reveal themselves in how people 'complete tasks, take and/or give orders, make decisions, plan, handle external and internal demands, take or give criticism, obey rules, take and delegate responsibility, and co-operate with people' (Oldham and Morris, 1991: 24). The antisocial, narcissistic, histri-onic, obsessive-compulsive, passive-aggressive and dependent types are particularly problematic in the workplace.

People with some personality disorders have difficulty expressing and understanding emotions. It is the intensity with which they express them and their variability that makes them odd, difficult and prone to derailment. More importantly, they often have serious problems with self-control.

Experts have tried to classify the disorders in various ways, but of most relevance to this chapter is the work of researchers who have understood the impact of personality dis-orders of those at work. Without doubt major credit should go to the Hogans. Hogan and

Hogan (1997) note that a 'view from the dark side', as they call the personality disorders, gives an excellent understanding of the causes of management derailment. They argue that there are obviously many 'mad' managers in organizations, and that helping people to identify potentially bad or derailed managers can help to alleviate a great deal of suffering. They see a measure of the disorders as a useful risk audit that might reveal how managers behave under stress, and their particular and peculiar vulnerabilities.

Hogan and Hogan also note from their reading of the literature that derailment is more about having undesirable qualities than not having desirable ones. This is because those responsible for selection are more concerned with select-in, rather than select-out, criteria. That is, they really look for what they do *not* want as opposed to what they *do* want. There is frequently no mechanism for, interest in or ability to look for potential signs of derailment, including personality disorders. The business of selection can be seen in a simple 2 × 2 matrix: Select/Reject and Good/Bad. The aim is to select the good candidates and reject the bad (inappropriate, less able, etc.). However, most selection involves the 'Select Good' box by specifying what abilities, competencies, experiences and motivations managers *should* have. They are rejected if they do not have 'enough' of these or fail to reach a standard. The flaw in this very common approach is not to look specifically for characteristics that should lead to rejection, that is, to seek evidence of traits that one does not want. Thus it may be important to specify both select-in and select-out criteria, and among the select-out criteria may be evidence of personality disorders.

The research of Hogan and Hogan in the area has led them to various specific conclusions. There is substantial (between-study) agreement regarding the dysfunctional dispositions/traits associated with management incompetence and derailment. Many derailed managers (especially those with narcissistic personality disorders) have impressive skills, which is why their disorders are not spotted at selection but only later by their subordinates. Bad managers are a major cause of misbehaviour (theft, absenteeism, turnover) by staff: it is poor treatment that often makes them resentful, vengeful and disruptive.

Hogan and Hogan have always argued that it is important to take the *observer's* view of personality – that is, the descriptions of the personality disorders given by those who deal with them. Thus it is less wise to rely on self-report in interview or by questionnaire as opposed to observer reports by colleagues, subordinates and clients. The problem for much research is that it can describe what derailed and derailing managers do rather than why they do it. Although the origin (in terms of learning or biology) is not clear for the personality disorders/derailment factors, their consequences are very apparent. The most obvious one is, quite simply, the inability to learn from experience. A second crucial consequence of the disorders is that they erode trust. Thus dysfunctional managers lose the trust of all those they deal with.

This chapter will examine three specific personality disorders ranked by prevalence and power to disrupt social functioning in the workplace.

The successful psychopath

There is a small but growing literature on the successful, that is, non-institutionalized, psychopath (Widom, 1978; Widom and Newman, 1985; Ishikawa et al., 2001). They are described as carefree, aggressive, charming and impulsively irresponsible. They have the essential personality characteristics of the psychopath but seem to refrain from serious antisocial behaviour. Researchers have identified many politicians and business leaders as non-criminal psychopaths. They are duplicitous but not illegally so. They show many patterns of misconduct but seem not to get caught. They seem brilliant at tactical impression management and are drawn to unstable, chaotic, rapidly changing situations where they can operate more easily. Successful, non-incarcerated psychopaths seem to have compensatory factors that buffer them against criminal behaviour, such as higher social class and intelligence. Thus the successful psychopath has a wider set of coping mechanisms than less privileged and able psychopaths, who soon get caught.

The term psychopath or sociopath is used to describe antisocial personality types whose behaviour is amoral or asocial, impulsive and lacking in remorse and shame. Once called 'moral insanity', it is found more commonly among lower socio-economic groups, no doubt because of the 'downward drift' of these types.

Self-report measures of the psychopathic personality give a clear indication of the sort of behaviours that are relevant (Benning et al., 2005). Impulsive nonconformity (reckless, rebellious, unconventional); blame externalization (blames others, rationalizes own transgressions); Machiavellian egocentricity (interpersonally aggressive and self-centred); carefree non-planfulness (excessive present orientation with lack of forethought or planning); stress immunity (experiencing minimal anxiety); fearlessness (willing to take risks, having little concern with potentially harmful consequences) and general cold-heartedness (unsentimental, unreactive to others' distress, lacing in imagination. These seem to factor into *two* dimensions: one related to high negative emotionality and the other low behavioural constraint. Further research by Benning et al. (2005) led these authors to think about two distinct facets of the psychopath: fearless dominance (glib, grandiose, deceitful, low stress) and impulsive antisociality (aggressive, antisocial, low control). This suggests that within the psychopath population one may be able to distinguish between the two groups.

Antisocial (psychopathic) managers show a blatant and consistent disregard for, and violation of, the rights of others. They often have a history of being difficult, delinquent or dangerous. They show a failure to conform to most social norms and frequently, if not bright or privileged, get into trouble with the law for lying, stealing and cheating. They are always deceitful, as indicated by repeated use of aliases and 'conning others' for personal profit or pleasure. They can be, in short, nasty, aggressive, con artists – the sort who often get profiled on business crime programmes. They are also massively impulsive and fail to plan ahead. They live only in, and for, the present. They show irritability and aggressiveness, as indicated by repeated physical fights or assaults. They manifest a surprising reckless disregard for the physical and psychological safety of self and others – or the business in general. In an environment that values risk taking they are clearly in their element. They are famous for being consistently irresponsible. Repeated failure to sustain consistent work behaviour or to honour financial obligations is their hallmark. Most frustrating of all, they show lack of remorse. They are indifferent to or cleverly rationalize having hurt, mistreated or stolen from another. They never learn from their mistakes. It can seem as if labelling them as antisocial is a serious understatement.

In his famous book, *The Mask of Sanity*, Cleckley (1976) set out ten criteria for the 'masks' that conceal insanity: superficial charm and intelligence; absence of anxiety in stressful situations; insincerity and lack of truthfulness; lack of remorse and shame; inability to experience love or genuine emotion; unreliability and irresponsibility; impulsivity and disregard for socially acceptable behaviour; clear-headedness with an absence of delusions or irrational thinking; inability to profit from experience; and lack of insight.

The book is indeed a classic in psychology and psychiatry because of its insights. Cleckley noted the slick but callous business person, the smooth-talking and manipulative lawyer and the arrogant and deceptive politicians as examples.

Antisocial, adventurous managers are not frightened by risk; they thrive on it. They love the thrill of adventure and are happy to put others' lives at risk as well as their own. They tend to be self-confident and not overly concerned with the approval of others. They live for the moment: they are neither guilty about the past nor worried about the future. They can be seriously reckless and tend not to tolerate frustration. They resist discipline and ignore rules. They have poor self-control and think little about the consequences of their actions. They need excitement all the time and are very easily bored. They can be successful entrepreneurs, journalists, bouncers, lifeguards.

It is an interesting question to try to identify in what sorts of jobs psychopathic traits might be, at least for a time, advantageous. This may refer both to the type of job but also a particular situation, such as when an organization is changing rapidly, in decline, or under investigation. They like outwitting the system – opportunistically exploiting whom and what they can. They usually hate routine and administration, which are seen as drudgery. No wonder people who work for them feel so demoralized.

They make bad bosses and bad partners because they are egocentric and only continue in a relationship as long as it is good for them. They rarely have long-lasting, meaningful relationships. They have two human ingredients missing which are crucial to a fully functioning person: conscience and compassion. They score very low on 'agreeableness' and 'conscientiousness'. Hence they can be cruel, destructive, malicious and criminal. They are unscrupulous, and are exploitatively self-interested with little capacity for remorse. They act before they think and are famous for their extreme impulsivity.

Oldham and Morris (1991) call these types 'Adventurous'. They describe the psychopath in popular terminology which makes it easier for non-specialists to spot them:

> The following eleven traits and behaviours are clues to the presence of the Adventurous style. A person who reveals a strong Adventurous tendency will demonstrate more of these behaviours more intensely than someone with less of this style in his or her personality profile:
> 1) *Noncomformity*: men and women who have the Adventurous personality style live by their own internal code of values. They are not strongly influenced by other people or by the norms of society.
> 2) *Challenge*: to live is to dare. Adventurous types love the thrill of risk and routinely engage in high-risk activities.
> 3) *Mutual independence*: they do not worry too much about others, for they expect each human being to be responsible for him- or herself.
> 4) *Persuasiveness*: they are silver-tongued, gifted in the gentle art of winning friends and influencing people.
> 5) *Adventurers relish sex*: they have a strong sex drive and enjoy numerous, varied experiences with different partners.
> 6) *Wanderlust*: they love to keep moving. They settle down only to have the urge to pick up and go, explore, move out, move on.
> 7) *Freelance*: adventurous types avoid the nine-to-five world. They prefer to earn an independent, freelance living, do not worry about finding work, and live well by their talents, skills, ingenuity and wits.
> 8) *Open purse*: they are easy and generous with money, believing that money should be spent and that more will turn up somewhere.
> 9) *Wild oats*: in their childhood and adolescence, people with the Adventurous personality style were usually high-spirited hell-raisers and mischief makers.

10) *True grit*: they are courageous, physically bold, and tough. They will stand up to anyone who dares to take advantage of them.
11) *No regrets*: adventurers live in the present. They do not feel guilty about the past or anxious about the future. Life is meant to be experienced now. (1991: 218)

Hogan and Hogan (2001) call the antisocial person 'mischievous'. They note that these types expect that others will like them and find them charming, and they expect to be able to extract favours, promises, money and other resources from other people with relative ease. However, they see others as merely to be exploited, and therefore have problems maintaining commitments and are unconcerned about social, moral and economic expectations. They are self-confident to the point of feeling invulnerable, and have an air of daring and sang-froid that others can find attractive and even irresistible. In industries where bold risk taking is expected they can seem very desirable for senior management positions.

Their self-deception, self-confidence and recklessness lead to many conflicts, but they have almost no ability to learn from experience. According to Hogan and Hogan (1997: 49):

> They tend to be underachievers, relative to their talent and capabilities; this is due to their impulsivity, their recklessness, and their inability to learn from experience. These people handle stress and heavy work loads with great aplomb. They are easily bored, and find stress, danger and risk to be invigorating – they actively seek it. As a result, many of these people become heroes – they intervene in robberies, they rush into burning buildings, they take apart live bombs, they volunteer for dangerous assignments, and they flourish in times of war and chaos. Conversely, they adapt poorly to the requirements of structured bureaucracies.

Babiak (1995) found five characteristics in the many studies of industrial psychopathy and various case studies. He has reported case studies of individuals and described how they succeed despite their predisposition. He has noted from a series of case studies:

> Comparison of the behaviour of the three subjects observed to date revealed some similarities: each a) began by building a *network of one-to-one relationships* with powerful and useful individuals, b) *avoided virtually all group meetings* where maintaining multiple facades may have been too difficult, and c) *created conflicts* which kept co-workers from sharing information about him. Once their power bases were established, d) *co-workers who were no longer useful* were abandoned and e) *detractors were neutralised* by systematically raising doubts about their competence and loyalty. In addition, unstable cultural factors, inadequate measurement systems, and general lack of trust typical of organizations undergoing rapid, chaotic change may have provided an acceptable cover for psychopathic behaviour. (1995: 184–5, emphasis added)

It is difficult to estimate the number of successful 'industrial' psychopaths. It is also sometimes difficult to explain why they 'get away with it' for so long. However, it is no mystery when enquiring from those who work or have worked with a successful psychopath how much misery or dysfunctionality they can bring to the workplace.

Babiak and Hare (2006) believe that psychopaths are indeed attracted to today's business climate. They devised a questionnaire to help people at work spot them. There are, according to the authors, ten markers of the problem. The successful, industrial psychopath is characterized by the following. He or she:

1. Comes across as smooth, polished and charming.
2. Turns most conversations around to a discussion of him or herself.
3. Discredits and puts down others in order to build up own image and reputation.
4. Lies to co-workers, customers, or business associates with a straight face.
5. Considers people he or she has outsmarted or manipulated as dumb or stupid.
6. Is opportunistic; hates to lose, plays ruthlessly to win.
7. Comes across as cold and calculating.
8. Acts in an unethical or dishonest manner.
9. Has created a power network in the organization and uses it for personal gain.
10. Shows no regret for making decisions that negatively affect the company, shareholders, or employees.

Psychopaths can easily look like ideal leaders: smooth, polished, charming. They can quite easily mesh their dark side – bullying, amoral, manipulative. In the past it may have been politics, policing, law, media or religion that attracted psychopaths, but increasingly it is now the fast-paced, exciting, glamorous world of business.

The narcissist (arrogant, self-confident, grandiose)
There is a fine line between healthy self-esteem and serious, self-defeating, narcissism. The latter is characterized by insatiable craving for adoration, feeling a special entitlement and right to be insensitive, even cruel, to others, but at the same time being either enraged, or crushed, by criticism. Narcissists feel that they deserve special treatment but are extremely upset if they are treated like any ordinary person. They are marked by grandiosity (in fantasy or behaviour), need for admiration and lack of empathy.

Narcissists have an excessive sense of self-importance, for example exaggerated achievements and talents, and expect to be recognized as superior without commensurate achievements. Most are preoccupied with fantasies of unlimited success, power, brilliance and money. They love honours, awards and media attention. They believe that they are 'special' and unique, and can only be understood by, or should associate with, other special or high-status people (or institutions). They may try to 'buy' themselves into exclusive circles. They request, and seem to require, excessive admiration and respect from everyone at work. They also have a sense of entitlement – that is, unreasonable expectations of especially favourable treatment or automatic compliance with their manifest needs. Worse, they always take advantage of others to achieve their own ends, which makes them very poor managers.

Further, like the antisocial personality, they lack empathy. All are unwilling to recognize or identify with the feelings and needs of others. They show arrogant, haughty behaviours or attitudes all the time, both at work and at home. It is, of course, extremely difficult to work for a narcissist. Their staff have to be more attentive to the narcissist's needs than their own work tasks.

Narcissists are always super-self-confident: they express considerable self-certainty. They are indeed 'self-people': self-asserting, self-possessed, self-aggrandizing, self-preoccupied, self-loving – and ultimately self-destructive. At work they tend to be outgoing, high-energy, competitive and very 'political'. They seem to make good leaders as long as they are not criticized, or made to share any glory. They seem to have an insatiable need to be admired, loved and needed. They are often a model of ambitious, driven, high-self-esteem, self-disciplined, socially successful people.

Narcissism is paradoxically a disorder of low self-esteem. Narcissists self-destruct because their self-aggrandizement blinds their personal and business judgement and perception. At work they exploit others to get ahead, yet they demand special treatment. Thus, unless feedback is positive, it is rejected. They nearly always shoot the messenger of any sort of criticism, however justified it may be. They aim to destroy that criticism, however well intentioned and useful. They are poor empathizers and thus have low emotional intelligence. They can be consumed with envy and disdain of others, and are prone to depression. They are manipulative, demanding and self-centred; even therapists do not like them!

Hogan and Hogan (2001) call these types 'Arrogant', 'the lord of the high chair': a two-year-old, sitting in its high chair demanding food and attention, and squealing in fury when his or her needs are not met. Narcissists expect to be liked, admired, respected, attended to, praised, complimented and indulged. Their most important and obvious characteristics are a sense of entitlement, excessive self-esteem and quite often an expectation of success that often leads to real success. They expect people to be so interested in them that books will be written about them, and then, when their needs and expectations are frustrated, they explode with 'narcissistic rage'.

What is most distinctive about narcissists is their self-assurance, which often gives them a particular type of charisma. Hogan and Hogan (1997) note that they are the first to speak in a group, and they hold forth with great confidence, even when they lack knowledge and are obviously wrong. They so completely expect to succeed, and take more credit for success than is warranted or fair, that they refuse to acknowledge failure, errors or mistakes. When things go right, it is because of their efforts but when things go wrong, it is someone else's fault. This is a classic but highly adaptive attribution error. Good things emanate from inside me; bad things are from outside. This leads to some problems with truth telling because narcissists always rationalize and reinterpret their failures and mistakes, usually by blaming them on others. Unlike those with antisocial personality disorder, they do know the difference between truth and lies. But in having such a strong desire to protect their fragile self-esteem, they are prone to telling untruths.

Narcissists can be energetic, charismatic, leader-like and willing to take the initiative to get projects moving. They can be successful in management, sales and entrepreneurship. However, they are arrogant, vain, overbearing, demanding, self-deceived and pompous. They are so colourful and engaging that they often attract followers.

Narcissists can handle stress and heavy workloads with ease; they are also quite persistent under pressure and they refuse to acknowledge failure. As a result of their inability to acknowledge failure or even mistakes and the way they resist coaching and ignore negative feedback, they are unable to learn from experience.

Oldham and Morris (1991: 80) note nine characteristics of these types they call 'Self-Confident':

1. *Self-regard*: Self-Confident individuals believe in themselves and in their abilities. They have no doubt that they are unique and special and that there is a reason for their being on this planet.
2. *The red carpet*: they expect others to treat them well at all times.
3. *Self-propulsion*: Self-Confident people are open about their ambitions and achievements. They energetically and effectively sell themselves, their goals, their projects and their ideas.
4. *Politics*: they are able to take advantage of the strengths and abilities of other people in order to achieve their goals, and they are shrewd in their dealings with others.

5. *Competition*: they are able competitors, they love getting to the top, and they enjoy staying there.
6. *Dreams*: Self-Confident individuals are able to visualise themselves as the hero, the star, the best in their role, or the most accomplished in their field.
7. *Self-awareness*: these individuals have a keen awareness of their thoughts and feelings and their overall inner state of being.
8. *Poise*: people with the Self-Confident personality style accept compliments, praise and admiration gracefully and with self-possession.
9. *Sensitivity to criticism*: the Self-Confident style confers an emotional vulnerability to the negative feelings and assessments of others, which are deeply felt, although they may be handled with this style's customary grace.

The business world often calls for and rewards arrogant, self-confident, self-important people. Yet such people may seek power and then abuse it. They thrive in selling jobs and those where they have to do media work. Further, as anyone who works with and for them knows, they can destabilize and destroy working groups by their deeply inconsiderate behaviour.

The central question must be the 'cut-off' point of self-esteem. In fact narcissists are masking low self-esteem, which is the real problem. A belief in self-worth and in the integrity of the self is fundamental to mental health: too little and the person can be paralysed by inactivity; too much and they can make too hasty, poorly informed decisions.

Most narcissists devise elaborate strategies to feed their obsession. Organizations can be required to devote considerable resources to support the vainglorious vagaries of senior managers who are too involved with themselves to make good staff and organizational decisions. Even the most supportive staff and organization cannot prevent the inevitable derailment which inevitably occurs.

The histrionic (colourful, dramatic)
The term is derived from the Latin *histrio*, meaning 'actor', but the original term was 'hysterical' from Greek via the Latin *uterus*, meaning 'womb'. This disorder is found more frequently in women. Histrionics are attracted to 'limelight' jobs and strive for attention and praise, but setbacks can lead easily to serious inner doubts and depression.

Histrionics are certainly emotionally literate, but they can change very quickly. These managers have excessive emotionality and attention-seeking behaviour. They are the 'drama queens' of the business world. Most are uncomfortable in situations in which they are not the centre of attention and try always to be so. They delight in making a drama out of a crisis. Their interaction with others is often characterized by inappropriate, sexually seductive or provocative behaviour. They display rapidly shifting and shallow expression of powerful emotions. Most use physical appearance (clothes) to draw attention to self. They certainly get a reputation in their office for their 'unique apparel'. This may be acceptable in the heady world of advertising and media, but very differently viewed in the cautious, serious world of banking and manufacturers.

Many histrionics have a style of speech that is excessively impressionistic and lacking in detail. They always show self-dramatization, theatricality and exaggerated expression of emotion – usually negative. Even the dullest topic is imbued with drama. They are easily influenced by others or circumstances, and are therefore both unpredictable and persuadable. Many consider relationships to be more intimate than they actually are. Being rather dramatic, they feel humdrum working relationships more intensely than others.

Histrionics deal with stress and heavy workloads by becoming very busy, enjoying high-pressure situations in which they can be the star. Breathless with excitement, they confuse activity with productivity and evaluate themselves in terms of how many meetings they attend rather than how much they actually get done. A key feature of these people that others may not appreciate is how much they need and feed on approval, and how hard they are willing to work for it. This explains why they persist in trying to be a star after their lustre has faded. To work with them, those who report to them have to be prepared to put up with missed appointments, bad organization, rapid change of direction and indecisiveness. This will never change, although it can be planned for.

Oldham and Morris (1991) noted seven characteristics of this type, which they call 'Dramatic': a person who reveals a strong 'Dramatic' tendency will demonstrate more of these behaviours more intensely than someone who has less of this style:

1) *Feelings*: Dramatic men and women live in an emotional world. They are sensation orien-tated, emotionally demonstrative, and physically affectionate. They react emotionally to events and can shift quickly from mood to mood.
2) *Colour*: They experience life vividly and expansively. They have rich imaginations, they tell entertaining stories, and they are drawn to romance and melodrama.
3) *Spontaneity*: Dramatic individuals are lively and fun. Their joie de vivre leads them to act on impulse to take advantage of the moment.
4) *Attention*: Dramatic people like to be seen and noticed. They are often the centre of atten-tion, and they rise to the occasion when all eyes are on them.
5) *Applause*: Compliments and praise are like food and water to persons with Dramatic style: they need them to go on.
6) *Appearance*: They pay a lot of attention to grooming, and they enjoy clothes, style and fashion.
7) *Sexual attraction*: In appearance and behaviour, Dramatic individuals enjoy their sexuality. They are seductive, engaging, charming tempters and temptresses. (1991: 126–7)

Managers with histrionic personality disorders are likely to be found in the more human-resource-oriented world. They can do very well in PR, marketing and training, particularly if they are talented. But they certainly remain hard work for those who report to them.

Histrionics, naturally, do not make good managers. They get impatient with and anxious about details and routine administrative function. They are certainly highly sociable and have intense relationships. They live to win friends and influence people, and can do so by being very generous with compliments, flattery and appreciation. They hate being bored: life with them is never staid and dull. They don't like being alone.

Interestingly, the definition of themselves comes from the outside: they see themselves as others say they see them. They are outer rather than inner emotional. They therefore lack a consistent sense of who they are. They need constant reassurance and positive feed-back from others. Because their heart rules their head, they can be impulsive, impetuous and impatient. They live not in the real world but in a storybook world of fantasy and success.

At work they can be persuasive and insightful. They enjoy the world of advertising, PR, sales and marketing, but need strong back-up for things such as plans, budgets and details. At work they are volatile and are known for being moody. They can be effusive with both praise and blame. Everything is an emotional drama, and emotionally they can be both child-like and childish. They have problems maintaining relationships, which means that with colleagues and subordinates they can be capricious, irascible and totally unpredictable. At work they need to be the star, the centre of attention, or else they can feel powerless or desperately unworthy. They are not introspective. Naturally they deal with failure particularly badly.

Hogan and Hogan (2001) call these types *colourful*: they seem convinced that others will find them interesting, engaging and worth paying attention to. They are good at calling attention to themselves – they know how to make dramatic entrances and exits, they carry themselves with flair, and self-consciously pay attention to their clothes and to the way that others react to them.

Histrionics are marked by their stage presence or persona, their self-conscious and distinctive aura – they perform extremely well in interviews, in assessment centres and in other public settings:

> They are great fun to watch, but they are also quite impulsive and unpredictable; everything that makes them good at sales (and selling themselves) makes them poor managers – they are noisy, distractible, overcommitted, and love to be the centre of attention. They are not necessarily extraverted, they are just good at calling attention to themselves. At their best, they are bright, colourful, entertaining, fun, flirtatious and the life of the party. At their worst, they don't listen, they don't plan, they self-nominate and self-promote, and they ignore negative feedback. (Hogan and Hogan, 2001: 49)

Other 'types'/disorders at work

It is possible that the particular characteristics of other disordered individuals can make them attractive or at least seem competent in certain other jobs. Thus people with mild paranoid personality disorder may be quite successful in the security business. Obsessive-compulsive personalities may succeed in many health and safety jobs.

It is important to bear in mind three factors with regard to personality-disordered people at work. First, it is crucial to take into consideration other factors such as physical appearance, level of cognitive ability and social skills. The brighter and more physically attractive people are, the more likely they are to be 'forgiven' various shortcomings. There is a vast literature in social psychology on the halo (and horns) effect which shows that attractive people are always judged more advantageously than less attractive people.

Second, it is indeed rare for an individual to have one 'clean and clear' personality disorder. Individuals have a *profile*, which means from a categorial perspective they reach 'caseness' scores in more than one disorder at the same time. Similarly, if one takes the psychological or dimensional approach, it is apparent that people have rich and complex profiles. Thus an antisocial personality may have a similar score on another dimension. Therefore one has to explain particular pathological behaviour at work by understanding the full profile of the individual.

Third, biographical details remain important. The middle-class antisocial personality will no doubt manifest very different traits from the working-class personality. Education and early work experiences can influence significantly how the disorders are manifested.

For social psychologists, Machiavellianism is a belief system, while for organizational psychologists it may be an index of managerial incompetence. It is, strictly speaking, not a personality disorder, though clearly related to the antisocial personality.

Machiavellianism may lead to destruction. It refers to people who are cynical, egocentric, controlling, distrustful and manipulative. They are deeply low on agreeableness and empathy. They are supposed to epitomize the philosophy of the Italian writer who advised: never show humility; morality and ethics are for the weak; it is better to be feared than loved. They *act* so as to gain advantage. Rather than rewarding loyalty and friendship and caring about decency, fair play and honour, they concentrate only on winning.

In the world of business Machiavellians employ tactics aimed at disarming or humiliating their enemies (Greenberg and Baron, 2003). These include neglecting/'forgetting' to share important information; always striving to make others look bad and incompetent to their seniors; failing to meet their contractual obligations and spreading false rumours.

However, technically Machiavellianism is considered an attitudinal, belief or stylistic variable, not a personality trait or disorder. However, it is very apparent from the aforementioned that there is considerable overlap with personality disorders, particularly the antisocial personality.

3.   Managing the disorders and extreme traits

What assessors and selectors must do, however, is look for signs of these behaviours before offering employment. Given the propensity of certain personality types to lying, exaggeration and attribution errors, this judgement has to be made by others/observers rather than the individual themselves. In other words, the interview will not suffice to gather data though it may give certain clues.

It is a strong recommendation and requirement for certain jobs that due diligence is taken. This may mean fairly extensive background searches to ensure that the work history of the individual is fully explored. This means contacting the bosses, colleagues and report staff at the various places where the candidate has claimed to work. It certainly means interviewing many more people than the candidate gave as referees. It also means probing very carefully the veracity of many claims.

Studies on CVs have shown that most people are prone to errors of both omission and commission: they forget and invent. Many of these sins are relatively minor and may amount to little more than impression management. Yet this is likely to be very different in the case of those investigated in carefully documented case studies, particularly of the antisocial personality at work. Indeed, the antisocial manager often leaves a rich and very noticeable destructive trail.

It is costly and time-consuming to do thorough checks. But in certain jobs it is a necessity. Further, it is possible to use self-report inventories which assess 'dark-side' personality disorders and train interviewers to look specifically for the 'tell-tale' evidence of particular problem types (Hogan and Hogan, 1997).

4.   Prevention and coping

It has been asserted that, using psychiatric criteria for the diagnosis of the personality disorders, it is possible to partly explain management derailment in terms of these disorders. It seems that many of these managers are on the borderline for diagnosis but may easily be 'pushed over' the brink by a set of particular circumstances. Thus an acute business problem or chronic issues may cause a number of crises and great stresses such that these individuals' 'dark side' emerges. Thus the disorders mentioned above, as long as not extreme (on the linear scale), could be considered 'potential risks for derailment'.

There are two important practical issues. The first is how to *identify* such individuals. The second is how to *prevent* such individuals getting into positions in organizations where they can cause great damage. Individuals are unlikely to self-diagnose or seek help. Whilst this may occur for some narcissists and histrionics, it is very unlikely to be the case with psychopaths. It is, however, quite probable that peers, subordinates and clients of psychopaths come to recognize their particular behaviours.

Therefore 360-degree ratings may prove particularly useful for picking up signs of pathology. Most such questionnaires concentrate on particular competency behaviours with regard to aspects such as teamwork, communication and innovation. Some of these could easily be rewritten to include consideration of the manifestations of disorders. Thus four or five items from each of the three personality disorders highlighted above maybe included in a 360-degree rating form. If there is both great disparity between the target manager (self-report) and his/her observers, be they boss, peers or customers, and if the observer ratings agree on the negative behaviours, then the person may warrant further attention.

The sort of behaviours to look for relate to various categories, such as management style (haughty, insincere, manipulative), interpersonal relations (shallow, back-stabbing, unskilled), job focus (impatient, erratic, unreliable) and other general 'dark-side' behaviours such as lying, cheating and bullying.

It is important to try to distinguish between 'normal' and 'abnormal' times and situations. Thus if the negative, risky or dangerous behaviours only manifest themselves when the manager is under great stress (not of his/her making) and these stress episodes are not overly frequent, then it may be that with some help the situation may be recovered.

The question remains at the organizational level: what should the organization do to prevent and then manage potentially derailing senior managers? An obvious start is to attempt to assess these issues at recruitment and selection. Thus one may use a 'select-out' set of criteria. Data on these could come from standard questionnaires (Hogan and Hogan, 1997), various checklists (Saulsman and Page, 2004) or, equally useful, reference checks. Clearly not enough organizations look actively for behaviours and traits that they don't want as opposed to competencies that they do.

A second series of issues relates to the situation where a manager is already in place in an organization and appears to be derailing because of evidence of one or more personality disorders. One obvious possibility is to try some sort of counselling or therapy. There remains some debate as to how amenable personality disorders are to treatment (Babiak and Hare, 2006; Kets de Vries, 1999). It is likely that some are more amenable to treatment than others (i.e. obsession versus psychopath), and that much depends on the nature of the treatment.

Another possibility is to try to limit or control the situations where 'risk-prone' managers are less likely to manifest problems or where they are less 'tempted' or provoked into inappropriate behaviour. This may mean trying to reduce their stress or moving them to jobs where they have fewer problems. Inevitably this suggests a ceiling beyond which they should probably not rise.

Another approach which appears to be advocated by Oldham and Morris (1991) is to educate those around these (correctly diagnosed) individuals to ensure than they understand and control rather than provoke and exacerbate this condition. This could also mean looking out for classic behaviours. Thus Babiak and Hare (2000) suggest that there is a common pattern when psychopaths join a company. They charm at assessment and through their honeymoon period. Soon they become manipulative and disparaging to others, and engage in flagrant-image enhancement. Then they confront by trying to neutralize enemies and abandoning those of little use to them. Finally, if successful, they tend to abandon their patrons as they move ever upward and onward. To be alerted to the possibility of this pattern may help to identify psychopaths before it is too late.

5.   Conclusion

As McCall (1998) points out, when talented people are promoted in organizations, their obvious abilities and strengths often mean that selectors ignore or downplay weaknesses and problems which return to haunt them in the form of the derailed senior manager.

This chapter has concentrated on three personality disorders and how 'successful' psychopathic, narcissists and histrionics behave at work. Many people assume that these pathological disorders will easily be diagnosed and that it is virtually impossible for such individuals to rise to important positions in business. That is simply not true, and there is increasing evidence that well-known and initially respected politicians, religious leaders, lawyers and business people turn out to be clearly diagnosable as having a disorder.

Further, this chapter asserts that, paradoxically perhaps, all three personality disorders discussed above may indeed help people in many business settings. The willingness to take risks on the part of the psychopath, the confidence of the narcissist and the emotional independence of the histrionic may make them particularly attractive for certain people in certain businesses.

The data on the prognosis for personality disorders are not hopeful. They are unlikely to be changed much, although they can be managed. There is no very clear cut-off point on the spectrum of these three disorders. People may be on the borderline and in the 'dangerous area', which clearly makes them less of a risk than if they were at the extreme of the spectrum.

The intelligent, educated, middle-class individual with one (or more) of these disorders no doubt fares better. They can even be seen as an asset at certain times in the business cycle. But over the long term they are likely to reap problems for themselves, their direct reports, their colleagues and their company. They can, as individuals, turn the happy efficient and functional workplace into one where people distrust each other, sabotage work and underperform. As powerful individuals they can often be seen as the root cause of the shift from a functional to a dysfunctional workplace.

References

American Psychiatric Association (1994), *Diagnostic and Statistical Manual of Mental Disorders*, 4th edn (DSM-IV), Washington, DC: American Psychiatric Association.
Babiak, P. (1995), 'When psychopaths go to work: a case study of an industrial psychopath', *Applied Psychology*, **44**, 171–88.
Babiak, P. and Hare, R. (2006), *Snakes in Suits*, New York: Regan Books.
Benning, S., Patrick, C., Bloniger, D., Hicks, B. and Iacono, W. (2005), 'Estimating facets of psychopathy from normal personality traits', *Assessment*, **12**, 3–18.
Cleckley, H. (1976), *The Mask of Sanity*, St Louis, MO: Mosley.
De Clercq, B. and De Fruyt, F. (2003), 'Personality disorder symptoms in adolescence: a five-factor model perspective', *Journal of Personality Disorders*, **17**, 269–92.
Durrett, C. and Trull, T. (2005), 'An evaluation of evaluative personality terms', *Psychological Assessment*, **17**, 359–68.
Farson, R. (1997), *Management of the Absurd*, New York: Touchstone.
Finkelstein, S. (2003), *Why Smart Executives Fail*, New York: Portfolio.

Furnham, A. (2004), *The Incompetent Manager*, London: Whurr.

Furnham, A. (2006), 'Personality disorders and intelligence', *Journal of Individual Differences*, **26**, 42–6.

Furnham, A. and Crump, J. (2005), 'Personality traits, types and disorders', *European Journal of Personality*, **19**, 167–84.

Greenberg, J. and Baron, R. (2003), *Behaviour in Organisations*, London: Pearson.

Gunter, B., Furnham, A. and Drakeley, R. (1993), *Biodata*, London: Methuen.

Hall, J. and Benning, S. (2005), 'The "successful" psychopath. Adaptive and subclinical manifestation of psychopathy in the general population', in C.J. Patrick (ed.), *A Handbook of Psychopathy*, New York: Guildford, pp. 459–78.

Hogan, R. and Hogan, J. (1997), *Hogan Development Survey Manual*, Tulsa, OK: Hogan Assessment Centres.

Hogan, R. and Hogan, J. (2001), 'Assessing leadership: a view from the dark side', *International Journal of Selection and Assessment*, **9**, 40–51

Ishikawa, S., Raine, A., Lenez, T., Bihrli, S. and Lacasse, L. (2001), 'Autonomic stress reactivity and executive functions in successful and unsuccessful criminal psychopaths from the community', *Journal of Abnormal Psychology*, **110**, 423–32.

Jakobwitz, S. and Egan, V. (2006), 'The dark triad and normal personality traits', *Personality and Individual Differences*, **40**, 331–9.

Kets de Vries, M. (1999), 'Managing puzzling personalities', *European Management Journal*, **17**, 8–19.

McCall, M. (1998), *High Flyers*, Boston, MA: Harvard University Press.

Miller, T. (1991), 'The psychotherapeutic utility of the five factor personality', *Journal of Personality Assessment*, **57**, 415–33.

Millon, T. (1981), *Disorders of Personality DSM-III: Axis II*, New York: John Wiley & Sons.

Oldham, J. and Morris, L. (1991), *The New Personality Self-Portrait*, New York: Banham.

Paulus, D. and Williams, K. (2002), 'The dark triad of personality', *Journal of Research in Personality*, **36**, 556–63.

Rolland, J.-P. and De Fruyt, F. (2003), 'The validity of FFM personality dimensions and maladaptive traits to predict negative affect at work', *European Journal of Personality*, **17**, 101–21.

Saulsman, L. and Page, A. (2004). 'The five factor model and personality disorder empirical literature: a meta-analytic review', *Clinical Psychology Review*, **23**, 1055–85.

Widiger, T.A., Costa, P.T. and McCrae, R.R. (2001), 'Proposals for Axis II: Diagnosing personality disorders using the five factor model', in P.T. Costa and T.A. Widiger (eds), *Personality Disorders and the Five Factor Model of Personality*, 2nd edn, Washington, DC: American Psychological Association, pp. 432–56.

Widiger, R.A., Trull, T.J., Clarkin, J.F., Sanderson, C. and Costa, P.T. (2002), 'A description of the DSM-IV personality disorders with the five-factor model of personality', in P.T. Costa and T.A. Widiger (eds), *Personality Disorders and the Five Factor Model of Personality*, 2nd edn, Washington, DC: American Psychological Association, pp. 89–99.

Widom, C.S. (1978), 'A methodology for studying non-institutionalised psychopaths', in R.D. Hare and D. Schalling (eds), *Psychopathic Behaviour: Approaches to Research* Chichester, UK: John Wiley & Sons, pp. 71–84.

Widom, C.S. and Newman, J.P. (1985), 'Characteristics of non-institutionalised psychopaths', in J. Gunn and D. Farrington (eds), *Current Research in Forensic Psychiatry and Psychology*, Vol. 2, New York: John Wiley & Sons, pp. 57–80.

3 Problems of employees with personality disorders: the exemplar of obsessive-compulsive personality disorder (OCPD)

Michael Kyrios, Maja Nedeljkovic, Richard Moulding and Guy Doron

1. Personality disorders and the exemplar of obsessive-compulsive personality disorder

Personality disorders involve longstanding, persistent and maladaptive ways of functioning that are associated with impairment in intrapersonal, social, occupational and academic functioning. Personality disorders are considered to have an onset in early adulthood, although most difficulties can be seen as traits from childhood. The diagnostic heading of personality disorder embraces a wide variety of presentations, with recognized diagnoses including dependent, histrionic, narcissistic, antisocial, schizoid, avoidant, borderline, paranoid, and obsessive-compulsive personality disorder.

This chapter will focus on obsessive-compulsive personality disorder (OCPD) as an exemplar of a personality disorder that represents a common problem affecting workplace performance. OCPD is a chronic and maladaptive pattern associated with excessive rigidity, preoccupation with perfection, overly stringent personal and moral standards, inflated concern about matters of control and order, extremes in emotional control and constriction, interpersonal reticence, and indecisiveness that affect all domains of an individual's life (Pfohl and Blum, 1991). The fourth edition of the *Diagnostic and Statistical Manual of Mental Disorders* (DSM-IV; American Psychiatric Association, 2000) lists eight personality traits that characterize OCPD: rigidity, perfectionism, hypermorality, overattention to detail, miserliness, an inability to discard worn or useless items, excessive devotion to work, and an inability to delegate tasks. Such characteristics can exert a negative influence on work performance, both in terms of the affected individual's capacity to work effectively and the quality of their relationships with co-workers. These issues can lead to significant challenges for individuals affected by OCPD, their co-workers and management, and a broad understanding of the condition is required in order to utilize effective strategies to maximize workplace performance. Many of the characteristics associated with OCPD, in milder degrees, may represent significant strengths for affected individuals and are often encouraged by the organizations in which they work (e.g. perfectionism, attention to detail, devotion to work). However, the disruptive effects of extremes in such characteristics support the need for furthering our understanding of OCPD within organizations, not only to help affected individuals, but also to maximize the performance of the organization and all its employees.

OCPD is one of the common personality disorders, affecting around 1–2 per cent of the population (Samuels et al., 2002; Torgersen et al., 2001), although prevalence rates of 8 per cent were reported in a recent large epidemiological study from the USA (Grant et al., 2004). OCPD has been noted more commonly in males and in married and working individuals (Nestadt et al., 1991). According to the American Psychiatric Association (APA, 2000),

OCPD accounts for up to 10 per cent of cases that present in clinical practice, and constitutes a major hurdle to successful treatment of clinical syndromes.

OCPD is not to be confused with obsessive-compulsive disorder (OCD), and numerous recent papers focus on the distinction between the two disorders (Eisen et al., 2006). For example, Black et al. (1993) concluded that the data do not support a specific relationship between OCPD and OCD, although there are similarities in their associated characteristics, particularly in the domains of perfectionism and the need for control. More recently, Eisen et al. (2006) examined the convergence between OCPD criteria and OCD using data from the Longitudinal Personality Disorders Study. They found that hoarding, perfectionism and preoccupation with details (i.e. three of eight OCPD criteria) were significantly more frequent in subjects with OCD than in subjects without OCD. Moreover, the relationship between OCD and these three OCPD criteria showed unique association relative to other anxiety disorders and major depressive disorder. Thus, although OCPD as a diagnostic classification may not be uniquely associated with OCD, certain features of OCPD are associated with OCD.

Millon (1996) differentiates eight characteristic patterns of individuals with OCPD: (a) a tendency for affected individuals to be highly regulated in their expressiveness and appearance (e.g. they appear tense and constrained, and have a serious demeanour), which hides an inner insecurity, ambivalence about most things, fear of disapproval and intense feelings of anger; (b) an interpersonal manner characterized by formality, social correctness, a high degree of outer respect for those in authority, and a highly developed sense of morality; (c) a highly regulated and rigid adherence to hierarchies, conventional rules and schedules; (d) adherence to a self-image typified by an inflated sense of personal responsibility and self-discipline, dedication to perfection and productivity and a reticence to participate in recreational activities; (e) defensiveness against the conscious experience of socially unacceptable intrusions (e.g. thoughts, images, impulses); (f) discomfort with negative emotional responses such as defiance, rebelliousness, resentment and anger, and the activation of a wide range of defences to control such emotions; (g) a compartmentalized morphological organization which tolerates little interaction between drive, memory and cognition (e.g. rigid compartmentalization of one's inner world to avoid the spilling over into consciousness of ambivalent images, feelings and attitudes); and (h) an overly sensitive or anhedonic temperament that could be constitutionally based. Such patterns fall on a continuum ranging from normal and adaptive through to pathological and maladaptive, although contextual factors define what constitutes dysfunction (Pollak, 1987).

Numerous OCPD subtypes have been identified which may present different challenges and may require differential management strategies. Millon (1996) discusses five adult subtypes: (a) the conscientious subtype who is generally willing to conform to rules and authority because of a fear of rejection or failure; (b) the puritanical subtype who is characteristically strict and punitive, highly controlled, self-righteous and extremely judgemental; (c) the bureaucratic subtype who is traditional and values formality, and who has a powerful identification with bureaucracy, which provides a set of rules, regulations and firm boundaries to contain feared inner impulses; (d) the parsimonious subtype who protects against the prospect that others might recognize the inner emptiness that they experience, and who is identifiable by a meanness and defensiveness against loss; (e) the bedevilled subtype who experiences discord, as their need to conform with the wishes of others clashes with a yearning to assert their own interests, leading to chronic feelings of resentment and conflict. While the identification of these subtypes may be useful, research has yet to establish their validity, the need for idiosyncratic interventions, or even their distinctive etiologies. Nonetheless, the profile of characteristics associated with each subtype may require that consideration is given to the placement of affected individuals within the workplace.

2.   Etiology of OCPD

Living and working with an individual affected by OCPD can be perplexing, especially if one has no overview of the factors associated with the etiology of the condition. Kyrios (1998) identified a range of etiological factors, including ethologically important instincts, biological dispositions and temperament; life experiences at strategic developmental stages; and dysfunctional schemas about oneself, others and the world. In particular, early attachments were conceptualized as leading to the development of at least five significant and interrelated core cognitive domains that contain various polarities of beliefs and hold strong affective associations. These domains involve beliefs about (a) self-worth and defectiveness; (b) the capacity to trust oneself and others; (c) the sense of control over oneself and the external environment; (d) the acquisition of specific roles that define one's identity; and (e) the specific role that adherence to ethical, religious or moral codes can play in the OCPD individual's sense of self. Basic trust in the world and others enables individuals to explore their environment, thereby facilitating the development of a sense of self-control and control over the external environment (Bowlby, 1973; Kyrios, 1998). Exploration in a safe environment also enables the individual to learn to deal effectively with increasing degrees of difficulty, complexity and uncertainty in the world (Bowlby, 1988). For instance, research suggests that securely attached children are more likely to explore their environment, facilitating the development of cognitive and social skills (Cassidy et al., 1996; Jacobsen and Hofmann, 1997; Verschueren and Marcoen, 1999). However, in the case of individuals with OCPD, basic emotional needs are not satisfied by their early experiences, thereby hampering the internalization of a sense of security and reliance on the self and the external world (Bowlby, 1973, 1988).

Such internal conflicts have a longstanding influence on individuals with OCPD. Within the workplace, conflicted individuals tend to underperform, and can also exert a negative influence on colleagues and the broader organization. Such individuals are rarely identified by standard assessment procedures, due to limitations associated with specific measures. Furthermore, many of the characteristics associated with OCPD are considered 'desirable' by some organizations (e.g. perfectionism, overly high moral concerns, overattention to detail). Often, it is only after employment has begun that problems begin to emerge due to the effects of the OCPD. The following section examines the assessment of OCPD, before we go on to discuss the detrimental effects of OCPD in more detail.

3.   Assessment of OCPD

The assessment of OCPD is complicated by issues relating to the distinction between personality and personality disorder. While numerous psychometrically satisfactory personality measures have been developed, these have mostly used a dimensional approach to conceptualization. This can be distinguished from the categorical approach traditionally seen in the assessment of personality disorder, which is limited by problems of reliability and validity. The relationship between dimensional and categorical approaches is not clear in the case of OCPD, and there may be differences in the nature of their relationships to outcomes in the workplace.

Most recent research on the influence of personality in the workplace has been conducted using the dimensional five-factor model (FFM; Costa and McCrae, 1992) of personality (openness, extraversion, neuroticism, conscientiousness and agreeableness). The FFM was initially developed to describe variation in the normal range of personality, but also accounts for considerable variance in personality pathology (Costa and Widiger, 2002). With respect to the workplace, a recent study found that agreeableness exhibited a direct relationship with interpersonal counterproductive work behaviours, whereas conscientiousness was directly associated with organizational counterproductive work behaviours, and job satisfaction was associated with both personality dimensions (Mount et al., 2006). A meta-analysis also found that agreeableness and conscientiousness were associated with job performance within teams (Peeters et al., 2006). Interestingly, OCPD has been associated with low agreeableness and high conscientiousness, as well as low extraversion and high neuroticism (de Fruyt et al., 2006). However, de Fruyt et al. (2006) reported that the FFM predicted far less of the variance in OCPD than personality measures based on Cloninger's (1987) psychobiological model (8 per cent versus 49 per cent, respectively). This supports the limited utility of more recent dimensional research using the FFM in the workplace with respect to understanding the effects of OCPD.

Measures of personality specifically designed to assess the pathological end of the spectrum may be more useful in the assessment of OCPD. Diagnostic interviews, such as the Structured Clinical Interview for DSM-IV Axis II Personality disorders (First et al., 1994), constitute the gold standard for the assessment of OCPD. However, while many questionnaire measures are useful in screening for personality disorder (e.g. the Symptom Check List [SCL-90-R]; Derogatis, 1983), the results of screening need to be verified with structured interviews to avoid the possibility of false negatives and false positives (Starcevic et al., 2000). Even well-validated self-report questionnaires such as the Minnesota Multiphasic Personality Inventory have been found to have questionable efficacy in distinguishing individuals with OCPD from others, even in inpatient units (Schotte et al., 1991). The various versions of the Personality Diagnostic Questionnaire (PDQ; Hyler et al., 1983; Hyler and Rieder, 1987; Hyler, 1994) have also demonstrated low agreement with structured interviews and overdiagnosed personality disorder (Fossati et al., 1998). Moreover, the OCPD scale from the most recent version of the PDQ (Hyler, 1994) demonstrated poor internal consistency, poor convergent validity, produced more false positives than false negatives, and showed relatively poor discriminant validity (Fossati et al., 1998). Furthermore, different measures of OCPD do not necessarily converge and may in fact assess different components of this personality syndrome (McCann, 1992). Such findings point to definitional variations, heterogeneity within the disorder, and differing symptomatic foci among the range of OCPD questionnaire measures.

In the absence of structured clinical interviews, such clinically based questionnaire measures are limited in their capacity to identify individuals with OCPD. However, measures that focus on normal personality traits, used more commonly in workplace contexts, are also ineffective in identifying at-risk individuals. Hence the assessment of OCPD within the workplace requires further research. The limitations of current assessments may explain why workplaces are slow to identify individuals with OCPD, and that some time passes before it becomes apparent that affected individuals impede organizational performance. Nonetheless, despite the limitations of existing assessment measures, the detrimental effects of OCPD are well documented. The following sections examine the general and specific workplace effects of OCPD.

4. General effects of OCPD

Individuals with OCPD present with a range of general difficulties, including increased disability across important life domains as well as an increased likelihood of specific psychological disorders. For instance, data from the Collaborative Longitudinal Personality Disorder Study (CLPDS; McGlashan et al., 2000) found that 75 per cent of individuals suffering from OCPD also suffered from major depressive disorder at some point in their lives. While recent evidence suggests that OCPD is associated with lesser degrees of disability than other personality disorders, in one study 90 per cent of individuals with OCPD were still found to have moderate or severe impairment in at least one area of functioning (Skodol et al., 2002). Furthermore, OCPD was associated with as much disability as major depression in areas relating to work and study.

Individuals with OCPD may present with a range of other psychological difficulties, including anxiety disorders, mood disorders, adjustment problems (particularly during stressful periods), physical symptoms, and somatoform disorders such as hypochondriasis. For instance, data from the CLPDS (McGlashan et al., 2000) suggest that more than 20 per cent of individuals diagnosed with OCPD reported symptoms consistent with general anxiety disorder (GAD) or OCD. With regard to substance abuse, the findings have been somewhat inconsistent. Nestadt et al. (1992) reported a decreased risk for alcohol abuse in a community study of OCPD, while Romach et al. (1995) reported that 45 per cent of chronic users of prescribed anxiolytics were diagnosed with a personality disorder, with 22 per cent diagnosed with OCPD specifically. Data from the CLPDS (McGlashan et al., 2000) found that around 29 per cent of individuals presenting with OCPD answered criteria for alcohol dependence or abuse and 25 per cent reported past or current drug dependence or abuse.

Intrapersonal and interpersonal difficulties are common among individuals with OCPD. For instance, affected individuals rarely experience a sense of security either internally or externally. Early life experiences that have linked mistakes and infringement of moral codes with parental rejection result in uncertainty about self-worth and fears about errors and imperfections (Guidano and Liotti, 1983; Millon, 1996). This results in inflexible adherence to ethical, religious or moral codes, and repeated attempts to prove one's worth by avoiding 'failure' and achieving 'perfection' (Beck and Freeman, 1990; Guidano and Liotti, 1983). The resulting perfectionism and intolerance for uncertainty increases vulnerability to a range of psychopathology (Flett and Hewitt, 2002; Tolin et al., 2003).

Individuals with OCPD are particularly challenged by the external world. They have a strong need to control their social and physical environment, and find it hard to trust others as they perceive them as irresponsible and incompetent (Beck and Freeman, 1990; Millon, 1996). Hostility towards others develops from an assumed coercion to accept the standards imposed by others, an assumption that is derived from their early experiences of constraint and discipline when they contravened parental rules (Millon and Davis, 1996). Fear of social disapproval evolves from such other-directedness and an assumption of rejection following any possible infringement of strict and restrictive moral codes. Hence, in order to resolve their ambivalence towards others, individuals with OCPD are likely to become preoccupied with socially prescribed perfectionism, self-control, social order, rules and regulations. As individuals with OCPD come to recognize that others do not share their own high standards and moral codes, they experience internal conflict between hostility towards others and a fear of social disapproval (Millon, 1996). Their perception of 'unsatisfactory' performance by others also results in feelings of frustration and anger, increased feelings of personal responsibility and the need to control the environment and themselves. However, individuals with OCPD also fear revealing their internalized hostility. They experience a fear that these feelings may spiral out of control and reveal their imperfections, resulting in their rejection by others (Millon, 1981). This internal struggle results in further attempts for control, rigidity of behaviour and affective restriction (McWilliams, 1994).

Individuals with OCPD compartmentalize many aspects of their lives (Millon, 1996). They rigidly allocate times for every task. In their attempts to maintain control they disregard their own emotional reactions to events and suppress memories. Such efforts for emotional and cognitive control result in lack of self-knowledge and difficulties with regulating their emotions. They may manage to avoid thinking about specific issues (e.g. relationships) during weekdays, which may be dedicated solely to work; however, they may consistently ruminate about these topics during weekends or at vacation times. Total absorption in the task at hand may result in a lashing out at any disturbance. In some cases, such compartmentalization may lead to extreme feelings of detachment from oneself, difficulties recalling recent important life events and a continuous sense of never 'feeling emotion' or 'being in the world'.

Individuals with OCPD show an excessive, dysfunctional devotion to achievement, activities of mastery, and work. Their basic insecurity, fear of exploration and intolerance for uncertainty hinders the development of a range of social roles. Rather than having several social roles, individuals with OCPD over-invest in socially sanctioned, structured social roles such as job competence. As a result of this excessive reliance on one social role, they become anxious, and overwhelmed by small changes in their work environment. They try to maintain control through excessive attention to detail, regulations and procedures. Again, their perfectionism and lack of trust in others results in a reluctance to delegate tasks. They may reject reactive solutions and assistance from others due to their mistrust and fear of novelty.

5. Workplace effects of OCPD

At a general level, many of the traits associated with OCPD are socially accepted and adaptive. For example, an individual with OCPD traits may present as a motivated and diligent worker, and be valued within the workplace. Research has suggested that OCPD traits, such as a dedication to work, perfectionism, adherence to rules, and avoidance of conflict, may be perceived as a boon to organizations. Furnham and Petrides (2006) used a vignette methodology to examine the influence of gender, ability, motivation and experience on perceived suitability of candidates for promotion. They found that work motivation was the most important of these variables for selection. Furnham (2002) investigated individuals' ratings of desired characteristics in a range of co-workers. Findings suggested that individuals most desired in organizations present as dedicated to their work, do not show obvious flaws, and are highly motivated.

By definition, however, OCPD refers to a personality disorder characterized by significant disruption and difficulty to the individual's life. In the workplace, OCPD may have a variety of negative effects. For the individual, it may present in a variety of forms, most notably perfectionism when conducting tasks, which in turn can be associated with workaholism or, conversely, procrastination and avoidance of tasks because of the high personal cost associated with attempts to maintain perceived 'perfection'. At an intrapersonal level, the general effects of OCPD transfer to the workplace; thus the individual may be at risk of depression and anger, and have a variety of personal issues such as feelings of defectiveness or a greater need for control. Such effects also manifest within interpersonal contact, for example relationships with work colleagues, behaviours within meetings and the ability to delegate tasks. Finally, other difficulties may be present, such as a lack of organization or over-organization, and possibly hoarding of items. Research relevant to these issues is detailed in the following sections.

Engagement in work tasks
The phenomenology of OCPD, involving perfectionism, rigidity, interpersonal control and orderliness, is similar to the characterization of individuals who are 'workaholics'. Porter (1996) suggested that workaholism is akin to an addiction, characterized by an excess of work hours to the exclusion of other roles; identity issues leading to the salience of work to bolster self-esteem; rigidity in thinking and perfectionism, high need for control and difficulty delegating to others. Little research has directly examined the relationship between OCPD and workaholism. Mudrack (2004), however, conducted a study that examined the relationship between job involvement, OCPD traits and workaholic behavioural tendencies. In this study, OCPD was operationalized as a multidimensional concept derived from psychodynamic research, with subcomponents consisting of obstinacy, orderliness, parsimony, perseverance, rigidity and superego involvement (morality), similar to Kyrios's (1998) contention that morality, control and trust are important in OCPD. Mudrack found that engaging in non-required work was related to an interaction between high work involvement coupled with high superego, and to high work involvement coupled with high obstinacy. Mudrack suggested that workaholism may function differently for these two patterns: in the case of high superego, individuals may use work to assuage feelings of guilt, whereas those with high obstinacy may be preoccupied with precision and order at work. Thus individuals who demonstrate difficulties with self-issues (worth/defectiveness, morality) and control can manifest in overcommitment to work activities.

Such workaholic tendencies have been associated with negative outcomes (e.g. burnout and stress), an important work management issue particularly for workplaces with high staff turnover or high staff training costs. Porter (2001) noted a division between positive and negative workaholism, where the former is due to enjoyment and fulfilment in work activity, and the latter due to the need to work in a compulsive, perfectionistic fashion. The latter category is relevant to OCPD, in its similarity to phenomenological descriptions of OCPD traits (Kyrios, 1998; APA, 2000). It has been suggested that this perfectionistic workaholism is associated with sensitivity to criticism and a tendency to judge oneself against elevated standards that ensure failure (Robinson, 1998). Such failures result in anger towards others that is used to justify low cooperation and communication with them.

Evidence has also supported the association between personality difficulties and vulnerability to burnout at work. In their review, Maslach et al. (2001) identified six aspects of person–environment fit that may relate to job burnout. They suggest that mismatches in workload, perceived control, perceived reward, community, fairness and values may contribute to the exhaustion, distancing and inefficacy dimensions of job stress. Such aspects are intimately related to the phenomenology of the individual with OCPD. In particular, if affected individuals experience an overload of work commitments, they are likely to exhaust their resources and ability to function. Similarly, if they feel they are responsible for producing results that they are not able to meet, they may experience burnout due to feelings of inefficacy. Those individuals with high moral values may experience burnout due to the conflict between the values of the workplace and their own values, which is especially pertinent to OCPD individuals' attempts to hide discord and personal flaws.

While some individuals with OCPD may react to their need for control through greater engagement in work tasks, others may react to perfectionism with the opposite tendency. For example, Flett et al. (1995) have suggested that procrastination is a response to a form of social evaluation that involves the perceived imposition of unrealistic expectations on the self. Flett et al. (2004) suggest that such procrastination is related to strong fear of failure due to perfectionistic standards. This fear of failure is either associated with, or a byproduct of, feelings of personal inferiority, inefficacy and low self-acceptance. While self-oriented perfectionism is associated with procrastination, socially prescribed perfectionism shows a more robust relationship, reflecting introjected beliefs regarding standards that others require one to meet. Flett and colleagues suggest that this relationship is mediated by automatic cognitions regarding perfectionism, stemming from schemas that the self should be ideal; this conception is similar to conceptions of OCPD as inflexibly adhering to ethical or moral codes with repeated attempts to prove self-worth through achieving 'perfection' and avoiding 'failure' (Guidano and Liotti, 1983). In an organizational setting, such avoidant tendencies would serve to place the individual in a high-stress position familiar to any student completing assignments, whereby the impending deadline for tasks serves to pressure the individual. Clinical descriptions of individuals with perfectionism or OCPD note that such individuals may never complete their assigned tasks. Such failure to perform tasks would further the lack of trust by the organization in the individual and feed into the affected individual's mistrust of others.

Workplace relationships
An important characteristic of personality disorders is their destructive effects on social relationships. Many personality disorders, by definition, are primarily concerned with social disruption, for example the extreme reaction of those with borderline personality disorder in response to perceived threats to attachment relationships. As noted previously, individuals with OCPD are characterized as having a higher need for control over themselves and the environment; perceptions of socially prescribed perfectionism; lack of trust and belief in others; rigidity in roles; and inflexible adherence to morality. All such beliefs interfere with relationships in general, and certainly translate to the work environment. Indeed, perfectionism and OCPD may have their greatest disruptive effects on the social fabric of the workplace. For example, Porter (1996) suggests that workaholic tendencies can be especially problematic if the individual is in a position of power. The individual

may set impossible standards for their workers, which gives the impression to the individual's superiors that they are striving for excellence, while leading to failure for their subordinates, who are then blamed for the failure. This tendency follows the individual's need for control, and may lead to frustration in co-workers. Porter also notes that if the individual does not trust others, then, through mutual interactions, the individual becomes seen as less trustworthy themselves. In most business organizations, this would have obvious impact on the ability of the group of workers to work cohesively towards shared goals. Porter (2001) found that workaholic individuals questioned the value of other individuals as people, not just as co-workers. Such an attitude would further exacerbate organizational mistrust and conflict.

From Maslach et al.'s (2001) conceptualization of variables affecting person–environment fit, social disruption is predominantly related to violations of community, rewards and fairness. In particular, these authors suggest that individuals who do not have a positive connection to others in the workplace are prone to burnout. If the individual fails to build positive relationships with others, they are likely to experience a lack of social support and sharing of positive emotion. As noted above, the difficult relationships between individuals with OCPD and their colleagues render them vulnerable to such burnout patterns. Further, if they view others as untrustworthy or incompetent, stemming from internal schemas of others, they may feel that there exists unfairness or mismatch of rewards within the workplace, contributing to their feelings of inefficacy. In particular, if the individual fails to achieve promotion due to the disruptive effects of OCPD, they may feel unjustly passed over for their 'more incompetent colleagues'. The resulting feelings of inefficacy are particularly problematic as individuals with OCPD also have a high need for control.

The schemas of individuals with OCPD will also probably hamper workplace effectiveness. For example, due to rigidity and perfectionism, it would be difficult and anxiety-provoking for the individual with OCPD to adapt within quickly changing environments, such as fast-paced workplaces, aspects of work that involve on-the-spot reactions (e.g. workplace meetings), or even periods of organizational restructuring. Beliefs relating to OCPD may also lead to difficulties in effectively delegating tasks. The individual may strive to maintain control over their work, or alternatively over their subordinates and colleagues, thus disrupting the ability of a workplace team to work together to maximize effectiveness. As noted above, the individual with OCPD may also be prone to unrealistic expectations of their employers or subordinates.

General organization

The individual experiencing OCPD may be relatively unable to plan and organize activities effectively. Individuals with extreme OCPD traits attempt to assert complete control over their lives or environment. Such attempts are doomed to failure, leading some individuals to become overwhelmed and less organized in their endeavours. Individuals with OCPD also focus on particular areas of their lives, leading to general neglect of others. They may overly focus on areas of workload in which they feel a degree of control or to which they particularly relate (e.g. tasks requiring attention to detail, solo tasks) to the detriment of tasks requiring creativity, flexibility and group interaction. In the workplace, this may lead to difficulty in effectively organizing time, tasks or the physical workplace, leading ultimately to a lack of effectiveness, which could combine with other difficulties such as an inability to delegate.

Finally, OCPD is associated with hoarding behaviours or the failure to discard items (Kyrios et al., 2002). In the workplace, the individual may demonstrate acquisition of, and failure to discard, items and knowledge, in order to fulfil a high need for control. Again, this would hamper the effective fulfilment of job requirements. Furthermore, hoarding of work documents will ultimately be associated with high degrees of clutter and disorganization, typically reaching a point where workspaces (including virtual workspaces on computers) are compromised in terms of their designated purpose.

6.   Management

An important issue for the workplace is the management of problems associated with personality disorders such as OCPD. Consistent with work-stress management literature (e.g. Kendall et al., 2000), interventions can be classified as primary (i.e. strategies that aim to prevent the occurrence of problems); secondary (i.e. activities designed to change the individual's reaction to stressors); and tertiary (i.e. approaches used to treat the problem). In addition, such interventions can occur at both the individual level (e.g. through group or individual interventions) and at the structural level (e.g. through improving workplace leadership and management). These levels of intervention are briefly described below.

Individual level

It is likely that most of the interventions at the individual level will occur at the secondary or tertiary stage (i.e. addressing problems and reactions to them) once difficulties start to manifest. However, primary prevention strategies can be incorporated as part of a screening strategy before employment, and as part of intervention in the form of a relapse prevention strategy (i.e. preventing future problems). The latter is particularly important when dealing with personality disorders such as OCPD, where individuals are likely to present only in acute crisis (Kyrios, 1998), usually with difficulties that may mask the personality disorder (e.g. adjustment disorder, major depression, anxiety disorders, relationship difficulties). In addition to management of the individual's response to stressors and the resultant symptoms, the interventions need to address the dysfunctional cognitive and behavioural processes. While a full discussion of psychotherapy interventions for OCPD is beyond the scope of this chapter (see Kyrios, 1998 for a more comprehensive discussion), a brief outline is presented below.

The individual who recognizes they have difficulties at the workplace will often present for counselling, with initial interventions likely to focus on management of acute symptoms. The individual is likely to present for treatment only when they are experiencing significant distress. Therefore, reducing negative mood states should be one of the priorities during early stages of management. Prescriptive behavioural techniques including relaxation, controlled breathing techniques, activity scheduling including activities of pleasure and mastery, and exercise can be effective in reducing the initial distress. The interventions can be provided on an individual basis or in groups. Mindfulness techniques (Segal et al., 2002), whereby the client is required to refocus attention to the moment, could be quite useful in reducing intense mood states, but also in allowing the client to expose themselves to feeling states as an observer and thereby increasing tolerance of mild negative affective states. Such techniques could prove useful for other personality disorders where management of negative emotions or tolerance of affective states is particularly important (e.g. borderline personality disorder). This can be done in conjunction with cognitive techniques that involve challenging the faulty beliefs surrounding the expression of emotions (e.g. 'emotions can and should be controlled'). Gestalt techniques (e.g. the empty chair technique) can also be useful in bringing the client's emotions to the 'here and now'.

Activity scheduling can be important in OCPD as it can improve mood through engagement in a range of pleasurable rewarding activities in the short term, but also from a primary preventive perspective in addressing the OCPD-related aversion for recreational activities, overemphasis on work and job over-involvement. It is now well recognized that one of the important aspects of mental well-being is the ability 'to gain satisfaction from a variety of sources' (Speller, 1998). The reward base of individuals with OCPD is often restricted to areas they perceive as productive. The scheduled pleasurable activities need to be initially structured and gently prescribed by the therapist, particularly as many of them (e.g. relaxation) may be viewed by the individual with OCPD as unproductive and unnecessary. Such interventions can easily be administered more generally within workplaces as part of 'cultural shift' strategies where the focus is on well-being of the workforce as distinct from a pure productivity-focused philosophy (i.e. at the structural level).

Such strategies counter the narrow and closed attention of the OCPD individual by providing experiences outside their usual routines, while increasing their ability to manage and tolerate affective states. This will be particularly important as the affected individual starts increasingly to encounter situations that are novel and subjectively threatening and that may have been previously avoided. In a psychotherapeutic context, it is important for difficulties and fears to be confronted in a structured and graded manner. Such techniques can involve the identification of 'high-risk' situations, predicted negative outcomes and responses, gradual exposure to the identified situation in an order of increasing risk, testing out the predictions and coping levels. Ultimately individuals develop skills in dealing with anxiety and discomfort in specific situations and, in addition, build up a sense of confidence in their ability to deal with threat and ambivalence. It is important that such techniques be accompanied by cognitive-behavioural strategies that challenge the dysfunctional beliefs leading to avoidance and maintaining the problem. In particular, the elevated perception of harm and threat often seen in OCPD needs to be challenged through the detailed examination of situations identified as risky by the individual, and estimating the likelihood and severity of negative outcomes. Affected individuals are made aware of their tendency to focus only on possible negative outcomes as well as the inconsistencies in their avoidance patterns. Socratic dialogue can be used to help individuals develop alternative ways of thinking. Similar strategies can be used to address the increased perfectionism in individuals with OCPD. Dysfunctional beliefs such as 'mistakes can have catastrophic consequences and should never be made' or 'everything must be done perfectly' can be challenged by exposing individuals to graduated purposeful mistakes to demonstrate that such beliefs are not supported by the emerging evidence. Alternatively, one can ask perfectionists to try harder to be 'more perfect' in order to demonstrate the futility of such strategies.

Individual interventions within the workplace could include giving consideration to the type of work that employees with OCPD might be best suited to. This may also entail changing the position or conditions of employees with OCPD who are not coping with current demands, although this may be difficult in small organizations or in work contexts with a narrow focus. Particular characteristics, such as those associated with specific subtypes, may provide clues about the most appropriate work. For instance, *the bureaucratic or conscientious subtypes* may be best suited to dealing with rules and regulations (e.g. health and safety). Individuals attuned to dealing with details may be better suited to developing manuals, dealing with data, or even detailed policy or actuarial development. Those who have relative limitations in dealing with the uncertainties of group activities may be better suited to individual projects while reporting to a benevolent authority figure. In cases where a change in employment conditions is not possible, counselling services may be required to help affected employees deal with changing circumstances and/or negative emotional responses. Appropriate placement of individuals with OCPD is not anathema to the strategies described above that aim to broaden their skills and comfort zone. In fact, as already noted, narrowing the focus to areas of work in which they feel control may be detrimental to other areas. However, a graded approach to the broadening of affected individuals' safety zones may be best implemented from the security of a work environment in which they feel competent.

Finally, individuals with OCPD may require support in dealing with their internal emotional states and the appropriate expression of emotion, particularly with respect to hostility and anger. For instance, assertiveness training and anger management are useful strategies for dealing with the internalized hostility that often threatens to break out in affected individuals. Furthermore, training in appropriate interpersonal skills (e.g. social skills, sensitivity and empathy training) can also be useful in circumventing the build-up of hostility.

In summary, psychotherapeutic interventions at the individual level aim to reduce negative mood states (e.g. lowered mood, irritability, anxiety, hostility) through a range of cognitive and relaxation strategies, and therefore develop a more adaptive response to stressors; increase emotional awareness and expressivity through monitoring strategies and by utilizing the therapeutic relationship to address affective and interpersonal difficulties; reduce avoidant tendencies and increase flexibility and tolerance of novelty through graded exposure techniques; improve interpersonal and emotional regulation skills; increase individuals' involvement in activities not related to work, particularly those viewed as 'unproductive' or a 'waste of time' (e.g. recreational, social, relaxation activities); and using cognitive restructuring techniques to address specific maladaptive cognitions (assumptions) that serve to maintain the maladaptive behaviours. While undertaking these strategies, particular focus should be given to maladaptive schematic processes that could impact on the treatment process. For example, difficulties with trust and emotional expressiveness could interfere with the quality of relationships and must be handled gently. Similarly, elevated need for control may make the client react more strongly to techniques that interfere with attacks on perceived control, for example relaxation strategies and the commencement of behavioural techniques such as exposure. Finally, such interventions can be integrated with the considered placement of affected individuals, so that they are given the opportunity to broaden their comfort zone from a secure base.

Structural level
Effective management of problems associated with OCPD should also include intervention at a structural or organizational level. It is now well recognized that work stress and associated mental health outcomes are a result of the interaction between environmental

and individual factors, for example aspects of the work environment or job and the personal and individual differences in reactions to, and coping with, stress at work (Siegrist, 1998). A study by Aust et al. (1997) demonstrated the beneficial effects on critical coping behaviour in highly stressed inner-city bus drivers following a brief programme that included interventions at both the individual and structural level. Some studies have indicated that organizational or work characteristics may have a greater impact than personal attributes (Maslach and Schaufeli, 1993) and that work stress may depend primarily on the way jobs are constructed and managed (Dollard and Winefield, 2002). Therefore interventions at the organizational level are necessary for effective management of the negative workplace effects of OCPD.

In accordance with the preventive stress management framework proposed by Quick et al. (1997), interventions at the structural level involve primary prevention strategies, which can include modification of work demands and stressors; secondary strategies aiming to change how individuals and organizations respond to the demands of work and organizational life; and tertiary strategies that would treat the distress that individuals and organizations may encounter. However, in terms of specific interventions to manage problems associated with OCPD, and personality disorders more generally, the research has been at best limited. This section offers some suggestions for structural management based on theory and research on OCPD treatment, theoretical frameworks of stress management and models of organizational management of workaholism.

First, an essential element of preventive or treatment intervention is the identification of potential problems or impediments in the workplace. In relation to OCPD, it is common for organizations to fail to acknowledge problematic behaviours until they escalate to a level where they cause considerable distress to the individual and impact on the effectiveness of the organization (e.g. through decline in individual performance, decrease in morale, or higher turnover rates). In addition, some of the behaviours that may become problematic may initially have been encouraged and fostered, and even rewarded within some organizational climates (e.g. job involvement, long working hours). It is essential for leaders and managers to be able to identify potentially problematic behaviours associated with particular positions (e.g. the tendency for workaholism and therefore burnout in air-traffic controllers) and recognize the signs or symptoms of maladaptive OCPD patterns in order to distinguish these from balanced work enthusiasm. Spence and Robbins (1992) distinguished between workaholics and work enthusiasts by noting that, while the two groups scored equally on measures of high job involvement, workaholics were more likely to report increased drive to work and low enjoyment of their work.

Several additional intrapersonal and interpersonal symptoms, which have been discussed earlier in the chapter (e.g. perfectionism, difficulties working in a team or delegating responsibility), can also be used as indicators of OCPD traits that could cause problems in the workplace. While general measures of OCPD have been found to be limited, more specific measures of particular characteristics could be used as part of selection batteries. For example, there are several measures of perfectionism or decision-making difficulties (e.g. Multidimensional Perfectionism Scale, Frost Indecisiveness Scale; see Martin et al., 2001) that could be useful in identifying at-risk individuals. Given that affected individuals might impede performance of other staff or damage the organizational climate, especially where team performance is important to organizational outcomes, early screening or identification may be a useful structural intervention. Furthermore, provision of educational and training programmes for leaders and managers regarding healthy working habits are an essential step in increasing their awareness of these potential problems, ensuring they do not promote the maladaptive patterns and increasing their ability to develop or implement strategies needed to counter the potential problems.

At the primary intervention level, the organizational climate may also require modifications to address the explicit and implicit messages that employees are given in terms of work hours (the value placed on quantity versus quality), job involvement and reward distribution. It is common for organizations to develop a culture where long hours and sacrifice are seen as essential for success and development (Porter, 1996). In such organizations, individuals working long hours may be more recognized, perceived as more dedicated and more frequently rewarded. This will not only impact on the OCPD individual by encouraging maladaptive workaholic patterns, but may also impact on other employees who spend fewer hours at work, but complete the job efficiently. According to Porter (1996), the effect of such patterns can impact on the ongoing interactions in the workplace both immediately and in the longer term (e.g. in terms of stress and burnout, decline in performance, absenteeism or higher turnover rates). Such patterns need to be recognized and changed at the organizational or leadership level. It is the leaders and managers of the organization who are instrumental in promoting more adaptive and balanced working patterns. This can be done through modelling and encouraging efficiency and teamwork over quantity of individual working time.

However, other aspects of how organizations function may be harder to change. For example, in organizations that are increasingly making use of advances in communications and technology (e.g. e-mails, mobiles, portable computers), workaholic behaviour is encouraged by blurring the line between the workplace and home. Moreover, organizational restructuring with more work for fewer staff, overlapping responsibilities and associated job insecurity further reinforce workaholic behaviour by providing justification for working longer. Setting concrete goals and tasks, clear deadlines and responsibilities may serve to reduce procrastination and increase efficiency. In the longer term, the inclusion of more collaborative work arrangements such as self-managing teams and more participation in decision making may be less conducive to workaholism and OCPD behaviours. On the other hand, greater self-responsibility and self-management may further encourage certain aspects of OCPD behaviour in the absence of deference to an authority figure. Many such interventions await empirical support, with ongoing research required to establish what type of organizational climates would discourage maladaptive patterns in OCPD and lead to more positive outcomes in the workplace. Nevertheless, considering the relative intolerance for novelty and changes to routine that individuals with OCPD demonstrate, any changes to the familiar organizational structure or function need to be instituted gradually to prevent escalation of stress.

Secondary interventions can be used in parallel to improve both the individual's and the organization's response to stresses and ongoing changes in the workplace. There are various roles and responsibilities for organizations and their leaders with respect to individuals with OCPD or OCPD traits, such as the need to make available group or individual stress management and skill training programmes, providing social and leisure opportunities to promote balanced working conditions; and promoting social support and team building. In particular, informal support systems may be more effective in shaping behaviour and avoiding distress. For instance, setting up mentoring schemes is one way by which an organization can encourage and reward interdependence and social support. As Quick et al. (1997) noted, organizations may sometimes emphasize independence to the extent that individuals are reluctant to seek support. To address this, leaders and managers need to reward appropriate assistance-seeking and supportive relationships at work. Such support would not only buffer against increasing work demands, but in the case of OCPD may provide valuable experience and opportunity for improving interpersonal functioning.

In addition, initiating and supporting regular social events or activities outside of work may serve to strengthen social interaction and at the same time promote a balanced approach to work and leisure activities. Strategies such as team building can be used to promote improvement of performance through cooperative, supportive relationships within a work group. Often, existing reward structures within organizations support individual performance. Redirecting the reward system to include rewards based on team performance may encourage development of a more cooperative approach towards teamwork. If problems do arise, organizations can take on the responsibility for ensuring referral to, or, depending on organizational size and contextual issues such as health insurance policies, the delivery of mental health services for distressed employees.

7. Conclusion

OCPD is one of many personality disorders that are associated with significant impairment in occupational and academic functioning, and in both intra- and interpersonal functioning. Specifically, OCPD is characterized by maladaptive patterns of rigidity, preoccupation with perfectionism and morality, overattention to detail, concerns about matters of control and order, emotional control and constriction, miserliness, interpersonal reticence, indecisiveness, an excessive devotion to work, and inability to delegate tasks. While such difficulties affect workplace performance, milder forms of the characteristics associated with OCPD are often encouraged by organizations and may represent significant individual strengths. Understanding OCPD may lead to more effective strategies to maximize workplace performance for not only the affected individuals, but more broadly for organizations. Biological dispositions, early developmental experiences, particularly early attachments, and dysfunctional thinking styles have been identified as important in the etiology and management of OCPD.

The management of problems associated with personality disorders such as OCPD is an important issue for the workplace. Interventions at the structural level could include some focused pre-employment assessment of specific characteristics known to undermine performance in particular work contexts; increasing awareness, monitoring and diagnosis of maladaptive patterns associated with OCPD through education and training programmes for the organization; adoption of a balanced work ethic that emphasizes reward efficiency and teamwork over extensive hours of work and isolation; increasing supports through individual, group and organizational training programmes on stress management; promotion of cooperative working relationships, social supports and team building; and provision of support and services to address distress among employees. While such interventions may help prevent or minimize the negative impact of OCPD on individuals and organizations, they are also likely to be associated with additional benefits to the organization and all individuals working within such organizations. With respect to individuals with OCPD, it is necessary to recognize and emphasize the positive contributions that affected individuals bring to the organization. The very characteristics that may present problems when at their extreme may, in milder degrees, represent significant strengths for both the individual and the organization. Individuals with OCPD can be dedicated, reliable, competent and committed employees. These strengths must be emphasized and built upon. Such an approach would serve to increase self-esteem, self-efficacy and competence, and lead to better adjustment. The challenge for leaders of organizations is to develop an organizational culture in which all employees are satisfied, productive and valued.

Overall, there is a paucity of research on the workplace and personality disorders, in general, and OCPD, specifically. Future research will need to establish the utility of specific measures of OCPD and OCPD traits as they relate to particular job specifications. Furthermore, the efficacy of screening procedures and other primary interventions, as well as secondary or tertiary interventions at the individual or structural levels with respect to improvement in individual and organizational performance, will require evaluation in specific employment contexts. This will require interdisciplinary endeavours, particularly between clinical and industrial/organizational psychologists. While the challenges are significant, the benefits for individuals and organizations may also be considerable.

References

American Psychiatric Association (2000), *Diagnostic and Statistical Manual of Mental Disorders*, 4th edn, text revision, Washington, DC: American Psychiatric Association.

Aust, B., R. Peter and J. Siegrist (1997), 'Stress management in bus drivers: a pilot study based on the model of effort–reward imbalance', *International Journal of Stress Management*, **4**(4), 297–305.

Beck, A.T. and A. Freeman (1990), *Cognitive Therapy of Personality Disorders*, New York: Guilford Press.

Black, D.W., R. Noyes Jr, B. Pfohl, R.B. Goldstein and N. Blum (1993), 'Personality disorder in obsessive-compulsive volunteers, well comparison subjects, and their first-degree relatives', *American Journal of Psychiatry*, **150**(8), 1226–32.

Bowlby, J. (1973), *Attachment and Loss Vol. 2, Separation: Anxiety and Anger*, New York: Basic Books.

Bowlby, J. (1988), *A Secure Base: Parent–child Attachment and Healthy Human Development*, New York: Basic Books.

Cassidy, J., S.J. Kirsh, K.L. Scolton and R.D. Parke (1996), 'Attachment and representations of peer relationships', *Developmental Psychopathology*, **32**(5), 892–904.

Cloninger, C.R. (1987), 'A systematic method for clinical description and classification of personality variants: a proposal', *Archives of General Psychiatry*, **44**, 573–88.

Costa, P.T. Jr and R.R. McCrae (1992), *Professional Manual: Revised NEO Personality Inventory (NEO-PI-R) and NEO Five-Factor Inventory (NEO-FFI)*, Odessa, FL: Psychological Assessment Resources.

Costa, P.T. Jr and T.A. Widiger (2002), *Personality Disorders and the Five-Factor Model of Personality*, Washington, DC: American Psychological Association.

De Fruyt, F., B.J. De Clercq, L. van de Wiele and K. van Heeringen (2006), 'The validity of Cloninger's psychobiological model versus the five-factor model to predict DSM-IV personality disorders in a heterogeneous psychiatric sample: domain facet and residualized facet descriptions', *Journal of Personality*, **74**, 479–510.

Derogatis, L.R. (1983), *SCL-90-R: Administration, Scoring and Procedures. Manual II*, Baltimore, MD: Clinical Psychometric Research.

Dollard, M.F. and A.H. Winefield (2002), 'Mental health: overemployment, underemployment, unemployment and healthy jobs', in L. Morrow, I. Verins and E. Willis (eds), *Mental Health Promotion and Work: Issues and Perspectives*, Melbourne, Australia: Auseinet/VicHealth, pp. 1–41.

Eisen, L., M.E. Coles, M.T. Shea, M.E. Pagano, R.L. Stout, S. Yen, C.M. Grilo and S.A. Rasmussen (2006), 'Clarifying the convergence between obsessive compulsive personality disorder and obsessive compulsive disorder', *Journal of Personality Disorder*, **20**(3), 294–305.

Flett, G.L. and P.L. Hewitt (2002), *Perfectionism: Theory, Research, and Treatment*, Washington, DC: American Psychological Association.

Flett, G.L., P.L. Hewitt and T.R. Martin (1995), 'Dimensions of procrastination and perfectionism', in J.R. Ferrari, J.L. Johnson and W.G. McCown (eds), *Procrastination and Task Avoidance: Theory, Research, and Treatment*, New York: Plenum Press, pp. 113–36.

Flett, G.L., P.L. Hewitt, R.A. Davis and S.B. Sherry (2004), 'Description and counseling of the perfectionistic procrastinator', in H.C. Schouwenburg, C.H. Lay, T.A. Pychyl and J.R. Ferrari (eds), *Counseling the Procrastinator in Academic Settings*, Washington, DC: American Psychological Association, pp. 181–94.

First, M.B., R.L. Spitzer, M. Gibbons, J.B.W. Williams and L. Benjamin (1994), *Structured Clinical Interview for DSM-IV Axis II Personality Disorders (SCID-II), (Version 2.0)*, New York: New York State Psychiatric Institute.

Fossati, A., C. Maffei, M. Bagnato, D. Donati, M. Donini, M. Fiorilli, L. Novella and M. Ansoldi (1998), 'Brief communication: criterion validity of the Personality Diagnostic Questionnaire-4+ (PDQ-4+) in a mixed psychiatric sample', *Journal of Personality Disorders*, **12**(2), 172–8.

Furnham, A. (2002), 'Rating a boss, a colleague and a subordinate', *Journal of Managerial Psychology*, **17**(8), 655–71.

Furnham, A. and K.V. Petrides (2006), 'Deciding on promotions and redundancies: promoting people by ability, experience, gender and motivation', *Journal of Managerial Psychology*, **21**(1), 6–18.

Grant, B.F., D.S. Hasin, F.S. Stinson, D.A. Dawson, S.P. Chou, W.J. Raun and B. Huang (2004), 'Co-occurrence of DSM-IV personality disorders in the US: results from the National Epidemiologic Survey on Alcohol and Related Conditions', *Comprehensive Psychiatry*, **46**(1), 1–5.

Guidano, V.F. and G. Liotti (1983), *Cognitive Processes and Emotional Disorders*, New York: Guilford Press.

Hyler, S.E. (1994), *Personality Diagnostic Questionnaire 4+ (PDQ-4+)*, New York: New York State Psychiatric Institute.

Hyler, S.E. and R.O. Rieder (1987), *PDQ-R: Personality Diagnostic Questionnaire – Revised*, New York: New York State Psychiatric Institute.

Hyler, S.E., R.O. Rieder, R. Spitzer and J.B.W. Williams (1983), *Personality Diagnostic Questionnaire (PDQ)*, New York: New York State Psychiatric Institute.

Jacobsen, T. and V. Hofmann (1997), 'Children's attachment representations: longitudinal relations to school behavior and academic competency in middle childhood and adolescence', *Developmental Psychology*, **33**(4), 703–10.

Kendall, E., P. Murphy, V. O'Neill and S. Burnsnall (2000), *Occupational Stress: Factors that Contribute to its Occurrence and Effective Management*, Canberra, Australia: Centre for Human Services, Griffith University.

Kyrios, M. (1998), 'A cognitive-behavioral approach to the understanding and management of obsessive-compulsive personality disorder', in C. Perris and P.D. McGorry (eds), *Cognitive Psychotherapy of Psychotic and Personality Disorders: Handbook of Theory and Practice*, New York: John Wiley & Sons, pp. 351–78.

Kyrios, M., G. Steketee, R.O. Frost and S. Oh (2002), 'Cognitions of compulsive hoarding', in R.O. Frost and G. Steketee (eds), *Cognitive Approaches to Obsessions and Compulsions: Theory, Assessment, and Treatment*, Amsterdam, Netherlands: Elsevier, pp. 139–64.

Martin, M.A., S.M. Orsillo and L. Roemer (2001), *Practitioner's Guide to Empirically-Based Measures of Anxiety*, New York: Kluwer Academic/Plenum.

Maslach, C. and W.B. Schaufeli (1993), 'Historical and conceptual development of burnout', in W.B. Schaufeli, C. Maslach and T. Marek (eds), *Professional Burnout: Recent Developments in Theory and Research*, Philadelphia, PA: Taylor & Francis, pp. 1–16.

Maslach, C., W.B. Schaufeli and M.P. Leiter (2001), 'Job burnout', *Annual Review of Psychology*, **52**, 397–422.

McCann, J.T. (1992), 'A comparison of 2 measures for obsessive-compulsive personality-disorder', *Journal of Personality Disorders*, **6**(1), 18–23.

McGlashan T.H., C.M. Grilo, A.E. Skodol, J.G. Gunderson, M.T. Shea, L.C. Morey, M.C.C. Zanarini and R.L. Stout (2000), 'The collaborative longitudinal personality disorders study: baseline axis I/II and II/II diagnostic co-occurrence', *Acta Psychiatrica Scandinavica*, **102**(4), 256–64.

McWilliams, N. (1994), *Psychoanalytic Diagnosis: Understanding Personality Structure in the Clinical Process*, New York: Guilford Press.

Millon, T. (1981), *Disorders of Personality*, New York: John Wiley & Sons.

Millon, T. (1996), *Disorders of Personality: DSM-IV and Beyond*, New York: John Wiley & Sons.

Millon, T. and Davis, R.D. (1996), 'An evolutionary theory of personality disorders', in J.F. Clarkin and M.F. Lenzenweger (eds), *Major Theories of Personality Disorder*, New York: Guilford Press, pp. 221–346.

Mount, M., R. Ilies and Johnson, E. (2006), 'Relationship of personality traits and counterproductive work behaviors: the mediating effects of job satisfaction', *Personnel Psychology*, **59**(3), 591–622.

Mudrack, P.E. (2004), 'Job involvement, obsessive-compulsive personality traits, and workaholic behavioral tendencies', *Journal of Organizational Change Management*, **17**(5), 490–508.

Nestadt, G., A.J. Romanoski, C.H. Brown, R. Chahal, A. Merchant, M.F. Folstein, E.M. Gruenberg and P.R. McHugh (1991), 'DSM-III compulsive personality disorder: an epidemiological survey', *Psychological Medicine*, **21**(2), 461–71.

Nestadt, G., A.J. Romanoski, J.F. Samuels, M.F. Folstein and P.R. McHugh (1992), 'The relationship between personality and DSM-III axis I disorders in the population: results from an epidemiological survey', *American Journal of Psychiatry*, **149**(9), 1228–33.

Peeters, M.A.G., H.F.J.M. van Tuijl, C.G. Rutte and I.M.M.J. Reymen (2006), 'Personality and team performance: a meta-analysis', *European Journal of Personality*, **20**, 377–96.

Pfohl, B. and N. Blum (1991), 'Obsessive-compulsive personality disorder: a review of available data and recommendations for DSM-IV', *Journal of Personality Disorder*, **5**(4), 363–75.

Pollak, J. (1987), 'Obsessive-compulsive personality: theoretical and clinical perspectives and recent research findings', *Journal of Personality Disorders*, **1**(3), 248–62.

Porter, G. (1996), 'Organizational impact of workaholism: suggestions for researching the negative outcomes of excessive work', *Journal of Occupational Health Psychology*, **1**(1), 70–74.

Porter, G. (2001), 'Workaholic tendencies and the high potential for stress among co-workers', *International Journal of Stress Management*, **8**(2), 147–64.

Quick, J.C., J.D. Quick, D.L. Nelson and J.J. Hurrell Jr (1997), *Preventive Stress Management in Organizations*, Washington, DC: American Psychological Association.

Robinson, B.E. (1998), *Chained to the Desk: A Guidebook for Workaholics, Their Partners and Children and the Clinicians Who Treat Them*, New York: New York University Press.

Romach, M., U. Busto, G. Somer, H.L. Kaplan and E. Sellers (1995), 'Clinical aspects of chronic use of alprazolam and lorazepam', *The American Journal of Psychiatry*, **152**(8), 1161–7.

Samuels, J., W.W. Eaton, O.J. Bienvenu III, C. Brown, P.T. Costa Jr and G. Nestadt (2002), 'Prevalence and correlates of personality disorders in a community sample', *British Journal of Psychiatry*, **180**(6), 536–42.

Schotte, C., D. Dedoncker, M. Maes, R. Cluydts and P. Cosyns, (1991), 'Low MMPI diagnostic performance for the DSM-III-R obsessive-compulsive personality-disorder', *Psychological Reports*, **69**(3), 795–800.

Segal, Z.V., J.M.G. Williams and J.D. Teasdale (2002), *Mindfulness-Based Cognitive Therapy for Depression*, New York: Guilford Press.

Siegrist, J. (1998), 'Adverse health effect of effort-reward imbalance at work–theory, empirical support and implication for prevention', in C.L. Cooper (ed.), *Theories of Organisational Stress*, Oxford: Oxford University Press.

Skodol, A.E., J.G. Gunderson, T.H. McGlashan, I.R. Dyck, R.L. Stout, D.S. Bender, C.M. Grilo, M.T. Shea, M.C. Zanarini, L.C. Morey, C.A. Sanislow and J.M. Oldham (2002), 'Functional impairment in patients with schizotypal, borderline, avoidant, or obsessive-compulsive personality disorder', *The American Journal of Psychiatry*, **159**(2), 276–83.

Speller, J.L. (1998), *Executives in Crisis: Recognising and Managing the Alcoholic, Drug-addicted, or Mentally-ill Executive*, San Francisco, CA: Jossey-Bass.

Spence, J.T. and A.S. Robbins (1992), 'Workaholism: definition, measurement and preliminary results', *Journal of Personality Assessment*, **58**(1), 160–78.

Starcevic, V., G. Bogojevic and J. Marinkovic (2000), 'The SCL-90-R as a screening instrument for severe personality disturbance among outpatients with mood and anxiety disorders', *Journal of Personality Disorders*, **14**(3), 199–207.

Tolin, D.F., J.S. Abramowitz, B.D. Brigidi and E.B. Foa (2003), 'Intolerance of uncertainty in obsessive-compulsive disorder', *Journal of Anxiety Disorders*, **17**(2), 233–42.

Torgersen, S., E. Kringlen and V. Cramer (2001), 'The prevalence of personality disorders in a community sample', *Archives of General Psychiatry*, **58**(6), 590–96.

Verschueren, K. and A. Marcoen (1999), 'Representations of self and socioemotional competence in kindergarteners: differential and combined effects of attachment to mother and father', *Child Development*, **70**(1), 183–201.

4   Tyrants and workplace bullying
Janice Langan-Fox and Michael Sankey

Bullies and the effects of bullying

Bullying is a widespread phenomenon in numerous countries. Studies suggest that as much as 10 per cent of the workforce is bullied (Hoel and Cooper, 2000; Vartia, 1996). Being bullied, then, is a 'normal' part of the working day for many people. Workplace bullies play out their 'foul game' (Neuberger, 1999) in organizations, engaging in punishment, self-aggrandizement and generally belittling subordinates (Ashforth, 1994). Bullies are especially prevalent in prisons, schools, young offenders' institutions and the armed forces. Bullies (a type of tyrant) are often 'leaders', and have devastating effects on their subordinates, causing tension (Baron, 1988), stress (Myers, 1977), helplessness (Ashforth, 1989), and work alienation (Clarke, 1985), as well as having more general effects on departmental or unit performance (Podsakoff and Schriesheim, 1985). It's difficult to put a cost on the effects of bullying to organizations because incidence is under-reported. For instance, some employees might not prefer to 'label' themselves as bullied by seeking organizational or professional assistance (Salin, 2001). However, given the consequences for individuals by way of stress, absenteeism, turnover, reduced productivity and other inefficiencies resulting from organizational dysfunction, the real cost must be staggering.

This chapter aims to document what we know about workplace bullying. We describe the incidence, extent and types of bullying that occur in workplaces, as well as its conceptualization. Second, we review the empirical work that has investigated bullying and what has been found. With bullying being increasingly perceived as an organizational issue (e.g. Liefooghe and Mackenzie Davey, 2001), this chapter focuses more specifically on organizational level influences, and their impact on bullying behaviour. Third, we examine the intervention literature which attempts to suggest actions and strategies that might be used by victims and organizations in order to prevent or combat bullying or mobbing.

Conceptualizations of workplace bullying

Bullying can be defined as behaviour that, on more than one occasion, is offensive, abusive, malicious, insulting or intimating; unjustified criticism on more than one occasion; punishment imposed without reasonable justification; and changes in the duties or responsibilities of the employee to the employee's detriment without reasonable justification (Lee, 2000, p. 596). Influenced by case-law definitions in racial and sexual harassment, definitions of bullying share three elements: its effect on the recipient; a negative effect on the victim; and bullying behaviour must be persistent and generally extend beyond six months (Quine, 1999). Workplace bullying is in the middle of a continuum: at one end is workplace homicide; physical violence at the next level; and in the middle, sexual harassment and bullying (Crawford, 1997). Bullying may incorporate incivility (breaches of etiquette), or forms of aggression (degradation), which can escalate into a conflict spiral (Andersson and Pearson, 1999; Felson, 1992) and is sometimes underwritten by judgements of 'appropriate' conduct and pressure to conform to gender-appropriate norms (Lee, 2002). The intention of perpetrators is to engage in concealed acts which cause humiliation, offence and distress (Lee and Brotheridge, 2006). For instance, Lee (2000: 604; original emphasis) described the following incident:

> *My supervisor got hold of me by my overalls. He pushed me against the workbench and verbally threatened me for no known reason. This attack took place when there was nobody else about.* ('George', electrician)

The potential danger to victims includes effects on their professional status, personal standing, being isolated, suffering overwork and being destabilized in the organization (Rayner and Hoel, 1997). 'Mobbing' (or 'shikato'), where groups of peers bully one person, has also been identified as common in schools and at work in Japan and Scandinavia but less so in the UK (Einarsen, 1999; Leymann, 1992). Bullying is a symptom of organizational dysfunction and is evidence of 'internal organizational conflicts which have bubbled to the surface . . . the conflict is either seeping to the surface or suddenly spills out' (Crawford, 1997: 221).

In general, bullying has been conceptualized as a combination of both individual and environmental factors. A general model of bullying has been provided by Ashforth's model of 'petty tyranny' (1994) (see Figure 4.1). This consists of individual predispositions (beliefs about the self, organization and subordinates, and preferences for action) interacting with situational facilitators, leading to petty tyranny (belittling subordinates, lack of consideration, discouraging initiative), and having effects on subordinates such as high frustration, low self-esteem etc. Behaviour may trigger a vicious circle. However, bullying has also been analysed from three different levels: the individual or person-oriented level, the dyadic or group level, and the organizational level. The need to recognize factors from all angles has been acknowledged by a number of researchers (Einarsen, 2000; Einarsen et al., 2003; Zapf, 1999).

Prevalence of workplace bullying

Bullying has commonly been associated with school playgrounds (Batch and Knoff, 1994). However, it was identified in Scandinavia as an adult issue in the 1980s, and, in the UK, in the 1990s. Workplace bullying is more common than previously thought. Of a sample of 7986, representing 14 different Norwegian surveys of a broad array of organizations and professions (Einarsen and Skogstad, 1996), as much as 8.6 per cent had been bullied at work in the recent past. Bullying was most prevalent in large, male-dominated organizations, and older workers were victimized more than younger workers. Similar proportions (10.1 per cent) have been reported by Vartia (1996), using Finnish municipal employees as participants. However, Quine (1999) found bullying more prevalent among health workers, with more than one-third of a sample of 1100 suffering bullying in the past year. These employees also reported low job satisfaction and high levels of job-induced stress. Even greater numbers were found by Leymann (1996), with roughly half of 2400 Swedish workers experiencing bullying. Similar numbers have been reported in research at Staffordshine University Business School, where Rayner (1997) found that 53 per cent of staff had experienced workplace bullying and 78 per cent had witnessed bullying of others. Rayner (1997) also found that 53 per cent of 1137 university students reported that

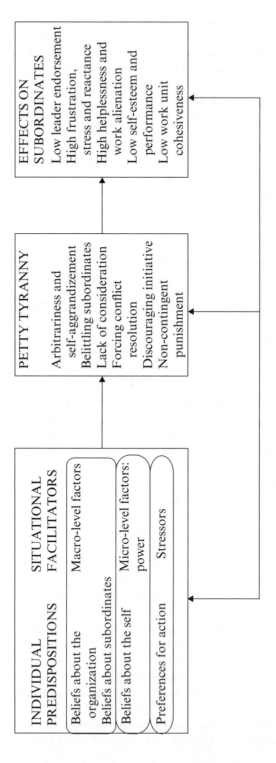

Note: The three ellipses reflect potential configurations of individual predispositions and situational facilitators that are likely to predict petty tyranny. It is not argued that tyrannical behaviour fully mediates the impact of the proposed antecedents on the proposed effects. It is recognized that certain antecedents may affect certain effects directly or through additional mediators.

Source: Reproduced with permission, from Ashforth (1994). Copyright (© The Tavistock Institute, London, UK, 1994) by permission of Sage Publications Ltd.

Figure 4.1 Proposed antecedents and effects of petty tyranny

they had been bullied during their working lives. Most people were bullied in groups, where bullying was more prolonged than in individual bullying, and were bullied immediately upon changing their jobs, accounting for 82 per cent of bullying onset. Other scenarios where bullying occurred was where an individual acquired a new manager. Women were bullied as much by men and women, but men were rarely bullied by women. Being bullied was associated with low use of support services, and leaving the job.

Job seniority does not provide immunity against bullying. Business professionals (managers and experts) also experience bullying. Salin (2001) found that 8.8 per cent of 377 respondent professionals (managers and experts) reported being bullied occasionally and 1.6 per cent weekly. Given the high-pressure, competitive nature of professional jobs, it was thought that this type of sample might be subjected to a different type of bullying. Compared to a British study (Hoel and Cooper, 2000) of professionals, Salin (2001) found that negative acts such as being given tasks with impossible targets or deadlines, having one's opinions and views ignored, and being given work clearly below one's level of competence were reported considerably more often. Particular industries and occupations where performance includes exacting tasks performed under time pressure are also situations where it is more likely that bullying will occur (Hillier, 1995).

Characteristics of the victim and the bully

The victim
Victims of bullying feel demoralization and defeat:

> *My own advice to anyone facing (bullying) is to resign straight away if you can and not to fight. . . .*
> *I have made a promise to myself that if I am faced with the same situation again I will leave straight*
> *away, after all life is too short.* (Crawford, 1997: 224; original emphasis)

The extent to which the personality of the victim is a contributing factor in bullying has been heavily debated. Early researchers (e.g. Leymann, 1996) were strongly opposed to the notion that victim personality might be a cause of bullying. However, many studies today suggest that victim personality cannot be ignored (e.g. Coyne et al., 2000; Zapf and Einarsen, 2003). Aquino et al. (1999) hypothesized that two groups of employees were particularly at risk of becoming victimized at work: the 'submissive' employee, and the 'proactive' employee. Typical 'submissive' victim characteristics include anxiety, low social competence, low self-esteem and low self-determination (Aquino et al., 1999; Coyne et al., 2000; Einarsen et al., 1994b; Vartia, 1996). Other victim characteristics found to be associated with bullying include a high level of social anxiety (Einarsen et al., 1994b), increased levels of sensitivity, anger and suspiciousness (Gandolfo, 1995), neuroticism (Vartia, 1996), disability, physical weakness, lack of friends, and introversion (Aquino and Lamertz, 2004; Smith et al., 2003). Research supports Aquino et al.'s claim that 'proactive' employees are likely to be targets of bullying. For example, Olweus (1993) used a sample of children in which a small group were characterized as 'proactive victims'. These victims were both anxious and aggressive, and were experienced by most other pupils as annoying and might provoke aggressive behaviours in others (Felson, 1992). In a similar vein, Brodsky (1976) described victims as overachievers with an unrealistic view both of their own abilities and resources and the demands of their work tasks. Such qualities may conflict with established group norms, causing frustration among colleagues who might then respond with hostility (Zapf and Einarsen, 2003).

One point of debate is whether, and to what extent, these characteristics should be considered causes of bullying or whether they are the end-product or result of the bullying process. While it could be claimed that the personality of the victim may provoke aggression in others, Leymann (1996) contends that victim characteristics need to be understood as a normal response to an abnormal situation. Specifically, observations of personality must not be seen as the cause, but instead the *consequence* of bullying (Leymann and Gustafsson, 1996). Similarly, Hoel and Cooper (2000) claim that exposure to bullying may affect the way an individual perceives the world and their ability to influence and control events. Since no longitudinal study has yet been presented, this explanation cannot be ruled out (Einarsen, 1999).

Certainly, individuals who possess a negative perception of life have been shown to be more vulnerable to workplace bullying. According to Watson and Clark (1984), persons with high negative affect are prone to focus on the negative aspects of their personal environment, are less happy with their lives, and may project a meek demeanour. Similarly, Coyne et al. (2003) and Jockin et al. (2001) also claim that a predisposition to negativity lends itself to a victim's perception – that once bullied, they will *always* be bullied. These claims are supported by the work of Einarsen and Skogstad (1996), who found victims with a long history of victimization to be attacked more frequently than those with a shorter victimization history. Examining a group of 268 Norwegian victims of bullying, they found the majority of those with a case history of more than two years reported being victimized on a weekly or daily basis. Only a small group of victims with a case history of less than 12 months reported being bullied this often. Demographic characteristics may also explain why certain employees are more likely to be targets of bullying. In particular, being different or belonging to a minority appears to be a risk factor. For example, both members of 'non-white' ethnic groups (Hoel and Cooper, 2000) and employees with disabilities (Leymann, 1992) show higher victimization rates. All of these characteristics leave the potential victim vulnerable and open for the more aggressive personality of the bully (Aquino and Byron, 2002).

The bully

Researchers have also examined the characteristics of a typical perpetrator, i.e. the bully. One popular school of thought places emphasis on the genetic and childhood experiences that lead to workplace bullying. Raine et al. (1994) describe biological 'causes' of aggressive bullying behaviour in the workplace. Some support has been shown for the assertion that the adult bully learned this behaviour in childhood, is unable to break the psychological cycle as he or she grows into adulthood, and thus mimics the destructive behaviour either at home or in the workplace (Haynie et al., 2001; Robinson and O'Leary-Kelly, 1998). Similarly, other research has given rise to the idea of a 'cycle of violence' (Tattum and Tattum, 1996; Randall, 1997), suggesting that bullying behaviour, cultivated in childhood and adolescence, continues to express and manifest itself in a variety of situations throughout life (Randall, 1997).

Research has identified a lack of social competency to be a common trait of perpetrators. For example, Zapf and Einarsen (2003) argued that both a lack of emotional control and 'thoughtfulness' could be contributing to abusive behaviour. Sheehan and Jordan

(2003) also argued that an inability to take responsibility for the expression and control of emotions may contribute to bullying. Moreover, they suggested bounded emotionality and personal mastery training were needed to curtail bullying behaviour.

Dyadic and group-level influences

On the dyadic level, it is emphasized that bullying consists of interactions between a victim and a perpetrator (or several perpetrators). This level of analysis emphasizes a dynamic process between the victim and the perpetrator (or perpetrators), with the victim construed as an active agent in the bullying process (Einarsen et al., 2003; Niedl, 1995). Research distinguishes between two forms of bullying: predatory and dispute-related bullying. Predatory bullying refers to those situations 'where the victim personally had done nothing provocative that may reasonably justify the behaviour of the bully' (Einarsen, 1999: 22). Predatory bullying is often identified as a public manifestation of power on the part of the perpetrator, or because the victim is part of an outgroup, i.e. an underrepresented sex or ethnic group. On the other hand, dispute-related bullying refers to those incidents of bullying that are connected with disagreement over work-related conflicts or violation of social norms. If conflicts remain unresolved, bullying behaviour may escalate and become increasingly personal.

Power differences should also be considered when analysing bullying on the dyadic level, as they are an inherent factor in bullying conflicts (Vartia, 1996). Differences in power are not necessarily due to the formal position of victims and perpetrators, but may be based on other situational and contextual characteristics (Cleveland and Kerst, 1993). Moreover, personality characteristics may also play a role in the development of such power imbalances between victim and perpetrator.

Organizational-level influences

The recent history of organizations shows environments that are fertile grounds for bullies to prosper. From the 1990s on, large organizations experienced vast changes which included restructures, downsizing, relocations, technological innovations (Langan-Fox, 2002, 2005) and a shift to more formal systems of appraisal to allow for accurate statistics, observance and monitoring of employee performance (Langan-Fox et al., 1998; Liefooghe and Mackenzie Davey, 2001). As a consequence, work conditions in large organizations are often fraught with uncertainties – prime environments that foster suspicion, competition, conflict and unsettling feelings about the future, resulting in an organizational environment that is tense and stress-filled.

Organizations with rigid hierarchical structures are more likely to have a culture where bullying can flourish, and where the power differential is handled without impunity. This appears to be the case especially in 'total institutions', such as the army (see Ashforth, 1994) or 'paramilitary' setting, such as the fire service (Archer, 1999). In Scandinavia, the quality of the organization's work and social environment has been seen as the main determinant of bullying. Leymann (1992) took a strong position in stating that work conditions 'alone' are the primary cause of bullying. Similarly, Vartia (1996) found that victims and observers of bullying felt that workplace deficiencies such as poor information flow, settling of conflicts and insufficient empowerment all contributed to bullying. Of a total of 2215 individuals in a labour union and employer's federation, Einarsen et al. (1994a) found that bullying was significantly correlated with measures of the work environment, including leadership, work control, workload, social climate and role conflict. This study showed that it was not only the victim who suffered from an ill-conditioned work environment, but also observers of bullying.

Workplace culture

Bullying has been shown to flourish in hectic and competitive environments, where employees are willing to sabotage or expel unwanted colleagues and subordinates in order to improve their own position within the organization (O'Moore et al., 1998; Salin, 2003a; Vartia, 1996). Certain reward systems may also facilitate micro-political behaviours and bullying by creating an atmosphere where colleagues or subordinates are considered as burdens or rivals (Kräkel, 1997; Sutela and Lehto, 1998). For example, a performance-based reward system may give an employee an incentive to bully a colleague if the remuneration is based on the relative ranking of the employees (Kräkel, 1997). This creates a situation where individuals may choose to sabotage the work of fellow employees to improve their own position. Team-based reward systems have also been shown to facilitate bullying behaviour. Sewell and Wilkinson (1992) suggested that teamwork may sometimes lead to oppressive control from peers. Collinson (1988) found that collective bonus systems motivated some workers' concern to discipline their colleagues. In accordance with this notion, Kräkel (1997) understood bullying to be a 'rent-seeking' behaviour, whereby perpetrators seek to benefit personally from their bullying activities. Advantages of engaging in workplace bullying may include higher pay, increased promotion opportunities, and improved performance appraisal (Salin, 2001). Gabriel (1998) also claimed that bullying serves the instrumental function of simultaneously establishing a pecking order and allowing for mobility within it. Some researchers have gone so far as describing bullying as 'personnel work with other means' (Zapf and Warth, 1997). That is, bullying may be used as a means to expel unwanted employees, whom it would be otherwise difficult to lay off. Salin (2003b: 40; original emphasis) described the following incident as an example of how bullying may be used as a way of obstructing or trying to eliminate rivals.

> *A supervisor, who is a colleague of mine, got a new subordinate, whom she obviously experienced as a threat to her own career. The new subordinate was not invited to common meetings, was publicly scoffed at, etc. When the subordinate had risen to the same hierarchical level, it was payback time. The former supervisor was slandered, was excluded from the work community, and it was generally considered that she was not capable of handling her work tasks.* (Woman, middle management)

Salin (2001) argued that a higher degree of bureaucracy, and stricter rules for laying off workers in the public sector, may increase the value of using bullying as a strategy for circumventing rules and eliminating unwanted persons. In these scenarios, bullying may be understood (by bullies) to be a more efficient method of managing difficult human resource issues!

Organizations characterized by an extreme degree of conformity and group pressure are also prone to bullying. Studies investigating the relationship between bullying and organizational culture have emphasized socialization processes whereby bullying behaviour has become normalized, reproduced or even considered institutionalized. In his study of bullying in the fire service, Archer (1999) investigated how bullying may become institutionalized and passed on as 'tradition'. A major reason for this prevailing culture lay in the induction to the service through basic recruit training. His study found the training process to be a powerful source of institutionalizing bullying behaviour which was passed on as tradition and thus not acknowledged as bullying behaviour. Bullying behaviour in the fire department, and other paramilitary institutions, is seen to be well ingrained and difficult to change. This is primarily due to the fact that superiors have been bought up within the same cultural tradition. Furthermore, the fact that many victims considered complaining about bullying to be an act of disloyalty emphasizes the potential strength and impact of the socialization processes at work (Archer, 1999).

Other studies have shown how bullying can be considered as being 'built into' or embedded within the organizational culture. In several work environments, bullying can be perceived as a 'normal' and acceptable way of getting things done. An environment that has frequently been associated with a high prevalence of bullying, often of a violent nature, is the kitchen of the gastronomic restaurant. A number of situational and societal factors, such as a hot and noisy workplace, and pressures to satisfy customers, can facilitate bullying behaviour (Anderson et al., 1996; Einarsen, 1996). Moreover, Johns and Menzel (1999) claim that increasing appeal in preparing food and cooking from the media has led to the achievement of a celebrity status for some chefs. Accordingly, the chef is often perceived as an artist, whose bullying and abusive behaviour is tolerated or explained as idiosyncratic behaviour born out of artistry and creativity (Johns and Menzel, 1999). There are some famous cases of chef bullying, as in the filming of Nigel Marriage, hitting and abusing a kitchen porter, with the rest of the kitchen staff performing their jobs as if nothing was happening. Peers, subordinates and immediate managers are often frightened and may experience self-doubt when faced with such a situation (Bowes-Sperry and O'Leary-Kelly, 2005; Delbecq, 2001). Similarly, Crawford (1997, p. 222) claims that bystander passivity is a consistent feature of bullying at work perhaps because nobody wants to get involved lest they become bullied too. Consequently, self-preservation appears to drive many observers into silence and acquiescence.

From the foregoing, it is clear that processes of learning and socialization exacerbate problems of workplace bullying. Discipline and subordination are fundamental mechanisms in which organizations get their employees to tolerate such behaviour as part of the workplace culture. In these environments, new employees and managers can also become socialized into treating bullying as a normal feature of working life: 'monkey see, monkey do' behaviour (Robinson and O'Leary-Kelly, 1998).

Support for bullying behaviour
Bullying behaviour may also flourish when individuals feel that such behaviour will go unpunished, due to a lack of policies or punishment (Einarsen, 1999; Rayner et al., 2002). Research suggests that employees will quickly come to view bullying behaviour as acceptable and 'normal' if they see others get away with it and are even rewarded for it (O'Leary-Kelly et al., 1996; Rayner et al., 2002). Bullying has been shown to be more frequent in large (Einarsen and Skogstad, 1996) and bureaucratic organizations (Thylefors, 1987), where the perpetrator is more invisible. In small and transparent organizations, both the perpetrator's risk of getting caught and the potential social consequences may be larger.

Einarsen (1999) claims that bullying is prevalent in organizations where employees and managers feel that they have the support, or at least implicitly the blessing, of senior managers to continue their bullying behaviour. In accordance with this notion, Brodsky

(1976: 83) argued that 'for harassment to occur, the harassment elements must exist within a culture that permits and rewards harassment'. Described as a 'sense of permission to harass', Brodsky claimed that bullying behaviour may be the result of a prevailing belief in industrial society that workers are most productive when exposed to a fear of harassment. In this sense, harassment is thus perceived as instrumental by management in achieving productivity or 'acceptable' performance from employees. Together, research suggests that, in some organizations, bullying may not be an integrated part of the culture, but is still indirectly 'permitted'.

In addition to giving tacit 'permission' for bullying, the culture in some organizations may be characterized by a heavy reliance on jokes and banter, which may border upon bullying behaviour. In some organizations, humiliating jokes, surprises and insults can also be part of the socialization process, whereby new members are tested to ensure compliance with shared norms. This behaviour is particularly prevalent in 'tough' male-dominated shopfloor environments, where harsh humour appears to be part of everyday life and an accepted part of the culture (Collinson, 1988; Einarsen and Raknes, 1997). However, as Einarsen and Raknes (1997) mention, in some cases it is possible that the target, for some reason, cannot defend himself or herself, or may not take such humour as a joke.

Job satisfaction and negative work environments
Research has uncovered a myriad of situational antecedents which have been shown to be associated with workplace bullying. Research suggests bullying behaviour to be more prevalent when employees are dissatisfied with the work environment. This includes bullies who are managers as well as those who are co-workers (Ishmael, 1999). In a Norwegian study among almost 2200 members of six different labour unions, both victims and observers of bullying at work reported being more dissatisfied than others with their work environment (Einarsen, 1999). This was attributed to a lack of constructive leadership, lack of possibilities to monitor and control their work tasks, and especially a high level of role conflict (Einarsen et al., 1994b). Furthermore, Einarsen et al. (1994b) found a higher number of bullying incidences in organizations with few challenges, less variety and less interesting work. Zapf (1999) also provided support for the view that bullying is associated with a negative work environment. He compared victims of bullying with a control group of non-victimized individuals. Victims assessed their environment more negatively than the control group on all features related to quality of work environment, including the work environment quality that existed before the onset of bullying. Other situational or psychosocial factors which have been found to provide a fertile ground for bullying include interpersonal conflicts, a lack of a friendly and supportive environment, poor information flow, authoritative ways of settling differences of opinion, lack of discussion about goals and tasks, insufficient possibilities to influence matters concerning oneself, organizational changes, low morale and vague supervision (Keashly and Jagatic, 2003; McCarthy, 1996; Seigne, 1998; Vartia, 1996).

Leadership style
Leadership style has been proven to be a fundamental precursor of workplace bullying. Together with role conflict, low satisfaction with leadership was a second organizational feature found to be most strongly identified with bullying in Einarsen et al.'s (1994) Norwegian trade union study. As indicated earlier, it has been found that a very 'tough'

and autocratic culture can be conducive to bullying (Archer, 1999; Johns and Menzel, 1999). Similarly, a very autocratic style of leadership has been shown to be correlated with higher reports of bullying (Hoel and Cooper, 2000; O'Moore et al., 1998; Vartia, 1996). Ashforth (1994) discussed potentially destructive sides of leadership and identified what he referred to as 'petty tyrants', i.e. leaders who exercise a tyrannical style of management, resulting in a climate of fear in the workplace. Such abusive leadership styles would thus be related to vertical bullying, i.e. superiors bullying their subordinates. Furthermore, Ashforth (1994) argued that entrepreneurs may be particularly at risk of becoming 'petty tyrants' because of their strong need for independence and control, their possible distrust of others, and their desire for approval. Although the prevailing literature suggests that abusive styles of management are dysfunctional, abdication of leadership (or a so-called *laissez-faire* style of management) may also provide a fertile ground for bullying between peers or colleagues (Einarsen et al., 1994b; Hoel and Cooper, 2000; Leymann, 1996). The association between a *laissez-faire* style of leadership and bullying behaviour may be attributed to the reluctance of superiors to recognize and intervene in bullying episodes, therefore conveying the impression that bullying is acceptable. This notion is substantiated by the work of Einarsen et al. (1994b), who found that dissatisfaction with the amount and quality of guidance, instructions and feedback provided to subordinates was associated with higher levels of bullying. In essence, bullying and leadership style seem to follow a curvilinear relationship, so that bullying is particularly frequent in cases of either very 'weak' (i.e. *laissez-faire*) or very 'tough' (i.e. autocratic) management styles. Observers reported an elevated level of conflict and dissatisfaction with the social climate and leaders of the organization, suggesting that a low quality of work environment is a prevailing characteristic of workplaces where bullying flourishes. Two out of five victims reported their immediate supervisor as the persecutor and 50 per cent reported that their co-workers were the bullies. Results of the study supported Brodsky's (1976) view that harassment elements must exist within a culture that permits and rewards harassment for harassment to occur. Thus harassment is inevitably associated with an organization's leadership. However, this study reinforced the notion that bullying cannot be exclusively explained in terms of work conditions. Work environment factors did not account for more than 24 per cent of the variance in bullying; overall only 10 per cent of bullying could be explained in terms of work environment conditions. Zapf et al. (1995) reported that organizational factors are indeed potential causes of mobbing at work. Mobbing was correlated with bad job content, bad social environment and poor psychological health (psychosomatic complaints, depression and irritation).

The phases of bullying
Empirical studies indicate that bullying is not an either–or phenomenon, but rather a gradually evolving process. Einarsen and Skogstad (1996) found that victims of long-lasting bullying were bullied with highest intensity, indicating that bullying takes the form of an escalating process: initially victims are attacked occasionally, with conflict escalating and increasing after some time, and then victims are attacked on a weekly basis. Models have been proposed to account for the escalation of conflict, such as that by Bjorkqvist (1992), which suggests a three-phase model of bullying: in the first phase indirect methods are used such as spreading rumours. These initial strategies are indirect, discreet, and aimed at degrading the victim. The second phase is more direct, where the

person is isolated or humiliated in public (e.g. becomes the butt of jokes), thereby justi-fying the behaviour of the bully. The third phase involves extreme aggression and power against the victim, for instance accusing them of being psychologically ill. Blackmail may also be used.

Leymann (1993, 1996) proposed that there is an initial critical event that triggers a con-flictual situation; the second phase consists of bullying and stigmatizing, on a more con-sistent basis. In the next phase, if the victim complains, personnel management may become involved although previous stigmatization, if it has been successful, can easily allow management to misjudge the situation. In the final phase, 'expulsion' occurs, but is precipitated by illness where the victim seeks medical or psychological help, but even at this stage, it's possible for the person to be misdiagnosed by professionals as 'character disturbance'. In Leymann's four-phase model, there is very little that the victim can do to solve the problem in becoming stigmatized, and expulsion is the completion of the victim's situation with the organization. In other words, the victim's attempts to solve the problem are unsuccessful. Both models predict that as bullying escalates, the situation deteriorates severely for the victim, leaving them powerless and unable to apply coping strategies that might end the conflict situation. Worse still, in many cases, research shows that the victim fails to seek support services, preferring instead to cope on their own. It is possible that a combination of shame, humiliation, self-doubt and isolation and the more severe forms of bullying disables any coping mechanisms a victim might employ. There are other models relevant to conflict escalation, outside the bullying literature (Glasl, 1994).

Outcomes of bullying

Bullying leads to stress. Lee (2000: 603; original emphasis) describes 'Sarah's' experience with her new line manager:

> *I had started having these terrible nightmares, I was dreaming about killing him, every time I put my head on the pillow I was killing him. I began to think I was going mad. I thought, I'm losing my marbles.*

Lee and Brotheridge (2006) found that among Canadian workers from the public service, a school hospital and mine, self-doubt was an important variable in mediating the rela-tionship between being bullied by others and burnout. Bullying affects self-confidence and a person's well-being:

> *I was working as a salesman in a Menswear shop in Worthing and the manager made my life a living hell from my first day. So much so that I stormed out after having been in the job for 10 weeks! After this experience I began to feel a great loss of confidence and for a long time was unemployed.* (Crawford, 1997: 221).

Using a random sample (1857) of Danish employees, Hogh and Dofradottir (2001) inves-tigated whether bullied respondents used the same coping strategies as non-bullied respondents. These authors estimated that about 2 per cent of employees in Denmark are bullied and that offenders were mostly colleagues. Nineteen per cent of the employees had been subjected to gossip and slander in the past 12 months and 6.5 per cent subjected to nasty teasing. Respondents seemed to use problem solving less often when exposed to negative workplace acts than those not exposed. Frank et al. (2006) reported that of 2316 medical students, 42 per cent of seniors reported experiencing harassment and belittlement during medical school. Medical students reporting harassment were significantly more likely to be stressed, depressed and suicidal, and significantly less likely to be glad they trained to become a doctor. Although few students characterized harassment and belittlement as severe, poor mental health was significantly correlated with these experiences. Bjorkqvist et al. (1994) found that as many as 30 per cent of men and 55 per cent of women at a Finnish university had been exposed to some form of harassment during the last year, and 32 per cent had been a witness to others being harassed at their workplace during the same period.

Coping with bullying-induced stress causes a depletion of emotional resources and the development of psychosomatic stress symptoms which include anxiety and depression (Lee and Brotheridge, 2006). In general, there is concrete evidence to indicate that individuals who are bullied or 'mobbed' are more likely to experience depression (Einarsen and Raknes, 1997); more psychosomatic and depressive symptoms than non-bullied persons (Papaioannou and Sjoblom, 1992); and higher levels of depression, anxiety, aggression and symptoms of post-traumatic stress disorder (PTSD) (Bjorkqvist et al., 1994). Severe degrees of PTSD have been shown to have effects comparable to PTSD in war or prison-camp experiences (Leymann and Gustafsson, 1996) and include problems related to cognition (memory disturbances), psychosomatic stress symptoms (nightmares), autonomic nervous system (heart palpitations), muscular tension (backache) and sleep problems.

Research has identified a number of other health-related consequences of bullying. Kivimäki et al. (2003) found victims of workplace bullying to be more likely to have chronic diseases such as asthma, rheumatoid arthritis, osteoarthritis, sciatica, diabetes or cardiovascular disease. It was also found that prolonged bullying was associated with the onset of cardiovascular disease, with victims 2.3 times more likely to acquire cardiovascular disease than non-victims after controlling for gender, age and income (Kivimäki et al., 2003). Furthermore, Kivimäki et al. (2003) reported a 4.8 odds ratio for bullying and depression diagnosed by a physician after controlling for gender, age and income.

Organizational repercussions of bullying have also been well documented, with bullying resulting in increased absenteeism and higher turnover of personnel, reduced commitment and productivity, and negative publicity (e.g. Ashforth, 1997; Hoel et al., 2003; Tepper, 2000). Given the severity and extent of problems associated with workplace bullying, prevention is a key.

Prevention of workplace bullying
Bullying appears to be a dynamic, interactive process with a multiplicity of causes. It is therefore unlikely that all forms of bullying will be completely eliminated in the workplace. In the words of Randall (1997: 107), 'the motivations for bullying are too complex, numerous and diverse for any organization to be completely free of such behaviour'. None the less, it is possible for an employer to significantly reduce the likelihood of this behaviour occurring and to detect bullying at a much earlier stage.

Leymann (1993) proposed specific features of organizations that contribute to bullying behaviour: deficiencies in work design, leadership behaviour, the socially exposed position of the victim/s, and low moral in the department are possibilities. Resch and Schubinski (1996) examined each of these causes as targets for organizational change. First, they argue that well-designed jobs with low strain, high job control and opportunities for decision making reduce the possibility of stress and scapegoating. Second, a new informed leadership style needs to permeate from the top down, with 'new leadership' learned on the job and management training evaluated through regular appraisals by employees. Third, grievance rules must be implemented that protect the individual even if he/she opposes the viewpoint of a group. Fourth, there needs to be a mutual understanding of acceptable behaviour of co-workers and of fairness or moral standard. In addition, the authors recommend a number of measures that need to be agreed upon that apply in the early, middle and late phases of the mobbing conflict.

Resch and Schubinski (1996: 296) claim that it takes 'a spectacular case to motivate the company to deal with a known but unacknowledged problem. Only if a worker dies from the consequences of alcohol abuse or a fatal accident happens does the company agree to confront the problem.'

Prevention measures need to be applied before mobbing becomes an issue. There is an 'early phase' when the conflict is still recognizable; a 'middle phase' where the participants no longer perceive a conflict but rather a problem with 'us and the person', and a 'late phase' when group or department borders are crossed and official measures are implemented, for instance warnings or transfers. Resch and Schubinski (1996) argue that there are probably two motivations for organizations to confront the problem of mobbing: first, public opinion against the company when a mobbing case becomes public and second, the pressure of the social service agency or trade union representatives. With underreporting a frequent phenomenon of bullying, research is needed into its onset and development (e.g. bullying spirals). Given that bullying is a persistent pattern of negative acts towards specific target/s, it needs to be determined if such behaviours are consistently directed at the *same person* over time (Lee and Brotheridge, 1997). People who are bullied have final reactions which include two destructive types, either through reducing commitment to the organization, or leaving permanently (Niedl, 1996). Either way, systems for preventing mobbing need to be instituted, with continued monitoring to prevent recurrences.

Future research
It is important to promote research directed at gaining a better understanding of the processes of change required to prevent mobbing in organizations. As Einarsen (2000: 396–7) has pointed out, 'the implementation of effective interventions may only be accomplished through the development of theoretical and empirically sound models of the causes and effects involved'. In addition, systematic and proper evaluation of preventive strategies is rare, and there are very few intervention programmes that offer empirical evidence of their effectiveness (Resch and Schubinski, 1996: 296).

Conclusion
This chapter has shown bullying to be a multifaceted, interactive and escalating process, which can negatively affect the victim's personal life, observers of bullying, relationships among group members, and ultimately the organization as a whole. Different types of bullying have been described, as well as different antecedents (i.e. individual, group and organizational), which may lead to workplace bullying. However, workplace bullying appears to be a relatively new area in the field of organizational behaviour, and there is an urgent need

for empirical work that investigates the contexts, causes and contingencies of bullying as well as its main consequences and ways of coping with it.

References

Anderson, C.A., Anderson, K.B. and Deuser, W.E. (1996), 'Examining an affective aggression framework: weapon and temperature effects on aggressive thoughts, affects and attitudes', *Personality and Social Psychology Bulletin*, **22**, 366–76.

Andersson, L.M. and Pearson, C.M. (1999), 'Tit for tat? The spiraling effect of incivility in the workplace', *Academy of Management Review*, **24**(3), 452–71.

Aquino, K. and Byron, K. (2002), 'Dominating interpersonal behavior and perceived victimization in groups: evidence for curvilinear relationship', *Journal of Management*, **28**, 69–87.

Aquino, K. and Lamertz, K. (2004), 'A relational model of workplace victimization: social roles and patterns of victimization in dyadic relationships', *Journal of Applied Psychology*, **89**, 1023–34.

Aquino, K., Grover, S., Bradfield, M. and Allen, D. (1999), 'The effects of negative affectivity, hierarchical status, and self-determination on workplace victimization', *Academy of Management Journal*, **42**(3), 260–72.

Archer, D. (1999), 'Exploring "bullying" culture in the para-military organization', *International Journal of Manpower*, **20**(1/2), 94–105.

Ashforth, B. (1989), 'The experience of powerlessness in organizations', *Organizational Behavior and Human Decision Process*, **43**, 207–42.

Ashforth, B. (1994), 'Petty tyranny in organizations', *Human Relations*, **47**(7), 755–78.

Ashforth, B. (1997), 'Petty tyranny in organizations: a preliminary examination of antecedents and consequences', *Canadian Journal of Administrative Sciences*, **14**(2), 216–40.

Baron, R.A. (1988), 'Negative effects of destructive criticism: impact on conflict, self efficiency and task performance', *Journal of Applied Psychology*, **73**, 199–207.

Batch, G.M. and Knoff, H.M. (1994), 'Bullies and their victims: understanding a pervasive problem in schools', *School Psychology Review*, **23**(2), 165–74.

Bjorkqvist, K. (1992), 'Trakassering forekommer bland anstallda vid AA' (Harassment exists among employees at Abo Academy), *Meddelanden fran Abo Akademi*, **9**, 14–17.

Bjorkqvist, K., Osterman, K. and Hjelt-Back, M. (1994), 'Aggression among university employees', *Aggressive Behavior*, **20**, 173–84.

Bowes-Sperry, L. and O'Leary-Kelly, A.M. (2005), To act or not to act: the dilemma faced by sexual harassment observers', *Academy of Management Review*, **30**, 288–306.

Brodsky, C.M. (1976), *The Harassed Worker*, Toronto: Lexington Books/D.C. Heath and Co.

Clarke, N.K. (1985), 'The sadistic manager', *Personnel*, **62**(2), 34–8.

Cleveland, J. and Kerst, M. (1993), 'Sexual harassment and perceptions of power: an underarticulated relationship', *Journal of Vocational Behavior*, **42**(1), 49–67.

Collinson, D.L. (1988), '"Engineering humour": masculinity, joking and conflict in shop-floor relations', *Organization Studies*, **9**(2), 181–99.

Coyne, I., Seigne, E. and Randall, P. (2000), 'Predicting workplace victim status from personality', *European Journal of Work and Organizational Psychology*, **9**(3), 335–49.

Coyne, I., Chong, P.S., Seigne, E. and Randall, P. (2003), 'Self and peer nominations of bullying: an analysis of incident rates, individual differences, and perceptions of the working environment', *European Journal of Work and Organizational Psychology*, **12**, 209–28.

Crawford, N. (1997), 'Bullying at work: a psychoanalytic perspective', *Journal of Community & Applied Social Psychology*, **7**, 219–25.

Delbecq, A.L. (2001), 'Evil manifested in destructive individual behaviour', *Journal of Management Inquiry*, **10**, 221–36.

Einarsen, S. (1996), 'Bullying and harassment at work: epidemiological and psychosocial aspects', Doctoral dissertation, Bergen: University of Bergen.

Einarsen, S. (1999), 'The nature and causes of bullying at work', *International Journal of Manpower*, **20**(1/2), 16–27.

Einarsen, S. (2000), 'Harassment and bullying at work: a review of the Scandinavian approach', *Aggression and Violent Behavior*, **4**(5), 379–401.

Einarsen, S. and Raknes, B.I. (1997), 'Harassment in the workplace and the victimization of men', *Violence and Victims*, **12**, 247–63.

Einarsen, S. and Skogstad, A. (1996), 'Bullying at work: epidemiological findings in public and private organizations', *European Journal of Work and Organizational Psychology*, **5**(2), 185–201.

Einarsen, S., Raknes, B.I. and Matthiesen, S.B. (1994a), 'Bullying and harassment at work and their relationships to work environment quality: an exploratory study', *European Work and Organizational Psychologist*, **4**(4), 381–401.

Einarsen, S., Raknes, B.I., Matthiesen, S.B. and Hellesøy, O.H. (1994b), *Mobbing og harde personkonflikter. Helsefarlig samspill på arbeidsplassen [Bullying and tough interpersonal conflicts. Health injurious interaction at the work place]*, Bergen: Sigma Forlag.

Einarsen, S., Hoel, H., Zapf, D. and Cooper, C.L. (2003), 'The concept of bullying at work: the European tradition', in S. Einarsen, H. Hoel, D. Zapf and C.L. Cooper (eds), *Bullying and Emotional Abuse in the Workplace*, London: Taylor & Francis, pp. 3–30.

Felson, R.B. (1992), 'Kick 'em when they're down: explanations of the relationship between stress and interpersonal aggression and violence', *Sociological Quarterly*, **33**, 1–17.

Frank, E., Carrera, J.S., Stratton, T., Bickel, J. and Nora, L.M. (2006), 'Experiences of belittlement and harassment and their correlates among medical students in the United States: longitudinal survey', *British Medical Journal*, **333**, 30 September, 682.

Gabriel, Y. (1998), 'An introduction to the social psychology of insults in organizations', *Human Relations*, **51**, 1329–54.

Gandolfo, R. (1995), 'MMPI-2 profiles of worker's compensation claimants who present with claimant of harassment', *Journal of Clinical Psychology*, **51**(5), 711–15.

Glasl, F. (1994), *Konfliktmanagement. Ein Handbuch fur Fuhrungskrafte und Berater* (Conflict Management: A Handbook for Managers and Consultants), 4th edn, Bern, Switzerland: Haupt.

Haynie, D.L., Nansel, T., Eitel, P., Crump, A.D., Saylor, K., Yu, K. and Simons-Morton, B. (2001), 'Bullies, victims, and bully/victims: distinct groups of at-risk youth', *Journal of Early Adolescence*, **21**, 29–50.

Hillier, C. (1995), 'On the record', *Hotel and Caterer*, 12 October, 40–42.

Hoel, H. and Cooper, C.L. (2000), *Destructive Conflict and Bullying at Work*, Manchester: Manchester School of Management.

Hoel, H., Einarsen, S. and Cooper, C.L. (2003), 'Organizational effects of bullying', in S. Einarsen, H. Hoel, D. Zapf and C.L. Cooper (eds), *Bullying and Emotional Abuse in the Workplace*, London: Taylor & Francis, pp. 145–61.

Hogh, A. and Dofradottir, A. (2001), 'Coping with bullying in the workplace', *European Journal of Work and Organizational Psychology*, **10**(4), 485–95.

Ishmael, A. (1999), *Harassment, Bullying and Violence at Work: a Practical Guide to Combating Employee Abuse*, London: The Industrial Society.

Jockin, V., Arvey, R.D. and McGue, M. (2001), 'Perceived victimization moderates self-report of workplace aggression and conflict', *Journal of Applied Psychology*, **86**, 1262–70.

Johns, N. and Menzel, P.J. (1999), ' "If you can't stand the heat!" . . . kitchen violence and culinary art', *Hospitality Management*, **18**, 99–109.

Keashly, L. and Jagatic, K. (2003), 'By another name: American perspectives on workplace bullying', in S. Einarsen, H. Hoel, D. Zapf and C.L. Cooper (eds), *Bullying and Emotional Abuse in the Workplace*, London: Taylor & Francis, pp. 31–61.

Kivimäki, M., Virtanen, M., Vartia, M., Elovainio, M., Vahtera, J. and Keltikangas-Järvinen, L. (2003), 'Workplace bullying and the risk of cardiovascular disease and depression', *Occupational and Environmental Medicine*, **60**, 779–83.

Kräkel, M. (1997), 'Rent-seeking in Organizationen – eine ökonomische analyse sozial schädlichen Verhaltens', *Schmalenbachs Zeitschrift für Betriebswirtschaftliche Forschung*, **49**(6), 535–55.

Langan-Fox, J. (2001), 'Women's careers and occupational stress', in C.L. Cooper and I.T. Robertson (eds), *Well-Being in Organizations*, Chichester, UK: John Wiley & Sons, pp. 177–208.

Langan-Fox, J. (2002), 'Communication in organizations: speed, diversity, networks and influence on organizational effectiveness, human health and relationships', in N. Anderson, D.S. Ones, H.K. Sinangil and C. Viswesvaren (eds), *Handbook of Industrial, Work and Organizational Psychology*, Vol. 2 London: Sage Publications, pp. 188–205.

Langan-Fox, J. (2005), 'New technology, the global economy and organizational environments: effects on employee stress, health and well-being', in C. Cooper and A.S. Antoniou (eds), *Research Companion to Organizational Health Psychology*, Cheltenham, UK and Northampton, MA, USA: Edward Elgar, pp. 413–29.

Langan-Fox, J., Waycott, J., Morizzi, M. and McDonald, L. (1998), 'Predictors of participation in performance appraisal: a voluntary system in a blue collar work environment', *International Journal of Selection and Assessment*, **6**(4), 249–60.

Lee, D. (2000), 'An analysis of workplace bullying in the UK', *Personnel Review*, **29**(5), 593–604.

Lee, D. (2002), 'Gendered workplace bullying in the restructured UK Civil Service', *Personnel Review*, **31**(1/2), 205–27.

Lee, R.T. and Brotheridge, C.M. (2006), 'When prey turns predatory: workplace bullying as a predictor of counteraggression/bullying, coping and well being', *European Journal of Work and Organizational Psychology*, **15**(3), 352–77.

Leymann, H. (1992), *Fran mobbning till utslagning I arbetslivet* (From Bullying to Expulsion from Working Life), Stockholm: Publica.

Leymann, H. (1993), *Mobbing – Psychoterror am Arbeitsplatz und wie man sich dagegen wehren kann* (Mobbing – Psychoterror in the Workplace and How One can Defend Oneself), Reinbeck, Germany: Rowohlt.

Leymann, H. (1996), 'The content and development of mobbing at work', *European Journal of Work and Organizational Psychology*, **5**(2), 165–84.

Leymann, H. and Gustafsson, A. (1996), 'Mobbing at working and the development of post-traumatic stress disorders', *European Journal of Work and Organizational Psychology*, **5**, 251–75.

Liefooghe, A.P.D. and Mackenzie Davey, K. (2001), 'Accounts of workplace bullying: the role of the organization', *European Journal of Work and Organizational Psychology*, **10**(4), 375–92.

McCarthy, P. (1996), 'When the mask slips: inappropriate coercion in organizations undergoing restructuring', in P. McCarthy, M. Shennan and D. Wilkie (eds), *Bullying: From Backyard to Boardroom*, Alexandria, VA: Millennium Books, pp. 55–72.

Myers, R.J. (1977), 'Fear, anger and depression in organizations: a study of the emotional consequences of power', unpublished doctoral dissertation, St. Johns University, New York.

Neuberger, O. (1999), *Mobbing: Ubel Mitspielen in Organisationen* (Mobbing – Foul Play in Organizations), (3rd rev. edn), Munich, Germany: Rainer Hampp Verlag.

Neuman, J.H. and Baron, R.A. (1998), 'Workplace violence and workplace aggression: evidence concerning specific forms, potential causes, and preferred targets', *Journal of Management*, **24**(3), 391–419.

Niedl, K. (1995), *Mobbing/bullying am Arbeitsplatz*. Munich, Germany: Rainer Hampp Verlag.

Niedl, K. (1996), 'Mobbing and well being: economic and personnel development implications', *European Journal of Work and Organizational Psychology*, **5**(2), 239–49.

O'Leary-Kelly, A.M., Griffin, R.W. and Glew, D.J. (1996), 'Organization-motivated aggression: a research framework', *Academy of Management Review*, **21**(1), 225–53.

Olweus, D. (1993), *Bullying at School. What We Know and What We Can Do*, Oxford: Blackwell Publishers.

O'Moore, M., Seigne, E., Mcguire, L. and Smith, M. (1998), 'Victims of bullying at work in Ireland', *Journal of Occupational Health and Safety – Australia and New Zealand*, **14**(6), 569–74.

Papaioannou, S. and Sjoblom, L. (1992), *Arbetsplatstrakassering i Kvinnodominerad vardmiljo*, Finland: Abo Akademi, humanistiska fakulteten, psykologiska institutionen.

Podsakoff, P.M. and Schriesheim, C.A. (1985), 'Field studies of French & Ravens bases of power: critique, reanalysis, and suggestions for future Research', *Psychological Bulletin*, **97**, 387–411.

Quine, L. (1999), 'Workplace bullying in NHS community trust: staff questionnaire survey. *British Medical Journal*, **318**, 23 January, 201–15.

Raine, A., Buchsbaum, S.J., Lottenberg, S., Abel, L. and Stoddard, J. (1994), 'Selective reductions in prefrontal glucose metabolism in murderers', *Biological Psychiatry*, **36**, 127–38.

Randall, P. (1997), *Adult Bullying: Perpetrators and Victims*, London: Routledge.

Rayner, C. (1997), 'The incidence of workplace bullying', *Journal of Community and Applied Social Psychology*, **7**, 199–208.

Rayner, C. and Hoel, H. (1997), 'A summary review of literature relating to workplace bullying', *Journal of Community and Applied Social Psychology*, **7**, 181–91.

Rayner, C., Hoel, H. and Cooper, C.L. (2002), *Workplace Bullying: What We Know, Who is to Blame, and What Can We Do?*, London: Taylor & Francis.

Resch, M. and Schubinski, M. (1996), 'Mobbing – prevention and management in organizations', *European Journal of Work and Organizational Psychology*, **5**(2), 295–307.

Robinson, S.L. and O'Leary-Kelly, A.M. (1998), 'Monkey see, monkey do: the influence of work groups on the antisocial behaviour of employees', *Academy of Management Journal*, **41**(6), 658–72.

Salin, D. (2001), 'Prevalence and forms of bullying among business professionals: a comparison of two different strategies for measuring bullying', *European Journal of Work and Organizational Psychology*, **10**(4), 425–41.

Salin, D. (2003a), 'Ways of explaining workplace bullying: a review of enabling, motivating and precipitating structures and processes in the work environment', *Human Relations*, **56**(10), 1213–32.

Salin, D. (2003b), 'Bullying and organizational politics in competitive and rapidly changing work environments', *International Journal of Management and Decision-Making*, **4**(1), 35–46.

Seigne, E. (1998), 'Bullying at work in Ireland', paper presented at the Bullying at Work Research Update Conference, Stafford.

Sewell, G. and Wilkinson, B. (1992), 'Empowerment or emasculation?', in X. Blyton and X. Turnbull (eds), *Reassessing Human Resource Management*, London: Sage, pp. 323–41.

Sheehan, M. and Jordan, P. (2003), 'Bullying, emotions and the learning organisation', in S. Einarsen, H. Hoel, D. Zapf and C. Cooper (Eds), *Bullying and Emotional Abuse in the Workplace: International Perspectives in Research and Practice*, London: Taylor & Francis, pp. 32–45.

Smith, P.K., Singer, M., Hoel, H. and Cooper, C.L. (2003), 'Victimization in the school and workplace', *British Journal of Psychology*, **94**, 175–88.

Sutela, H. and Lehto, A.M. (1998), Henkinen vakivalta on koko tyoyhteison ongelma (Bullying is a problem of the whole work unit), *Hyvinvointikatsaus*, **3**, 18–24.

Tattum, D. and Tattum, E. (1996), 'Bullying: a whole school response', in P. McCarthy, M. Sheehan and W. Wilke (eds), *Bullying: From backyard to boardroom*, Alexandria, Australia: Millennium Books, pp. 13–23.

Tepper, B.J. (2000), 'Consequences of abusive supervision', *Academy of Management Journal*, **43**, 178–90.

Thylefors, I. (1987), *Syndabockar – om utstötning och mobbning i arbetslivet* (Scapegoats – about exclusion and bullying in work life), Stockholm: Natur och Kultur.

Vartia, M. (1996), 'The sources of bullying: psychological work environment and organizational climate', *European Journal of Work and Organizational Psychology*, **5**(2), 203–14.

Watson, D. and Clark, L.A. (1984), 'Negative affectivity: the disposition to experience aversive emotional states', *Psychological Bulletin*, **96**, 465–90.

Zapf, D. (1999), 'Organisational, work group related and personal causes of mobbing/bullying at work', *International Journal of Manpower*, **20**(1/2), 70–85.

Zapf, D. and Einarsen, S. (2003), 'Individual antecedents of bullying', in S. Einarsen, H. Hoel, D. Zapf and C.L. Cooper (eds), *Bullying and Emotional Abuse in the Workplace*, London: Taylor & Francis, pp. 165–84.

Zapf, D. and Gross, C. (2001), 'Conflict escalation and coping with workplace bullying: a replication and extension', *European Journal of Work and Organizational Psychology*, **10**(4), 497–522.

Zapf, D. and Warth, K. (1997), 'Mobbing: Subtile Kriegsführung am Arbeitsplatz', *Psychologie Heute*, **20**; 28–9.

Zapf, D., Knorz, C. and Kulla, M. (1995), 'On the relationship between mobbing factors, and job content, social work environment, and health outcomes', *European Journal of Work and Organizational Psychology*, **5**(2), 215–37.

5 The struggle of the self: identity dysfunctions in the contemporary workplace
Glen E. Kreiner

Introduction
Employment relationships are changing dramatically in the contemporary workplace. The new employment contract has redefined work arrangements of the past and ushered in a new era of organizational complexity (Rousseau, 1997). These changes bring about new challenges and tensions in the worker–workplace interface. As societies, organizations, families and individuals each become more complex, the interactions among them magnify in complexity as well. This new complexity calls for a richer understanding of existing constructs in the organizational literature – research that mirrors the intricacy and nuance experienced by the modern worker. In this chapter, I provide one such approach by examining several of the identity and identification dysfunctions in the modern workplace. Specifically, I examine how the 'struggle for self' (Baumeister, 1986) manifests itself in often dysfunctional ways in the workplace. I do so by examining eight specific dysfunctions, four of which derive from imbalanced identity boundaries, and four of which are suboptimal identification states. I then end the chapter by suggesting ways that individuals and organizations might work toward reducing identity dysfunctions in the workplace.

I have two goals with this chapter. First, for those readers not intimately familiar with the identity and identification literatures, I hope to orient you toward how these areas of research can be linked with yours to better understand the common identity-based dysfunctions in the modern workplace. Second, for those who do toil in the identity and identification areas of research, I hope to present a framework for how we might understand the linkages between what we research and the broader issues of dysfunctions in the workplace.

Identity and identification
The concepts of identity and identification have proven to be fertile ground for exploring the dynamics of self-definition via a multitude of contexts and situations (Haslam et al., 2003; Hogg and Terry, 2001; Sedikides and Brewer, 2001). Yet, despite their popularity, confusion remains around the meanings and uses of the terms 'identity' and 'identification' (Pratt, 1998). Hence a brief review is in order here. Individual 'identity' consists of two dimensions: (1) personal identity, which comprises *unique* aspects of the self that differentiate a person from others; and (2) social identity, which comprises *shared* aspects with some social group that depersonalize the self by emphasizing group membership (Brewer, 1991).

'Identification' is the degree to which a person embraces a given social identity (Tajfel and Turner, 1986). Hence we speak of identification with any social group (an organization, a team, a church, a gender, an age group, an ethnicity, etc.) as the extent to which the definition of self comprises that particular social identity. Identification processes can occur early on in a person's relationship with the social group, and can change throughout that relationship (Pratt, 1998). Organizational identification, for example, might even begin to occur before a person is hired, if that person has preconceived ideas about the organization and potential value congruence. More typically, though, the hiring process and subsequent socialization are the first major processes through which identification with the organization unfolds. As such, many of the dysfunctions described below might actually start during, or be exacerbated by, hiring and socialization processes. Oversocializing newcomers or hiring individuals with a lack of fit toward organizational values can be precursors to the full-blown dysfunctions outlined below.

Perhaps because of its centrality to modern living, the workplace now constitutes a considerable source of identity and identification for individuals. The prominent role of organizations in our lives results in a number of potential identity-based dysfunctions for the individual, which I explore herein. I divide the dysfunctions into two types: those dealing with identity, and those dealing with identification. Accordingly, each section below comprises two parts – first, a description of a dysfunction that arises relating to individual *identity*, followed by a description of a dysfunctional *identification* state that is likely to result from the identity problem. This two-part approach will allow for an exploration into identity dysfunction that illustrates how individual identity and organizational identification work in tandem. This linkage is often advocated, but rarely provided, in the research literature.

Identity boundaries
In order to better explore potential identity dysfunctions, as well as the linkages between identity and identification, I shall call upon the lens of *identity boundaries*. This perspective, which has been invoked in recent years, has proved to be a particularly useful lens for understanding identity dynamics (Hartmann, 1991; Kreiner et al., 2006b; Paulsen, 2003). Identity boundaries have been referred to as 'self-boundaries' (Whitfield, 1993) or 'ego boundaries' (Freud, 1923). Though labels vary, the basic idea is the same: individuals create cognitive, physical or temporal boundaries around themselves that serve to demarcate where the self begins and ends. Hence a boundary separates an individual from other individuals and from collectives such as groups and organizations. Zerubavel (1991: 13) applies the notion of an identity boundary when he writes, 'The manner in which we isolate supposedly discrete "figures" from their surrounding "ground" is also manifested in the way we come to experience ourselves. It involves a form of mental differentiation that entails a fundamental distinction between us and the rest of the world. It is known as our sense of identity.' Hence an important part of understanding oneself involves identity boundaries. Creating and maintaining healthy identity boundaries requires work, and individuals are prone to numerous pitfalls or dysfunctions as they engage in this 'identity work' (Kreiner et al., 2006a). Family, school, work and other social environments affect individual identity boundary development. Identity theorists generally argue that identity formation occurs throughout one's life, beginning in infancy and occurring (though typically less dramatically) throughout adulthood (Harter, 2003).

Identity and identification dysfunctions

Identity dysfunction 1: weak identity boundaries
The first type of identity boundary dysfunction is what I shall term a 'weak identity boundary'. This refers to an individual who lacks a sufficiently robust self-concept,

leaving him- or herself overly vulnerable to the influences of others and to the demands of the workplace. An examination of various treatments of personal identity and the potential for the weak identity boundary follows, with the intent of further articulating the dysfunction of a weak identity boundary.

Although they do not use this terminology *per se*, the notion of identity boundaries can be traced back to ancient philosophers and religious leaders. Lao-tzu, for example, referred to attachments outside the self as the '10,000 things' (Lao-tzu, 1997), and the Buddha advocated the separation and detachment of self from the external world. Consider the symbolic boundaries of the roof and the island in these passages by the Buddha: 'An unreflecting mind is a poor roof. Passion, like the rain, floods the house. But if the roof is strong, there is shelter' (Bancroft, 1997: 36). Similarly, 'By watching and working, the master makes for himself an island, which the flood cannot overwhelm' (ibid.: 39). Implicit in each of these early approaches to understanding identity is the preference for strong identity boundaries – the individual taking charge of his or her boundaries in relation to the outside world, standing willfully independent of the forces and influences of nature, custom and society.

Modern psychology in the twentieth century has frequently used the concept of boundaries to illustrate mental health issues. Freud (1923) spoke of the *Reizschutz*, a protective shield or barrier against the outside world important to all organisms, and noted, 'We describe as traumatic the excitations from outside which are powerful enough to break through the protective shield' (Freud, 1920: 29). He referred to this shield as a 'body ego' (Freud, 1923), but his followers developed the concept of 'ego boundary' to refer to the division between ego and the outside world (see Federn, 1952, for an example).

Much of modern psychotherapy assumes that healthy individuals know what is inside or outside themselves, whereas psychotic individuals lack these basic distinctions (Hartmann, 1991). However, some sociologists have noted that modern society dissolves the boundaries of self, as social pressures and influences blur the once-clear border between public and private lives (Bensman and Lilienfeld, 1974). And in observing other world cultures, countries such as Japan tend to celebrate the permeability of individual identity through fostering collectivist versus individualist norms (Hofstede, 1984).

Similar to ancient and historical writings dealing with boundaries, modern psychology implicitly (and sometimes explicitly) argues that strong identity boundaries are superior to weak ones, that a clear sense of self as being – and staying – distinct and separate from others is a crucial part of mental health. Katherine (1991: 70–72) put it this way:

> Weak boundaries equal a weak self-image; a healthy self-image equals healthy boundaries. Boundaries without a self would be like a punctured balloon. It collapses when nothing is inside. A self without boundaries is like air without a balloon, shapeless, formless, diffused . . . A clean, clear boundary preserves your individuality, your youness. You are an individual, set apart, different, unique. Your history, your experiences, personality, interests, dislikes, preferences, perceptions, values, priorities, skills – this unique combination defines you as separate from others.

Hence, from ancient philosophy to modern psychology, an admonition for healthy identity boundaries has been given. Weak identity boundaries leave the individual susceptible to excessive influence from other people and social domains. If you don't know who you are, the logic goes, someone (or something) else will tell you. This susceptibility is particularly problematic in regard to workplace dysfunction, as organizations, occupations and other workplace social groups can be particularly 'greedy' in their demands on individuals (Kreiner et al., 2006a). Without a strong sense of self to counteract the greed, one's individuality is further lost. An example of how this occurs can be found in overidentification.

Identification dysfunction 1: overidentification
The first dysfunctional identification state is *overidentification*, which has been defined as an extreme case of identification 'where the self gets lost, the identity of the organization replaces self, and little of the self is left – there is little or no perceived uniqueness or differentiating factors' (Dukerich et al., 1998: 247). Individuals with weak identity boundaries represent an interesting individual difference that, I believe, makes them particularly prone to overly embrace the identity provided by an organization. That is, if an individual lacks a clear self-concept, and the organization has a particularly strong identity, the individual is more likely to become overidentified. (I should note here that, although my focus is on identification issues with the organization, overidentification and other dysfunctions can also occur with other targets, such as the occupation or the work group. Indeed, dysfunction related to any entity can spill over into an unhealthy relationship with the organization.)

Overidentification is a kind of addiction, which is any substance or process that has taken over one's life (Reber, 1995). In this case, the 'addict' over-relies on the organization to fulfill his or her identity needs and to replace the emptiness that accompanies weak identity boundaries. In their work, Schaef and Fassel (1990) label organizations as a potentially addictive substance. They wrote about their research studies:

> We were seeing something more than the organization as a setting for addictive behavior: in many instances, the organization was itself the addictive substance. It was both setting *and* substance . . . Nothing in and of itself is addictive. *Anything* can be addictive when it becomes so central in one's life that one feels that life is not possible without the substance or the process . . . We recognized that for many people, the workplace, the job, and the organization were the central foci of their lives. Because the organization was so primary in their lives, because they were totally preoccupied with it, they began to lose touch with other aspects of their lives and gradually gave up what they knew, felt, and believed. (Ibid.: 118–19)

While it is clear to see how overidentification can be dysfunctional for the individual, it is also important to consider how collective overidentification among a workforce can be dysfunctional for the organization. First, overidentification may very well lead to a homogenization of the workplace, resulting in a lack of diversity and creativity. This impedes the organization's ability to recognize and respond to environmental changes. Second, the homogenization from collective overidentification may lead to impaired decision making, such as has been documented with groupthink (Janis, 1982). Third, as Dukerich et al. (1998) note, overidentifiers may be more inclined to break rules and laws for the organization's benefit, as well as be more likely to cover up the wrongdoing of others in the organization. Hence managing identification processes becomes important for healthy diversity, innovation and an ethical climate.

Identity dysfunction 2: work–self intrusion
The second type of identity dysfunction is *work–self intrusion*, which was articulated by Kreiner et al. (2006b) as occurring when an individual perceives that his or her otherwise

healthy identity boundaries are being breached or penetrated in an unwanted fashion by the organization. For example, an organization with a strong culture might attempt to change its employees' personal values or individuality, seemingly asking them to give up a sense of their own personal identity in order to fit in with others and/or support the organizational mission or culture. In response to such a demand, the individual may perceive that he or she has had to give up a valuable part of him- or herself. The person experiences an identity boundary conflict as his or her personal boundary is intruded upon by the organization. In work–self intrusion, the organization 'punctures' the individual identity. Note the key difference here between work–self intrusion and a weak identity boundary – with the latter, the individual does not have a healthy concept of self, whereas in the former, his/her healthy sense of self is disturbed or violated by the organization.

Identification dysfunction 2: disidentification
The second dysfunctional identification state is *disidentification*, which occurs when an individual's self-definition is based on an active separation between individual identity and organizational identity (Elsbach and Bhattacharya, 2001). In other words, individuals who disidentify see themselves as not having the same attributes that define the organization. This disconnection from the organizational identity is thought to enhance an individual's social identity by separating him or her from the negatively evaluated organization (Elsbach, 1999). I believe that one path to disidentification results from individuals having experienced work–self intrusion. When an individual has a strong sense of self and perceives that the organization is trying to change that identity, he or she is likely to resent such actions. This would be particularly the case when the individual perceives an incongruity in the values of the identities. This resentment can be the seed or the spark leading to festering or accelerating disidentification. Further, I suspect that a strong organizational identity (normally required for intrusion) is also a typical prerequisite for a person to strongly disidentify; it's hard to feel strongly about an organization that doesn't have a clear identity.

There are, of course, other paths to disidentification. For example, Pratt (2000) found that Amway distributors who disidentified with the organization were those who had initially embraced the ideology of the company but later became disenchanted with it. Hence strong initial identification can be a precursor to disidentification, as opposed to disenchantment simply leading to neutral identification. Other documented antecedents to disidentification include a negative organizational reputation, psychological contract breach and negative affectivity (Kreiner and Ashforth, 2004).

Of course, disidentification is dysfunctional for the individual and the organization. Disidentification 'can become all-consuming, paralyzing the individual and dominating his or her actions in the organization' (Dukerich et al., 1998: 250). Disidentification also likely exhausts more cognitive and emotional resources than identification, draining the individual of energy and the organization of a potential resource (Dukerich et al., 1998; Kreiner and Ashforth, 2004). Disidentifiers could create instability in work groups, as they would be perceived (both by themselves and others) as misfits. Disidentifiers will be more likely to engage in behaviors that harm the organization, such as speaking out against it or performing acts of sabotage (Dukerich et al., 1998). They would also be less likely to form trusting relationships within the organization or build interdependencies in a team, as the disidentification with the organization spills over or trickles down into subgroups and individuals within the organization.

Identity dysfunction 3: work–self distance

The third type of identity boundary dysfunction is *work–self distance*. It occurs when the individual perceives that the organization has been too distant or uninvolved in the identity sensemaking process experienced at work (Kreiner et al., 2006b). When an individual feels that the organization has not provided him or her with adequate ideologies or identity, distance conflict is experienced. We can therefore speak of distance conflict as the result of an individual who desires an organization to provide him or her with a stronger identity boundary than is available. So, in contrast to work–self intrusion, work–self distance leaves the individual 'high and dry' in terms of being provided a useful identity at work.

Kreiner et al. (2006a) argue that both work–self intrusion and work–self distance will result in negative individual and organizational consequences, primarily as a result of an imbalance between the desired and the actual level of organizational identity provided to the individual. This assertion has important implications for understanding the management of identity in order to avoid dysfunction: identity needs will vary among individuals; and managers should be wary of either inflicting an unwanted identity (which would lead to intrusion) or not providing a sought-after identity (which would lead to distance). Kreiner et al. (2006b) advocate that managers work toward providing 'work–self balance', wherein an optimal equilibrium between organizational and individual identities is found. Note that this is a similar argument often made by work–family researchers – that workplaces should attempt to balance the segmentation or integration of work and life aspects rather than either forcing an artificial separation or inflicting unwanted work aspects into the non-work environment (Kirchmeyer, 1995).

Identification dysfunction 3: neutral identification

Let's consider now how work–self distance might affect identification. I believe work–self distance is one of many paths to what has been called *neutral identification* (Elsbach, 1999; Kreiner, 2001; Kreiner and Ashforth, 2004) or *underidentification* (Dukerich et al., 1998), which occurs when individuals neither identify nor disidentify with the organization. It 'does not instantiate an identity, and the absence of such an identity proves dysfunctional' (ibid.: 248). Since employees are not receiving the level of organizational identity they desire, yet there is no strong organizational identity with which to disidentify, this anemic state results. Neutral or underidentification is dysfunctional for the individual and organization. For the individual, the extreme detachment can result in intense anxiety (Baumeister, 1986), suboptimal distinctiveness (Brewer, 1991) and a sense of disconnectedness (Glynn, 1998). For the organization, it loses valuable resources in this worker, who would be far less likely to engage in superior performance or extra-role behaviors (Kreiner and Ashforth, 2004). Further, the underidentified employee will likely need extrinsic incentives in order to perform, costing the organization additional resources.

Identity dysfunction 4: incongruent multiple identities

While the preceding sections focus on boundaries of the self and their relation to the organization, this section examines identity boundaries *within* an individual. These internal boundaries demarcate parts of the individual as separate from one another. Hence we can speak of the thickness of *internal identity boundaries* as a proclivity toward either integrating or segmenting parts of one's identity into subidentities (also called roles). This notion of internal boundaries has been variously conceptualized as division of 'life space', 'self aspects' and 'multiple identities'. These approaches have a common thread: that the placing and maintaining of internal boundaries is an individual difference. In order to show how multiple identities can lay a foundation for identity dysfunction, I now give a brief history of various approaches to internal individual boundaries.

William James (1920: 9) gave detailed descriptions of two types of 'temperament' in individuals – rationalist and empiricist: rationalists were described as 'starting from the whole or universals, making much of the unity of things', while empiricists were described as 'starting from the parts', not the whole. Lewin (1938) used the notion of a 'life space' to describe the psychological environment created and lived in by individuals. Individuals carve out different patterns in their life space and differentiate aspects of their lives by creating and maintaining boundaries of varying permeability. Some regions of the self may be highly permeable to others (allowing flow between them), while some are rigid and isolated from other regions. A similar notion is found in the definition of compartmentalization, a word psychologists use to describe 'the isolation of various . . . thoughts, feelings, and beliefs from each other' (Reber, 1995: 142).

The concept of multiple identities has also been used to explain how individuals partition elements of themselves. A person's identity has been conceptualized as a collection of role identities, which are essentially role-specific self-descriptions made up of the characteristics a person ascribes to him/herself in a particular social role (Stryker and Serpe, 1982). Hence individuals have 'multiple selves' that are created by a person's self-conceptions derived from various social domains. These can be thought of as subcomponents of one's global identity, or 'subidentities'.

Similarly, some theorists (see Showers, 2000 for an example) have conceptualized individuals as comprising many 'self-aspects' (reflecting roles, the self in specific situations, personality traits and so on) that may be more or less compartmentalized. Nippert-Eng (1996) found wide variation in the degree to which individuals integrated or segmented home and work domains, even when in the same occupation and/or organization. That is, they differed in the integration or segmentation of their subidentities or roles. Some individuals would separate the two worlds (subidentities) by keeping separate calendars and key chains, and not discussing the events of one domain with the participants of the other. Conversely, others would display pictures of family at work, bring co-workers home for dinner, etc. Extreme segmentation and extreme integration can both be dysfunctional for the individual. High integration makes boundary preservation difficult, while high segmentation makes role transitions challenging (Ashforth et al., 2000).

While most theorists on multiple identities agree that the degree of segmentation will vary among individuals, Deaux and Perkins (2001: 302) argue that for everyone, 'the various forms of self-representation are inextricably linked to one another through shared attributes or components of self. Thus . . . the structure of self is one in which the attributes are always linked and thus, on every occasion, are potentially coactors in self-definition and in action.' In other words, even those who segment and compartmentalize will interrelate their subidentities in some way. This has important implications for potential identity dysfunction. Specifically, it implies that if one element of identity is dysfunctional, that element can bleed into other elements and circumstances, suggesting that the 'whole self' must be understood and managed, not merely the part of the self that is typically invoked during the work day.

Of course, the interplay among multiple identities can be functional as well as dysfunctional, and debate lingers about the psychological costs and benefits of multiple identities (Ashforth and Johnson, 2001; Thoits, 1987). Shorto (1999) argues that the collapse of internal boundaries can be either a transcending experience (as is documented by Shorto of early Christian saints) or a destructive experience (as is the case for severe mental collapses). Dysfunctions that have been documented as a result of competing multiple identities include increased role conflict and a sense of self-fragmentation (Showers and Zeigler-Hill, 2003).

Identification dysfunction 4: ambivalent identification

So, how might multiple identities affect possible identification dysfunction? Previous research has shown that multiple identities (individual or organizational) can lead to *ambivalent identification*, which is the presence of both strong identification and strong disidentification (Elsbach, 1999; Kreiner and Ashforth, 2004; Pratt, 2000; Pratt and Doucet, 2000). This is particularly salient when the multiple identities are clearly in conflict with one another (Kreiner and Ashforth, 2004). Ambivalent identification can result from incongruence at the individual identity level, the organizational identity level, or both. First, when *individual* aspects of identity are in conflict, different parts of the individual would respond differently to the same organizational identity. For example, an individual with a strong identity component of 'star employee' could deeply identify with a 'greedy' culture that demands much of his or her time; yet that same person could have a strong identity component of 'parent' that disidentifies with the organization because it routinely takes him or her away from important family opportunities.

The second path to ambivalence occurs when *organizational* aspects of identity are in conflict. In this case, an individual may identify with some aspects of the organizational identity (that are in alignment with the individual) while disidentifying with other aspects (that are not in alignment) (Kreiner and Ashforth, 2004). In what Pratt (2001) calls 'multiple organizational identity environments' (MOIEs), the organization has two or more important identities that vie for employees' attention. At least two identity dysfunctions can often be seen in individuals and groups working in MOIEs. First, an individual can experience conflict as he or she tries to 'choose' or prioritize which identity is most important (Elsbach, 2001; Pratt and Foreman, 2000). For example, because family businesses often have strong identities linked to family roots, but also have a strong business function, family members are often torn between the two identities (Sundaramurthy and Kreiner, in press).

Second, different groups within an organization (e.g. departments) often assign conflicting salience to different identities. For example, Pratt and Rafaeli (1997) found three competing identities among groups of nurses in a rehabilitation hospital (an example of an MOIE): 'rehabilitation identity', 'acute care identity' and 'nurse as public servant identity'. Another example of an MOIE results from the merger or acquisition of two companies, which leaves groups with at least three potential challenges: (1) one group (i.e. one of the two organizations) might be required to 'shift' identities and identifications to align with the dominant identity; (2) both groups might face a newly created superordinate identity; or (3) the two previous identities continue to coexist in the new organization. These scenarios can create confusion and identity dysfunction among workers as groups are either asked to change their previous conceptualizations and attachments or work in a newly defined (or ill-defined) environment. Hence multiple organizational identities can lead to strong ambivalence in workers as they are torn between different aspects of the organization. The upshot of this research is that multiple organizational identities must be managed to avoid dysfunctional individual identities and ambivalent identification. (See Pratt and Foreman, 2000 for an excellent typology of managerial responses to multiple organizational identities.)

Toward resolving identity/identification dysfunctions

Thus far, I have been guilty of airing quite a bit of dirty laundry, in terms of identity in the workplace, without suggesting much in the way of remedy. So, in this section I begin a modest attempt to outline some of the possible paths toward resolving identity dysfunctions in the workplace. While this goal might be 'easier said than done', my intention is to lay out strategies at the individual, organizational and societal levels that may prove useful in ameliorating identity dysfunctions. Hence employees, managers, consultants or human resources specialists might find value in adapting these strategies to their own circumstances to prevent, reduce or intervene regarding these dysfunctions. The three strategies are: invoking identity work tactics; adjusting one's need for organizational identification; and reenergizing nonwork domains.

Invoking identity work tactics

Much of my own research has focused on how individuals in highly problematic occupations manage to have healthy identities. My work with Blake Ashforth and other colleagues, for example, has examined how those in dirty work professions are often able to construct very positive individual identities in the face of stigma and taint (Ashforth and Kreiner, 1999; Ashforth et al., 2007; Kreiner et al., 2006). Similarly, my work with Elaine Hollensbe and Mathew Sheep has demonstrated how those in a particularly 'greedy' occupation (Episcopal priests) can still maintain a sense of self despite strong demands on their identities (Kreiner et al., 2006a). The upshot of these research projects has been that individuals do not need to be mere passive recipients of the identity conditions of their workplace and/or occupation. Rather, they can quite actively negotiate the identity demands by invoking various cognitive and behavioral tactics. I review some of these below, with the aim to provide practical solutions to some of the aforementioned identity dysfunctions.

In our work on Episcopal priests, we identified three broad classifications of identity work tactics that respondents used to help maintain a positive identity (Kreiner et al., 2006a). These include (1) segmenting tactics (which separated the personal and social identity), (2) integrating tactics (which blended the personal and social identity in order to be more like a 'typical' priest), and (3) dual-function or neutral tactics that could be used to either segment or integrate. We uncovered five segmenting tactics. The first, *separating role from identity*, involves marking the difference between the functional approach to the occupation ('this is what I do') and the ontological approach to the occupation ('this is who I am'). With the second, *setting limits*, individuals acknowledge their capacity and human limitations to perform the occupational demands; this allows an escape when pressures get too high, as in 'I've reached my limits and that's OK.' The third, *creating an identity hierarchy*, involves creating a clear order of identities, such as 'family first' or 'take care of myself first, then others'. This allows for a pecking order that is used to make decisions about how and when to spend time and cognitive resources for the job. The fourth, *enacting ephemeral roles*, is accomplished by stepping into an entirely different role from that of work, such as coaching soccer, joining a club, etc. By immersing – temporarily – in a role that is unrelated (and sometimes counter to) the work identity, the individual can escape the pressures of the work role. The fifth segmenting tactic, *flipping the on–off switch*, involves consciously choosing to make the work identity explicit or implicit at a given time. This can be done either intrapersonally (saying to oneself, 'you are *not* at work now') or interpersonally (saying to others, 'I don't want to talk shop while we're at dinner'). The common theme among the segmenting tactics is that the person can consciously separate – whether temporarily or longer-term – their work social identity from their personal identity.

Conversely, we also uncovered three tactics that were meant to combine work identity with personal identity. These were undertaken as a means to draw closer to work and gain deeper meaning from it. The first integrating tactic, *merging role with identity*, involves consciously blending work and personal identity and not treating 'self' and 'role' as separate at all. To invoke the second tactic, *infusing self aspects into task*, unique elements of self (personal identity, personality, life history) are incorporated into elements of the job, bringing one's own individuality to the task at hand. The third, *casting self as emblem*, involves framing oneself as a symbol or representative of the occupation or the ideologies inherent in it; this enables the individual to feel like a more meaningful part of the occupation.

In addition to the tactics that were clearly segmenting or integrating, we discovered three tactics that could be used to perform either function as needed in the moment. The first of these dual-function tactics, *seeking refreshment*, is accomplished by seeking renewal of important individual aspects for a sense of self-preservation or respite, or to avoid burnout. The second, *involving other people*, involves allowing or asking others to help with identity work; this can include family members, stakeholders, friends, or therapists who help the individual work through identity challenges. The third, *tapping spiritual resources*, involves using non-secular approaches, such as consulting a spiritual director or searching for answers to identity dilemmas through prayer, meditation, scripture or worship. While our sample consisted of priests, these spiritual approaches are of course practiced more widely than merely by those in religious occupations.

In addition to these tactics from my own research, Philipson (2002) gives several specific suggestions for avoiding identity dysfunctions such as workaholism. (See also Burke and McAteer, Chapter 10 in this volume.) These include: setting clear boundaries before a dilemma arrives; leaving work at a particular time each day rather than working as late as 'needed'; setting aside time every day to pause and reflect, accomplishing no 'regular' work; establishing limits on 'electronic leashes' by not checking emails, answering phones, etc.; ensuring that one has close friends who are not colleagues; taking vacations; and communicating with oneself via journals and with others via email or conversations about what is happening at work.

Adjusting one's need for identification
While much work on identification has focused on factors of the organization, more recent attention has been given to how individuals vary in their 'need for organizational

identification' or 'nOID' (Glynn, 1998). nOID is defined as 'an individual's need to maintain a social identity derived from membership in a larger, more impersonal general social category of a particular collective' (ibid.: 238–9). Note that nOID differs from McClelland's (1987) need for affiliation in that nOID necessarily implicates an identity-based relationship between the person and the organization, whereas affiliation need not invoke identity processes. An individual's nOID comprises such issues as feeling incomplete without a meaningful organization to work for; sensing that an important part of self would be missing if one didn't define the self through work; desiring to find a higher purpose of life through one's organization; or having a sense of emptiness filled by an organization (Kreiner and Ashforth, 2004). A person's own identity needs can dramatically affect what type of attachment he or she experiences in the workplace. That is, overly strong needs for such attachment can lead to an unhealthy dependence on the organization for one's own identity and perceived survival. Such highly dysfunctional levels can be a precursor to deviant behaviors such as fostering corruption in order to help the organization at any cost (Anand et al., 2004).

While nOID is defined as an individual difference, it is interesting to note that in my work with Blake Ashforth, we found in a highly diverse sample of university alumni that the mean score for our measure of nOID was 3.49 on a scale of 1–5 (SD = 0.64) (Kreiner and Ashforth, 2004). This suggests that the need to identify is rather high *generally*. This might be a symptom of the modern cultural norms (found in many countries) of high importance placed on work in relation to other social spheres, discussed in the next section. We also found a significant correlation between nOID and being a supervisor or manager. Two possible inferences can be drawn from this finding. First, those with higher levels of nOID worked their way higher up the organization to become more vested with the organization identity sought after, thereby fulfilling their identity need. Second, once individuals were promoted, their preferences were actually changed, perhaps because the identity provided them became more meaningful (e.g., 'now that I have this, I need it').

So, how might we apply this work to identity dysfunction? First, identifying and labeling a phenomenon can give individuals power over it. That is, understanding what nOID is and that it varies among people can help workers and managers to be more aware of their own underlying need that might be driving a considerable amount of their own behaviors (e.g. working too many hours, trying desperately to climb the corporate ladder, sacrificing time with family). Second, this awareness can lead to a conscious attempt to reduce one's need for the organization and identifying with it. And while it's hard to imagine an nOID '12-step program' *per se*, awareness of a problem is the proverbial 'first step' toward change.

Re-energizing non-work life

The modern world presents us with identity challenges that did not exist decades or centuries ago (Baumeister, 1986). It is therefore important to understand how certain sociological trends are increasing workplace identity dysfunctions. Of particular note is the trend that the modern organization has increasingly replaced the traditional social and identity functions of family and other life domains. I argue that many of today's workplace identity dysfunctions stem from these changes. That is, as the importance of family and nonwork social institutions has waned, the salience of organizational life for individual identity has waxed stronger.

We find evidence of these trends both in psychological and sociological literature. As background to understand these trends, it is helpful to think of a person's life as comprising of three domains: 'home', 'work' and 'third places' (Ashforth et al., 2000; Oldenburg, 1997). *Third places* include anything that is not home (first place) or work (second place), such as community groups, formal religious organizations, social clubs, neighborhood gathering places, etc. Oldenburg (1997) calls these 'the great good places' where people can gather together and set aside their worries from home and work. However, Oldenburg (1997) argues, modernity has largely pushed aside such 'great good places' in favor of less personable ones – such as chain stores and fast-food restaurants that offer a faster, impersonal and non-intimate social experience. These social domains, which previously provided interaction and meaning for people's lives, are on the decline. As Putnam (2000) wrote, 'we have been pulled apart from one another and from our communities over the last third of the century'.

In addition to the decline in the importance of third places, sociological and demographic research clearly documents shifts in family and home life over the past decades. Some of these shifts point to decreasing stability in what was considered 'traditional' family structure; these include higher divorce rates, a smaller percentage of individuals getting married, and fewer children being born per family (Robertson, 2000; Rothausen, 1999; Stebbins, 2001; Whitehead, 1996). Other trends point to less enriching lives within families; these include increases in private (versus family) television viewing at home, increases in Internet usage, increases in children being left home alone, decreases in family mealtime, and decreases in family activities (Philipson, 2002; Robertson, 2000). The net result is often a less meaningful home life. Coupled with a less meaningful social life (i.e. non-work, non-home), the influence of the workplace on individual identity can dramatically increase to fill the void. Organizations often promise things that people are not getting in their families and personal lives (e.g. caring, recognition, approval, affiliation) thereby increasing the organization's addictive power (Schaef and Fassel, 1990). Hence the consequences of these societal shifts are evidenced as identity dysfunctions in individuals: the organization becomes increasingly important as a proportion of individual identity. As Philipson (2002: 74–5) notes:

> Not only do we have less to come home to and less to go out to, we have less of a means for anchoring ourselves and evaluating our circumstances and experiences. As we live more of our lives outside of institutional shelters where we are long-term witnesses to each other's lives, where we experience a shared history and a collective memory, we lack reference points for understanding ourselves and what goes on around us. In this denuded landscape, the workplace can seem like one's only mooring, providing emotional shelter, meaning, and direction.

What does all this imply for addressing the problem of workplace identity dysfunction? I argue that a re-energizing of nonwork domains is an important – if not daunting – goal. Clearly, this is a complex suggestion that requires a multi-level approach for maximum impact. Hence I offer some sample strategies for individuals, employers and community leaders. *Individuals* can reach out to others in order to become less isolated and less dependent on the workplace to fill identity needs. This might manifest itself, for example, by individuals joining or starting clubs or social groups with neighbors, friends or fellow churchgoers. It might also entail a recommitment to investment in family time and depth of familial relationships. *Employers* can strive to safeguard the workplace boundaries, helping to reduce work-to-home spillover (Kossek and Lambert, 2005). Further, they can work to create what Kirchmeyer (1995) calls the 'respecting workplace' – a workplace that is neither overly greedy (too involved in workers' lives and demanding of time, passion or attention), nor overly agnostic about the well-being of its workforce. Respecting workplaces provide work–life balance resources for individuals (e.g. flextime, job sharing) without overstepping the bounds and encroaching upon private lives (e.g. requiring employees to be 'on call' with cell phones and email when it's not truly essential). Given the shift over the past two decades in the overall psychological/employment contract of the workforce, this necessitates a rethinking of what claims on identity contemporary organizations can declare as legitimate. As organizations promise less in terms of long-term benefits (e.g. job security, pensions), we should expect to see a commensurate reduction in the expectations of long-term or deeply held attachment from their employees (e.g. via identification) (Rousseau, 1998). Finally, Oldenburg (1997) offers several suggestions for how *community leaders* can take steps to re-energize third places: these include zoning more common/open spaces that can be used for social gathering, and designing new neighborhoods around interesting gathering places and shopping within walking distance of homes. Recent trends in city planning echo this perceived need: 'new urbanism', for example, blends modern lifestyles with older designs to create beauty and functional third places (Grant, 2006). The upshot is that 'great good places' can be fostered and reinvented in modern life, and home life can be strengthened, to provide bulwarks against the identity demands of greedy workplaces.

Conclusion

Indeed, myriad identity and identification dysfunctions are present in the modern workplace. I can envision future research on identity dysfunctions that seeks to accomplish the following goals: (1) more thoroughly document the antecedents and consequences of the identity and identification dysfunctions outlined in this chapter; (2) examine the impact of individuals' usage of identity work tactics as means to ameliorate these dysfunctions; (3) document how consciously adjusting one's need for organizational identification alleviates identity dysfunction; (4) exploring how individuals, employers and community leaders can effectively reinvigorate aspects of nonwork life. In sum, this research agenda suggests that workers, managers and scholars can each play a role to better understand and reduce the negative effects of contemporary organizations' excessive influence on individual identity.

References

Anand, V., B.E. Ashforth and M. Joshi (2004), 'Business as usual: the acceptance and perpetuation of corruption in organizations', *Academy of Management Executive*, **18**(2), 39–53.

Ashforth, B.E. and S.A. Johnson (2001), 'Which hat to wear? The relative salience of multiple identities in organizational contexts', in M.A. Hogg and D.J. Terry (eds), *Social Identity Processes in Organizational Contexts*, Ann Arbor, MI: Taylor & Francis, pp. 31–48.

Ashforth, B.E. and G.E. Kreiner (1999), ' "How can you do it?": dirty work and the challenge of constructing a positive identity', *Academy of Management Review*, **24**, 413–34.

Ashforth, B.E., G.E. Kreiner, M.A. Clark and M. Fugate (2007), 'Normalizing dirty work: managerial tactics for countering occupational taint', *Academy of Management Journal*, **50**, 149–74.

Ashforth, B.E., G.E. Kreiner and M. Fugate (2000), 'All in a day's work: boundaries and micro role transitions', *Academy of Management Review*, **25**, 472–91.

Bancroft, A. (ed.) (1997), *The Dhammapada*, Rockport, MA: Element.

Baumeister, R.F. (1986), *Identity: Cultural Change and the Struggle for Self*, New York: Oxford University Press.
Bensman, J. and R. Lilienfeld (1974), *Between Public and Private: The Lost Boundaries of the Self*, New York: Free Press.
Brewer, M.B. (1991), 'The social self: on being the same and different at the same time', *Personality and Social Psychology Bulletin*, **17**, 475–82.
Deaux, K. and T.S. Perkins, (2001), 'The kaleidoscopic self', in C. Sedikides and M.B. Brewer (eds), *Individual Self, Relational Self, Collective Self*, Philadelphia, PA: Psychology Press, pp. 299–313.
Dukerich, J.M., R.M. Kramer and J. McLean Parks (1998), 'The dark side of organizational identification', in D.A. Whetten and P.C. Godfrey (eds), *Identity in Organizations: Building Theory through Conversations*, Thousand Oaks, CA: Sage, pp. 245–56.
Elsbach, K.D. (1999), 'An expanded model of organizational identification', *Research in Organizational Behavior*, **21**, 163–200.
Elsbach, K.D. (2001), 'Coping with hybrid organizational identities: evidence from California legislative staff', *Advances in Qualitative Organization Research*, **3**, 59–90.
Elsbach, K.D. and C.B. Bhattacharya (2001), 'Defining who you are by what you're not: organizational disidentification and the National Rifle Association', *Organization Science*, **12**, 393–413.
Federn, P. (1952), *Ego Psychology and the Psychoses*, New York: Basic Books.
Freud, S. (1920), 'Beyond the pleasure principle', in J. Strachey (ed.), *The Standard Edition of the Complete Psychological Works of Sigmund Freud*, Vol. 10, London: Hogarth Press, pp. 25–38.
Freud, S. (1923), 'The ego and the id', in J. Strachey (ed.), *The Standard Edition of the Complete Psychological Works of Sigmund Freud*, Vol. 10, London: Hogarth Press, pp. 167–89.
Glynn, M.A. (1998), 'Individuals' need for organizational identification (nOID): speculations on individual differences in the propensity to identify', in D.A. Whetten and P.C. Godfrey (eds), *Identity in Organizations: Building Theory through Conversations*, Thousand Oaks, CA: Sage, pp. 238–44.
Grant, J. (2006), *Planning the Good Community: New Urbanism in Theory and Practice*, New York: Routledge.
Harter, S. (2003), 'The development of self-representations during childhood and adolescence', in M.R. Leary and J.P. Tangney (eds), *Handbook of Self and Identity*, New York: Guilford Press, pp. 610–42.
Hartmann, E. (1991), *Boundaries in the Mind: A New Psychology of Personality*, New York: Basic Books.
Haslam, S.A., D. van Knippenberg, M.J. Platow and N. Ellemers (eds) (2003), *Social Identity at Work: Developing Theory for Organizational Practice*, New York: Psychology Press.
Hofstede, G. (1984), *Culture's Consequences: International Differences in Work-related Values*, Newbury Park, CA: Sage.
Hogg, M.A. and D.J. Terry (eds) (2001), *Social Identity Processes in Organizational Contexts*, Philadelphia, PA: Taylor & Francis.
James, W. (1920), *Collected Essays and Reviews*, ed. by R.B. Perry, New York: Russell & Russell.
Janis, I.L. (1982), *Groupthink*, 2nd edn. Boston, MA: Houghton-Mifflin.
Katherine, A. (1991), *Boundaries: Where You End and I Begin*, New York: Parkside Publishing.
Kirchmeyer, C. (1995), 'Managing the work–nonwork boundary: an assessment of organizational responses', *Human Relations*, **48**, 513–36.
Kossek, E.E. and S.J. Lambert (eds) (2005), *Work and Life Integration: Organizational, Cultural, and Individual Perspectives*, Mahwah, NJ: Lawrence Erlbaum Associates.
Kreiner, G.E. (2001), 'On the edge of identity: boundary conflict and workplace fit', unpublished doctoral dissertation, Arizona State University, Tempe, AZ.
Kreiner, G.E. and B.E. Ashforth (2004), 'Evidence toward an expanded model of organizational identification', *Journal of Organizational Behavior*, **25**, 1–27.
Kreiner, G.E., B.E. Ashforth and D.M. Sluss (2006), 'Identity dynamics in occupational dirty work: integrating social identity and system justification perspectives', *Organization Science*, **17**, 619–36.
Kreiner, G.E., E.C. Hollensbe and M.L. Sheep (2006a), 'Where is the "me" among the "we"? Identity work and the search for optimal balance', *Academy of Management Journal*, **49**, 1031–57.
Kreiner, G.E., E.C. Hollensbe and M.L. Sheep (2006b), 'On the edge of identity: boundary dynamics at the interface of individual and organizational identities', *Human Relations*, **59**, 1315–41.
Lao-tzu (1997), *Tao Te Ching: A Book About the Way and the Power of the Way*, transl. U.K. Le Guin, Boston, MA: Shambhala.
Lewin, K. (1938), *The Conceptual Representation and the Measurement of Psychological Forces*, Durham, NC: Duke University Press.
McClelland, D. (1987), *Human Motivation*, Cambridge, UK: Cambridge University Press.
Nippert-Eng, C.E. (1996), *Home and Work: Negotiating Boundaries through Everyday Life*, Chicago, IL: University of Chicago Press.
Oldenburg, R. (1997), *The Great Good Place: Cafés, Coffee Shops, Community Centers, Beauty Parlors, General Stores, Bars, Hangouts and How They Get You Through the Day*, 2nd edn, New York: Marlowe.

Paulsen, N. (2003), '"Who are we now?"': Group identity, boundaries, and the (re)organizing process', in N. Paulsen and T. Hernes (eds), *Managing Boundaries in Organizations: Multiple Perspectives*, New York: Palgrave Macmillan.

Philipson, I. (2002), *Married to the Job: Why We Live to Work and What We Can Do About It*, New York: Simon & Schuster.

Pratt, M.G. (1998), 'To be or not to be? Central questions in organizational identification', in D.A. Whetten and P.C. Godfrey (eds), *Identity in Organizations: Building Theory Through Conversations*, Thousand Oaks, CA: Sage, pp. 171–207.

Pratt, M.G. (2000), 'The good, the bad, and the ambivalent: managing identification among Amway distributors', *Administrative Science Quarterly*, **45**, 456–93.

Pratt, M.G. (2001), 'Social identity dynamics in modern organizations: an organizational psychology/ organizational behavior perspective', in M.A. Hogg and D.J. Terry (eds), *Social Identity Processes in Organizational Contexts*, Philadelphia, PA: Psychology Press, pp. 13–30.

Pratt, M.G. and L. Doucet (2000), 'Ambivalent feelings in organizational relationships', in S. Fineman (ed.), *Emotion in Organizations*, 2nd edn, London: Sage, pp. 204–26.

Pratt, M.G. and P.O. Foreman (2000), 'Classifying managerial responses to multiple organizational identities', *Academy of Management Review*, **25**, 18–42.

Pratt, M.G. and A. Rafaeli (1997), 'Organizational dress as a symbol of multilayered social identities', *Academy of Management Journal*, **40**, 862–98.

Putnam, R. (2000), *Bowling Alone: The Collapse and Revival of American Community*, New York: Simon & Schuster.

Reber, A.S. (1995), *The Penguin Dictionary of Psychology*, 2nd edn, London: Penguin Books.

Robertson, B. (2000), *There's No Place Like Work: How Business, Government, and our Obsession with Work have Driven Parents from Home*, Dallas, TX: Spence Publishing Company.

Rothausen, T.J. (1999), '"Family" in organization research: a review and comparison of definitions and measures', *Journal of Organizational Behavior*, **20**, 817–36.

Rousseau, D.M. (1997), 'Organizational behavior in the new organizational era', *Annual Review of Psychology*, **48**, 515–46.

Rousseau, D.M. (1998), 'Why workers still identify with organizations', *Journal of Organizational Behavior*, **19**, 217–33.

Schaef, A.W. and D. Fassel (1990), *The Addictive Organization: Why We Overwork, Cover Up, Pick Up the Pieces, Please the Boss, and Perpetuate Sick Organizations*, San Francisco, CA: Harper & Row.

Sedikides, C. and M.B. Brewer (eds) (2001), *Individual Self, Relational Self, Collective Self*, Philadelphia, PA: Taylor & Francis.

Shorto, R. (1999), *Saints and Madmen: Psychiatry Opens its Doors to Religion*, New York: Henry Holt.

Showers, C.J. (2000), 'Self-organization in emotional contexts', in J.P. Forgas (ed.), *Feeling and Thinking: The Role of Affect in Social Cognition*, New York: Cambridge University Press, pp. 283–307.

Showers, C.J. and V. Zeigler-Hill (2003), 'Organization of self-knowledge: features, functions, and flexibility', in M.R. Leary and J.P. Tangney (eds), *Handbook of Self and Identity*, New York: Guilford Press.

Stebbins, L.F. (2001), *Work and Family in America: A Reference Handbook*, Santa Barbara, CA: ABC-CLIO.

Stryker, S. and R.T. Serpe (1982), 'Commitment, identity salience, and role behavior: theory and research example', in W. Ickes and E. Knowles (eds), *Personality, Roles and Social Behavior*, New York: Springer-Verlag, pp. 192–218.

Sundaramurthy, C. and G.E. Kreiner (in press), 'Governing by managing identity boundaries: the case of family businesses', accepted for publication in *Entrepreneurship Theory and Practice*.

Tajfel, H. and J.C. Turner (1986), 'The social identity theory of intergroup behavior', in S. Worchel and W.G. Austin (eds), *Psychology of Intergroup Relations*, 2nd edn, Chicago, IL: Nelson-Hall, pp. 7–24.

Thoits, P.A. (1987), 'Negotiating roles', in F.J. Crosby (ed.), *Spouse, Parent, Worker: On Gender and Multiple Identities*, New Haven, CT: Yale University Press, pp. 174–89.

Whitehead, B.D. (1996), *The Divorce Culture: Rethinking our Commitments to Marriage and Family*, New York: Vintage Books.

Whitfield, C.L. (1993), *Boundaries and Relationships: Knowing, Protecting, and Enjoying the Self*, Deerfield Beach, FL: Health Communications.

Zerubavel, E. (1991), *The Fine Line: Making Distinctions in Everyday Life*, New York: Free Press.

6 Why bad leaders stay in good places
Debra L. Shapiro and Mary Ann Von Glinow

Studies of leadership traits or actions/behaviors that are linked to more rather than less effective performance by individual employees, teams and/or the organization as a whole (McShane and Von Glinow, 2007) are an important if not overwhelming part of the management literature. The importance of understanding antecedents to leader effectiveness is due to the fact that the destination, or fate, of organizations depends on who is in the 'driver's seat' – that is, on who is leading. Of course, leaders cannot alone control their organization's fate due to the inherently interdependent nature of organizational life (Weick, 1995). However, as 'captains of their ship', so to speak, leaders are expected to carefully select responsible and skilled 'crew members', to ensure that their ship's technological operations are properly functioning, and that resources such as those related to procuring, training and developing, monitoring, controlling and communicating are readily available in the event of operational disruptions in order to limit such disruptions' frequency and impact. When disruptions are due to 'human error', such as the recent tilting of a new luxury cruise ship, *Crown Princess*, on a calm day 11 miles off the Florida coast near Port Canaveral injuring hundreds of passengers (see Martinez, 2006), we look to the captain for explanation. As well, leaders are expected to discipline the culprits to minimize the damage that unintended or intended human error can cause. The need for leaders to be cognizant of, and reactive to, structural and human-related elements is why leader roles have been said to include those that vary in terms of actions that are controlling and flexibility-enhancing (e.g. nurturing) and in terms of actions that involve internal and external scrutiny (see Cameron and Quinn, 1999). Of course these labels are variants on task-oriented and people-oriented leader behaviors which have permeated the leadership literature since the 1960s.

But what happens when leaders are the disruptive force in their organizations? Are they removed from the 'driver's seat' or less strictly disciplined? Or do they keep driving? Surprisingly, the management literature is virtually mute on this issue. Litzky et al. (2006: 100) share this observation, stating:

> While the popular press has devoted a significant amount of time and energy to reports of ethical misconduct among top corporate executives, deviance scholars have yet to explore how deviant behaviors at the executive level are similar or different from employee deviant behaviors. Research indicates that fraudulent behaviors by executives cause a median loss of $900,000 per incident, which is 14 times higher than the average loss caused by employees. Similarly, the focus in the deviance literature has been on non-supervisory employees.

The management literature's silence regarding dynamics pertaining to operational disruptions caused by top managers is in stark contrast to the vividness with which scandals have been linked to corporate leaders in the last several years, especially following the fall of Enron and Arthur Andersen in 2002. Even the American Competitiveness and Corporate Accountability Act of 2002 (i.e. Sarbanes–Oxley, or SOX), which was a response to these financial and accounting scandals, has skirted the specific role of the leader and has homed in on the establishment of audit committees, and the establishment of rules regarding the reporting of insider transactions, conflicts of interest, document destruction and whistleblower protection. The role that the leader plays is subsumed within those provisions and generally includes the establishment of a code of ethics for the firm.

There are two possible explanations for why the management literature has generally been silent about dynamics relating to *leader* misbehavior. First, as Dirks and Ferrin (2002: 612) point out in their meta-analysis of the leadership literature, the terms '*leaders*' and '*managers*' are often used interchangeably, a practice that they also opted to follow; on the other hand, this tendency does not change the fact that empirical assessments of various types of deviance are typically taken from employees at lower levels of the organizational hierarchy (see Litzky et al., 2006). A second possible explanation for why leader misbehavior has generally escaped examination by management scholars is that theories of leadership tend to take a 'relationship-based perspective' or a 'character-based perspective'. Dirks and Ferrin (2002) explain that the relationship-based perspective emphasizes relational issues, such as the perceived quality of the social exchange between leaders and their followers, whereas the character-based perspective emphasizes dynamics associated with character-based assessments of leaders such as their perceived trustworthiness. In both of these perspectives, the leader's actual behavior, including the leader's actual level in the hierarchy and privileges (and possible abuses) of power associated with that, are beyond theoretical and empirical scope. The leadership literature that has emerged thus informs us about dynamics associated with followers' perceptions of leaders, and about perceptions that pertain – not to deviance, but – to the quality of social exchanges and to the quality of leaders' character. Presumably, character assessments are guided by the behaviors enacted by those being assessed; but as we have noted, the behaviors typically assessed in leadership studies do not pertain to deviance by high-ranking officials.

The purpose of this chapter is to address this gap. Toward this end we will focus on the dynamics associated with employees' hierarchical status (such as a CEO) and note how stature alone is associated with various sources of power (e.g. coercive and reward power) that enable employees who are highly seated in organizations to remain there possibly long past it is appropriate to remove them. We will illustrate the dynamics we propose via sequential causal models that culminate in a 'leader-deviance framework'. The theoretically grounded relationships depicted in our models, and succinctly integrated in our leader-deviance framework, promise to assist future empirical work. Minimally, our framework identifies variables that need to be measured and relationships that need to be tested. Additionally, with our focus on hierarchical status as the 'trigger', our theorizing promises to ensure that future studies of deviance will target participants whose rank is relatively high rather than low in their organization. We conclude with practical and theoretical implications.

Do bad leaders stay in good places?

Before we attempt to explain why bad leaders stay in good places – that is, stay in control of their title and all the resources associated with this (e.g. status, job autonomy, subordinates, job-related perks including top salary) – it is important that we substantiate this claim. Interestingly, such substantiation is difficult to make since judging a leader as 'bad' is itself a challenging task. We recognize that the word 'bad' has two distinct connotations, the antecedents and consequences of which stem from different schools of thought. The first interpretation of 'bad' refers to a descriptor of the person, which could also carry descriptions such as evil, despotic, brutal. Tyrants such as Hitler, Milosevic and Saddam Hussein fit this category in their attempts to expunge huge segments of the population. However, a second interpretation of 'bad' can also refer to the leader's actions or behaviors quite apart from his/her innate goodness or badness. Examples of leaders behaving badly include President Bill Clinton, Martha Stewart and Kenneth Lay. For two reasons our chapter's focus will be on the latter case – when 'bad' is an attribute of the leaders' *actions*. First, it is difficult *a priori* to identify a leader as innately bad; sadly, there are several world leaders including Noriega, Saddam Hussein, and even Osama Bin Laden that the USA thought were good before learning via their actions that they were bad (Solomon, 2005: 10–11). Second, it is our view that leaders behaving badly, thus suggesting that good people sometimes act badly (see Lutzer, 2001), represents the far more common case and offers greater opportunity for managerial intervention. For this reason and throughout this chapter, we define bad leaders as those leaders who behave or act badly and, thereby, bring harm to their organization.

The challenge in evaluating leaders as 'acting badly' remains, however. This is due to the fact that their job descriptions, especially if they are truly at the top of their organization such as CEOs, are highly complex and long term in nature. For example, CEOs are typically evaluated by the board of directors, and this is true for all firms whether for profit or not for profit, with the exception of the very small Mom-and-Pop enterprises. It could be argued that their very survival is the first proxy for performance. However, organizational performance is not the sum of performances of any specific team, department or business unit or region, but rather of the entire company. The abundance of influences on company performance, many of which are external and outside the control of the leader, make it difficult unequivocally to blame leaders for poor organizational performance. Consistent with this, Salancik and Meindl (1984: 238) wrote:

> powerful environmental forces and a variety of interest groups affect an organization's functioning (Pfeffer & Salancik, 1978). These interests hold management accountable for their actions and will withdraw support if they go unsatisfied, *even though management often cannot control the factors that determine outcomes.* (Emphasis added)

Internal influences on poor organizational performance include the layers of employees upon whom blame can be, and often is, laid for miscommunications and acts of disobedience, as evidenced by descriptions of why Enron fell from grace (Eichenwald, 2005) and by descriptions of why the tragedy of torture and inhumane treatment of prisoners at Abu Ghraib in Iraq occurred – attributed to intelligence failures, lies and a culture of corruption (Hersh, 2004). Importantly, leaders or top managers are not alone in blaming poor and/or unethical practices on 'culture'; indeed, Callahan (2004) reviews countless examples where a 'cheating culture' is identified as the reason employees at all levels give for the unethical actions they take. Our point here, and throughout our chapter, is that employees at higher rather than lower levels of the hierarchy have an easier time identifying external factors, including but not limited to culture, as the blameworthy source. External influences on company performance include, for example, competitor actions globally as well as locally, international crises such as oil shortages caused by acts of war or terrorism, and natural disasters such as hurricanes, earthquakes, tsunamis and wild-fires that also cause economic (as well as human) casualty. Devastating conditions, especially when oil supplies seem threatened by them, create 'market uncertainty' which then feeds 'market sell-offs' that cause organizations' share prices to fall, even plummet. When an organization 'sinks' or dies, this is typically attributed to one or more of these internal or external factors; after all, the organization's leader is only one person and, according to ecological management models (Freeman, 1982) as well as intuition, is unable alone to determine the organization's fate.

Anecdotal support for how top leaders escape responsibility for organizational failures occurs in almost every industry spawning a dizzying array of consulting services designed to get to the root of the problem. Frequently attributed to mission/vision myopia, organizational failures and indeed industry failures are documented for the railroad industry, the typewriter industry and across much of US manufacturing industry. In all of these examples the top leaders of organizations (in their respective industries) stayed as top leaders long after their organization first began showing signs of trouble. Thus we believe that there is sufficient anecdotal evidence to support our conclusion that bad leaders can, and do (at least relative to bad employees), stay in good places. Next, we turn our attention to why it is so difficult to unseat top leaders who are performing badly.

Why bad leaders stay in good places

A cognitive explanation
To guide our thinking about why bad leaders stay in good places, we consulted literature regarding antecedents to punitive evaluations. This is because the question we are asking can be rephrased as 'Why are bad leaders not penalized?' Perceived responsibility and outcome severity are key determinants of people's punitiveness toward others who have caused harm. Specifically, the greatest punitiveness is typically expressed toward those whose actions have caused serious rather than trivial harm and whose harm-doing seems either intentional or preventable. Harm-doing that is intentionally evil casts doubt on the integrity of the actor, whereas harm-doing that seems preventable typically casts doubt on the actor's competence. Although less anger is typically associated with judgments of others' incompetence rather than low integrity (Kim et al., 2006), those whose competence is questioned are typically *not* trusted (Mayer et al., 1995), hence *not* placed or held long in positions requiring trust. But in the previous section we explained why leaders' actions are less clearly linked to them as opposed to the myriad of others and/or other factors that influence the organization. As a result, blaming leaders for harm-doing – and thus judging leaders as low in competence or integrity – is more difficult to do, even though the late-night comics have a field day with both attributions of our leaders, from President Bush to Kenneth Lay. Figure 6.1 illustrates the relationships we have posited thus far. Specifically, we have noted that higher-level employees, especially the CEO, have jobs of greater complexity (illustrated in Figure 6.1 by the positive sign on Arrow A), and this in turn reduces the ease of measuring the employee's performance success (illustrated in Figure 6.1 by the negative sign on Arrow B). Finally, because we tend to attribute responsibility to behaviors that are observable, hence measurable (as illustrated by the positive sign on Figure 6.1's Arrow C), Figure 6.1 helps to explain why higher- rather than

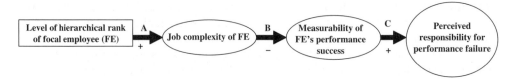

Figure 6.1   Cognitive-based explanation for why bad leaders stay in place

lower-ranking employees more easily escape perceived responsibility for performance failure. The greater job complexity of higher-ranking employees makes it less clear whether we ought to blame them (or *only* them) for performance failures that occur 'on their watch'. Indeed, the latter expression is often used by leaders, especially political ones, to indicate that they cannot (at least solely) be blamed for events that occur while they are in office. Consistent with our thinking, Salancik and Meindl (1984: 242) wrote: 'Unfortunately, management's control is not measurable.'

While we believe the relationships shown in Figure 6.1 help to explain why bad leaders stay in good places, we recognize that they are simplistic. Their simplicity is due to the fact that the relationships shown there are all cognitive in nature; missing from Figure 6.1 is recognition of the emotional dynamics that keep bad leaders often securely in place. For this reason, we turn next to 'an emotional explanation' for why bad leaders stay in good places. We will argue that *leaders have many sources of power that shield them from negative evaluations*. Their shield, we will argue, is emblazoned by the strong positive emotions (e.g. loyalty, trust) and even negative emotions (fear) that leaders, especially charismatic ones, often engender in their followers. Just as emotions generally cloud judgment (Janis and Mann, 1977), we will argue that these *emotions blind followers from seeing 'bad' in what leaders do*.

An emotional explanation
By definition, leaders control things. At a minimum, leaders control the allocation of resources in their organization, including hiring, firing and salary decisions, etc. As a result, employees often feel dependent upon leaders – good or bad. The adage 'don't bite the hand that feeds you' or 'kick down, kiss up' helps explain why employees will probably be more reluctant to report a top leader rather than a peer or subordinate for performing poorly. We say this because a leader's choice to cease providing important resources that others depend on (including employment) carries negative consequences. The reflections of US Supreme Court Justice Sandra Day O'Connor (2004) in her memoir support our belief that employees will be reluctant to judge critically those they depend on for positive evaluation and resources. In Justice O'Connor's explanation for why the US Supreme Court can indeed act independently rather than as puppets for government or industry, she notes:

> The first, and perhaps foremost, method of ensuring judicial independence is to place judges' salaries and positions beyond the reach of outside forces. Judges cannot perform their function with the necessary disregard for the government's preferred outcomes if the government has the ability to punish them. The reason that judges in the United States, unlike many countries, need not fear the displeasure of the government is that they are guaranteed their offices during good behavior and receive compensation that cannot be diminished while they are in office . . . Safeguards for *both* position and compensation are essential, because unless both are protected, the safeguard is empty. (Ibid.: 252–3)

Of course, it would be impractical to structure all employee contracts the way the contracts of US Supreme Court judges are structured (i.e. with lifelong job security and salary protection). But, at the same time, it is impractical to expect employees who are vulnerable to the evaluation and resource provisions of their leaders to act as judges – hence to report misconduct of the leaders on whom they depend.

Interestingly, it is precisely this dependence on leaders for resources that also explains why the removal of bad-performing leaders is often resisted. At least during transition, leader removal puts the safety of the 'ship' (to return to the ship analogy) into question. But even after a new leader potentially 'takes the helm', there is often uncertainty and fear associated with this regarding whether the new leader will be better or worse than his/her scandalous predecessor. The adage 'Better the Devil you know than the one you don't' explains why bad leaders remain the captains of their organizations long after initial signs of trouble appear. Put differently, if punishing or removing leaders is feared to hurt the *punishers*, then no penalizing action will be taken. Sadly, this is probably why attributions of wrongdoing are more frequently linked to employees who are more rather than less dispensable (i.e. subordinates) and why only 'slaps on the wrist' seem to go to top-performing athletes, especially those needed in an upcoming championship game, who have transgressed. Virtually every sport has been plagued with scandalous behavior of top athletes – from basketball's Kobe Bryant to baseball's Barry Bonds, and in many of these cases, their celebrity shields them from penalty.

Since leaders indeed 'feed' others resources they need, leaders have reward power over followers (French and Raven, 1960). Since rewards give us pleasure, this in turn suggests that leaders can and do influence the extent to which employees feel *positive* emotions. Consistent with this, most of the early studies on leader effectiveness measured employees' satisfaction with their leaders. During the 1970s and 1980s, satisfaction with leadership was often taken as a proxy for satisfaction with leader performance. Coincidentally, in the 1970s House and his colleagues (House, 1977) identified feelings of strong adoration for leaders, or 'charisma', as a characteristic of some leaders. The adage 'love is blind' explains why charismatic leaders often escape negative evaluation by their followers.

In summary, up to this point we have argued that leaders exert both cognitive and emotional pulls on followers, and as such can easily blind them from recognizing or punishing bad behaviors, thereby shielding them from negative evaluations. Figure 6.2 reflects the emotional dynamics we have added to the cognitive-oriented explanations we initially offered for why bad leaders often go unseated or even disciplined. Specifically, Figure 6.2 shows that employees who are higher in the organization's hierarchy, especially the CEO, have more ability than those seated lower to exert coercive power and reward power over others; this is illustrated by this figure's Arrows A and B, respectively. Those with greater levels of coercive and reward power typically evoke fear and adoration from others they (can) manipulate with these power sources, as illustrated in Figure 6.2 by Arrows C and D, respectively. Finally, Figure 6.2 shows that a reduced likelihood of higher-ranked employees being reported for misconduct exists when such employees are adored (as illustrated by Arrow E) and when such employees are feared (illustrated by Arrow F). As noted earlier, such fear stems from the resource withholding that coercive power-wielding leaders may choose to do if they become scornful toward others and/or from the negative consequences that may result from leader removal.

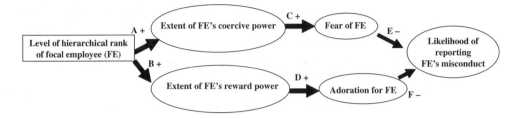

Figure 6.2   Emotion-based explanation for why bad leaders stay in place

Empirical support for Figure 6.2 abounds. First, in a survey study conducted during the time when former US President Bill Clinton was under impeachment for lying about his extramarital affair with an intern, Monica Lewinsky, we found that significantly more forgiveness for President Clinton was expressed by those feeling more rather than less personally benefited by policies (such as the Family Leave Act) that were initiated by the Clinton Administration (McLean Parks et al., 2000). Consistent with this, during the time of his impeachment hearings, President Clinton noted in his memoir that 'voters responded positively when told about the family leave law, the 100,000 new police in the crime bill, the education standards and school reform, and our other achievements' (Clinton, 2004: 628). Similarly, studies regarding antecedents to punitiveness have demonstrated that less harshness toward transgressors is typically expressed by those who have benefited rather than suffered from transgressors' actions (e.g. Shapiro, 1991). Such findings support Figure 6.2's suggestion that there will be a positive relationship between employees' ability to provide others with valued resources and the extent to which such employees receive 'adoration' or support (and similarly, less punitiveness and/or more forgiveness when they transgress). Consistent with our thinking, President Clinton (2004: 634–6) notes in his memoir how much less harshly the Republicans judge transgressions by political leaders when it helps rather than hurts them. Clinton states:

> Newt [Gingrich] said that America had been a great country until the sixties, when the Democrats took over and replaced absolute notion of right and wrong with more relativistic values. He pledged to take us back to the morality of the 1950s, in order to 'renew American civilization' . . . I kept waiting for Gingrich to explain how the Democrats' moral bankruptcy had corrupted the Nixon and Reagan administration and led to the crimes of Watergate and Iran-Contra. I'm sure he could have found a way. When he was on a roll, Newt was hard to stop.

Anecdotally, there are also numerous examples supporting Figure 6.2's suggestion that coercive power by leaders enhances the likelihood of 'silence' when it comes to reporting them for acting wrongfully (intentionally or not). For example, the outing of secret US CIA agent Valerie Plame Wilson via leaks that have been linked to US White House officials in both the Vice-President's and President's office has been attributed to the fact that Ms Wilson is the wife of former US Ambassador to Iraq Joe Wilson, who publicly questioned, *prior to* the 2002 Iraq War, the wisdom of starting the war due to his knowledge that intelligence information suggesting that Saddam Hussein 'was seeking to buy uranium ore from Niger for its alleged nuclear weapons program' (Wilson, 2005: xiv) was false. From Joe Wilson's perspective, he was retaliated against for publicly stating this. The fear of being retaliated against for questioning the Bush Administration, especially publicly, is why some suggest investigative reporters are historically more reticent than ever (see Thomas, 2006; Boehlert, 2006).

While we believe the relationships shown in Figure 6.2 help to explain why bad leaders stay in good places, we recognize that they are still too simplistic. Their simplicity is due to the fact that the relationships shown there all presume that *followers'* cognitions and emotions determine leaders' fate. Missing from Figure 6.2 is recognition of networking dynamics *among top managers* that keep bad leaders often securely in place. For this reason, we turn next to 'a network explanation' for why bad leaders stay in good places.

A network explanation
The cognitions and emotions that employees have about organizational leaders – indeed, about any aspect of their organization's culture – are socially influenced. The classic study by Asch (1951) in which people more often in the company of others rather than alone identified line lengths as similar when they were clearly different vividly illustrated years ago how susceptible people's judgments are to others' expressed opinions. Studies demonstrating the phenomenon of 'emotional contagion' (Barsade, 2002) illustrate that what we feel is also strongly socially guided. Importantly, though, people's reliance on social cues has generally been found to be stronger in circumstances that are more rather than less ambiguous (Festinger, 1954; see Shapiro and Kirkman, 2001, for a review). Similarly, the more ambiguous (subjective) performance data are, the more prone performance evaluations are to the 'confirmatory bias' (Snyder and Swann, 1978) introduced by others' opinions and by one's own first impressions or stereotype-guided expectations, which cause people to generally see what they expect to see (see Elaad et al., 1994; Siegall, 1992). Our tendency to rely on social cues in more rather than less ambiguous circumstances suggests that wrongdoers may more easily escape blame when: (1) there is *ambiguity* about the wrongfulness of their action and (2) there are *social cues that favor the wrongdoer's claim of innocence* (or at least unintended harm-doing). Such social cues include supportive others who express their support 'loudly' in verbal or print form. Put differently, *a network of supporters* – in the form of speakers and writers for public consumption – surely helps wrongdoers escape blame. Such a network thus consists of media personnel and people influential enough to capture media attention. Given the tendency for homogeneity to characterize networks (Brass et al., 2004), leaders surely have more access than do their subordinates to high-ranking others inside and outside the organization; hence the positive sign on Arrow A in Figure 6.3. Given the increasing tendency for investigative reports to engage in 'celebrity journalism' (Moyers, 2005), the greater celebrity status of leaders relative to their subordinates also explains why leaders probably have more accessibility to the media, as illustrated by the positive sign on Figure 6.3's Arrow B. Additional reasons why those with more rather than less organizational stature have easier access to high-ranking insiders and outsiders, including media personnel, include the greater levels of reward and coercive power of top managers, as we discussed previously. Leaders' sources of both coercive and reward power create dependence on leaders' approval, hence incentives for others to sing the praises of the leaders whose approval they seek. Consistent with this, Helen Thomas (2006), the dean of the White House press corps, provides countless examples where journalists have apparently chosen, in the interest of

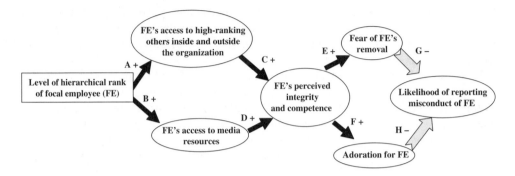

Figure 6.3   Network-based explanation for why high-ranking leaders stay in place

seeking fame and fortune, to highlight praiseworthy acts and ignore (at least as long as possible) worrying acts on the part of business and governmental leaders today. Moyers (2005: 124) suggests that the very definition of 'news' today is greatly distorted by the fact that 'Today, just six companies [AOL, Time Warner, Viacom, CBS, Disney, ABC] dominate what America reads in books, magazines, and newspapers and watches on television and at the movies.' Moyers explains that businesses' ownership in multimedia services resulting from the mergers between AOL and Time Warner, between Viacom and CBS, and between Disney and ABC makes questionable how truly independent journalists can be when reporting on the actions of the businesses whose leaders control their fate. Consistent with this, Boehlert (2006: 3) suggests that the traditional role of public watchdog on the part of investigative reporters has weakened due to key factors that include 'the consolidated media landscape in which owners [are] increasingly – almost exclusively – multinational corporations; the same corporations anxious to win approval from the Republican-controlled federal government to allow for even further ownership consolidation.' Regardless of how independent journalism is from the preferences of leaders in business or government, one thing is certain: leaders, especially in the highest seats of these organizations, have more access than do their subordinates to journalists and media personnel in general.

Because networks comprising public speakers and/or writers for public consumption shape 'public opinion', these networks ultimately shape perceptions regarding whether any wrongdoing was ever committed. Consistent with this, sociologists have long noted that 'deviance' is socially defined. At a minimum, for an act of deviance to occur, an agreed-upon norm must be perceived to have been violated (Becker, 1978). Similarly, then, for a leader to be perceived as 'bad', there must be consensus that s/he has committed a norm-violating act. For several reasons, such a consensus is unlikely to occur in the case of leaders. First, we have already noted the difficulty in evaluating the quality of leaders' work given the complexity and long-term nature of leaders' tasks. Second, we have already noted that leaders have coercive and reward power, making followers unlikely to 'bite the hand that feeds them' and likely to fall prey to 'love is blind' and thus see no evil. Third, we have just noted that leaders have access to a network of supporters – in both publicly verbal and written forms. But what do supporters say to assist bad leaders in staying securely seated? We turn our attention to this next.

What leaders' networks say to keep leaders in place
Managers' desire to create or maintain a positive image, such as perceived fairness, hence ethicality, and their tendency to do this with various verbal strategies (e.g. excuses, justifications), has been noted elsewhere (Greenberg, 1990). Our theorizing is meant to reinforce this and highlight that: (1) leaders' image management strategies are *not* only verbal where the focus of impression management strategy research has tended to be; and (2) leaders' access to media networks greatly eases their ability to remake 'the truth' as they wish others to see it. Next, we identify the communications in verbal and print form that have previously been linked to obfuscating dark truths and/or creating more favorable truths and, ultimately, to winning the hearts and minds of leaders' followers.

Tactic 1. The Devil made me do it, but henceforth the Devil is controllable   Attributing negative events to external factors (e.g. actions of others) rather than to internal factors (e.g. one's own actions or intentions) has long been linked to lower levels of punitive evaluation. This is true for contexts involving poor employee performance (Mitchell et al., 1981), managers' delivery of unfavorable decisions such as resource refusals (Bies and Shapiro, 1987; Bies et al., 1988), and employees' explanation for providing false information on a loan application (Shapiro, 1991). Undesirable actions that are unintended and externally caused are less likely than intended (internally motivated) actions to be viewed as maliciously motivated and/or likely to repeat themselves; this is one of the reasons given for why external attributions tend to have punitive-minimizing effects (see Bies, 1987; Wong and Weiner, 1981). When the external attributions refer to reasons that have stable (ongoing) rather than unstable (one-time or temporary) qualities, then the ameliorating effect of external relative to internal attributions is less significant. Consistent with this, in their qualitative study of 18 US corporations' annual reports to stockholders over 18 years, Salancik and Meindl (1984) observed that the causal attributions for corporate performance most frequently found in the reports were of a nature that enhanced management's 'image of control'. More specifically, the causal attributions in these corporate reports tended to be external versus internal when the performance being explained was failure versus success, respectively. Salancik and Meindl reasoned, too, that 'management trying to assure constituencies that it controls the firm's outcomes would be ill-advised to blame too many of its troubles on external circumstances' (ibid.: 242). Similarly, they suggested that 'by accepting blame for negative outcomes, they communicate that hitherto unfavorable circumstances are understood and, by implication, under control' (ibid.: 239). Salancik and Meindl (1984: 239) explain that the attribution pattern in CEOs' annual reports is due, at least in part, to the fact that

> [CEOs'] attributional accounts are political statements that reassure constituents or induce them, when necessary, to participate in the organization's affairs. Managers, needing to suggest they can cope with an unruly environment, may use attributions to do so.

Importantly, this presentational bias was predicted by Salancik and Meindl to occur more on the part of CEOs of unstable rather than stable firms due to the greater ease of credibly blaming external events under unstable circumstances; indeed, this is what they found. More recently, Dirks and his associates (Kim et al., 2004) have found that apologies versus excuses for wrongdoing (hence internal versus external attributions, respectively) tend to be significantly more likely to mitigate punitive reactions toward the wrongdoer when the apology regards actions that are explained to be within (rather than outside) the apologizer's control.

In summary, the findings described above suggest that in corporate as well as interpersonal exchanges, more sustained support tends to be directed at those who explain negative events (e.g. mistakes, poor performance, and even wrongdoing) when the explainers' attributions enable the 'harm-doer's' integrity and competence (control over the environment) to be viewed positively. Not surprisingly, then, this is the response that we have seen by the Bush Administration in 2006 in the wake of repeated calls for the resignation of US Secretary of Defense Donald Rumsfeld regarding his (mis)handling of the Iraq War. Specifically, the Bush Administration has frequently referred to the historically volatile times in which we live (an external attribution) and to events in Iraq as proceeding as expected (hence presumably under control), since the movement from tyranny to democracy does not happen overnight (14 April 2006, BBC News). This fervently-held belief by the Bush Administration is also why President Bush twice rejected Secretary Rumsfeld's offer to resign over the Abu Ghraib scandal, which itself reinforces Bush's message that Iraq-War-related problems are due to external, not internal, factors (ibid.).

Essentially, then, the explanations given for leaders' actions by high-ranking others and the media tend to emphasize that the leaders have acted with integrity and have the competence needed to ensure that good things (rewards) will occur ultimately, if not immediately. This is illustrated by the positive signs on Arrows C and D in Figure 6.3, respectively. With the leader's perceived integrity and competence firmly reinforced, followers are likely to again fear that leader's removal, as illustrated by Figure 6.3's Arrow E, and to feel strongly loyal to the leader's continued reign, as illustrated by Figure 6.3's Arrow F; again, these feelings keep others from reporting leaders' misconduct, as illustrated by Figure 6.3's Arrows G and H.

Tactic 2: There is reasonable doubt   The US legal system requires that a verdict of 'guilty' be delivered only when there is the absence of reasonable doubt regarding the accused party's culpability. This is why an accused party is innocent until proven guilty and the burden of proof is shouldered by the accuser. Not surprisingly, then, those who are accused of wrongdoing, and those who represent them (e.g. lawyers, witnesses for the defense, network supporters) tend to do all they can to create reasonable doubt about the accused party's supposed wrongdoing.

Typically, the doubt that defenders aim to create relate to whether the accused party's action was indeed immoral or unlawful and whether the accused party's motive was a moral rather than sinister one. Because there can be conflicting standards for assessing morality, including law versus moral judgment, such doubt can be stirred by highlighting the standards that seem to conflict with each other. Not surprisingly, then, this is indeed what defenders do. For example, news reported on 1 April 2006 at 7:59 a.m. by WTOP radio, and now available on this radio station's website, regarded the call made to the US Senate Judiciary Committee by President Richard Nixon's White House lawyer John W. Dean for current US President George W. Bush to be impeached or, at a minimum, censured for wiretapping domestic phone calls. Dean said:

> President Bush's domestic spying exceeds the wrongdoing that toppled his former boss [Richard Nixon] . . . Had the Senate or House, or both, censured or somehow warned Richard Nixon, the tragedy of Watergate might have been prevented . . . Hopefully the Senate will not sit by while even more serious abuses unfold before it.

A response to Dean's remark that came from Republican Senator Lindsey Graham illustrates the tactic we have been describing here about the strategic value of highlighting conflicting moral standards. Specifically, on its website, WTOP News states that 'Graham said that the comparison to Watergate is "apples and oranges" because Nixon's actions were more about saving himself and his presidency than national security.' The implication, then, is that the President's authorization of the warrantless surveillance of Americans without the court approval required by law – even if this is illegal or in violation of the Constitution, as some claim – is necessary for enhancing national security during the war against terrorism. This in turn suggests that there is a moral dilemma between adhering to law versus putting the security of his country's citizens at risk which excuses any violator, such as Bush, for choosing one moral act over the other. Disagreement over whether indeed the warrantless domestic spying program poses a moral dilemma that absolves Bush from being held accountable for violating the law and/or the Constitution remains unresolved today. While the debate rages on, President Bush remains in place, and undisciplined.

A second way typically used to create doubt regarding the wrongfulness of an accused party's action is to question whether the action is discrepant with established and practiced norms. The importance of this relativistic assessment is that 'deviance' is itself defined, at least by sociologists (Becker, 1978) and management scholars (see Robinson and Bennett, 1995, 1997), as a violation of a normative practice. This means that cheating is deviant, hence wrong, only if it is *not* the norm. The normative practice of acting deceptively (or bluffing) in poker as well as in negotiation is why deception in either of these circumstances is typically *not* judged as wrongdoing (see Shapiro and Bies, 1994). Similarly, Callahan (2004) explains that the normative practice of cheating in the workplace has also placed in question how wrong it is for employees to engage in deceptive practices at work – in part, because employees can arguably say that they had no choice but to cheat if they were to keep their job. Essentially, then, making an organization's *culture* blameworthy of 'cheating' or 'corruption' makes wrongdoing or deviance the norm and, in turn, creates doubt about who the corrupt party is – the employee or the system. As the fall of Enron vividly illustrates, such a culture ultimately costs an organization's viability (Eichenwald, 2005). But more than a century ago, President Theodore Roosevelt (1906) explained why creating doubt about everyone in one's culture has the potential to ultimately destroy an entire country. Roosevelt said:

> If the whole picture is painted black there remains no hue whereby to single out the rascals for distinction from their fellows. Such painting finally induces a kind of moral color blindness; and people affected by it come to the conclusion that no man is really black, and no man really white, but they are all gray. In other words, they neither believe in the truth of the attack, nor in the honesty of the man who is attacked; they grow as suspicious of the accusation as of the offense . . . There results a general attitude either of cynical belief in and indifference to public corruption or else of a distrustful inability to discriminate between the good and the bad. Either attitude is fraught with untold damage to the country as a whole.

A third way to create doubt regarding the wrongfulness of an accused party's action is to describe events relating to the action in ways that allow the accused party to have plausible deniability. For example, in a simulated negotiation study, Shapiro and Bies (1994) found that negotiators who were identified after an initial transaction as having provided false information to their partner received significantly more positive evaluation and cooperation from their partner in a subsequent negotiation when 'rumor' rather than 'fact' was the way negotiators referred to the information that was later learned by their partner to be false. This led Shapiro and Bies to conclude, as they had predicted, that there is strategic value in cloaking one's information in ambiguity if the information's veracity is unsure or known by the communicator to be false. Another example of how dubious language can help relieve those suspected of wrongdoing is illustrated by the way a Senate report describes the distribution of the CIA intelligence report containing Ambassador Joe Wilson's politically unpopular finding on his trip to Niger that no evidence existed to support a link between Iraq and Niger's uranium ore. The Senate report stated that this report was 'widely distributed in routine channels' yet also stated that the 'CIA's briefer did not brief the Vice President on the report, despite the Vice President's previous question about the issue' (Wilson, 2005: xxiii). Investigative reporter Russ Hoyle, in his foreword to Wilson's memoir, states (ibid.):

> Had Cheney read the report? His office later denied it. By marginalizing Wilson's findings on the CIA-sponsored trip to Niger and broadcasting that the report was distributed through routine channels, Agency analysts handed Vice President Cheney that old executive-branch plum, plausible deniability. Yet the Senate committee also reported that the CIA report on Wilson was widely distributed, suggesting that the vice president could not possibly have missed it.

In summary, the tactic of creating reasonable doubt about the morality of an accused party's action and/or about one's motive – indeed, about one's awareness of an action whose ethics is in question in the first place – places doubt, ultimately, on whether the accused party has indeed acted badly. This tactic is thus used by accused leaders and/or by such leaders' network of supporters to help leaders stay in place, despite whatever wrongdoing they may be suspected of committing. Although this tactic may assist leaders in maintaining their position (which of course is important for leaders who are innocent but dangerous for organizations whose leaders are engaging in wrong), it has the potential to harm organizations as a whole *and society at large* since it highlights competing moral standards that may, in turn, confuse message receivers including employees about what ought to be morally guiding their actions.

Tactic 3. The harm-doer/leader is in actuality the victim (of politics)   People typically wish to see harm-doers or wrongdoers punished – that is, to see 'retributive justice' (Alicke, 1992). But the degree of punishment they typically deem appropriate is that which is proportional to the harm that has been done. For this reason, 'proportional justice' is what people generally seek; indeed, it is also a hallmark of the US justice system. When extreme punishment is foisted upon harm doers, judgments become blurred about who is the 'victim': is it those harmed by the accused party's action, or is the victim the accused party as a result of prosecutors' or punishers' strong-arm tactics? The recent war between Israel and Lebanon, started after Lebanon took unprovoked aggression against Israel by repeatedly firing rockets into its cities and kidnapping two Israeli soldiers, vividly illustrates how judgments about who is the 'victim' change as punishers' responses become increasingly aggressive. Sympathy tends to be directed at victims; not surprisingly, then, identifying oneself as a victim is a strategy that has been found to help people accused and even found guilty of wrongdoing to receive less punitive judgment.

Consistent with this, Solomon (2005: 98) notes that 'the inversion of victimizer and victim is common in wartime media coverage . . .' and that support for decisions to act militarily is generally higher when the aggressor is perceived as the victim in need of military defense. Relatedly, support for wrongdoers is generally higher when they are viewed as victims. For example, McLean Parks et al. (2000) found that evaluations of President Bill Clinton during the time of his impeachment hearings resulting from the Lewinsky scandal were more supportive on the part of those who more rather than less strongly perceived Clinton to be *a victim* of prosecuting attorney Kenneth Starr's unethical tactics. Leaders' support networks are generally quick to say that accusations against the leader are politically motivated, thereby suggesting that the accused leader is a victim of politics (see Thomas, 2006). Such statements not only increase the perceived victimization of the accused party, but also reduce the credibility of the accuser. This returns us to the risk journalists take when they report concerns, or ask concerning questions, regarding the actions of top leaders in government or business.

Business leaders, not only politicians, have illustrated how networks can assist them in shaping perceptions and evaluations in a desired direction. For example, as we noted earlier, CEOs use corporate annual reports, as well as the assistance of many employees who actually do the writing and data-related substantiating needed to create these, to explain corporate performance in ways that enhance the likelihood of continued shareholder support (see Salancik and Meindl, 1984). Additionally, Conlon and Shapiro's (2002) content analysis of managers' replies to employees' postings on an electronic bulletin board during a time of employee layoffs demonstrates that managers explain good news versus bad news differently – namely, the length and 'readability', as measured by the Flesch (1951) score, is worse (i.e. longer and less understandable) for the communications containing negative content. Because leaders control the substance that gets printed and/or posted to management-supervised electronic bulletin boards, including removing postings (even websites) that harm the corporation's image (see Shapiro and Kulik, 2004), leaders' access to supportive networks – in verbal and print form – exceeds the network accessibility of their subordinates. As a result, leaders have a greater ability than lower-level or non-supervisory employees to loudly and widely 'shout' their innocence or lack of intended harm-doing.

In summary, our explanations for why bad leaders stay in good places thus far share a common assumption – namely, that the leader has indeed acted badly but this truth can be shielded by interpersonal mechanisms that are cognitive-, emotional- and/or network-based. *All of the latter actions would be taken only by a leader who believes s/he is guilty or may be perceived as guilty.* As such, the explanations we have offered for why bad leaders stay in place fail to consider the possibility that a bad leader may stay in place *not* because s/he is shielding him/herself from punitive evaluation – and, thus, *not* because s/he is doing things to actively influence others' attributions of responsibility, positive or negative emotions, or public-oriented communications. Next, we consider the final reason why bad leaders stay in good places: they feel no guilt or concern about their actions and, as such, continue boldly to do whatever actions have been ethically questioned by others. Firmly believing themselves to be performing good deeds, continuing unabated to do these deeds, and communicating their conviction via their supportive networks (described above), such leaders essentially define their actions so that they and eventually others, even skeptics, see them only as good.

A self-oriented explanation: the leader feels guiltless
There are several reasons why leaders may feel no guilt about whatever harm or wrong they may be committing. First, as noted earlier, 'deviance' is consensually defined; as a result, it is possible that if cheating is normative, the leader who is doing this may see this as 'the way we do business'. Second and relatedly, as we have noted in the previous section, leaders may believe they are victims with little choice but to do as they are doing. For example, if they are victims of a corrupt culture, as apparently some top-ranking employees at Enron believed themselves to be (Eichenwald, 2005), they may believe they have no choice but to conform (see Callahan, 2004). If they believe they are victims of unfair pay or other unfair work practices, they may believe they 'deserve' to steal harmlessly from the organization (see Greenberg, 1990). Third, they may believe that their actions are *not* harmful since in the long run (if not the short run) their actions will be beneficial to their organization and all of its stakeholders. And lastly, related to some of the issues we have already examined, perhaps one of the easiest explanations for why the leader feels guiltless is due to perceived media hypocrisy. A recent article challenges the cabal-like dynamics of Karl Rove, Bob Novak and others who have been excoriated in the press, when in fact it was the CIA who actually blew Plame's cover over a decade ago (McCarthy, 2005). The specifics of this argument, while fascinating, point to the fact that many leaders who have been hauled over the coals in the court of public opinion don't pay any further attention to media reporting they perceive to be skewed in the wrong direction. Here the leader feels guiltless due to bias in media coverage. Enron's CEO Kenneth Lay has similarly been described as one who disbelieved the business reports he was receiving prior to that company's collapse (see Eichenwald, 2005).

Relatedly, the leader feels guiltless because followers are unwilling or unable to intervene (Kellerman, 2004). Kellerman notes that bad leadership is as ubiquitous as it is insidious – and that leaders, followers and context are all comingled such that cause and effect are questioned. When this happens, we argue, bad leaders continue to behave badly.

Other reasons offered for why bad leaders feel guiltless include attributes discussed earlier such as incompetence, corruption and sheer evilness. To this, Kellerman (2004) adds rigidity, callousness and insularity, all attributes that serve to inure the leader to guilt.

A framework for why bad leaders stay in good places
Taken together, the relationships posited in the figures we have presented thus far, and the logic accompanying these, culminate in the framework we offer in Figure 6.4 for why bad leaders tend to remain in place long past the time when they might optimally go.

As shown in Figure 6.4, the hierarchical level of the employee influences how aware others will be of the employee's misconduct (as shown via Arrow A) and how willing others will be to report the employee's misconduct (as shown via Arrow B). We arrive at these conclusions guided by the theorizing we presented earlier about the greater job complexity of higher- relative to lower-ranking employees and, relatedly, the more complex and long-term metrics typically associated with complex jobs. Low levels of awareness regarding a high-ranking employee's misconduct and little (if any) willingness to report it in turn influence the likelihood that that employee will remain in place (as shown via Arrows C and D, respectively). If, indeed, this framework is valid – a question for future leadership researchers – then it has several important practical as well as theoretical implications. We next turn our attention to these, in turn.

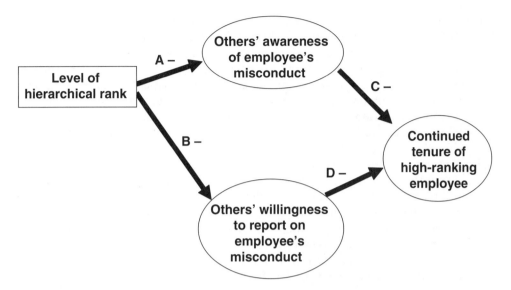

Figure 6.4   Cumulative framework regarding why high-ranking leaders stay in place

Practical and theoretical implications for managing 'bad' leaders

Practical implications

There are several practical implications associated with the relationships shown in the cumulative framework we offer in Figure 6.4 regarding why bad leaders stay in good places. First, there is a need for organizations to rethink what they are doing to enable others to be aware of what *leaders* are doing. Interestingly, the typical human resource management system is designed to enable leaders to assess what their subordinates are doing, yet very little attention is given to telling subordinates what leaders are doing, short of face-to-face staff meetings. In other words, performance appraisal data of leaders are seldom revealed to subordinates even though it is quite common to have one-on-one reviews for subordinates. Even less observed in most HR systems is the type of upward appraisal that academics discuss (Gomez-Mejia et al., 2007). Moreover, in many firms, it is considered disloyal for employees to 'go over the head' of their immediate supervisor and communicate with someone further up the chain of command (ibid.). This insularity of leaders can simultaneously create and be created by barriers to upward communication channels. Practically speaking, organizations should reinforce two-way 'line of sight' arguments generally aimed at ensuring low-level employees know/understand and act on the leader's mission and vision (WatsonWyatt.com, 2004).

A second practical implication of our framework offered in Figure 6.4 is that there is a need for organizations to rethink what they are doing to enable others to feel willing to report misconduct that they may be aware of on the part of *leaders*. We recognize that the latter action carries risk for the reporters, evidenced vividly by well-known whistleblower Jeffrey Wigand who lost his marriage as well as his job with a big tobacco company after 'he revealed that executives of the tobacco companies knew that cigarettes were addictive and the firms added carcinogenic ingredients to the tobacco' (Thomas, 2006: 92). Such risk surely explains why whistleblowing tends to be a low base-rate phenomenon (Miceli and Near, 1992). Consequently, minimizing this risk is something that organizations need to do if they are to help employees feel 'safe' in reporting the misconduct they know about. While the latter insight is *not* new and has been noted previously by scholars studying employee-reporting behavior (see Shapiro et al., 1995), the latter studies regarded *peer*-reporting behavior and thus have insights that may *not* necessarily generalize to interventions that may help employees report higher-ups. Although Sarbanes–Oxley provides whistleblower protections, and although ethics officers in organizations tell us that they routinely assure employees that their reports of misconduct will be treated with confidentiality, anecdotal evidence as well as preliminary evidence from a survey-study by Shapiro et al. (2006) demonstrates that such assurances are generally *not* believed due to the fact that co-workers (not just organizational authorities) are feared agents of retaliation.

A third practical implication regards the fact that the dynamics described in this chapter and illustrated in Figure 6.4 begin with, simply, the hierarchical level of the employee. This alone suggests that organizations may need to rethink what the effect of 'legitimate power' (i.e. employees' rank) may be on the behavior of others who have less of this. Perhaps it is because the USA is deemed a 'low-power distance culture', at least relative to Asian countries where deference to authority is more the norm (Hofstede, 1980), that management scholars have generally ignored the effect of this structural variable. However, cultures of high- versus low-power distance and of other types of cultural values are increasingly likely to mix as the nature of work (even domestically) becomes increasingly internationally diverse due to organizations' reliance on global virtual teams (Shapiro et al., 2002), expatriates (Kumar et al., 2005), and other internationally expanding activities involving the use of teams and/or organizations as a whole (see Shapiro et al., 2005, for a review of this literature). This reinforces the need for managers to rethink how legitimate power may be affecting the perceptions, emotions and actions of their employees.

The last point suggests that the only source of power that higher-ranking employees have over others is legitimate in nature. Our chapter has highlighted the reward- and coercive-based sources of power that employees' rank enables them to have, as shown in Figure 6.3. Consequently, a fourth important implication for managers is to monitor how higher-level employees are using the sources of power available to them, or at least more available to them than to those lower in the hierarchy. For example, Sarbanes–Oxley provisions require transparency with respect to financial statements or audits, and provides penalties for senior executives who attempt to influence, coerce, manipulate or mislead any auditor. By analogy, leaders should not abuse their sources of power for their own personal gain.

Theoretical implications
There are several theoretical implications associated with the relationships shown in the cumulative framework we offer in Figure 6.4 regarding why bad leaders stay in good places. First, with respect to the 'transformational leadership perspective', care should be taken *not* to define transformational leadership in terms of the leader's success, of which tenure may be a proxy. Furthermore, transformational leadership should not be viewed as universal, which is how it has been taken until very recently (Pawar and Eastman, 1997; Egri and Herman, 2000). Transformational leadership should be viewed from a situationalist perspective in that this type of leadership may be more appropriate

in some situations than others, and some cultures rather than others (McShane and Von Glinow, 2007). Employee awareness of misconduct and willingness to report such misconduct is quite likely to be situational and cultural. For example, Butterfield et al. (2006) studied academic dishonesty and discovered that peer behavior had the greatest impact on whether or not students cheated; penalties and policies had little effect. Thus we would predict that, based on our model, willingness to report misconduct may well be influenced more by the situation and less by the leader, even if that leader is engaged in transformational or even charismatic leader behaviors. We would also assert that the cultural context makes a difference as well. For example, employee misconduct can be considered along a numeric continuum of less to more, but that does not mean that 'less' or 'more' is bothersome in some cultures.

Second, it should be noted that the leadership literature has historically looked at the traits, competencies, behaviors and so on of *good* rather than *bad* leaders. Given the recent corporate scandals, our model would suggest that it is time to start studying *bad leaders* (a) because there are a lot more of them; (b) their degree of badness has significantly impacted the study of organizational behavior; and (c) recent research suggests that business graduate students, more than any other discipline, are more likely to engage in cheating (Butterfield et al., 2006). Taken as a whole, our view is that the study of why bad leaders stay in good places is woefully under-researched.

Third, if our model suggests that situations and cultures play a role, it may be that everyone regardless of level plays a role in abetting misconduct by the leader. Should this be the case, then the network analysis discussed earlier should include a myriad of others from board members, to advisors, to customers/clients to government relations. All may play a role in determining why bad leaders stay in good places (Kellerman, 2004).

Conclusion

In conclusion, we believe bad is good. This is to say that the study of bad leadership should require focused research attention as much as, if not more than, what constitutes good leadership. Influence tactics have more recently been scrutinized and increasingly US-based corporate governance structures mandate codes of conduct. However, if the values of a society, culture, organization or any other socially constructed entity dictate 'how things are done around here', then it is no wonder that simple awareness of inappropriate behavior, much less willingness to report it, are met with a blind eye and go begging.

References

Alicke, M.D. (1992), 'Culpable causation', *Journal of Personality and Social Psychology*, **63**, 368–78.
Asch, S. (1951), 'Effects of group pressure upon the modification and distortion of judgment', in M.H. Guetzkow (ed.), *Groups, Leadership and Men*, Pittsburgh, PA: Carnegie, pp. 117–90.
Barsade, Sigal G. (2002), 'The ripple effect: emotional contagion and its influence on group behavior', *Administrative Science Quarterly*, **47**, 644–75.
Becker, H.S. (1978), 'Outsiders', in E. Rubinton and M.S. Weinberg (eds), *Deviance: The Interactionist Perspective*, 3rd edn, New York: Macmillan, pp. 11–14.
Bies, R.J. (1987), 'The predicament of injustice: the management of moral outrage', in L.L. Cummings and B.M. Staw (eds), *Research in Organizational Behavior*, Vol. 9, Greenwich, CT: JAI Press, pp. 289–319.
Bies, R.J. and Shapiro, D.L. (1987), 'Interactional fairness judgments: the influence of causal accounts', *Social Justice Research*, **1**, 199–218.
Bies, R.J., Shapiro, D.L. and Cummings, L.L. (1988), 'Causal accounts and managing organizational conflict: is it enough to say it's not my fault?', *Communication Research*, **15**, 381–99.

Boehlert, E. (2006), *Lapdogs: How the press rolled over for Bush*, New York: Free Press.

Brass, D.J., Greve, J., Galaskiewicz, H.R. and Tsai, W. (2004), 'Taking stock of networks and organizations: a multilevel perspective', *Academy of Management Journal*, **47**, 795–819.

Butterfield, K., McCabe, D. and Trevino, L. (2006), 'Academic dishonesty in graduate business programs: prevalence, causes, and proposed action', *Academy of Management Learning and Education*, **5**(3), 294–305.

Callahan, D. (2004), *The Cheating Culture: Why More Americans are Doing Wrong to Get Ahead*, New York: Harcourt.

Cameron, K.S. and Quinn, R.E. (1999), *Diagnosing and Changing Organizational Culture: Based on the Competing Values Framework*, New York: Addison-Wesley.

Clinton, B. (2004), *My Life*, New York: Alfred A. Knopf.

Conlon, D.E and Shapiro, D.L. (2002), 'Employee postings and company resources to downsizing inquiries: implications for managing, and reacting to, organizational change', in J. Wagner III, J. Bartunek and K. Elsbach (eds), *Advances in Qualitative Research*, Vol. 4, Greenwich, CT: JAI Press, pp. 39–67.

Day O'Connor, S. (2004), *The Majesty of the Law*, New York: Random House.

Dirks, K.T. and Ferrin, D.L. (2002), 'Trust in leadership: meta-analytic findings and implications for research and practice', *Journal of Applied Psychology*, **87**(4), 611–28.

Egri, C.P. and Herman, S. (2000), 'Leadership in the North American environmental sector: values, leadership styles and contexts of environmental leaders and their organizations', *Academy of Management Journal*, **43**(4), 571–604.

Eichenwald, K. (2005), *Conspiracy of Fools: A True Story*, New York: Broadway Books.

Elaad, E., Ginton, A. and Ben-Shakhar, G. (1994), 'The effects of prior expectations and outcome knowledge on polygraph examiners' decisions', *Journal of Behavioral Decision Making*, **7**, 279–92.

Festinger, L. (1954), 'A theory of social comparison processes', *Human Relations*, **7**, 117–40.

Flesch, R. (1951), *How to Test Readability*, New York: Harper & Row.

Freeman, J. (1982), 'Organizational life cycles and natural selection', in B.M. Staw and L.L. Cummings (eds), *Research in Organizational Behavior*, Vol. 4, Greenwich, CT: JAI Press, pp. 1–32.

French, J.P.R. Jr and Raven, B. (1960), 'The bases of social power', in D. Cartwright and A. Zander (eds), *Group Dynamics*, New York: Harper & Row, pp. 607–23.

Gomez-Mejia, L., Balkin, D. and Cardy, R. (2007), *Managing Human Resources*, Upper Saddle River, NJ: Pearson/Prentice-Hall.

Greenberg, J. (1990), 'Employee theft as a reaction to underpayment inequity: the hidden cost of paycuts', *Journal of Applied Psychology*, **75**, 561–8.

Hersh, S. (2004), *Chain of Command: The Road from 9/11 to Abu Ghraib*, New York: HarperCollins.

Hofstede, G. (1980), *Culture's Consequences: International Differences in Work-related Values*, Beverly Hills, CA: Sage.

House, R. (1977), 'A 1976 theory of charismatic leadership', in J.G. Hunt and L. Larson (eds), *Leadership: The Cutting Edge*, Carbondale, IL: Southern Illinois University Press.

Janis, I.L. and Mann, L. (1977), *Decision Making: A Psychological Analysis of Conflict, Choice, and Commitment*, New York: The Free Press.

Kellerman, B. (2004), *Bad Leadership: What it is, How it Happens, Why it Matters*, Boston, MA: Harvard Business School Press.

Kim, P.H., Dirks, K.T., Cooper, C.D. and Ferrin, D.L. (2006), 'When more blame is better than less: the implications of internal vs. external attributions for the repair of trust after a competence- vs. integrity-based trust violation', *Organizational Behavior and Human Decision Processes*, **99**(1), 49–65.

Kim, P.H., Ferrin, D.L., Cooper, C.D. and Dirks, K.T. (2004), 'Removing the shadow of suspicion: the effects of apology versus denial for repairing competence- versus integrity-based trust violations', *Organizational Behavior and Human Decision Processes*, **89**(1), 104–18.

Kumar, K., van Fenema, P. and Von Glinow, M.A. (2005), 'Intense collaboration in globally distributed work teams: evolving patterns of dependencies and coordination', in D.L. Shapiro, M.A. Von Glinow and J. Cheng (eds), *Managing Multinational Teams: Global Perspectives*, Amsterdam: Elsevier, pp. 125–55.

Litzky, B.E., Eddleston, K.A. and Kidder, D.L. (2006), 'The good, the bad, and the misguided: how managers inadvertently encourage deviant behaviors', *The Academy of Management Perspectives*, **20**(1), 91–103.

Lutzer, E.W. (2001), *Why Good People Do Bad Things*, Nashville, TN: Thomas Nelson.

Martinez, A. (2006), 'Injury total on tilted cruise ship up sharply', posted on www.thestate.com/mld/thestate/news/nation/15081966.htm, originally reported in *The Miami Herald*, 20 July.

Mayer, R.C., Davis, J.H. and Schoorman, F.D. (1995), 'An integrative model of organizational trust', *Academy of Management Review*, **20**, 709–34.

McCarthy, A. (2005), 'Did the CIA "out" Valerie Plame?' *National Review Online*, 18 July.

McLean Parks, J., Shapiro, D.L. and Von Glinow, M.A. (2000), 'Love is blind and forgiveness divine: reactions to a leader's transgressions', paper presented as part of an All-Academy Showcase Symposium entitled 'Puzzles and Paradoxes of Organizational Justice Research' at the annual meeting of the Academy of Management.

McShane, S. and Von Glinow, M.A. (2007), *Organizational Behavior Essentials*, New York: McGraw-Hill/Irwin.

Miceli, M. and Near, J. (1992), *Blowing the Whistle: The Organizational and Legal Implications for Employees*, New York: Lexington Books.

Mitchell, T.R., Green. S. and Wood, R. (1981), 'An attributional model of leadership and the poor performing subordinate: development and validation', in B.M. Staw and L.L. Cummings (eds), *Research in Organizational Behavior*, Vol. 3, Greenwich, CT: JAI Press, pp. 197–234.

Moyers, B. (2005), *Moyers on America: A Journalist and his Times*, New York: Random House.

Pawar, B.S. and Eastman, K.K. (1997), 'The nature and implications of contextual influences on transformational leadership: a conceptual examination', *Academy of Management Review*, **22**, 80–109.

Robinson, S.L. and Bennett, R.J. (1995), 'A typology of deviant workplace behaviors: a multidimensional scaling study', *Academy of Management Journal*, **38**, 555–72.

Robinson, S.L. and Bennett, R.J. (1997), 'Workplace deviance: its definition, its manifestations, and its causes', *Research in Negotiations*, **6**, 3–27.

Roosevelt, T. (1906), *The Man with the Muck Rake*, presidential speech, 15 April.

Salancik, G. and Meindl, J.R. (1984), 'Corporate attributions as strategic illusions of management control', *Administrative Science Quarterly*, **29**, 238–54.

Shapiro, D.L. (1991), 'The effect of explanations on negative reactions to deceit', *Administrative Science Quarterly*, **36**, 614–30.

Shapiro, D.L. and Bies, R.J. (1994), 'Threats, bluffs, and disclaimers in negotiation', *Organizational Behavior and Human Decision Processes*, **60**, 14–35.

Shapiro, D.L. and Kirkman, B.L. (2001), 'Anticipatory injustice: the consequences of expecting injustice in the workplace', in J. Greenberg and R. Cropanzano (eds), *Advances in Organizational Justice*, Stanford, CA: Stanford University Press, pp. 152–78.

Shapiro, D.L. and Kulik, C. (2004), 'Disputing with faceless opponents: new challenges for conflict management research', in M.J. Gelfand and J.M. Brett (eds), *Handbook of Negotiation and Culture*, Palo Alto, CA: Stanford University Press, pp. 177–92.

Shapiro, D.L., Decelles, K.A. and Trevino, L.K. (2006), 'Reporting misconduct: the effects of fear, futility, moral outrage and positive organizational support', paper presented at the annual meeting of the Academy of Management.

Shapiro, D.L., Furst, S., Spreitzer, G. and Von Glinow, M.A. (2002), 'Teams in the electronic age: is team identity and high-performance a risk?', *Journal of Organizational Behavior*, **23**, 455–68.

Shapiro, D.L., Trevino, L. and Victor, B. (1995), 'Correlates of employee theft: a multidimensional justice perspective', *The International Journal of Conflict Management*, **6**(4), 404–14.

Shapiro, D.L. Von Glinow, M.A. and Cheng, J. (2005), *Managing Multinational Teams: Global Perspectives*, Amsterdam: Elsevier.

Siegall, M. (1992), 'The effect of rater expectations on the evaluation of a hypothetical subordinate', *The Journal of Psychology*, **126**(5), 453–63.

Solomon, N. (2005), *War Made Easy: How Presidents and Pundits Keep Spinning us to Death*, New York: John Wiley & Sons.

Snyder, M. and Swann, W.B. Jr (1978), 'Hypothesis-testing processes in social interaction', *Journal of Personality and Social Psychology*, **36**, 1202–12.

Thomas, H. (2006), *Watchdogs of Democracy? The Waning Washington Press Corps and How it has Failed the Public*, New York: Scribner.

WatsonWyatt.com (2004), WorkUSA2004 Study.

Weick, K.E. (1995), *Sensemaking in Organizations*, Thousand Oaks, CA: Sage.

Wilson, J. (2005), *The Politics of Truth: Inside the Lies that Put the White House on Trial and Betrayed My Wife's CIA Identity*, New York: Carroll and Graf.

Wong P. and Weiner, B. (1981), 'When people ask "why" questions, and the heuristics of attributional search', *Journal of Personality and Social Psychology*, **40**(4), 650–63.

www.wtop.com. (2006), 'John Dean blasts warrantless eavesdropping', 1 April.

7 Leadership and ethics: the darker side of management

Marc J. Schabracq and Iva Embley Smit

Introduction

This chapter examines management and leadership in their relation to ethics. As an example, the role of the Christian main virtues in regulating management is explored, together with the development of ethics in dialogue. The relation between ethics and management is further examined by analyzing the social context of ethics, as well as the role of emotion, empathy and reflection in ethics.

Due to a number of recent scandals in government and business (Bakan, 2004; Glasbeek, 2002; Huffington, 2003; Usher, 2006), the relation between ethics, or rather the absence of ethics, and leadership has yet again become an issue. The costs of unethical leadership and inadequate management – the darker side of management – are enormous, both at the organizational and personal level. To examine the relations between leadership and ethics, we investigate the following topics:

- Good leadership
- Ethics
- The social context of ethics
- Integrity
- The emotional process inherent in ethics
- The role of empathy in ethics
- Reflection in ethics
- Dialogue.

What is good leadership?

In German, the verb 'to lead', 'leiten' (in Dutch: 'leiden'), has the intransitive counterpart 'leiden' (in Dutch: 'lijden'), which means to suffer, to undergo, to be subjected to, and to go. The old English forms of 'lead', 'lidan' and 'lithan' also mean to go. Leading thus becomes the causative of experiencing or going. Though in English this is not expressed as harshly as in Dutch and German – where to lead essentially stands for making someone suffer – leading in English determines where someone else goes (or does not go), and thereby what that person is subjected to and experiences. It is obvious that ethics must play a part here, for the well-being of the 'led' as well as the leader and other stakeholders is at stake.

Ideally, a leader reflects the 'soul' of a group (Chopra, 2006, personal communication). He or she[1] tunes into its motives and into the potential of its members. He represents them to the outside world, orchestrates their actions, and strives for their actualization. Leading then boils down to sensing the explicit as well as tacit needs of the group and transforming them into an effective approach, without cronyism and without drawing too much attention to itself. Discerning where the group needs to go and guiding it on its way

110

presupposes skills in sensing and observing, connecting with others, and clarifying their motives and needs. It also demands taking responsibility, organizing resources, and sensing the right moment for actions (Chopra, 2006, personal communication). Leadership is thus about realizing, both in the sense of becoming aware of, and of fulfilling and actualizing, motives and potentials. To succeed, a leader – as Gandhi stated (Nair, 1997) – must be morally courageous and willing to serve unselfishly and truthfully.

Essentially, being a 'good' leader is following what Handy (1996) has termed the 'subsidiarity principle', i.e. being a servant to your people to enable them to do their job as well as possible. Such leadership can start a virtuous cycle, called the 'loyalty effect' (Reichheld, 1996): this leads to more motivated employees and consequently to more satisfied customers and happier stockholders (see also Rosenbluth and McFerrin Peters, 1992).

As leaders reflect the motives of the group members, the group members are to a degree responsible for what the leader does. Ethically speaking, a group gets the leader it deserves. Accordingly, Chopra (2006, personal communication) explicitly stated that American citizens shouldn't complain too much about having Bush for president.

Reflecting the 'soul' of the group is not enough for being a good leader. In order not to mis-lead the group, the leader also has to consider the group's environment. First, he should ensure that the group's motives take into account the ethics of the environment. Second, to prevent phenomena such as groupthink and distorted perception, he should remain open to independent external information.

To conclude, as a leader governs the conduct of the group, good leadership must, by definition, be firmly rooted in ethics.

What is ethics about?

We argue that ethics is about the regulation of the interactions among human beings, as well as the interactions with their further environment. Essentially, its function is the joint optimization of the quality of life of the individuals and groups involved.

As such, ethics consists of a body of suppositions, values and rules that govern the conduct of the involved actors. In addition, there are virtues – the standards of moral excellence – which provide guidelines and criteria for good behavior, and sins, which inform us of exemplary bad behavior. Practicing these virtues and sins is exemplified in all the stories about heroes and villains. Ethics addresses issues such as conduct, custom, manners, prescription, free will, choices, infractions, self-esteem and honor. Further, ethics investigates the underlying principles of conduct, their structure and application in specific domains. Acting morally then involves what Williams (1985) referred to as:

- feeling an obligation,
- acting autonomously,
- acting from a certain 'station' or position,
- the actor's free will (which boils down to being free to do what is right; Schabracq, 1991),
- an idea that this is for the best,
- the power of right judgment.

Ethics comes into being by interaction: when a certain new form of interaction turns out to be successful, that is when its outcomes are favorable to all parties involved, its forms tend to be repeated. These forms gradually get a prescriptive quality: they in turn help to shape future interactions. In this way, ethics is embedded in action and practices. In the words of Usher (2006: 136): 'ethical behaviour is not a matter of applying codes because ethics is immanent, it is *always already* in practices'.

The ensuing cyclical process of interactions being first shaped by and then shaping other interactions usually happens tacitly, outside of awareness. The process consists of almost automatic tuning in to situated rules by all participants, so that they, for the time being, inhabit a shared reality. Here the participants exchange some information, which makes them even more alike, as they now share not only the situated reality, but also some additional knowledge (Schabracq, 1991). In this context, it is interesting to note that the word 'communication' stems from the Latin 'communis facere', or to make common. Once established, the common forms of interactions tend to stay in place for a long time, even if their outcomes are no longer favorable.

To be able to deal with the fast and great changes in the societal environment, ethics cannot be completely unchanging. Still, to remain trustworthy, rules about good and evil cannot be entirely relative and flexible either. Ethics is developing, but in such a way that the underlying suppositions and values are not really affected. This development often takes the form of 'non-zero-sum' solutions (Wright, 2001), i.e. solutions to interpersonal and intergroup disagreements that benefit all parties and are based on an alignment of underlying suppositions where at the behavioral level differences of opinion seem to be insurmountable. Ethics can even be conducive to reaching such alignment, as we shall illustrate in the final section.

To give an example of the regulatory role of ethics, we look at the system of ethics exemplified by the Christian main virtues such as coined by the apostle Paul. This is about the virtues of faith, hope, love, temperance, courage (or vigor), prudence and justice. The latter four, which Paul has taken from Plato, are called the cardinal virtues. Cardinal originates from 'cardo' (hinge), the virtues that serve as the hinge from which everyday reality hangs and around which it revolves (Schabracq, 1991).

For the regulatory part of ethics, it is easy to see that following the guidelines of virtues in everyday life has much to offer, also from a secular point of view. Interacting along these lines is not only morally rewarding, but also makes our interactions more functional, as there are few conflicts. There is less unnecessary stress and misery. The perceived safety of most situations is greater and most situations inspire more trust. There are more positive interpersonal feelings, as those involved can attune their goals better to each other and their environment, so that these goals are more easily attainable, with less waste and environmental damage (for a further elaboration see Schabracq, 1991). Nonetheless, virtues obviously do not always find their way into everyday practice. Let us investigate what can happen if a manager doesn't subscribe to some of these virtues.

First, let us consider the case of a manager who has insufficient faith in what he and the organization are doing. Such a person does not occupy himself with the longer term, makes only *ad hoc* decisions focused on immediate gains, without any consistency over time, and behaves without bearing in mind any ethical considerations. In short, this manager acts like a psychopath[2] (Hare, 1993; Stout, 2005), and, unless stopped by others, brings disaster upon the organization or department.

A manager who is without hope in what he and the organization are doing has a very undesirable impact too. He never attains the loyalty effect (Reichheld, 1996). Instead, he spreads pessimism, and undermines the meaning of what his employees are doing by obscuring their goals. His attitude implies a negative self-fulfilling prophecy, starting a vicious cycle of despair, which paralyzes the employees, the department and even the organization as a whole. Such effects of hopelessness or pessimism are well documented by Seligman (2000).

A manager who treats his colleagues and other stakeholders of the organization without respect can also considerably damage his department or organization. He does not recognize the abilities of his employees and arrests their development. This makes their work unchallenging and can negatively influence their client-friendliness. Moreover, such a manager does not provide social support, so that stress and burnout can ensue (Winnubst and Schabracq, 1996). The effects on clients, shareholders and other parties involved, not to mention the environment, are equally devastating.

In a similar way we can demonstrate that the absence of any of the other main Christian virtues – temperance, courage, prudence and justice – in a manager would be just as disastrous for the organization or department. All in all, it is obvious that ethics, exemplified in Christian virtues, has an all-important regulatory function in management and leadership.

Does that mean that management essentially is a Christian affair? Not at all. First, these virtues are not exclusively Christian. Christianity shares them with other religions such as Judaism and Islam, while we've already mentioned that Paul derived four of them from Plato. In addition, more virtues are involved, such as sincerity, creativity, wisdom and so on.

Ethics as a cultural phenomenon

Ethics transcends the here and now, and is much bigger than an individual person, even if this person is an influential leader. Ethics is a cultural phenomenon: it is shared by members of an organization, trade or society. Ethics here refers to what you may and must do, as well as to what you must abstain from. As far as this system of assumptions and rules is successful, it governs what you do and how you do it. In many instances, it comes close to custom or manners. In fact, the ancient Greek word 'ethos' (ηθος) means 'custom' or 'customary place to be'. This meaning of ethos is also used in 'ethology', the biology of behavior.

To operate ethically, we must take part in an external cultural reality that was already there before we were born and will be there when we are gone. Functioning within this reality provides feedback about how we are doing, reinforces certain lines of conduct and extinguishes or punishes others. This happens mostly 'bottom–up', by vicarious learning, by copying successful others. Occasionally, however, the learning can take place 'top–down', in a form of an explicit instruction or code (Allen et al., 2005). So we build up proficiency in many different rule-steered domains and situations, which we must explore and learn to know in order to 're-cite' and 're-present' them (Moscovici, 1984).

The cultural context also encompasses agencies and systems that are more specifically focused on guarding ethical behavior: explicit codes of behavior, legislation, a juridical system and a police force. Without these provisions, ethical functioning is vulnerable. In organizational settings this requires that a manager should practice sufficient monitoring and auditing, including – i.e. when possible – of outcomes and not only of procedures. This is part of ethics also, just as is applying rightful rewards and sanctions. In Einstein's words, 'The world is a dangerous place to live in, not because of the people who are evil, but because of the people who don't do anything about it' (Stout, 2005: 106).

Moreover, it is advisable to minimize secrecy in organizations, as secrecy is responsible for much distrust (Nair, 1997). More concretely, minimization of secrecy leads to managerial questions such as 'Is the payment on the face of an invoice?' and 'Would it embarrass the recipient to have the gift mentioned in the company newspaper?' (Cadbury, 1983: 6). Benjamin Franklin, for instance, made it a rule 'to be concerned in no affairs that I would blush to have made public' (Rogers, 1990: 155).

A wise leader, then, explicates the values of his organization, takes a clear position regarding them, and reinforces them (Gellerman, 1983). Robert Haas, interviewed by Howard (1983), stated that values can act as guidelines and controls for behavior on the work floor. Further, he argues that values provide a common language for aligning a company's leadership and people. Essentially, this is the logic behind mission statements and corporate philosophies. Of course, this works only if the values and assumptions behind the mission statements reverberate with the desires and motives of the group. By actualizing values in this sense, a leader enables people at all organizational levels to make their own choices, and empowers them to use their creativity and problem-solving capacities optimally, without unnecessary supervision.

Integrity

Ethics is not only a cultural phenomenon, but also a personal one. Personal ethics boils down to *choosing* to behave appropriately in specific situations, actually *behaving* so, and building a *repertory* of such conduct. This approach, which is largely internalized, involves a great deal of repetition: each time an actor enters the same situation with the same purpose – which happens surprisingly often, as 'right' conduct tends to produce desirable outcomes – he assumes the same appropriate attitude, in both its mental and bodily sense (Schabracq, 2006). Such an attitude is an internalized disposition of action, desire and feeling. This is how Aristotle defined virtue (Williams, 1985). Besides repetition, building up a repertory of virtues also involves a strict discipline of attention: it is essential to attend only to what must be attended to in a given situation and ignore the rest. In this way the mind is kept free to handle optimally the situation at hand and to attain the goals involved (Schabracq, 2003a). As it is, vices can be learned in a comparable way, especially if the societal feedback is not functioning appropriately.

The appropriate attitudes are mainly 'appropriated' by mimesis, i.e. by copying from other people in a never-ending, mostly tacit, history of assimilation and adaptation. The resulting set of attitudes not only helps to structure one's life, behavior and experiences, but also installs consistency over time. In addition, various attitudes from different situations can be related to each other, enriching the repertory of conduct even further (Schabracq, 2006). All of this results in what we call 'integrity', a term that points both to wholeness and being moral. Integrity involves a system of ethics that acts as a whole, in the sense that an infraction on a part of it activates the whole system (Schabracq, 2003b; Williams, 1985). At the same time, integrity implies a sense of self (Damasio, 2000), and involves a familiar background feeling of personal 'sameness' against which feelings and thoughts can be perceived.

Essentially, consistency and wholeness are about staying on Aristotle's way of the middle, the narrow path of virtue (Schabracq et al., 2001; Nair, 1997). On the other hand, the *absence* of such a consistency and wholeness is characteristic for psychopaths. This lack of consistency implies that they are completely rooted in the present, and as such are unable to resist any good opportunity presenting itself. Moreover, lack of consistency makes casual lying – another key characteristic of psychopaths – very easy (Hare, 1993).

Integrity can be then seen as the basis for work and life. If well developed, it forms a comfort zone that provides control over one's living space and reality. It enables working without interference, keeps risks at bay, and affords safety, peace of mind and acceptance by others. In the longer term, it incites trustworthiness, self-esteem and honor (Branden, 1987; Stout, 2005). Building integrity, however, takes effort. Spinoza saw this effort to preserve oneself as the unique foundation of virtue (Spinoza, 1677/1952, part IV, proposition 22).

It is good to contemplate one's integrity from time to time, to check whether it is still the intact source of one's actions. If not, extra attention is needed. This is of special importance to managers, as they find themselves in a rather lonely position, especially when they have to make decisions involving opposing interests. The deliberate use of mental silence, for example by meditation techniques or running, can be of help here.

Contemplating one's integrity ultimately leads to the explication of a personal theme, a personal mission, a task that makes life worth living. Such a theme or task can give direction to both professional and personal life, and can be used as a touchstone to examine whether one is still on the right track. Although we speak about a *personal* mission, to be meaningful, it must explicitly include at least some reference to others and their well-being. For instance, considering the unfriendliness, even hostility, that unfortunately prevails in many organizations, an example of such a mission would be to learn about adverse environments and how to deal with them, so that this skill could be passed on to others. Another example is learning about not being accepted – perhaps because of having unusual or unpopular opinions – and dealing with such 'disqualifications' constructively. This can be of great value when an unacceptable 'solution' of an ethical issue is leading the group astray. Moreover, the ability to demonstrate a different attitude can immensely improve problem solving and counteract groupthink. For instance, how many successful inventions have seen the light only because their creators went on in spite of others' disapprovals?

Managers can improve their and others' integrity by refining the goals at hand, and by making them as motivating and challenging as possible. The most important point here is that the goals should closely fit the selected theme and strong points of the people involved. Other criteria to improve the goals are their:

- ethical characteristics;
- expression in positive terms;
- specificity, concreteness and measurability;
- acceptability to relevant others;
- realism and appropriate level of challenge, i.e. being neither too high nor too low;
- independence of circumstances that cannot be influenced.

Once you have appropriately refined a goal, connect yourself strongly with it and let it sink in really deeply, for example by a simple self-suggestion technique: formulate the goal as concisely as possible, put yourself in a state of mental quiet and then drop 'the' goal into that quiet. In difficult times evoke the goal explicitly, and ensure that your activities are in line with it.

Integrity has a strong spatial component. It takes place in one's own niche in reality, partly self-selected, self-designed and self-furnished, though its forms are obviously cultural. The spatial characteristics of integrity include, for instance, the space of one's own office, and the rules that specify its accessibility; one's personal space, with its different zones for intimate, personal, social and public communication (Hall, 1966); and lastly one's rights, privacy, privileges and claims. This niche recalls an animal's territory, the area in and from which an animal lives, and which it defends and takes care of (Emlen, 1958; Kaufman, 1971). Here lie the beginnings of the concepts of mine and thine that underlie the ideas of division, exchange etc. Here also is the biological source of all kinds of set points defining infractions and intrusions, and the emotions triggered by passing them (Frijda, 1986).

Consequently, one's immediate environment at work must meet certain criteria not to interfere with integrity. Only then is it possible to work effectively. This should involve appropriate – neither too low nor too high – levels of orderliness, social embedding and compatibility of norms and rules. A too high compatibility of norms and rules with the work environment, for example, would rob us of our limits and would leave us open to every demand from the organization, while a too low one would imply that we are forced to do things that go against our own norms and values. In the longer term, both can result in burnout (see Schabracq, 2003b). The criterion that determines whether these levels are appropriate is the functionality of the workplace: can the required work be done here without unnecessary disturbance or diversion, and does it feel safe to do so? Ensuring that the work environment satisfies these criteria involves the following steps, which essentially are valid for employees at all levels of the organization, including the CEO.

First, be aware of your own needs. Select, design and furnish your own territory to your own preferences. Think about the right degrees of orderliness, social embedding and compatibility of rules and norms. Set your limits and guard them. Second, if applicable, be aware of the needs of your employees in this respect. Are they able to design and furnish their own niches? Do you give them enough autonomy, room to move? Let them set their own limits, then recognize and respect these. Are the orderliness, social embedding and compatibility of norms and rules in their niche appropriate? Coach them in attaining this objective. Third, keep in touch with your external environment. That is, stay open to its signals and communicate with it. Several exercises are useful here. They involve purposefully centering yourself, appreciating your environment with all your senses without prioritizing one of them and enlarging your limits until they encompass the whole environment and you feel at one with it. In fact, connecting yourself with entities greater than yourself in a loving way by eliminating borders is one of the principles underlying all ethics (Sato, 2003).

The emotional process inherent in ethics

Although not all philosophers agree, in our opinion ethics is to a considerable degree a matter of emotions and feelings. Saint Jerome, the fourth-century church father, spoke in this context of 'syndresis', the innate God-given ability to sense the difference between good and evil (Stout, 1995). What kind of sense did he mean? Ideally, acting ethically feels good, and sometimes may even involve a feeling of flow, the feeling of coinciding with one's activity (Csikszentmihalyi, 1988). Other times there is not much feeling at all. Moreover, trying to be good may even feel forced, a little bit priggish (Williams, 1985).

In everyday life, ethics only tends to come to the fore when something threatens to go wrong according to our ethical standards. So (the threat of) an infraction or transgression of ethical rules does evoke feelings, mostly rather aversive ones. It activates an emotional process (Frijda, 1986), more specifically a stress process, which links ethics to the extensive stress research literature (Schabracq, 2003a). Is it a coincidence that the media treat stress phenomena as modern manifestations of evil? However, not everybody can adequately sense ethical transgressions. Psychopaths, for example, probably cannot. Yet, when it is socially desirable, they make up for the lack of affect by making a facsimile based on a cognitive approach (Hare, 1993).

The emotional process triggered by rule infraction involves readiness to a highly energetic action, that is to fight the unethical act, fly from it, or freeze and postpone more drastic actions. Of course, this readiness for action also pertains to more figurative forms of the accompanying patterns, and goes hand in hand with specific feelings such as anger, indignation, fear, anxiety, disgust, shock or terror. These feelings we call primary alienation, i.e. the feeling that something is wrong (Schabracq and Cooper, 2003).

The second stage of this process starts with the realization that the unethical influence is there to stay; nothing can be done about it. This stage involves diverting one's attention and suppressing the readiness to respond to the original unethical act and the feelings it evoked. This is achieved by switching off the whole feeling capacity. As the feelings evoked by the original act were unpleasant, their denial, i.e. suppressing them and diverting one's attention, is rewarding. This not feeling what one was about to feel we call secondary alienation (Schabracq and Cooper, 2003). Secondary alienation can also lead to impersonal and rude behavior, which is mostly aimed at keeping the other person at a distance, as is amply documented in the burnout literature (e.g. Schaufeli and Buunk, 2003).

Switching off one's feeling capacity deprives oneself of the signal that something is wrong, and takes away the responsibility for what happens. It also implies not meeting the challenges laid on one's path, and not acting as a full person, or as a full manager, for that matter. According to Branden (1987), such a withdrawal negatively affects self-esteem. Essentially, it is a breakdown of morality, an act of bad faith, according to Sartre (1966). Still, it is obvious that secondary alienation is far from uncommon in organizational life, where often everything is subjugated to the goal of making profit. Yet – surprising as it may sound – maximizing profits is only a company's second priority. The first is ensuring its survival, and acting in unethical ways may very well jeopardize this primary goal (Gellerman, 1983).

Preventing and solving secondary alienation requires regularly checking your feelings in this respect. This involves the so-called focusing technique, that is paying special attention to your bodily feelings and examining the mental content that the focusing evokes (Gendlin, 1981; Hendricks, 1998). In addition, you can systematically examine your imagination (Glouberman, 1989). Next, go back mentally to the original event that triggered the secondary alienation. Admit the accompanying feeling again, face it and work it through. In a way, this is akin to confession: facing sin and repenting (Schabracq and Cooper, 2003).

Ethics and empathy

Most human beings have the faculty of empathy, feeling what the other feels. By fully or subliminally imitating the other within ourselves physically, we more or less automatically feel what the other feels and, to a certain degree, thinks. We assume the other's attitude in its mental as well as bodily meaning, and fully or subliminally examine how he feels. In German this is expressed by the verbs 'verhalten' (in Dutch: 'verhouden') and 'verstehen' (in Dutch: 'verstaan'), which mean, respectively, to relate and to understand, but which literally mean to change attitude and stance, i.e. take the attitude or stance of the other. This is a very ancient faculty, which we share with many other species that live in groups. During the first years of our life, we are heavily influenced by this mechanism. Learning to partially or fully inhibit the automatic assumption of the stance of another person, so that it no longer controls us, is one of the major developmental tasks around our second birthday. Failing this task can condemn one to the predicament of being completely overwhelmed by the feelings of others. Something similar can happen in the case of damage in the pre-frontal lobes of the brain. This concerns the phenomena of echopraxia and echolalia, that is involuntarily copying the movements and speech utterances of any person entering one's focus of attention (Schabracq, 1991).

That most human beings have the faculty of empathy is not to say that everybody always practices it. As we have seen, it is a faculty that can be switched off in the case of secondary alienation. Moreover, psychopaths probably are not able to use this faculty fully, and have to seek refuge in cognitively constructing or reconstructing the other's mental state (Hare, 1993). But still, the combination of the emotional process in ethics, discussed in the last section, and the human faculty of empathy lies at the base of much of ethical functioning, as the following basic rules express (Stout, 2005):

- 'Do unto others as you would have them do unto you.' (Jesus)
- 'Do not do to others what you do not want done to you.' (Confucius)
- 'What is hateful to you, do not to your fellow man. This is the law: all the rest is commentary.' (Jewish proverb)

According to Stout (2005), there are two kinds of mistakes one can make here. The first is the desire to be personally in control of others and of the world. This motivation involves the illusion that domination in itself is a worthwhile goal. Managers have power over employees, and using this power well can be difficult, especially when a manager finds this kind of power personally important. The second mistake is moral exclusion. This happens in siding too much with other managers and seeing other employees as representatives of a lesser kind. Incredible as that may sound, it can have very real consequences. One example is being unduly harsh to employees; another is the frequently occurring phenomenon that managers increase each others' salaries by a much higher percentage than that of the other workers.

Managers can prevent such mistakes by staying in close contact with their employees, and working hard to genuinely see the employees and their good qualities and possibilities. This also implies seeing the employees' annoying qualities as a surplus of an intrinsically good thing, for example seeing someone's nagging as simply too much of a healthy, critical attitude. Other approaches are: attentive listening (what is he really saying?), using all sensory modalities without prioritizing one of them (sensing), intentionally taking the perspective of the other party (role reversal) and maybe exaggerating that a little (role exaggeration). What also helps is entering into a dialogue. Full-person treatment, that is not seeing the other as lesser person, could also be made into the subject of a separate training module.

Such approaches also help to learn about problems early, by being told about them by the employees. This, however, requires trust between the involved parties, for people usually hide their failures to protect themselves. Staying in contact with one's employees also involves keeping them informed, providing accurate feedback, explaining decisions and policies, being candid about one's own problems, and resisting the temptation to hoard information as a tool or reward. As it is, a decline in information flow – in both directions! – is often a first sign of trouble (Bartolomé, 1983).

Ethics and reflection
Ethical functioning is not just an emotional process; it also involves reflection. This is what Thomas Aquinas called 'conscientia', human reason – mistake-prone as it is – struggling to reach decisions about behavior, a mental debate about how to behave (Stout, 2005). Reflection consists of looking to ourselves and our feelings and activities, and those of others by the faculty of empathy. Essentially, reflection boils down to asking ourselves questions. As such, it implies the presence of an autonomous and judging agent inside ourselves, who is able to observe, ask questions, interpret answers, apply ethical standards, ask further questions, make choices and take decisions about our own functioning. Reflection is also about free will. That is, we can reflect at will and we can act according to its outcomes. Though this free will applies mostly to the selection of our goals, it also gives us choices about our own actions and our reactions to the actions of others. We can always say yes or no, and take the consequences (Frankl, 1978). As such, reflection is basic to ethical functioning as well.

In general, it is more than worthwhile to reflect on the ethical aspect of one's managing. Where Socrates stated that the unexamined life is not worth living (Williams, 1985), Gandhi saw a daily period of reflection as a necessity, which doesn't draw time from work, as it supports the mind and heightens the intensity and quality of work (Nair, 1997).

So, if reflection is a matter of asking questions, what questions may be relevant here? A few examples (based on Gellerman, 1983):

- Is this an ethical issue? And if so, what are the consequences of different approaches?
- What points of view are relevant here? Who are the stakeholders involved?
- Do I mask my feelings?
- Am I putting the interest of the organization above my own sense of right and wrong?
- How would I feel if I were found out?
- Did I choose not to investigate bad news?
- Am I doing it only because I think that the company thinks it would be OK and will even protect me?
- Will this bring me in jeopardy? Will it bring (the survival of) my organization in jeopardy?

Other examples could be:

- What are my choices here and what are their consequences?
- Is this a fair exchange? Is this a hit-and-run approach? Am I trying to get something for nothing?
- Am I staying within reasonable ethical and legal limits here?
- Do I respect the other person? Did I order him to do something irrespective of his limits and of how he felt?
- Am I being as courageous as I should be?
- Am I being honest here?

Dialogue

When one wants to pay more attention to ethical issues, a logical way to start is to organize a work conference for the top management. A logical objective would be a plan to jointly optimize performance quality and ethical quality. Coming to a real dialogue is then an appropriate way to realize this. Dialogue is a technique to reach innovative agreements, which involves some definite ethical development (Dixon, 1998). It consists of learning to know each other's presuppositions, and finding a non-zero-sum or win–win solution to satisfy all parties involved. As such, dialogue is used in business and politics to work out solutions for disagreements and conflicts that cannot be solved otherwise. To make dialogue successful, all its participants must practice certain virtues. Because we described this approach extensively elsewhere (Schabracq, in press), we confine ourselves here to a further examination of the role of the Christian main virtues mentioned earlier. The idea is that development of these and other virtues would greatly enrich everyday management practice.

Dialogue presupposes willingness to look at other people's good and strong points, as well as their possibilities. If we don't, we will not find out much about others' underlying suppositions and will take a too passive, defensive or indifferent stance to be successful in dialogue. This willingness can be regarded as a form of *love* for our fellow men, as accepting the others, seeing their good characteristics, having compassion for their weaker sides, and intending to assist them and make their life pleasant. Thomas Aquinas, the thirteenth-century Italian philosopher and theologian, stated in this respect: 'the plurality and consequently the inequality among things provides the occasion for the performance of good acts. Charity is the more perfect when we love things different from ourselves' (Long, 2005: 60).

Dialogue also is a matter of *faith* or *belief*, particularly belief in our ability to create, re-create and inhabit our own world (Freire, 1970, in Dixon, 1998). This belief relates especially to our assumptions. It is the belief that appropriate assumptions enable us to found a reality we can inhabit and understand, a reality that manifests itself to us as if of its own accord (Heidegger, 1991; James, 1890/1950), a reality that we share with others. Such a belief resounds also in Anselm of Canterbury's saying: 'I believe in order that I understand' (Schisskoff, 1978). When all parties believe in the common assumptions and the resulting reality, we are on firm ground. If that is not the case, there is work to be done. In everyday life, when assumptions are not questioned, this belief comes easily and is self-evident. In dialogue, however, when assumptions must be suspended or even uprooted, this belief has to be transformed into the more abstract faith that the enterprise undertaken is worthwhile, can be taken to a good end, and in time will give rise to proper new beliefs. This involves a serious test of faith. Not subjecting ourselves to the faith test equals signing off: one is no longer a partner in dialogue. Moreover, when we merely pretend to believe, our mind is unable to execute the required mental operations.

Another virtue is *hope*, namely, hope that the dialogue will succeed, that a solution that works for all will be found. This hope refers to the idea that the group is smart enough to come up with solutions. Entertaining such hope is well founded for several reasons. First, it is a fact of experience that success is definitely possible, as the alignment of diverging values has been achieved numerous times before. Second, it can be defended that assumptions underlying any reality have always a positive goal deep down: to keep us out of trouble and get where we want to be. The same goes for other people's assumptions. So, the chances are that these seemingly incompatible goals can be integrated in an and–and solution that enriches all parties involved. Lastly, once hope kicks in, it operates as a self-fulfilling prophecy: if we think that we can accomplish something, we are much more open to opportunities to do so, and put in effort to succeed. In this way hope protects us from the vicious cycle of thinking that nothing will work out, missing out on opportunities and consequently not putting in any effort at all.

The openness that dialogue requires demands acceptance of the other person, and suspension of a part of our assumptions and behavioral repertory can be painful and threatening. We must expose ourselves and give away control to somebody we do not trust. Also, we have to go into unknown territory without a ready-made repertory, not knowing what to expect. Moreover, dialogue involves allowing ourselves to fully realize that the other is different and has different views on things. It also means that we let that different material sink in, which is difficult and sometimes painful. Further, to fully explore and map the differences with the other, we must bear this long enough to gain a clear understanding of what is different, because only then can we shape a new reality together. All in all, dialogue demands from us that we willingly and knowingly enter a situation with painful and threatening moments, a situation which we do not control, and the outcomes of which we don't know in advance. That asks for *courage* and strength. Abstaining from openness or making a false show of openness is incompatible with a successful dialogue, or with any form of real communication.

Another crucial element of dialogue is to call forth our and others' assumptions, with their similarities and differences, without deterring or hurting the other party. This demands *carefulness*. Carefulness is crucial in inquiry, in asking questions without making the other feel unduly observed, attacked or misunderstood. It also plays a role in advocacy, that is in explaining our own ideas as a means to invite the other to comment on them and to point out lacunas, exaggerations and distortions in them (Dixon, 1998). The term 'caution' applies here as well, also in the sense of circumspection, looking for possible risks and pitfalls, such as may result from possible sensitivities of the other person. Acting in a gross way in inquiry and advocacy obviously has devastating effects on the progress of the dialogue.

Another threat to dialogue consists of overstressing one or more virtues at the cost of the others. This would endanger the whole ethical fabric (Berlin, 1998). For instance, too much carefulness interferes with courage, too much faith becomes fanaticism and interferes with carefulness, and so on. Overstressing one virtue constitutes a lack of *moderation* or temperance, the sin of *intemperantia*. Lack of moderation not only jeopardizes dialogue, but all forms of communication and action. Inflating one of the virtues can also be used as a weapon. We do this by making ourselves ethically superior by focusing on our favorite virtue and accusing others of not living up to our standard. This assigned 'lack of virtue' is then also a handy pretext for punishing the other, while we ourselves come out smelling of violets and roses.

Lastly, in dialogue, we should see to it that nobody is mistreated or cheated out of something, as this always jeopardizes the end result. Essentially, we are talking here about *justice*, the right application of the whole ethical system. Justice results in rules about the exchange and division of property, hierarchical position, rights and attention, and rules about the ranking of rules and about their applicability (see also Storrs Hall, 2000). This is what Socrates called the only true virtue (Williams, 1985). An important point here is that such a system should be more or less equally applied to all involved. So no person or group of persons should be preferentially or unfairly treated. Organizational examples here are to be found in differences in increases in compensation between management and shopfloor. Another issue stems from all kinds of IT applications, which employ computational techniques to judge performances, often within the context of performance or competence management. This may even have consequences for individual compensation. There are several other problems here. One is the use of too narrow or downright invalid performance criteria; another is the blind application of these judgments to different individuals in different circumstances. The delegation of decisions to computers can lead to ethical negligence and malpractice, as it obscures or even covers up the judgmental tasks. In general, it is the task of the leader to explicate the ethical system, truthfully spelling out the dilemmas, implications and choices.

All in all, the example of applying and explicating the Christian main virtues in dialogue shows that virtues not only act as regulatory principles, but also play a pivotal role in the development of the ethical system.

Of course dialogue is not the only intervention possible. Others are improvements in policy (see for example Nair, 1997), coaching and work progress meetings. In addition, many different training programs and workshops address the specific knowledge, skills and attitudes involved in ethics (Schabracq, in press).

Conclusion
Organizations operate in an increasingly complex and turbulent environment, which makes it more and more difficult for them to prosper and even to survive. Delivering the required results under these circumstances puts the highest demands on the continuous development of the coordination of all stakeholders involved, inside and outside the organization. Such coordination is essentially a matter of good leadership and carefully concerted governance of conduct. In fact, as we have argued in this chapter, we may conclude that good leadership, that is a leadership that successfully takes on the challenges arising from the organization and its environment, is almost by definition of an ethical nature.

Clegg and Rhodes (2006: 4) state that 'in recent years the study of business ethics has been particularly critical of the assumption that organizations can collapse ethics into systems of rules, codes or administrative procedures'. Ethical codes, which merely provide rules and regulations, are of no great help here, as they cannot remedy all behavioral difficulties (Cohen, 2006). Apart from their window-dressing functions, they serve at best as a top–down disciplining tool. As organizations by themselves are not particularly ethical by nature – Bakan (2004) compares the corporation's legal 'personality' with that of a psychopath – leaders play a crucial role here. Essentially, leadership always boils down to individual feelings, reflections and choices in a moral maze. Here the difference is made between the darker and the brighter side of management.

Notes

1. For reasons of readability, in the remainder of this chapter, we will use 'he' in place of 'he or she'.
2. We refer to the characteristics of psychopaths here, and in other places in the chapter, because they represent the epitome of unethical behavior. For more detailed examination of psychopathy, we refer the reader to Chapter 2.

References

Allen, C., Smit, I. and Wallach, W. (2005), 'Artificial morality: top–down, bottom–up, and hybrid approaches', *Ethics and Information Technology*, **7**(3), 149–55.

Bakan, J. (2004), *The Corporation: The Pathological Pursuit of Profit and Power*, New York: Free Press.

Bartolomé, F. (1983), 'Nobody trusts the boss completely – Now what?', in *Ethics at Work*, Boston, MA: HBS Press, pp. 15–22.

Berlin, I. (1998), *The First and the Last*, London: Granta Books.

Branden, N. (1987), *How to Raise Your Self-Esteem*, New York: Bantam Books.

Cadbury, A. (1983), 'Ethical managers make their own rules', in *Ethics at Work*, Boston, MA: HBS Press, pp. 3–7.

Clegg, S.R. and Rhodes, C. (2006), 'Introduction: questioning the ethics of management practice', in S.R. Clegg, and C. Rhodes (eds), *Management Ethics: Contemporary Contexts*, London/New York: Routledge, pp. 1–9.

Cohen, S. (2006), 'Management ethics, accountability and responsibility', in S.R. Clegg, and C. Rhodes (eds), *Management Ethics: Contemporary Contexts*, London/New York: Routledge, pp. 113–34.

Csikszentmihalyi, M. (1988), 'Introduction', in M. Csikszentmihalyi and I.S. Csikszentmihalyi (eds), *Optimal Experiences*, Cambridge: Cambridge University Press.

Damasio, A. (2000), *The Feeling of What Happens*, London: Vintage.

Dixon, N.M. (1998), *Dialogue at Work*, London: Lemos & Crane.

Emlen, J.T. Jr. (1958), 'Defended area? A critique of occasion, territory concept and of conventional thinking', *Ibis*, **99**, 352.

Frankl, V.E. (1978), *De Zin van het Bestaan* (*The Meaning of Existence*), Rotterdam: Ad. Donker.

Freire, P. (1970), *Pedagogy of the Oppressed*, New York: Seabury Press.

Frijda, N.H. (1986), *The Emotions*, Cambridge: Cambridge University Press.

Gellerman, S.W. (1983), 'Why "good" managers make bad ethical choices', in *Ethics at Work*, Boston, MA: HBS Press, pp. 9–14.

Gendlin, E. (1981), *Focusing*, New York: Bantam.

Glasbeek, H. (2002), *Wealth by Stealth: Corporate Crime, Corporate Law, and the Perversion of Democracy*, Toronto: Between the Lines.

Glouberman, D. (1989), *Life Choices and Life Changes through Image Work*, London: Grafton Books.

Hall, E.T. (1966), *The Hidden Dimension*, Garden City, NY: Doubleday.

Handy (1996), *The Empty Raincoat*, London: Arrow Business Books.

Hare, R.D. (1993), *Without Conscience*, New York/London: Guilford Press.

Heidegger, M. (1991), *Over Denken, Bouwen, Wonen. Vier Essays* (*About Thinking, Building, Dwelling. Four essays*) Nijmegen, Netherlands: Sun.

Hendricks, G. (1998), *The Ten-Second Miracle*, San Francisco, CA: Harper.

Howard, R. (1983), 'Values make the company', in *Ethics at Work*, Boston, MA: HBS Press, pp. 55–61.

Huffington, A. (2003), *Pigs at the Trough. How Corporate Greed and Political Corruption are Undermining America*, New York: Crown Publishers.

James, W. (1890/1950), *The Principles of Psychology*, New York: Dover.

Kaufman, J.H. (1971), 'Is territoriality definable?', in A.H. Esser (ed.), *Behavior and Environment*, New York: Plenum Press, pp. 36–40.

Long, R.J. (2005), 'Aquinas and Franciscan nature mysticism', *Logos*, **8**, 56–64.

Moscovici, S. (1984), 'The phenomenon of social representation', in R.M. Farr and S. Moscovici (eds), *Social Representations*, Cambridge: Cambridge University Press, pp. 3–69.

Nair, K. (1997), *A Higher Standard of Leadership: Lessons from the Life of Gandhi*, San Francisco, CA: Berrett-Koelher.

Reichheld, F.F. (1996), *The Loyalty Effect*, Boston, MA: HBS Press.

Ridley, M. (1996), *The Origins of Virtue*, London: Viking.
Rogers, G.L. (ed.) (1990), *Benjamin Franklin's The Art of Virtue*, Eden Prairie, MN: Acorn Publishing.
Rosenbluth, H.F. and McFerrin Peters, D. (1992), *The Customer Comes Second*, New York: W. Morrow & Co.
Sartre, J.-P. (1966), *Being and Nothingness*, New York: Pocket Books.
Sato, T. (2003), *Rhythm, Relationship and Transcendence*, New York: Writers Club Press.
Schabracq, M.J. (1991), *De Inrichting van de Werkelijkheid* (*The Design of Reality*), Amsterdam/Meppel: Boom.
Schabracq, M.J. (2003a), 'Everyday well-being and stress in work and organisations', in M.J. Schabracq, J.A.M. Winnubst and C.L. Cooper (eds), *Handbook of Work and Health Psychology*, 2nd rev. edn, Chichester, UK: John Wiley & Sons, pp. 9–36.
Schabracq, M.J. (2003b), 'Organisational culture, stress and change', in M.J. Schabracq, J.A.M. Winnubst and C.L. Cooper (eds), *Handbook of Work and Health Psychology*, 2nd rev. edn, Chichester, UK: John Wiley & Sons, pp. 37–62.
Schabracq, M.J. (2005), 'Stress, alienation and leadership', in A.-S. Antoniou and C.L. Cooper (eds), *Research Companion to Organizational Health Psychology*, Cheltenham, UK and Northampton, MA: Edward Elgar, pp. 122–31.
Schabracq, M.J. (2006), 'Leadership and organizational culture', in R.J. Burke and C.L. Cooper (eds), *Inspiring Leaders*, New York: Routledge, pp. 212–33.
Schabracq, M.J. (in press), *Changing Organizational Culture*, Chichester, UK: John Wiley & Sons.
Schabracq, M.J. and Cooper, C.L. (2003), 'To be me or not to be me. About alienation', *Counselling Psychology Quarterly*, **16**, 53–79.
Schabracq, M.J., Cooper, C.L., Travers, C. and Maanen, D. van (2001), *Occupational Health Psychology*, Leicester, UK: British Psychological Society.
Schaufeli, W.B. and Buunk, B.P. (2003), 'Burnout', in M.J. Schabracq, J.A.M. Winnubst and C.L. Cooper (eds), *Handbook of Work and Health Psychology*, 2nd rev. edn, Chichester, UK: John Wiley & Sons, pp. 383–425.
Schisskoff, G. (Schmidt, H.) (1978), *Philosophischer Wörterbuch*, Stuttgart: Kröner Verlag.
Seligman, M.E.P. (2000), 'Optimism, pessimism, and mortality', *Mayo Clinical Proceedings*, **75**, 133–4 (www.mayoclinicproceedings.com/inside.asp?AID=1374&UID=23777).
Spinoza, B. (1677/1952), *Ethica* (Dutch translation), Amsterdam/Antwerpen: Wereld-Bibliotheek.
Storrs Hall, J. (2000), 'Ethics for machines', www.discuss.foresight.org/~josh/ethics.html.
Stout, M. (2005), *The Sociopath Next Door*, New York: Broadway Books.
Usher, R. (2006), 'Management ethics and organizational networks', in S.R. Clegg and C. Rhodes (eds), *Management Ethics: Contemporary Contexts*, London/New York: Routledge, pp. 135–54.
Williams, B. (1985), *Ethics and the Limits of Philosophy*, Cambridge, MA: Harvard University Press.
Winnubst, J.A.M. and Schabracq, M.J. (1996), 'Social support, stress and organization', in M.J. Schabracq, J.A.M. Winnubst and C.L. Cooper (eds), *Handbook of Work and Health Psychology*, Chichester, UK: John Wiley & Sons, pp. 87–102.
Wright, R. (2001), *Nonzero*, London: Abacus.

8   Employee loss of trust in management: surviving in a new era
Roger C. Mayer

Opportunities for gain via organizational trust

While trust was sporadically recognized as important in the management literature, until the mid-1990s the topic was often mentioned, but then attention was turned to other more manageable topics (Gambetta, 1988). In contrast, the last decade has seen a great deal of attention turned to the topic of trust in the workplace (Kramer and Tyler, 1996; Dirks and Ferrin, 2002). Sadly, there is no credible evidence that the new interest in trust has translated into higher trust levels in the workplace. Corporate scandals such as those seen at Enron, WorldCom and Tyco may have actually taken trust in management in the opposite direction.

Over four decades ago, Argyris (1964) theorized that organizations in which members trusted the leaders would perform better than those whose leaders garnered less trust. Surprisingly little empirical evidence of this proposed performance improvement has been published. Dirks (2000) found that National Collegiate Athletics Association basketball teams who had higher levels of trust in their respective coach amassed better win/loss records than those whose coaches garnered less trust. Davis et al. (2000) found that in a chain of restaurants, those in which the facility's general manager was more trusted had significantly higher overall sales and net profits than those where the manager was less trusted. The fact that these differences were statistically significant was particularly striking, given that with only nine stores in the study there was very little statistical power. To achieve statistical significance with such a modest sample size suggests that something rather powerful was operating.

A simple keyword search of Social Science Citation Index or Google Scholar reveals that many hundreds of papers on trust and related topics have been published in the organizational sciences within the last decade. Many of them have studied levels of trust in various levels of the management ranks, including supervisors (e.g. Konovsky and Pugh, 1994), general managers of a facility (e.g. Davis et al., 2000), and top management (e.g. Mayer and Gavin, 2005). During that same period, a much smaller number of researchers have been exploring employee behaviors from a less traditional viewpoint. Scholars have examined such topics as employee deviance, looking at employee behaviors that might be considered as counter-organizational (see Becker and Bennett, Chapter 9, this volume). Their research has considered employee reactions that are very much in contrast to employees trusting in management. Rather, the behaviors might be seen as ways of acting out against the organization when there is a lack of trust. The current chapter considers factors that lead to loss of trust in management as well as some potential remedies.

If trust can enable higher levels of organizational performance as some of the research above suggests, then it seems reasonable to assume that cultivating higher levels of trust would be a worthwhile goal for managers to pursue. In addition to potentially higher performance for the organization, working in a more trusting environment is likely to reduce employees' stress levels. Stress is known to be related to a number of serious negative medical conditions such as heart disease and cancer. If companies can build a more trusting environment that lowers the level of stress that employees experience, one might expect not only positive medical benefits for the employees but also a reduction in loss of resources for the employers. Not only might medical and insurance costs be driven down, but scheduling problems might also be avoided if fewer employees take medical leave. While this tie has not often been considered in the organizational literature, it is a hidden cost of a low-trust environment. Incremental improvements in intra-organizational trust levels might bring not only immediate gains in productivity and teamwork, but also long-term financial benefits from lower healthcare costs for the organization.

This chapter will first consider how employees find themselves at risk in their work arrangements. This risk comes from a variety of sources, both inside and outside the organization. Next, I consider how the past and anticipated future length of the relationship affects trust and the employment relationship. Taken together, these perspectives lead to questions about why an employee *should* trust management. Following that, the potential role of catharsis in rebuilding broken trust as well as insights from classical conditioning relevant to the repair of broken trust are considered. At the conclusion of the chapter are some general approaches to managing trust in an organizational setting.

Referents of trust
Despite the gains in productivity and reductions in costs that may be made via organizations' efforts to develop higher trust levels, a variety of forces tends to inhibit trust within a work organization. To gain a clear understanding of these, two points about trust are important. First, it is critical to understand the relationship of risk with trust. While one can hold some level of trust in a party without ever being called on to take any risk, it is when a risky decision must be made that the level of trust becomes relevant. In other words, whether or not one trusts one's manager doesn't matter until one is in a position where one must choose how much to willingly put oneself at risk at one's manager's hands. At that point in time, trust becomes crucial because it is an important determinant of the actual risk taking (Mayer et al., 1995). Thus, understanding where and how employees are in a position to take risks as part of their jobs is important, as trust will be a key determinant of their risk taking.

Second, it must be recognized that in an organization there are multiple important specific referents of trust. A commonly considered referent is an employee's direct supervisor, as in the example above. The relationships that expose an employee to risk, however, go far beyond the employee's supervisor. Within the formal organization, top management makes decisions that affect the direction of the company, its prosperity, and thus its long-term viability as a provider of security for an employee. The general manager of an employee's facility is often in a middle management position with responsibility for many decisions about scheduling, hiring and firing, staffing levels, and promotions within the organization. All of these decisions have a significant impact on the employee.

Aside from the line managers above the employee in the organization, many others also affect the employee's well-being. For example, those who work in the human resources function within the organization develop and implement policies having to do with compensation and benefits policies that clearly affect the employee. In a unionized firm, the board of directors may ultimately determine the stance that the company will take in forging contracts with the union.

In addition to these specific tangible trust referents, employees often tend to think about the organization itself as a trust referent (see Robinson, 1996). Eisenberger and colleagues (Eisenberger et al., 1986, 1997) developed the idea that people perceive the organization itself as an entity that can provide a greater or lesser perceived level of support, despite the fact that this construct reflects decisions made by a number of different people within the organization. In the same way that people see the entity as a sentient being that can make either more or less supportive decisions, consistent with Robinson and others I contend that people commonly view their employing organization as an important refer-ent of trust. Over time, different people move into and out of managerial roles. Because of this, ownership of decisions that affect an employee may remain unknown. Over a period of time, the employee cannot determine who made the decision that had an adverse impact on him or her. He or she is simply aware that things happened over which someone within the organization had control. In other words, someone in the organization whose identity may or may not be known made a decision that hurt the employee. After seeing people come and go in the various important positions, it occurs to the employee that it is not necessarily the particular person who occupies the role that matters. The focus of the referent becomes nebulous, and the attribution is made in the employee's mind that 'the organization' did something to him or her. While in reality the organization is not a sentient being capable of making decisions about how trustworthy to be, to the extent that an employee thinks about the organization as sentient, the employee will react to it as if it is.

Employees can be vulnerable to their co-workers and to their subordinates as well. One's teammates, for example, jointly determine the success of projects assigned to the whole group. An employee's subordinates have a substantial impact on his/her performance as well, since their collective level of performance largely constitutes their manager's level of performance. For completeness, it is important to note that an employee can also be vul-nerable to parties outside the organization such as customers, governmental officials, and former employers and employees, to name a few. Such parties can create risk in the employment relationship for a wide variety of reasons (e.g., non-compete lawsuit from a former employer because of the nature of the employee's involvement with the current employer). Consideration of risk involving these outside parties is, however, beyond the scope of this chapter.

Sources of risk in the employment relationship

Consideration in this chapter of the sources of risk that affect an employee begins with a broad external view. The past several decades have seen a major shift in the US labor market. In the 1950s and 1960s, the rate of technological change was very slow compared to the present rate. The inventor and futurist Kurzweil (Kurzweil and Meyer, 2006) pro-jects that the twenty-first century alone will account for more technological change than did the previous 20,000 years. As such, in decades past the reasons for changes in an employer's labor needs were based on relatively simple factors such as business volume, a new product, or on an occasional change in strategy. While the intent here is not to minimize the complexity involved in these decisions, the reasons for change in workforce needs for a company in this new age have become far more complex. Such issues as outsourcing, new manufacturing technologies, the advent and growth of the Internet, and the growth in importance of the global labor market have made firms' employment needs much more turbulent over time. Employees whose parents had stable employment with a given company for 30 or 40 years or more joined the company expecting to do the same, only to find that, unlike those of their parents, their skills became obsolete. The tasks they performed were either no longer needed, were replaced by machines or robots, or were moved offshore to be performed by less expensive labor.

This phenomenon is certainly not new to the last several decades. The invention of the cotton gin over two centuries ago in 1793, for example, had much the same effect on the workers who performed the laborious task of removing the seeds from raw cotton. What has changed is how widespread across industries these changes happen, the speed at which they occur, and the extent to which people with higher skill levels are also affected by the developments.

Some companies have been very open about these changes. General Electric's (GE's) legendary chairman Jack Welch, for example, made it clear to employees that GE could not offer job security to a worker, as job security implies that a given job would continue on into the future. Instead, he said that GE was committed to offering *employment* security. The thrust of this idea was that GE was committed to helping an employee continuously upgrade his or her skills such that if the person's skills became no longer needed at GE, he or she could go on to another job at a different company which was as good as or better than their current job at GE. The idea that Welch was pushing his workforce to accept is that the days of expecting to work for the same company for an entire career were probably gone, and that they should respond by continually upgrading their skills to make certain that they always possessed a skill set that was contemporary and valuable. In essence, this approach forces employees to think about the labor market much as free agents do in sports: develop strong skills, then market and sell them to the highest bidder at a point in time. Professional sports in the USA are becoming full of examples of athletes who move from organization to organization every few years.

One might argue that GE was in an atypical situation compared to most firms. Being one of the world's largest corporations, GE had the resources to commit to continuous development of their employees. This idea of employment security and 'free agency' is more feasible for large companies with deep pockets than for smaller or less profitable firms or those competing in less profitable industries. Such firms cannot afford to pay a premium to attract the necessary current skills, or to continually invest in helping their employees reinvent themselves.

Another pressure that contributes to undermining the relationship between employers and employees is the short-term expectations of Wall Street. It seems that analysts have little patience for investments in areas such as building positive relations and morale in the workforce. While these endeavors tend to play very positively in the eyes of employees, persuading Wall Street of their value is a different matter. The pressure to continually generate quarterly earnings, and to either meet or beat the expectations of Wall Street analysts, puts many managers in a perceived position that they must make short-term oriented decisions. Moves such as downsizing in response to economic downturns or slowdowns in demand for current products may play well to Wall Street analysts, but they threaten the most basic security of employees and their ability to support their families. Maslow (1943) pointed out half a century ago that threatening fulfillment of such basic needs will have a major impact on employee motivation and the focus of their attention.

In sum, there are numerous reasons for employees to be wary about expecting a long-term relationship with their employers. Wall Street and investors put tremendous pressure on companies to maintain short-term profits. Structurally, a given company needs the flexibility to evolve its skill set continually. Releasing employees who do not have the needed skills to hire employees that do seems to present a viable solution to companies that need to continually evolve their skill sets while maintaining even short-term profits. These pressures come from sources outside the firm, but have a major influence on decisions within the firm that affect employees. Given these factors that entice an employer to take a short-term orientation toward employees, the next section considers the effect of longevity of the relationship on its outcomes.

Length of the relationship

Trust is a fundamental dimension of a relationship between parties. Its presence allows the parties to deal with one another in situations where they perceive risks either to what they might gain or what they might lose. It is common that the parties in a relationship do not have full information about the risks involved or the likelihood of success. It is under these conditions that the parties need to have trust in one another in order to cope with this uncertainty. The length of the relationship has at least two important effects. One is the basis for judgments about the other party, the other is a basis for future expectations.

In a new relationship where one does not have information about the other party, the nature and extent of trust is tenuous at best. Some have referred to this stage of the relationship as having deterrence-based trust (e.g. Shapiro et al., 1992; Lewicki and Bunker, 1996), in that a party would only take the level of risk that is appropriate given the level of control or deterrence that can be had over the other party via such external mechanisms as the law or contracts. Mayer et al. (1995) suggested that in such situations a person is forced to rely on what they termed propensity to trust. This is the person's general tendency to trust others, which, by definition, is how much they trust a person of unknown characteristics. Kramer (1999) suggested that a trustor accounts for the group to which someone belongs as providing some information about relevant trustworthiness characteristics. For example, knowing only that someone is a politician, used-car salesman, policeman, bank teller or manager moves a person from having no data about the trustee (wherein Mayer et al. suggest one must rely on their propensity to trust) to having only category-based data. Still, this information is at best a sketchy basis for making a risky decision. In sum, each of these describes a very tenuous basis on which to trust another party. In each case, the main ingredient that is lacking is information about the trustee developed through repeated interactions over time. Mayer et al. explain that such interactions provide data about the trustee, allowing for a more data-based judgment of trustworthiness. Lewicki and Bunker (1996) refer to this stage of the relationship as having knowledge-based trust.

In addition to the length of the relationship between parties affecting both the bases of their trust in one another and its stability in the face of reasons to question it, there is an important forward-looking component in the relationship as well. Parties in a relationship are cognizant of how much they expect to continue to deal with one another into the future. Negotiation experts point out the importance of the relationship itself in choosing a strategy for negotiation (see Lewicki et al., 2006). They recommend avoiding distributive negotiations, where one party's gain will be at the other's loss, when one expects to have to deal with the other party in the future. Any 'wins' for a focal party in the negotiation are likely to come at the expense of the quality of the relationship with the negotiation partner. When the parties must deal with one another again in the future, a party who feels that the other has taken unfair advantage will likely remember the past interaction and be less likely to cooperate. People have a tendency to behave fundamentally differently based on their expectations of how much they will have to deal with the other in the future. Those who do not expect to deal with the other party commonly engage in a so-called 'end-game strategy' of maximizing current gain without concern for any damage that might be done to the relationship. If there is no expectation of dealing with the other in the future, there is no offsetting cost in the relationship to taking any immediate gain possible. Patterns of cooperative behavior by a party often halt abruptly if the interaction is known to be at an end. Thus, in a typical end-game scenario a previously cooperative partner is suddenly willing to defect on the last exchange upon learning that there will be no further opportunities for exchange.

So far this chapter has considered risk to employees and perspectives on time. Putting the two lines of thought together produces a disturbing situation. First, a case was put forward that companies face considerable external pressure to take a short-term orientation toward the employment relationship. Employees can see from the reactions of the labor market, with downsizing, outsourcing and the increased pace of the need for new skills, that unless they are very adaptive and learn new skills very quickly, their security is clearly at risk. When one considers this new-age employment relationship in light of what is known about actions of parties who do not expect to continue in a relationship, it should not be surprising to find employees reacting to the relationship in a negative way.

The perspectives on time orientation and its effect on the relationship provide reasons for serious concern on the part of those who seek to make organizations run effectively over time. These concerns are exacerbated when attention is also given to other outside forces that affect employees' evaluations of the relationship with the employer. The next section considers some of these other factors.

Coping with risk: can you ignore that elephant?
Mayer et al. (1995) clarified the relationship between risk and trust. They proposed that the two interact to determine actual risk taking in the relationship by the trustor. In order to understand the effect of trust, they defined risk in terms of the likelihood of gains or losses *outside of issues related to the trustee*. By conceptualizing risk in this fashion, in their model, if there is enough trust to overcome the height of the threshold of risk, the trustor will engage in the risk-taking action. If there is insufficient trust to overcome the threshold of risk, the trustor will avoid engaging in the risk. Based on this analysis, then, there are two basic approaches that can get a trustor to engage in a risky behavior if the risk inherent in the action exceeds the level of trust the trustor has in the trustee. Either the level of trust in the trustee must rise, or some other factors must come into play to control the level of risk to the trustor. Conversely, if events transpire that either lower the level of trust in the trustee or raise the perceived risk inherent in the situation, the trustor will be less likely to engage in risk-taking actions.

Recent years have seen several noteworthy examples of major abuses and scandals by corporate executives that serve to heighten employees' awareness that their security is at risk. Among the most heinous examples was the fall of Enron. At the time of this writing, top executives were being found guilty of major wrongdoing that was clearly designed for self-gain. This fosters a perception among many employees that those on the top are there to serve only themselves. The chasm of compensation levels between high-level executives and lower-level employees makes fertile ground for this perception to grow. As if these executives' abuses of their power for self-gain were not enough to pique the perception of risk for employees, it was learned that the highly respected auditing firm of Arthur Andersen was aware of and allowed the accounting fraud to persist in order to preserve its company's lucrative consulting contracts with Enron. The lessons for employees were that not only can you not trust the executives, but you cannot trust those responsible for keeping the executives' potential greed and opportunism in check.

This is by no means meant to imply that all or even most executives are not trustworthy and good stewards of the companies and resources placed in their charge. The point here is that the magnitude of the scandals at companies such as Enron and WorldCom raises questions for employees of many other firms – even large, well-respected ones. Few employees of Enron saw its collapse coming, and the employees were certainly devastated after it happened. Not only did they lose their jobs, but what were the employment prospects for an employee who reentered the job market with years of experience at 'The Crooked E'? Not only did employees lose their financial security, they also saw their employability take a serious hit. If it could happen at a highly respected firm like Enron while a large prestigious auditing firm like Arthur Andersen was overseeing it, an employee is left to wonder if the same thing *could* happen or perhaps *is* happening in his or her own firm.

The picture painted so far in this chapter is rather bleak. Even in a firm where the executives have done no wrong, the pressures for taking a short-term orientation, the firm's need to be able to change skill sets quickly and cheaply, and the surprising and salient examples of executive opportunism in these and other well-publicized debacles all suggest to employees that their futures are substantially at risk. What's more, given the information asymmetry in large organizations, it is virtually impossible for the employees to accurately assess the extent to which they are at risk.

The text above presents a case that demonstrates that it is difficult in today's environment for organizations to build trust even in the best of circumstances. Rather than questioning why employees don't seem to trust their employers, perhaps we would do better to ask why employees *should* trust their employers. With this as a starting point, what happens if an organization's leader makes a self-serving decision that affects the company and the security of the employees? Can trust from employees be rebuilt, or is the executive's errant behavior the straw that broke the camel's back for the already wary employees? At the time of this writing, the topic of repairing broken trust is beginning to gain attention among organizational researchers. An upcoming issue of *Academy of Management Review* (Dirks et al., eds) will be focused on precisely that issue. The next section examines some factors that could have a positive effect on rebuilding broken trust.

The role of catharsis

When a party behaves in ways that damage trust, the experience can be anywhere from illuminating to heartbreaking for the violated party. Lewicki and Bunker (1996), among others, have pointed out that destroying trust is much faster and easier than is building it initially. Mayer and Fuller (2002) extended this reasoning to suggest that it is even harder to rebuild trust after it has been broken. Following that work, it is suggested here that the process of rebuilding may be somewhat different conceptually from initially building trust.

A well-accepted proposition in employee selection is that one of the best predictors of future performance is past performance. By the same token, one of the best predictors of future trustworthiness is past trustworthiness. A party with a developed pattern of trustworthy behavior is likely to continue that pattern in successive interactions. Lewicki and Bunker (1996) recognize this, referring to that phase of the development of the relationship as having knowledge-based trust.

While this supports the gradual incremental building of trust, the importance of a violation of trust becomes very large. If a party violates trust in a significant way, the violation can become extremely important as a predicting event. A large or salient violation may take on such importance to the violated party that it precludes rebuilding trust merely through acting subsequently in a trustworthy fashion. In these circumstances, in order for trust to be rebuilt, an intervening event or process may be needed that provides a discontinuity between the past and the future. Since the best predictor of the party's future behavior is past behavior, a salient trust violation may become the best predictor of what to expect in the future. Thus, an important first step in rebuilding trust is to get the violated party to move beyond preoccupation with the risk that will be involved in once again becoming vulnerable to the other party.

The intervening event that divorces the past from the future was referred to by Mayer and Fuller (2002) as catharsis. Catharsis is a cleansing, and has been found to be important in other domains. For example, the well-known twelve-step program used by Alcoholics Anonymous for moving people from dependence on alcohol to an alcohol-free lifestyle begins with a public admission of having a problem and a desire to change to a new lifestyle. This is a form of catharsis, as it divorces the person from feeling that the past will necessarily continue. It represents turning from the past to a new and different pattern of expectations of self.

By the same token, rebuilding trust after a large and salient violation necessitates that events of the past be divorced from expectations of the future. Without catharsis, the best predictor of future behavior will be past experiences. Unless there is an event to provide a discontinuity in the expectations, the same action that violated trust in the first place will make rebuilding it solely through subsequent trustworthy behavior very difficult. The following section describes how rebuilding trust after a major violation can be precluded via classical conditioning.

The violator as a conditioned stimulus

In some circumstances, the likelihood of rebuilding trust after a violation is small or zero (Robinson et al., 2004). Pavlov's famous experiments and a wealth of subsequent research demonstrated that a neutral stimulus presented along with some naturally stimulating cue can associate the neutral stimulus with a physical reaction. This makes the inherently neutral cue a 'conditioned' stimulus to which the subject will respond in much the same fashion as to the natural stimulus. In Pavlov's case, a bell and the presentation of food were paired, which led to a dog salivating in response to merely hearing the bell – which had become a conditioned stimulus. In some cases, a transgressor may become a conditioned stimulus leading to a negative emotional reaction from violated trust (see Morrison and Robinson, 1997). This is likely to be particularly true if the trustee has violated trust repeatedly or where the violation of trust is severe and salient. Seeing or hearing the voice of the violator – or perhaps even just hearing the violator's name – can be sufficient to evoke strong emotional reactions that preclude the violated party from considering being vulnerable to the violator again.

The strength of the emotional pain suffered by the violated party as well as attributions about the reasons for broken trust (Tomlinson and Mayer, 2006) will be related to the extent to which that party needs catharsis to rebuild trust. Consider the experience of Enron employees under the late CEO Kenneth Lay, who was found in court to have had a high level of responsibility for the well-known scandal. The CEO, by sight and name, becomes associated with the emotional turmoil associated with the trust violation. Consider the reaction of the employees if Enron had somehow survived as a company with the same CEO, who then began to act in a completely trustworthy fashion. There are, at that point, too many cues about the CEO that are paired with the violation of trust and the emotional turmoil it brought to be overlooked. In such a situation, some form of catharsis may be necessary before trust can be rebuilt to any significant extent.

While classical conditioning is usually associated with repeated pairings of the conditioned stimulus with the unconditioned stimulus (e.g. the bell paired with presentation of food), repetition is not necessary. An undergraduate psychology of learning demonstration pairs an animal's ingesting sugarwater for the first time (which is normally attractive to an animal) with injection of a noxious drug that sickens the animal for several hours. This classical conditioning of a taste aversion can be effective after only a single pairing of the conditioned and unconditioned stimulus. After only one taste of sugarwater and then experiencing subsequent illness, the animal will refuse the (normally attractive) sweet liquid in the future.

Classical conditioning may help to explain why leaders sometimes must be replaced in order to rebuild trust in management. Interestingly, this Pavlovian association might also extend to potential trustees who are similar to someone in a trustor's memory. Similarities in such innocuous issues as appearance, voice quality or mannerisms may be enough to trigger negative reactions. Furthermore, rebuilding trust may involve more than the violating party. It may include the context, such as the office or the position. Thus, once the office (e.g. that of the CEO) has violated trust, those who follow in the position inherit that legacy despite the fact that they personally have done nothing to violate trust. In such severe situations, replacing the leader may be the only practical option to restore trust in the leader's office. Given the cues surrounding the violator, even that remedy may have less than the desired effect in providing catharsis to enable rebuilding trust.

Conclusion

Why is trust necessary? Why does a lack of trust cause the workplace to be dysfunctional? It is because there are so many areas of uncertainty in an employment relationship. An employee cannot know what information his/her supervisor has when conducting a performance appraisal, or what his/her supervisor will do with those insights or with his or her personal feelings. Likewise, an employee cannot know whether top executives are being good stewards (Davis et al., 1997) of the organization's resources, or if they are making decisions that will increase their own net worth regardless of the potential consequences to the organization and its employees. Thus risk is very salient to the employee when the employee has reason to believe management might be self-serving and won't have the employee's interests in mind. If one does not trust, then 'CYA' (cover your ass) and the other mechanisms discussed in Mayer and Gavin (2005) will become important to protect one's self-interest if the person cannot leave that to the protection of the manager.

Can anything be done to foster a recovery of trust in organizations? At the time of this writing, a special issue of *Academy of Management Review* is in progress which is focused on rebuilding broken trust. Clearly, persuading managers of the importance of acting in trustworthy ways would be very helpful, but a clear and complete understanding of what that means for them would be necessary. Due to differences in such issues as demands of their roles and individual perceptions, various parties will have different views about the trustworthiness of a given party. Formal mechanisms such as 360-degree evaluations can help a manager to understand how other relevant parties view him or her, and thus provide a basis for planning how to change behaviors to appear more trustworthy in the eyes of those others.

As described in this chapter, employees find themselves at risk for a variety of reasons. Risk can come from sources both inside and outside the organization. In addition to attempting to increase trust in management, there is a variety of actions the organization can take to reduce the perceived levels of risk to the employees. Some of these involve changing formal systems to increase their transparency to employees (e.g. Mayer and Davis, 1999). Others involve helping employees stay prepared for environmental changes that might affect their current employment, such as continuous development of their skill sets. One of the most valuable ways to identify good strategies is to ask the employees themselves what issues stand in the way of trusting management. Further examination of these strategies and a plan for when it is best to use which would provide a helpful roadmap for managers who want to help their employees deal with the growing risk of the twenty-first-century work environment and to heal the dysfunctional workplace.

References

Argyris, C. (1964), *Integrating the Individual and the Organization*, New York: John Wiley & Sons.
Davis, J.H., Schoorman, F.D. and Donaldson, L. (1997), 'Toward a stewardship theory of management', *Academy of Management Review*, **22**, 20–47.
Davis, J.H., Schoorman, F.D., Mayer, R.C. and Tan, H.H. (2000), 'The trusted general manager and business unit performance: empirical evidence of a competitive advantage', *Strategic Management Journal*, **21**, 563–76.
Dirks, K.T. (2000), 'Trust in leadership and team performance: evidence from NCAA basketball', *Journal of Applied Psychology*, **85**, 1004–12.
Dirks, K.T. and Ferrin, D.L. (2002), 'Trust in leadership: meta-analytic findings and implications for research and practice', *Journal of Applied Psychology*, **87**, 611–28.
Eisenberger, R., Huntington, R., Hutchison, S. and Sowa, D. (1986), 'Perceived organizational support', *Journal of Applied Psychology*, **71**, 500–507.
Eisenberger, R., Cummings, J., Armeli, S. and Lynch, P. (1997), 'Perceived organizational support, discretionary treatment, and job satisfaction', *Journal of Applied Psychology*, **82**, 812–20.
Gambetta, D.G. (1988), 'Can we trust trust?', in D.G. Gambetta (ed.), *Trust*, New York: Basil Blackwell.
Konovsky, M.A. and Pugh, S.D. (1994), 'Citizenship behavior and social exchange', *Academy of Management Journal*, **37**, 656–69.
Kramer, R.M. (1999), 'Trust and distrust in organizations: emerging perspectives, enduring questions', *Annual Review of Psychology*, **50**, 569–98.
Kramer, R.M. and Tyler, T.R. (eds) (1996), *Trust in Organizations: Frontiers of Theory and Research*, Thousand Oaks, CA: Sage.
Kurzweil, R. and Meyer, C. (2006), 'Understanding the accelerating rate of change', www.kurzweilai.net/articles/art0563.html?printable=1 (downloaded 1 November).

Lewicki, R.J. and Bunker, B.B. (1996), 'A model of trust development and decline', in R. Kramer and T. Tyler (eds), *Trust in Organizations: Frontiers of Theory and Research*, Thousand Oaks, CA: Sage.

Lewicki, R.J., Saunders, D.M. and Barry, B. (2006), *Negotiation*, 5th edn, Boston, MA: McGraw-Hill Irwin.

Maslow, A.H. (1943), 'A theory of human motivation', *Psychological Review*, **50**, 370–96.

Mayer, R.C. and Davis, J.H. (1999), 'The effect of the performance appraisal system on trust for management: a field quasi-experiment', *Journal of Applied Psychology*, **84**, 123–36.

Mayer, R.C. and Fuller, M.A. (2002), 'Re-establishing trust: the importance of catharsis in the trust rebuilding process', presented in an All-Academy Symposium: 'Theory, evidence, and an agenda for future research on rebuilding trust', Academy of Management annual meeting, Denver.

Mayer, R.C. and Gavin, M.B. (2005), 'Trust in management and performance: who minds the shop while the employees watch the boss?', *Academy of Management Journal*, **48**, 874–88.

Mayer, R.C. and Davis, J.H. and Schoorman, F.D. (1995), 'An integrative model of organizational trust', *Academy of Management Review*, **20**, 709–34.

Morrison, E.W. and Robinson, S.L. (1997), 'When employees feel betrayed: a model of how psychological contract violation develops', *Academy of Management Review*, **22**, 226–56.

Robinson, S.L. (1996), 'Trust and breach of the psychological contract', *Administrative Science Quarterly?*, **41**, 574–99.

Robinson, S.L., Dirks, K.T. and Ozcelik, H. (2004), 'Untangling the knot of trust and betrayal', in R.M. Kramer and K.S. Cook (eds), *Trust and Distrust in Organizations: Dilemmas and Approaches*, New York: Sage, pp. 327–41.

Shapiro, D., Sheppard, B.H. and Cheraskin, L. (1992), 'Business on a handshake', *Negotiation Journal*, **8**, 365–77.

Tomlinson, E.C. and Mayer, R.C. (2006), 'The role of causal attribution dimensions in trust repair', unpublished manuscript.

9 Employee attachment and deviance in organizations
Thomas E. Becker and Rebecca J. Bennett

Workplace deviance refers to intentional acts initiated by employees that violate norms of the organization and have the potential to harm the organization or its members (Bennett and Robinson, 2000, 2003). The yearly costs of deviance in the USA are staggering: $4.2 billion for violence (Bensimon, 1997), $50 billion for employee theft and fraud (Sandberg, 2003), and $54 billion for corporate cyberloafing (Conlin, 2000). Add to this the costs of sabotage (Ambrose et al., 2002) and slowed productivity (Dunlop and Lee, 2004), and it becomes obvious that organizational deviance constitutes an extremely serious problem for employees, employers and society.

Much has been learned about types of deviance and their antecedents and consequences (see Bennett and Robinson, 2003; Berry et al., in press), but less is known about how misbehavior might be reduced. Researchers have studied organizational deviance as an effect of (a) frustration, perceived injustice and other reactions to organizational experiences (e.g. Greenberg and Alge, 1998; Spector, 1997), (b) personality traits such as dispositional aggressiveness and anger (e.g. Deffenbacher, 1992; James, 1998), and (c) norms, modeling and other aspects of social context (e.g. Bennett et al., 2005; Giacalone et al., 1997; Robinson and O'Leary-Kelly, 1998). These antecedents suggest that there are a number of ways that deviance might be reduced in the workplace. For instance, selection processes may be used to screen for hostile applicants, abusive supervision might be ameliorated by careful training, and performance management systems may be designed to apply clear and apt consequences for deviant acts. However, not all aggressive applicants are likely to be screened out of the applicant pool, and not all hostility is a function of individual characteristics. Further, abusive supervision is sometimes more a matter of motivation than insufficient knowledge or skills, so training won't always be the answer. Finally, although providing formal consequences for deviance is a noble goal, one must first know that deviance occurred, who was involved, and who was at fault – not always simple matters. We assert that because behavior in organizations occurs in a social context, and because deviance requires interaction among people, the degree and target of employee attachment are likely to be additional drivers of deviance. Like other deterrents, attachment will not be a panacea. But as we explain in the following sections, elucidating the attachment–deviance relation has potential for enhancing the scientific understanding of employee deviance and better managing deviant actions.

The premise of this chapter is that one promising route to understanding employees' social contexts lies in the phenomenon of employee attachment – in particular, workplace commitment and identification. Employee commitment is one's psychological bond to various social foci (e.g. supervisors, work groups, the organization) (Becker, 1992; Bishop and Scott, 2000; Reichers, 1985; Siders et al., 2001) and non-social foci (e.g. goals, jobs, change programs) (Klein et al., 2001; Herscovitch and Meyer, 2002; Morrow, 1993).

Given the topic of this chapter, our focus will be on commitment to social foci. Widely studied forms of commitment to such foci include affective commitment (a positive emotional bond), normative commitment (a sense of obligation to maintain membership), and continuance commitment (an awareness of the perceived costs of leaving) (Meyer and Allen, 1997). Employee identification is an individual's perceptions regarding membership in a collective (Ashforth and Mael, 1989), and the attitudes and behaviors adopted in order to have a satisfying, self-defining relationship with the collective (Becker et al., 1996; O'Reilly and Chatman, 1986).

Compared to the variables mentioned earlier, employee attachment may be easier to influence. For example, commitment is positively affected by transformational leadership, role clarity, fair treatment, and employees' perceptions of the degree to which the organization values their contributions and cares about their well-being (Meyer et al., 2002; Rhoades and Eisenberger, 2002). Given that these processes are largely under the control of organizational decision makers, they appear promising as counterweights to organizational deviance. Indeed, indirect evidence suggests that both commitment and identification may lessen organizational deviance. For example, higher levels of both variables are positively related to in-role performance and organizational citizenship behaviors, and negatively associated with absenteeism and turnover (Cooper-Hakim and Viswesvaran, 2005; Meyer et al., 2002; Riketta, 2005). Therefore, it would seem that commitment and identification should be negatively correlated with deviant behaviors such as intentionally restricting one's performance (shirking), engaging in antisocial behaviors such as aggressively competing with co-workers or spreading rumors about the company, and voluntarily violating attendance norms such as taking regular two-hour lunches or leaving early.

However, a deeper consideration of the link between attachment and deviance suggests that the relationship may not be so straightforward. For instance, supervisors don't always share the norms of the wider organization, and in these situations commitment to the supervisor may have a dominant influence on employees' behavior (Becker et al., 1996). If the supervisor's values run counter to the welfare of the organization (e.g. 'In this department, the boss encourages unethical activity'), commitment to the supervisor would likely promote organizational deviance. As another example, the form of commitment may be consequential. Unlike affective and normative commitment, continuance commitment is positively related to absenteeism and low performance (Cooper-Hakim and Viswesvaran, 2005; Meyer et al., 2002). These behaviors are considered to be 'deviant' if they are intentional. As a final example, several authors (Glomb and Liao, 2003; Robinson and O'Leary-Kelly, 1998) have demonstrated that group social context influences individual interpersonal aggression. This has been called a modeling or social learning effect, but we would expect that an individual's identification with their work group would exacerbate the relation between social context and aggression.

Because employee attachment seems to be a promising means for better understanding and more effectively managing organizational deviance, we believe the time has come to focus greater effort on examining the link between these two variables. In the following section, we provide our initial ideas on deviance and attachment as a means of setting the stage for subsequent theory development. Next, we draw upon a mature, validated motivational model, the theory of planned behavior, to elucidate the link between attachment and deviance. This approach serves as the basis for 12 specific and testable propositions. We end with a discussion of the implications of our perspective for science and practice.

Preliminary thoughts on employee deviance and attachment

Employee deviance

Workplace deviant behavior (WDB) is based on the violation of organizational norms, i.e. standards established by the dominant coalition of an organization (Robinson and Bennett, 1995). Although the norms of other entities (e.g. supervisors, work teams, customers) also influence WDB, behaviors that violate other entities' norms but not organizational norms are not WDB. Nonetheless, they may be considered deviant by the entity, and may have implications for organizational constituencies and the organization overall. Thus we will address the causes of such behavior and will answer the question of why an employee may violate the norms of a given entity while following organizational norms, or vice versa.

Bennett et al. (2005) investigated the origins of norms regarding acceptable behavior. They suggested that new employees are socialized by organizational leaders to adopt the appropriate role behaviors defined by the organization's culture. As a result of this socialization process, employees may internalize organizational norms, and subsequent violations produce guilt and shame and a desire to correct the deviant behavior. In the case of other workplace entities, socialization also identifies what behaviors are considered deviant. For example, new members of a work group quickly pick up on written and unwritten rules of appropriate behavior (Feldman, 1984; Levine and Moreland, 1998; Moscovici, 1985). Members either adapt to the norms or experience discomfort. If the latter, they may leave the situation (e.g. seek a transfer from the work group). The leadership of a collective (e.g. department, union, work unit) is likely to have a significant effect on the collective's culture, norms and socialization practices. If the norms of the collective are different from the norms of the organization, employees will probably experience conflict. In such situations, we propose that which norms more strongly affect employee behavior depend upon certain aspects of employee commitment.

Employee commitment and identity

Commitment   Commitment is a psychological bond between an individual and a social or non-social target, and to a course of action relevant to that target (Meyer et al., 2004). This definition reflects that an individual's bond with a target commits the person to behaviors pertinent to that target, and implies that commitment can vary in degree (see Becker and Kernan, 2003, and Meyer and Herscovitch, 2001, for further discussion). As mentioned earlier, we concentrate on social foci because we believe these are an essential part of the social context in which deviance occurs. In this section we further restrict our discussion to within-target comparisons (i.e. where identity and commitment involve the same collective). In a later section, we broaden this discussion to include the relationship between commitment and identity across collectives.

The links between commitment and behavior vary as a function of the mindsets accompanying commitment. More specifically, employees maintain attachments to foci because they want to (affective commitment), because they think they should (normative commitment), or because they have too much to lose by leaving (continuance commitment) (Meyer and Allen, 1997). As Meyer et al. (2002) reported, affective commitment generally has relatively strong and positive relationships with behaviors such as employee retention, extra-role activities and performance; normative commitment has weaker positive relationships with these behaviors; and continuance commitment has negative or no relationships with these behaviors.

Identity   The essence of a social identity is inclusion of group membership as part of one's self-concept (Riketta, 2005). That is, having a social identity means seeing oneself as part of a larger whole (Rousseau, 1998; Tajfel, 1978). Because social identities can be specific to situations or take on a trait-like character, Rousseau (1998) suggested distinguishing between two kinds of identity. *A situated identity* arises when contextual cues indicate that an individual shares interests with a collective. Thereafter, the identity is dependent on those cues and exists only as long as the cues persist. On the other hand, a *deep-structure identity* involves changing one's self-concept to incorporate attributes (e.g. interests, values) of the collective. Once created, deep-structure identities are relatively enduring and impervious to situational cues.

Many employees belong to multiple collectives, such as teams, unions and organizations. Therefore employees can form multiple social identities, one or more of which may be dominant at a given time (Van Dick et al., 2005). In addition, social identities are composed of cognitive, emotional and evaluative elements (Van Dick, 2001). The mindsets associated with a social identity typically include a cognitive awareness of membership in a collective, an evaluation of the collective and oneself as a member, and an emotional response to that evaluation (Harris and Cameron, 2005). Finally, social identities have implications for behavior. For instance, social identification has been tied to stereotyping, ingroup favoritism and susceptibility to social influence, all of which have ramifications for group dynamics (Ashforth and Mael, 1989; Blanton et al., 2002).

In sum, as Meyer et al. (2006) have argued, although both commitment and identification are forms of attachment, they differ in terms of their defining characteristics. That is, social identification involves defining 'self' as part of a collective, while commitment involves the binding of self to a target and a course of action. Also, the two concepts differ in terms of the corresponding mindsets and behavioral implications. We turn now to the development of a model explicating the relationships between identification, commitment and deviance.

Attachment, deviance and the theory of planned behavior

Our model of attachment and employee deviance is illustrated in Figure 9.1. In beginning our analysis, the theory of planned behavior (Ajzen, 1991) seemed to us a reasonable starting point. We chose this theory due to its parsimony and demonstrated ability to enrich the prediction and explanation of motivated behavior. The theory of planned behavior is an extension of the well-known theory of reasoned action (Fishbein and Ajzen, 1975), which holds that a person's intention to engage in a behavior is the most proximate determinant of that behavior. Behavioral intention is, in turn, determined by attitude toward the behavior and subjective norms regarding it. Attitude toward the behavior is the degree to which a person has a favorable or unfavorable evaluation of the given behavior. This attitude is a function of the expectation that engaging in the behavior will lead to certain consequences and the person's evaluation of those consequences. Subjective norms are the perceived social pressure to engage in the behavior. They are a function of the belief about whether others think the person should engage in the behavior and the motivation to comply with others.

Although the theory of reasoned action has demonstrated predictive utility in many situations and across a large variety of behaviors (Prestholdt et al., 1987; Sheppard et al.,

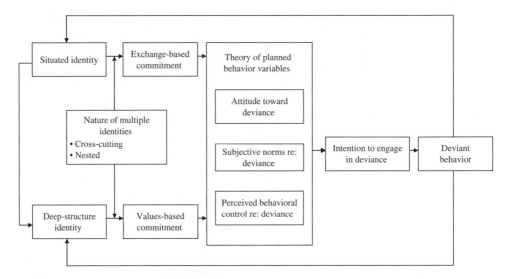

Figure 9.1   The theory of planned behavior as the linking pin between employee attachment and organizational deviance

1988), it does not fare so well with respect to behaviors (e.g. smoking cessation) that are influenced less by volition and more by other factors (Ajzen, 1989). In such cases an additional variable, perceived behavioral control, is helpful. Perceived behavioral control is the degree to which a person believes he or she has the resources (personal, social and material) necessary to engage in the behavior. It is a function of the person's belief that certain resources are present and the person's evaluation of the usefulness of these resources. The only difference between the theory of reasoned action and the theory of planned behavior is that the latter includes perceived behavioral control while the former does not.

The theory of planned behavior performs especially well in situations where there are constraints on volition (Ajzen, 1991), such as starting a business (Kolvereid, 1996; Krueger et al., 2000), using new technology (Harrison et al., 1997; Venkatesh et al., 2000), preventing industrial pollution (Cordano and Frieze, 2000), and – perhaps most relevant to our topic – ethical decision making (Chang, 1998; Flannery and May, 2000). Because deviant behavior can be facilitated or constrained by broad structural and sociological factors such as societal norms (Bennett et al., 2005; Dietz et al., 2003), organizational culture (Trevino, 1986; Vardi and Weitz, 2004), workplace policies (Leatherwood and Spector, 1991; Schat et al., 2005) and other situational variables, we believe the theory of planned behavior is preferable to the theory of reasoned action for predicting and explaining deviance in organizations.

Most likely, the theory of planned behavior has superior validity in the above conditions because constraints on behavior are often open to interpretation, and because the same events are not equally constraining for everyone. For example, one person, low on perceived behavioral control, might start a new business and view competitors and the need for financing as overwhelming constraints. But another person, high on perceived control, might see the same 'constraints' as challenges to be overcome on the path to success. The varied perceptions of the two people would be a matter of real or imagined differences in available, relevant resources.

A legitimate application of the theory of planned behavior requires adherence to the principle of compatibility, that is, that all of the elements (attitude, subjective norms, perceived behavioral control, intention and behavior) have an identical focus (Ajzen, 1991). Because the focal behavior of current interest is deviance, the relevant determinants are:

- *Intention to engage in workplace deviance*: the extent to which an employee aims to engage in deviant behavior at work.
- *Attitude toward workplace deviance*: the degree to which an employee has a favorable or unfavorable evaluation of deviant behavior at work. This attitude is a function of the expectation that engaging in deviance will lead to certain consequences (e.g. material goods from theft, getting fired) and the actor's evaluation (positive or negative) of those consequences.
- *Subjective norms regarding workplace deviance*: the perceived social pressure to engage in deviant behavior at work. These subjective norms are a function of the employee's belief about whether others (e.g. managers, peers) think the employee should engage in deviance, and the employee's motivation to comply with the others.
- *Perceived behavioral control regarding workplace deviance*: the degree to which an employee believes he or she has the resources necessary to engage in deviant behavior at work. This variable is a function of the employee's belief that personal resources (e.g. knowledge of how to get away with a deviant act, a sense of justified outrage), social resources (e.g. sympathetic peers) and other resources (e.g. opportunity) are present, and the person's evaluation of how useful these resources are.

In summary, the theory of planned behavior applied to the current context suggests that workplace deviance will occur when employees intend to engage in deviant acts. This intention will exist when employees believe workplace deviance will result in positive outcomes (and/or help avoid negative ones), when they are inclined to comply with others who favor deviance, and when they believe the necessary resources are available. Therefore we offer the following propositions:

Proposition 1: The best predictor of deviant behavior is the intent to engage in deviance.
Proposition 2: A more positive attitude toward deviance (the perceived probability that deviance will lead to desired, rather than undesired, outcomes) leads to a greater intent to engage in deviance.
Proposition 3: Subjective norms favorable to deviance (based on the motivation to comply with others' favorable judgments regarding deviance) lead to a greater intent to engage in deviance.
Proposition 4: High perceived behavioral control regarding deviance leads to a greater intent to engage in deviant behavior.

Exchange-based and values-based commitments and deviance
In attempting to integrate work on social identities and commitment, and explain how these affect workplace behavior, Meyer et al. (2006) developed several key points relevant to this chapter. The first is that some forms of commitment (value-based commitment) are more potent than others (exchange-based commitment), in that the former have a

broader effect on work behaviors. Earlier, Meyer et al. (2004) argued that employees with a strong affective commitment to a collective act on the basis of a volitional, positive attachment, and that they thus want to engage in positive actions relevant to the collective. Meyer et al. (2006) added that the same is true of employees whose bond with a collective is driven by an uncoerced desire to fulfill moral obligations, a form of attachment they labeled 'normative commitment as moral imperative'. For both types of 'value-based commitments', employees are likely to experience autonomous self-regulation (Ryan and Deci, 2000), the sense that one is freely choosing his or her course of action. Because action is experienced as freely chosen, and because it is predicated on strong, positive attachments to the given collective, the employee is likely to engage in both non-discretionary and discretionary actions relevant to the collective. For example, if the collective is the organization, such an employee would be inclined to perform both in-role and extra-role behaviors with a similar degree of vigor. On the other hand, employees with strong continuance commitment, or normative commitment based on a resigned obligation to repay a debt (normative commitment as indebted obligation), experience a greater feeling of being controlled. They therefore restrict their efforts to required, non-discretionary behaviors.

With respect to workplace deviance, the above analysis suggests that employees who have a high level of value-based commitment to a target other than the organization are most likely to engage in workplace deviance. This is especially true when the target (e.g. boss, work team) is characterized by norms and values that are not in the organization's best interests. For example, the first author once worked as a waiter in a restaurant where the maitre d' told servers that 'A good waiter never goes hungry!' Not surprisingly, most dining-room employees assumed this to mean that stealing food was acceptable – which, since nobody was ever punished for such theft, was a reasonable assumption. Given the above, employees who were emotionally attached to the maitre d' (e.g. who liked and admired him), or who shared his ideal for an employee-initiated profit-sharing plan, were most likely to have stolen from the restaurant. The theory of planned behavior suggests that this is because, compared to other employees, these individuals were either more likely to have a positive attitude about theft (e.g. because we often adopt the attitudes of those to whom we're committed), a more favorable subjective norm regarding stealing (e.g. because we are motivated to comply with the norms of those to whom we're affectively committed), higher perceived behavior control (e.g. because we believe those to whom we are affectively committed – such as the maitre d' – will protect, or at least not condemn, us), or because we hold some combination of these beliefs.

This is not to suggest that exchange-based commitment cannot lead to deviant behavior. For instance, one could label overcommitment to a course of action a type of deviant behavior. In the classic 'knee deep in the Big Muddy' scenario (Staw, 1976), individuals continue to contribute to a losing cause long after it is clear that this is a tremendous waste of money. This behavior may be influenced, in part, by sunk costs, in that the amount lost can make it difficult for a person to halt irrational investments. However, this overcommitment is volitional in the sense that it is not required and participants can choose to stop. Assuming that the norms of the organization do not support the senseless disposal of profits, overcommitment driven by sunk costs seems deviant by definition. The same is true of an accountant completing illegal transactions due to perceived obligations to top management or to a lack of alternatives. Thus, while value-based commitment appears likely to produce a more enthusiastic, ostensibly autonomous deviant, exchange-based commitment can probably lead to deviance too. Therefore we offer the following propositions:

Proposition 5: When emotional attachment or moral ideals favor deviance, value-based commitment to non-organization foci leads to cognitions (theory of planned behavior cognitions) conducive to deviance. This form of commitment typically has a stronger relation with deviance than does exchange-based commitment.

Proposition 6: When sunk costs, a sense of indebted obligation, or a lack of alternatives favor deviance, exchange-based commitment leads to cognitions conducive to deviance.

Situated and deep-structure identities and deviance

Another key point made by Meyer et al. (2006) is that some kinds of social identities (deep-structure identities) have a greater effect on the more potent types of commitment than do others (situated identities). According to Rousseau (1998), situated identities are interest-based and cue-dependent, whereas deep-structure identities involve the internalization of characteristics of the collective into one's self-concept. Situated identities, such as those typically formed by contingent and marginal workers, are likely to contribute to the development of exchange-based commitment. This is because these employees may perceive the existence of a transactional contract with the organization (Rousseau, 1995), one that involves a mutual, time-bound, *quid pro quo* relationship. On the other hand, deep-structure identities, like those typically formed by dedicated, long-term employees, are likely to foster values-based commitment. The internalization and sharing of values, characteristic of deep-structure identities, are a basis of affective commitment (Becker and Billings, 1993; Kristof-Brown et al., 2005), and this should be true of other forms of values-based commitment too. Finally, it should be noted that employees' desires for security and belongingness may facilitate the transition from situated to deep-structure identities (Meyer et al., 2006), especially for those whose self-concept is rooted in membership in a given collective. Hence we offer the following:

Proposition 7: Deep-structure identities lead to values-based commitments which, under the right circumstances (Proposition 6), increase the likelihood of deviance. Situated identities lead to exchange-based commitments which, under the right circumstances (Proposition 5) can also increase the likelihood of deviance.

Norms, the informal rules that collectives adopt to regulate behavior, are an essential mechanism by which collectives influence members, and members who strongly identify with the collective are particularly affected by its norms. An organization is usually composed of multiple constituencies (e.g. work teams, union, departments), and may have strong associations with others (e.g. professions, customers), including non-work-related ones (e.g. families, activist groups). For employees, these constituencies can serve as the bases for one or more foci of commitment. Further, although the norms of a given constituency can be congruent with organizational norms and, therefore, may benefit the organization, this is not always necessarily the case. Norms develop through explicit statements, critical events and history, and normative control focuses on behaviors that ensure survival of the collective, increases predictability of members' behavior, avoids embarrassing interpersonal situations, or gives expression to the collective's central values (Feldman, 1984). It seems clear that norm development of a constituency can work against organizational norms, and may even operate to harm the organization. For example, a work group that has experienced massive layoffs could attempt to ensure the group's survival by creating norms supporting sabotaging other groups or engaging in hostile office politics.

When these kinds of deviance norms evolve, members with deep-structure identities are most likely to promote and enforce them. For these employees, the norms of the collective are fully consistent with their self-concept and reflect their personal goals and values. While those with a situated identity may comply with the norms, their actions are driven by situational cues rather than internal values. The corresponding lack of emotional attachment with the collective would make their related beliefs and actions less fervent.

Hence we offer:

Proposition 8: The effects of identification on deviance are mediated by commitment and the theory of planned behavior variables.

Proposition 9: When norms of a collective favor deviance, a deep-structure identity *vis-à-vis* the collective leads to more, and more severe, deviance motivation and behavior than does a situated identity.

Multiple identities, commitments and deviance

Finally, Meyer et al. (2006) acknowledged that employees can identify with and commit to many different work-relevant foci, and discussed the attitudinal and behavioral implications of the nature of such commitments. In this section we extend this analysis to deviance-related attachment and behavior. Due to space constraints, we limit our focus to relatively stable identities and two fundamental types of relations among foci: nested and cross-cutting.

Among the many work-related foci that may engender important and stable identities are organizations, departments, teams and specific individuals (e.g. supervisor, friend at work). However, what determines the relative strength of these identities? How do they relate to one another, and what implications does this have for deviant behavior? Ellemers and Rink (2005) identified two configurations of multiple identities. The first is nested collectives, whereby membership in one (e.g. team) requires membership in the other (e.g. organization). Although identical variables influence identities at all levels of nesting, the corresponding forces tend to be stronger and more salient at proximal (lower) levels. Thus identities are usually stronger at these levels (Becker et al., 1996; Riketta and Van Dick, 2005). For example, most employees come into more regular contact with specific local members of their department (e.g. the immediate supervisor) than they do with more general, global representatives of the organization (e.g. top management). Therefore the distinctiveness and meaningfulness of employees' associations with department members are likely to be stronger. Further, while it has been argued that commitment to the organization must mediate the effects of more proximal commitments (Hunt and Morgan, 1994), research has demonstrated that this is not the case: relationships between commitment to teams and other foci and behavior exist even after commitment to the organization is controlled (Maertz et al., 2002).

Ellemers and Rink (2005) also described a second configuration of attachment to foci that they called 'cross-cutting'. Cross-cutting collectives have no necessary dependencies, and therefore employees may have to choose among their loyalties. To borrow an example from Meyer et al. (2006), employees can identify with their profession, the organization in which they work, or both. Further, Ellemers and Rink suggest that these identities can have reinforcing or diluting effects. Reinforcing effects occur when values and norms are compatible. In such cases, employees might identify most with, and show the greatest favoritism toward, others who share the same profession and who work in their own department. With diluting effects, values and norms are incompatible, and the strength of an employee's identity with one likely undermines identification with the other.

In light of the evidence provided by Ellemers and Rink (2005) and the logic outlined in the development of our previous propositions, we offer the following propositions concerning the impact of multiple identities on commitment and deviance:

Proposition 10: Individuals with multiple identities in nested collectives identify most strongly with the lower-level collective and develop stronger value-based commitment to that collective and its deviance norms than they do to the higher-level collective.

Proposition 11: Individuals with multiple identities in cross-cutting collectives develop value-based commitment to the collective and its deviance norms in proportion to the strength of their identity *via-à-vis* these collectives. When identities are reinforcing, employees experience value-based commitment to both collectives, and deviance norms are strengthened. When identities are diluting, employees develop a stronger values-based commitment to that collective, and its deviance norms, with which they identify most strongly.

Reciprocal effects of deviance on identity

Finally, although identities are important antecedents of commitment, motivation and behavior, there may also be a reciprocal influence of behavior on social identities. For example, according to Bandura's social cognitive theory of self-regulation (1991), we learn about ourselves in part through observing our own behavior. Therefore, engaging in positive discretionary behavior directed toward a collective might be interpreted as indicating that the collective is important to the person, thereby leading to an increase in deep-structure identity. In contrast, restricting one's activities to non-discretionary task performance might help to maintain one's perception that membership in a collective is conditional (i.e. situated). Applying this rationale to deviance in organizations, we offer:

Proposition 12: The perception of voluntarily engaging in deviant behavior on behalf of a collective creates or enhances deep-structure identity with respect to that target. The perception of involuntarily engaging in deviant behavior on behalf of a collective creates or enhances situated identity with respect to the target.

In the preceding pages, we have described what we believe to be a tenable and testable model of employee attachment, motivation and deviance in organizations. We now turn our attention to discussion of specific implications of our approach for advancing knowledge in this area, and for facilitating the management of deviance.

Implications for theory and practice

Implications for theory
Our theory has implications for prior approaches to understanding WDB, including social psychological perspectives, models of perceived organizational support, and research on interpersonal treatment. First, we believe our model of attachment contributes to social psychological perspectives of modeling, information processing in groups, and social contagion (for discussion of these models, see Dietz et al., 2003; Ferguson, 2006; Glomb and Liao, 2003; and Robinson and O'Leary-Kelly, 1998). Although the related research provides insights into WBD, it doesn't provide the specific, detailed connections to motivation and behavior that is possible with the theory of planned behavior and that is reflected in our 12 propositions. Further, because they do not distinguish between different forms of commitment and do not consider the social identities of the deviant employees, these theories are at a disadvantage in explaining and predicting motivational processes pertinent to employee deviance.

Perceived organizational support has also been found to affect WDB (Colbert et al., 2004; Eder and Eisenberger, 2006; Stamper and Masterson, 2002). That is, if perceived organizational support is low (i.e. the employee experiences a thwarted sense of belongingness), the employee may exhibit *more* WDB than when perceived support is high (Thau et al., 2006). This effect may be mediated through affective commitment and identification with the supervisor and other commitment foci. The inclusive model of attachment proposed in this chapter would further explain why perceived support may have varying effects depending on employees' attachments to other nested and cross-cutting collectives. For instance, if supervisors' norms encourage engagement in WDB but organizational norms do not, employees may typically act according to supervisors' norms (Becker and Kernan, 2003). If, however, employees have high perceived organizational support, they may identify more strongly with the organization and hence be better able to avoid engaging in the WDBs encouraged by individual supervisors. Thus our model implies a more complex but more significant role of perceived organizational support in the deviance process.

Finally, interpersonal treatment has received considerable support as an antecedent for WDB (e.g. Aquino et al., 1999; Colquitt et al., 2001; Dineen et al., 2006). We suspect that interpersonal justice, behavioral integrity and trust affect values-based commitment which, in turn, often discourages engaging in WDB. On the other hand, unjust treatment and a lack of integrity by supervisors, and corresponding mistrust on the part of employees, are likely to result in greater WDB because of a reduction in values-based commitment. Further, we anticipate that cross-cutting and nested identities may moderate the effect of interpersonal mistreatment on WDB. For example, if a supervisor is verbally abusive of employees but co-workers treat one another with respect, WDB may depend on whether employees are most attached to the supervisor or to each other. We suggest that studying these dynamics will contribute to the understanding of workplace justice, employee trust and other areas of interpersonal treatment.

Implications for practice
Our model implies that there are several attachment-related triggers for modifying deviant behavior. For purposes of discussion, we make two assumptions: that our model and propositions are sound, and that organizational norms are legal and ethical. The first

trigger is employees' social identities. To foster desirable employee identities, organizational decision makers should encourage deep-structure identities with the organization, with entities nested within the organization (supervisors, work groups, etc.), or both. To benefit the organization, the nested entities would need to share the organization's norms against deviance. Promoting this condition would likely require targeted hiring practices (to screen for inclinations toward deviance), training (to inform employees about core norms and values and impress upon them the seriousness with which management holds them), and an effective incentive system (to reward ethical behavior and punish WDBs).

The second trigger is employee commitment, a variable that is affected not only by social identification, but also by personal, job and organizational characteristics (Mathieu and Zajac, 1990). Take, for example, a situation in which an exchange-based commitment has been created due to an anti-organizational situated identity (e.g. a clique of contingent workers). As discussed previously, under the right conditions this would be expected to produce employee deviance. However, this outcome might be ameliorated by increasing values-based commitment to the organization or organization-friendly foci. One way to do this would be to provide additional material or psychological resources, thereby enhancing perceived organizational support. As noted above, perceived organizational support appears to be an important driver of affective commitment (Rhoades and Eisenberger, 2002), so it would be expected to foster other forms of values-based commitment as well. Similar arguments could be made for other antecedents of commitment, such as job autonomy, role clarity and leadership behaviors.

The final trigger for reducing deviance is via the theory of planned behavior variables. Even when identity and commitment favor deviance, it is possible that management can to some degree counteract this tendency by attempting to influence employee attitudes, subjective norms or perceived behavioral control. For instance, attitudes favoring deviant behavior could be discouraged by offering valued material or social rewards for acting according to organizational norms. Subjective norms supporting deviance could be undermined by hiring more independent thinkers who value productivity and ethical behavior. These employees, low in self-monitoring and need for approval, would provide an excellent fit in organizations holding these same values, and would not be motivated to comply with foci holding deviant norms. Regarding perceived behavioral control, we suspect the major resources needed for deviant behavior are skill in accomplishing specific deviant acts (e.g. ability to cleverly cover up theft), social support (e.g. the sanction of one's peers) and opportunity (e.g. keys to the store room). The first two resources can likely be reduced by the hiring, training and socialization tactics discussed previously. In addition, treating employees fairly has been shown to reduce the motivation to act deviantly (Greenberg and Alge, 1998). We suspect that promoting justice may similarly reduce the tendency to sanction deviance. Reducing opportunities for deviance will necessarily require an analysis of direct causes (e.g. Joe has keys to the store room) and development of corresponding solutions (e.g. take the keys away from Joe, fire Joe).

Conclusion
We have presented a model of employee attachment, motivation and deviant behavior in the workplace, and have argued that the corresponding propositions add to previous theory on employee deviance. Before implications of the model are put into practice, it is imperative that a research program be designed and implemented to test propositions and

determine to what extent the model fits reality. This will involve both conceptual and empirical challenges. Conceptually, it is clear that the model should not be applied to deviant behavior that may be driven by unconscious, non-intentional actions. As its name implies, the theory of planned behavior is relevant only to planned courses of action. However, distinguishing WBDs that are intentional versus more spontaneous or automatic may sometimes be difficult, and more research is needed to differentiate these domains. Empirically, there will certainly be challenges in developing deviance-specific measures of planned behavior variables, and in creating an approach to testing the model that is not plagued by method variance and purely cross-sectional data. Nevertheless, the statistics on workplace deviance provided at the beginning of this chapter lead us to believe the trouble will be worth the effort.

References

Ajzen, I. (1989), 'Attitude structure and behavior', in H. Pratkanis, S.J. Breckler and A.G. Greenwald (eds), *Attitude Structure and Function*, Hillsdale, NJ: Lawrence Erlbaum Associates, pp. 241–74.

Ajzen, I. (1991), 'The theory of planned behavior', *Organizational Behavior and Human Decision Processes*, **50**, 179–211.

Ambrose, M., M. Seabright and M. Schminke (2002), 'Sabotage in the workplace: the role of organizational justice', *Organizational Behavior and Human Decision Processes*, **89**, 947–65.

Aquino, K., M. Lewis and M. Bradfield (1999), 'Justice constructs, negative affectivity and employee deviance: a proposed model and empirical test', *Journal of Organizational Behavior*, **20**, 1073–91.

Ashforth, B.E. and F. Mael (1989), 'Social identity theory and the organization', *Academy of Management Review*, **14**, 20–39.

Bandura, A. (1991), 'Social cognitive theory of self-regulation', *Organizational Behavior and Human Decision Processes*, **50**, 248–87.

Becker, T.E. (1992), 'Foci and bases of commitment: are they distinctions worth making?', *Academy of Management Journal*, **35**, 232–44.

Becker, T.E. and Billings, R.S. (1993), 'Profiles of commitment: an empirical test', *Journal of Organizational Behavior*, **14**, 177–90.

Becker, T.E. and M. Kernan (2003), 'Matching commitment to supervisors and organizations to in-role and extra-role performance', *Human Performance*, **16**, 327–48.

Becker, T.E., R.S. Billings, D.M. Eveleth and N.W. Gilbert (1996), 'Foci and bases of commitment: implications for performance', *Academy of Management Journal*, **39**, 464–82.

Bennett, R.J. and S.L. Robinson (2000), 'Development of a measure of workplace deviance', *Journal of Applied Psychology*, **85**, 349–60.

Bennett, R.J. and S.L. Robinson (2003), 'The past, present, and future of workplace deviance research', in J. Greenberg (ed.), *Organizational Behavior: The State of the Science*, 2nd edn, Mahwah, NJ: Lawrence Erlbaum Associates, pp. 247–81.

Bennett, R.J., K. Aquino, A. Reed, II and S. Thau (2005), 'The normative nature of employee deviance and the impact of moral identity', in S. Fox and P. Spector (eds), *Counterproductive Work Behavior: Investigations of Actors and Targets*, Washington, DC: American Psychological Association, pp. 107–25.

Bensimon, H. (1997), 'What to do about anger in the workplace', *Training and Development*, 28–32.

Berry, C., D. Ones and P. Sackett (in press), 'Interpersonal deviance, organizational deviance, and their common correlates: a review and meta-analysis', *Journal of Applied Psychology*.

Bishop, J.W. and K.D. Scott (2000), 'An examination of organizational and team commitment in a self-directed team environment', *Journal of Applied Psychology*, **85**, 439–50.

Blanton, H., C. Christie and M. Dye (2002), 'Social identity versus reference frame comparisons: the moderating role of stereotype endorsement', *Journal of Experimental Social Psychology*, **38**, 252–67.

Chang, M.K. (1998), 'Predicting unethical behavior: a comparison of the theory of reasoned action and the theory of planned behavior', *Journal of Business Ethics*, **17**, 1825–34.

Colbert, A., M. Mount, J. Harter, L.Witt and M. Barrick (2004), 'Interactive effects of personality and perceptions of the work situation on workplace deviance', *Journal of Applied Psychology*, **89**, 599–609.

Colquitt, J., D. Conlon, M. Wesson, C. Porter and K. Ng (2001), 'Justice at the millennium: a meta-analytic review of 25 years of organizational justice research', *Journal of Applied Psychology*, **86**, 425–45.

Conlin, M. (2000), 'Workers, surf at your own risk', *Business Week*, 12 June, 105.

Cooper-Hakim, A. and C. Viswesvaran (2005), 'The construct of work commitment: testing an integrative framework', *Psychological Bulletin*, **131**, 241–59.

Cordano, M. and I.H. Frieze (2000), 'Pollution reduction preferences of U.S. environmental managers: applying Ajzen's theory of planned behavior', *Academy of Management Journal*, **43**, 627–41.

Deffenbacher, J.L. (1992), 'Trait anger: theory, findings, and implications', in C.D. Spielberger and J.N. Butcher (eds), *Advances in Personality Assessment*, Vol. 9, Hillsdale, NJ: Lawrence Erlbaum Associates, pp. 177–201.

Dietz, J., S. Robinson, R. Folger, R. Baron and M. Shultz (2003), 'The impact of community violence and an organization's procedural justice climate on workplace aggression', *Academy of Management Journal*, **46**, pp. 317–26.

Dineen, B., R. Lewicki and E. Tomlinson (2006), 'Supervisory guidance and behavioral integrity', *Journal of Applied Psychology*, **91**, 622–35.

Dunlop, P. and K. Lee (2004), 'Workplace deviance, organizational citizenship behavior, and business unit performance: the bad apples do spoil the whole barrel', *Journal of Organizational Behavior*, **25**, 67–80.

Eder, P. and R. Eisenberger (2006), 'Perceived organizational support: overcoming work group deviance', working paper, University of Delaware.

Ellemers, N. and F. Rink (2005), 'Identity in work groups: the beneficial and detrimental consequences of multiple identities and group norms for collaboration and group performance', *Advances in Group Processes*, **22**, 1–41.

Feldman, D.C. (1984), 'The development and enforcement of group norms', *Academy of Management Review*, **9**, 47–53.

Ferguson, M. (2006), 'From bad to worse: a social contagion model of organizational misbehavior', working paper, Vanderbilt University.

Fishbein, M. and I. Ajzen (1975), *Belief, Attitude, Intention, and Behavior: An Introduction to Theory and Research*, Reading, MA: Addison-Wesley.

Flannery, B.L. and D.R. May (2000), 'Environmental decision making in the U.S. metal-finishing industry', *Academy of Management Journal*, **43**, 642–62.

Giacalone, R.A., C.A. Riordan and P. Rosenfeld (1997), 'Employee sabotage: toward a practitioner–scholar understanding', in R. Giacalone and J. Greenberg (eds), *Antisocial Behavior in Organizations*, Thousand Oaks, CA: Sage, pp. 109–29.

Glomb, T.M. and H. Liao (2003), 'Interpersonal aggression in work groups: social influence, reciprocal, and individual effects', *Academy of Management Journal*, **46**, 486–96.

Greenberg, J. and B. Alge (1998), 'Aggressive reactions to workplace injustice', in R.W. Griffin, A. O'Leary-Kelly and J. Collins (eds), *Dysfunctional Behavior in Organizations: Vol. 1. Violent Behavior in Organization*, Greenwich, CT: JAI Press, pp. 119–45.

Harris, G.E. and J.E. Cameron (2005), 'Multiple dimensions of organizational identification and commitment as predictors of turnover intentions and psychological well-being', *Canadian Journal of Behavioral Science*, **37**, 159–69.

Harrison, D.A., P.P. Mykytyn, Jr and C.K. Riemenschneider (1997), 'Executive decisions about adoption of information technology in small business: theory and empirical tests', *Information Systems Research*, **8**, 171–95.

Herscovitch, L. and J.P. Meyer (2002), 'Commitment to organizational change: extension of a three-component model', *Journal of Applied Psychology*, **87**, 474–87.

Hunt, S.D. and R.M. Morgan (1994), 'Organizational commitment: one of many commitments or key mediating construct?', *Academy of Management Journal*, **27**, 1568–87.

James, L.R. (1998), 'Measurement of personality via conditional reasoning', *Organizational Research Methods*, **1**, 131–63.

Klein, H.J., M.J. Wesson, J.R. Hollenbeck, P.M. Wright and R.P. DeShon (2001), 'The assessment of goal commitment: a measurement model meta-analysis', *Organizational Behavior and Human Decision Processes*, **85**, 32–55.

Kolvereid, L. (1996), 'Prediction of employment status choice intentions', *Entrepreneurship Theory and Practice*, **21**, 47–57.

Kristof-Brown, A.L., R.D. Zimmerman and E.C. Johnson (2005), 'Consequences of individual's fit at work: a meta-analysis of person–job, person–organization, person–group, and person–supervisor fit', *Personnel Psychology*, **58**, 281–342.

Krueger, N.F., Jr, M.D. Reilly and A.L. Carsrud (2000), 'Competing models of entrepreneurial intentions', *Journal of Business Venturing*, **15**, 411–32.

Leatherwood, M. and P. Spector (1991), 'Enforcements, inducements, expected utility and employee misconduct', *Journal of Management*, **17**, 553–69.

Levine, J.M. and R.L. Moreland (1998), 'Small groups', in D.T. Gilbert, S.T. Fiske and G. Lindzey (eds), *The Handbook of Social Psychology,* Vol. 2, 4th edn, New York: McGraw-Hill, pp. 415–69.

Maertz, C.P., D.C. Mosley and B.L. Alford (2002), 'Does organizational commitment fully mediate constituent commitment effects? A reassessment and clarification', *Journal of Applied Social Psychology*, **32**, 1300–313.

Mathieu, J.E. and D.M. Zajac (1990), 'A review and meta-analysis of the antecedents, correlates, and consequences of organizational commitment', *Psychological Bulletin*, **108**, 171–94.

Meyer, J.P. and N.J. Allen (1997), *Commitment in the Workplace: Theory, Research, and Application*, Newbury Park, CA: Sage.

Meyer, J.P. and L. Herscovitch (2001), 'Commitment in the workplace: toward a general model', *Human Resource Management Review*, **11**, 299–326.

Meyer, J.P., T.E. Becker and C. Vandenberghe (2004), 'Employee commitment and motivation: a conceptual analysis and integrative model', *Journal of Applied Psychology*, **89**, 991–1007.

Meyer, J.P., T.E. Becker and R. Van Dick (2006), 'Social identities and commitments at work: toward an integrative model', *Journal of Organizational Behavior*, **27**, 665–83.

Meyer, J.P., D.J. Stanley, L. Herscovitch and L. Topolnytsky (2002), 'Affective, continuance and normative commitment to the organization: a meta-analysis of antecedents, correlates, and consequences', *Journal of Vocational Behavior*, **61**, 20–52.

Morrow, P.C. (1993), *The Theory and Measurement of Work Commitment*, Greenwich, CT: JAI Press.

Moscovici, S. (1985), 'Social influence and conformity', in G. Lindzey and E. Aronson (eds), *The Handbook of Social Psychology*, Vol. 2, 3rd edn, New York: Random House, pp. 347–412.

O'Reilly, C.A. III and J. Chatman (1986), 'Organizational commitment and psychological attachment: the effects of compliance, identification, and internalization on prosocial behavior', *Journal of Applied Psychology*, **71**, 492–9.

Prestholdt, P.H., I.M. Lane and R.C. Mathews (1987), 'Nurse turnover as reasoned action: development of a process model', *Journal of Applied Psychology*, **72**, 221–7.

Reichers, A.E. (1985), 'A review and reconceptualization of organizational commitment', *Academy of Management Review*, **10**, 465–76.

Rhoades, L. and R. Eisenberger (2002), 'Perceived organizational support: a review of the literature', *Journal of Applied Psychology*, **87**, 698–714.

Riketta, M. (2005), 'Organizational identification: a meta-analysis', *Journal of Vocational Behavior*, **66**, 358–84.

Riketta, M. and R. Van Dick (2005), 'Foci of attachment in organizations: a meta-analytic comparison of the strength and correlates of workgroup versus organizational identification and commitment', *Journal of Vocational Behavior*, **67**, 490–510.

Robinson, S.L. and R.J. Bennett (1995), 'A typology of deviant workplace behaviors: a multidimensional scaling study', *Academy of Management Journal*, **38**, 555–72.

Robinson, S.L. and A.M. O'Leary-Kelly (1998), 'Monkey see, monkey do: the influence of work groups on the antisocial behavior of employees', *Academy of Management Journal*, **41**, 658–72.

Rousseau, D.M. (1995), *Psychological Contracts in Organizations: Understanding Written and Unwritten Agreements*, Thousand Oaks, CA: Sage.

Rousseau, D.M. (1998), 'Why workers still identify with organizations', *Journal of Organizational Behavior*, **19**, 217–33.

Ryan, R.M. and E.L. Deci (2000), 'Self-determination theory and the facilitation of intrinsic motivation, social development, and well-being', *American Psychologist*, **55**, 68–78.

Sandberg, J. (2003), 'Workplace klepto culture squanders key resources', www.careerjournal.com/columnists/cubicleculture/20031121-cubicle.html, *21 November*.

Schat, A., S. Desmarais and E. Kelloway (2005), 'Effects of organizational tolerance on the incidence and consequences of workplace aggression', paper presented at the National Academy of Management Meetings, Honolulu, Hawaii.

Sheppard, B.H., J. Hartwick and P.R. Warshaw (1988), 'The theory of reasoned action: a meta-analysis of past research with recommendations for modifications and future research', *Journal of Consumer Research*, **15**, 325–43.

Siders, M.A., G. George and R. Dharwadkar (2001), 'The relationship of internal and external commitment foci to objective job performance measures', *Academy of Management Journal*, **44**, 580–90.

Spector, P.E. (1997), 'The role of frustration in antisocial behaviour at work', in R.A. Giacalone and J. Greenberg (eds), *Antisocial Behavior in Organizations*, Thousand Oaks, CA: Sage, pp. 1–17.

Stamper, C. and S. Masterson (2002), 'Insider or outsider? How employee perceptions of insider status affect their work behavior', *Journal of Organizational Behavior*, **23**, 875–94.

Staw, B.M. (1976), 'Knee-deep in the Big Muddy: a study of escalating commitment to a chosen course of action', *Organizational Behavior and Human Performance*, **16**, 27–44.

Tajfel, H. (1978), 'Social categorization, social identity, and social comparison', in H. Tajfel (ed.), *Differentiation between Social Groups: Studies in the Social Psychology of Intergroup Relations*, London: Academic Press, pp. 61–76.

Thau, S., K. Aquino and M. Portvleit (2006), 'Self-defeating behaviors in organizations: the relationship between thwarted belonging and interpersonal work behaviors', working paper, London Business School.

Trevino, L. (1986), 'Ethical decision making in organizations: a person–situation interactions model', *Academy of Management Review*, **11**, 601–17.

Van Dick, R. (2001), 'Identification in organizational contexts: linking theory and research from social and organizational psychology', *International Journal of Management Reviews*, **3**, 265–83.

Van Dick, R., U. Wagner, J. Stellmacher and O. Christ (2005), 'Category salience and organizational identification', *Journal of Occupational and Organizational Psychology*, **78**, 273–85.

Vardi, V. and E. Weitz (2004), *Misbehavior in Organizations: Theory, Research and Management*, Mahwah, NJ: Lawrence Erlbaum Associates.

Venkatesh, V., M.G. Morris and P.L. Ackerman (2000), 'A longitudinal field investigation of gender differences in individual technology adoption decision-making processes', *Organizational Behavior and Human Decision Processes*, **84**, 33–60.

10 Work hours and work addiction: work now, pay later[1]

Ronald J. Burke and Teal McAteer

This chapter offers a selective review of the literature addressing work hours and workaholism or work addiction and their effects. Although these two bodies of literature deal with the same topics, they have historically been considered quite separately (Burke, 2006). Work is a vital and potentially enjoyable event which provides us with monetary and non-monetary benefits. Work can give us a sense of achievement and success. Yet how much work is too much? This chapter will explore motives for working long hours, the associated work and well-being outcomes, as well as possible modifiers affecting the relationship between work hours and well-being.

The importance of focusing on work hours is multifaceted. First, a large number of employees are unhappy about the number of hours they work (Jacobs and Gerson, 1998). Second, the amount of time demanded by work is an obvious and important way in which work affects other parts of one's life (Dembe, 2005; Shields, 1999). Third, work hours are a widely studied structural output of employment. Fourth, the study of work hours and well-being outcomes has produced some inconsistent and complex results (Barnett, 1998).

Because of technological advances and flexible work arrangements, it might be assumed that working time was getting progressively shorter. However, this is one trend that varies from country to country and even within countries by gender, occupation, race and time period (Figart and Golden, 1998). Beginning in the nineteenth century with the Industrial Revolution, workers fought to get policies enacted to restrict hours of work, especially by women and children (Figart and Golden, 1998). In the mid-twentieth century, the USA began to implement employment legislation that reduced the number of hours worked (Hinrichs et al., 1991). A new employment arrangement emerged after World War II, which provided stable and lifelong employment in addition to a family wage. This was an era of stability for North American households; however, it and the employment arrangement have disintegrated. Economic, technological and cultural factors have influenced working time, making it extremely variable (Figart and Golden, 1998).

Recently there has been a rise in the number of hours worked in North America. Jacobs and Gerson (1998) found that professionals and highly educated individuals have seen an increase in their hours worked. In contrast, it was also found that less educated workers have seen a decline. It is also believed that professionals and highly educated persons tend to have more responsibility and are under more stress, with larger workloads (Jacobs and Gerson, 1998). Within the USA, large numbers of people are working very long hours, in both paid overtime and salaried positions (Figart and Golden, 1998). Overtime, which has been used as an indicator of an expanding economy and tight labor markets, has been increasing since 1970 (Glosser and Golden, 1997). In addition, Glosser and Golden (1997) found that the number of those working excessive hours, described as 49 hours per week or more, has also been on the rise, especially for higher-educated white men (Hedges,

1993). Conversely, work hours, both weekly and annually, in Western Europe have decreased (Figart and Golden, 1998). This could be due to a number of factors, including work legislation and standards on overtime hours. However, specifically in the Netherlands, Belgium and West Germany, from 1960 to 1985 there was an annual reduction of 20 percent of work hours (Figart and Golden, 1998). There has been a slight decrease in work hours across Canada as well, which is said to be due to increased vacation time and the expansion of part-time jobs (ILO, 1995).

Work hours and their effects
People have expected an association of long working hours and adverse consequences for over 100 years. Concerns were raised in 1830 during the Industrial Revolution and in later years, and efforts were made to legislate limits in working hours to 10 hours per day at that time (Figart and Golden, 1988). Most studies of long work hours have been conducted in Japan where 'karoshi', sudden death due to long hours and insufficient sleep, was first observed (Kanai, 2006).

A variety of outcome measures have been examined in connection with working long hours (van der Hulst, 2003). Several hypotheses have also been advanced to explain the relationship between long work hours and adverse health outcomes. Working long hours affects the cardiovascular system through chronic exposure to increases in blood pressure and heart rate (Buell and Breslow, 1960; Iwasaki et al., 1988; Uehata, 1991). Working long hours produces sleep deprivation and lack of recovery leading to chronic fatigue, poor-health-related behaviors, and ill health (Ala-Mursjula et al., 2002; Defoe et al., 2001; Liu and Tanaka, 2002). Working long hours makes it more difficult to recover from job demands and the stress of long work hours. Finally, working long hours has been associated with more errors and accidents (Gander et al., 2000; Loomis, 2005; Nachreiner et al., 2000; Schuster and Rhodes, 1985).

More specifically, the research literature suggests that long hours are associated with adverse health effects and increased safety risk (Harrington, 1994, 2001; Cooper, 1996; Kirkcaldy et al., 1997; Spurgeon et al., 1997). Long work hours have been found to be associated with poor psychological health (Kirkcaldy et al., 2000; Sparks et al., 1997; Borg and Kristensen, 1999; Worrall and Cooper, 1999), excessive fatigue (Rosa, 1995) and burnout (Barnett, et al., 1999). Several studies have also reported that long working hours are associated with more work–family conflict (Staines and Pleck, 1984), fatigue, worrying and irritability (Grzywicz and Marks, 2000; Kluwer et al., 1996; Geurts et al., 1999).

Van der Hulst (2003) found that long work hours were associated with adverse health, particularly cardiovascular disease, disability retirement, self-reported ill health and fatigue. She concluded that working more that 11 hours per day was associated with a threefold risk of coronary heart disease and a fourfold risk of diabetes. In addition, working 60 or more hours a week was associated with a threefold risk of disability retirement.

Dembe et al. (2005) examined the impact of overtime and extended working hours on the risk of occupational injuries and illnesses in a representative sample of working adults in the USA. They estimated the relative risk of long working hours per day, extended hours per week, long commute times, and overtime schedules on reporting a work-related injury or illness after controlling for age, gender, occupation, industry and region. Data were collected from 10 793 workers between 1987 and 2000. After adjusting for these control factors, they found that working in jobs with overtime schedules was associated with a 61 percent higher injury hazard rate compared to jobs without overtime. Working at least 12 hours per day was associated with a 32 percent increased hazard rate and working at least 60 hours per week was associated with a 23 percent increased hazard rate. A strong dose–response effect was observed, with the injury rate increasing in correspondence with the number of hours per day (or per week) in the worker's customary schedule. Job schedules with long working hours were not more risky because concentrated in inherently hazardous industries or occupations, or because people working long hours have more total time at risk for a work injury.

Van der Hulst et al. (2006) considered overtime, work characteristics (job demands, job control), and need for recovery in a large sample (N=1473) of Dutch municipal administration employees working full time. Van der Hulst's (2003) review showed that long work hours were associated with poorer physiological recovery; working long hours was also associated with fewer hours of sleep. The effort–recovery model (Meijman and Mulder, 1998) proposes that negative consequences of long working hours for health and well-being depend on the opportunities for recovery during the work day (internal recovery) and after work (external recovery). Working overtime reduces the time available for recovery. In addition, external recovery may be poor due to the spillover of work demands to one's home life. Finally, overtime is more likely to occur in demanding jobs, limiting opportunities for internal recovery. They examined four types of jobs: *low strain* – low demands, high control; *passive* – low demands, low control; *active* – high demands, high control; and *high strain* – high demands, low control. Overtime was common for a majority of employees and in jobs making high demands. While there was no relationship between working overtime and need for recovery in the total sample, there was a significant and positive relationship between overtime hours and need for recovery in high-strain jobs (high demands, low control); there was also a relationship between overtime and need for recovery in active jobs (high demands, high control). Working conditions (high-demand jobs) influenced the relationship between overtime and need for recovery.

Van der Hulst (2003) suggested two possible pathways between long hours and health: insufficient recovery and poor lifestyle behaviors. Long work hours are believed to be associated with lifestyle choices such as smoking, coffee and alcohol consumption, lack of exercise and a poor (unhealthy) diet. These unhealthy behaviors produce physiological changes (e.g. high blood pressure, high levels of cholesterol, obesity, diabetes) and higher risk of coronary heart disease and poorer health in general.

Caruso et al. (2004) reviewed the accumulating research evidence on the influence of overtime and extended work shifts on worker health and safety as well as worker errors, considering 52 studies in total. Overtime has increased in the USA from 1970 to 2000 (Rones et al., 1997; Hetrick, 2000). Overtime was defined as working more than 40 hours per week; extended work shifts are defined as shifts longer than 8 hours. They found, in a majority of studies of general health, that overtime was associated with poorer perceived general health, increased injury rate, more illness and increased mortality. A pattern of reduced performance on psychophysiological tests and injuries while working long hours, particularly very long shifts, and when 12-hour shifts combined with over 40 hours of work per week, was also noted. When 12-hour shifts are combined with more than 40 hours of work per week, more adverse effects were evident. Hänecke et al. (1998), in a study of 1.2 million German workers, found that the risk of workplace accidents increased during the latter portion (after the eighth hour) of a long work shift.

Rissler (1977) studied the effects of high workload and overtime on heart rate and hormone levels during rest and work hours. High workload was associated with higher levels of adrenaline and heart rate during evenings at home (rest periods) as well as feelings of fatigue and irritation. His results also indicated an accumulation effect of overtime on adrenaline levels. That is, it takes several weeks to return to normal (resting) values following several weeks of overtime.

Van der Hulst and Geurts (2001), in a study of 525 full-time employees of the Dutch Postal Service, found that working overtime was associated with negative work–home interference. Employees working overtime and reporting low rewards indicated greater burnout, negative work–home interference, and slower recovery. Employees working overtime and with high pressure to do so, coupled with low rewards, had poorer recovery, more cynicism and negative work–home interference.

Rosa (1995) reported that overtime and fatigue were found to be associated with increases in back injuries, hospital outbreaks of bacterial infection, a threefold increase in accidents after 26 hours of work, and increased risk of safety violations in nuclear power plants, showing that long work hours do not just negatively affect the worker; they put a strain on overall workplace safety. Shimomitsu and Levi (1992) found that two-thirds of Japanese workers complain of fatigue, with 'karoshi', or death from overwork, an important social concern. Moruyama et al. (1995) found long work hours associated with poor lifestyle habits such as heavy smoking, poor diet and lack of exercise. Sparks et al. (1997) undertook a meta-analysis of 21 samples and found small but significant correlations between hours of work and health symptoms, physiological and psychological health symptoms. Qualitative analyses of 12 other studies supported the findings of a positive relationship between hours of work and health.

Motivations for working long hours
Porter (2004) distinguishes two motivations for long hours of work, both of which could have different moderating effects. A person can work long hours because of the joy in their work. This is a constructive, highly committed achievement-oriented style. A person can also put in long hours in a compulsive, perfectionist fashion, driven to achieve unrealistic standards. Such individuals react to criticism with hostility and resentment, experience frustration from failing to meet superhuman standards, and express anger and competition with colleagues in the workplace. These individuals may also experience the adverse impacts of stress and burnout. Tucker and Rutherford (2005) argued that some individuals may work longer hours because they enjoy their job and derive pleasure from succeeding at it, enjoy the associated benefits, or want to enrich their job or quality of life. This is contrasted with someone who works longer hours to avoid job insecurity or negative sanctions from a superior. Although there might be pressure on an employee to overwork, it is ultimately their choice.

Brett and Stroh (2003) examined why some managers work 61 or more hours per week. They considered four explanations: the work–leisure trade-off; social contagion; work as an emotional respite from home; and work as its own reward. Data were collected from a sample of 595 male and 391 female MBA alumni of the same university. The males were all married with children at home and a smaller percentage of the females were married and had children. More men than women worked 61 or more hours per week (29 percent versus 11 percent). Men worked 56.4 hours per week and women worked 51.5 hours per week. Of the four explanations considered by Brett and Stroh, work as its own reward was the only one supported for males, with hours worked significantly connected with job involvement and intrinsic satisfaction. For females, the work–leisure trade-off and social contagion hypotheses were supported. However, hours worked did not correlate with job involvement, income or job satisfaction for females.

For some samples, such as blue-collar workers, money may be a more important moderator of the hours worked and health relationship. Brett and Stroh (2003), in their sample of MBA graduates in managerial and professional jobs, found that extrinsic (financial) and intrinsic job rewards were associated with working longer hours. How many hours a person works involves weighing the costs (more fatigue, impact on family and social life) against the benefits (income, recognition). People with good social support may be better able to deal with the costs of long work hours; rewards will be more attractive to these individuals.

Choosing to work long hours as opposed to being pressured to work long hours is an important moderating consideration. One may choose to work long hours for more pay, to get the job done, to prove one is committed, and to position oneself for advancement. One can also work long hours or overtime to avoid sanctions and increase one's job security. Barnett et al. (1999) found that discrepancies between actual and desired hours are associated with negative health outcomes. In their study of 141 married physicians, the relationship between number of hours worked and burnout depended on the extent to which work schedules met the needs of the employee, his or her partner and their children. Physicians working more or fewer hours than they and their partners preferred, and whose work hours were distributed differently than they and their partner preferred, scored higher on burnout measures.

Moderators of the work hours–well-being relationship
The literature has attempted to study possible moderators in relationship between work hours and the variety of outcomes identified. Tucker and Rutherford (2005) examined the relationship of work hours and self-reported health as moderated by the reasons for working long hours (or overtime), by work schedule autonomy and by the degree of social support experienced at home and at work. They collected data from 372 train drivers in the south of England. Respondents lacking both schedule autonomy or control and social support demonstrated positive relationships between hours worked and physical health symptoms. Negative relationships were found among drivers reporting low schedule autonomy and high social support. No such interactions were found with fatigue and psychological health, however.

Addressing work hours
Legislative and structural policy changes may have moderating effects worth considering. Figart and Mutari (1998) argue that the expansion of overtime for men and part-time jobs for women reinforces the skewed division of domestic labor and occupation segregation. Gender typing of jobs was prevalent before many equality policies were enacted in the 1960s and 1970s. These statutes and legislation broke down barriers for women to enter the labor force; however, they did not address the larger social structures (Figart and Mutari, 1998).

Strategies for preventing work injuries should consider changes in scheduling practices, job redesign, and health promotion programs for people working in jobs involving overtime and extended hours. Van der Hulst and Geurts (2001) suggest that compensation may also reduce adverse effects of work hours. In addition, length of vacation and commuting time may also affect the relationship of overtime with health and safety. More days of vacation allow for more rest and many lessen the impact of overtime; longer commute times may add additional job stressors to the effects of working hours. Workers' ability to exert control over work schedules may have influenced the effects of work hours on health (Barton, 1994; Smith et al., 1998).

A number of other initiatives could be undertaken by organizations and their employees to minimize the potential adverse effects of long work hours. These include the following:

- encourage governments to regulate the length of work schedules, as is already the case in many countries in Europe;
- increase worker control of work hours;
- utilize ergonomic job design;
- increase worker training;
- develop capable supervision;
- establish a workplace culture that promotes health and safety;
- employ more people working fewer hours;
- use more rest breaks (Tucker et al., 2003);
- redesign work to avoid the need for overtime;
- offer health promotion counseling about the risks of long work schedules; and
- provide medical examinations for at-risk workers.

Workaholism
Although the popular press has paid considerable attention to workaholism (Kiechel, 1989a, 1989b; Klaft and Kleiner, 1988) very little research has been undertaken to further our understanding of it (McMillan et al., 2003). It should come as no surprise, then, that opinions, observations and conclusions about workaholism are both varied and conflicting (McMillan et al., 2001). Some writers view workaholism positively from an organizational perspective (Garfield, 1987; Korn et al., 1987; Machlowitz, 1980; Sprankle and Ebel, 1987). Machlowitz (1980) conducted a qualitative interview study of 100 workaholics and found them to be very satisfied and productive. Others view workaholism negatively (Killinger, 1991; Schaef and Fassel, 1988; Oates, 1971). These writers equate workaholism with other addictions and depict workaholics as unhappy, obsessive, tragic figures who are not performing their jobs well and are creating difficulties for their co-workers (Porter, 1996, 2001). The former would advocate the encouragement of workaholism; the latter would discourage it.

Definitions of workaholism
Research on workaholism has been hindered by the absence of acceptable definitions and measures. Mosier (1983) defined workaholism in terms of hours worked; workaholics were those who worked at least 50 hours per week. Machlowitz (1980: 11) defines workaholics as people 'who always devote more time and thoughts to their work than the situation demands . . . what sets workaholics apart from other workers is their attitude toward

work, not the number of hours they work'. Killinger (1991: 6) defines a workaholic as 'a person who gradually becomes emotionally crippled and addicted to control and power in a compulsive drive to gain approval and success'. Robinson (1998: 81) defines workaholism 'as a progressive, potentially fatal disorder, characterized by self imposed demands, compulsive overworking, inability to regulate work habits and an over-indulgence in work to the exclusion of most other life activities'.

Oates (1971: 4), generally acknowledged as the first person to use the word 'workaholic', defined it as 'a person whose need for work has become so excessive that it creates noticeable disturbance or interference with his bodily health, personal happiness, and interpersonal relationships, and with his smooth social functioning'. Most of these definitions have a negative connotation.

Spence and Robbins (1992: 62) define the workaholic as a person who 'is highly work involved, feels compelled or driven to work because of inner pressures, and is low in enjoyment at work'. Most writers view workaholism as a stable individual characteristic (Scott et al., 1997; Spence and Robbins, 1992) and use the terms excessive work, workaholism and work addiction interchangeably.

Types of workaholics
Some researchers have proposed the existence of different types of workaholic behavior patterns, each having potentially different antecedents and associations with job performance, work and life outcomes. Scott et al. (1997) suggest three types of workaholic behavior patterns: compulsive-dependent; perfectionist; and achievement-oriented. They hypothesize that compulsive-dependent workaholism will be positively related to levels of anxiety, stress, physical and psychological problems and negatively related to job performance and job and life satisfaction. Perfectionist workaholism will be positively related to levels of stress, physical and psychological problems, hostile interpersonal relationships, low job satisfaction and performance and voluntary turnover and absenteeism. Finally, achievement-oriented workaholism will be positively related to physical and psychological health, job and life satisfaction, job performance, low voluntary turnover and pro-social behaviors.

Spence and Robbins (1992) propose three workaholic types based on their workaholic triad notion. The workaholic triad consists of three concepts: work involvement; feeling driven to work; and work enjoyment. Profile analyses were undertaken, resulting in the emergence of three workaholism types. Several other studies (e.g. Buelens and Poelmans, 2004; Kanai et al., 1996), using the same three scales, have produced essentially these same types: work addicts (WAs); enthusiastic addicts (EAs); and work enthusiasts (WEs). WAs score high on work involvement and feeling driven to work, and low on work enjoyment. WEs score high on work involvement and work enjoyment, and low on driveness. EAs score high on all three components. A consideration of types of workaholics may help to reconcile conflicting findings.

Research findings
The following sections review research findings that compare the three types of workaholics proposed by Spence and Robbins (1992) on personal demographic and work situation characteristics, job behaviors, work outcomes, personal life and family functioning and indicators of psychological health.

Personal demographic and work situation characteristics

A critical question involves potential differences between the three workaholism types on both personal demographic and work situation characteristics, including hours worked per week. If the workaholism types were found to differ on these (e.g. organizational level, marital status, hours worked per week), these differences would account for any differences found on work and health outcomes.

A number of studies (Spence and Robbins, 1992; Burke, 1999a; Burke et al., 2002; Bonebright et al., 2000) have reported essentially no differences between the workaholism types on a variety of personal and work situation characteristics. The workaholism types work the same number of hours and extra hours per week; the workaholism types working significantly more hours per week and more extra hours per week than the non-workaholism types. In addition, these three workaholism types were similar on age, gender, marital and parental status, level of education, job and organizational tenure, income and organizational size.

Job behaviors

There has been considerable speculation regarding the job behaviors likely to be exhibited by workaholics. This list includes perfectionism, job stress, non-delegation of job respon-sibilities to others, job performance and interpersonal conflict. There is empirical research which examines some of these hypothesized relationships (Porter, 2001).

Both Spence and Robbins (1992) and Burke (1999a) provide evidence of the concurrent validity of the Spence and Robbins workaholism types. Both studies showed that WAs exhibited higher levels of perfectionism, non-delegation and job stress than did the two other workaholic profiles (WEs and EAs). Kanai et al. (1996), using the Spence and Robbins measures, also reported that EAs and WAs scored higher than WEs on measures of job stress, perfectionism and non-delegation.

Antecedents of workaholism

Three potential antecedents of workaholism have received some conceptual and research attention. One, personal beliefs and fears, is the result of socialization practices within families and society at large. The second, Type A behavior, is a learned response to envi-ronmental demands. The third, organizational norms and expectations for work–personal life imbalance, represents organizational values and priorities.

Personal beliefs and fears Burke (1999b) examined the relationship of personal beliefs and fears, a reflection of values, thoughts and interpersonal styles and workaholism types. Measures of three beliefs and fears developed by Lee et al. (1996) were used. One, 'Striving against others', had six items (e.g. 'There can only be one winner in any situation'). A second, 'No moral principles', had six items (e.g. 'I think that nice guys finish last'). The third, 'Prove yourself', had nine items (e.g. 'I worry a great deal about what others think of me'). A total score was also obtained by combining these three scales.

Burke compared the three Spence and Robbins workaholic types on these measures of beliefs and fears. First, all three beliefs and fears were significantly correlated with mea-sures of feeling driven to work (positively) and work enjoyment (negatively). Second, com-parisons of workaholism types showed significant type effects on all three measures of beliefs and fears as well as on their composite. More specifically, WAs scored significantly higher than WEs and EAs on measures of 'Striving against others' and 'No moral principles', as well as on the composite measure. In addition, WAs scored higher on the need to prove self than did WEs. WAs scored higher on the composite measure than both WEs and EAs. Workaholism thus emerges as work behaviors in response to feelings of low self-worth and insecurity. This is best reflected in managers' feelings of being driven to work because of inner needs.

Type A behavior   Type A behavior has been shown to be associated with levels of job stress, psychological distress and coronary heart disease. Pred et al. (1987) factor-analyzed the Jenkins Activity Survey, a self-report measure of type A behavior, producing two independent factors: 'Achievement striving' (AS), which they found to be predictive of positive work attitudes and performances, and 'Impatience–Irritation' (II), found to be predictive of psychological distress. Burke et al. (2004), in a study of 171 Norwegian owners and senior managers of construction companies, found that WAs scored higher than WEs on II, while EAs scored higher than WEs on AS. Impatience–Irritation has been shown to be predictive of psychological distress.

Organizational values   Burke (1999c) compared perceptions of organizational values supporting work–personal life imbalance among the Spence and Robbins workaholism types. Organizational values encouraging work–family imbalance were measured by scales proposed by Kofodimos (1993). Organizational values encouraging balance were measured by nine items (e.g. 'Setting limits on hours spent at work'). Organizational values supporting imbalance were measured by eight items (e.g. 'Traveling to and from work destinations on weekends'). A total imbalance score was obtained by combining both scales, reversing the balance scores.

There was considerable support for the hypothesized relationships. WEs reported greater organizational balance values than did both WAs and EAs. WAs reported greater imbalance values than both WEs and EAs. In summary, WAs see their workplaces as more supportive of work–personal life imbalance than two other workaholism types.

Work outcomes

The relationship between workaholism and indicators of job and career satisfaction and success is difficult to specify. It is likely that different types of workaholics will report varying work and career satisfactions (Scott et al., 1997). Burke (1999d) compared levels of work and career satisfaction and success among the workaholism profiles observed by Spence and Robbins (1992). Four work outcomes, all significantly intercorrelated, were used. 'Intent to quit' was measured by two items (e.g. 'Are you currently looking for a different job in a different organization?') This scale had been used previously by Burke (1991). 'Work satisfaction' was measured by a seven-item scale developed by Kofodimos (1993). One item was 'I feel challenged by my work'. 'Career satisfaction' was measured by a five-item scale developed by Greenhaus et al. (1990). One item was 'I am satisfied with the success I have achieved in my career'. 'Future career prospects' was measured by a three-item scale developed by Greenhaus et al. (1990). One item was 'I expect to advance in my career to senior levels of management'.

WAs scored lower than WEs and EAs on job satisfaction, career satisfaction and future career prospects and higher than WEs on intent to quit. Interestingly, all three workaholic profiles (WAs, EAs, WEs) worked the same number of hours per week and had the same job and organizational tenure.

Psychological well-being
There is considerable consensus in the workaholism literature on the association of workaholism and poorer psychological and physical well-being (McMillan et al., 2003). In fact, some definitions of workaholism incorporate aspects of diminished health as central elements. It is not surprising that this relationship has received research attention.

Burke (1999e) compared the three workaholism types on three indicators of psychological and physical well-being. Data were obtained from 530 employed women and men MBAs using questionnaires. Psychosomatic symptoms was measured by 19 items developed by Quinn and Shepard (1974). Respondents indicated how often they experienced each physical condition (e.g. 'headaches') in the past year. Lifestyle behaviors was measured by five items developed by Kofodimos (1993). One item was 'I participate in a regular exercise program'. Emotional well-being was measured by six items developed by Kofodimos (1993). One item was 'I actively seek to understand and improve my emotional well-being'.

The comparisons of the workaholism types on the three measures of psychological and physical well-being provided considerable support for the hypothesized relationships. Thus WEs and EAs had fewer psychosomatic symptoms than did WAs; WEs had more positive lifestyle behaviors than did WAs; WAs had more psychosomatic symptoms than both WEs and EAs and poorer physical and emotional well-being than did WEs.

Other researchers have shown similar results. Kanai et al. (1996), using the workaholism triad components developed by Spence and Robbins in a sample of 1072 Japanese workers from ten companies, found that both WAs and EAs reported more health complaints than did WEs. There were no differences between these three groups on measures of smoking, alcohol consumption and serious illness, however. Spence and Robbins (1992), in a sample of men and women social work professors, noted that WAs indicated more health complaints than did individuals in their other profiles.

Extra-work satisfactions and family functioning
A number of writers have hypothesized that workaholism is likely to impact negatively on family functioning (Killinger, 1991; Porter 1996; Robinson, 1998). Empirical examinations of this hypothesis are unfortunately few. Robinson and Post (1995) report data from a sample of 107 self-identified workaholics (members of Workaholics Anonymous chapters in North America) who completed the Work Addiction Risk Test (WART) and a family assessment instrument. Three levels of WART scores representing increasing levels of workaholism were compared. High scores differed from low and medium scores on six of the seven family assessment scales indicating lower (poorer) family functioning in all cases.

Robinson (1990) also reviewed the literature on children of workaholics. Robinson and Kelley (1998) asked 211 young adults (college students) to think back to their childhoods and rate the workaholism of their parents on the WART. Participants also completed measures of depression, anxiety, self-concept and locus of control. College students who perceived their parents as workaholics scored higher on depression and external locus of control. Children of workaholic fathers scored higher on anxiety than did children of non-workaholic fathers. Interestingly, mothers' workaholism had no effect on these outcomes. Burke (1999f) considered the relationship of workaholism types identified by Spence and Robbins (1992) and extra-work satisfactions. Three aspects of life or extra-work satisfaction were included. Family satisfaction was measured by a seven-item scale developed by Kofodimos (1993). One item was 'I have a good relationship with my family members'. 'Friends satisfaction' was measured by three items developed by Kofodimos (1993). One item was 'My friends and I do enjoyable things together'. 'Community satisfaction' was measured by four items also developed by Kofodimos (1993). A sample item was 'I contribute and give back to my community'.

The comparisons of the workaholism types on the three measures of life or extra-work satisfactions provided moderate support for the hypothesized relationships. First, WAs reported less family satisfaction than did the two other types. Second, WAs reported less friend satisfaction than WEs. Third, WAs and EAs reported less community satisfaction than did WEs. Thus WAs reported less satisfaction on all three measures than did WEs and less satisfaction on one (family) than did EAs.

Evaluating workaholism components
The two workaholism measures used in two or more research studies (i.e. Robinson, 1998; Spence and Robbins, 1992) each contain components or factors. Do each of these factors have similar and independent relationships with particular outcomes? Or might they have opposite relationships with some outcomes and no relationship with others?

Burke (1999g) considered whether the workaholism triad components had different consequences. A research model was developed to guide both variable selection and analysis strategy. There have been suggestions that both personal and work-setting factors are antecedents of workaholic behaviors (Scott et al., 1997; Schaef and Fassel, 1988). Thus both individual difference characteristics and organizational factors were included for study. Five panels of predictor variables were considered. The first consisted of individual demographic characteristics (e.g. age, gender, marital status). The second consisted of three measures of personal beliefs and fears (Lee et al., 1996). The third consisted of work situation demographic factors (e.g. years with present employer, size of organization). The fourth included measures of perceived organizational values supporting work–life imbalance (Kofodimos, 1993). The fifth included the workaholism triad components (work involvement, feeling driven to work, work enjoyment). The important questions were whether the workaholism triad components would add significant increments in explained variance on particular work and personal well-being measures, and if they did, which of the workaholism triad components accounted for these increments.

Outcome measures included job behaviors indicative of workaholism (e.g. hours worked, job stress, perfectionism) aspects of work satisfaction (e.g. job satisfaction, career satisfaction, future career prospects, intent to quit), psychological well-being (psychosomatic symptoms, emotional well-being, lifestyle behaviors) and elements of life satisfaction (e.g. family satisfaction, friends satisfaction, community satisfaction).

An examination of the relationships among specific workaholism components and the various types of outcome variables revealed an interesting, and complex, pattern of findings. First, work enjoyment and feeling driven to work were significantly related to every job behavior measure, while work involvement was significantly related to about half of them. Respondents scoring higher on the workaholism components also scored higher on job behaviors reflecting workaholism, with one exception – difficulty in delegating. In this instance, respondents scoring higher on work involvement and feeling driven to work, and lower on work enjoyment reported greater difficulty in delegating. Second, joy in work was the only workaholism component related to work outcomes. Respondents reporting greater work enjoyment also reported more job satisfaction, more optimistic future career prospects and more career satisfaction to date. Third, both work enjoyment and feeling driven to work were related to indicators of psychological well-being but in opposite directions. Respondents reporting greater work enjoyment and lesser feelings of being driven to work indicated more positive psychological well-being. Finally, workaholism components had a significant effect on only one of the three measures of extra-work satisfactions. Respondents reporting greater work involvement and lesser feelings of being driven to work reported greater community satisfaction.

Although work enjoyment and feeling driven to work had consistent and similar effects on job behaviors reflecting workaholism, these two workaholism components had different effects on work outcomes and psychological well-being. One, work enjoyment, was associated with positive outcomes; the other, feeling driven to work, was associated with negative outcomes. Finally, none of the workaholism components showed consistent relationships with measures of extra-work satisfactions.

Conclusions and implications

This chapter compared the job behaviors, work and non-work outcomes, psychological well-being and personal values among three types of workaholics, all of whom work equally long hours. A generally consistent pattern of findings emerges from the literature. Work addicts reported job behaviors likely to be associated with reduced contribution (job stress, perfectionism, difficulty delegating) in comparison with work enthusiasts and enthusiastic addicts. Work addicts also indicated lower levels of psychological health than the two other types. And work addicts indicated less non-work satisfactions.

Why would three types of managers working the same hours per week at the same organizational levels, having the same family structures, the same job and organizational tenure and earning the same incomes, indicate such different work and life experiences? The findings shed some light on this. First, work addicts held values and beliefs indicative of greater needs to prove themselves, greater insecurity (lower self-esteem) and a less supportive and trusting environment in general. Second, work addicts described their organizational values as less supportive of work–personal life balance. Third, they scored higher on feeling driven to work because of inner needs, certainly related to their beliefs and values. Fourth, they worked in ways that created higher levels of work stress for themselves and others, being perfectionistic and non-delegating. Thus it was not a question of how hard they worked, but why (their motivations) and how (their behaviors) they worked hard that mattered.

WAs are addicted to the process of work; outcomes are important only as they supply external rewards for temporarily enhancing self-esteem. Work addicts strive for increasing accomplishments to achieve self-worth. They are given to rigid thinking and perfectionism. They have difficulty delegating, which limits the development of others around them – work addicts are likely not effective team contributors. They strive to be in control, in control of their work activities and of other people around them. As a consequence they increase the chances of ill health, poor relationships and diminished leadership contribution – theirs and others around them.

Addressing workaholism

How can employers help workaholics and workaholics help themselves? Schaef and Fassel (1988) offer the following suggestions. Employers should pay attention to the performance and work habits of employees and be alert to warning signs of workaholism. They should not reward addictive behavior, but recognize those employees who are productive but also lead balanced lives. They should ensure that employees take vacation time away from work. Finally, job insecurity, work overload, limited career opportunities and lack of control can make employees feel compelled to work longer. If these factors exist, employers should try to minimize their impact on the atmosphere within the organization.

Haas (1991) also highlights the role that managers can play in assisting their workaholic employees to change. Workaholic employees should be referred to an employee assistance program or a recovery program to start treatment processes. Managers should help prioritize projects for employees as long-term and short-term assignments. Workaholics must be encouraged and helped to delegate their work. At the end of each day, the manager should meet with the employee to discuss what has been accomplished during that day and to plan (down to short intervals) for the following day. The employee should be given specific times to take breaks and to leave work so that positive terms may be acquired through training. It may also be possible to reduce the negative effects of workaholism, particularly well-being and health consequences, through stress management training.

The development of workplace values which promote new, more balanced priorities and healthier lifestyles will support those workaholism types that want to change their behaviors.

There is an old saying that 'hard work never killed anybody'. Our research bears this out. Hard work that provides feelings of accomplishment and joy, undertaken for noble not selfish motives, is likely to enrich a person's life. It is not how hard you work, but why and how you work hard that matters.

Note

1.   Preparation of this chapter was supported in part by the Schulich School of Business, York University and the DeGroote School of Business, McMaster University. Several colleagues contributed to our research, including Zena Burgess, Lisa Fiksenbaum, Fay Oberklaid and Astrid Richardsen. Louise Coutu prepared the manuscript.

References

Ala-Mursjula, L., Vahtera, J., Kivimaki, M., Kevin, M.V. and Penttij, J. (2002), 'Employee control over working times: associations with subjective health and sickness absences', *Journal of Epidemiology and Community Health*, **56**, 272–8.

Barnett, R.C. (1998), 'Towards a review and reconceptualization of the work/family literature', *Genetic Social and General Psychology Monograph*, **124**, 125–82.

Barnett, R.C., Gareis, K.C. and Brennan, R.T. (1999), 'Fit as a mediator of the relationship between work hours and burnout', *Journal of Occupational Health Psychology*, **4**, 307–17.

Barton, J. (1994), 'Choosing to work at night: a moderating influence on individual tolerance to shift work', *Journal of Applied Psychology*, **79**, 449–54.

Bonebright, C.A., Clay, D.L. and Ankenmann, R.D. (2000), 'The relationship of workaholism with work–life conflict, life satisfaction and purpose in life', *Journal of Counseling Psychology*, **47**, 476–7.

Borg, V. and Kristensen, T.S. (1999), 'Psychosocial work environment and mental health among traveling sales people', *Work and Stress*, **13**, 132–43.

Brett, J.M. and Stroh, L.K. (2003), 'Working 61 plus hours a week: why do managers do it?', *Journal of Applied Psychology*, **88**, 67–78.

Buelens, M. and Poelmans, S.A.Y. (2004), 'Enriching the Spence and Robbins typology of workaholism: demographic, motivational and organizational correlates', *Journal of Organizational Change Management*, **17**, 446–58.

Buell, P. and Breslow, L. (1960), 'Mortality from coronary heart disease in Californian men who work long hours', *Journal of Chronic Disease*, **11**, 615–26.

Burke, R.J. (1991), 'Early work and career experiences of female and male managers: reasons for optimism?', *Canadian Journal of Administrative Sciences*, **8**, 224–30.

Burke, R.J. (1999a), 'Workaholism in organizations: measurement validation and replication', *International Journal of Stress Management*, **6**, 45–55.

Burke, R.J. (1999b), 'Workaholism in organizations: the role of beliefs and fears', *Anxiety, Stress and Coping*, **13**, 1–12.

Burke, R.J. (1999c), 'Workaholism in organizations: the role of organizational values', *Personnel Review*, **30**, 637–45.

Burke, R.J. (1999d), 'Are workaholics job satisfied and successful in their careers?', *Career Development International*, **26**, 149–58.

Burke, R.J. (1999e), 'Workaholism in organizations: psychological and physical well-being consequences', *Stress Medicine*, **16**, 11–16.

Burke, R.J. (1999f), 'Workaholism and extra-work satisfactions', *International Journal of Organizational Analysis*, **7**, 352–64.

Burke, R.J. (1999g), 'It's not how hard you work but how you work hard: evaluating workaholism components', *International Journal of Stress Management*, **6**, 225–39.

Burke, R.J. (2006), *Research Companion to Working Hours and Work Addiction*, Cheltenham, UK and Northampton, MA, USA: Edward Elgar.

Burke, R.J., Burgess, Z. and Oberklaid, F. (2002), 'Workaholism job and career satisfaction among Australian psychologists', *International Journal of Management Literature*, **2**, 93–103.

Burke, R.J., Richardsen, A.R. and Mortinussen, M. (2004), 'Workaholism among Norwegian managers: work and well-being outcomes', *Journal of Organizational Change Management*, **17**, 459–70.

Caruso, C., Hitchcock, F., Dick, R., Russo, J. and Schmitt, J.M. (2004), *Overtime and Extended Work Shifts: Recent Findings on Illness, Injuries and Health Behaviors*, Publication No. 2004–143, Cincinnati, OH: NIOSH Publications.

Cooper, C.L. (1996), Editorial, 'Working hours and health', *Work and Stress*, **10**, 1–4.

Defoe, D.M., Power, M.L., Holzman, G.B., Carpentieri, A. and Schulikin, J. (2001), 'Long hours and little sleep: work schedules of residents in obstetrics and gynecology', *Obstetrics and Gynecology*, **97**, 1015–18.

Dembe, A.E. (2005), 'Long working hours: the scientific bases for concern', *Perspectives on Work*, Winter, 20–22.

Dembe, A.E., Erickson, J.B., Delbos, R.G. and Banks, S.M. (2005), 'The impact of overtime and long work hours on occupational injuries and illnesses: new evidence from the United States', *Occupational and Environmental Medicine*, **62**, 588–97.

Figart, D.M. and Golden, L. (1998), 'The social economics of work time: introduction', *Review of Social Economy*, **4**, 411–24.

Figart, D.M. and Mutari, E. (1998), 'Degendering work time in comparative perspective: alternative policy frameworks', *Review of Social Economy*, **4**, 460–80.

Gander, P.H., Merry, A., Millar, M.M. and Weller, J. (2000), 'Hours of work and fatigue-related error: a survey of New Zealand anaesthetists', *Anaesthetic and Intensive Care*, **28**, 178–83.

Garfield, C.A. (1987), *Peak Performers: The New Heroes of American Business*, New York: William Morrow.

Geurts, S., Rutte, C. and Peeters, M. (1999), 'Antecedents and consequences of work–home interference among medical residents', *Social Science and Medicine*, **48**, 1135–48.

Glosser, S.M. and Golden, L. (1997), 'Average work hours as a leading economic variable in US manufacturing industries', *International Journal of Forecasting*, **13**, 175–95.

Greenhaus, J.H., Parasuraman, S. and Wormley, W. (1990), 'Organizational experiences and career success of black and white managers', *Academy of Management Journal*, **33**, 64–86.

Grzywicz, J.G. and Marks, N. (2000), 'Reconceptualizing the work–family interface: an ecological perspective on the correlates of positive and negative spillover between work and family', *Journal of Occupational Health Psychology*, **5**, 111–26.

Haas, R. (1991), 'Strategies to cope with a cultural phenomenon – workaholism', *Business and Health*, **36**, 4.

Hänecke, K., Tiedemann, S., Nachreiner, F. and Grzech-Sukalo, H. (1998), 'Accident risk as a function of hour at work and time of day as determined from accident data and exposure models for the German working population', *Scandinavian Journal of Work, Environment and Health*, **24**, 43–8.

Harrington, J.M. (1994), 'Working long hours and health', *British Medical Journal*, **308**, 1581–82.
Harrington, J.M. (2001), 'Health effects of shift work and extended hours of work', *Occupational and Environmental Medicine*, **58**, 68–72.
Hedges, J.N. (1993), 'Worktime levels and trends: differences across demographic groups', *Industrial Relations Research Association, 45th Proceedings*, pp. 321–5.
Hetrick, R. (2000), 'Analyzing the recent upward surge in overtime hours', *Monthly Labor Review*, **123**(2), 30–33.
Hinrichs, K., Rochem, W. and Sirianni, C. (1991), *Working Time in Transition: The Political Economy of Working Hours in Industrial Nations*, Philadelphia, PA: Temple University Press.
International Labour Office (ILO) (1995), *Working Time Around the World: Conditions of Work Digest*, **14**, Geneva: ILO.
Iwasaki, K., Sasaki, T., Oka, T. and Hisanaga, N. (1998), 'Effect of working hours on biological functions related to cardiovascular system among salesmen in a machinery manufacturing company', *Industrial Health*, **36**, 361–7.
Jacobs, J.A. and Gerson, K. (1998), 'Who are the overworked Americans?', *Review of Social Economy*, **56**, 442–59.
Kanai, A. (2006), 'Economic and employment conditions, Karoshi (Work to Death) and the trend of studies on workaholism in Japan', in R.J. Burke (ed.), *Research Companion to Working Time and Work Addiction*, Cheltenham, UK and Northampton, MA, USA: Edward Elgar, pp. 158–72.
Kanai, A., Wakabayashi, M. and Fling, S. (1996), 'Workaholism among employees in Japanese corporations: an examination based on the Japanese version of the workaholism scales', *Japanese Psychological Research*, **38**, 192–203.
Kiechel, W. (1989a), 'The workaholic generation', *Fortune*, 10 April, 50–62.
Kiechel, W. (1989b), 'Workaholics anonymous', *Fortune*, 14 August, 117–18.
Killinger, B. (1991), *Workaholics: The Respectable Addicts*, New York: Simon & Schuster.
Kirkcaldy, B., Trimpop, R. and Cooper, C. (1997), 'Working hours, job stress, work satisfaction and accident rates among medical practitioners, consultants and allied personnel', *International Journal of Stress Management*, **4**, 79–87.
Kirkcaldy, B.D., Levine, R. and Shephard, R.J. (2000), 'The impact of working hours on physical and psychological health of German managers', *European Review of Applied Psychology*, **50**, 443–9.
Klaft, R.P. and Kleiner, B.H. (1988), 'Understanding workaholics', *Business*, **33**, 37–40.
Kluwer, E.S., Heesink, J.A.M. and van der Vliert, E. (1996), 'Marital conflict about the division of household labor and paid work', *Journal of Marriage and the Family*, **58**, 958–69.
Kofodimos, J. (1993), *Balancing Act*, San Francisco, CA: Jossey-Bass.
Korn, E.R., Pratt, G.J. and Lambrou, P.T. (1987), *Hyper-performance: The A.I.M. Strategy for Releasing your Business Potential*, New York: John Wiley & Sons.
Lee, C., Jamieson, L.F. and Earley, P.C. (1996), 'Beliefs and fears and Type A behavior: implications for academic performance and psychiatric health disorder symptoms', *Journal of Organizational Behavior*, **17**, 151–78.
Liu, Y. and Tanaka, H., The Fukuoka Heart Study Group (2002), 'Overtime work, insufficient sleep, and risk of non-fatal acute myocardial infarction in Japanese men', *Occupational Environmental Medicine*, **59**(7), 447–51.
Loomis, D. (2005), 'Long work hours and occupational injuries: new evidence on upstream causes', *Occupational and Environmental Medicine*, **62**, 585.
Machlowitz, M. (1980), *Workaholics: Living with Them, Working with Them*, Reading, MA: Addison-Wesley.
McMillan, L.H.W., O'Driscoll, M.P., Marsh, N.V. and Brady, E.C. (2001), 'Understanding workaholism: data synthesis, theoretical critique, and future design strategies', *International Journal of Stress Management*, **8**, 60–92.
McMillan, L.H.W., O'Driscoll, M.P. and Burke, R.J. (2003), 'Workaholism in organizations: a review of theory, research and future directions', in C.L. Cooper and I.T. Robertson (eds), *International Review of Industrial and Organizational Psychology*, New York: John Wiley & Sons, pp. 167–90.
Meijman, T.F. and Mulder, G. (1998), 'Psychological aspects of workload', in P. Dreuth, H. Thierry and C. Dewolff (eds), *Handbook of Work and Organizational Psychology*, 2nd edn, Vol. 2. *Work Psychology*, Hove, UK: Psychology Press, pp. 5–33.
Moruyama, S., Kohno, K. and Morimoto, K. (1995), 'A study of preventive medicine in relation to mental health among middle-management employees. Part 2. Effects of long working hours on lifestyles, perceived stress and working-life satisfaction among white-collar middle-management employees', *Nippon Elseigaku Zasshi (Japanese Journal of Hygiene)*, **50**, 849–60.
Mosier, S.K. (1983), 'Workaholics: an analysis of their stress, success and priorities', unpublished Masters Thesis, University of Texas at Austin.
Nachreiner, F., Akkermann, S. and Hanecke, K. (2000), 'Fatal accident risk as a function of hours into work', in S. Hornberger, P. Knauth, G. Costa and S. Folkard (eds), *Shift Work in the 21st Century*, Frankfurt: Peter Lang, pp. 19–24.

Oates, W. (1971), *Confessions of a Workaholic: The Facts about Work Addiction*, New York: World.

Porter, G. (1996), 'Organizational impact of workaholism: suggestions for researching the negative outcomes of excessive work', *Journal of Occupational Health Psychology*, **1**, 70–84.

Porter, G. (2001), 'Workaholic tendencies and the high potential for stress among co-workers', *International Journal of Stress Management*, **8**, 147–64.

Porter, G. (2004), 'Work, work ethic, work excess', *Journal of Organizational Change Management*, **17**, 424–39.

Pred, R.S., Hemreich, R.L. and Spence, J.T. (1987), 'The development of new scales for the Jenkins Activity Survey measure of the TABP construct', *Social and Behavioral Science Documents*, **16**, 51–2.

Quinn, R.P. and Shepard, L.J. (1974), *The 1972–73 Quality of Employment Survey*, Ann Arbor, MI: Institute for Social Research, University of Michigan.

Rissler, A. (1977), 'Stress reactions at work and after work during a period of quantitative overload', *Ergonomics*, **20**, 13–16.

Robinson, B.E. (1990), 'Workaholic kids', *Adolescent Counselor*, **2**, 24–47.

Robinson, B.E. (1998), *Chained to the Desk: A Guidebook for Workaholics, their Partners and Children and the Clinicians who Treat Them*, New York: New York University Press.

Robinson, B.E. and Kelley, L. (1998), 'Adult children of workaholics: self-concept, anxiety, depression, and locus of control', *American Journal of Family Therapy*, **26**, 35–50.

Robinson, B.E. and Post, P. (1995), 'Work addiction as a function of family or origin and its influence on current family functioning', *The Family Journal*, **3**, 200–206.

Rones, P.L., Ilg, R.E. and Gardner, J.M. (1997), 'Trends in hours of work since the mid-1970s', *Monthly Labor Review*, **120**, 3–14.

Rosa, R.R. (1995), 'Extended workshifts and excessive fatigue', *Journal of Sleep Research*, **4**, 51–6.

Schaef, A.W. and Fassel, D. (1988), *The Addictive Organization*, San Francisco, CA: Harper & Row.

Schuster, M. and Rhodes, S. (1985), 'The impact of overtime work on industrial accident rates', *Industrial Relations*, **24**, 234–46.

Scott, K.S., Moore, K.S. and Miceli, M.P. (1997), 'An exploration of the meaning and consequences of workaholism', *Human Relations*, **50**, 287–314.

Shields, M. (1999), 'Long working hours and health', *Health Reports*, **11**, 33–48.

Shimomitsu, T. and Levi, L. (1992), 'Recent working life changes in Japan', *European Journal of Public Health*, **2**, 76–96.

Smith, L., Hammond, T., Macdonald, I. and Folkard, S. (1998), '12-h shifts are popular but are they a solution?', *International Journal of Industrial Ergonomics*, **21**, 323–31.

Sparks, K., Cooper, C., Fried, Y. and Shirom, A. (1997), 'The effects of hours of work on health: a meta-analytic review', *Journal of Occupational and Organizational Psychology*, **70**, 391–408.

Spence, J.T. and Robbins, A.S. (1992), 'Workaholism: definition, measurement, and preliminary results', *Journal of Personality Assessment*, **58**, 160–78.

Sprankle, J.K. and Ebel, H. (1987), *The Workaholic Syndrome*, New York: Walker Publishing.

Spurgeon, A., Harrington, J.M. and Cooper, C. (1997), 'Health and safety problems associated with long working hours: a review of the current position', *Occupational and Environmental Medicine*, **54**, 367–75.

Staines, G.L. and Pleck, J.H. (1984), 'Non standard work schedules and family life', *Journal of Applied Psychology*, **69**, 515–23.

Tucker, P. and Rutherford, C. (2005), 'Moderators of the relationship between long work hours and health', *Journal of Occupational and Health Psychology*, **10**, 465–76.

Tucker, P., Folkard, S. and Macdonald, I. (2003), 'Rest breaks reduce accident risk', *Lancet*, **361**, 680.

Uehata, T. (1991), 'Long working hours and occupational stress-related cardiovascular attacks among middle-aged workers in Japan', *Journal of Human Ergonomics*, **20**, 147–53.

Van der Hulst, M. (2003), 'Long work hours and health', *Scandinavian Journal of Work, Environment and Health*, **29**, 171–88.

Van der Hulst, M. and Geurts, S. (2001), 'Associations between overtime and psychological health in high and low reward jobs', *Work and Stress*, **15**, 227–40.

Van der Hulst, M., van Veldenhoven, M. and Beckers, D. (2006), 'Overtime and need for recovery in relation to job demands and job control', *Journal of Occupational Health*, **48**, 11–19.

Worrall, L. and Cooper, C.L. (1999), 'Working patterns and working hours: their impact on UK managers', *Leadership and Organizational Development Journal*, **20**, 6–10.

11 Feedback phobia? Why employees do not want to give or receive performance feedback

Jeanette N. Cleveland, Audrey S. Lim and Kevin R. Murphy

Performance appraisal (PA) information is used as a basis for a variety of critical organizational and individual decisions (Murphy and Cleveland, 1995). Organizations use PA information to decide who receives salary increases, promotions or key assignments or will be reprimanded or terminated from employment. Employees use PA feedback to gauge their performance compared to co-workers, assess interpersonal relationships with their supervisors, and make career development choices (Murphy and Cleveland, 1995). Representative quotes from leading researchers in this area reinforce the belief that feedback is both utilized and beneficial to employees. For example, London (2003: 1) notes that 'Meaningful feedback is central to performance management. Feedback guides, motivates, and reinforces effective behaviors and reduces or stops ineffective behaviors.' He further indicates that 'Even when someone who shies away from seeking feedback directly may still crave it' (ibid.: 12). Ashford and Cummings (1985: 67) claim that 'It is generally acknowledged that feedback and knowledge of results provide mechanisms for increasing employee performance'.

Performance appraisal and feedback systems in most organizations often rest upon three assumptions: (1) employees want feedback about their performance; (2) supervisors can and will give useful feedback; and (3) timely and accurate feedback will lead to positive changes in employees' behavior. Unfortunately, none of these assumptions is likely to be warranted. Supervisors and subordinates often approach performance evaluations and feedback with equal amounts of dread and cynicism; dissatisfaction with performance appraisal and feedback is endemic in many organizations (Boswell and Boudreau, 2000; Harris, 1994; Murphy and Cleveland, 1995; Steelman and Rutkowski, 2004). The purpose of this chapter is to examine why supervisors are often unwilling to give and subordinates unwilling to accept and act on feedback about their performance. We begin by explaining the importance of examining feedback avoidance and discuss three PA feedback assumptions. We then identify the characteristics of individuals, organizations and situations that can lead to the success or failure of performance appraisal and feedback systems. In particular, we examine factors that influence the likelihood that supervisors and subordinates will be willing or unwilling to give, receive and act on performance feedback.

Why is it important to understand unwillingness to give or receive performance feedback?
The consequences of not receiving performance feedback can be dire. Two powerful anecdotes clearly illustrate this (Moss and Sanchez, 2004). NASA engineers heatedly debated the potential for wing damage the day before the space shuttle *Columbia* disintegrated, but they never provided feedback to their superiors for fear of the way this feedback would be received (Associated Press, 2003). Government officials in Guandong, China appear to have hampered the spread of prevention information concerning Severe Acute

Respiratory Syndrome (SARS) because employees were fearful of supervisory reprisal (Flor Cruz, 2003). In both cases, the fear that supervisors would receive negative feedback led to catastrophic consequences.

Giving feedback to employees can have a range of adverse consequences. Employee aggression is particularly likely after receiving negative performance feedback (Geddes and Baron, 1997). Extreme workplace violence, in which disgruntled employees shoot their colleagues and supervisors, is also sometimes linked to negative feedback (Neuman and Baron, 1998). Potential causes of such aggression often include the perception of unfair treatment (Neuman and Baron, 1997), which can enhance the likelihood of aggressive behavior towards superiors. Unfair treatment can also lead to acts of deviance. Performance appraisal feedback can lead to perceptions of unfair treatment (Vardi and Weitz, 2004), and employees may retaliate by engaging in organizational misbehavior ranging from interpersonal infractions, such as incivility, aggression, harassment and bullying.

Affective explanations play an important role in understanding why employees may be unwilling to provide accurate feedback to their bosses (Moss and Sanchez, 2004). Specifically, there are emotional costs in the seeking of feedback. There is fear of appearing incompetent to one's boss as well as fear of peer criticism. Conversely, managers may respond emotionally when the feedback is negative. Managers who avoid conflict may be uncomfortable with their subordinates' emotional responses. Hence the potential for very negative affective responses from both the manager and the employee may adversely influence feedback seeking and giving.

Assumptions about feedback

As we noted at the beginning of this chapter, research and practice in the area of performance management is based on assumptions that feedback is wanted, accurate and necessary for improvement in employee performance. We examine each of these assumptions in greater detail below.

Employees want feedback

Employees often do want feedback, as long as the feedback is positive. However, employees may not want to risk seeking feedback unless they are confident that the information will be positive (London, 2003). There is significant literature on evaluation apprehension (e.g. Leary, 2004) showing that evaluation by others is generally stressful and is unlikely to be seen as purely beneficial. We do not enjoy failing and avoid interactions where we believe negative information about our behavior will be forthcoming from others.

Why do employees avoid feedback? Prior to entering the workforce, we are likely to realize that people will often disagree in their evaluations of performance. The performance appraisal literature certainly bears out this observation. Agreement in evaluations of job performance is disappointingly low, regardless of the source of the evaluation (Conway and Huffcutt, 1997; Viswesvaran et al., 1996). Further, we are likely to understand that other people's evaluations of our performance will tend to be less positive than self-evaluations. Again, research on performance evaluations in organizations supports this conclusion. Self-ratings of performance are usually higher, or more lenient, than ratings obtained from supervisors and peers (Farh and Werbel, 1986; Harris and Schaubroeck, 1988; Thornton, 1980). This self-serving bias in evaluation is quite robust, and has been empirically confirmed in a number of settings (Bracken et al., 2001).

Finally, it is not completely clear whether people *evaluate* their performance in an unrealistically positive fashion, or whether they merely *report* high performance in situations where there are clear motivations to do so (e.g. in performance evaluations). There is little research comparing private self-assessments with more public discussions of performance that are required when organizations request self-ratings. Much of the available research on feedback is written from the supervisory or organizational perspective rather than the employee perspective. There are surprisingly few studies asking employees directly about their preferences for feedback. It is unlikely that employees want or will act on feedback about many aspects of their job performance. For example, I may invite or seek feedback in areas where I believe I am capable of making meaningful changes, for example, time management or self-development. I may be less receptive to feedback on tasks that depend on skills, knowledge or abilities that are difficult to change (e.g. interpersonal or leadership skills).

With the increasing attention given to 360-degree feedback (Atwater et al., 2002), employees are provided with potentially huge amounts of performance information from multiple sources. Employees may not desire performance feedback because the volume of information may reduce its apparent usefulness and value. When an employee receives multisource feedback, (s)he must make sense of it, decide what information can be used, what behaviors can realistically be modified or improved and how to implement these changes. The information overload produced by some current multisource performance management systems may make feedback seem overwhelming, leading employees to avoid performance feedback rather than struggle with complex and sometimes confusing performance management systems.

Supervisors can and will give useful feedback
The only task more difficult than *receiving* performance feedback is *giving* performance feedback. Managers often see little practical value in providing feedback because they anticipate a largely aversive situation, especially when constructive or negative feedback is offered. Managers also may avoid providing positive feedback because it can lead to unrealistic expectations that valued rewards will flow from such evaluations (London, 2003). Regardless of the content, providing one-to-one feedback is generally regarded as an uncomfortable situation where supervisors either feel embarrassed (providing positive information) or apprehensive (in providing negative information).

Further, supervisors may believe that they have little control over the performance of their employees, especially poor-performing employees. Employees who are performing poorly tend to avoid performance feedback (Larson, 1989), even though it is precisely these employees who need to improve their behaviors. Feedback avoidance often means that poor performers will perform even worse over time. Baron (1988) found that as performance problems persist, the supervisor is likely to see the problem as more significant and become increasingly angry and resentful toward the employee, diminishing the likelihood of constructive feedback.

Finally, the task of evaluating employee performance is a complex one. For accurate judgments, the process requires a number of factors that may or may not be present within a work situation or relationship. For example, accurate evaluation requires full and effective acquisition of information about employee performance, often through observation of relevant employee behaviors and outcomes; encoding of the behaviors; storing the information in memory and then retrieving it when the appropriate time comes to record it within the organization (Murphy and Cleveland, 1995). Raters who understand the complexity of their task and the potential inaccuracy of the feedback they provide may take the conservative strategy and provide as little concrete feedback as possible.

Timely and accurate feedback will lead to positive changes in employee behavior
It is widely assumed that performance feedback helps to motivate and direct behavior change, and that high-quality feedback will lead to performance improvements (Kluger and DeNisi, 1996; London, 2003). Empirical assessments of feedback effects suggest otherwise. Even when feedback is provided, there is not consistent evidence of positive improvements in performance. Performance following feedback sometimes improves (Atwater et al., 1995; Reilly et al., 1996), but it is unclear why and whether or not it is the results of the feedback *per se*. A widely cited meta-analysis by Kluger and DeNisi (1996) showed that in many situations, especially those in which feedback focused on personal characteristics rather than task behaviors, performance deteriorated rather than improved following feedback.

Self-enhancement and self-identity theory predicts that employees will react more positively to favorable feedback. However, although positive feedback may be perceived as more accurate and acceptable to the recipient, it is generally viewed as providing the least information about developmental needs. Thus there continues to be a question about whether or not feedback (positive or negative) is likely to lead to constructive changes in employee performance.

Theoretical frameworks for understanding feedback
Organizational researchers have developed a number of different theoretical frameworks for studying performance feedback including control theory, expectancy theory and variations of justice and goal-setting frameworks. These theories provide insights about how feedback works (or should work) and how feedback could be improved. Notably, the willingness to give feedback is either assumed or ignored in most of these models (models of feedback seeking being an exception), but nevertheless, understanding how feedback is supposed to function may shed light on the variables that influence how it actually works or fails to work in organizational settings.

Many feedback models are variations of control theory, in which feedback is the result of a discrepancy between the present state of a system and the desired state. Feedback is designed to reduce that discrepancy (Brief and Hollenbeck, 1985; Sandelands et al., 1991). In this tradition, feedback might be part of a self-regulation process or part of a process in which regulation of behavior is largely determined by external demands. In all control theories, there is an emphasis on learning about discrepancies between actual and desired states and taking actions to reduce these discrepancies. Some theories suggest that feedback can be used to modify goals (or desired states) as well as to reduce discrepancies between present and desired states (Murphy et al., 2001b). Other models examine sequences of decisions, in which feedback from previous decisions might be used to help determine future decisions (Lant and Hurley, 1999).

Expectancy theory suggests that feedback can change both goals and perceptions of the feasibility of attaining these goals (Pavett, 1983). Studies based on expectancy theory often focus on anticipated rewards and punishments that might accompany different choices in responding to feedback. Goal orientation research suggests that in addition to external rewards and punishments, there are individual differences in the extent to which people are willing and able to expend effort in order to reach key goals (Cron et al., 2005; VandeWalle, 2003). Some models are concerned with the perceived fairness of feedback (e.g. Alder and Ambrose, 2005), which presumably affects willingness to receive feedback. Others focus on the reasons why people might or might not be willing to seek feedback (Ashford, 1986). Feedback that is inconsistent with self-assessments or self-images (e.g. Stets, 2005) is of particular interest in both of these research streams, because one's willingness to accept feedback, believe it is fair and act on it is likely to vary as a function of how much the feedback threatens one's own assessments of performance and success.

While few feedback models directly address rater willingness to give feedback, they do provide some useful insights. In particular, feedback is most difficult to provide when there is a large discrepancy between the feedback the supervisor wants to give and his or her *perceptions* of the subordinate's self-assessments. For example, it will be harder for a supervisor to give a person negative feedback when the supervisor believes the employee thinks his or her performance is good than when the supervisor believes the employee already knows that his/her performance is substandard. Research examining performance feedback over a series of decisions (e.g. Lant and Hurley, 1999) suggests that supervisor's previous feedback can directly affect the supervisor's willingness to give feedback in the future. In particular, when a supervisor has given positive feedback in the past, the history of positive feedback will make it more difficult for the supervisor to give negative feedback in the future, especially when the trend in performance is not so dramatic as to make it easy to change the evaluation. Finally, goal orientation models suggest that a supervisor's beliefs about whether or not subordinates will incorporate the feedback and change their behavior are likely to influence willingness to provide feedback.

Factors that affect willingness to give and receive feedback
Figure 11.1 presents a model of the factors that are likely to affect the willingness to give and/or receive feedback. The content and structure of this model is based in large part on recent reviews of the performance appraisal and feedback literature (Anseel and Lievens, 2002; Ashford et al., 2003). This figure suggests that characteristics of raters, ratees and organizations influence the willingness to give or receive feedback. Our review of the literature suggests that seven specific characteristics of raters and ratees (i.e. rater and ratee demographic factors; personality; performance or competence levels; rater–ratee relationships; rates affect; impression management or motives; and perceptions of organization) and two characteristics of organizations (i.e. performance management systems, feedback climate) are particularly important influences on the willingness to give and receive feedback. It is likely that there are several other attributes of raters, ratees and organizations that are also important, but these nine have been most heavily researched. A review of this research suggests that the dynamics of performance feedback are quite complex, and that a number of characteristics of persons and organizations combine to make it quite difficult to give or receive feedback.

Rater and ratee characteristics
Various rater and ratee characteristics can affect both seeking and providing feedback, including demographic factors such as gender, ethnicity and culture, personality, competence levels and ratee PA motives.

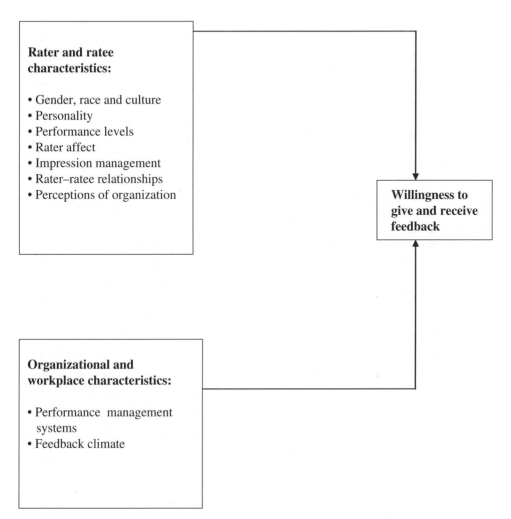

Figure 11.1   Factors affecting feedback seeking and feedback avoidance

Gender, race, and culture   Women have reported stronger intentions than men to alter their behavior based on feedback (Johnson and Hegelson, 2002). However, these differences are accounted for by male–female differences in job status. That is, individuals with lower job status, not women *per se*, reported the greatest tendency to alter their behavior after feedback. In a study on race, being the only African American in the workplace was predictive of stereotype threat perceptions (Roberson et al., 2003). That is, solo African-American subordinates were the most likely to feel threatened by the expectation that their supervisors did not expect them to succeed, and therefore were less likely to welcome feedback. Further, employees who experienced stereotype threat were likely to discount performance feedback provided by superiors as well as more likely to rely on monitoring others as an indirect mode of feedback seeking. Race also appears to influence supervisors' behavior. African-American managers employ monitoring as a strategy more often than white male managers (Lovelace and Rosen, 1996). Monitoring and discounting are often less successful inquiry methods (than direct inquiry) and reliance on these indirect methods of obtaining feedback may have a negative impact on job performance.

Cultural differences across individuals may also affect the way in which feedback is sought. Morrison et al. (2004) compared newcomers in the USA and Hong Kong in feedback seeking and found that newcomers in the USA tend to indicate more feedback seeking. They found that such differences were associated with cultural variations in power distance and self-assertiveness. Power distance indicates the extent to which there is unequal power distribution, while self-assertiveness within individualistic societies is the tendency to be direct in communication (Markus and Kitiyama, 1991). Both perceptions of low power distance and self-assertiveness appear to be related to feedback-seeking behavior.

Research also suggests that the extent to which employees agree with their supervisors on performance ratings may differ across cultures and that this, in turn, may impact how feedback is used. Fletcher and Perry (2002) outline a theoretical framework examining the impact of two cultural dimensions, power distance and individualism–collectivism, on the performance appraisal process. Specifically, they note the differences that may be expected between cultures with different levels of power distance and with different individualism–collectivism orientations. For example, supervisors in cultures with small power distances may be more likely to start the feedback process (Fletcher and Perry, 2002). At the same time, employees may be more willing to approach their supervisors for feedback as well as to disagree with them. Related to this, Korsgaard et al. (2004) found that employees who tended to be more other-oriented also demonstrated higher levels of rating agreement with their supervisors. Further, these results also suggest that other-oriented employees demonstrated less leniency (i.e. they gave lower performance ratings) as compared to the rating of their supervisors. This suggests that other-oriented employees were more open to receiving negative feedback from their direct supervisors.

Personality   The personality of a rater and ratee appears to influence performance appraisals and performance feedback. Raters who are high in agreeableness tend to give more lenient or elevated performance ratings (Bernardin et al., 2000). Elevated ratings are especially likely to occur when raters high in agreeableness expect a face-to-face meeting (Yun et al., 2005). Individuals who are low in conscientiousness are also more likely to provide higher ratings (Levy and Williams, 2004). This finding suggests that low levels of conscientiousness may be associated with relatively careless ratings and with low standards of performance.

Research looking at the relationship between personality and willingness to receive feedback can be summarized with reference to the five-factor model of personality (see Smither et al., 2005, for a review). Leaders who are open to new experiences have a greater tendency to be receptive to feedback, while those who are more emotionally stable are more motivated to actually use the feedback (Smither et al., 2005). Interestingly, leaders who are more extraverted and open to experience have a greater tendency to see the value of negative feedback, and to seek further feedback after initial criticism.

Overall, the relationships between personality and responses to feedback are complex. Research on core self-evaluation illustrates this complexity. Core self-evaluations reflect an individual's evaluation of the self that is enduring (Judge et al., 1997). Four broad traits are identified as being indicative of an individual's core self-evaluation: self-esteem; generalized self-efficacy; locus of control; and emotional stability. For individuals with high core self-evaluations, developmental goal commitment is stronger when self-ratings are higher than other-ratings than when self- and other-ratings are the same (Bono and Colbert, 2005). On the other hand, for individuals with low core self-evaluations, goal commitment is highest when self- and other-ratings agree. Other research shows that individuals with high levels of self-efficacy tend to be less accepting of repeated negative feedback, while individuals with low self-efficacy did not alter their levels of acceptance (Nease et al., 1999).

There are a number of limitations to the research on personality, feedback and performance changes. First, few studies include job- or task-related feedback from actual work contexts (Bono and Colbert, 2005). Second, our understanding of how recipient characteristics affect feedback processes is limited. Finally, strong theoretical development regarding the use of personality variables in feedback research is needed (VandeWalle, 2003).

Performance levels   Performance levels may be one factor that affects beliefs held about feedback received or about the outcomes of feedback. Research has examined the feedback management strategies of both good and poor performers. Moss et al. (2003) discuss the application of three feedback management strategies (seeking, mitigating and avoiding) in two different contexts: when the employee is performing well, and performing badly. When seeking feedback, employees may use entitlements or enhancements as tactics (Moss et al., 2003). Entitlements allow the employee to be recognized for their work while enhancements serve to heighten the supervisor's perception of the work quality. When mitigating negative feedback, employees may apologize for poor performance or even present the employer with evidence of their poor performance to short-circuit the supervisor's emotional response. Finally, in feedback avoidance, the employee seeks to reduce the possibility of the supervisor even acknowledging poor performance. In a longitudinal field study on helicopter pilot trainees, there were higher levels of feedback eliciting when performance was rated poorly (Fedor et al., 1992). These results support Ashford's (1986) model which posits that when performance improvement is needed, feedback is regarded as an asset.

In terms of providing feedback to poor performers, supervisors tend to explain subordinates' poor performance in terms of low effort or ability (Ilgen et al., 1981). However, Ilgen et al. (1981) also suggest that when outcomes for the supervisor are affected by the subordinate's low performance, there is a tendency for the supervisor to regard poor performers better and respond in a more helpful way. Overall, employees who perform at different levels may have different ways of managing feedback. Snyder et al. (1984) note that subordinates who viewed the relationship they had with their leaders in a favorable light tended to respond positively to the performance feedback process. At the same time, employees who had a more favorable response to performance feedback also tended to report more role clarity and experienced less role conflict. Finally, the more the employee was perceived as being competent, the more favorable the response to performance feedback.

A caveat should be noted, however. Assessments of performance levels may be systematically biased for several reasons, including the purpose of performance appraisal. It is generally recognized that administrative ratings (e.g. ratings used to make salary or promotion decisions) tend to be lenient or more positive than ratings provided for the purpose of developmental feedback. Jawahar and Williams's (1997) meta-analytic review suggests that performance ratings for administrative purposes were one-third standard deviation higher than performance ratings obtained for developmental purposes. Higher ratings under administrative conditions may be used to motivate an employee who is not performing well (Murphy and Cleveland, 1995), allow the supervisor to avoid negative outcomes, including providing negative feedback, or simply used to attain positive outcomes such as pay increments for the employee. Conversely, more accurate (and lower) ratings are likely to occur in developmental appraisals. Such situations provide an opportunity for the supervisor to help the subordinate work on performance deficiencies. These caveats should be borne in mind when feedback management strategies of different levels of performers are considered.

Rater–ratee relationships   One way of perceiving the relationship between the rater and the ratee may be through the leadership lens. Different leadership styles may affect feedback seeking in different ways. Levy et al. (2002) use a vignette study to examine the relationship between leadership styles and feedback-seeking intentions. Participants showed a greater intention to seek feedback when they were exposed to a transformational leader, rather than a transactional leader (transformational leadership involves inspiring employees whereas transactional leadership involves working out favorable bargains with employees). At the same time, certain leader characteristics, specifically the extent of individual consideration, could explain intention to seek feedback above and beyond a particular leadership style. Individual consideration refers to a leader's ability to develop an empowering work environment by taking into consideration how their followers may be different, as well as seeking to develop each follower taking into account individual differences. Individuals who are skilled in providing individual consideration are more likely to provide feedback, and their feedback is more likely to be accepted.

The influence of rater affect   Research examining the relationship between leaders and their followers in feedback contexts has examined the effects of the method of delivering negative feedback on ratees. There is a tendency for raters to display negative emotions such as anger and disgust when delivering failure feedback (Baron, 1988, 1990). The emotion leaders display during feedback can also influence subsequent follower perceptions of leader effectiveness and performance perceptions. Using affective events theory as a theoretical framework in an experimental study, Gaddis et al. (2004) found that when a leader displayed negative emotions, subordinates viewed the leader as being lower in effectiveness than when the same feedback was provided with a display of positive emotions. Furthermore, groups with leaders who display negative affect when giving feedback subsequently perform more poorly than groups with leaders who displayed positive affect. In fact, workers who receive a combination of negative feedback and negative emotions performed worse than they did prior to the feedback.

When subordinates have performed badly, Moss and Martinko (1998) note that leaders tend to avoid giving feedback. In addition to delaying the provision of feedback, leaders distort it to reduce its negativity. However, when leaders' outcomes are linked to subordinates' performance, feedback tends to be more immediate, frequent and directive. However, when leaders' outcomes were dependent on subordinate performance and when attributions were made regarding low levels of effort, feedback tended to be more negative and immediate (Moss and Martinko, 1998).

Interview research suggests the possibility of a dynamic exchange between employee feedback-seeking strategies and the delivery of feedback by the supervisor (Larson, 1989). In particular, feedback and support provided by a supervisor between formal appraisal sessions is likely to influence satisfaction with supervision. When performance feedback is provided informally and regularly, employees may be more receptive to feedback received during their formal appraisal and feedback sessions.

Impression management: ratee motives   Ratees may have multiple goals in performance appraisal interviews, including obtaining feedback, influencing the impressions of raters and developing good relationships with raters (Ashford and Cummings, 1983; Murphy and Cleveland, 1995). Impression management consists of attempts to control how an individual comes across to other people (Morrison and Bies, 1991) and has been identified as an important component in the feedback-seeking process.

Impression management is not necessarily a strategy to bias ratings upwards; it is probably best thought of as a defensive strategy against criticism. Negative appraisals can be a source of threat to the ratee's self-esteem, and ratees will engage in proactive efforts to reduce negative feedback. Morrison and Bies (1991) suggest a three-stage model of feedback inquiry, taking into account motives of impression management, ego-protection and information, while Villanova and Bernardin (1991) outline possible means, motives and opportunities to engage in impression management.

It should be noted that the impact of impression management behaviors on performance appraisals is not necessarily large (Villanova and Bernardin, 1991), in part because supervisors usually have access to information about subordinate performance that is not directly under ratees' control. Nevertheless, ratees are often strongly motivated to do what they can to encourage positive feedback and discourage negative feedback by influencing the information that is available to raters when evaluating their performance.

Several impression management tactics have been identified and include tactics used to either repair a negative impression or to establish a positive identity. Kacmar and Carlson (1999) review the effectiveness of impression management tactics across several human resource situations. The same tactics may not be equally effective across different situations. For example, self-promotion appears effective in an interview context but is believed to lead to negative outcomes in performance evaluation. Nevertheless, there is evidence that individuals who engage in impression management tend to receive higher performance evaluations than those who avoid impression management (Wayne and Liden, 1995).

Job-focused impression management (Wayne and Ferris, 1990) refers to efforts aimed at self-enhancement by ensuring that the supervisor is aware of work accomplishments; supervisor impression management includes ingratiatory tactics such as complimenting supervisors. Gender dissimilarity and network centrality appear to strengthen the positive association between supervisor-focused impression management and performance appraisal (Barsness et al., 2005). That is, supervisor-focused impression management is most likely to be successful when supervisor and subordinate gender differs and when the subordinate is strongly placed in a workplace network. On the other hand, gender dissimilarity between supervisors and subordinates strengthens the negative relationship between job-focused impression management and performance appraisal.

Rater perceptions of organizations   Drawing on models and hypotheses presented by Murphy and Cleveland (1995), Tziner and his colleagues conducted a series of studies examining the relationships among perceptions of organizations, personnel systems and performance ratings (Tziner and Murphy,1999; Tziner et al., 2001; Tziner et al., 1998). These studies suggest that rater attitudes toward organizations influence performance ratings. For example, raters who perceive a participative organizational climate and a more positive affective commitment to the organization tend to: (1) give higher ratings; (2) make smaller distinctions among the subordinates they evaluate; and (3) make stronger distinctions among the strengths and weaknesses of their subordinates. One implication of these findings is that the feedback subordinates receive may depend, in part, on whether or not the rater views the organization positively. Supervisors who are strongly invested in the organization and in the concept of participation may be more lenient and less discriminating. On the other hand, raters who are disengaged and authoritarian may be harsher and more judgmental.

Tziner and his colleagues suggest that more proximal attitudes (i.e. perceptions of human resource systems and of the performance appraisal process) have a stronger effect on performance evaluations. In particular, supervisors' beliefs about the way performance evaluations are used in organizations (purpose of rating) and about the way their colleagues conduct performance appraisals (performance appraisal politics) seem particularly important. Supervisors who believe that performance evaluations will be used to make important decisions about their subordinates (e.g., raises, promotions) are likely to inflate ratings. Similarly, supervisors who believe their colleagues manipulate ratings to accomplish political ends (e.g. maintaining harmony in the work group, making the supervisor look good) are likely to inflate ratings. Again, these findings imply that the performance feedback one receives is the result not only of actual employee performance levels, but also of the supervisor's confidence or lack of it, (e.g. trust) in other supervisors in the organization and of his or her perceptions of the links between performance ratings and values outcomes and rewards.

The supervisor's trust in the PA process can also influence the ratee's trust and acceptance of PA feedback. Supervisors who do not trust appraisal systems (because they believe that other supervisors manipulate ratings) are unlikely to give useful feedback, particularly to poor performers. Murphy and Cleveland (1995) suggest that these same poor performers are often least receptive to feedback. When supervisors and subordinates do not trust the appraisal system, it becomes very difficult to give and receive negative feedback. Murphy and Cleveland (1995) suggest that the tendency to avoid painful feedback will be especially strong when trust in the performance appraisal system is low.

There are several reasons to believe that trust in supervisors and in performance management systems is an important determinant of one's willingness to accept performance feedback. First, there is evidence that trust in one's supervisor directly affects perceptions of the fairness and accuracy of performance appraisals (Fulk et al., 1985). There is a clear tendency for individuals to discount negative feedback, and this tendency is likely to be stronger when the source of the feedback is not trustworthy. Second, there is evidence that trust in the source of feedback affects one's willingness to make meaningful changes in behavior (London, 2003). If the supervisor is viewed as untrustworthy, it is likely that the advice he or she gives about improving performance will also be viewed as suspect.

Organizational and workplace characteristics
A number of contextual variables are thought to affect the feedback-seeking process. A sample of such context factors include supervisory support and politics, feedback in group settings, career transitions, decision standards, multisource feedback systems and feedback climate. Rosen et al. (2006) proposed a theoretical model of relationships between percep-tions of organizational politics, morale and job performance that includes the construct of feedback environment, defined in terms of the value and usefulness of daily, informal feed-back provision at the workplace (Steelman et al., 2004). Rosen et al. (2006) found that higher-quality feedback environments are related to reduced levels of perceived politics within the organization. When information is available to employees regarding what is appropriate behavior and performance in the workplace, there is a decline in organiza-tional politics perceptions and also improved employee performance. Further, employees seek more feedback when both supervisors and peers are perceived as supportive.

Feedback seeking is also likely to occur in groups. Robinson and Weldon (1993) provide a theoretical perspective of this process, outlining potential motives that may drive feed-back seeking in groups. Further, they describe how employee motives can affect the feedback-seeking process in terms of whether the feedback is at the individual or group level, whom to seek feedback from, and whether to seek feedback in private or in public. In one study on work groups, the tendency to seek and receive feedback depended on the overall performance level of the work group and not on differences in active or passive feedback-seeking behaviors (Wijngaard et al., 2000).

Feedback seeking is especially likely during career transitions. Career transitions are especially important times for both the organization and employee as they lay the foun-dation for how long an employee may stay with an organization. Callister et al. (1999) note that career transitions are times where employee feedback seeking is especially helpful in terms of obtaining role information about their new environment (Ashford and Black, 1996), in particular how well they are attaining objectives (Ashford, 1986). In a lon-gitudinal study, Callister et al. (1999) found that employee observational monitoring for feedback from supervisors and peers was constant across time. Employees' direct requests for feedback from supervisors also remained stable across time. However, direct requests for feedback from peers reduced across time. As employees' role clarity increased, there was also a decline in direct requests for feedback from peers.

The decision or comparison standard used to evaluate an employee may also affect sub-sequent employee-helping behavior (Klein, 2003). Besides being more pleased with their performance, individuals who received positive feedback were more likely to provide helpful hints to another participant on a subsequent task. This relationship was strongest when the feedback provided compared the employee to that other participant or to an 'average person'. The relationship was weaker when the comparison was made to an objective criterion or to the performance of a person other than the person receiving the help. Klein (2003) noted that, overall, individuals tend to be more responsive to feedback when the comparison is made to an average person.

Current research suggests that that organizational contexts and workplace characteristics do affect the nature of feedback seeking in terms of how the feedback is sought as well as the frequency with which it is sought.

Multi-source performance feedback systems   Traditionally, performance appraisals and feedback have followed a strict top–down model, in which supervisors evaluate their subordinates. Indeed, one of the defining features of a supervisory role is the power and the responsibility to evaluate the performance of one's subordinates. However, it has long been recognized that there are many potential sources of performance evaluations and feedback (e.g. self-ratings, peer ratings, upward feedback), and it is quite likely that the source of feedback will influence the nature of that feedback and the willingness of recipients to act on it. The increasing use of multi-source feedback systems in organizations (Bracken et al., 2001) highlights the importance of considering both who evaluates one's performance and how these evaluations are obtained and communicated.

There is a growing literature documenting the effects of multi-source feedback systems (Atwater and Brett, 2005; Atwater et al., 2002; Bailey and Fletcher, 2002; Funderburg and Levy, 1997). These systems are popular, well regarded by users and widely lauded in the business press, but it is still far from clear whether the use of multi-source feedback leads to better outcomes (e.g. performance improvements) than traditional top–down systems (Atwater et al., 2002; Smither et al., 2005a). It seems likely, however, that multi-source feedback systems do have potential to address many of the barriers to feedback giving and acceptance encountered in traditional top–down systems. In particular, a good multi-source feedback system might help address raters' fear of negative consequences (especially if ratings are less positive than hoped), and ratees' concerns about the credibility and bias of supervisory evaluations (Harris, 1994; Rutkowski and Steelman, 2005). Because ratings are usually collected from and aggregated across many individuals, the likelihood that any single individual can be blamed for a low evaluation, or that a negative evaluation can be written off on the basis that a particular supervisor is biased or unfair, is reduced. In theory, therefore, multi-source feedback systems should increase the rater's willingness to give and the ratee's willingness to receive and accept feedback.

The potential Achilles' heel of multi-source systems is their potential for providing feedback that is inconsistent and unclear. Murphy et al. (2001a) argue that disagreement will often be the norm when performance is evaluated by multiple sources. For example, supervisors see different behaviors than are seen by peers, and are likely to evaluate them from a different frame of reference. Similarly, peers see different behaviors and evaluate them differently than subordinates (Murphy and Cleveland, 1995). Even if we focus solely on raters who are at a comparable level in the organization (e.g. ratings from multiple supervisors), it is likely that different individuals will, as a result of their position in the organization, work assignments etc., see different samples of behavior. Unfortunately, as Murphy et al. (2001a) note, inconsistency and disagreement often lead recipients to dismiss the feedback they receive, especially if it is negative.

Feedback climate and environment   McDowall and Fletcher (2004) suggest that perceptions of fairness are associated with the perceived feedback climate. Leung et al. (2001) suggest that even when negative feedback is delivered, if it is done with a sense of interpersonal fairness there is greater acceptance of the feedback as well as more positive reactions towards the supervisor and the organization. Interpersonal fairness entails an attentive, respectful and supportive attitude towards the recipient of such feedback. Leung et al. (2001) argue that fairness in interpersonal treatment softens the impact of negative feedback by lessening negative dispositional attributions made to the supervisor delivering the criticism as well as drawing forth positive attributions. As noted by Leung et al. (2001), when treated fairly, individuals make positive attributions and think that the person in authority has acted appropriately.

Apart from perceived fairness, trust is also an important aspect of the feedback climate and affects both raters as well as ratees. Trust in the appraisal process has been conceptualized as the extent to which a rater thinks that appraisals are both fair and accurate (Bernardin and Orban, 1990). Raters who express less trust in the average supervisor tended to provide higher performance ratings. Employee trust in the source of feedback as well as perceived importance of feedback has also been found to partially mediate the influence of feedback on performance (Earley, 1986).

Research has also demonstrated the importance of trust in the ability of management and accountability via performance appraisal to be among the factors that are predictive of employee participation in behavior-based safety processes (DePasquale and Geller, 1999). Given the heavy reliance on technology in organizations today, the use of computers to gather, analyze and report on individual or group performance is not unusual. Even then, the perceived fairness of such monitoring is affected by feedback attributes. For example, there were higher levels of perceived fairness using such computer monitoring when constructive feedback was provided, rather than destructive feedback. At the same time, perceived fairness of computer monitoring was also higher when individuals had their feedback delivered face to face, rather than through a computer medium.

A recent conceptualization of the feedback climate has also looked at the feedback environment, that is, contextual features pertaining to supervisors and colleagues who are the source of feedback. Steelman et al. (2004) define the feedback environment as the contextual aspects of daily interactions pertaining to feedback between supervisors and subordinates. An environment conducive to feedback facilitates the communication and use of feedback, while an environment unfavorable to feedback limits the acceptance and use of feedback information. Specifically, seven dimensions have specifically been highlighted: source availability, source credibility, feedback delivery, feedback quality, diagnostic favorable feedback, diagnostic unfavorable feedback, and the extent to which feedback seeking is promoted (Steelman et al., 2004). Initial work on this construct has found that when employees are able to be informed about what is acceptable and deemed desirable in the office, political perceptions decline and work outcomes improve (Rosen et al., 2006). Higher-quality feedback environments are inversely associated with reduced perceptions of organizational politics.

Overall, fairness and trust are important across several contexts of feedback. Recent conceptualizations of climate issues include the feedback environment where contextual features pertaining to the daily interactions of supervisors and subordinates are emphasized.

Practical alternatives to traditional performance appraisal and feedback
There are many reasons why supervisors may be reluctant to give and subordinates may be reluctant to receive performance feedback, even when the feedback is positive. Are there reasonable alternatives to traditional performance appraisal and feedback systems

that might work better? We see two broad approaches that might improve matters. First, it might be possible to tweak current systems to make it easier to give and receive useful feedback (in line with former US President Clinton's 'mend it, don't end it' approach). For example, we might focus on giving people more detailed, objective feedback about their performance. Some performance appraisal problems can be traced to inconsistencies between the feedback that is given and the target's subjective understanding and interpretation of that feedback (Moore and Kuol, 2005). Increasing the level of detail and the amount of relevant objective information in feedback might reduce these conflicts between the feedback the supervisor thinks he or she has given and the target's interpretation of that feedback. Another possibility for reducing supervisor–subordinate differences in the interpretation of performance feedback would be to use frame of reference training, or some variation on this method, to provide a uniform perspective from which to view and interpret feedback (Sulsky et al., 2002). If supervisors and subordinates at least spoke a common language and knew what phrases such as 'average performance' or 'acceptable performance' actually meant, the potential value of performance feedback would probably increase.

Instead of changing the feedback or changing the sender and the recipient of the feedback, we might try changing the environment within which performance feedback is typically given and received. In particular, there is evidence that perceptions of the degree to which political factors affect performance appraisals influence the perceived value and trustworthiness of performance feedback (Rosen et al., 2006; Tziner et al., 1998). If we can make the rating environment less political (which can sometimes be accomplished by increasing everyone's access to information), we might expect better, more useful feedback.

Murphy and Cleveland (1995) had a more radical suggestion – that organizations should consider doing away with performance appraisal and feedback systems altogether. There are sometimes compelling legal or administrative reasons for retaining performance appraisal systems, but it is often hard to point to concrete benefits to the organization, the raters or the ratees that come as a result of performance appraisal and feedback. We suspect that if more organizations took Murphy and Cleveland's (1995) suggestion to compare the problems associated with performance appraisal and feedback systems with the benefits these systems provide, their assessments of pain versus gain would quickly lead to the abandonment of performance appraisal and feedback systems as we currently know them.

Suppose we dropped the sort of top–down system (or its 360-degree variant) currently used to provide performance feedback. What would we put in its place? One possibility is to put more emphasis on giving people the tools, the information and the motivation to realistically evaluate their own performance. Leadership in organizations too often takes the form of telling people what to do, but when leaders can establish relationships with their subordinates that allow them to serve as valued mentors rather than as judges and juries, the likelihood that subordinates will care about and realistically evaluate their own performance may increase. Self-evaluations are rarely trusted in organizations, but there is good reason to believe that changing the relationships between supervisors and subordinates could turn self-evaluations into a valuable tool. In most organizations, self-evaluations, if they are requested at all, are given in a context where employees are motivated to inflate their own ratings and where they expect that others' evaluations will not be accurate or trustworthy.

Despite the many reasons for distrusting and avoiding performance feedback, there are many people who actively seek feedback about their performance (Anseel and Lievens, 2002; Ashford and Cummings, 1983, 1985). There are situations in which feedback is both sought and welcomed (e.g. safety-related feedback; Sasson and Austin, 2004). There are organizations in which performance appraisal and feedback systems seem to work well (Ash, 1994). As organizations move toward increasingly decentralized structures and approaches, one significant challenge will be to better equip individual employees to function without requiring detailed input from supervisors. It may be time to identify and develop possible substitutes for performance appraisal and feedback systems as currently used in organizations.

References

Alder, G.S. and Ambrose, M.L. (2005), 'An examination of the effect of computerized performance monitoring feedback on monitoring fairness, performance, and satisfaction', *Organizational Behavior and Human Decision Processes*, **97**, 161–77.

Anseel, F. and Lievens, F. (2002). 'Feedback seeking behavior in organizations: a review of the literature and directions for future research', *Gedrag en Organisatie*, **15**, 294–319.

Ash, A. (1994), 'Participants' reactions to subordinate appraisal of managers: results of a pilot', *Public Personnel Management*, **23**, 237–56.

Ashford, S.J. (1986), 'Feedback-seeking in individual adaptation: a resource perspective', *Academy of Management Journal*, **29**, 465–87.

Ashford, S.J. and Black, J.S. (1996), 'Proactivity during organizational entry: the role of desire for control', *Journal of Applied Psychology*, **81**, 199–214.

Ashford, S.J. and Cummings, L.L. (1983), 'Feedback as an individual resource: personal strategies of creating information', *Organizational Behavior and Human Performance*, **32**, 370–98.

Ashford, S.J. and Cummings, L.L. (1985), 'Proactive feedback seeking: the instrumental use of the information environment', *Journal of Occupational Psychology*, **58**, 67–79.

Ashford, S.J., Blatt, R. and VandeWalle, D. (2003), 'Reflections on the looking glass: a review of research on feedback-seeking behavior in organizations', *Journal of Management*, **29**, 773–99.

Associated Press (2003), 'Engineers feared shuttle wing burning', CNN.com, 26 February.

Atwater, L.E. and Brett, J.F. (2005), 'Antecedents and consequences of reactions to developmental 360-degree feedback', *Journal of Vocational Behavior*, **66**, 532–48.

Atwater, L., Rousch, P. and Fischthal, A. (1995), 'The influence of upward feedback on self- and follower ratings of leadership', *Personnel Psychology*, **48**, 35–59.

Atwater, L.E., Waldman, D.A. and Brett, J.F. (2002), 'Understanding and optimizing multisource feedback', *Human Resource Management*, **41**, 193–200.

Bailey, C. and Fletcher, C. (2002), 'The impact of multiple source feedback on management development: findings from a longitudinal study', *Journal of Organizational Behavior*, **23**, 853–67.

Baron, R.A. (1988), 'Negative effects of destructive criticism: impact on conflict, self-efficacy, and task performance', *Journal of Applied Psychology*, **73**, 199–207.

Baron, R.A. (1990), 'Countering the effects of destructive criticism: the relative efficacy of four interventions', *Journal of Applied Psychology*, **75**, 235–45.

Barsness, Z., Diekmann, K.A. and Siedel, M.-D.L. (2005), 'Motivation and opportunity: the role of remote work, demographic dissimilarity, and social network centrality in impression management', *Academy of Management Journal*, **48**, 401–19.

Bernardin, H.J. and Orban, J.A. (1990), 'Leniency effect as a function of rating format, purpose for appraisal, and rater individual differences', *Journal of Business and Psychology*, **5**, 197–211.

Bernardin, H.J., Cooke, D.K. and Villanova, P. (2000), 'Conscientiousness and agreeableness as predictors of rating leniency', *Journal of Applied Psychology*, **85**, 232–6.

Bracken, D. Timmreck, C. and Church, A. (2001), *Handbook of MultiSource Feedback*, San Francisco CA: Jossey-Bass.

Brett, J.F. and Atwater, L.E. (2001), '360-degree feedback: accuracy, reactions, and perceptions of usefulness', *Journal of Applied Psychology*, **86**, 930–42.

Brief, A.P. and Hollenbeck, J.R. (1985), 'An exploratory study of self-regulating activities and their effects on job performance', *Journal of Occupational Behavior*, **6**, 197–208.

Bono, J. and Colbert, A.E. (2005), 'Understanding responses to multisource feedback: the role of core self-evaluations', *Personnel Psychology*, **58**, 171–203.

Boswell, W.R. and Boudreau, J.W. (2000), 'Employee satisfaction with performance appraisals and appraisers: the role of perceived appraisal use', *Human Resource Development Quarterly*, **11**, 283–99.

Callister, R., Kramer, M.W. and Turban, D.B. (1999), 'Feedback seeking following career transitions', *Academy of Management Journal*, **42**, 429–38.

Conway, J.M. and Huffcutt, A.I. (1997), 'Psychometric properties of multisource performance ratings: a meta-analysis of subordinate, supervisor, peer, and self-ratings', *Human Performance*, **10**, 331–60.

Cron, W.L., Slocum, J.W. Jr, VandeWalle, D. and Fu, Q. (2005), 'The role of goal orientation on negative emotions and goal setting when initial performance falls short of one's performance goal', *Human Performance*, **18**, 55–80.

DePasquale, J.P. and Geller, E.S. (1999), 'Critical success factors for behavior-based safety: a study of twenty industry-wide applications', *Journal of Safety Research*, **30**, 237–49.

Early, P.C. (1986), 'Trust, perceived importance of praise and criticism, and work performance: an examination of feedback in the United States and England', *Journal of Management*, **12**, 457–73.

Farh, J.L. and Werbel, J.D. (1986), 'Effects of purpose of the appraisal and expectation of validation on self-appraisal leniency', *Journal of Applied Psychology*, **71**, 527–9.

Fedor, D.B., Rensvold, R.B. and Adams, S.M. (1992), 'An investigation of factors expected to affect feedback seeking: a longitudinal field study', *Personnel Psychology*, **45**, 779–805.

Fletcher, C. and Perry, E.L. (2002), 'Performance appraisal and feedback: a consideration of national culture and a review of contemporary research and future trends', in N. Anderson, D.S. Ones, H.K. Sinangil and C. Viswesvaran (eds), *Handbook of Industrial, Work and Organizational Psychology*, Vol. 1, London: Sage, pp. 127–44.

Flor Cruz, J. (2003), 'Pressure on China over SARS bug', CNN.com, 2 April.

Fulk, J., Brief, A.P. and Barr, S.H. (1985), 'Trust-in-supervisor and perceived fairness and accuracy of performance evaluations', *Journal of Business Research*, **13**, 301–13.

Funderburg, S.A. and Levy, P.E. (1997), 'The influence of individual and contextual variables on 360-degree feedback system attitudes', *Group & Organization Management*, **22**, 210–35.

Gaddis, B., Connelly, S. and Mumford, M.D. (2004), 'Failure feedback as an affective event: influences of leader affect on subordinate attitudes and performance', *The Leadership Quarterly*, **15**, 663–86.

Geddes, D. and Baron, R.A. (1997), 'Workplace aggression as a consequence of negative performance feedback', *Management Communication Quarterly*, **10**, 433–54.

Harris, M.M. (1994), 'Rater motivation in the performance appraisal context: a theoretical framework', *Journal of Management*, **20**, 737–56.

Harris, M.M. and Schaubroeck, J. (1988), 'A Meta-analysis of self-supervisory, self-peer, and peer-supervisory ratings', *Personnel Psychology*, **41**, 43–62.

Ilgen, D.R., Mitchell, T.R. and Fredrickson, J.W. (1981), 'Poor performers: supervisors' and subordinates' responses', *Organizational Behavior and Human Performance*, **27**, 386–410.

Jawahar, I.M. and Williams, C.R. (1997), 'Where all the children are above average: the performance appraisal purpose effect', *Personnel Psychology*, **50**, 905–25.

Johnson, M. and Hegelson, V.S. (2002), 'Sex differences in response to evaluative feedback: a field study', *Psychology of Women Quarterly*, **26**, 242–51.

Judge, T.A., Locke, E.A. and Durham, C.C. (1997), 'The dispositional causes of job satisfaction: a core evaluations approach', *Research in Organizational Behavior*, **19**, 151–88.

Kacmar, K.M. and Carlson, D.S. (1999), 'Effectiveness of impression management tactics across human resource situations', *Journal of Applied Social Psychology*, **29**, 1293–315.

Kacmar, K.M., Wayne, S.J. and Wright, P.M. (1996), 'Subordinate reactions to the use of impression management tactics and feedback by the supervisor', *Journal of Managerial Issues*, **8**, 35–53.

Klein, W.M.P. (2003), 'Effects of objective feedback and "single other" or "average other" social comparison feedback on performance judgments and helping behavior', *Personality and Social Psychology Bulletin*, **29**, 418–29.

Kluger, A.N. and DeNisi, A. (1996), 'The effects of feedback interventions on performance: a historical review, a meta-analysis, and a preliminary feedback intervention theory', *Psychological Bulletin*, **119**, 254–84.

Korsgaard, M.A., Meglino, B.M. and Lester, S.W. (2004), 'The effect of other orientation on self-supervisor rating agreement', *Journal of Organizational Behavior*, **25**, 873–91.

Lant, T.K. and Hurley, A.E. (1999), 'A contingency model of response to performance feedback: escalation of commitment and incremental adaptation in resource investment decisions', *Group & Organization Management*, **24**, 421–37.

Larson, J.R. Jr (1989), 'The dynamic interplay between employees' feedback seeking strategies and supervisors' delivery of performance feedback', *Academy of Management Review*, **14**, 408–22.

Leary, M.R. (2004), 'The self we know and the self we show: self-esteem, self-presentation and the maintenance of interpersonal relations', in M. Brewer and M. Hewstone (eds), *Emotion and Motivation. Perspectives on Social Psychology*, Malden, MA: Blackwell Publishing, pp. 204–24.

Leung, K., Su, S. and Morris, M.W. (2001), 'When is criticism not constructive? The role of fairness perceptions and dispositional attributions in employee acceptance of critical supervisory feedback', *Human Relations*, **54**, 1155–87.

Levy, P.E., Cober, R.T. and Miller, T. (2002), 'The effect of transformational leadership perceptions on feedback-seeking intentions', *Journal of Applied Social Psychology*, **32**, 1703–20.

Levy, P.E. and Williams, J.R. (2004), 'The social context of performance appraisal: a review and framework for the future', *Journal of Management*, **30**, 881–905.

London, M. (2003), *Job Feedback: Giving, Seeking, and Using Feedback for Performance Improvement*, 2nd edn, Mahwah, NJ: Lawrence Erlbaum Associates.

Lovelace, K. and Rosen, B. (1996), 'Differences in achieving person–organization fit among diverse groups of managers', *Journal of Management*, **22**, 703–22.

Markus, H. and Kitiyama, S. (1991), 'Culture and the self: implications for cognition, emotion, and motivation', *Psychological Review*, **98**, 224–52.

McDowall, A. and Fletcher, C. (2004), 'Employee development: an organizational justice perspective', *Personnel Review*, **33**, 8–29.

Moore, S. and Kuol, N. (2005), 'Students evaluating teachers: exploring the importance of faculty reaction to feedback on teaching', *Teaching in Higher Education*, **10**, 57–71.

Morrison, E.W. and Bies, R.J. (1991), 'Impression management in the feedback-seeking process: a literature review and research agenda', *Academy of Management Review*, **16**, 522–41.

Morrison, E.W., Chen, Y.-R. and Salgado, S.R. (2004), 'Cultural differences in newcomer feedback seeking: a comparison of the United States and Hong Kong', *Applied Psychology: An International Review*, **53**, 1–22.

Moss, S.E. and Martinko, M.J. (1998), 'The effects of performance attributions and outcome dependence on leader feedback behavior following poor subordinate performance', *Journal of Organizational Behavior*, **19**, 259–74.

Moss, S.E., Valenzi, E.R. and Taggart, W. (2003), 'Are you hiding from your boss? The development of a taxonomy and instrument to assess the feedback management behaviors of good and bad performers', *Journal of Management*, **29**, 487–510.

Moss, S.E. and Sanchez, J.I. (2004), 'Are your employees avoiding you? Managerial strategies for closing the feedback gap', *Academy of Management Executive*, **18**, 32–44.

Murphy, K.R. and Cleveland, J.N. (1995), *Understanding Performance Appraisal: Social, Organizational, and Goal-based Perspectives*, Thousand Oaks, CA: Sage.

Murphy, K., Cleveland, J. and Mohler, C. (2001a), 'Reliability, validity and meaningfulness of multisource ratings', In D. Bracken, C. Timmreck and A. Church (eds), *Handbook of Multisource Feedback*, San Francisco, CA: Jossey-Bass, pp. 130–48.

Murphy, P.R., Mezias, S.J. and Chen, Y.R. (2001b), 'Adapting aspirations to feedback: the role of success and failure', In T.K. Lant and Z. Shapira (eds), *Organizational Cognition: Computation and Interpretation*, Mahwah, NJ: Lawrence Erlbaum Associates, pp. 125–46.

Nease, A.A., Mudgett, B.O. and Quinones, M.A. (1999), 'Relationships among feedback sign, self-efficacy, and acceptance of performance feedback', *Journal of Applied Psychology*, **84**, 806–14.

Neuman, J.H. and Baron, R.A. (1997), 'Type A behavior pattern, self-monitoring, and job satisfaction as predictors of aggression in the workplace', in G. Chao (chair), *Counterproductive Job Performance and Organizational Dysfunction*, Symposium conducted at the meeting for the Society for Industrial and Organizational Psychology, St Louis, MO.

Neuman, J.H. and Baron, R.A. (1998), 'Workplace violence and workplace aggression: evidence concerning specific forms, potential causes, and preferred targets', *Journal of Management*, **24**, 391–419.

Pavett, C.M. (1983), 'Evaluation of the impact of feedback on performance and motivation', *Human Relations*, **36**, 641–54.

Reilly, R.R., Smither, J.W. and Vasilopoulos, N.L. (1996), 'A longitudinal study of upward feedback', *Personnel Psychology*, **49**, 599–612.

Roberson, L., Deitch, E.A., Brief, A. and Block, C.J. (2003), 'Stereotype threat and feedback seeking in the workplace', *Journal of Vocational Behavior*, **62**, 176–88.

Robinson, S. and Weldon, E. (1993), 'Feedback seeking in groups: a theoretical perspective', *British Journal of Social Psychology*, **32**, 71–86.

Rosen, C., Levy, P.E. and Hall, R.J. (2006), 'Placing perceptions of politics in the context of the feedback environment, employee attitudes, and job performance', *Journal of Applied Psychology*, **91**, 211–20.

Rutkowski, K.A. and Steelman, L.A. (2005), 'Testing a path model for antecedents of accountability', *Journal of Management Development*, **24**, 473–86.

Sandelands, L., Glynn, M.A. and Larson, J.R. (1991), 'Control theory and social behavior in the workplace', *Human Relations*, **44**, 1107–30.

Sasson, J.R. and Austin, J. (2004), 'The effects of training, feedback, and participant involvement in behavioral safety observations on office ergonomic behavior', *Journal of Organizational Behavior Management*, **24**, 1–30.

Smither, J.W., London, M. and Reilly, R.R. (2005a), 'Does performance improve following multisource feedback? A theoretical model, meta-analysis and review of empirical findings', *Personnel Psychology*, **58**, 33–66.

Smither, J.W., London, M. and Richmond, K.R. (2005b), 'The relationship between leaders' personality and their reactions to and use of multisource feedback: a longitudinal study', *Group & Organization Management*, **30**, 181–210.

Snyder, R.A., Williams, R.R. and Cashman, J.F. (1984), 'Age, tenure, and work perceptions as predictors of reactions to performance feedback', *The Journal of Psychology*, **116**, 11–21.

Steele, C.M. and Aronson, J. (1995), 'Stereotype threat and the intellectual test performance of African Americans', *Journal of Personality and Social Psychology*, **69**, 797–811.

Steelman, L.A., Levy, P.E. and Snell, A.F. (2004), 'The Feedback Environment Scale (FES): Construct definition, measurement and validation', *Educational and Psychological Measurement*, **64**, 165–84.

Steelman, L.A. and Rutkowski, K.A. (2004), 'Moderators of reactions to negative feedback', *Journal of Managerial Psychology*, **19**, 6–18.

Stets, J.E. (2005), 'Examining emotions in identity theory', *Social Psychology Quarterly*, **68**, 39–74.

Sulsky, L.M., Skarlicki, D.P. and Keown, J.L. (2002), 'Frame-of-reference training: overcoming the effects of organizational citizenship behavior on performance rating accuracy', *Journal of Applied Social Psychology*, **32**, 1224–40.

Thornton, G.C. III (1980), 'Psychometric properties of self-appraisals of job performance', *Personnel Psychology*, **33**, 263–71.

Tziner, A. and Murphy, K. (1999), 'Additional evidence of attitudinal influences in performance appraisal', *Journal of Business and Psychology*, **13**, 407–19.

Tziner, A., Murphy, K.R. and Cleveland, J.N. (2001), 'Relationships between attitudes toward organizations and performance appraisal systems and rating behavior', *International Journal of Selection and Assessment*, **9**, 226–39.

Tziner, A., Murphy, K.R., Cleveland, J.N., Beaudin, G. and Marchand, S. (1998), 'Impact of rater beliefs regarding performance appraisal and its organizational contexts on appraisal quality', *Journal of Business and Psychology*, **12**, 457–67.

VandeWalle, D. (2003), 'A goal orientation model of feedback-seeking behavior', *Human Resource Management Review*, **13**, 581–604.

Vardi, Y. and Weitz, E. (2004), *Misbehavior in Organizations: Theory, Research, and Management*. Mahwah, NJ: Lawrence Erlbaum Associates.

Villanova, P. and Bernardin, H.J. (1991), 'Performance appraisal: the means, motive, and opportunity to manage impressions', in R.A. Giacalone and P. Rosenfeld (eds), *Applied Impression Management: How Image-making Affects Managerial Decisions*, Vol. 135, Thousand Oaks, CA: Sage, pp. 81–96.

Viswesvaran, C., Ones, D.S. and Schmidt, F.L. (1996), 'Comparative analysis of the reliability of job performance ratings', *Journal of Applied Psychology*, **81**, 557–74.

Waldman, D.A. and Atwater, L.E. (2001), 'Confronting barriers to successful implementation of multisource feedback', in D.W. Bracken, C.W. Timmreck and A.H. Allan (eds), *The Handbook of Multisource Feedback: The Comprehensive Resource for Designing and Implementing MSF Processes*, San Francisco, CA: Jossey-Bass, pp. 463–77.

Wayne, S.J. and Ferris, G.R. (1990), 'Influence tactics, affect, and exchange quality in supervisor–subordinate interactions: a laboratory experiment and field study', *Journal of Applied Psychology*, **75**, 487–99.

Wayne, S.J. and Liden, R.C. (1995), 'Effects of impression management on performance ratings: a longitudinal study', *Academy of Management Journal*, **38**, 232–60.

Wijngaard, O., Hoekstra, H.A. and Emans, B.J.M. (2000), 'Feedback in work groups: a description of actively seeking and passively receiving feedback in work groups', in M. Vartiainen, F. Avallone and N. Anderson (eds), *Innovative Theories, Tools, and Practices in Work and Organizational Psychology*, Ashland, OH: Huber Publishers, pp. 141–54.

Yun, G.J., Donahue, L.M., Dudley, N.M. and McFarland, L.A. (2005), 'Rater personality, rating format, and social context: implications for performance appraisal ratings', *International Journal of Selection and Assessment*, **13**, 97–107.

12 Everybody hurts, sometimes: the language of emotionality and the dysfunctional organization

Anjana Anandakumar, Tyrone S. Pitsis and Stewart R. Clegg

My illness – a trigger for changes, obviously, in my personal life – also set in motion my thinking about the kinds of hidden forces that determine our well-being, even to the point of acquiring disease. And in particular, how the behavior in organizations and the people in them can affect the health of individuals. (Frost, 2003b: 2)

In memory of Professor Peter J.C. Frost
30 August 1939 – 18 October 2004

Introduction

The Chambers English Dictionary defines dysfunction as: '*n.* impairment or abnormality of the functioning of an organism'. To be a functional human being means that one can operate in one's daily life in an ordered, structured, efficient, useful and practical way. The term dysfunctional, therefore, refers to an inability to consistently operate in 'functional' ways. Put simply, dysfunction implies that something is not working properly. Applying this logic to organizations, we can argue that workplace organizations are predicated on the assumption that everything is 'working' properly, or that there is a normal mode of functioning. Organizations, when they work well, are places where people come together to communicate and interact in order to achieve organizational objectives, achieve self-actualization, solve problems, provide goods and services, and generate and sustain organizational survival.

What happens when working well is results-oriented in such a way that notions of self-actualization are interpreted almost entirely in terms of the selves at the top of the organization's hierarchy? What is, and is not, meant to be achieved or pursued organizationally is dictated, almost always, from the top down. To this end, only management and leadership get to define what 'functional' and 'dysfunctional' mean organizationally. What is deemed functional or dysfunctional is typically operationalized from very rational and dualistic assumptions. Against this rationalism we argue for a non-dualist interpretation of 'dysfunction'. We believe that organizations can be both functional and dysfunctional simultaneously; that is, they may pursue functional objectives but in ways that are dysfunctional for the well-being of those who are charged with delivering this functionality. When the individual employee is faced with a tension between external, functional and rational constraints and they experience these constraints as personally dysfunctional, we argue that the emotional life of the person becomes the conduit through which tensions are displayed and sometimes resolved. Thus the coexistence of functionality and dysfunctionality can be best explained through the expression of emotions in the workplace.

Using rich ethnographic research, we investigate the relationships and functioning of staff within a leading neo-natal intensive care unit (NICU). Specifically, we explore how nursing staff operate and make sense of the functional and dysfunctional aspects of their work through their emotions. We chose the NICU because we knew that it is a highly emotionally charged workplace context, where matters of life and death dominate everyday working lives. Drawing upon positive psychology, especially the late Professor Peter Frost's work on toxic emotions, we show how dysfunctional workplaces are typified by divergence in emotions felt towards one's workplace, co-workers and management. We then discuss these findings with specific reference to understanding and managing workplace dysfunctions.

Setting the scene

Hospitals are extraordinary spaces in which rich tapestries of everyday life – and death – unfold, as life starts for some and ends for others, as people struggle with all kinds of illnesses, as families and friends rejoice and grieve. Yet, between the spaces of all the stories that comprise this rich tapestry, people do their jobs. It takes a massive division of labour and knowledge to maintain the everyday life of an organization as complex as a major hospital. Indeed, few organizations concentrated on one site are as complex, and almost none, if any, are as emotionally charged. Even universities, equally professionalized and divided, only have to contend with success and failure in several of life's small tournaments, not the success and failure of living itself.

Within the extraordinariness of life and death, seemingly mundane acts of organizing, managing and working continue. Cleaners clean, nurses nurse, administrators administer and doctors prescribe. Hospitals are ideal contexts within which to study many of the issues raised within the chapters of this book. Hospitals are emotionally laden spaces in which the functionality of the patients' well-being is predominant. We enter this functional – and emotional – space where one of its most vulnerable and joyful rituals occurs: birth and its immediate aftermath. Specifically, we examine a neo-natal intensive care unit in which are placed new-born babies with life-threatening complications. In this chapter, however, we are not concentrating on these tiny patients but on those people that work and manage in the unit.

The neo-natal intensive care unit (NICU) not only looks after critically ill babies but also attends to the emotional well-being of the babies' parents. Primarily, the responsibility for critical care and parent interaction falls on nurses, who also have the additional role of coaching the new parents and other family members in caring for the new baby and integrating it back into the family. A key component of a nurse's work is being able to cope with the emotions of the baby's family members, who are often highly emotional. It is a context in which, after the joy of birth, there is sometimes the grief of death, of a little life stilled before it has barely begun. The babies' illnesses and conditions are serious; otherwise they would not be in NICU, and, thus, deaths are inevitable. Subsequently, nurses must cope personally with these deaths after having been primary care givers for these babies. At the same time they are also expected to assist the family in coping emotionally and mentally.

Nursing anywhere is a stressful, complex and emotionally charged profession (Boyle and Healy, 2003). Nurses in health care systems that are subject to frequent reorganization and change, often as a result of political pressures outside of their everyday work, face the additional stresses of not merely the job but also the changing context in which it can be done. The New South Wales health system has consistently been the focus of print and television media attention that is highly politically charged. In part this is because of the fact that while health care is a state responsibility, the funding that sustains it is derived from the federal tier of government. Shortcomings that are exposed by media attention can always be blamed by one tier of government on the inadequacies of the other tier. Recent *causes célèbres* have included a focus on nurse 'whistleblowers' exposing alleged medical and hospital managerial incompetence, the pervasiveness of nursing shortages, health system mismanagement, insufficient beds creating long queues for surgery, problems of death due to hospital negligence, and many other undesirable outcomes.

Still, the everyday life of the hospital must go on. Added to the political pressures, nursing is a profession involving high levels of emotional investment and labour, as nurses deal with illness and death almost daily. Nursing has been a growing area of management research and theory (Diers, 2004), in part because of its relatively recent incorporation as a discipline in universities. Because of this, careers are developing that are premised on the social scientific research into nursing. Such research shows that organizational responses to conflictual and contentious public issues increasingly create highly stressful, unproductive and unsustainable working environments, in which nursing managers seek proactively to support nurses in their coping with these work stressors so that they remain in the nursing profession in the long term (Cohen-Katz et al., 2004). We believe such observations make nursing and hospitals ideal contexts within which the discipline of positive psychology can provide insight into how such emotionally charged professions and organizations function.

The positive psychology of emotional labour

Nursing as emotional labour
For over a decade there has been a growing interest in how one can best manage staff working in roles that are emotionally demanding – which has been commonly labelled as emotional labour. Ashforth (1993: 1) defines emotional labour as

> the display of expected emotions by service agents during service encounters. It is performed through surface acting, deep acting, or the expression of genuine emotion. Emotional labour may facilitate task effectiveness and self-expression, but it also may . . . trigger emotive dissonance and self-alienation.

Much of the work on emotional labour focuses on service industries, such as customer service officers, call centres and so on (Higgs, 2004). Nursing as a profession is commonly referred to as emotional labour and involves two aspects: the care of the sick and tending to the entire environment within which such care happens (Diers, 2004). Nursing in a neonatal intensive care unit is doubly emotionally charged, given nurses deal with illness and death, as well as the emotions of parents and carers, on a daily basis. In other words, these NICU nurses are required to perform emotional work within a context that is itself deeply embedded emotionally (Boyle and Healy, 2003).

The emotional context within which nurses work is compounded by changes such as the recent restructuring of the healthcare industry to meet the growing needs of the public; the increasing politicization of healthcare; calls for increases in numbers of foreign nurses to address staff shortage; and growing public discontent with the health system and an associated increase in media interest. Anecdotally one would assume that working under such conditions would be highly stressful, uncertain and complex (Zapf et al., 1999: 372).

The New South Wales health system has seen a trend towards hospitals being run more like a profit-and-loss making business, where managerial skills are now centred on allocating budgets, on strategically rational planning and managing of resources based on quantitative outcomes. Any management that is oriented to the numbers, to quantitative performance indicators, runs the risk of neglecting that which is being managed in favour of that which is being reported against. Realizing this, positive organizational scholarship suggests that in order to ensure the health and longevity of a productive workforce, there needs to be a shift in management and organizational practices towards developing positive psychological strengths, such as optimism, hope and resilience (Seligman and Csikszentmihalyi, 2000; Luthans, 2002a, 2002b; Weick, 2003; Clair and Dufresne, 2004; Snyder and Lopez, 2007). By respecting meaningful aspects of people's lives, managers can nurture in employees a more positive connection to their organization. In doing so, they help employees develop a stronger sense of purpose in work than when they are treated merely in terms of their achievement of targets.

There is a further important point that emerges from the positive organization scholarship literature. Sometimes, the organizations in which we work and the things that we are required to do in them can be deeply disturbing; they can, literally, cause us pain. In this spirit, Peter Frost (2003b) suggests that managers should recognize that emotional pain is an inevitable and sometimes necessary part of working life. However, a key to building sustainable workplace practices as well as a 'happy' workforce is to 'handle' this pain in ways that result in growth, learning and increased organizational identity for employees. Moreover, he suggests that handling pain is a major responsibility of managers. He presents a model that identifies seven causes of organizational pain so that managers can use this understanding to address pain within their organizations (albeit that the model has not been subjected to much empirical validation). While Frost acknowledges that negative consequences result from the seven causes of pain, he does not identify the specific consequences of each cause. Consequently, management have at times ignored the centrality of the issues that unavoidably arise when those people whom they supervise are in pain. Left unresolved, with management focused on metaphorical and quantitative bottom lines, the culmination of leaving such issues unaddressed and unresolved is that job dissatisfaction, turnover and industrial actions can escalate, and morale sinks (Chan, 2001).

Nurses are particularly vulnerable to such stresses. Nursing has changed greatly in a relatively short time; nurses now have far more managerial responsibility than they did a few years ago, when their job was premised more on on-the-job training and workplace knowledge (Clegg and Chua, 1989, 1990). As nurses have become better educated, their ability to contribute to patient diagnosis and care has grown, as have the expectations and demands put upon them by management. It is no surprise that the emotional demands on nursing staff often prove to be overwhelming (Diers, 2004). Indeed, research has highlighted the adverse effects of unmanaged emotional stress on health workers who are no longer able to manage their emotions adequately while interacting with others. The main affect is 'burnout', which includes emotional exhaustion, alienation and reduced motivation to accomplish tasks (Zapf et al., 1999). Since nurses confront emotional stress as part of their daily work, they are especially prone to manifesting symptoms of burnout. The outcomes of emotional stressors in nursing can even manifest themselves as crisis situations, such as patient death or serious errors in judgement (Kohn and Henderson, 2002). Nursing managers need to develop managerial competencies to help their nurses, as long-term patient carers who deal regularly with traumatic events, to maintain effective functioning (Cohen-Katz et al., 2004).

Being surrounded by traumatic events, nurses are particularly prone to negative psychological states. Nursing managers need to guide nurses towards focusing purposefully on positive psychological states if they are to counteract negativity. That emotionally charged workplaces need not necessarily be seen as having negative psychological and emotional consequences is one of the tenets of positive psychology (PP). Research by Clair and Dufresne (2004) has found that constructive outcomes can result from environments typified by challenging events, such as those that nurses deal with every day. These outcomes include: greater feelings of organizational identity; heightened insight and awareness of the organization's vulnerabilities; greater insight into addressing issues relevant to leadership of the team; and an enhanced sense of emotional, spiritual and existential aspects of organizational life. How leaders manage, develop and mentor people during emotionally demanding contexts is the key to whether subjectively negative events can have positive outcomes (Dunphy and Pitsis, 2003; Frost, 2003b; Pitsis and Clegg, 2007). Thus a better understanding of the possible effects of traumatic workplace events, and the role managers play in such events, is required if managers are to foster the experience of positive outcomes for their employees, themselves and their organizations.

The tradition of positive psychological research
Positive organizational behaviour (POB) applies the principles of PP directly to management practice. The growing interest in positive psychology is associated with the special issue of the *American Psychologist* (2000) edited by Martin Seligman and Mihaly Csikszentmihalyi. The key feature of positive psychology is the argument that psychology should refocus on its original mission: investigating how one can achieve and live a psychologically healthy life. Seligman and Csikszentmihalyi (2000) argue that originally psychology concentrated on positive aspects, such as strength of character, happiness and optimism, virtues, resiliency and other related areas. However, mainstream psychology shifted focus to investigating psychological maladjustment, deviance and abnormality. In short, psychology moved away from investigating what makes people happy towards what makes them sad. Seligman and other positive psychologists believe a more successful approach seeks systematically to build competencies, rather than correcting weaknesses. Therefore, positive psychology is the development of the science of human strength (Seligman and Csikszentmihalyi, 2000; Snyder and Lopez, 2007). There are several human strengths that shield people from mental illness; examples include courage, future-mindedness, optimism, interpersonal skill, faith, work ethic, hope, honesty and perseverance.

As a division of PP, positive organizational behaviour (POB)[1] is the study and application of positively oriented human resource strengths and psychological capacities that can be effectively managed for performance improvement in the workplace (Luthans, 2002a). POB recognizes that in order to apply human strengths consistently and effectively, managers need to have a systematic and proactive attitude to incorporating them in both daily interactions and long-term planning with employees. Founders of POB believe that focusing on positive attributes of our lives can lead to enhanced psychological health, which, in turn, can have benefits for the organization's performance. POB argues that successful organizational leadership is achieved by: focusing on enhancing what is being done well while things are going well; working to enhance, improve and transfer those strengths to those areas of potential weakness; and always being mindful of *what* is working *when* it is working (Gollan, 2000; Seligman and Csikszentmihalyi, 2000; Luthans, 2002b). The field of POB applies a theory- and research-driven perspective to management practice: understanding and application of those factors that allow individuals, groups, organizations and communities to thrive and prosper (Luthans, 2002a, 2002b; Weick, 2003; Clair and Dufresne, 2004). Its mission is to educate managers on how to nurture both themselves and employees so that, as a team, they are well equipped in both physical- and knowledge-based resources, as well as emotional strength, organizational loyalty and the determination to work through adverse occurrences.

POB suggests that nurturing employee loyalty and commitment is achieved by building positive social, human and psychological capital within the organization (Luthans, 2002b; Bagozzi, 2003; Fredrickson, 2003). In other words, by placing a greater emphasis on the more meaningful aspects of employees' lives, such as family, or connection to nature, managers can nurture a more positive connection in employees to their organization and also develop in them a stronger sense of purpose with their work. Luthans and Youssef (2004) have added another component to leadership termed positive psychological capital management. The role of psychological capital management is to develop and enhance employees' psychological strengths such as hope, optimism, self-efficacy and resiliency, achieved by acknowledging the life experiences that everyone brings to the workplace as well as the ways in which the current workplace events shape an employee's confidence, hope, resiliency and optimism. Organizations that make opportunities to build and strengthen human capital, by understanding that their employees are malleable and flexible to positive change and renewal, are said to be acting in socially sustainable ways (Dunphy and Pitsis, 2003; Luthans and Youssef, 2004; Clegg et al., 2005: 254–7). A sustainable, productive and fulfilling working life, therefore, is seen as a hallmark of POB, and for these reasons it can have a significant impact upon the profession of nursing (Shirey, 2006).

Positive psychology and workplace sustainability
A key concern for POB scholars is how the majority of interactions between co-workers and managers can be made positive and uplifting (Dutton and Heaphy, 2003; Luthans and Avolio, 2003). The concept of sustainability has been used to characterize such positive relationships (Gladwin and Kennelly, 1995; Dunphy and Benveniste, 2000), which Dunphy and Benveniste (2000: 9) define as 'development that meets the needs of the present without compromising the ability of future generations to meet their own needs'. While the concept of sustainability has been widely applied, used in the human context it refers to the building of human capability and skills for high-level organizational performance that, either directly or indirectly, benefits community well-being (Dunphy and Benveniste, 2000). One should not be surprised to find that although management places strong emphasis on providing satisfactory remuneration, training opportunities and working conditions, people are still unhappy in their workplace (Dunphy and Benveniste, 2000; Goleman, 2003; Bolman and Deal, 2003). The stress on developing sustainable

human resource relations is less concerned with exploiting people as resources and more with reorienting to a primary emphasis on shared humanity that focuses on the emotional and psychological needs, potential and aspirations of employees.

Luthans and Youseff (2004) illustrate that employees draw strength, creativity and inspiration from multiple sources, as well as their place of employment. However, in organizations, a lack of importance is often accorded to individual and community values in preference to those directly related to monetary wealth (Bolman and Deal, 2003; Neal et al., 1999; Dunphy and Pitsis, 2003). Corporate cultures are created that leave employees feeling isolated and dispirited, leading to high absenteeism, burnout, political manipulation, padding of budgets and turnover as well as low staff morale and a general distrust of management (Cavanagh, 1999; Garcia-Zamor, 2003). Issues pertaining to human relationships at work need to be restored to the agenda to counter these adverse tendencies (Cameron et al., 2003).

POB, as a division of PP, is not without its critics: one major criticism is that it promotes research abandoning a focus on failure, to focus entirely instead on the positive. Success and failure are subjectively interdependent, as Lazarus (2003) argues, such that the processes of coping and improvement cannot be understood adequately without addressing both facilitative and restrictive factors in coping and improvement. For Lazarus, focusing on the positive over the negative makes little sense. Given that experience is highly subjective, what is positive for one person might be negative for another. Similar arguments are made about the term 'positive', and this criticism has been applied equally to positive psychology and its underlings, positive organizational scholarship and positive organizational behaviour. 'Positive' as a word has strong symbolic connotations and meanings attached to it.[2] How society comes to understand and define terms such as positive is socially constructed and experienced (Fineman, 2006; Pitsis, 2007). The term has moral and ethical underpinnings because a positive term will be experienced differently by different societies, groups and individuals.

In our view, the former criticism is not as valid as the latter because the main proponents of PP, POS and POB have never sought to deny the importance, affect and force of the negative upon people, organizations and communities. Indeed, PP is often the study of how people cope and thrive after 'negative' events in their lives, and how they can facilitate growth and healing through the practice of compassion during times of stressful events (see, for example, Kanov et al., 2004). Where a real issue does exist, however, is in the use of the term positive by PP scholars, and the seeming lack of acceptance that how the term is used and defined is highly intersubjective – or socially sensed – and therefore biased towards the person(s) defining and conceptualizing it as a dependent variable upon which to conduct research. For example, there is still no common agreement as to what happiness means. How does the happiness a person feels when her child is born, even though she forwent her chance of successful professional career, differ from the happiness she feels when she gets a promotion at work, even though she sacrificed having children. Clearly, the answer to both cases will be value laden.

For such reasons, one of the most intellectually appealing approaches for explaining how managers can foster a positive and sustainable workplace in highly emotional conditions was that offered by Peter Frost. Frost covertly addressed the criticism of POB by examining the sources of negativity in organizations to understand how these could be managed to realize positive outcomes for both employees and organizations. Frost's

(2003b) work on toxic emotion integrates a concern with highly emotional conditions caused either by events or people, especially managers; he directly applied the principles of positive organizational behaviour to such situations, focusing directly on the conditions that foster sustainable social and psychological capital at work.

Frost's toxicity and sustainability
Frost (2003a, 2003b) acknowledges the emotional effects of work life on employees and asserts that psychological capital and emotional capital are intertwined in the concepts of hope, optimism, self-efficacy and resiliency. For example, in discussing the notion of resiliency, Frost explains that the extent to which members feel connected to their organization is the key. Hence the achievement of resiliency and the other POB concepts need to be created and nurtured on both a psychological and emotional level.

For Frost (2003a, 2003b), leaders by their very nature will inevitably cause emotional pain. Thus it is not the avoidance of pain, but rather how pain is managed that determines the strength and sustainability of an organization's workforce. Frost notes that in most companies it is not the manager that plays this role, but rather another employee with whom other employees feel comfortable and safe. However, if there is not an open forum for communication with the manager, then the problems that become identified are most likely to remain unresolved, and become exacerbated over time. Moreover, toxicity is contagious, so when employees choose to vent their pain to other employees, the toxicity spreads among employees with devastating results (Barsade, 2003).

We argue that there is a need for organizational leaders proactively to handle pain. Often it can be a manager's job to cause pain for their employees. Asking an employee to work harder or work in a new situation or with new people can sometimes be a source of anxiety, fear and doubt. These directives need not remain a source of negativity if they are managed appropriately. Implicit in being a manager is the role of providing support and guidance to employees in such situations. By helping employees learn how to manage such potentially toxic-emotion-causing situations, managers can yield positive outcomes for individuals, teams and the organization.

Enter Toxic Emotions at Work
In his book, *Toxic Emotions at Work*, Frost (2003b) discusses the inevitability of emotional pain within organizations. In fact, it is often the job of a manager to create pain by pushing employees outside of their comfort zone. Leaders who are responsive to the pain that they create or encounter in the workplace are better able to develop and sustain the loyalty of those they lead. According to Frost (2003b), if left alone or managed poorly, pain can become toxic and have detrimental effects on organizational efficiency and sustainability. Emotions that are toxic are negative: fear, anger, betrayal and stress are the most usual, counteracting and interfering with the development of hope, optimism, resiliency and self-confidence. Toxicity occurs systematically in organizations for many reasons, such as company restructures, demanding bosses and clients, as well as retrenchments, for instance. In his book, *Toxic Emotions at Work*, Frost (2003b) identifies seven sources of toxicity within organizations termed the 'seven deadly INs': *intention, incompetence, infidelity, insensitivity, intrusion, institutional forces* and *inevitability*. Frost focuses on managerial behaviour that results in creating each of the 'seven deadly INs'. Each of these INs will be discussed in what follows.

Intention refers to those managers who purposely or maliciously create pain in others. Behaviour consistent with 'intention' may be exhibited in various ways such as the use of derogatory names or threats, explosive outbursts, public ridicule, or withholding information (Zellars et al., 2002). There is increasing literature that suggests that employees who report being mistreated also report greater job and life dissatisfaction, have greater incidence of intentions to quit their jobs, display role conflict and psychological distress, than those who have not been treated in this way (Zellars et al., 2002). There are various reasons for such abuse in the workplace, including managers' psychological need to control others, personal prejudices, or a mistaken belief that fear motivates people. 'Intention' can have serious ramifications for employees, such as reduced self-confidence, as well as increased fear, anger, resentment and mistrust towards the perpetrator. In turn, these emotional responses affect worker performance levels, morale and organizational loyalty.

Incompetence refers to those managers who gain their position due to technical expertise rather than an ability to work with people. Many managers lack people skills and adequate management training on how to create productive relationships with staff. The Karpin Report demonstrated that Australian managers were strong in operational and technical skills, but weak in relationship-building-skills:

> The Report found that in general, while Australian managers have acknowledged strengths, they also have distinct weaknesses, and that these tend to cluster in those areas which are most critical for the successful manager and business profile for the 21st century. These areas include leadership including teamwork and empowerment, people skills including management of a diverse workforce, strategic skills, a learning focus, and international orientation. In short, Australian managers have strong functional skills (business efficiency and technical skills) but lack cross-functional, strategic and corporate skills. They have depth but lack breadth. (Australian Local Government Information Service, 27/11/04: 1)

In today's 'corporate' health system, managers' performance tends to be measured on a cost-efficiency basis. Managers often are not monitored on non-cost areas, such as their ability to foster and nurture relationships at work. Thus one should be cautious in labelling managers as incompetent when they display characteristics that might be perceived as incompetent in terms of managing people, given that their organizations do not expect them to perform in such non-cost areas. Management incompetence manifests itself in various ways, such as indecisiveness and overcontrolling behaviour or an overriding concern for production and efficiency at the expense of people. Frost's (2003b) concept of 'incompetence' has parallels with behavioural-based theories of leadership, such as the difference between transactional and transformational leadership. Transactional leaders are task-focused and perform well in areas such as budgeting and scheduling, but lack proficiency in people management skills, such as motivating, encouraging confidence, and building effective social relationships (Clegg et al., 2005). POB argues that it is the people management and social networking skills that distinguish outstanding leaders from effective leaders (Luthans, 1988, 2002b).

Infidelity is the betrayal of an employee's trust by a manager. Trust acts as a bonding agent between organizational members and can eliminate the barriers that hinder long-term relationships, open communication, knowledge sharing and continuous feedback, which can facilitate creativity, efficiency and improvement (Luthans and Youssef, 2004).

Therefore it is an essential component in creating and nurturing the psychological and emotional commitment of employees towards their employer (Atkinson, 2004; Gillespie and Mann, 2004). POB literature highlights the importance of establishing and strengthening the employee's psychological contract with both managers and organization.

> According to Robinson and Rousseau (1994), a psychological contract is defined as one's own belief in the reciprocal nature of the exchange relationship between oneself and a third party, based on the promises made or implied in their interactions. Much of Rousseau's work has shown that once a psychological contract is broken, re-building the relationship is extremely difficult. (Pitsis et al., 2004: 58)

Frost's examples of 'infidelity' include cases where an employee confides in a manager about a co-worker and the manager discusses this with someone else; when a manager deliberately misleads an employee to believe that s/he will be promoted and then gives the promotion to someone else, or where managers take credit for the ideas of their employees. Betrayal results in long-term mistrust, bitterness and fear within the manager–employee relationship (Frost, 2003b).

Insensitivity is a source of toxicity that stems from those individuals who are emotionally unintelligent; they are unable to gauge the emotional impact of their own actions on others. Emotional intelligence comprises personal and social competence. Personal competence refers to an individual's ability to understand their own feelings – or their self-awareness – and their ability to manage those feelings effectively – their self-management (Luthans, 2002b; Goleman, 2004; Lubit, 2004). Social competence refers to the capacity to understand what others feel and then respond accordingly (Luthans, 2002b; Goleman, 2004; Lubit, 2004). Individuals who lack one or both of these competencies behave in ways that insult and hurt those around them. In particular, managers who display 'insensitivity' can make decisions or behave in ways that devalue others or that lack empathy and as such are counterproductive to the development of positive psychological and emotional capital (Luthans, 2002b; Luthans and Avolio, 2003; Lubit, 2004).

Intrusiveness can be described as the downside of charismatic leadership. According to Frost, charismatic leaders are able to inspire others towards organizational goals but also use that charisma to manipulate them into working longer hours and taking on more than reasonable workloads. Often these leaders use their relationships with other employees to create 'guilt' or 'fear' that has them working beyond agreed-upon hours (Frost, 2003b). 'Intrusiveness' abuses the goodwill between manager and employee; employees, in their eagerness to please their charismatic boss, may allow themselves to be persuaded to behave in ways that they would not normally.

Institutional forces refer to company rules, policies and procedures that employees must adhere to. Rules govern conditions of work and specify standard processes for carrying out tasks. Their purpose is to provide a standardized approach that ensures similar situations are dealt with consistently across the organization (Bolman and Deal, 2003). Toxicity can arise when employees do not agree with company rules or protocol. Being forced to comply with rules can cause negative emotions such as resentment, and can influence employees' attitude towards their work and the company. Another aspect of 'institutional' toxicity occurs when there are discrepancies between a stated company policy and what actually happens. In such situations employees can feel demoralized and lose faith in management and trust in their company (Frost, 2003b).

Inevitability refers to trauma resulting from situations such as unexpected downsizing or externally caused situations, such as fires, earthquakes, terrorist attacks and so on. For the nursing profession, especially nurses in the NICU, 'inevitability' comes in the form of sick and dying babies and the emotional pain of their parent and families. As this is a daily inevitability of NICU, managing the emotional trauma from such events is crucial to maintaining the emotional and psychological health and well-being of the nurses to ensure they are willing and able to work in the NICU over the long term.

Methodological approach: ethnographic case study
Frost (2003b) identified seven potential sources of toxicity within organizations that can be manifested in various ways detrimental to employees, on a personal and organizational level. Although Frost's 'toxic emotions' have great intellectual appeal, there is little research that applies such concepts empirically. Therefore this study will investigate how and if these sources of toxicity are manifest within the NICU of a children's hospital. Frost explains that there are negative consequences of toxic emotions at work that affect organizations, managers and employees. Applying Frost's model to investigate the nurses' situation at NICU is particularly relevant, given that the nurses claim to be satisfied with their pay, training opportunities and job tasks, but still report unhappiness at work and serious thoughts about leaving their workplace. Managing a sustainable workforce has to be built on the basis of an understanding of how toxic tendencies are, and are not, managed.

Nursing occurs under conditions of high emotionality, generally, and this point, along with the nature of the research aims, strongly influenced the choice of methodology. The NICU is a particularly emotional context that provides a unique and ethnographically rich context in which to investigate workplace emotionality. The research takes an exploratory approach, allowing the nurses to tell their own story, thereby providing a socially constructed description of emotions at work (Strauss and Corbin, 1998). As such, we contribute an understanding of how managers can foster a positive and fulfilling working relationship with, and for, nurses working under conditions of high emotionality.

An ethnographic approach enables the researcher to gather data that are rich in description and go beyond surface-level understanding by allowing the research subjects to tell their own story (Schneider et al., 2002). A case study is an empirical enquiry that investigates a contemporary phenomenon within its real-life context, especially when the boundaries between phenomenon and context are not clearly evident (Yin, 2003). Ethnography allows the in-depth study of a phenomenon within its cultural context. In the tradition of ethnography, we used semi-structured interviews that rely on the researcher establishing strong rapport with research subjects. The questions were theoretically informed by the positive psychology approaches expounded by Peter Frost and other theorists to help guide the recognition of emerging themes (Muecke, 1994). As Eisenhardt (1989) suggests, *a priori* concepts can help researchers focus the research process.

Data collection: embracing the NICU culture
One researcher spent several hours within the NICU simply observing and talking with the nurses about their jobs and explaining the themes for our research. The time spent in the ward provided insight into the interactions between the nurses, managers, patients and their families, allowing us to understand those topics requiring sensitivity when engaging in talk about the occurrence of specific events, such as the death of babies.

The role of the interviewer was to introduce topics for discussion and then let the interviewees proffer their opinions and tell their story (Kvale, 1996; Collis and Hussey, 2003). Instead of seeking a breadth of understanding by interviewing a representative sample of NICU nurses, we chose to focus on depth (Pratt and Rosa, 2003). Of the 60 NICU nursing staff, 17 volunteered to participate, including the nursing unit manager and 16 nurses. All volunteers were female, and 11 were senior nursing staff (six or more years at NICU), while five were junior nurses. Deep conversations, for thick descriptions, were developed with this sample (Geertz, 1973).

Analysis

Each answer was deconstructed into those individual concepts that represented a specific phenomenon. Each phenomenon was labelled, comparing each emergent concept from the totality of the transcripts, so that similar phenomena were given the same name. Phenomena with similar labels were then grouped into categories that captured emerging themes of toxicity. The consequences ascribed to each issue by the interviewees were also analysed and coded, using the same open coding process. Finally, these themes and issues were examined for patterns or commonalities.

Results: emergent themes

Analysis of the data highlighted two emergent themes relative to the NICU. One emergent theme centred on issues of emotionality. Under this theme are categorized issues of inter- and intrapersonal emotionality because they involve aspects of emotional responses directly caused by person-to-person interactions (inter-) or responses emerging from one's own internalized thinking or feelings (intra-). These include the inability to manage one's own emotions, ignorance about staff's emotions, and emotional bullying. The second theme centred on issues emerging from the tasks, roles and responsibilities of working in the NICU. So, broadly speaking, the first set of issues relates to people interacting with others while the second relates to people interacting with their work, its rules, systems and policies. Moreover, as indicated in the methodology, for each of the emergent issues, the specific consequences resulting from the causes of toxicity were also analysed.

Theme: inter- and intrapersonal emotionality

Emotional management

Emotional management refers to the nurses' perception that their manager allowed her mood to determine the nature of their interactions. The majority of nurses interviewed (12 out of 16) reported that interactions between themselves and management were mediated by the nursing unit manager's (NUM) mood at the time. For example: *'when she's in a good mood, she's very helpful. Certainly with problems, she's very helpful, but depending on her mood, you can really get a slap in the face' (nurse 1).* Similarly, *'I mean my NUM isn't approachable . . . She needs to not be judgmental and not so abrupt. She needs to take the time to listen to you and not say "I haven't got time, just email me" . . . She needs to not dismiss you from the start . . . it depends what sort of mood she is in' (Nurse 2).* Another 10 nurses had similar views, making mood a dominant and important issue.

Indeed, the NUM herself acknowledged both that she allowed her personal emotions to have an impact on how she interacted with the nurses and that her behaviour lacked consistency: *'with me, it depends on what sort of mood I'm in . . . Because if I'm pee'd off with them, then they'll be a bit anxious about who I am actually angry with and what I'm going to say. But if I'm travelling ok then the ward travels ok.'*

Consequences of emotional management

Given that the majority of nurses mentioned the moodiness of the manager as a source of negativity in the NICU, and that the manager also recognized it as a problem, it is important to highlight what are the consequences of such behaviours. The manager was reported as being unapproachable, with nurses feeling nervous, stressed and afraid to voice opinions in her presence. Such behaviour was regarded by the nurses as unprofessional and created a gap between them and management. A few nurses stated that they had considered leaving the NICU, mentioning that they thought the NUM should be held accountable for her behaviour through the hospital's formal appraisal system, so that she would be motivated to change this aspect of her management style. In order to cope with the manager's behaviour, some nurses reported that they tried to avoid face-to-face interactions by avoiding her when they saw her in the ward, using email to communicate, or trying not to work during the same shifts as the NUM. Overall the nurses consistently stated that the NUM's mood directly shaped the atmosphere on the ward and the quality of their working day, exemplified by the following quotes:

> *I try not to work weekdays. I was thinking about becoming full time, but then I knew I would have to work weekdays . . . and I don't want to. Other people have thought about quitting. I know someone else is thinking of going part time so she doesn't have to work as many weekdays to have that much involvement with her [NUM] . . . (Nurse 7)*

> *I don't want to tell her something or I delay telling her something 'cause I don't feel like getting a negative response when I'm trying to deal with the day to day activity and keep in a positive frame of mind. (Nurse 12)*

> *I think people tend to be wary of the particular ward manager who is very up and down as far as emotional stability . . . Because you're not sure how what you say to this person is going to be received, you tend to either not go there or be walking on egg shells a little bit . . . and that's fairly universal. (Nurse 1)*

Emotional ignorance

Nurses reported that management, when responding to a situation or making decisions, was often inconsiderate towards their feelings: whether the working climate was 'comfortable' or 'uncomfortable' was based upon the manager's mood on a given day. The emotionally ignorant manager does not care or try to regulate her behaviour and intentionally ignores staff's feelings and concerns.

Examples of emotional ignorance included:

- Management not standing by the nurses when parents challenged nurses' decisions: *'The thing is now it's set up as "us" vs. "them" and we're always at fault. No matter what happens nurses are always at fault. If something goes wrong it's automatically our fault' (Nurse 6).*
- Management being more concerned with providing counselling for the families in the ward after a baby's death but not acknowledging that the nurses were also grieving, and expecting them to carry on as if nothing occurred: *'I think if they had more*

counselling for staff with death it would be good. They [only] address how the parents, who are around when the baby died, were feeling . . . not the staff' (Nurse 11).

- Lack of appreciation and acknowledgement by immediate and general management: '*You work your hardest. I have missed meals, gone home late so many times and never asked for a cent in return and if you leave half an hour early one day, you're docked. That's not respect. We often give a lot more than we get in return and it's that simple exchange for management to realize that "I know you people work hard, so half an hour is not a big deal." . . . Simple examples like that' (Nurse 6).*

Consequences of emotional ignorance

A recurring theme from the nurses was that that their feelings and needs seemed to go unacknowledged by management on significant occasions. The nurses reported that they felt that they were shown disrespect, that they were unsupported and taken for granted by management. They also stated that this made them feel angry and hurt:

The fact was that management had taken the side of the parents without saying that this person has worked for you for a number of years and you haven't had a complaint before . . . so why all of a sudden are they complaining? Don't just automatically blame the nurse. If you've been working for a number of years you expect not to be automatically blamed. It really irritates me. That's not respect. (Nurse 6)

It made me feel that they thought more about the parents than the actual staff and didn't really care about your needs. (Nurse 11)

Emotional bullying

The majority (14 out 16) of the nurses reported either observing, or being involved in, incidents where they perceived the NICU management to be forceful, threatening, unfair and callous. For example:

One of the girls recently broke her arm . . . the NUM made her feel so bad for not coming to work and said to her 'why can't you come to work? Why can't you come to work?' . . . she needed staff that badly, that she actually made her cry on the telephone, making her feel so bad that she had broken her arm . . . it's just the way she goes about things. (Nurse 7)

the hierarchy or the head honcho's don't have families. They have no understanding of what they expect of us to come in on our off days. And we're tight for staff at the moment. I think they expect more than just our general work . . . So I've been abused because I haven't come in on the extra days when they've rung me. It really doesn't matter what's going on in your life . . . and I've been told that. (Nurse 2)

That criticism was offered in a way that wasn't necessarily constructive or it occurred in an environment which wasn't appropriate; maybe in front of a family . . . and physically, she's quite intimidating and she has a loud voice etc. (Nurse 4)

Consequences of emotional bullying

When management was aggressive in interactions with staff, the nurses reported that this undermined their self-confidence, heightened their sense of grievance, and led them to view the NUM as unprofessional. Often, the nurses expressed these feelings by complaining to each other in the tea room and at other staff functions. The junior nurses, in particular, felt vulnerable and sought other people on the ward to talk about problems, bypassing management altogether. Four of the junior nurses had considered leaving this particular NICU because they feel intimidated by the NUM, but were afraid to do so in case the NUM gave them a poor reference. The nurses attributed the emotional bullying as a significant cause for the gap that existed between the NICU management and the nurses.

The nurses' transcripts consistently revealed that they believed management did not understand or respect their lives outside the NICU, resulting in anger and frustration with management:

> *Sometimes if we don't do the extra nights we're reprimanded. I think a lot of us don't understand that or find that we're not appreciated for what we do while we're there. (Nurse 2)*

> *I do think there is a perception that a lot of the nurses on our staff feel that management doesn't understand the stress that they're under and are less than sympathetic to the workload demands . . . I think that's an issue in our unit . . . because people verbalize mainly in the tearoom. They don't do it in the unit and they do it at social functions outside work, away from work. That's where you really get to hear how distressed people can be. (Nurse 10)*

Trust breaking

The nurses reported incidences of when they had worked especially hard towards a particular goal and the agreed-upon or promised reward was not provided by the manager. For example:

> *Every Christmas and Easter the nurses have a hamper to raffle and we bring in items to donate for the hamper and we raffle it. That's to raise money for the unit to buy equipment for the babies or things for the staff to make their life a little bit easier. So we raise the money with this raffle and the money goes into a bank account and is never seen again. (Nurse 10)*

> *The government recognizes that all hospitals are meant to be promoting the upgrading of the qualifications of its entire staff and the hospital tries to meet certain quotas each year. So that when I went to Jenny last year and said 'I'm doing Bachelor of Nursing', she was ecstatic. She kissed me on the cheek! That was really surprising because it meant that it had sorted out another problem for her in meeting quotas on a report. The hospital subsequently has withdrawn all tertiary funding for assisting nurses to do training, and there's not been any apology . . . And instead of getting 60% of funding for uni I get zilch now. (Nurse 5)*

Almost half the nurses interviewed reported similar incidences relating to broken promises or expectations.

Consequences of trust breaking

Trust breaking was reported by the nurses to have devastating consequences, leaving them feeling undervalued, unappreciated and less motivated, as well as more cynical and resentful towards not only their managers but also their jobs and even colleagues. Betrayal of trust is a strong source of toxicity, as illustrated in the following quotes:

> *People tend to feel a bit demoralized. You think 'what's the point? Where's the equipment that we've bought with the money we've raised from these raffles?' We haven't got it. (Nurse 10)*

> *I do not feel quite as positive about my work. When you're encouraged to do something and it's almost a verbal agreement that says 'We will back you up in this practical way', and then it's withdrawn half way through, then you feel not to think it's such a trustworthy agreement, do you? (Nurse 5)*

Misdirected energies

Nursing managers become immersed and committed to issues related to their own performance, such as budgets, quotas, deadlines, but to an extent that is disproportionate to their care for their staff. All care seems to be oriented to the performance indicators – not the performers. The majority of nurses at the NICU perceived that the NUM had become too removed from the day-to-day operations of the ward. They felt that she had become so focused on budgets and quotas that she did not care to address people management issues that affect the NICU nurses on a daily basis. For example:

> We don't deal with the bullying because it's a time constraint . . . there's no time to effectively deal with problems. (Nurse 4)

> It [management of the ward] could be better. I'm not used to the nurse manager just doing all the managerial stuff. Normally they come and help in the ward in other hospitals but here they don't at all, even to relieve nurses for meal breaks. (Nurse 11)

> I'm not sure that they're necessarily as available as they'd like to think they are . . . If you try to contact them that are not always possible . . . They're busy too . . . I don't have a lot of contact with the managers; I get the feeling that they're more looking over your shoulder than giving you help. (Nurse 2)

> There's that difference in objectives. The bedside nurses are very much focused on the bedside outcome and they're not so focused on 'Am I fitting in with that wider hospital framework and adhering to a budget?' (Nurse 5)

Consequences of misdirected energies

There was a perception among the nurses that management did not allocate enough time or energy to managing people within the NICU. Subsequently, the nurses felt that the NUM was unavailable to them, that she did not understand the daily demands of their work. They felt that management did not care about their needs and that the people issues in the ward were managed on a crisis basis that could be managed better.

> I think they've lost touch with what we're doing at night. I think that they think that even though the work is done that somehow we've got all this idle time. (Nurse 2)

> I do think there is a perception that a lot of the nurses on our staff feel that management doesn't understand the stress that they're under . . . and are less than sympathetic to the workload demands . . . I think that's an issue in our unit. (Nurse 10)

Selectivity (in group/out group)

Not only was management perceived to have misdirected their energies away from managing people; they were also seen as being selective in terms of which staff they paid more attention to. Such attention might be in the form of preferential treatment for some, or negative treatment for others; irrespective, it created feelings of inequity in the NICU. According to the nurses interviewed, the manager's behaviour was biased in favour of those who were in the manager's 'ingroup'. Typically this group consisted of senior nurses. Nurses who saw themselves as members of both the 'ingroup' and 'outgroup' reported the existence of these cliques as a source of contention within the department. While those nurses in the 'ingroup' acknowledged the benefits of preferential treatment by their managers, they reported that the managers' favouritism towards certain staff members was noticeable and unfair to other nurses in the ward. They craved a more formally rational and less emotionally prejudiced environment, one in which everyone's emotional needs were acknowledged and managed fairly.

Examples of selectivity include:

> *I'm lucky that my personal relationship with her [NUM] helps me achieve what I want to achieve professionally. I feel guilty if I generalize and say that [she has favourites] because for me personally, I'm very lucky. I don't have this, but I see it. I'm speaking of my experience through other staff. I've witnessed it . . . I've had to pick up the pieces, but provide reassurance or act as an intermediary. (Nurse 4).*

> *the coordinators are ok, but there's one that can take an instant dislike to you and will give you a really hard time and watch everything that you do and give you a really hard time, instead of helping you get through all of that, will just prefer to yell at you about it, give you a hard time and make your life quite miserable . . . In fact she's made two people cry today already. (Nurse 15)*

Consequences of selectivity (in group/out group)

Those nurses who were not given preferential treatment felt unsupported by management and would not voice their opinion for fear of reprimand. Overall, feelings of unfairness and inequity had the flow-on consequence of making nurses feel resentful. Interestingly, the nurses who acknowledged that they received preferential treatment also reported this as a problem for the NICU, suggesting that it contributed to emotional stress and the gap between management and staff:

> *They seek out people that they find are more approachable, who may not necessarily know the answers to their questions. So, it's a double-edged sword as well. (Nurse 4)*

> *It depends on who it was that was giving them a hard time. I don't think that the NUM gives the coordinators a rap across the knuckles . . . I don't know if she ever pulls them in and tells them that she knows and to fix what they're doing. (Nurse 13)*

> *If they're too scared to talk to NUM, they may talk to Julie . . . or they may not even want to talk to Julie . . . but I don't think they'd talk to anybody . . . and that's probably why they go home crying. (Nurse 15).*

Organizational and occupational triggers

Another set of emergent themes was grouped around feelings associated with the job at hand, including role, structure, policies and procedures, a theme labelled 'organizational and occupational triggers'. While these triggers had intra- and interpersonal emotional consequences similar to the intra- and interpersonal issues, their sources were quite different.

Role-based emotion (sick and dying babies)

Nurses made it clear that death, illness and sadness are 'part of the job', and accept that some kind of emotional pain is unavoidable. Understandably, all 16 nurses identified role-based emotion as a source of distress which affected them on both a professional and a personal level. For example:

> *I have been affected before. I've gotten too close to certain families. And it's like you've lost that child. (Nurse 3)*

> *We are trying to have this environment which is caring for the sick babies and the families and I don't believe that people who are not cared for can care for people. (Nurse 12)*

Consequences of role-based emotion (sick and dying babies)

The emotional and sometimes sad nature of the nurses' work at NICU was a contributor to toxic emotions within NICU. All the nurses acknowledged that the majority of patient outcomes were positive but that sadness associated with sick new-born babies and occasional patient deaths takes an emotional toll. They reported feelings of sadness, personal loss and emotional trauma. Some said that they were able to separate their work-related emotions from their home life whereas others reported that the sadness overflowed into interactions with people outside of work. Some nurses also reported that they wanted more accessible and effective grief counselling to be made available to them so as to help them cope:

> *More regular de-briefings would probably be really good for us because we get upset. (Nurse 10)*

> *We don't have any good or working structure to help people debrief. I don't think they've tapped on to the best way to deal with it . . . there's a lot of grief that the nurses are left to deal with it. (Nurse 1).*

Most nurses reported that their coping mechanisms for the tension caused by deaths and patient suffering were as simple as talking with family and friends and displacement through pursuing hobbies outside work. All reported that trying to maintain clearly defined temporal, physical and emotional boundaries between home and work life played a key part in limiting the negative impact of emotional labour on other aspects of their lives. Examples of this include:

> *I think that's because I keep quite clearly defined work hours and they are fairly regular. So when I'm not working I just switch off to another person, and I feel that keeps me strong really. I feel as though I just take off my nursing hat and put on my home hat . . . and the busy-ness of the kids and doing a wide range of other activities stops me from thinking about work. I find I often don't start thinking about it until it's coming around to going back to work. (Nurse 1)*

> *It's just nice to come to work, do the best you can and do the best for those kids and those families and then go home and don't take it with me . . . Before I go home from a shift I make sure I've done everything that I've needed to do for that day . . . if I haven't completed something, then hand it over. Make sure that the person who's taking over from me knows that I haven't finished that, so that it will be done . . . and then that's it, go home. I'm no longer responsible. (Nurse 3)*

Some less frequently mentioned, but important, consequences of role-based emotion reported by a few of the nurses were that being around sick babies and death had made them more appreciative of their family and friends. The senior nurses reported that they had become better at coping with the emotional nature of the job over time and empathized with new nurses for whom the trauma must be harder to deal with. Older nurses or nurses with children who have grown up and are able to take care of themselves reported that the emotional toll of their work was easier to cope with now that they did not worry as much about their own children.

Issues of bureaucracy and hierarchy

The hospital has a stated policy of thanking staff through letters, afternoon teas, and award ceremony dinners, which means that the nurses were dealt with in a routinized, bureaucratic way. In fact, they all had a cynical perception of the intention behind and value of the token gestures of thanks by immediate and general hospital management, and saw them as nothing but symbolically weak gestures from those higher up the bureaucratic chain. Nurses felt that a simple 'thank you' from their NUM would mean much more than these impersonal, formalized and standardized 'thank you' attempts. Failure by the NUM to ensure nurses were personally thanked added to the nurses' cynicism. For example:

> *They have what they call the service awards. They've been having these little ceremonies where people who've been there for 10, 15, 20 years get hauled up and they get presented with a little certificate and this dinky badge. It's about 50 cents worth of brass with a number on it. And you think 'That's the best they can do? 50 cents worth of tin for 15 years of service?' I find that a bit crass. (Nurse 5)*

> *it always seems to be those days when you've had the crappiest day, and you walk out thinking 'Gosh, if only someone had recognized that you've done a good job'. (Nurse 15)*

> *In an institution, it all seems production line like . . . You know they have a morning tea, which is sometimes held at an inconvenient time for you to attend. It's in a tea room 500m from the nursery, which is a pain to leave. At a hospital infrastructure level we don't really get any reward. The director of nursing doesn't come and say 'Gosh. You girls do a good job'. (Nurse 4)*

Consequences of bureaucracy and hierarchy
Nearly all the nurses interviewed expressed that they felt unappreciated and that the attempts to reward them by immediate and hospital management were insincere and mechanical.

> *Everything seems so . . . tokenism. Well that means 'jack' to me because it is mass produced and nobody ever came down and said 'Wow that was a good job'. (Nurse 4)*

> *I know that sometimes they try and they have these afternoon teas and things like that but I think I've gotten to the point where I'm so jaded . . . because it's been so long time in coming, these sorts of rewards and appreciation, I've become cynical towards them now . . . it's like the proverbial pat on the head and 'there, there' everything is alright. (Nurse 6)*

The nurses also expressed how much they value genuine praise and thanks from management:

> *I think it [encouragement] is very important. You can't come to work on a daily basis unless you know that what you're doing makes a difference. That the people around you think that you make a difference and that there is mutual respect amongst team members. That's really important. (Nurse 8)*

Positive aspects of work
Despite the causes of toxicity discussed above, all nurses interviewed reported that the type of work they did with the NICU was the reason they have stayed there. In response to questions regarding personal values and the meaning of life, the NICU nurses reported that their work helped them find meaning which was congruent with their values and beliefs. They all expressed a love of being able to work with babies and families as a source of satisfaction: helping people through their work contributed to their self-confidence and self-esteem. For example:

> *My family appreciate what I do and I think it builds me up and makes me feel that I'm a good person; that I'm doing a good thing by working here . . . I've got a lot of support so that even when I do have horrible days here and I'm very tired, I've got something else to go home to and something else to look forward to . . . so it's not all negative . . . I came back because I enjoy it . . . for the money, of*

> *course, but for the stimulation, the friendship, to catch up with people and have the everyday social side of it . . . I came back because I enjoy it and because it makes up a big part of me. (Nurse 13)*

All 16 nurses stated that they were happy with the level of pay and the opportunities for training and skill development provided by the NICU. While 3 of the 16 nurses reported shift work as being one aspect that they found exhausting to cope with, the other 13 said that having varied working hours was a benefit of the job, as it provided variety in their week and allowed flexibility for family responsibilities.

Functioning and dysfunctioning at work

Analysis revealed that the individual incidences of toxicity could be categorized into two broad themes: 'inter- and intrapersonal emotionality' and 'organizational and occupational triggers'. Within these themes a number of issues emerged that the nurses describe as causing toxic emotions in the NICU – 'emotional management', 'emotional ignorance', 'emotional bullying', 'trust breaking', 'misdirected energies', 'selectivity', 'role-based emotion' and 'policies, procedures and regulations'. Overall, these emerging issues were consistent with the sources of toxicity as defined by Frost (2003b).

Inter- and intrapersonal emotionality

Emotional management

We all experience a range of moods. However, our ability to regulate these moods when interacting with other people affects the nature of these interactions. The NICU nurses described how the unit manager (NUM) allowed her moods to affect the way in which she interacted with staff and how this directly affected the overall atmosphere within the NICU. From the NUM's own comments, she appeared to be able to recognize her own mood changes; however, such recognition did not prevent her moods affecting the way she interacted with staff.

There are some similarities between 'emotional management' and 'insensitivity' as defined by Frost (2003b). 'Insensitivity' stems from managers who are emotionally unintelligent. Goleman (2004) identifies one of the keys to effective leadership as having a capacity for self-regulation: managers able to modulate their behaviour such that it is appropriate to the situation and sensitive to the feelings of others are better able to establish positive psychological and emotional connections with employees (Goleman et al., 2002; Luthans and Avolio, 2003). The NICU nurses stated that the moodiness of their manager had a negative impact on their desire to be around her and their willingness to communicate openly with her. The NUM's lack of self-regulation had a deleterious effect on the atmosphere of the NICU that, by its nature, was already quite serious and sad. Upbeat moods make people view other people and events in a more positive light, in turn making them feel more optimistic about their own abilities at work (Goleman et al., 2002). Given the frequency of upsetting events in the NICU, an improvement in the NUM's 'emotional management' would have been particularly beneficial to the emotional well-being and longevity of the nurses' careers.

Emotional ignorance

Many managers feel the pressures of meeting deadlines and having to please many people external to their team. Consequently, some managers do not always consider the repercussions of their behaviour and decisions on members of their team. NICU management was also 'insensitive' to emotional needs in this respect. The current management assumption is that parents of babies are always in the right if they complain. Nurses feel betrayed and unsupported when they are not afforded the opportunity to present their perspective before being accused of poor performance. The NUM's focus on meeting budgets to maintain a positive image for the NICU among management meant that she behaved in ways that made the nurses feel unappreciated, misunderstood and undervalued. Research by POB scholars suggests that ensuring that employees feel that their work is valued is vital for cultivating individual and team resiliency, confidence and optimism (Emmons, 2003; Luthans and Youssef, 2004).

Emotional bullying

Bullying is repeated and unprovoked verbal or physical aggressive behaviour by one individual towards another. Workplace bullying is the infliction of a hostile work environment upon an employee through verbal and non-verbal behaviours (Vickers, 2001). Not all bullying is intentional. Some bullies are ignorant that their bullying behaviour is wrong. Some may be stressed, because of increasing managerial pressures imposed by sources external to their team, resulting in uncharacteristic bullying behaviour (Vickers, 2001), which seemed to be the case with the NICU management. The nurses perceived their manager to be, generally, a good person. However, they reported that, in her role as a manager, she often bullied them, bringing hostility to their work environment. The bullying at NICU was primarily manifest in the use of guilt and a threatening tone to coerce nurses to work extra shifts and take on more than reasonable workloads. In this way management encroached on the nurses' non-work domains.

'Emotional bullying' within the context of the NICU is consistent with Frost's sources of toxicity of 'intrusiveness', which occurs when leaders use emotional capital to manipulate the behaviour of employees for the benefit of the organization (Frost, 2003b). However, Frost's focus is on the charismatic leader using their own personality and charm to create emotional ties to persuade the employee to work harder. Instead this manager used her legitimate authority, and the emotionality of dealing with sick babies to impose guilt on nurses to take extra shifts. In this way she coerced her nurses into compromising other aspects of their life, such as family time. It has been shown that when people feel forced into behaviours, they are less likely to approach the behaviour with a positive attitude (Goleman, 2003). Additionally, coercive techniques result in feelings of resentment and frustration towards the perpetrator, as shown in the case of the NICU nurses.

Trust breaking

Interpersonal trust is essential to sustaining effective teams, and it is leaders who are primarily responsible for establishing and developing trust in teams (Gillespie and Mann, 2004). Frost (2003b) defines 'infidelity' as the betrayal of an employee's trust by a manager. The nurses reported various situations in which they felt their trust was abused by management. Thus they were reluctant to invest extra effort in their work or into developing the NICU. Moreover, this created emotional and psychological distance between the nurses and management. 'Infidelity' in the NICU was another cause of the toxic emotions of feeling undervalued and unsupported by management. Moreover, the nurses report that, if betrayed once, they were less inclined to trust managers again and were more cynical towards management intentions and decisions.

Misdirected energies
'Misdirected energies' was one aspect of 'incompetence' as defined by Frost (2003b). Often managers were so preoccupied with running from meeting to meeting or with managing relationships with clients or members of the wider organization that they did not take time to focus on their own employees' concerns or needs. Over time this built resentment that depleted employee loyalty to the hospital and the manager. The NUM had been with the NICU for years as a nurse and had progressed to management level over time. As such, she had been successful in rising through the hospital ranks because of her strong nursing technical skills. However, according to the nurses, she was ineffective in areas of management such as managing and nurturing relationships (Luthans, 1988).

Selectivity (in group/out group)
Leader–member exchange (LMX) theory is a well-established theory that states that those employees who are considered part of a manager's ingroup have high-quality exchanges. Managers give theses employees preferential treatment, such as increased information, latitude and discretion (Gomez and Rosen, 2001; Davis and Gardener, 2004). Some employees are empowered while the converse happens to those in the manager's outgroup. The perceived injustice of this favouritism by those in the outgroup, in turn, leads to a perception that the psychological contract has been broken (Davis and Gardener, 2004). LMX research shows that ingroup members are chosen by managers based on their assessment of employees skills, motivation to assume greater responsibility, and the extent to which they think employees' can be trusted (Gomez and Rosen, 2001). The nurses report that NICU management had obvious favourites, and displayed distinct preferential treatment towards these employees in terms of patient allocation, assistance with career development, and by her general manner of interaction. The nurses reported that the NUM's ingroup consisted mostly of senior nurses, creating a feeling of mistrust in the junior nurses and a reluctance to communicate openly with the NUM.

Organizational and occupational triggers

Role -based emotion (sick and dying babies)
The NICU nurses must deal with the emotional implications of engaging in highly emotional work on a daily basis. Frequently, being faced with the sadness associated with the death and illness of babies has significant repercussions for nurses' psychological and emotional well-being. The NICU nurses acknowledge that this is implicit in their work but are unhappy with the fact that management seem to expect them to remain unaffected by babies' deaths. They feel there is little emotional counselling and assistance to help them process their grief and sadness. The result is that nurses cope by themselves by debriefing with friends, family and other nurses, or often bottle up their emotions. As Luthans and Youssef (2004) explain, there are many potential team benefits that well-managed crises can have for an organization, such as greater feelings of organizational identity, heightened insight and awareness of the organization's vulnerabilities, greater insight into addressing issues relevant to leadership of the team, and an enhanced sense of emotional, spiritual

and existential aspects of organizational life (Luthans and Youssef, 2004). Hence there is the opportunity for NICU management to foster team unity and encourage organizational loyalty by proactively helping the nurses to deal with traumatic events as a team.

Bureaucracy and hierarchy

Toxin can flow from everyday practices, often unintentionally. It can be exacerbated when management is insensitive to the ways it affects employees who try to make the system work. The hospital's attempts to show the nurses gratitude was another source of toxicity that resonated repeatedly among the nurses. The hospital's HRM policies ensure that there are official recognition procedures for staff. Examples include staff recognition ceremonies and official hospital thank-you letters. The nurses feel that these efforts are insincere and only pay lip-service to their hard work; because management rarely offer personal thanks, the nurses are actually offended by these systematized 'thank yous'. Thus toxicity occurs when day-to-day interactions with management are not consistent with such institutionalized acts of gratitude. Being forced to comply with rules can cause negative emotions, such as resentment, and can influence employees' attitude towards their work and organization. Another aspect of 'institutional' toxicity is when there are discrepancies between a stated company policy and what actually happens: employees feel demoralized and lose faith in management and trust in the organization. Given that nurturing others is part of their job description and that they work in an emotionally intense context, being shown that they are valued is very important for their own self-worth and emotional well-being (Diers, 2004).

Table 12.1 summarizes the key specific consequences of each source of toxicity identified within the NICU. As Frost (2003b) points out, events are not toxic in and of themselves but become sources of negativity due to the way in which they are managed – or

Table 12.1   Consequences of NICU toxicity

NICU sources of toxicity	Consequence
Emotional management	Reported thoughts of quitting, nervousness, fear of voicing opinion, management is unapproachable
Emotional ignorance	Feeling that one is afforded insufficient respect, is taken for granted, becoming angry and hurt
Emotional bullying	Reported thoughts of quitting, avoidance of communication with management, complain to each other, gap between manager and staff
Trust breaking	Feeling devalued, less motivated at work, cynical and resentful towards management
Role-based emotion	Wanting more counselling
Issues of bureaucracy and hierarchy	Feeling unappreciated and cynical towards management
Misdirected energies	Feeling uncared for and unimportant
Selectivity (ingroup/outgroup)	Those in the outgroup are afraid to voice their opinion; they perceive inequity and unfairness at work, and experience a gap between management and staff

mismanaged, as was evident in the interviews with the nurses. Occurrences at work only became sources of toxicity for the nurses when they were mismanaged. It is important to note that not all of the nurses who reported some incidences were actually involved in them; however, being a witness had an impact upon their opinions and feeling towards management and their job. Most reported that even one negative incident between management and a nurse can have a significant and toxic impact on the overall morale of the nurses in NICU, which speaks to Frost's notion that toxicity spreads throughout organizations with devastating results (Barsade, 2003; Frost, 2003b).

Implications for NICU management

NICU management does not seem to be aware, or even seem to acknowledge, that nurses perceive staff turnover as resulting from the NUM's mismanagement of issues important to them. The NUM attributes the staff turnover primarily to reasons such as marriage, travel and moving interstate or overseas. The question raised here is whether the NUMs' acknowledge that issues raised by the nurses about management are important. If they fail to acknowledge their role in the creation of problems at NICU it is quite possible that they may not recognize the issues raised herein. The study highlights that nurses perceive NICU management as causing toxicity, which acts as a major trigger in their thoughts about leaving the ward. The implication for management is that if they want to address the issues as stated by their nurses, they will need to accept some ownership of the causes and consequences of toxic emotions. Thus, by taking some ownership of the issues, the NICU management can directly address the toxicity being caused and have greater control over issues affecting staff retention, or at least nurses' thoughts about leaving the NICU.

The NUM needs to be aware that her actions are particularly significant for the junior nurses, who report that they struggle to cope with the already highly emotional environment of the NICU when they first start. The extent to which they do or do not feel initially supported by management is especially relevant to how secure they feel at work, which in turn affects their intention to stay within the NICU. As reported by the nurses, the 'emotional bullying' and 'emotional management' toxins stemming from the NUM are particularly difficult to cope with. Especially for newer staff, with many questions, it can be difficult when they are afraid to approach their NUM for assistance or clarification. Research studies into bullying at work affirm these findings and have shown that employees who perceive their supervisor to be abusive are more likely to quit their jobs. Those who remain in their jobs are associated with lower levels of job and life satisfaction, commitment to work, conflict between work and family and higher psychological distress (Tepper, 2000).

Another important concern that NICU managers need to re-evaluate is the emphasis they place on creating and building trust with the nurses. Employees' trust in their managers has been related to a range of productivity-related processes and outcomes, such as the quality of communication, problem-solving discretionary effort, organizational commitment, citizenship behaviour and the rate of employee turnover (Gillespie and Mann, 2004). As shown in the results section, incidences of betrayal of trust result in the nurses feeling less motivated and more cynical towards management actions. In turn, this impedes the cultivation of an open communication culture in the NICU. Given the nature of their work and the importance of the daily work decisions the nurses need to make regarding patient care, nurses must be able to trust each other and their managers. NICU management is directly responsible for promoting and encouraging trust among the nurses.

The NICU nurses reported that feeling unappreciated and undervalued by management was detrimental to their feelings about working at the NICU. POB studies show that displays of gratitude and a gratitude culture can improve individual well-being and lower toxic emotions, such as resentment, in the workplace. Moods are important determinants of efficiency, success, productivity and employee loyalty. Recent studies have demonstrated that employee happiness and well-being are positively associated with absenteeism, turnover and burnout (Emmons, 2003). It also quite notable that the nurses reported that issues within the theme of 'intra- and interpersonal emotionality' triggered thoughts or intentions to leave the NICU, rather than the organizational or role-based issues. This further highlights the importance of managing emotions at work. Frost's (2003b) work on toxic emotions emphasizes the importance of 'toxic handling'. This study reiterates the need for managers proactively to manage toxins within the workplace. Indeed, as Luthans (1988) points out, this is the difference between successful and effective managers, and those that are incompetent.

Another implication of this study is that management would greatly benefit from training in people management skills. As mismanagement of emotionality seems to be the key trigger for nurses' thoughts about leaving the NICU, such training could help in fostering sustainable work practices. The nurses report they are very happy with the work itself, the opportunities for training and remuneration. Therefore, these are strengths the managers can use to create and enhance relationships between the nurses and the NICU, as well as at wider levels of the hospital. As the POB literature emphasizes, central to fortifying worker performance and job satisfaction is proactive enhancement of strengths.

The nurses have a strong personal desire and respect for the work they do. Being able to assist patients and families in times of crisis is a motivating factor for the nurses to stay with the NICU. Management has significant opportunity to focus the role-based emotionality of NICU nursing to strengthen team unity, self-efficacy and organizational identity (Clair and Dufresne, 2004). It is particularly important for NICU management to be aware of this due to the frequency of traumatic events that occur in the NICU. If mismanaged or left unmanaged, workplace-related trauma can easily result in dissonance between nurses, their co-workers and their managers.

Implications for management researchers

For management researchers the present report adds value to the initial studies by Frost on 'toxic emotions at work', by providing a socially constructed theory that confirms Frost's notions of toxicity and toxic handling. Additionally these findings contribute to Frost's study by positing a relationship between specific consequences and sources of toxicity. Management informed by toxic handling theory would be better able to focus training, development and managerial effort on recognizing the consequences of toxicity (as a symptom) and to locate the cause. Frost's work has been extended by discovering ways of identifying specific toxin causes. With this knowledge, managers can then develop targeted strategies to manage specific sources of toxicity.

Table 12.2 summarizes the parallels between Frost's 'seven deadly INs' and the sources of toxicity that emerged from analysis of the nurses.

Table 12.2   Comparison of Frost's 'INs' with NICU sources of toxicity

Frost's corresponding 'IN'	NICU sources of toxicity
Insensitivity	Emotional management, emotional ignorance
Infidelity	Trust breaking
Intrusiveness	Emotional bullying
Inevitability	Role-based emotion
Incompetence	Misdirected energies
Intention	Selectivity (ingroup/outgroup)
Institutional	Bureaucracy and hierarchy

Functions and dysfunctions as complex spaces

Our research in this case study has highlighted that perceptions of functionality and dysfunctionality in the workplace are always open to interpretation. Sometimes there is little coherence between staff, and even less coherence between staff and management in terms of functional organizational behaviour. How staff experience dysfunction can often differ from how management experiences dysfunction; hence issues and problems may often go unreconciled. Sometimes, these differences manifest themselves in ways that apparently have little implication for organizational performance. That is, nurses will hardly cease their duty of care towards an ill baby. To this extent organizational functioning may appear 'normal'. However, the increasing level of dissent, turnover, anger and frustration is a manifestation of serious organizational dysfunction. As we have seen in our analysis, these dysfunctions are experienced as negative emotions, cognitions and behaviours that fit Frost's (2003) concept of toxic emotions at work. The implication is that managers are experiencing, interpreting and assessing one idea of organizational dysfunction, while staff are experiencing, interpreting and assessing an entirely different idea. In other words, there is a lack of voice, shared sensemaking and collaborative behaviour.

Moreover, our study did not look into some other important issues about workplace functionality and dysfunctionality. In this chapter we have given the impression that the experience of functionality and dysfunctionality was one expressed solely through manager/subordinate relations. To present such an impression is false. There were similarly 'functional' and 'dysfunctional' relationships between the nurses, as there were functional and dysfunctional relationships between managers, although we have had insufficient space or occasion to stress these in the confines of this chapter. In other words, the experience of workplace functionality and dysfunctionality was omnipresent and not restricted to management and their staff. Future research might look at these different experiences.

Conclusion

There is an important lesson to be learnt about humans working in emotionally intensive and stressful conditions. Experience of pain and adversity affects workers' spirits, and these results demonstrate that the key to successful emotional management is to understand and respect staff, rather than exploit their pain. As such, managers should be toxic handlers and be skilled in managing human relationships at work, with all that that entails. The NICU nurses are remarkable examples of how resilient, patient, caring and generous people can be pushed to their limits by managers lacking strength and abilities in people management from a humanist, positive psychological perspective. As positive organizational behaviour literature and research suggests, placing focus on these human strengths is the key to ensuring a healthy and stable workforce. Frost's (2003b) acknowledgement of the need to take a positive approach towards the potentially negative elements of working life certainly provides great insight into the skills and abilities that need to be taught to managers of the future. They must learn not only how to manage reporting upwards in terms of performance indicators, but also reconcile such adequacy with their capacity to manage other people in humane and respectful ways. In this regard, management, and management education, still seems to have a long journey ahead of it, if even in 'caring professions' so little care can be routinely exhibited.

Notes

1. Positive organizational behaviour (POB) and positive organizational scholarship (POS) both evolved out of positive psychology (PP). While some attempts have been made to differentiate POB from POS, the distinction is for the most part quite trivial. Hence, for brevity we treat both terms the same. This is not to say the POB and POS will not evolve into distinct entities, but presently they have not.
2. Moreover, there is also a great deal of conceptual baggage in the social sciences' use of the term positive, reaching back as far as Comte and St Simon in their eighteenth-century quest for a positive science of society, which becomes transmogrified in some twentieth-century organizational theory into positivist science (Donaldson, 1996).

References

Ashforth, B. (1993), 'Emotional labour in service roles: the influence of identity', *Academy of Management Review*, **18**(1), 88–116.

Atkinson, S. (2004), 'Senior management relationships and trust: an exploratory study', *Journal of Managerial Psychology*, **19**(6), 571–87.

Australian Local Government Information Service (2004), 'The Karpin Report', www.parklane.com.au/austext/karpin.htm, (accessed 27/11), p. 1.

Bagozzi, R. (2003), 'Positive and negative emotions in organizations', in K. Cameron, J. Dutton and R. Quinn (eds), *Positive Organizational Scholarship: Foundations of a New Discipline*, San Francisco, CA: Berrett Koehler, pp. 176–93.

Barsade, S.G. (2003), 'The ripple effect: emotional contagion and its influence on group behaviour', *Administrative Science Quarterly*, **47**(4), 644–76.

Bolman, L.G. and Deal, T.E. (2003), *Reframing Organizations: Artistry, Choice and Leadership*, 3nd edn, San Francisco, CA: Jossey-Bass.

Boyle, M.V. and Healy, J. (2003), 'Balancing mysterium and onus: doing spiritual work within an emotion-laden organizational context', *Organization Articles*, **10**(2), 351–73.

Cameron, K., Dutton, J., Quinn, R. and Wrzesniewski, A. (2003), 'Developing a discipline of positive organizational scholarship', in K. Cameron, J. Dutton and R. Quinn (eds), *Positive Organizational Scholarship: Foundations of a New Discipline*, San Francisco, CA: Berrett Koehler, pp. 361–70.

Cavanagh, G. (1999), 'Spirituality for managers: context and critique', *Journal of Change Management*, **12**(3), 84–195.

Chan, C. (2001), 'Implications of organizational learning for nursing managers from the cultural, interpersonal and systems thinking perspectives', *Nursing Inquiry*, **8**(3), 196–9.

Clair, J.A. and Dufresne, R.L. (2004), 'Phoenix rising: positive consequence arising from organizational crisis', presented at Academy of Management Conference.

Clegg, S.R. and Chua, W.-F. (1989), 'Contradictory couplings: occupational ideology and organizational context in nursing', *The Journal of Management Studies*, **26**(2), 103–28.

Clegg, S.R. and Chua, W.-F. (1990), 'Professional closure: the case of British nursing', *Theory and Society*, **19**, 135–72.

Clegg, S.R., Kornberger, M. and Pitsis, T.S. (2005), *Managing and Organizations: An introduction to theory and practice*, London: Sage.

Cohen-Katz, J., Wiley, S.D., Capuano, T.B. and Shapiro, S. (2004), 'The effects of mindfulness-based stress reduction on nurse stress and burnout', *Holistic Nursing Practice*, **18**(6), 302–9.

Collis, J. and Hussey, R. (2003), *Business Research: A Practical Guide for Undergraduate and Postgraduate Students*, 2nd edn, New York: Palgrave Macmillan.

Davis, W.D. and Gardener, W.L. (2004), 'Perceptions of politics and organizational cynicism: an attributional and leader–member exchange perspective', *Leadership Quarterly*, 15(4), 439–65.

Diers, D. (2004), *Speaking of Nursing: Narrative of Practice, Research, Policy and the Profession*, Boston, MA: Jones and Bartlett.

Donaldson, L. (1996), *For Positivist Organization Theory*, London: Sage.

Dunphy, D. and Benveniste, J. (2000), 'An introduction to the sustainable corporation', in D. Dunphy, J. Benveniste, A. Griffiths and P. Sutton (eds), *Sustainability – The Corporate Challenge of the 21st Century*, Melbourne: Allen & Unwin, pp. 5–10.

Dunphy, D. and Pitsis, T.S. (2003), 'This wisdom of leadership', in C. Barker and R. Coye (eds), *7 Heavenly Virtues of Leadership*, Melbourne: McGraw-Hill, pp. 166–97.

Dutton, J.E. and Heaphy, E.D. (2003), 'The power of high-quality connections', in K. Cameron, J. Dutton and R. Quinn (eds), *Positive Organizational Scholarship: Foundations of a New Discipline*, San Francisco, CA: Berrett Koehler, pp. 263–78.

Eisenhardt, K.M. (1989), 'Building theories from case study research', *Academy of Management Review*, 14(4), 532–50.

Emmons, R.A. (2003), 'Acts of gratitude in organizations', in K. Cameron, J. Dutton and R. Quinn (eds), *Positive Organizational Scholarship: Foundations of a New Discipline*, San Francisco, CA: Berrett Koehler, pp. 81–93.

Fineman, S. (2006), 'On being positive: concerns and counterpoints', *Academy of Management Review*, 31(2), 270–91.

Fredrickson, B.L. (2003), 'Positive emotions and upwards spirals in organizations', in K. Cameron, J. Dutton, and R. Quinn (eds), *Positive Organizational Scholarship: Foundations of a New Discipline*, San Francisco, CA: Berrett Koehler, pp. 163–75.

Frost, P. J. (2003a), 'The hidden work of leadership', *Leader to Leader*, Fall, 13–18.

Frost, P.J. (2003b), *Toxic Emotions at Work*, Boston, MA: Harvard Business School Press.

Garcia-Zamor, J. (2003), 'Workplace spirituality and organizational performance', *Public Administration Review*, 63(3), 355–63.

Geertz, C. (1973), *The Interpretation of Cultures*, New York: Basic Books.

Gillespie, N.A. and Mann, L. (2004), 'Transformational leadership and shared values: the building blocks of trust', *Journal of Managerial Psychology*, 19(6), 588–607.

Gladwin, T.N. and Kennelly, J.J. (1995), 'Shifting paradigms for sustainable development: implications for management theory and research', *Academy of Management Review*, 20(4), 874–908.

Goleman, D., Boyatzis, R. and McKee, A. (2002), *The New Leaders: Transforming the Art of Leadership into the Science of Results*, London: Time Warner Paperbacks.

Goleman, D. (2003), *Destructive Emotions, and how we overcome them*, London: Bantam Dell.

Goleman, D. (2004), 'What makes a leader?', *Harvard Business Review*, 82(1), 82–91.

Gollan, P. (2000), 'Human resources, capabilities and sustainabilities', in D. Dunphy, J. Benveniste, A. Griffths and P. Sutton (eds), *Sustainability – The Corporate Challenge of the 21ˢᵗ Century*, Melbourne: Allen Unwin, pp. 55–77.

Gomez, C. and Rosen, B. (2001), 'The leader–member exchange as link between managerial trust and employee empowerment', *Group & Organization Management*, 26(1), 53–69.

Higgs, M. (2004), 'A study of the relationship between emotional intelligence and performance in UK call centres', *Journal of Managerial Psychology*, 19(4), 442–54.

Kanov, J.M., Maitlis, S., Worline, M.C., Dutton, J.E., Frost, P.J. and Lilius, J. (2004), 'Compassion in organizational life', *American Behavioral Scientist*, 47(6), 808–27.

Kohn, C. and Henderson, C.W. (2002), 'Study looks at nurse workloads', *Managed Care Weekly Digest*, 25 November, pp. 12–14.

Kvale, S. (1996), *InterViews: An Introduction to Qualitative Research Interviewing*, Thousand Oaks, CA: Sage.

Lazarus, R.S. (2003), 'Does the positive psychology movement have legs?', *Psychological Inquiry*, 14(2), 93–109.

Lubit, R. (2004), *Coping with Toxic Managers, Subordinates and Other Difficult People*, Upper Saddle River, NJ: Prentice Hall.

Luthans, F. (1988), 'Successful vs. effective managers', *Academy of Management Executive*, 2(2), 127–33.

Luthans, F. (2002a), 'The need for and meaning of positive organizational behaviour', *Journal of Organizational Behaviour*, 23(6), 635.

Luthans, F. (2002b), 'Positive organizational behaviour: developing and managing psychological strengths', *Academy of Management Executive*, 16(1), 1–11.

Luthans, F. and Avolio, B. (2003), 'Authentic leadership development', in K. Cameron, J. Dutton and R. Quinn (eds), *Positive Organizational Scholarship: Foundations of a New Discipline*, San Francisco, CA: Berrett Koehler, pp. 241–58.

Luthans, F. and Youssef, C.M. (2004), 'Human, social and now positive psychological capital management: investing in people for competitive advantage', *Organizational Dynamics*, **33**(2), 143–60.

Muecke, M. (1994), 'On the evaluation of ethnographies', in J.M. Morse (ed.), *Critical Issues in Qualitative Research Methods*, Thousand Oak, CA: Sage, pp. 187–209.

Neil, J.A., Lichtenstein, B.M.B and Banner, D. (1999), 'Spiritual perspectives on individual, organizational and societal transformation', *Journal of Organizational Change Management*, **12**(3), 175–86.

Pitsis, T.S. (2007), 'Project life: the pragmatic phenomenological psychology of project based organizing', in S.R. Clegg and C. L. Cooper (eds), *The Handbook of Macro-Organizational Behavior*, Thousand Oaks, CA: Sage.

Pitsis, T.S., Kornberger, M. and Clegg, S. (2004), 'The art of managing relationships in interorganizational collaboration', *Management*, **7**(3), 47–67.

Pitsis, T.S. and Clegg, S.R. (2007), 'Beware the words of the wise: managerial wisdom and influence', in Eric H. Kessler and James R. Bailey (eds), *Handbook of Organizational and Managerial Wisdom*, Thousand Oaks, CA: Sage.

Pratt, M.G. and Rosa, J.A. (2003), 'Transforming work–family conflict into commitment in network marketing organizations', *Academy of Management Journal*, **46**(4), 395–418.

Schnieder, Z., Elliott, D., LoBiondo-Wood, G. and Haber, J. (2002), *Nursing Research: Methods, critical appraisal and utilisation*, 2nd edn, Sydney: Elsevier, pp. 186–7.

Seligman, M. and Csikszentmihalyi, M. (2000), 'Positive psychology: an introduction', *American Psychologist*, **55**(1), 5–14.

Shirey, M.R. (2006), 'Authentic leaders creating healthy work environments for nursing practice', *American Journal of Critical Care*, **15**, 256–68.

Snyder, C.R. and Lopez, Shane J. (2007), *Positive Psychology: The Scientific and Practical Explorations of Human Strengths*, Thousand Oaks, CA: Sage.

Strauss, A. and Corbin, J. (1998), *Basics of Qualitative Research: Techniques and Procedures for Developing Grounded Theory*, 2nd edn, Thousand Oaks, CA: Sage.

Tepper, B.J. (2000), 'Consequences of abusive supervision', *Academy of Management Journal*, **43**(2), 178–91.

Vickers, M.H. (2001), 'Bullying as unacknowledged organizational evil: a researcher's story', *Employee Responsibilities and Rights Journal*, **13**(4), 205–16.

Weick, K.E. (2003), 'Positive organizing and organizational tragedy', in K. Cameron, J. Dutton and R. Quinn (eds), *Positive Organizational Scholarship: Foundations of a New Discipline*, San Francisco, CA: Berrett Koehler, pp. 66–80.

Yin, R.K. (2003), *Case Study Research: Design and Methods*, 3rd edn, Thousand Oaks, CA: Sage.

Zapf, D., Vogt, C., Seifert C., Mertini, H. and Isic, A. (1999), 'Emotion work as a source of stress: the concept and development of an instrument', *European Journal of Work and Organizational Psychology*, **8**(3), 317–400.

Zellars, K., Tepper, B. and Duffy, M. (2002), 'Abusive supervision and subordinates' organizational citizenship behaviour', *Journal of Applied Psychology*, **87**(6), 1068–76.

13 Humor in organizations: no laughing matter
Robert E. Wood, Nadin Beckmann and Fiona Pavlakis

Introduction

The positive effects of humor have provided justification for the increasing use of humor interventions in customer services, leadership, problem solving, teams and coping with stress, to name a few applications. These prescriptions ignore the fact that much of the humor in organizational behavior is negative and likely to have detrimental effects on individuals and groups. We outline a multidimensional conceptualization of humor and link the four different types (affiliative, self-enhancing, aggressive and self-defeating humor) to individual differences in the production and reactions to humor. We then discuss negative forms of humor as a type of dysfunctional organizational behavior that is related to health risk behaviors, unproductive cultural norms, exclusion of individuals from groups, maintenance of status differentials and negative team cultures. The implications for future research and the need for research on negative humor, along with other forms of dysfunctional organizational behavior, as a counterbalance to the positive psychology research agenda in organizational behavior are discussed.

Humor can be either a coping mechanism for people confronting dysfunctional organizational behavior or a type of dysfunctional behavior that generates stress and other dysfunctional outcomes. The apparently contradictory relationships between humor and dysfunctional behavior are explained by the different types of humor and their differing effects in organizations. In this chapter, we define dysfunctional organizational behavior as behavior that has dysfunctional consequences for individuals and social relationships within organizations. Thus we use 'dysfunctional' to refer to behavior that has deleterious effects rather than behavior that has null or unintended effects. When humor makes a person feel inadequate, lowers self-confidence or causes stress, we consider those dysfunctional outcomes and the humor that produced them dysfunctional behavior. Similarly, humor that excludes individuals from interpersonal relationships and groups or supports cynical cultural beliefs is treated as dysfunctional. Most research has tended to focus on the potentially positive effects of humor, with relatively little attention being given to negative humor and its dysfunctional outcomes.

Humor is a pervasive, naturally occurring behavior in organizational life. Jokes and other sources of humor are communicated face to face, via memos, written reports and other documents and, increasingly, via email and other forms of electronic communication. In organizations, humor has unique properties. For example, as a form of communication, humor cuts across authority and status boundaries, flows in all directions, moves much more rapidly than formal communication, and is largely unfiltered (Barsoux, 1996). Humor also tends to illuminate the paradoxes, ambiguities and contradictions that inevitably arise in organizations despite management's attempts to maintain rational, structured patterns of action (Hatch and Ehrlich, 1993). Humor also brings together cognitive and emotional processes of organizations in a single frame.

Despite the pervasiveness of humor in organizations, there has been very little study of humor in management or organizational settings. The surge of interest in humor that was evident in the psychological literature in the 1980s (Foot, 1991) has not been evident in the writings on management or organizational behavior. The available literature can be divided into prescriptive arguments, which treat humor as a critical organizational resource that can facilitate communication, creativity, problem solving and tolerance (e.g. Boverie et al., 1994), and descriptive studies of conditions, such as paradox and ambiguity, that give rise to humor in organizations (Hatch and Ehrlich, 1993). Very few studies speak to the issues of the effects of humor in organizations.

The lack of evidence notwithstanding, there are many prescriptions and organizational programs based on the assumption that humor is a positive organizational behavior. Such activities, are, for example: establishing a humor room (Kodak Eastman, Hewlett Packard), hiring corporate comedians (American Cancer Society, American Academy of Physician Assistants), clowns (therapeutic clowning in disaster management, Red Nose Response, Inc.), and humor consultants (Owens–Corning Fiberglass used humor consultants to run workshops for their employees when they laid off 40 percent), including humor in the mission statement (Grimes Aerospace, Highway Insurance, Zapatec Software), stressing the utilization of humor in customer service (from a SouthWest Airlines employee: 'There may be 50 ways to leave your lover, but there are only 4 ways out of this airplane'), and implementing fun at work through programs, such as a bring-your-animal-to-work program (Autodesk Software).

The justifications for these interventions were based on claims that humor in organizations is energizing, breaks up boredom and fatigue, and increases attention levels (e.g. laughter releases endorphins into the body, increases oxygen intake, burns up calories), facilitates communication and breaks up conflict and tension, builds relationships, enhances staff cohesion and team work, increases creativity, enhances productivity, provides new perspectives and reduces stress, enhances learning and creates a positive culture. Many of these claims can be backed up by research evidence from areas outside of organizational behavior. However, as we argue in later sections of this chapter, the positive view of humor presented ignores the dysfunctional effects of negative forms of humor, including sarcasm, aggressive and mean-spirited humor and self-defeating humor.

In the following sections, we first describe different types of humor within a two-by-two typology that differentiates humor in terms of valence (positive or negative) and the target (self or other) and links the four different types of humor to personal characteristics and organizational outcomes, with specific attention to gender-related differences. This is followed by a section in which we review and discuss the research that points to the dysfunctional effects of negative humor. In the final section we present our conclusions and some suggestions on future research into the role of humor in dysfunctional organizational behavior.

Humor is more than happy hah hah

As with many psychological constructs, there has been considerable debate over what exactly constitutes humor and the definitions have changed both over time and as a function of the specific issues being investigated. From an individual perspective, humor is a complex mental ability based on the interplay of multiple cognitive–affective processes (Shammi and Stuss, 1999). Neuropsychological research suggests that the right frontal region mediates humor comprehension. Damage in the right frontal lobe – an area related to integrating cognitive and affective information – disrupts the ability to appreciate humor (Shammi and Stuss, 2003). Measures of a range of basic cognitive functions (working memory, visual scanning, focus on detail) and more complex cognitive abilities (verbal intelligence, creativity) have repeatedly been found to correlate with humor cognition tested in clinical samples (patients with brain lesions) and non-clinical samples of students and other participants (Shammi and Stuss, 1999, 2003; Feingold and Mazzella, 1991). Feingold and Mazzella (1991), however, argue that the humor ability can be distinguished from verbal intelligence. While humor reasoning is related to verbal intelligence, no relation has been found between verbal intelligence and memory for humorous material. Shammi and Stuss (1999) also distinguished humor comprehension from affective humor appreciation. In their study, elderly respondents showed a deficit in the cognitive comprehension of humor – arguably based on diminished cognitive abilities with aging – but not in the affective appreciation of humor (Shammi and Stuss, 1999).

Some authors focus on the positive communicative function of humor and conceptualize it as a social skill that leads to greater acceptance and influence in interpersonal relations (e.g. Dews et al., 1995; Sala, 2000). Observations of joking behavior in various work contexts (e.g. meetings) suggest that humor can provide flexibility in the communication of messages that might otherwise be rejected. Thus humor can be used to critique in socially acceptable ways (Grugulis, 2002; Holmes and Mara, 2002), to point out ambiguity (Grugulis, 2002) or deviations from expectations (Ullian, 1976), or to suggest alternative perspectives within a problem space (Grugulis, 2002; Hatch, 1997). The only experimental study on communicative functions of humor revealed that ironic criticism was perceived as funnier and less insulting than literal criticism, and that irony damaged the addressee–addressor relationship less than literal criticism (Dews et al., 1995). In follow-up qualitative analyses the authors identified a self-protective function of irony. Irony regarding poor performance protected the addressee's face; irony regarding offensive behavior protected the addressor's face (Dews et al., 1995).

Humor is also defined in terms of its effects on the recipient (e.g.Weaver and Cotrell, 1987: 177), with a particular emphasis on laughing, smiling, or a feeling of amusement. The focus on these three responses is due to their recognized benefits. Laughing, that is, genuine laughter, engages positive affect or emotion via the sympathetic nervous system and is the basis of much of the research on humor and its effects. It is also noteworthy that forced laughter, as may occur in a group audience, can also increase positive affect, whereas suppressed laughter, which can occur in group or one-on-one contexts, appears to render the recipient's perception of humor as being less funny, although it is not clear whether suppressed laughter reduces positive affect (Cetola and Reno, 1985). A second response to humor, smiling, is short of laughing but it can, with the often-accompanying body relaxation, via efferent feedback from the muscles, intensify positive affect (Laird, 1974). On the other hand, suppressed smiling, as may occur in 'serious' management situations, can reduce felt affect (Lanzetta et al., 1976; Petty et al., 1983; see also Zillmann, 1991). The third response to humor, a feeling of amusement, should really be referred to as a perception of amusement, that is, the cognitive apprehension that humor has occurred. This perception can occur without felt affect. Laughter, smiling and feelings of amusement are most reliably elicited by some form of perceived incongruity (such as a deliberate joke) but can also be elicited, although less consistently, in situations of failure or disappointment, relief from a threat, or elation at mastering a task (Boverie et al., 1994).

A limitation of the typical conceptualizations of humor described above is their narrow focus on humor as an adaptive response with positive benefits for the individuals involved. They ignore the potential for negative or maladaptive outcomes, such as might arise when one person is the target of an ethnic joke that others find funny. More recently, researchers have begun to define humor as a multidimensional construct that can be either positive or negative in tone and effects (Kirsh and Kuiper, 2003; Martin et al., 2003) and targeted at either the self or some other person (Martin et al., 2003). Positive and negative humor are considered adaptive and maladaptive (i.e. dysfunctional), respectively, in their consequences for the target. The four types of humor and different manifestations of each type are shown in Figure 13.1. The two types of adaptive or functional humor (shown in Quadrants 1 and 2 of Figure 13.1) can be effective mechanisms for coping with dysfunctional organizational behavior. The two types of maladaptive humor shown in Quadrants 3 and 4 of Figure 13.1 can be examples of dysfunctional organizational behavior.

The first of the two adaptive forms (positive-self) is shown in Quadrant 1 and includes self-enhancing humor that is used to cope with potentially stressful events and situations.

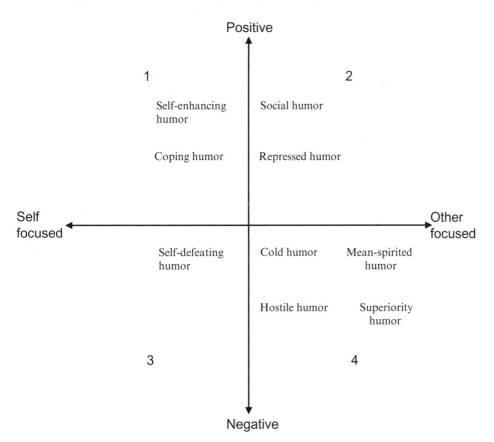

Figure 13.1   Two-dimensional model of workplace humor

Self-enhancing or coping humor helps minimize negative emotional reactions to stressors while maintaining a realistic perspective on problems.

Quadrant 2 (positive-other) is a socially adaptive style of affiliative humor that is used to enhance interpersonal and social relationships through the non-hostile use of jokes and banter that reduce interpersonal tensions. Affiliative humor is employed to raise group morale, identity and cohesiveness by reducing conflicts and increasing others' feelings of well-being (Kuiper et al., 2004). Affiliative humor is often spontaneous and creates a feeling of belonging to a common, if temporary, community among those individuals who share in the joke.

The two types of maladaptive or dysfunctional humor are shown in Quadrants 3 and 4 of Figure 13.1. Quadrant 3 (negative-self) includes humor that is expressed in a self-deprecating manner, often at a high personal cost. Kuiper et al. (2004) describe Quadrant 3 style humor as 'strained and obsequious'. Dysfunctional, self-targeted humor is evident in the excessive use of self-disparaging and ingratiating comments made during what are generally considered inappropriate attempts to fit into social groups or to gain the approval of others. High levels of self-defeating humor may also be used to mask negative feelings and anxieties or to avoid dealing constructively with a problem (Martin et al., 2003; Kuiper et al., 2004). Quadrant 3 humor is associated with avoidance, emotional neediness and low self-esteem.

Quadrant 4 (negative-other) includes boorish humor and aggressive use of humor in which the source displays a lack of concern or respect for others through coarse or vulgar displays or through mean-spirited and sarcastic comments (Kuiper et al., 2004). Aggressive humor includes a variety of negative techniques, such as teasing, ridicule, sarcasm and disparagement. The aim of Quadrant 4 humor is to denigrate and put down others and is executed without regard for its potential negative impact on the target(s). Continual use of aggressive humor against the same target(s) will eventually alienate the individual(s) targeted and seriously impair social and interpersonal relationships with them (Kuiper et al., 2004).

Studies of the relationships between humor and leadership behavior provide support for the argument that positive humor and negative humor (self and other-directed) have differential effects on organizational behavior. The use of positive humor or similarly 'warm humorous conduct' (Priest and Swain, 2002), and a 'hedonic tone' of humor (Cooper, 2003) is related to the behavior and effectiveness of leaders, evaluations of the leader by subordinates and leader–member relationships. Leaders who use more positive humor in their interactions with staff and peers tend to also receive higher ratings from subordinates for both task-oriented behavior and relationship-oriented behaviors and to be valued as more effective in their roles (Decker and Rotondo, 2001). Positive (functional) humor has also been found to be positively related to subordinates' evaluation of leader effectiveness (Priest and Swain), and leader–member exchange quality (Cooper, 2003). The amount of negative (dysfunctional) humor, including aggressive, deprecating and boorish humor, used by a leader is related to lower ratings of the leader's task behaviors and relationship behavior by his or her subordinates (Decker and Rotondo, 2001).

Correlational studies have also shown that some of the different types of humor in Figure 13.1 are associated with different organizational outcomes. In a study by Susa (2002), superiority humor (Quadrant 4) was negatively related to organizational climate, job satisfaction, commitment, creativity, performance and attendance, whereas the more positive incongruity humor and relief humor (Quadrants 1 and 2) were positively related to the same organizational variables.

Responses to the different types of humor shown in Figure 13.1 also can vary as a function of the target's motivation for the task being performed and the context in which the humor occurs. In school settings, for example, students with a low motivation for academic tasks had a greater preference for negative, hostile and self-defeating humor than for more positive self-enhancing and affiliative humor (Saroglou and Scariot, 2002). The preference for negative forms of humor was not evident for more highly motivated students. In addition, the cultural background of employees needs to be considered when making assumptions about preferred types of humor. For example, American employees reported higher usage of self-enhancing and self-defeating humor than did Arabic employees (Kalliny et al., 2006).

In summary, humor is becoming an increasingly popular organizational intervention, but the prescriptions are not based on any strong body of evidence of the proclaimed effects from organizational research. In addition, justifications for humor interventions in organizations are based exclusively on positive forms of humor (i.e. self-enhancing and affiliative humor), and the beneficial physiological and psychological effects that are related to the laughing, smiling and amusement produced by positive humor. To this point, negative dysfunctional forms of humor (i.e. self-defeating and aggressive humor) and their consequences have received relatively little attention.

Individual differences
Individuals differ in their mental and emotional responses to situations, including humor, and these differences could be expected to moderate both the production and the effects of different types of humor. The encoding of a message as humorous or funny, which will often be an automatic, subconscious process, will influence the individual's internal reactions, including the experience of positive affect and feelings of amusement or joy, and overt behavior, including smiling and laughter. Alternative interpretations, such as 'obvious', 'offensive', 'disgusting' or 'sick' will produce very different internal responses. These may be feelings of dissatisfaction, embarrassment, incompetence, anger or disgust and any number of associated behavioral responses, but not normally spontaneous smiling or laughter. However, circumstances do frequently arise when the recipient's overt behavior includes laughter or smiling but the internal affective reactions are neutral or negative. For example, a person may laugh at a joke that he or she finds personally offensive, because of deference to the teller or to avoid the embarrassment or conflict that may arise from a more critical response.

Jokers and killjoys
While it is generally accepted that people differ in their appreciation of and reactions to different types of humor, studies of humor as a personality trait have not yet identified a psychometrically valid measure that can effectively differentiate those who have a sense of humor from those who don't. Self-report measures for sense of humor have been found to have only weak correlations with behavioral measures of humor conduct, which is at least partly due to the weak psychometric properties of the scales used to measure sense of humor (Köhler and Ruch, 1996). Also, behavioral data on humor conduct show that humor appreciation can be distinguished from humor production (Köhler and Ruch, 1996).

Table 13.1   Humor usage and personality factors

		Direction	
		Self	Other
Valence	Positive	*e.g. self-enhancing* • Openness (+) • Agreeableness (+) • Agency • Communion • Self-esteem (+)	*e.g. affiliative* • Openness (+) • Agreeableness (+) • Agency • Communion • Self-esteem (+)
	Negative	*e.g. self-defeating* • Conscientiousness (−) • Emotional stability (−) • Agency • Communion • Security in attachment (−) • Self-esteem (−)	*e.g., aggressive* • Conscientiousness (−) • Agreeableness (−) • Agency • Communion

While there is a lack of support for a valid measure of a humor trait, research correlating humor responses with other more valid measures of personality and demographic variables, specifically gender, have identified more systematic individual differences in the production and/or responses to different types of humor.

Preferences for the four types of humor in Figure 13.1 have been shown to have significant relationships with a range of indicators of personality and well-being, which basically follow the pattern in Table 13.1 (based on findings reported in Martin et al., 2003; Saroglou and Scariot, 2002). Openness and agreeableness are associated with a positive (self- and other-directed) sense of humor, whereas neuroticism and lack of conscientiousness are associated with a negative (self- and/or other-directed) sense of humor (Saroglou and Scariot; see Table 13.1). Extraversion is related to high humor production behavior. Positive aspects of the higher-order personality factors agency and communion were related to a positive sense of humor (adapt and socially skilled humor), whereas negative aspects of agency and communion were related to a negative sense of humor (Kirsch and Kuiper, 2003). Agency and communion have also been established as moderators for the facilitative effect of humor on well-being (Kuiper and Borowicz-Sibenik, 2005; see Kuiper et al., 2005, 2004).

Men and women may be different
One individual difference that frequently arises as a moderator of both the production and effects of different types of humor is the gender of the participants in the study. Men and women produce different amounts of and respond differently to positive and negative humor. However, while differences between men and women are reported in several studies of humor production and problem-solving processes, they are not the product of any systematic theory or research program. Therefore, because there are no clear discernible patterns in the results reported, the interpretation of the results, while interesting, is largely speculative at this stage.

Several organizational studies have reported differences between the levels of humor used by male and female leaders and in the impacts of the different types of humor when it is used by men versus women. In a study of executive level leadership roles, Sala (2000) found that female executives employed more overall humor than male executives, but male executives employed more negative (dysfunctional) humor than their female counterparts. Thus the greater production of total humor, positive and negative, by female executives was due to their significantly greater use of positive humor compared to male executives. Decker and Rotondo (2001), however, found that male managers used more humor (negative and positive) compared to female managers. The gender of the manager also moderated the impact of humor use on leadership ratings of the manager by their subordinates. Female managers received higher leadership ratings than male managers when using positive humor, but lower ratings than male managers when using negative humor (Decker and Rotondo, 2001).

Gender differences have been found in the production of humor in difficult social situations in several studies. Male students are significantly more likely to react with humor in socially awkward situations than female students; female students are more likely to show a helping response (e.g. Cox et al., 1990).

Studies of different problem-solving processes have identified several male–female differences in reactions to and the use of information when humor is included as part of the task presentation. For example, gender has been shown to moderate the impact of humor on the recall and use of information. Recent experimental studies support the assumption that presenting material in a humorous way facilitates its recall (Schmidt, 2002; Thompson, 2001; Fischer and Thussbas, 2000). Within a classroom setting Casper (1999) analyzed the impact of two different humorous learning contexts on performance. Female students outperformed male students when the material was presented with a humorous message that was irrelevant to the material to be learned, and when no laughter was involved. Under laughter conditions, however, male students outperformed female students.

Humor also has been shown to have more beneficial effects for women than men in some, but not all, cognitive abilities tests. After reviewing studies of the effects including humor in testing materials, McMorris et al. (1997) concluded that gender, along with anxiety and humor appreciation, should be included as a potential moderator of humor effects on test performance. For example, the inclusion of humor in test materials had differential effects for men and women in their performance of analogy tasks used to assess reasoning skills. The inclusion of humor slowed the responses of men but not of women (Belanger et al., 1998). In the same study the inclusion of humor produced faster responses by both men and women on mental rotation tasks.

One of the often-mentioned benefits of humor in problem-solving processes is its potential role as a mechanism for coping with anxiety and other sources of negative arousal that can interfere with information processing. The effectiveness of humor as a coping mechanism for anxiety has been found different for men and woman in a study by Abel and Maxwell (2002). In their study, trait humor was related to lower anxiety for women but not for men. Also, the effects of a humor induction on anxiety and mood reactions differed for men and women, depending on the stressfulness of the problem situation. Humor led to lower anxiety and more positive mood reactions by women under low stress conditions, whereas introduction of humor had more beneficial effects on anxiety and mood for men under high stress conditions (Abel and Maxwell, 2002). However, in a later experimental study by Filipowicz (2006) manipulations of humor had more benefi-cial effects for men than for women. Male participants showed broader affective reactions to the humorous stimuli in a video and increased their performance more on a subsequent creativity task compared to female participants (Filipowicz, 2006). Stress was not manip-ulated in the Filipowicz study and the problem solving was therefore under conditions that would approximate the low stress condition in the Abel and Maxwell study. Without access to the videotape used for the humor induction it is not clear if the humor presented was positive, negative, or some combination of the two. Therefore we cannot rule out the type of humor as a possible explanation for the male–female differences.

In summary, measures of a sense of humor have not been validated to the point that they are reliably related to the actual production and reactions to humor, but preferences for different styles of humor are related to other psychometrically valid measures of per-sonality, particularly the five-factor model. Male–female differences keep popping up in studies but the results are rarely based on theory, show no clear pattern of differences, and are sometimes contradictory. The implications of these findings are taken up in the dis-cussion, following a consideration of humor as a form of dysfunctional organizational behavior.

Humor as dysfunctional organizational behavior
The almost universal emphasis on the positive functions of humor in research studies and popular prescriptive accounts of humor in organizations ignores the potential negative cognitive and emotional effects of humor that are apparent to anyone who has been the target of the superior, aggressive, mean-spirited and deprecating types of humor that are represented in Quadrant 4 of Figure 13.1. Many jokes represent an attack on the identity of individuals who are members of groups that are targeted in jokes. Ethnic jokes are an obvious example, but identity threats in the form of jokes within organizations can be tar-geted at occupations, age cohorts, organizational level, gender and many other groups. Humor that is used to include members within a group or community can also be used to exclude people.

In the discussion that follows we will first highlight some findings where humor has been found to have some unexpected negative effects: unexpected because the studies were conducted within the narrow conceptualization of humor as a coping mechanism that only leads to positive effects. In particular we focus on evidence for negative humor as a potential health risk behavior. This is followed by a discussion of research illustrating the effects of negative forms of humor in organizational culture, in group formation processes, relationships between high- and low-status individuals and group performance. This review is necessarily selective because most research has focused on positive humor and a brief review of indicative findings from that research is presented at the end of the section for reasons of balance.

While there is evidence that humor can ameliorate the experienced effects of self-reported everyday life stressors (Abel, 2002; Kuiper et al., 1993) and experimentally induced stress (Kuiper et al., 1995), there is very little evidence that these effects get trans-lated into better health outcomes, the many claims for the positive health effects of humor notwithstanding. The first longitudinal study of the causal effects of humor usage on health and well-being found no evidence for a facilitative effect of humor in a three-year study of Finnish police officers (Kerkkänen et al., 2004). Neither self-reported nor peer-rated sense of humor predicted subsequent health and well-being of the Finish police officers in the study. In a follow-up longitudinal study, the same authors report that humor was, unexpectedly, positively related to health risk behaviors, such as smoking, and developing a high body mass index (BMI) (Kerkkänen et al., 2004). Kuiper and Borowicz-Sibenik (2005) suggest that the higher-order personality factors of agency and communion may moderate the effect of humor on health outcomes.

An alternative possible explanation for the findings of the Kerkkänen et al. (2004) studies and for other studies that have failed to find a relationship between humor and health outcomes is that health effects depend upon the type as well as the level of humor that is commonly used by the people being studied. If the prevailing type of humor used by officers in the police departments studied by Kerkkänen et al. (2004) was aggressive and self-deprecating, then the humor may have been a cause of the increased smoking and other negative health effects; or negative humor is a health risk behavior that occurs together with other risk behavior such as smoking. In support of this argument is correlational research, mainly with student samples, in which the different types of humor are identified in the measurement process. These studies show that negative forms of humor are negatively related to a range of health and well-being indicators. Those who use aggressive and, particularly, self-deprecating types of humor are more likely to report higher levels of anxiety, depression and negative self-judgments and lower levels of self-esteem and security in attachments (self-focused maladaptive humor, Kuiper et al., 2004; hostile and self-defeating humor, Saroglou and Scariot, 2002).

Further support for the hypothesis that negative humor can be a health risk behavior comes from studies of the relationships between sense of humor and depression (Overholster, 1992; Kuiper and Borowicz-Sibenik, 2005). While positive-self-focused forms of humor, such as coping humor and self-enhancing humor, have been found to be negatively related to depression, negative-self-focused forms of humor, such as self-defeating humor, have been found to be positively related to depression (Kuiper et al., 2004).

Even positive humor may be dysfunctional for certain targets in certain circumstances. Humor has been identified as a defining characteristic of work cultures in organizations and teams (Holmes and Marra, 2002). This insight has led to many attempts to create fun cultures at work, such as that exemplified by South West Airlines, where a sense of humor is one of the selection criteria used when hiring staff and the pervasive sense of fun at work is seen as a cultural attribute that contributes to the competitive advantage of the company (Hallowell, 1996). However, there are also risks associated with attempts to create or support a humorous organizational work culture. Fleming (2005) reported increased cynicism among employees in one analyzed company when the management supported a 'fun' culture.

Organizational culture can also include negative humor and other forms of dysfunctional organizational behavior as norms. Taylor and Bain (2003) observed that among employees of two call centres subversive satire was a cultural norm and was used to weaken the managerial authority. Roy's (1960) classic participant observation study of work culture, indexed by the 'times' and 'themes' of the informal social interactions among a small group of machine operators within a factory, highlighted the role of negative humor in organizational culture. The 'times' were breaks that punctuated the working day and were built around practical jokes in which one member was the target. The banana time of the title was a daily ritual in which one member of the group would consume the banana brought by another for his own lunch, always announcing 'banana time'. The 'themes' communicated through humor covered racial tensions and status differentials. Qualitative work of the type done by Roy (1958) may be the only way to effectively study the role of negative humor in organizational culture. This point is taken up in the discussion.

Negative humor and the selective use of positive humor also serve a power function that benefits some and not others in relationships, such as occur in relationships between in-group and out-group members and organizational members of differing status. When humor is used to create a sense of community between group members and foster group cohesion, the process of socialization often includes negative humor to exclude people whom the group rejects and to strengthen the sense of identity among the in-group (e.g. Vinton, 1989). An example of negative humor in the socialization processes comes from a qualitative study by Terrion and Ashford (2002), who studied participants during a six-week executive development program. One of their findings was that when participants were placed in work groups they used negative put-down humor against other participants in the program to promote the identity of their newly established group. Studies of established work teams have also identified the emergence of humor networks in which negative humor is used to exclude out-group members and to form a stronger sense of community amongst in-group members (Duncan and Feisal, 1989).

Negative humor is used by both high- and low-status people in their relationships with one another, but the specific forms of humor vary with the status of the individual and the specific work setting (Duncan, 1985). Negative humor is often used by high-status individuals to control and maintain differentials between them and lower-status individuals (e.g. Vinton, 1989). For low-status individuals, negative humor (e.g. subversive humor) can be used to challenge authority (e.g. Brown and Keegan, 1999; Holmes and Marra, 2002). Other studies point to the fact that the use of humor in relationships between low- and high-status individuals varies from organization to organization. For example, Duncan (1985) found high- and low-status individuals in health care work teams were part of the same humor network and had no extra humor status, whereas high-status individuals (managers) in business groups were less often the focus of positive or negative humor.

Studies that attempt to link humor with group performance outcomes will often report a positive impact on the affective reactions of participants but a null effect for subsequent performance (e.g. Filipowicz, 2002). In an earlier review of studies of the relationship between humor and performance, Pollio and Bainum (1983) attributed mixed results of manipulated humor effects on group performance (group problem solving) to the humor index employed. If 'total seconds of laughter' was considered as a measure of group humor, positive effects of group humor on group performance (anagram tasks) were found; no effects were found, however, if 'number of jokes' was considered as a measure of group humor. Findings also suggest that different effects of humor can be expected for different types of tasks. While positive effects were reported for anagram tasks, no effects were found for decision-making tasks (Pollio and Bainum, 1983). Another possible explanation is that the effects of humor on many work group performance outcomes are more cumulative and influence performance through causal pathways than the affective responses to jokes. Over time, humor can become embedded in various cultural norms that may influence group performance (e.g. Roy, 1960). As was illustrated in our earlier discussion of culture, positive and negative humor may give rise to or reinforce different norms with different implications for group performance.

The leadership of groups is also affected by the types of humor used. While there is evidence that effective leaders use more humor than ineffective leaders (Priest and Swain, 2002; Holmes and Marra, 2006; Sala, 2000; Aviolo et al., 1999); it is the type of humor used that seems to define its effects. Specifically, negative humor is associated with low leadership performance. Managers who used negative humor received poor ratings in leadership outcome variables, such as task and relationship behavior, especially for female leaders (Decker and Rotondo, 2001). Also the use of negative humor by a leader is likely to be reciprocated by the members of the group (Decker and Rotondo, 1999), thus initiating a cycle that can lead to the creation of a negative and potentially less productive work culture.

In summary, although the current state of evidence is more suggestive than conclusive, negative humor has the potential to be a dysfunctional form of organizational behavior that is related to health risk behaviors, unproductive cultural norms, exclusion of individuals from groups, maintenance of status differentials and negative team cultures. As with the earlier results reported for gender differences, more research is needed on occurrence, determinants and outcomes of negative humor to establish the causal dynamics and generalizability of these relationships.

It's not all bad – laughter is good medicine

Our discussion of humor as a dysfunctional organizational behavior has been based on a necessarily selective review of the literature. While this has served to highlight the potential for dysfunctional effects of humor and the relative lack of research on those effects, it does not reflect the findings from the extensive body of research on positive humor and its effects. In summary, positive humor has been shown to have many beneficial effects, including:

1. Lower experienced stress in response to stressors (e.g. Abel, 2002; Kuiper et al., 1993; Lefcourt et al., 1995), including quicker physiological adaptation (e.g. reduction in systolic blood pressure) to stressful situations (e.g. Lefcourt et al., 1995).
2. More positive mood and emotional responses (e.g. Abel and Maxwell, 2002; Lehman et al., 2001; Moran and Massam, 1999; Szabo et al., 2005).
3. Reduction of anxiety levels (Szabo et al., 2005; Abel and Maxwell, 2002).
4. Lower levels of exhaustion and burnout in stressful occupations (e.g. Killian, 2005; Mesmer, 2001; Talbot, 2000).
5. Higher levels of psychological well-being and lower frequency of psychosomatic illnesses (e.g. Fry, 1995; Cavanaugh, 2002; Sanders, 2004; Francis et al., 1999).
6. Higher self-esteem (e.g. Martin et al., 2003).

This summary of findings is illustrative of the many benefits that can flow from self-enhancing, affiliative and other forms of positive humor. What emerges from the research is that positive humor helps people to cope better with stressful situations, both psychologically and physiologically, and to maintain a positive sense of self-worth. At the risk of overstatement, it should be stressed that attributing these outcomes to humor, rather than to positive humor, is misleading.

Conclusion
Our aim in this review has not been to question the potential beneficial effects that laughter, smiling and amusement can bring to people at work. Humor that produces these effects in members of the target audience has clear psychological and physiological benefits. However, not all humor is funny for all people all of the time and not all humor produces positive effects. In particular, much humor is negative in tone and has potentially detrimental effects for the individuals, groups and organizations, and therefore can rightly be considered a form of dysfunctional organizational behavior. Our review highlights for us the need for further research that examines the occurrence, determinants and effects of negative humor in organizations, in order to provide a balanced perspective on the role of humor in organizational behavior and to craft interventions that both minimize the potential negative effects while seeking to enhance the beneficial effects that can flow from positive forms of humor. To this end, we would like to comment on the conceptualization of the role of humor in organizations and the methods that are likely to be most effective in the study of negative humor in organizational behavior.

One clear implication of our review is that organizational researchers need to conceptualize humor as a multidimensional construct that includes both negative and positive forms of humor. In addition a dynamic conceptualization of the construct will need to take account of norm formation and other social factors, such as status differentials, that will interact with humor displays to affect the outcomes. It is possible, for example, that the frequent but so far incoherent gender differences in reactions to humor are the product of differential humor norms that are held by and about males and females. One hypothesis worthy of examination is that humor norms for females support greater use of positive, particularly affiliative, forms of humor when dealing with others and more self-defeating humor in self-regulatory activities. By way of contrast, male norms might support greater use of aggressive and self-enhancing forms of humor. These hypotheses could be extended into predictions of cultural norms about humor for male- versus female-dominated occupational groups and organizations and about the consequences of cultural fit (or misfit) for males and females.

In order to progress a research agenda of humor as dysfunctional organizational behavior, the current research points to the importance of qualitative field research designs for identifying the occurrence and outcomes of negative humor. In the Roy (1960) and Terrion and Ashford (2002) studies, participants were observed unobtrusively over an extended period. In both cases the pattern of negative humor and its functions only became evident over time. Also, it was probably the case that displays of negative humor, which may present an unflattering view of the person being studied, are more likely to be constrained when data collection is obviously focused on displays of humor. This social desirability effect, plus the fact that human ethics committees may be reluctant to approve studies with inductions of negative humor, may account for the bias toward positive humor, at least in experimental studies.

In concluding, we would like to highlight what we see as the risk to the field of organizational behavior in the application of positive psychology (e.g. Luthans, 2005; Turner et al., 2002; Wright, 2003), which we see as including the biases and limitations that we have identified in the humor research through our analysis of the dysfunctional effects of humor. Humor research, with its bias toward positive humor, is both an exemplar and source of ideas for the newly emerging field of positive psychology, which focuses on the study of individual, social and institutional determinants of human happiness (e.g. Seligman and Csikszentmihalyi, 2000). On his website 'Authentic Happiness', the founder of positive psychology, Martin Seligman, proclaims that 'his research has demonstrated that it is possible to be happier – to feel more satisfied, to be more engaged with life, find more meaning, have higher hopes, and probably even laugh and smile more, regardless of one's circumstances', and that 'he is now turning his attention to training Positive Psychologists, individuals whose practice will make the world a happier place'. Not surprisingly, the application of positive psychology within organizational behavior (Luthans, 2005; Turner et al., 2002; Wright, 2003) shows the same positive bias. As our review of humor research shows, the risk of focusing on positive organizational behavior is that it ignores the dysfunctional organizations' behavior and the many negative outcomes that this can produce for individual, groups and organizations.

References

Abel, M.H. (2002), 'Humor, stress, and coping strategies', *Humor: International Journal of Humor Research*, **14**(9), 365–81.

Abel, M.H. and Maxwell, D. (2002), 'Humor and affective consequences of a stressful task', *Journal of Social and Clinical Psychology*, **21**(2), 165–90.

Aviolo, B.J., Howell, J.M. and Sosik, J.J. (1999), 'A funny thing happened on the way to the bottom line: humor as a moderator of leadership style', *Academy of Management Journal*, **42**(2), 219–28.

Barsoux, J.L. (1996), 'Why organizations need humor', *European Management Journal*, **14**(5), 500–508.

Belanger, H.G., Kirkpatrick, L.A. and Derks, P. (1998), 'The effects of humor on verbal and imaginal problem solving', *Humor: International Journal of Humor Research*, **11**(1), 21–31.

Boverie, P., Hoffman, J.E., Klein, D.C., McClelland, M. and Oldknow, M. (1994), 'Humor in human resource development', *Human Resource Development Quarterly*, **5**(1), 75–91.

Brown, R.B. and Keegan, D. (1999), 'Humor in the hotel kitchen', *Humor: International Journal of Humor Research*, **12**(1), 47–70.

Casper, R. (1999), 'Laughter and humor in the classroom: effects on test performance (arousal, memory, gender differences)', *Dissertation Abstracts International: Section B: The Sciences and Engineering*, **60**(6-B), 3014.

Cavanaugh, R.E. (2002), 'An analysis of the relationship between humor styles and perceived quality of life among university faculty', unpublished dissertation, Southern Illinois University, Carbondale.

Cetola, H.W. and Reno, R.R. (1985), 'The effects of laughter on humor and humor on mood', paper presented at the Annual Meeting of the Midwestern Psychological Association, Chicago, USA.

Clinton, T.A., Jr (1995), 'An experimental study of the effects of humor and a conventional lesson on the divergent thinking of undergraduate students', *Dissertation Abstracts International Section A: Humanities and Social Sciences*, **55**(8-A), 2322.

Cooper, C.D. (2003), 'No laughing matter: the impact of supervisor humor on leader–member exchange (LMX) quality', *Dissertation Abstracts International Section A: Humanities and Social Sciences*, **64**(6-A), 2161.

Cox, J.A., Read, R.L. and Van Auken, P.M. (1990), 'Male X female differences in communicating job-related humor: an exploratory study', *Humor: International Journal of Humor Research*, **3**(3), 287–95.

Decker, W.H. and Rotondo, D.M. (1999), 'Use of humor at work: predictors and implications', *Psychological Reports*, **84**(3), 961–8.

Decker, W.H. and Rotondo, D.M. (2001), 'Relationships among gender, type of humor, and perceived leader effectiveness', *Journal of Managerial Issues*, **13**(4), 450–65.

Dews, S., Kaplan, J. and Winner, E. (1995), 'Why not say it directly? The social functions of irony', *Discourse Processes*, **19**(3), 347–67.

Duncan, W. (1985), 'The superiority theory of humor at work: joking relationships as indicators of formal and informal status patterns in small, task-oriented groups', *Small Group Behavior*, **16**(4), 556–64.

Duncan, W. and Feisal, J. (1989), 'No laughing matter: patterns of humor in the workplace', *Organizational Dynamics*, **17**(4), 18–30.

Feingold, A. and Mazzella, R. (1991), 'Psychometric intelligence and verbal humor ability', *Personality and Individual Differences*, **12**(5), 427–35.

Filipowicz, A.M. (2002), 'The influence of humor on performance in task-based interactions', *Dissertation Abstracts International Section A: Humanities and Social Sciences*, **63**(4-A), 1437.

Filipowicz, A. (2006), 'From positive affect to creativity: the surprising role of surprise', *Creativity Research Journal*, **18**(2), 141–52.

Fischer, K. and Thussbas, C. (2000), 'The effect of humorous-episodic element in television commercials on memory performance and brand evaluations. An experimental study', *Medienpsychologie: Zeitschrift fuer Individual- und Massenkommunikation*, **12**(1), 51–68.

Fleming, P. (2005), 'Workers' playtime? Boundaries and cynicism in a "culture of fun" program', *Journal of Applied Behavioral Science*, **41**(3), 285–303.

Foot, H. (1991), 'The psychology of humor and laughter', in R. Cochrane and D. Caroll (eds), *Psychology and Social Issues. A Tutorial Text*, London: Taylor & Francis, pp. 1–13.

Francis, L., Monahan, K. and Berger, C. (1999), 'A laughing matter? The uses of humor in medical interactions', *Motivation and Emotion*, **23**(2), 155–74.

Fry, P. (1995), 'Perfectionism, humor, and optimism as moderators of health outcomes and determinants of coping styles of women executives', *Genetic, Social, and General Psychology Monographs*, **121**(2), 211–45.

Grugulis, I. (2002), 'Nothing serious? Candidates' use of humor in management training', *Human Relations*, **55**(4), 387–406.

Hallowell, R. (1996), 'The relationships of customer satisfaction, customer loyalty, and profitability: an empirical study', *International Journal of Service Industry Management*, **7**(4), 27–42.

Hatch, M.J. (1997), 'Irony and the social construction of contradiction in the humor of a management team', *Organization Science*, **8**(3), 275–88.

Hatch, M.J. and Ehrlich, S.B. (1993), 'Spontaneous humor as an indicator of paradox and ambiguity in organizations', *Organization Studies*, **14**(4), 505–26.

Holmes, J. and Marra, M. (2002), 'Over the edge? Subversive humor between colleagues and friends', *Humor: International Journal of Humor Research*, **15**(1), 65–87.

Holmes, J. and Marra, M. (2006), 'Humor and leadership style', *Humor: International Journal of Humor Research*, **19**(2), 119–38.

Kalliny, M., Cruthirds, K.W. and Minor, M.S. (2006), 'Differences between American, Egyptian and Lebanese humor styles: implications for international management', *International Journal of Cross Cultural Management*, **6**(1), 121–34.

Kerkkänen, P., Kuiper, N.A. and Martin, R.A. (2004), 'Sense of humor, physical health, and well-being at work: a three-year longitudinal study of Finnish police officers', *Humor: International Journal of Humor Research*, **17**(1/2), 21–35.

Killian, J.G. (2005), 'Career and technical education teacher burnout: impact of humor-coping style and job-related stress', *Dissertation Abstracts International Section A: Humanities and Social Sciences*, **65**(9-A), 3266.

Kirsh, G.A. and Kuiper, N.A. (2003), 'Positive and negative aspects of sense of humor: associations with the constructs of individualism and relatedness', *Humor: International Journal of Humor Research*, **16**(1), 33–62.

Köhler, G. and Ruch, W. (1996), 'Sources of variance in current sense of humor inventories: how much substance, how much method variance?', *Humor: International Journal of Humor Research. Special Issue: Measurement of Sense of Humor*, **9**, 363–97.

Kuiper, N.A. and Borowicz-Sibenik, M. (2005), 'A good sense of humor doesn't always help: agency and communion as moderators of psychological well-being', *Personality and Individual Differences*, **38**(2), 365–77.

Kuiper, N.A., Grimshaw, M., Leite, C. and Kirsh, G.A. (2004), 'Humor is not always the best medicine: specific components of sense of humor and psychological well-being', *Humor: International Journal of Humor Research*, **17**(1/2), 135–68.

Kuiper, N.A., Martin, R.A. and Olinger, L. (1993), 'Coping humor, stress, and cognitive appraisals', *Canadian Journal of Behavioral Science*, **25**(1), 81–96.

Kuiper, N.A., McKenzie, S.D. and Belanger, K.A. (1995), 'Cognitive appraisals and individual differences in sense of humor: motivational and affective implications', *Personality and Individual Differences*, **19**(3), 359–72.

Laird, J.D. (1974), 'Self-attribution of emotion: the effects of expressive behavior on the quality of emotional experience', *Journal of Personality and Social Psychology*, **29**, 475–86.

Lanzetta, J.T., Cartwright-Smith, J. and Kleck, R.E. (1976), 'Effects of nonverbal dissimulation on emotional experience and autonomic arousal', *Journal of Personality and Social Psychology*, **33**(3), 354–70.

Lefcourt, H.M., Davidson, K., Shepherd, R., Phillips, M., Prkachin, K. and Mills, D. (1995), 'Perspective-taking humor: accounting for stress moderation', *Journal of Social and Clinical Psychology*, **14**(4), 373–91.

Lehman, K.M., Burke, K.L., Martin, R., Sultan, J. and Czech, D.R. (2001), 'A reformulation of the moderating effects of productive humor', *Humor: International Journal of Humor Research*, **14**(2), 131–61.

Luthans, F. (2005), 'The need for and meaning of positive organizational behavior', *Journal of Organizational Behavior*, **26**, 695–706.

Martin, R.A., Puhlik-Doris, P., Larsen, G., Gray, J. and Weir, K. (2003), 'Individual differences in uses of humor and their relation to psychological well-being: development of the Humor Styles Questionnaire', *Journal of Research in Personality*, **37**, 48–75.

McMorris, R.F., Boothroyd, R.A. and Pietrangelo, D.J. (1997), 'Humor in educational testing: a review and discussion', *Applied Measurement in Education*, **10**(3), 269–97.

Mesmer, P.J. (2001), 'Use of humor as a stress coping strategy by para-professional youth care workers employed in residential group care facilities', *Dissertation Abstracts International: Section B: The Sciences and Engineering*, **62**(1-B), 587.

Moran, C.C. and Massam, M.M. (1999), 'Differential influences of coping humor and humor bias on mood', *Behavioral Medicine*, **25**(1), 36–42.

Overholster, J.C. (1992), 'Sense of humor when coping with life stress', *Personality and Individual Differences*, **13**(7), 799–804.

Petty, R.E., Cacioppo, J.T. and Schumann, F. (1983), 'Central and peripheral routes to advertising effectiveness: the moderating role of involvement', *Journal of Consumer Research*, **10**, 134–48.

Pollio, H.R. and Bainum, C.K. (1983), 'Are funny groups good at solving problems? A methodological evaluation and some preliminary results', *Small Group Behavior*, **14**(4), 379–404.

Priest, R.F. and Swain, J.E. (2002), 'Humor and its implications for leadership effectiveness', *Humor: International Journal of Humor Research*, **15**(2), 169–89.

Roy, D.F. (1960), '"Banana Time". Job satisfaction and informal interaction', *Human Organization*, **18**, 158–68.

Sala, F. (2000), 'Relationship between executives' spontaneous use of humor and effective leadership', *Dissertation Abstracts International: Section B: The Sciences and Engineering*, **61**(3-B), 1683.

Sanders, T. (2004), 'Controllable laughter: managing sex work through humor', *Sociology*, **38**(2), 273–91.

Saroglou, V. and Scariot, C. (2002), 'Humor Styles Questionnaire: personality and educational correlates in Belgian high school and college students', *European Journal of Personality*, **16**(1), 43–54.

Schmidt, S.R. (2002), 'The humor effect: differential processing and privileged retrieval', *Memory*, **10**(2), 127–38.

Seligman, M.E.P. and Csikszentmihalyi, M. (2000), 'Positive psychology: an introduction', *American Psychologist*, **55**, 5–14.

Shammi, P. and Stuss, D. (1999), 'Humor appreciation: a role of the right frontal lobe', *Brain: A Journal of Neurology*, **122**(4), 657–66.

Shammi, P. and Stuss, D. (2003), 'The effects of normal aging on humor appreciation', *Journal of the International Neuropsychological Society*, **9**, 855–63.

Susa, A.M. (2002), 'Humor type, organizational climate, and outcomes: the shortest distance between an organization's environment and the bottom line is laughter', *Dissertation Abstracts International: Section B: The Sciences and Engineering*, **63**(12-B), 6131.

Talbot, L.A. (2000), 'Burnout and humor usage among community college nursing faculty members', *Community College Journal of Research and Practice*, **24**(5), 359–73.

Taylor, P. and Bain, P. (2003), '"Subterranean Worksick Blues": Humor as subversion in two call centres', *Organization Studies*, **24**(9), 1487–509.

Terrion, J.L. and Ashford, B.E. (2002), 'From I to we: the role of putdown humor and identity in the development of a temporary group', *Human Relations*, **55**(1), 55–88.

Thompson, J.L.W. (2001), 'Funny you should ask, what is the effect of humor on memory and metamemory?' *Dissertation Abstracts International: Section B: The Sciences and Engineering*, **61**(8-B), 4442.

Turner, N., Barling, J. and Sachaatos, A. (2002), 'Positive psychology at work', in C. Snyder and S.J. Lopez (eds), *Handbook of Positive Psychology*, New York: Oxford University Press, pp. 715–30.

Ullian, J.A. (1976), 'Joking at work', *Journal of Communication*, **26**(3), 129–33.

Vinton, K.L. (1989), 'Humor in the workplace: is it more than telling jokes?', *Small Group Behavior*, **20**(2), 151–66.

Weaver, R.L. and Cotrell, H.W. (1987), 'Lecturing: essential communication strategies', *New Directions for Teaching and Learning*, **32**, 57–69.

Wright, T.A. (2003), 'Positive organizational behavior: an idea whose time has truly come', *Journal of Organizational Behavior*, **24**, 437–42.

Zillmann, D. (1991), 'Empathy: affect from bearing witness to the emotions of others', in J. Bryant and D. Zillmann (eds), *Responding to the Screen: Reception and Reaction Processes*, Hillsdale, NJ: Lawrence Erlbaum Associates.

PART II

MANAGING ORGANIZATIONAL MAYHEM

14 The role of organizational practices and routines in facilitating normalized corruption
Mahendra Joshi, Vikas Anand and Kevin Henderson

Introduction

In this chapter we argue that firms become highly susceptible to normalized corruption when organizational practices that are essential for the functioning of the firm assume a taken-for-granted character. When mindlessly enacted, many common practices are likely to increase the probability that employees will rationalize unethical acts, that newcomers will be easily socialized into ongoing corruption, and that corruption will become institutionalized in organizational processes and routines. For example, some compensation characteristics can lock in employees to develop standards of living that cannot be maintained easily in other jobs and force them to rationalize their immoral acts; certain types of organizational structures may distance employees from the affected stakeholders and increase chances of employees engaging in unethical behaviors without conscious thought about their actions; an imperfectly communicated code of ethics can proliferate corruption instead of reducing it; and finally the ways of handling the discovery of immoral acts can influence whether the organization is likely to face an ongoing corruption in future. We highlight these issues and suggest ways in which organizations can guard themselves against the harmful unethical consequences of routine organizational practices.

In the wake of several recent corporate scandals, we have witnessed a tremendous amount of scholarly work in improving our understanding of organizational corruption. Several researchers have offered frameworks that help us understand how corruption sets in and perpetuates within firms. For example, recently, Ashforth and Anand (2003) pointed out that corrupt practices can prevail in organizations for a long time because otherwise ethical people can engage in corrupt activities and convince themselves that such activities are ethical in nature. Terming this process 'the normalization of corruption', they proposed that three factors contributed to perpetuating unethical activities for a prolonged period: institutionalization, rationalization and socialization. Corruption is institutionalized when deviant practices become part of an organization's memory – i.e. are embedded in organizational routines and practices (e.g. Anand et al., 1998; Nelson and Winter, 1982). Rationalization refers to mental tactics that are used by individuals to portray their unethical acts as acceptable (Adams and Balfour, 1998; Coleman and Ramos, 1998). Socialization refers to practices used by veterans in corrupt units to introduce and involve newcomers in ongoing corruption (Darley, 2001; Sherman, 1980).

Because of the mutually reinforcing patterns of these three mechanisms, organizations with normalized corruption find it extremely difficult to reverse the process and put things in order again (Ashforth and Anand, 2003). This is evident in many recent instances of normalized corruption where firms realized too late that their moral well-being had deteriorated beyond repair. Since it is not easy to reverse normalized corruption, firms *need to emphasize prevention* by ensuring that the system is on a constant vigil to nip corruption in its budding stages.

A critical step in preventing normalization involves understanding how some of the very basic practices within organizations,[1] if taken for granted, can facilitate the onset of normalized corruption. Many of these practices are essential for the normal functioning of a firm and include efforts to create suitable organizational structures, employee compensation and rewards, interactions with stakeholders, and policies regarding employee conduct. In addition to the day-to-day function of the organization, these practices are also critical for obtaining legitimacy and scarce resources, and to develop a competitive advantage (DiMaggio and Powell, 1983; Pfeffer and Salancik, 1978; Scott, 2001). However, if practices in a complex organization are not implemented with care, they can increase the likelihood of normalized corruption becoming endemic within the organization (Perrow, 1984).

In this chapter we examine four organizational practices which, while usually very valuable for the firm, can also act as key catalysts fostering organizational corruption. We focus on four key practices: organizational compensation and rewards; organizational structure; ethical codes of conducts; and systems and procedures for handling the discovery of corrupt acts. We start with a brief review of the literature on the rationalization, socialization and institutionalization of corruption. Following this, we explain how the above-mentioned four organizational practices can induce normalization of corruption in firms. We simultaneously discuss how these practices can be effectively used to prevent the normalization of corruption while keeping their economic viability. Finally, we conclude by suggesting areas of future research and managerial implications.

Normalization of corruption in organizations

Ashforth and Anand (2003) proposed a framework that suggests that corruption becomes embedded in organizational structures and processes and is internalized by organizational members as permissible or even desirable through three mechanisms – institutionalization, socialization and rationalization. We provide a brief review of these mechanisms in the following section since we extensively use this framework to build our further arguments.

Institutionalization of corruption

Corruption is institutionalized when corrupt practices are enacted by organizational members as a matter of routine without significant thought given to the nature of the behavior. Institutionalization of corruption is manifested through three phases: (1) the initial decision to act; (2) embedding corruption in structures and processes; and (3) routinization of corruption. These three phases are explained below.

An organizational member's initial decision to act in a corrupt manner is prompted by the permissive ethical climate of the organization. For instance, a significant emphasis on financial goals in an organization, without an assessment of how those goals are met, presents several opportunities for members to act immorally. One factor that plays a huge role in developing a permissive climate is the leadership within the organization. Supervisors not only serve as role models but also have the authority to both reward and condone subordinates' behaviors. Thus, when supervisors explicitly or tacitly act in promiscuous ways (such as focusing exclusively on financial goals without appraising how those goals are met), it sends a clear signal to subordinates that the unethical means used to achieve the ends is less likely to be punished when the immediate financial goals are met. Organizational structures and processes also insulate managers from responsibility toward such acts of unethical means. For example, many organizations institute the concept of 'a vice-president responsible for going to jail' for unethical activities (Braithwaite, 1984), allowing other managers to easily remain blind to corrupt practices.

Corruption gradually gets embedded in organizational structures and processes by making its way into organizational memory. Activities stored in organizational memory – a metaphor used to describe the process through which an organization acquires, stores and uses the knowledge that is applied to its activities (Anand et al., 1998) – obtain legitimacy and are often performed by organizational members without them being consciously aware of the context in which they were performed. Thus previous unethical decisions and positive outcomes accompanying those decisions validate the use of unethical means in the future.

As corrupt practices get embedded in organizational routines, a deviant culture tends to emerge that normalizes corruption. The deviant culture insulates its actors from a wider culture where a premium is placed on socializing with insiders, condemning outsiders, and strongly identifying with the in group. These practices further amplify a group member's engagement in corrupt activities as they are seen to be in accordance with group norms and necessary for in-group identification (Mars, 1994). Finally, as corrupt practices become institutionalized and repeatedly enacted, they become routinized and habitual (Benson, 1985). This routinization is further enhanced because organizational members keep performing their specialized tasks without being aware of how their individual actions, in conjunction with the actions of others, contribute to the enhancement of a corrupt practice.

Rationalization of corruption
Interestingly, individuals involved in organizational corruption tend not to view themselves as corrupt. Instead, these individuals use various rationalizing strategies in not only countering the negative connotations of their acts but also positively articulating and justifying their corrupt behavior (Ashforth and Anand, 2003). There appear to be at least eight types of rationalizations, which are described below.

A common form of rationalization is excusing oneself of corrupt practices on the grounds that they are *not actually illegal*. Since many decisions concerning corrupt behavior are quite ambiguous in nature and few specific rules exist to prescribe or proscribe the behavior, individuals often use this rationalization tactic to absolve themselves of having done anything wrong.

In addition, corrupt actors frequently employ three types of denial strategies to rationalize their misdemeanors. In *denying their responsibility*, actors construe that they have no choice due to circumstances beyond their control such as management order and peer pressure. In *denial of injury*, actors construe that no one was harmed, and thus, when the actual damage is insignificant, the organization doesn't appear to care. In the third form of rationalization – *denial of victim* – actors either justify their acts of corruption by arguing that the victims deserved their fates, or psychologically distance themselves by moral excluding themselves from the acts of corruption.

In a different form of rationalization – *social weighting* – actors engage in impugning the legitimacy of those who would cast the act as corrupt. Thus the corrupt may characterize a law or a norm as vague or inconsistent, thereby rejecting its legitimacy in governing an individual's behavior.

Individuals also make use of *appealing to higher loyalties* in rationalizing their corrupt acts. For instance, a strong sense of group loyalty can force individuals to bend or break rules that may jeopardize the existence or image of the group. Individuals are also likely sometimes to act in corrupt ways to uphold the moral principles of their group. For instance, a group may act counter to universal ethical norms if they regard those laws as an obstacle to particular principles.

Socialization into corruption

Socialization can also be extremely effective in inducing newcomers to participate in existing corrupt practices. Specifically, organizations make use of three different socialization tactics – cooptation, incrementalism and compromise – to introduce ongoing corrupt acts to newcomers. In *cooptation*, rewards are utilized to induce newcomers toward corrupt behavior. Rewards act in a very subtle way by inducing newcomers to resolve the ambiguity prevailing in business scenarios while suiting their own self-interests. Consequently, newcomers often remain unaware of their engagement in unethical activities.

Incrementalism, the second process of newcomer socialization into corrupt activities, acts in a different fashion. Newcomers are induced to engage in small acts of corruption, which may seem harmless as well as possibly explicit and irrevocable. The acts can create some cognitive dissonance which is resolved by different types of rationalization techniques that the organizational culture makes available for newcomers (Festinger, 1957). Gradually, newcomers overcome the guilty feelings associated with the act and become more open to enacting corrupt practices of more severe magnitudes.

Finally, *compromise* is the third avenue to corruption through socialization. Under pressing dilemmas, role conflicts or other problems, individuals (often in good faith) essentially revert to corruptive tendencies. Birnbaum (1992), for instance, describes how some politicians have to act against their ethical principles when they seek power by currying favors and cutting deals, often causing them to support actors they may usually avoid.

Each of the three pillars of corruption – institutionalization, rationalization and socialization – also reinforce each other in normalizing corruption in organizations. For instance, institutionalized corrupt beliefs are reinforced through the rationalizing tactics of individuals and the social cocoon of socialization which helps reduce any dissonance observed by individuals into acceptance of corruption. In a similar way, socialization of newcomers into corrupt activities is aided when there are leaders and organizational structures in place that ease a newcomer's acceptance and subsequent engagement in immoral activities. Institutionalization also supports rationalization by creating easily acceptable objective accounts of a reality that shrouds the unethical practices associated with the acts involved in such a reality. It helps individuals to rationalize (e.g. appeal to higher loyalties) their acts while avoiding pangs of conscience.

Coercion into corruption or the threat of negative consequences, such as ostracism and demotions, can also induce individuals to grudgingly accept unethical means in organizations. Coercion can be blatant or subtle. Blatant coercion forces individuals to either accept rationalizations in order to comply with the corrupt directives or react in resentment and reactance against the source of coercion. However, in subtle coercion, where for example a manager casually suggests a subordinate lie to a client, the perceived ambiguity about the situation increases for the subordinate. In these ambiguous situations, rewards that foster cooptation are likely to induce the subordinate to corrupt actions.

The development of the three 'pillars' of normalization is in turn facilitated by the development of a 'social cocoon' within the organization (Ashforth and Anand, 2003). In a social cocoon, the firm or sub-unit creates a micro-culture where the norms are very different from those valued by the society members. Members prize their association with the group, identify strongly with the group's values and practices, and actively seek to compartmentalize themselves from external influences. Inside the cocoon, the veterans model the corrupt behavior, newcomers are encouraged to bond with and emulate the veterans, and newcomers are subjected to strong, consistent ideologies, so that they accept and practice the prevalent corrupt acts and view them in a positive light.

An unfortunate outcome of the cocoon formation is that even though the ethical climate of the sub-unit gradually erodes, the members remain oblivious of it. Ethical climate refers to the 'prevailing perceptions of typical organizational practices and procedures that have ethical content' (Victor and Cullen, 1988). The existing members are already socialized, so they tend to view the group in a positive light, easily rationalizing the unethical practices. However, newcomers, who feel the initial pangs of corrupt practices, may also engage in self-censorship and reason that their own misgivings are overblown because the unethical acts are routine and the veterans espouse these behaviors. As a result, members in the cocoon focus on goal attainment without a corresponding focus on the means used to achieve those goals (Trevino, 1990). In the following sections we discuss how some valued practices in organizations can lead to such cocoon formation when their ethical implications are not carefully examined.

Taken-for-granted practices and their effect on normalized corruption
The above discussion illustrates how the three mechanisms – institutionalization, rationalization and socialization – can gradually relegate a firm towards normalized corruption. Once corruption sets in, the three processes mutually reinforce each other, resist change, and are facilitated by a cocoon formation. Thus it is extremely difficult to root corruption out of the system at that stage. An implication of this line of research is to make all too clear to managers that it is vital to understand the normalization process so that it may be prevented.

In this chapter, we highlight four such practices, which if implemented carelessly, can gradually push the organization into the irreversible realm of embedded corruption. Our selection of practices is based on an extensive review of the literature. We believe that these are four key practices that can increase the likelihood that normalized corruption will prevail in organizations. However, we do not intend this list to be complete or exhaustive. Our discussions about these practices emphasize the importance of a careful examination of any practice from an ethical viewpoint prior to implementation in organizations.

Compensation
Compensation has emerged as a widely used organizational tool to recruit and retain executives and to manage their behaviors. While the role of compensation in inducing unethical employee behaviors has been discussed previously (Kerr, 1975; Sims, 1992; Schwartz, 2001), we focus on two specific elements that can aid in the onset of normalized

corruption: (1) fixed pay levels and (2) the incentive mix (such as annual bonuses, incentives, etc.). Fixed pay levels refer to the guaranteed component of employee pay – the annual pay that does not include any incentives. We also use the term fixed pay to include benefits such as medical reimbursement, retirement plans, etc. that are not part of the cash paid to employees. High fixed pay levels are increasingly used as inducements to attract individuals to high-risk jobs or to undesirable locations (Beatty and Zajac, 1994). While often a desirable (and sometimes the only) way to ensure that the firm employs competent executives, the use of higher than market pay can create 'lock-ins' for employees. Individuals receiving above-market pay may develop standards of living that cannot be maintained easily in other jobs. When such employees are exposed to corrupt events, they often find themselves in a bind. Given the risks and uncertainties fraught in whistle blowing (Brief et al., 2001; Haddad and Barrett, 2002; Janis, 1983), such employees may be paralyzed into inaction – they cannot leave because they may have mortgages and other expenses to cover and are unable to find other jobs with similar pay levels. The reduced exit opportunities create strong dissonance brought on by prolonged exposure to the ongoing corruption (Festinger, 1957). Since most individuals cannot sustain dissonance for significant lengths of time (Clore et al., 1994; Clark and Isen, 1982), the salve offered by socialization and rationalization tactics may prove irresistible.

For instance, institutionalized sexual harassment likely continued at Mitsubishi's Normal plant for as long as it did because there were no other employment opportunities in the region that offered similar pay (Weimer and Thorton, 1997). Employees who were victims of the practice, or uncomfortable with it, kept silent and stayed with the organization because of a lack of other opportunities. Similarly, Zekany et al. (2004) point out that WorldCom's top executives were compensated above organizational and industry norms. Such employees were hesitant to jeopardize income levels that could not be earned elsewhere – indeed, as in Normal, Illinois, where Mitsubishi's plant was located, there were few comparable opportunities for WorldCom employees in Jackson, Mississippi. Therefore employees encountered exit barriers and, rather than face persistent dissonance at continually observed ethical deviances, such individuals were likely to adopt rationalizations or succumb to socialization tactics. Zekany et al. (2004) also speculate that board members avoided confrontations with then WorldCom CEO Ebbers because they were lavished with a large number of perks not normally provided to board members by other companies.

Note that we are not necessarily arguing against the use of above-market compensation. Indeed, in many cases such compensation may be a necessity or an integral part of firm strategy. However, we do point out that such compensation creates situations that make it easier for normalized corruption to set in. While we focus on the fixed component of compensation creating a lock-in for employees, incentive pay can also create such situations for employees. For instance, in many organizations, it is a practice to link large amounts of long-term incentives to long vestment periods – thus employees receive incentives only if they've stayed with the organization for a specific length of time. Alternately, while incentives may appear to be contingent on performance, many incentives are so designed that receiving them becomes a virtual certainty. For example, even before the lengthy 'boom market' of the 1990s, Lambert et al. (1991) calculated that the probability of an 'at-the-money' option with a ten-year maturity finishes 'in-the money' (assuming that the stock market return and volatility parameters do not vary in the period) is 0.943.

Similarly, based on the same assumption, but using other parameters, Hall and Murphy (2000) obtained a probability of 0.79. In other words, incentive pay in many cases can be treated as fixed pay – and if it is very large, it locks in employees, making them more susceptible to ongoing normalized corruption.

While incentive pay can lock in employees to the organization, a prime objective of short- and long-term incentives is to align shareholder and executive preferences by linking executive pay to firm or sub-unit performance (Eisenhardt, 1989). A key aspect here is the linkage of incentive pay. Do executives receive the pay based on some objectively determined criteria (such as sales growth, profitability, etc.) or do they receive the incentive pay based on a subjective evaluation of their performance (Beatty and Zajac, 1994; Wiseman and Gomez-Mejia, 1998)? Objective evaluations are typically used in firms where employee behaviors have a strong impact on unit performance or in diversified firms where supervisors have insufficient knowledge about what constitutes appropriate and effective behavior in their subordinates. Subjective evaluations are more likely to be used in highly turbulent and unpredictable environments where several unanticipated factors may muddy up the relationship between executive behavior and performance (Beatty and Zajac, 1994).

While unavoidable in some cases, the use of subjective evaluations to grant incentive pay to employees can make them more susceptible to elements of normalized corruption. In order to achieve subjective rewards, employees at least have to exhibit behaviors that are consistent with the prevalent organizational norms. In such organizations, employees are likely to wear façades of conformity that are 'false representations created by employees to appear as if they embrace organizational values' (Hewlin, 2003: 634). As Lifton's (1986) study of Nazi doctors in Hitler's concentration camps shows, such façades, when repeated over time, lead to routinized behavior and the adoption of rationalizations that allow actors to justify unethical acts to themselves – indeed he found many such rationalizations continued to be used decades after the end of World War II. In a longer run, the façades no longer remain a pretense; employees willfully de-emphasize, compartmentalize, or suppress their acts of corruption in favor of normatively redeeming features of their work or workplace (Ashforth and Kriener, 1999; Wegner, 1989).

Another consequence of conformity generated by subjective determinations of incentive pay (or other forms of rewards, for that matter) may be the appearance of social cocoons within organizations. Subcultures emerge with multiple employees who are tied together by their common behaviors in the pursuit of desired rewards. A clear ingroup is created, with non-conformists being ostracized and left out of organizational activities. For instance, in their book *Final Accounting*, Toffler and Reingold (2005) detail the subculture that was prevalent in Arthur Andersen before its demise – specific norms of dressing, need to conform with lengthy hours of work, eating in 'company-sanctioned' restaurants and so on. The development of such a subculture creates an environment where individuals bond and socialize increasingly with other unit members, and develop their own specialized language. While there are positive aspects to such strong subcultures, they also create a fertile environment for the emergence of a social cocoon and the development of euphemistic language – factors that greatly enhance the likelihood of normalized corruption (Ashforth and Anand, 2003; Anand et al., 2004).

In summary, we expect that compensation designs that create exit barriers by paying above-market levels, and/or have large amounts of incentive pay based on subjective performance criteria, increase the likelihood of the onset of normalized corruption in organizations.

Codes of ethics

In the wake of recent corporate scandals around the world, organizations have become far more proactive in the development of ethics codes and compliance procedures, and the adoption of various other policies such as providing confidential access to ombudspersons for employees (Adams et al., 2001). This is clearly a positive development. The presence of an ethics code in an organization signals organizational commitment to avoid unethical practices. In some cases, it also provides employees with a uniform set of values with which to evaluate their decisions. For instance, after examining organizations with and without ethics codes, Bowen (2002: 275) argues that in organizations without ethics codes, the 'actual belief system used to make decisions could be any number of things and could lead to inconsistent and problematic decisions'. On the other hand, in a recent interview, George Hermann, Vice President and Chief Financial Officer at Jefferson Wells International, commented about ethical codes and other internal control procedures:

> too many companies fall into a 'check the box' mentality regarding corporate governance and internal controls. In other words, there is a lot of focus on the externals, such as board composition, and [Sarbanes–Oxley Section] 404 compliance, at the exclusion of whether honesty, integrity and respect for the stakeholders are actually alive in the organization. (Anon, 2003: 22)

From the point of view of normalized corruption, the presence of an ethical code statement, in the absence of a company-wide supporting initiative, can become just another rationalization tactic. Any ethical uncertainty associated with a decision could be quelled by relying on the presence of the company's ethics code. The ethics code itself may create in the organization an illusion of morality that allows employees to decide that certain unethical decisions are, in fact, quite legitimate (Anand et al., 2004). For instance, McKendall et al. (2002) found that the presence of ethical codes and compliance procedures was positively related to the number of Occupational Safety and Health Act (OSHA) violations. Thus the ethics codes could have been used as merely window dressing or be in place to lessen the impact of sentencing due to the violations. Similarly, Weaver et al. (1999) point out that while a large majority of American companies have adopted ethics codes and statements, the intent may be symbolic since many of these firms have not followed up with more intensive efforts to ensure that there is ethical decision making in firms. Obviously, the mere presence of an ethics code is unlikely to foster ethical behavior. However, previous research suggests that codes of ethics are far more effective in increasing employees' propensity to behave ethically when there is strong management commitment toward ethical behavior (Adams et al., 2001; Trevino and Ball, 1992).

Ethics codes and compliance procedures can help prevent normalized corruption in two ways: (1) building awareness among employees about the firm's ethics codes and helping them appreciate that ethical issues exist in almost every major decision; and (2) encouraging employees willingly to speak up against rationalization and socialization tactics they may encounter in an organization. As awareness of the ethics code increases, there is a higher likelihood that employees believe that the organization places some value on ethical behavior and that unethical behavior is likely to be punished (Valentine and

Barnett, 2003). Positive and negative reinforcements in the firm regarding ethical behavior can discourage easy rationalizations of corrupt acts and also help morally upright employees bring unethical activities to the attention of others.

Awareness of an ethics code must also be supplemented by an understanding and acceptance that most strategic decisions have moral implications. Indeed, normalized corruption happens not because employees are evil, looking for opportunities to engage in unethical acts, but because individuals have either not recognized ethical issues or have used subtle cognitive mechanisms to eliminate ethical considerations from the decision (Ashforth and Anand, 2003). For instance, in the Ford Pinto recall decision, managers converted the injuries and deaths due to the Pinto's exploding fuel tanks into dollar amounts and associated probabilities for their occurrence. Subsequent decisions to withdraw the car were then based on a cost–benefit analysis that was completely separated from the ethical issues involved in continuing to sell a product that endangered human lives (Gioia, 1992). Similarly, in their study of Exxon-Mobil's decision to dump (as allowed by law) hazardous waste in a small community waste-fill, Hamilton and Berken (2005: 399) point out that

> Exxon as a company was committed to efficiency. Middle and lower managers who faced a conflict between cost efficiency and the ethical treatment of people would have chosen efficiency. Efficiency is a hard criterion . . . ethics is a soft criterion difficult to measure in short term costs . . . unless managers know that ethical behavior is rewarded and unethical behavior punished in annual evaluations, pay, and advancement, the priority assigned to ethics will remain ambiguous . . .

And every time a decision is made favoring efficiency over ethics in an organization, it increases the likelihood of normalization because past precedent is a strong predictor of routinization (Ashforth and Anand, 2003).

An effective ethics code and compliance program can also generate normalization-thwarting behaviors by increasing employee willingness to speak up against rationalization and socialization tactics they may encounter in an organization. A good example of such a program is provided in some of the changes initiated by Tyco International after ousting its scandal-plagued CEO, Dennis Kozlowski. E.M. Pillmore (2003), Tyco's Chief Ethics Officer, writing in the *Harvard Business Review*, describes the program as one whose intent was not 'simply to teach people to spot right answers to obviously worded questions but rather to acknowledge that the issues involved are often nuanced and complex. How will you know if you're moving into territory where ethical judgment is required? How will you notice when things begin to smell bad?' They developed vignettes that highlighted such issues and produced several short videos dramatizing the situations and showed them to all employees. Such active intervention probably creates confidence among employees in challenging rationalization and socialization tactics when they encounter them. At the very least, they increase the likelihood that the cognitive dissonance created when an employee first encounters a rationalized unethical act or is socialized into a corrupt practice will be large and difficult to overcome.

In sum, then, we argue that ethics codes and compliance programs can help reduce the likelihood of normalized corruption occurring in an organization, as long as such programs are strongly supported in the organization and not developed for mere window dressing. On the other hand, if the sole purpose of such programs is to create documents that can be shown to external stakeholders, then they may actually increase the likelihood of normalized corruption becoming endemic in an organization. It is indeed interesting that Enron Corporation had a very strongly worded ethics code (a portion out of the 64-page booklet is described below), but unfortunately, it was a mere document.

> Employees of Enron Corp., its subsidiaries, and its affiliated companies are charged with conducting their business affairs in accordance with the highest ethical standards. An employee shall not conduct himself or herself in a manner which directly or indirectly would be detrimental to the best interests of the Company or in a manner which would bring to the employee financial gain separately derived as a direct consequence of his or her employment with the Company. Moral as well as legal obligations will be fulfilled openly, promptly, and in a manner which will reflect pride on the Company's name. (Bastone, 2006)

The disconnect between employees and stakeholders

A third organizational issue that we consider as likely to affect the onset of normalized corruption is that of employee–stakeholder disconnect (ESD). We define employee–stakeholder disconnect as the degree to which organizational actors are separated from individuals and entities who are affected by the ethical implications of their decisions. Traditional organizational theorists such as Thompson (1967) have argued that efficient organizations have a technical core that comprises individuals and practices that perform key throughput functions. The technical core is, or ought to be, surrounded by boundary spanners who interact with the organization's environment, and provide needed inputs to the technical core. This suggests a duality in the organization where some units are distanced from stakeholders, while others are in touch with them. As we move into the twenty-first century, these traditional structures have been replaced to some extent by more flexible forms such as matrix and network organizations that create greater interaction between organizational units and their stakeholders (Lee et al., 2001; March, 1994; Markides, 1997). However, sub-units within organizations are still likely to vary in the extent to which their employees are connected or disconnected with stakeholders.

We argue that there are two ways in which greater ESD increases the chances of normalization of corruption. First, a greater distance from affected stakeholders allows decision makers in organizations or sub-units to depersonalize the affected individuals, to deny responsibility for the final outcomes of their decisions, or even to take more aggressive stances towards victims of their unethical decisions (Ashforth and Anand, 2003). Thus various rationalization strategies can be easily used by employees to excuse themselves of the corrupt acts. Second, it is likely that employees are not even aware of the ethical implications of their jobs on stakeholders. For instance, an increase in ESD can reduce 'heedful interrelating' (Weick and Roberts, 1993; Weick et al., 1999), which exists when individuals in complex systems understand how the system has been configured to achieve some goal or the big picture. With an increase in heedfulness, employees are aware of how their jobs and tasks are related with other activities in the organization and how these jobs affect the overall interests of the organization as well as its stakeholders. As the distance from stakeholders increases, employees are less likely to understand how their individual jobs affect organizational stakeholders (see Bunderson, 2001), thus reducing the chances of employees making decisions while keeping the stakeholders in mind.

In most cases organizational ability to reduce employee–stakeholder distance is likely to be constrained for a variety of reasons. First, as tasks are increasingly complex in today's knowledge-based environments, there is an increased need for specialization among employees (Anand et al., 1998). This often prevents employees from performing a complete task and thus confronting the outcomes of their unethical acts – these, in turn, are factors that facilitate the adoption of denial of responsibility and denial of victim rationalizations (Ashforth and Anand, 2003), for example, medical detail-men who provide doctors with large (and illegal) incentives to prescribe higher-priced drugs, and are oblivious to the hardship caused to impoverished patients who struggle to pay for them. As another example, Enron energy traders were caught on tape shouting 'Burn baby, burn' as forest wildfires raged in California and worsened its energy crisis in 2001 (McLean, 2006). So distant from reality were the traders that they failed to see the hardship endured by individuals who could not afford to pay for utilities in record-setting heat.

In organizations with a large distance from stakeholders, socialization efforts aimed at inducing newcomers to buy into rationalizations are also likely to be much easier since the distance from affected individuals reduces any qualms that employees may have about their actions. For instance, Munro (1998) refers to Bauman's (1991) study of the Nazi era crimes and points out that individuals involved in the mass murder of Jews were able to justify (at least to themselves) their actions based on their distance from victims and the final outcome of the events they participated in. Thus individuals who were responsible for loading Jews into trains that took them to concentration camps justified their personal actions by claiming that they were only responsible for transporting the Jews and that if they did not do so, it might lead to disruption of train schedules. While there were rumors that Jews were subjected to evils at their destination, there was no guarantee that they would not be subjected to evil at the rail station itself if they were not boarded on trains.

A second reason for an organization's constrained ability to reduce employee–stakeholder distance may lie in the large numbers of stakeholders affected by employee decisions. For instance, consumer product or utility firms may have millions of customers, and at best employees may know a minuscule fraction of the total employees. Given limited cognitive information-processing abilities, employees will be forced to use categorization processes in thinking about consumers, thus distancing them from the customers' individual personalities. Furthermore, categories can easily be depersonalized, vividly demonstrated recently by Danley (2005) in his re-evaluation of the Pinto case. He points out that at the time the Pinto was under development, Ford issued the Grush–Suanby report that opposed enactment of regulations that required increased safety features in cars. Arguing that the cost of compliance was $137 million (at $11 per vehicle), and assuming that the cost of a person killed was $200 000 and that of a burn victim $67 000, Ford argued that complying with the safety regulations would thus have a societal cost of $49.5 million (assuming 180 deaths and 180 burn victims). Indeed, the large distance from the millions of potential buyers easily allowed Ford executives to think about possible victims in dollar terms rather than seeing them as parents or breadwinners in families. Had they done so, perhaps their final decisions would have been different. Yet another example of the problems inherent in employee–stakeholder distancing was demonstrated in the recently released tapes of Enron traders who were found to be manipulating electricity generation during California's power crisis in 2001. In response to a fellow trader's quip asking how many Grandmas he had bilked in California (due to higher energy prices), an Enron trader responded: 'Yeah, Grandma Millie, man. But she's the one who couldn't figure out how to vote on the butterfly ballot' (Rose, 2004: 1).

In effect, normalized corruption is much more likely to occur where organization structure, organization strategy, or industry environment has created a distance between employees and affected stakeholders. While organizational decisions are often complex and creating distance may be the only way of making hard decisions while separating the emotions involved, organizations need to bear in mind that there are negative consequences of such large distances between employees and stakeholders. It is possible for organizational efforts to reduce distance and, thus, protect against normalization, but often times organizations increase employee–stakeholder distance at the first whiff of an ethical breakdown. For instance, Hamilton and Berken (2005) detail the story of Exxon-Mobil and the Grand-Bois Community in Louisiana. Exxon-Mobil had moved hazardous waste to the community of Grand-Bois and when the first reports of individuals being affected surfaced, no efforts were made by any company employees to visit the disaster first hand. In fact, the local manager who received a letter from a community leader did not respond to the letter, stating in a subsequent media interview that he had referred the letter to legal counsel. While legal advice may have been behind Exxon-Mobil's decision, it ultimately ended up costing them large amounts of animosity and bad press, and ultimately led to a reversal of the decision.

Handling the discovery of unethical acts
In all organizations, there is always the likelihood of isolated unethical acts by rogue employees. While such acts are almost impossible to eliminate in totality, organizational responses to the discovery of such acts can significantly influence whether normalization could prevail in the future. Organizational reactions can range from denial to acceptance to punishment. For instance, between 1977 and 1982, Beech-Nut Corporation had sold a chemical concoction comprising just sugar and chemicals as apple juice in the USA (Queenan, 1988). The company stonewalled when investigators tried to question the firm. Beech-Nut went to the extent of shipping the adulterated juice out of a plant in New York to Puerto Rico during the night in order to put it beyond the jurisdiction of federal investigators (Kindel, 1989). Clearly the message given to employees was to avoid detection rather than avoid unethical behavior – and this could potentially sow the seeds for future normalization if Beech-Nut had gotten away with their actions.

In a similar instance but with a completely different response, Crane (2005) describes how Procter and Gamble discovered that some of its executives had employed private investigators to rummage through Unilever's trash cans to obtain information about its hair care business. When top management learnt of this, they reacted by publicly acknowledging the wrongdoing, issuing an apology to Unilever, and then agreeing to an out-of-court compensatory settlement of about 10 million dollars. In doing so, P&G clearly indicated to its managers that unethical actions were unacceptable, and created an environment that made it more difficult for employees, to rationalize their acts. The discovery of an unethical act, while damaging in and of itself, provides a great opportunity for organizational leaders to communicate organizational values and priorities to employees, and especially to newcomers. Accepting a mistake, punishing the perpetrators, and taking action to prevent future occurrences embolden newcomers and employees to question unethical practices when they encounter them. On the other hand, if discovery of an unethical act is addressed by denial and cover-up (as in the Beech-Nut example above), employees will feel discouraged in reporting unethical acts and are more likely to become susceptible to rationalization and socialization in the future.

However, just knowing that it is important to handle the discovery of unethical acts in an appropriate manner is not sufficient. Such discoveries, if not part of a systematic process of corrupt acts in an organization, almost always catch top executives by surprise (Nicholson and Miller, 2005). Subsequent to the initial discovery of such acts, and especially if the act becomes public knowledge, events unfold at a rapid pace. There is uncertainty about whether the act is unethical and/or illegal, there is a need to discuss liability issues, there is a need to identify what needs to be communicated to key stakeholders – key decisions that must be made at breakneck speed in circumstances that are fraught with emotion and often unfold under the glare of media publicity. Right intentions in such circumstances do not necessarily lead to right actions, and one wrong decision may be sufficient to lead the organization down a slippery, irreversible path.

Handling the discovery of unethical acts is an increasingly specialized task that needs advanced thought and training. We believe that proper reactions to the discovery of unethical acts are possible only if organizations have thought about these issues in advance. Ideally, firms will have laid out the specific procedures to be followed in case of an unethical discovery. A team that can handle such an occurrence needs to be identified in advance, and team members assigned specific responsibilities (e.g. who will investigate, who will take on the communication role, and so on) and trained to discharge those responsibilities. Firms that have put such procedures in place are likely to handle ethics breakdowns better and thus reduce the likelihood of normalized corruption in the future.

Implications and conclusion

In this chapter we have discussed how some organizational practices, when taken for granted, can cause the normalization of corruption. In the absence of a proper understanding of the ethical implications of these practices, these practices are likely to induce rationalizations of corrupt acts, easily socialize newcomers into organizational corruption, and institutionalize corruption in organizational processes and routines. As discussed, some compensation characteristics (such as fixed pay, subjective rewards) can lock in employees and force them to accept rationalization and socialization techniques to reduce their dissonance with the organizational norms. Organizational structures that distance sub-units or organizations from the affected stakeholders increase chances of employees engaging in unethical behaviors without conscious thought about their propriety. Imperfectly communicated codes of ethics can propagate corruption instead of reducing it because employees are either unaware of the codes or they are unable to judiciously use them in their decision making. Finally, the ways of handling the discovery of immoral acts can influence whether an organization is likely to face ongoing corruption in future.

All our conclusions provide fertile ground for future organizational research. For example, while many researchers have argued that compensation characteristics affect employee behaviors, very few studies have actually examined how different types of compensation practices influence the ethical behavior of employees. As we argued earlier, future research can evaluate how subjective rewards influence employee tendencies to engage in some of the rationalization techniques. Similarly, above-market pay and different incentive mixes are likely to promote rationalization behaviors and socialization techniques. Further research needs to examine the dynamics involved in these factors.

Organizational structure has also been one of the key areas of research in business strategy and policy. However, research in this area lacks frameworks that help us understand which types of structures are likely to ease institutionalization and rationalization of corruption. One good start in this line of research may be an evaluation of the employee–stakeholder disconnect (ESD) created by the organizational structure and its influence on normalization of corruption within the firm. As we have argued earlier, it is likely that sub-units or organizations that are distanced from the affected stakeholders become easy grounds for rationalization and socialization of corrupt acts. Future investigations of this phenomenon can be undertaken at both organizational as well as sub-unit levels.

As against compensation and organizational structure, codes of ethics have received a significant amount of scholarly research. However, we still need grounded frameworks that allow us to predict when the codes of ethics are likely to offset normalized corruption. We have provided two key arguments regarding this. We believe that along with codes of conduct, organizations must create a suitable atmosphere where employees can raise their voice regarding unethical activities. In the absence of organizational thrust behind actually maintaining an ethical climate, the mere presence of codes of ethics will not be effective. Future research needs to test these arguments empirically.

Finally, how organizations handle the discovery of unethical acts has received minimal attention in the current literature on business ethics. Several factors may influence whether organizations are likely to engage in denial, acceptance or punishment of corrupt officials. It is possible that firms that develop the NIH (not invented here) syndrome are more likely to keep justifying their behaviors in the event of the discovery of unethical acts because of their overtly inward focus and consequent formation of a social cocoon within the firm. Firms in industries that have high exit costs are also likely to deny unethical acts because acceptance may jeopardize the very existence of the organization.

In terms of managerial implications, we suggest that executives should realize that several practices, which are no doubt essential for the firm's functioning, may also provide breeding grounds for unethical activities. Organizational practices, therefore, cannot be viewed in isolation from ethical implications emanating from their adoption. While discussing these practices and their influence over organizational corruption, we have argued that managers need to consistently focus on *prevention of corruption* because it is extremely diffcult to reverse the normalized corruption once unethical activities get embedded in organizational routines and processes. Thus, in the case of organizational corruption, prevention may not be better than cure – it probably is the only cure. Throughout our discussion we have highlighted several ways in which managers can reduce the potential threat of normalized corruption arising from different practices.

To conclude, we believe that organizational practices and ethics go hand in hand. The practices, if taken for granted, can provide easy grounds for rationalization, socialization and institutionalization of corruption. While it is obviously a welcome sign that organizations are becoming more sensitive to ethical issues, we need better understanding of how the very practices that build a firm can bring it down by breeding corruption. Our chapter provides ideas and opens a few new potential areas for future research in this direction.

Note

1. Corrupt practices can exist in either a sub-unit or the entire organization. Therefore, unless otherwise specified, we use the term organization to refer to both a complete organization and a sub-unit.

References

Adams, G.B. and D.L. Balfour (eds) (1998), *Unmasking Administrative Evil*, Thousand Oaks, CA: Sage.
Adams, J.S., A. Taschian and T.H. Shore (2001), 'Codes of ethics as signals for ethical behavior', *Journal of Business Ethics*, **29**(3), 199–211.
Anand, V., C.C. Manz and W.H. Glick (1998), 'An organizational memory approach to information management', *Academy of Management Review*, **23**(4), 796–809.
Anand, V., B.E. Ashforth and M. Joshi (2004), 'Business as usual: the acceptance and perpetuation of corruption in organizations', *Academy of Management Executive*, **18**(2), 39–53.
Anon (2003), 'Transparency at the top', *Financial Executive*, 20–23.
Ashforth, B.E. and G.E. Kriener (1999), ' "How can you do it?": dirty work and the challenge of constructing a positive identity', *Academy of Management Review*, **24**(3), 413–34.
Ashforth, B.E. and V. Anand (2003), 'The normalization of corruption in organizations', in R.M. Kramer and B.M. Staw (eds), *Research in Organizational Behavior*, Vol. 25, Oxford: Elsevier, pp. 1–51.
Bastone, W. (ed.) (2006), 'Enron's code of ethics', www.thesmokinggun.com/enron/enronethics5.htm, 30 January.
Bauman, Z. (1991), 'The social manipulation of morality: moralizing actors, adiophorizing action', *Theory, Culture and Society*, **8**(1), 137–51.
Beatty, R.P. and E.J. Zajac (1994), 'Managerial incentives monitoring, and risk bearing: a study of executive compensation ownership and board structure in initial public offerings', *Administrative Science Quarterly*, **39**(2), 313–35.
Benson, M.L. (1985), 'Denying the guilty mind: accounting for involvement in a white-collar crime', *Criminology*, **23**, 583–607.
Birnbaum, J.H. (ed.) (1992), *The Lobbyists: How Influence Peddlers Work their Way in Washington*, New York: Times Books.
Bowen, S.A. (2002), 'Elite executives in issues management: the role of ethical paradigms in decision making', *Journal of Public Affairs*, **2**(4), 270–83.
Braithwaite, J. (1984), *Corporate Crime in the Pharmaceutical Industry*, London: Routledge & Kegan Paul.
Brief, A.P., R.T. Buttram and J.M. Dukerich (2001), 'Collective corruption in the corporate world: toward a process model', in M.E. Turner (ed.), *Groups at Work: Theory and Research*, Mahwah, NJ: Lawrence Erlbaum Associates, pp. 471–99.
Bunderson, J.S. (2001), 'Normal injustices and morality in complex organizations', *Journal of Business Ethics*, **33**(3), 181–90.
Clark, M.S. and A.M. Isen (1982), 'Toward understanding the relationship between feeling states and social behavior', *Cognitive Social Psychology*, 73–108.
Clore, G.L., N. Schwarz and M. Conway (1994), 'Affective causes and consequences of social information processing', in R.S. Wyer, Jr and T.K. Srull (eds), *Handbook of Social Cognition, Vol. 1: Basic Processes*, Hillsdale, NJ: Lawrence Erlbaum Associates, pp. 323–417.
Coleman, J.W. and L.L. Ramos (1998), 'Subcultures and deviant behavior in the organizational context', in P.A. Bamberger and W.J. Sonnenstuhl (eds), *Research in the Sociology of Organizations*, Vol. 15, Stamford, CT: JAI Press, pp. 3–34.
Crane, A. (2005), 'In the company of spies: when competitive intelligence gathering becomes industrial espionage', *Business Horizons*, **48**(3), 233–40.
Danley, J.R. (2005), 'Polishing up the Pinto: legal liability, moral blame, and risk', *Business Ethics Quarterly*, **15**(2), 205–36.
Darley, J.M. (2001), 'The dynamics of authority influence in organizations and the unintended action consequences', in J.M. Darley, D.M. Messick and T.R. Tyler (eds), *Social Influences on Ethical Behavior in Organizations*, Mahwah, NJ: Lawrence Erlbaum Associates, pp. 37–52.
DiMaggio, P. and Walter W. Powell (1983), 'The iron cage revisited: institutional isomorphism and collective rationality in organizational fields', *American Sociological Review*, **48**(2), 147–60.
Eisenhardt, K.M. (1989), 'Making fast strategic decisions in high-velocity environments', *Academy of Management Journal*, **32**, 543–76.
Festinger, L. (1957), *A Theory of Cognitive Dissonance*, Oxford: Row, Peterson.
Gioia, D.A. (1992), 'Pinto fires and personal ethics: a script analysis of missed opportunities', *Journal of Business Ethics*, **11**(5/6), 379–89.
Haddad, C. and A. Barrett (2002), 'A whistle-blower rocks an industry; Doug Durand's risky documentation of fraud at drugmaker TAP is prompting wider probes', *Business Week*, 3788, 126.

Hall, B.J. and K.J. Murphy (2000), 'Optimal exercise prices for executive stock option', *American Economic Review*, **90**, 209–14.

Hamilton, J.B. and E.J. Berken (2005), 'Exxon at Grand Bois, Louisiana: a three level analysis of management decision making and corporate conduct', *Business Ethics Quarterly*, **15**(3), 385–408.

Hewlin, P.A. (2003), 'And the award for the best actor goes to . . .: facades of conformity in organizational settings', *Academy of Management Review*, **28**(4), 633–42.

Janis, I.L. (1983), *Groupthink: Psychological Studies of Policy Decisions and Fiascoes*, 2nd edn, Boston, MA: Houghton Mifflin.

Kerr, S. (1975), 'On the folly of rewarding A while hoping for B', *Academy of Management Journal*, **18**(4), 769–83.

Kindel, S. (1989), 'Bad apple for baby', *Financial World*, **158**, 48.

Lambert, R.A., D.F. Larcker and R.E. Verrecchia (1991), 'Portfolio considerations in valuing executive compensation', *Journal of Accounting Research*, **29**, 129–49.

Lee, C., K. Lee and J.M. Pennings (2001), 'Internal capabilities, external networks, and performance: a study on technology-based ventures', *Strategic Management Journal*, **22**(6/7), 615–40.

Lifton, R.J. (1986), *The Nazi Doctors: Medical Killing and the Psychology of Genocide*, New York: Basic Books.

McKendall, M., B. DeMarr and C. Jones-Rikkers (2002), 'Ethical compliance programs and corporate illegality: testing the assumption of the corporate sentencing guidelines', *Journal of Business Ethics*, **37**(4), 367–83.

McLean, B. (2006), 'A feisty utility fends off Enron's big bad creditors', *Fortune*, **154**(2), 32.

March, J.G. (1994), *A Primer on Decision Making: How Decisions Happen*, New York: The Free Press.

Markides, C.C. (1997), 'To diversify or not to diversify', *Harvard Business Review*, **75**(6), 93–9.

Mars, G. (1994), *Cheats at Work: An Anthropology of Workplace Crime*, Aldershot, UK: Dartmouth.

Munro, R. (1998), 'Ethics and accounting: the dual technologies of self', in M. Parker (ed.), *Ethics and Organizations*, Thousand Oaks, CA: Sage, pp. 198–220.

Nelson, R.R. and S.G. Winter (1982), *An Evolutionary Theory of Economic Change*, Cambridge, MA: Belknap Press.

Nicholson, A. and T. Miller (2005), 'Life after scandal', *Corporate Legal Times*, June, 40–49.

Perrow, C. (1984), *Normal Accidents: Living with High Risk Technologies*, New York: Basic Books.

Pfeffer, J. and G.R. Salancik (1978), *The External Control of Organizations: A Resource Dependence Perspective*, New York: Harper & Row.

Pillmore, E.M. (2003), 'How we're fixing up Tyco', *Harvard Business Review*, **81**(12), 96–103.

Queenan, J. (1988), 'Juice Men: ethics and the Beech-Nut sentences', *Barron's National Business and Financial Weekly*, **68**, 37–8.

Rose, C.D. (2004), 'Tapes reveal market-rigging discussions at Enron', *Knight Ridder Tribune Business News*, 3 June.

Schwartz, M. (2001), 'The nature of the relationship between the corporate codes of ethics and behavior', *Journal of Business Ethics*, **32**(3), 247–62.

Scott, W.R. (2001), *Institutions and Organizations*, 2nd edn, Thousand Oaks, CA: Sage.

Sherman, L.W. (1980), 'Three models of organizational corruption in agencies of social control', *Social Problems*, **27**, 478–91.

Sims, R.R. (1992), 'The challenge of ethical behavior in organizations', *Journal of Business Ethics*, **11**(7), 505–13.

Thompson, J.D. (1967), *Organizations in Action*, New York: McGraw-Hill.

Toffler, B.L. and J. Reingold (2003), *Final Accounting: Ambition, Greed and the Fall of Arthur Andersen*, New York: Broadway Books.

Trevino, L.K. (1990), 'A cultural perspective on changing and developing organizational ethics', *Research in Organizational Change and Development*, **4**, 195–230.

Trevino, L.K. and G.A. Ball (1992), 'The social implications of punishing unethical behavior: observers' cognitive and affective reactions', *Journal of Management*, **18**(4), 751–68.

Valentine, S. and T. Barnett (2003), 'Ethics code awareness, perceived ethical values, and organizational commitment', *Journal of Personal Selling and Sales Management*, **4**, 359–67.

Victor, B. and B.C. Cullen (1988), 'The organizational bases of ethical work climates', *Administrative Science Quarterly*, **33**, 101–25.

Weaver, G.R., L.K. Trevino and P.L. Cochran (1999), 'Corporate ethics practices in the mid-1990's: an empirical study of the Fortune 1000', *Journal of Business Ethics*, **18**(3), 283–94.

Wegner, D.M. (1989), *White Bears and Other Unwanted Thoughts: Suppression, Obsession, and the Psychology of Mental Control*, New York: Viking.

Weick, K.E. and K.H. Roberts (1993), 'Collective mind in organizations: heedful interrelating on flight decks', *Administrative Science Quarterly*, **38**(3), 357–81.

Weick, K.E., K.M. Sutcliffe and D. Obstfeld (1999), 'Organizing for high reliability: processes of collective mindfulness', in B. Staw and R. Sutton (eds), *Research in Organizational Behavior*, Vol. 21, pp. 81–123.

Weimer, D.A. and E. Thornton (1997), 'Slow healing at Mitsubishi: it's clearing up sex-harassment charges, but ill will lingers', *Business Week*, 3545, 22 September, 74–6.

Wiseman, R.M and L.R. Gomez-Mejia (1998), 'A behavioral agency model of managerial risk taking', *Academy of Management Review*, **23**(1), 133–53.

Zekany, K.E., L.W. Braun and Z.T. Warder (2004), 'Behind closed doors at WorldCom: 2001', *Issues in Accounting Education*, **19**(1), 101–17.

15 The dysfunction of territoriality in organizations
Graham Brown and Sandra L. Robinson

Alex was the team leader in charge of developing a new program for WARE Inc. He had worked numerous months with his team of software engineers to develop this new program. Although he knew it was common for programs to be cancelled, he was still upset to learn that the company had decided that the product he developed was not viable. Fortunately, the code he was developing could be used as the base of a new program that the company decided was more lucrative and they wanted Alex to lead that new effort. But Alex refused to turn over the code, even when the organization threatened him with a demotion. The company was faced with an awkward situation. What was going on?

At first glance, it appears Alex was manipulating the politics of the situation for personal gain. Much like the machine experts identified by Pfeffer (1981), who binned the manuals to ensure they were the irreplaceable sole operators of their machines, Alex was holding onto a valuable scarce resource. Yet, clearly, this could not explain it all. The company provided lucrative incentives, and Alex was going to lead the new program regardless. Moreover, Alex faced major repercussions from his actions and he knew his behavior was negatively impacting his reputation. The company was at a loss to deal with this predicament. Alex had produced the code using company resources, in company time, and was paid well by the company. The company owned the code. Or did they? Academics are paid to write papers and represent their employers when they publish their work. But who owns it? When the work is published, it becomes the journal's proprietary, legal claim. But does this lessen the felt ownership of the writer over the paper?

Alex's situation and, more specifically, the dilemma faced by his organization can be best understood from the perspective of territoriality. Territoriality involves feelings of ownership over things at work, and behaviors used to mark and defend our claims over those things that we believe belong to us. The refusal of Alex to allow his code to be modified or used reflects his attachment to the original idea that he helped create. What was important to Alex was to control use of that code which he felt belonged to him, even if he was not legally entitled to it.

Territoriality is an important, prevalent and overlooked aspect of work in organizations. Territoriality reflects and fulfills basic human needs of ownership and, as such, it can be functional to individuals and groups. Despite their benefits, territorial feelings and behaviors have both direct and indirect negative side effects in organizations. As such, it is critical for organizations to understand, recognize and effectively manage territorial issues inherent in the workplace.

In this chapter we discuss the nature of territoriality in organizations, and the myriad of negative implications of this phenomenon for individuals, groups and organizations. We begin by introducing the concept of territoriality and its key concepts, including territorial feelings, territorial behaviors and territorial infringement. For each of these aspects of territoriality, we address their negative implications. That is, we identify some of the key problems associated with territorial feelings, behavior and infringement. In the final section we discuss how the misunderstanding and mismanagement of territoriality may contribute to its dysfunctionality and then we offer practical advice to help managers cope more effectively with the potential dysfunction of territoriality.

The nature of territoriality

Territoriality was first observed and studied in animals (Edney, 1975; Sundstrom and Altman, 1974) in the early twentieth century. The early animal research was focused mostly on biological determinants of territories and did not generate much interest for study in human populations. However, in the mid-1970s scholars began to view human territoriality over physical space and objects as a means to organize people so that violence, aggression and overt domination were unnecessary. In a review of the field published shortly after this shift in focus, Stokols (1978: 271) argued that 'recent analyses have emphasized the cognitive and social–organizational functions of human territoriality rather than its biological (reproductive and survival-related) aspects'.

The shift in focus toward the cognitive and social functions of territoriality led to a proliferation of research, most highlighting its functionality (Brown, 1987; Malmberg, 1980). For example, territoriality over the physical world was found to be linked to identity construction (Altman and Chemers, 1980; Tuan, 1980), conflict management (Altman and Haythorn, 1967; Rosenblatt and Budd, 1975), safety (Brown, 1983), social cohesion (Altman, 1975; Brown and Werner, 1981; Lewis, 1979) and improved group effectiveness (Sundstrom and Altman, 1989). Relatedly, feelings of ownership over physical space have been found to be associated with more responsibility for (Rodgers and Freundlich, 1998) and positive evaluations of the object itself (Nuttin, 1987).

In recent years, the study of territoriality has moved into the organization. This organizational perspective takes a much broader focus, no longer limited to territoriality over physical space and objects. Indeed, we now know from recent research that individuals and groups can experience territorial feelings and behavior over all aspects of organizational life, such as roles, tasks, relationships, ideas, products, and even time (Brown et al., 2005; Brown and Robinson, 2006; Pierce et al., 2001, 2003).

Formally, we define territoriality in organizations as the behaviors people use to express their feelings of ownership toward physical or social entities. Embedded in the idea of territoriality are both feelings of possessiveness and action oriented towards claiming, communicating and protecting our claims of ownership. Territoriality involves attachment or territorial feelings toward an object or social entity, which in turn leads to the social construction of it as a territory through processes of signaling and defending it *vis-à-vis* others. These feelings and behaviors over possessions are reinforcing, such that feelings lead to behaviors, and yet engaging in territorial behaviors also reinforces one's territorial feelings.

To understand the phenomenon of territoriality more generally, and to explore its negative implications more specifically, it is useful to consider territorial feelings, behaviors and infringement separately. Below we discuss each of these in turn.

Territorial feelings

Prior research has identified a number of factors that influence the feelings of ownership that an individual will develop with regard to a particular object or social entity. The most obvious, or 'rational' factor, impacting a sense of ownership is the centrality or value of the object to the individual. The psychological or intrinsic value of an object or entity is important to a sense of ownership (Taylor and Stough, 1978), but so too is its value as a strategic or political resource that brings extrinsic rewards to its possessor (Clegg, 1989). Indeed, a basic component of power in organizations is the role that valued resources pay in extracting benefits to the controller of those resources (Pfeffer and Salancik, 1978).

Although the value of entities plays a role in developing a sense of ownership over them, territoriality is about much more than 'rational' or strategic control of valued resources. The development of proprietary attachment to things at work is not so much reflective of a rational calculus of the costs and benefits of ownership, but rather of naturally occurring psychological mechanisms and needs.

As Pierce and colleagues have argued, individuals have an inherent need to attach themselves to objects and entities, and to acquire a sense of ownership over facets of their environment (Pierce et al., 2001, 2003; Pierce et al., 1991). In any context, individuals' sense of ownership fulfills basic fundamental needs, including the need to express one's identity and to have a sense of control or efficacy over one's environment (see Pierce et al., 2003 for a review).

Research shows that organizational members are more likely to develop proprietary attachment to objects or entities at work that enable them to express, construct or maintain their social identity at work (Brown and Altman, 1981; Dittmar, 1992). Objects vary in terms of how important they are to individuals' identity construction (Altman and Chemers, 1980; Ashforth and Mael, 1989; Goffman, 1959; Tuan, 1980). For some organizational members, identity expression through proprietary relationships with things in the organization may be a key strategy for establishing who they are in relation to others in the organization and for creating impressions for themselves and others (Brown and Werner, 1985).

Individuals are also more likely to attach themselves to objects or social entities into which they have invested their self (Czikszentmihalyi and Rochberg-Halton, 1981; Pierce et al., 2001). Investments of self include time, effort, ideas, expertise or attention (Pierce et al., 2001). They might include, for example, extended effort to get a marketing project off the ground, sacrifices made to gain a senior position in the firm, or time taken to obtain a coveted parking pass.

Finally, the amount of time or degree of interaction one has had with a particular object will strengthen one's sense of ownership over it (Brown et al., 2005). By interacting or using the object, one gains information or knowledge about it (Beggan and Brown, 1994; Rudmin and Berry, 1987), gains greater familiarity with it, and thus deepens one's relationship to it (Pierce et al., 2001).

This research suggests that attachment to an object or entity is a function of variety of psychological mechanisms, many of which cannot be explained by simple reference to the objective value of the object. Though numerous external factors may alter the strength of ownership feelings, the need to own will persist.

Given the role of such attachments, it is tempting to conclude that such feelings are functional to the individual organizational member. Indeed, previous research supports the notion that territoriality is important. Despite the functionality and inevitability of such feelings, they also pose several challenges or problems. We shall now discuss some of those challenges.

The dysfunction of territorial feelings
As we will discuss below, territorial feelings, though potentially beneficial to the individual, can undermine organizational effectiveness in a number of ways. Although attachment in degrees is useful, it poses challenges to sharing, cooperation and collective efforts toward organizational goals, potentially hurting the individual and the organization.

Ineffective knowledge sharing   From an organizational perspective, it is critical for individual members, groups and divisions to openly share and exchange knowledge, ideas, information and work output to achieve organizational goals. Understandably, organizations promote and encourage such sharing and exchange, and in many cases ensure their rightful ownership and control over intellectual capital through policies and contracts. Despite these forces, individual organizational members invariably develop a sense of attachment, if not ownership, over their creations of knowledge and intellectual products. The ideas, knowledge and information created by individuals and groups tend to be particularly reflective of those individuals and groups. Products of the mind or group activity are intimately known to the creators, and their source is clear. Thus knowledge, information and ideas are likely to be intensely felt territories. Given these divergent feelings of ownership over ideas and knowledge, it is likely that this territorial terrain is fraught with tension.

This tension around knowledge territory creates two potential problems for the organization. One prominent challenge is that despite the importance of knowledge sharing and idea cooperation to organizational goals and organizational efforts to enhance it, individuals and groups of the organization may resist such sharing. Indeed, recent research demonstrates that individuals actually hide information, and are reluctant to share it when asked (Connelly et al., 2006), or given the opportunity (Robinson and Brown, 2006).

Moreover, one can speculate that the more that norms and formal policy dictate knowledge sharing, and the more pressure that is created for such cooperation, the worse this problem may become. Under such circumstances, resistance will become covert and underground and thus less possible for management to know about and influence. Also, prior research shows that resistance to sharing may be stronger when one feels others are demanding it. In an interesting series of studies by Ruback (Ruback and Juieng, 1997; Ruback and Snow, 1993; Ruback et al., 1989), it was found that if people sense others are waiting to use public resources, such as a parking space or a phone booth, they spend more time with that resource than they would otherwise. Extrapolating this effect to knowledge sharing in the workplace, individuals may be even more reluctant to share their knowledge and ideas when pressured to do so than when left to their own free will.

Another problem posed by feelings of territoriality over knowledge is that the individuals or groups who create them may believe they have a right to use or share that information however they wish. Thus, for example, they may convey sensitive information to professional colleagues in competing firms (Brodt and Sitkin, 2006), or use that knowledge to start their own ventures (Brown and Menkhoff, 2007). These efforts not only run counter to the organization's beliefs and legal claims over such knowledge, but obviously conflict with the organization's interests.

Resistance to change   Another potential challenge posed by territorial feelings is evident during organizational change efforts. Organizational change, by placing aspects of the organization in flux, potentially threaten an individual's or group's sense of ownership over a wide swath of territories, such as the nature of specific roles, relationships, workspaces and status. When feelings of ownership are threatened, organizational members may resist change and engage in a variety of behaviors to protect their proprietary attachments. Organizational members with territories in the existing organizational structure or system will be reluctant to embrace change efforts that may undermine these attachments. Indeed, many of the struggles facing organizational change efforts may be better understood by using the lens of territoriality.

Change involving shifts in the social structure may be particularly problematic from a territoriality perspective because it undermines shared social understandings of the territorial boundaries that exist. An influx of new organizational members, for example, means that too many people are unaware of the invisible but social boundaries around ownership. These new individuals also have to carve out their own territories among the pre-existing ones. As such, newcomers shift boundaries of perceived ownership and with that, renegotiation, tension and potential conflicts emerge in the environment.

Territoriality can also hamper change efforts involving succession. In such cases, due to territorial feelings, leaders and founders may struggle to let go of the companies or units or products they have built. Thus, even when it is strategically or financially wise to loosen the reins, those who had prior proprietary ownership over something that belonged to them may consciously (or not so consciously) resist such moves. This effect will be especially strong if the duration of ownership has been long, or the owner's identity is embedded in that which they must give up.

Limits on creativity and decision making   Feelings of territoriality can also impede creativity and decision making by limiting the possible options considered, or by fueling escalation of commitment to a bad decision or losing course of action. To the extent that individuals or groups invest in, and identify with, particular choices they make, or ideas they share, the less willing they are to concede the lack of value in those ideas or abandon them altogether for better ones. Thus, to the extent that we are more tied to our own ideas and creations, we are less willing to take on and endorse others ideas, even if they may be superior.

Territorial behavior
Territorial feelings lead to territorial behaviors. The stronger one's attachments, the more one feels a need to communicate that ownership to others, to identify and communicate boundaries around that ownership, and to regulate the use of that territory by others. In a previous paper we (Brown et al., 2005) outline several key territorial behaviors that people use to mark, claim and defend objects that they feel are theirs. We discuss each of these behaviors below.

Control-oriented marking
Control-oriented marking involves actions and symbols that communicate to others the boundaries around a territory and, most importantly, one's psychological ownership over it (Altman, 1975; Becker and Mayo, 1971; Smith, 1983). Examples might include putting a sign on one's door, or telling others about one's idea in a meeting. Such marking serves to communicate that someone has claimed a territory so that other people are discouraged from accessing or using the territory as their own.

Identity-oriented marking
Identity-oriented marking, or personalization, is the deliberate decoration or modification of an object by its owners to reflect the owner's identity (Sommer, 1974; Sundstrom and Sundstrom, 1986). Examples might include putting pictures of one's family on one's desk, or changing the birthday celebration ritual once it becomes one's role. Identity-oriented marking serves to enable individuals to construct and express their identities to themselves and to others through the ownership of things at work. It allows individuals to influence how others see them and what they are associated with.

Anticipatory defenses
Although marking demarcates territorial boundaries and indicates the relationship between a territory and an individual, the socially defined nature of these boundaries and attachments means they will sometimes be subject to differing interpretations (Brown and Altman, 1981, 1983; Lyman and Scott, 1967; Wollman et al., 1994). As a result, individuals may engage in anticipatory defenses, actions designed to thwart infringements that might be made in the future by others (Dyson-Hudson and Smith, 1978; Edney, 1975, 1976; Knapp, 1978). Examples of anticipatory defenses include a lock on a door, a password on computer files, or even planted ideas that are useless, but prevent someone from stealing the valid ones.

Reactionary defenses
Reactionary defenses are responses to infringement attempts by others: how one reacts if someone uses or takes that which they see as belonging to them (Brown et al., 2005; Wollman et al., 1994). Examples include confronting the individual, taking the issue to higher-ups, or putting up greater barriers. Such reactions can serve a variety of purposes, from a simple expression of frustration to undermining the infringement, or to preventing future attempts.

The dysfunction of territorial behaviors
We have considered how feelings of territoriality can create potential problems for individuals and the organizations in which they work. Territorial behaviors may protect valued territories, but such behaviors also come with costs, both direct and indirect. We now examine how the territorial behaviors noted above may be detrimental to individuals and their organizations.

Injured reputation   Individuals naturally gravitate toward a sense of ownership over a wide range of objects at work, often without conscious thought. In work organizations, employees often come to treat communal resources as their own private territories. For example, communal space often gets taken over by particular individuals or groups. From the psychology of ownership and territoriality, such behavior is natural and often functional for those engaging in it. Yet, to those observing territorial behavior, it is viewed as petty, political behavior, or resource hoarding. Those seen as behaving territorially can be labeled as uncooperative or non-team players. Indeed, co-workers tend to negatively evaluate territorial individuals, especially those who engage in anticipatory defenses (Brown, 2006). Thus marking and defending one's territory may have negative effects on the territorial individual and may negatively impact their reputation among others. A good example of this effect is what happened to the fictional Les Nessman from WKRP. Les did not have an office yet he would mark the walls of an imaginary office with tape and require people to 'knock' before answering. His fellow co-workers interpreted this behavior as a sign that Les was 'strange'.

Isolation   Territorial behaviors may protect valued territories, but the creation and protection of one's territory requires significant energy and resources. For example, the direct costs of constructing anticipatory defenses around a physical location not to be used by others may include the cost of installing and maintaining physical mechanisms, such as locks, doors, surveillance cameras or alarm systems. Social boundary mechanisms for the same purpose, such as secretaries and receptionists, are also costly.

On the side of softer social costs, individual employees who seek to protect their turf may find additional overlooked long-term costs. Thus, while they may win the battle in terms of protecting a valued asset, they may lose the war in terms of social relations at work and in sharing of the cooperative bounty of workplace life.

The individual preoccupied by territoriality may lose out in communication opportunities or the benefits that come from sharing and exchanging resources with others (Szilagyi and Holland, 1980). Those deemed non-team players may be overlooked for promotion or other benefits bestowed by management. Among peers, the territorial employee may be ostracized, ridiculed, or even excluded from formal and informal opportunities because of a lack of trust. For example, the sessional instructor who demands ownership over a particular course because they taught it in the past may ultimately get to keep that course, but the department chair may be reluctant in the future to award additional courses to them, given their attitude.

Although the development of territorial boundaries can facilitate coordination, at times it may also impede needed interaction when individuals and groups are overly sensitive about issues of territoriality. Such boundaries create areas that employees do not enter, groups they will not seek to join, or projects they will not go near, all out of respect for unspoken but assumed territorial boundaries which they do not want to infringe. Such unspoken respect for territories may undermine collaboration, interaction and the achievement of organizational goals. To illustrate with an example, one of us authors recalls the unspoken but shared understanding among PhD students in graduate school around students working with faculty. Out of respect and fear of infringing each other's territory, students avoided working with faculty that they felt were already 'taken' by other students. This unspoken understanding, not known to faculty, was entirely counterproductive to student development and the betterment of the PhD program in general.

Psychological discomfort   Engaging in territorial behaviors should and does increase the security of one's claims and reduce uncertainty in the workplace. By marking a territory as one's own, one gains confidence that others share that understanding and will respect their proprietary claim. By implementing anticipatory defenses, the individual fearing possible intrusion or threat may instead feel confident that if attempted, an infringement will be unsuccessful. Thus, engaging in territorial behaviors may create psychological safety.

In contrast, however, territoriality may actually reduce the psychological safety of those who have to navigate the minefield of invisible ownership. If employees feel cut off, excluded, or stressed from territorial boundaries, they themselves will be less committed to the organization. Unfortunately, as the following example illustrates, sometimes the organization is responsible for creating this type of discomforting and detrimental situation. A service firm in the Netherlands was trying to maximize space usage. A group of employees, each with their own personal workspace, only worked four days a week. The organization hired an additional employee but rather than assign them their own workspace, they let them rotate through the other available spaces when not occupied. Although the existing employees agreed to this arrangement, in practice it did not work when on occasion the unoccupied workspace became reoccupied by an unexpected employee coming in on a day off. Not surprisingly this environment created sufficient psychological discomfort for the new employee that it ultimately led to their resignation.

Conflict   Territorial behavior has implications for conflict in organizations. Some territorial behaviors, such as control-oriented marking and anticipatory defenses, may reduce the level of conflict among organizational members if and when they lead to a shared understanding of who controls what resources and how they may be used. Prior research has shown that the territoriality of physical space is related to managing conflict (Altman and Haythorn, 1967; Edney, 1974; Freedman, 1979; Rosenblatt and Budd, 1975) and thus we would expect territoriality over other facets of organizational life to also facilitate the management of conflict. For example, the establishment of boundaries helps people to regulate access to each other, which can facilitate task accomplishment, social cohesion (Altman and Haythorn, 1967; Altman et al., 1971), and smooth functioning within social units (Rosenblatt and Budd, 1975; Altman et al., 1972). Markings clarify boundaries and the proprietary nature of territories (Becker and Mayo, 1971; Brown, 1987) and both animals and humans tend to respect those boundaries and search for resources or space somewhere else, in order to avoid the practical and emotional costs of conflict. Along similar lines, the construction of anticipatory defenses that limit the potential for infringement on others' territories will also mute conflict. Locks on doors, policies restricting who can belong to what group, and 'created by' stamps all work to minimize the degree to which territory holders need to deal directly with those who might want to use that which belongs to them (Knapp, 1978; Sundstrom and Sundstrom, 1986).

Although conflict may be reduced when territorial behaviors create agreed-upon territories, we contend that territorial behavior can actually *increase* conflict if it involves territory that is not agreed upon or if, over time, disagreement over ownership arise. Territorial behaviors may increase conflict by highlighting or escalating disagreements over territory. Marking and defense behaviors may make explicit a disagreement over territories that was previously only implicit or unacknowledged, and consequently increase the level of conflict. Moreover, the act of marking or defending territory that one sees as one's own will lead to a sense of infringement by another if that other also feels proprietary attachment to that territory. At the extreme end of the scale, invaded territories may be major triggering events for workplace violence (Buchanan, 1998). The conflict inherent in reacting may damage future relations between the organizational members involved. Thus there is a paradox of marking and defending territories.

The above sections outline some of the potential problems associated with having territorial feelings and the territorial behavior that emanates from them. Our discussion also underscores the value that organizational members place on their territories, given the efforts they go to in order to protect them. Yet, despite attempts to mark and defend one's territories, these efforts are not always successful. In such cases, infringement occurs and such infringement also has negative implications for individuals and organizations.

Territorial infringement

Lyman and Scott (1967) describe the act of encroaching on another person's territory or property as an infringement. Infringement is a common occurrence for several reasons. First, the subjective, socially constructed nature of territories means inadvertent infringements can occur. When co-workers claim the same territory or fail to recognize the boundaries of another's territory, it increases the likelihood that at least one will take, use or seek control over another's territory, believing it is free to be claimed as their own. Another reason why infringement occurs is that stakes in territories have value to organizational members. As previously noted, territories serve a number of valuable functions. Thus, despite protective actions on the part of the individual who claims a territory in an organization, there may also be competing incentives for others to infringe and claim or use it as their own territory.

The dysfunction of territorial infringement

Infringements undermine one's claim and control over one's proprietary attachment to something at work. The inability to control that which belongs to oneself, be it space, belongings, roles, identity or relationships, can have a variety of detrimental effects. Infringement can lead to feelings of frustration, fear and even grief for the loss of control of one's possession. Formanek (1991) notes that the loss of possessions can lead to feelings of depression. Related research in the area of social undermining indicates that undermining events evoke emotional reactions such as distress and reduced subjective well-being (e.g. Finch et al., 1989; Rook and Pietromonaco, 1987). Additionally, people may perceive their inability to adequately control their environment as symbolic of their role, value or contribution in the organization (Steele, 1986).

Though research is limited on the experience of infringement regarding the wide range of territories in the workplace, prior empirical work has examined the infringement of physical space, one very common type of territory in organizations. Oldham and Brass (1979) and Zalesny and Farace (1987) both report that a change from private offices to an open office plan led to increased intrusions by others and reduced satisfaction and motivation. Similarly, people who share offices are less able to regulate access to themselves and their space, and more likely to perceive territorial invasions (Wollman et al., 1994). With reduced privacy, workers also experience reduced work satisfaction, involvement and motivation (Dean, 1977; Marans and Spreckelmeyer, 1981). Sutton and Rafaeli (1987) also report a negative relationship between satisfaction and workstation intrusions by others.

Related research on place attachment suggests that loss of place confers significant psychological damage on the individual (Brown and Perkins, 1992). Loss of place means a potential loss of identity, of something one has invested in, and a venue for self-expression. As James (1890: 291–2) notes, our perceptions of our self can go up or down depending on our possessions:

> a man's Self is the sum total of all that he CAN call his, not only his body and his psychic powers, but his clothes and his house, his wife and children, his ancestors and friends, his reputation and

works, his land, and yacht and bank account. All these things give the same emotions. If they wax and prosper, he feels triumphant; if they dwindle and die, he feels cast down.

Moreover, the loss of possessions can lead to 'shrinkage of our personality, a partial conversion of ourselves to nothingness' (ibid.: 178).

This loss of identity emanating from infringement is a major issue and not just one that is restricted to individuals. An excellent example of the importance of territoriality for groups and its relevance to identity comes from Richards and Dobyns's classic article in *Human Organization* (1957). They describe a team of employees who worked in an area called 'The Cage'. Workers in this unit were engaged in filing and locating for a large insurance company. The external boundaries were clearly defined: one of the walls was enclosed in steel mesh and blocked from the view of other employees through the use of large filing cabinets. Pasteboard boxes piled on top of these filing cabinets further obstructed the view of other employees from this unit. One door from this unit led to the audit unit of which they were a part; the other door led to an outside corridor. They developed strong territorial claims to the items in the cage and their belonging to this unit and space. In this cage they established a territory and were physically and psychologically protected. However, at a later point, the company relocated two divisions together on one floor and the cage was changed. The members of the original group remained a unit but they were no longer afforded the territorial claim of a particular place. The external boundaries of this territory became permeable, affecting the social and working autonomy of this once-cohesive group. The results were nearly catastrophic as employee morale declined rapidly, and work efficiency dropped drastically. Psychological stress resulted. There was a loss of freedom and control.

Another potential problem as a result of infringement, or even perceived infringement, includes the reactions that ensue. These reactions may include detrimental conflict, pulling away from a focus on work performance, or negative behaviors such as sabotage, aggression or retaliation (Allen and Greenberger, 1980; Brown and Robinson, 2006; Greenberger and Strasser, 1986). Examples might include sabotaging the infringer's work, or rebuffing the infringer on future work projects. When top management or organizations are seen as responsible for the infringement, retaliation may take many forms of destructive behavior aimed at the organization (Robinson and Bennett, 1997).

An extreme and humorous example illustrating the dysfunctional reactions to infringement occurs in the film *Office Space*. The territory in question was a simple stapler but the employee's attitude towards the stapler was strong. His reaction to continual infringement by his manager taking 'his' stapler ultimately resulted in the employee burning down the office headquarters after, of course, reclaiming his stapler.

Managing territoriality

Territoriality is prevalent and inevitable in organizations. Yet the above discussion on the dysfunctional side of territoriality underscores the fact that managers and organizations have a huge issue to deal with. Unfortunately, it is not uncommon for organizations or their managers to deny territoriality; that is, to make decisions as though territoriality and a sense of ownership do not exist, that they are not important, or that they can be driven away by policy. We contend that managerial strategies that disregard or minimize employee's opportunities for ownership will be counterproductive. Both Ardey (1966) and Altman (1975) cautioned that serious consequences will arise if people's fundamental needs for a sense of ownership are suppressed. Additionally, as we suggested at the outset of this chapter, there are many benefits to having territories in organizations, so to thwart territories is to throw out the baby with the bath water. Rather than simply deny, dismiss or take away a sense of ownership, we argue that organizations and managers need to acknowledge its existence and value, and then be proactive in dealing with it. The organizations' and managers' goals should be to accentuate and harness the benefits of territoriality, while mitigating and eliminating some of the negative repercussions. In this section we offer several suggestions regarding how to more effectively manage territoriality.

The first and most critical step is to acknowledge and correctly identify territoriality as underlying many behaviors and 'problems' in organizations. It is likely common for managers and employees to attribute issues of territoriality to other things for several reasons. One reason is that individuals with territorial feelings or motivations are unlikely to admit it to themselves, let alone to management. Few are willing to acknowledge, or able to explain, why ownership just for the sake of ownership is so important to them. They worry they will be seen as petty, unprofessional or manipulative. Thus organizational members will couch such feelings and behavior in other terms that look more rational or acceptable. So, for example, individuals might argue they are against a change in policy because it will affect performance when in fact they only fear losing their status or they may claim they are the only one who knows how to do a job, when really they do not want to lose ownership over a role.

As our example of Alex at the beginning of this chapter illustrates, understanding that an issue involves territoriality helps managers to correctly address it. This means more research is needed to better understand territoriality, but we also need more dialogue in organizations. Sweeping these feelings of ownership under the carpet will only serve to frustrate employees' needs and will itself result in some of the dysfunction we have discussed above. Rather than ignoring the issue, organizations can explicitly encourage and provide opportunities for ownership.

Second, organizations should put more emphasis on the development of group territories. Brown and Menkhoff (2007) use examples of territoriality in collectivist societies to suggest that one way to reduce individual territoriality and increase sharing is by encouraging people to view objects and entities as secondary territories shared by many. For instance, collectivist cultures are assumed to be less territorial because employees more strongly identify with the larger organization and thus put more effort into trying to help, improve or defend the organization (Nonaka, 1991). Yet this same orientation can exist outside of collectivist societies. Constant et al. (1994: 400) found that a belief in organizational ownership of work encourages and mediates attitudes favoring sharing. Similarly, Salari et al. (2006) found evidence suggesting that territoriality can be lessened if members view the entire organization as a territory, rather than specific areas within it. To the extent that the culture of the organization encourages people to view ideas, spaces and relationships as shared or belonging to the whole organization, rather than to the individual, some of the problems associated with sharing and cooperation can be addressed.

Organizations in non-collectivist environments can create this shared mentality by changing their culture, which can be accomplished through several means. First, repeated messages in various forms from all levels of management can overtly signal the importance and value of such shared or secondary territories. Second, reward structures that encourage behaviors reflecting the sharing of territories can be emphasized. Although such action may be initially prompted by external rewards, it can also establish a pattern of behavior that sustains an understanding that most organizational resources are shared ones.

Perhaps the most important thing that management can do to shift the culture in the right direction is to model the sharing of resources. Thus, rather than emphasize their own territorial claim over floors, policy making and parking spaces, they can lower such boundaries and instead model more open sharing of organizational resources, treating the whole organization as a shared territory for all organizational members to use.

Yet, even within a culture that emphasizes group territories, organizational members may need the opportunity to have a place of their own – to feel proprietary attachment over some things at work. This ability to control something, however small, is a basic human need (Wrzesniewski and Dutton, 2001). To the extent that people have territorial attachment to a place at work, they may commit and feel more attached to the organization. In contrast, if an individual cannot form a territorial attachment they may feel less connected to and satisfied with the organization (Brown, 2006).

In a recent study, Salari and colleagues (2006) argued that people may become more territorial if they lack control in other situations or areas. This has important implications for the management of territoriality in that it suggests that employees will be less territorial if they have a sense of control or ownership over some facets of their work environment. Perhaps organizations can facilitate and provide individual territories in respect of things at work that are less consequential to the functioning of the overall organization. For example, providing physical objects such as lockers and workspaces may allow people to satisfy their ownership needs. Giving individuals opportunities to personalize their workspaces, computers and such may also fulfill those needs. Personalizing spaces gives employees the chance to have control over some aspect of their work, and enables them to feel more connected and satisfied with the organization (Wells, 2000). Research shows that workplaces that encourage individual personalizations benefit from decreased turnover and absenteeism (Becker, 1981; Steele, 1986; Wells, 2000).

The recent trend toward 'hotelling' provides a good example of the dysfunction of territoriality but also suggests ways that it can be mitigated or managed better. Hotelling is the situation where employees do not have a fixed space but instead book space on an as-needed basis for the days they are in the office. Hotelling policies are intended to save organizational resources, but resistance by employees undermines the cost savings. Although one study found that over a quarter of companies that introduced flexible workspace suffered drops in morale (Nathan, 2002), there have been several successful cases which suggest that the downside can be mitigated in several ways. For example, many employees tend to seek the same space repeatedly (Katz-Stone, 1999) and may mark the space with personalizations. There are even stories of several workers collaborating on a coordination effort with regard to a particular office, ensuring only they share the space and respect one another's personalizations of it. Some organizations further support this by encouraging employees to personalize these temporary spaces, or provide small spaces for employees to place personal belongings (Katz-Stone, 1999). These creative solutions allow for more limited space requirements by the organization but also facilitate a sense of ownership of space among employees.

Although we need to learn much more about territoriality in organizations so as to more effectively manage this phenomenon, we can see several means by which managers can do a better job in this regard. Although territoriality can have its downsides, it should not, and cannot, be eliminated; rather it is critical to recognize it, and redirect it in ways that help rather than hinder the organization.

Conclusion

Territoriality is an inevitable and important aspect of organizational life. Where you find people interacting together over time, you will find natural territorial feelings and territories emerging. Although prior research and theorizing on territoriality has identified its numerous benefits, as this chapter has illustrated, it also has the potential to be dysfunctional. Territorial feelings, territorial behavior and the experience of territorial infringement pose problems to individuals and the organizations in which they work.

It would be dangerous for us to dismiss territoriality as trivial, limited to a few, or necessary to avoid. All organizational members have an inherent need for a sense of ownership and will naturally react to protect that which they see as theirs. As such, the effective acknowledgment and management of territoriality in the workplace is essential. Eliminating territories at work would not be possible, and even if it were, it would only undermine commitment to the organization. The key for future research is to learn under what conditions the positive and negative consequences are realized and how the benefits of territoriality can be realized without incurring dysfunction. Fortunately this is a new and growing area, with many fascinating questions still to be explored by researchers in our field.

Acknowledgment

This chapter was supported by a grant from the Social Sciences and Humanities Research Council of Canada.

References

Allen, V.I. and D.B. Greenberger (1980), 'Destruction and perceived control', in A. Baum and J.E. Singer (eds), *Advances in Environmental Psychology*, vol. 2, *Applications of Personal Control*, Hillsdale, NJ: Lawrence Erlbaum Associates, pp. 85–109.

Altman, I. (1975), *Environment and Social Behavior: Privacy, Personal Space, Territory, and Crowding*, Monterey, CA: Brooks/Cole.

Altman, I. and M.M. Chemers (1980), *Culture and Environment*, Monterey, CA: Brooks/Cole.

Altman, I. and W.W. Haythorn (1967), 'The ecology of isolated groups', *Behavioral Science*, **12**, 168–82.

Altman, I., P.A. Nelson and E.E. Lett (1972), *The Ecology of Home Environments: Catalog of Selected Documents in Psychology*, Washington, DC: American Psychological Association.

Altman, I., D.A. Taylor and L. Wheeler (1971), 'Ecological aspects of group behavior in social isolation', *Journal of Applied Social Psychology*, **1**, 76–100.

Ardey, R. (1966), *The Territorial Imperative*, New York: Atheneum.

Ashforth, B.E. and F. Mael (1989), 'Social identity theory and the organization', *Academy of Management Review*, **14**, 20–39.

Becker, F.D. (1981), *Workspace: Creating environments in organizations*, New York: Praeger.

Becker, F.D. and C. Mayo (1971), 'Delineating personal space and territoriality', *Environment and Behavior*, **3**, 375–81.

Beggan, J.K. and E.M. Brown (1994), 'Association as a psychological justification for ownership', *Journal of Psychology*, **128**, 365–80.

Brodt, S. and S. Sitkin (2006), 'The paradox of secrecy norms in organizations', paper presented at the Society for Industrial Organizational Psychology, Dallas, TX, May.

Brown, B.B. (1983), 'Territoriality, street form, and residential burglary: social and environmental analyses', unpublished doctoral dissertation, University of Utah.

Brown, B.B. (1987), 'Territoriality', in D. Stokols and I. Altman (eds), *Handbook of Environmental Psychology*, vol. 2, New York: John Wiley & Sons, pp. 505–31.

Brown, B.B. and I. Altman (1981), 'Territoriality and residential crime: a conceptual framework', in P.J. Brantingham and P.L. Brantingham (eds), *Environmental Criminology*, Beverly Hills, CA: Sage, pp. 55–76.

Brown, B.B. and I. Altman (1983), 'Territoriality, defensible space and residential burglary: an environmental analysis', *Journal of Environmental Psychology*, 3, 203–20.

Brown, B.B. and D.D. Perkins (1992), 'Disruptions in place attachment', in I. Altman and S. Low (eds), *Place Attachment*, vol. 3, New York: Plenum, pp. 279–304.

Brown, B.B. and C.M. Werner (1985), 'Social cohesiveness, territoriality, and holiday decorations: the influence of cul-de-sacs', *Environment and Behavior*, 17, 539–65.

Brown, G., T. Lawrence and S.L. Robinson (2005), 'Territoriality in organizations', *Academy of Management Review*, 30, 577–94.

Brown, G. (2006), ' "Mine" and "not yours": the impact of psychological ownership and territoriality in organizations', paper presented at the Academy of Management Conference, Atlanta, GA, August.

Brown, G. and T. Menkhoff (2007), 'Territoriality over knowledge: towards a cross-cultural perspective', in T. Menkhoff, E.F. Pang and H.D. Evers (eds), *The Power of Knowing: Studies of Chinese Business in Asia*, special issue of the *Journal of Asian Business* (2007 forthcoming).

Brown., G. and S.L. Robinson (2006), 'Reactions to territorial infringement', paper presented at the Academy of Management Conference, Atlanta, GA: August.

Buchanan, J. (1998), 'The hot spot: the anatomy of anger in the office', *Office Systems*, February.

Clegg, S.R. (1989), *Frameworks of Power*, London: Sage.

Connelly, C.E., D. Zweig and J. Webster (2006), 'Knowledge hiding in organizations', paper presented at the Society for Industrial Organizational Psychology, Dallas, TX, May.

Constant, D., S. Kiesler and L. Sproull (1994), 'What's mine is ours, or is it? A study of attitudes about information sharing', *Information Systems Research*, 5(4), 400–421.

Csikszentmihalyi, M. and E. Rochberg-Halton (1981), *The Meaning of Things*, New York: Cambridge University Press.

Dean, A.O. (1977), 'Evaluation of an open office landscape: A.I.A. headquarters', *A.I.A. Journal*, 66, 40–46.

Dittmar, H. (1992), *The Social Psychology of Material Possessions: To Have is To Be*, New York: St. Martin's Press.

Dyson-Hudson, R. and E.A. Smith (1978), 'Human territoriality: an ecological reassessment', *American Anthropologist*, 80, 21–41.

Edney, J.J. (1974), 'Human territoriality', *Psychological Bulletin*, 81, 959–75.

Edney, J.J. (1975), 'Territoriality and control: a field experiment', *Journal of Personality and Social Psychology*, 31, 1108–15.

Edney, J.J. (1976), 'Human territories: comment on functional properties', *Environment and Behavior*, 8, 31–47.

Finch, J., J.A. Okun, M. Barrera, A. Zautra and J.W. Reich (1989), 'Positive and negative social ties among older adults: measurement models and the prediction of psychological distress and well-being', *American Journal of Community Psychology*, 17, 585–605.

Formanek, R. (1991), 'Why they collect: collectors reveal their motivations', in F.W. Rudmin (ed.), *To Have Possessions: A Handbook on Ownership and Property*, special issue, *Journal of Social Behavior and Personality*, 6(6), 275–86.

Freedman, D.G. (1979), *Human Sociobiology*, New York: Free Press.

Goffman, E. (1959), *The Presentation of Self in Everyday Life*, New York: Doubleday.

Greenberger, D.B. and S. Strasser (1986), 'Development and application of a model of personal control in organizations', *Academy of Management Review*, 11, 164–77.

James, W. (1890), *The Principles of Psychology*, New York: Holt.

Katz-Stone, A. (1999), 'Office as hotel', *Washington Business Journal*, 29 January–4 February.

Knapp, M.L. (1978), *Non-verbal Communication in Human Interaction*, New York: Holt, Rinehart and Winston.

Lewis, C.A. (1979), 'Comment: healing in the urban environment', *Journal of the Institute of American Planners*, 45, 330–38.

Lyman, S.M. and M.B. Scott (1967), 'Territoriality: a neglected sociological dimension', *Social Problems*, 15, 236–49.

Malmberg, T. (1980), *Human Territoriality*, New York: Mouton.

Marans, R.W. and K.F. Spreckelmeyer (1981), *Evaluating Built Environments: A Behavioral Approach*, Ann Arbor, MI: Institute for Social Research.

Nathan, M. (2002), 'The work foundation', *Space SIG*, London: Peter Runge House.

Nonaka, I. (1991), 'The knowledge-creating company', *Harvard Business Review*, **69**(6), 96–104.

Nuttin, J.M. Jr (1987), 'Affective consequences of mere ownership: the name letter effect in twelve European languages', *European Journal of Social Psychology*, **17**, 381–402.

Oldham, G.R. and D.J. Brass (1979), 'Employee reactions to an open-plan office: a naturally occurring quasi-experiment', *Administrative Science Quarterly*, **24**(2), 267–84.

Pfeffer, J. (1981), *Power in Organizations*, Marshfield, MA: Pitman.

Pfeffer, J. and G.R. Salancik (1978), *The External Control of Organizations: A Resource Dependence Perspective*, New York: Harper & Row.

Pierce, J.L., S.A. Rubenfeld and S. Morgan (1991), 'Employee ownership: a conceptual model of process and effects', *Academy of Management Review*, **16**, 121–44.

Pierce, J.L., T. Kostova and K.T. Dirks (2001), 'Toward a theory of psychological ownership in organizations', *Academy of Management Review*, **26**, 298–310.

Pierce, J.L., T. Kostova and K.T. Dirks (2003), 'The state of psychological ownership: integrating and extending a century of research', *Review of General Psychology*, **7**, 84–107.

Richards, C.B. and H.F. Dobyns (1957), 'Topography and culture: the case of the changing cage', *Human Organization*, **16**, 16–20.

Robinson, S.L. and R.J. Bennett (1997), 'Workplace, deviance: its definitions, its manifestations, and its clauses', *Research on Negotiations in Organizations*, **6**, 3–27.

Robinson, S.L. and G. Brown (2006), 'Territoriality in organizations: impediment to knowledge sharing', paper presented at the Society for Industrial Organizational Psychology, Dallas, TX, May.

Rodgers, L. and F. Freundlich (1998), 'Nothing measured, nothing gained', *Employee Ownership Report, XVIII, No. 1*. Oakland, CA: National Center for Employee Ownership. www.ownershipassociates.com/nothingm.html.

Rook, K.C. and P.A. Pietromonaco (1987), 'Close relationships: ties that heal or bind?', in W.H. Jones and D. Perlman (eds), *Advances in Personal Relationships: A Research Annual*, Greenwich, CT: JAI Press, pp. 1–35.

Rosenblatt, P.C. and L.G. Budd (1975), 'Territoriality and privacy in married and unmarried cohabitating couples', *Journal of Social Psychology*, **97**, 67–76.

Ruback, R.B. and D. Juieng (1997), 'Territorial defense in parking lots: retaliation against waiting drivers', *Journal of Applied Social Psychology*, **27**(9), 821–34.

Ruback, R.B. and J.N. Snow (1993), 'Territoriality and nonconscious racism at water fountains: intruders and drinkers (Blacks and Whites) are affected by race', *Environment and Behavior*, **25**, 250–67.

Ruback, R.B., K.D. Pape and P. Doriot (1989), 'Waiting for a phone: intrusion on callers leads to territorial defense', *Social Psychology Quarterly*, **52**, 232–41.

Rudmin, F.W. and J.W. Berry (1987), 'Semantics of ownership: a free-recall study of property', *The Psychological Record*, **37**, 257–68.

Salari, S., B.B. Brown and J.C. Eaton (2006), 'Conflicts, friendship cliques and territorial displays in senior center environments', *Journal of Aging Studies*, **20**, 237–52.

Smith, H.W. (1983), 'Estimated crowding capacity, time, and territorial markers: a cross-national test', *Sociological Inquiry*, **53**, 95–9.

Sommer, R. (1974), *Tight Spaces: Hard Architecture and How to Humanize It*, Englewood Cliffs, NJ: Prentice-Hall.

Steele, F. (1986), *Making and Managing High Quality Workplaces: An Organizational Ecology*, New York: Teachers College Press.

Stokols, D. (1978), 'Environmental psychology', *Annual Review of Psychology*, **29**, 253–95.

Sundstrom, E. and I. Altman (1974), 'Field study of territorial behavior and dominance', *Journal of Personality and Social Psychology*, **30**, 115–24.

Sundstrom, E. and I. Altman (1989), 'Physical environments and work-group effectiveness', in L.L. Cummings and B.M. Staw (eds), *Research in Organizational Behavior*, vol. 11, Greenwich, CT: JAI Press, pp. 175–209.

Sundstrom, E. and M.G. Sundstrom (1986), *Work Places: The Psychology of the Physical Environment in Offices and Factories*, New York: Cambridge University Press.

Sutton, R.I. and A. Rafaeli (1987), 'Characteristics of work stations as potential occupational stressors', *Academy of Management Journal*, **30**, 260–76.

Szilagyi, A. and W. Holland (1980), 'Changes in social density: relationships with functional interaction and perceptions of job characteristics, role stress, and work satisfaction', *Journal of Applied Psychology*, **65**, 28–33.

Taylor, R.B. and R. Stough (1978), 'Territorial cognition: assessing Altman's typology', *Journal of Personality and Social Psychology*, **36**, 418–23.

Tuan, Y. (1980), 'The significance of artifact', *Geographic Review*, **70**, 462–72.

Wells, M.M. (2000), 'Office clutter or meaningful personal displays: the role of office personalization in employee and organizational well-being', *Journal of Environmental Psychology*, **20**, 239–55.

Wollman, N., B.M. Kelly and K.S. Bordens (1994), 'Environmental and intrapersonal predictors of reactions to potential territorial intrusions in the workplace', *Environment and Behavior*, **26**, 179–94.

Wrzesniewski, A. and J.E. Dutton (2001), 'Crafting a job: revisioning employees as active crafters of their work', *The Academy of Management Review*, **26**, 179–201.

Zalesny, M.D. and R.V. Farace (1987), 'Traditional vs. open offices: a comparison of sociotechnical, social relations, and social meaning perspectives', *Academy of Management Journal*, **30**, 240–59.

16 Towards a relational model of workplace aggression
M. Sandy Hershcovis and Julian Barling

In a national study of the prevalence of workplace aggression in the USA, Schat et al. (2006) found that 41 percent of workers experience some type of psychological aggression at work, and 6 percent of workers experience some form of physical violence. Workplace aggression is a ubiquitous and insidious feature of many organizations, and studies have shown that such aggression, even in its mildest forms, has detrimental effects on the well-being of its victims.

Although researchers have examined the effects of workplace aggression, little research exists that conceptualizes aggression as a function of a *relationship* between a perpetrator and a victim. More emphasis on the nature of this relationship is important because the enactment of aggression as well as the victim's experience of aggression is likely to depend on the perpetrator/victim relationship. This chapter sets out first to provide an overview of the literature on workplace aggression by examining its predictors and consequences. We then consider how the relationship between the perpetrator and the victim might affect both the enactment of aggression by perpetrators, and the experience of aggression by victims. Finally, we consider the constraints in existing methods that prevent us from examining the perpetrator/victim relationship, and make some suggestions for how future studies can overcome these constraints.

Over the past decade, a burgeoning literature has emerged that focuses primarily on two streams of workplace aggression research. The first stream examines the *predictors* of enacted workplace aggression; this literature considers aggressive acts to be a reaction to other organizational stressors (e.g. injustice, abusive supervision, role stressors; Bowling and Beehr, 2006; Hershcovis et al., 2007), or the outcome of individual dispositions (e.g. trait anger, negative affectivity; Douglas and Martinko, 2001).

The second stream of research studies the *outcomes* of experienced workplace aggression. Researchers who study the consequences of workplace aggression consider it to be a stressor that leads to a range of attitudinal, behavioral and health-related strains. These include lower levels of job satisfaction, affective commitment, psychological and physical health, and higher levels of turnover intentions and counterproductive work behavior (Bowling and Beehr, 2006; Lapierre et al., 2005; Hershcovis and Barling, 2005).

This chapter is divided into three sections. The first section will discuss existing conceptualizations of workplace aggression including five issues around which these conceptualizations vary. The second section examines the predictors of enacted aggression, followed by the consequences of experienced aggression. In the third and final section we will examine some potential new directions for future research in workplace aggression, with an aim to widen the scope of research in this field.

Conceptualizing workplace aggression
Research in the field of workplace aggression has developed over the past 15 years, and during that time, several researchers have simultaneously conceptualized and examined

overlapping forms of workplace aggression (Fox and Spector, 2005). Due to these different types of aggression, its definition varies widely (Neuman and Baron, 2005). For example, in some definitions, workplace aggression and violence are separated: workplace aggression refers to psychological harm inflicted on an individual (e.g. verbal and psychological abuse), while workplace violence refers to physical harm or a threat of physical harm (e.g. Greenberg and Barling, 1999). In other research, workplace aggression includes all intentional acts of harming another person within an organization, with both psychological aggression and physical violence subsumed under this definition (e.g. Latham and Perlow, 1996).

Multiple conceptualizations of similar phenomena have resulted in several variations on how researchers define and label workplace aggression. These variants likely derive from at least one or more of five sources: (1) the researchers' assumptions regarding workplace aggression; (2) the conceptualization of aggression; (3) the target and severity of aggression under examination; (4) the perspective under examination (i.e. actor versus victim/target); and (5) intentionality.

First, ideological assumptions about the act of workplace aggression have resulted in different conceptualizations across researchers. Many researchers (e.g. Bennett and Robinson, 2000; Fox and Spector, 2005; Robinson and O'Leary-Kelly, 1998) adopt a manager-centered perspective by presupposing that aggression is counternormative (Bies and Tripp, 2005). These researchers define workplace aggression as an act that threatens the well-being of the organization and its members, and therefore label their aggression construct as deviant, counterproductive and antisocial. In contrast, Bies and Tripp (2005) adopt an employee-centered approach, and argue that workplace aggression is not necessarily counternormative in all circumstances. Rather, they suggest that aggression is often a result of negative situational factors within the organization, such as injustice and poor leadership, which lead employees to act out in an effort to eliminate these negative factors. Thus, Bies and Tripp (2005) argue that aggression can be pro-social, productive and beneficial, and that a manager-centered label precludes this possibility.

A second and related variation in the definition of workplace aggression concerns its conceptualization. For example, Skarlicki and Folger (1997) conceptualize aggression as a form of retaliation against the organization and its members for an array of perceived injustices. By conceptualizing aggression as retaliatory, they measure the retaliation construct as aggressive acts against the organization and the people within the organization (e.g. purposefully damaged equipment, disobeyed supervisors' instructions, spread rumours about co-workers) in response to a particular provocation. In contrast, Robinson and Bennett (1995) defined workplace deviance as voluntary behavior that violates organizational norms and threatens the well-being of the organization and/or its members. In this conceptualization, the act of aggression is considered counternormative rather than retaliatory, implicitly suggesting that workplace aggression may result more from a difficult employee than a particular provocation. The measurement of this form of aggression, however, largely overlaps with Skarlicki and Folger's (1997) measure, the primary difference being that Bennett and Robinson (2000) separated interpersonal aggression (targeted at a co-worker or supervisor) from organizational aggression (targeted at the organization). Therefore, despite the variation in conceptualization, one might not necessarily appreciate this difference from the operationalization of these constructs.

In addition, the predictors investigated in studies examining these two conceptualizations are largely similar, and results suggest that these factors predict both retaliation and deviance. To add to the confusion, similar conceptualizations of deviant behavior have been given different labels such as antisocial (e.g. Robinson and O'Leary-Kelly, 1998), counterproductive (e.g. Fox and Spector, 2005), incivility (Andersson and Pearson, 1999; Lim and Cortina, 2005), and organizational misbehavior (Vardi and Weiner, 1996). In short, while there are many diverse labels given both to substantively different and substantively similar conceptualizations of aggression, the measurement and indeed the predictors and outcomes are largely the same. We argue that researchers should not conceptualize workplace aggression *a priori* as either retaliatory or deviant. Workplace aggression may occur for multiple reasons, and confounding the construct with its potential predictors adds to the conceptual ambiguity.

The third difference in definition and label concerns the target and severity of aggression. Robinson and Bennett (1995) found that workplace aggression varied on two dimensions, namely target (i.e. interpersonal versus organizational), and severity (minor versus major). Interpersonal aggression refers to aggression targeted at a particular person within the organization (e.g. yelling at someone, spreading gossip), whereas organizational aggression refers to aggression aimed to harm the organization (e.g. damaging equipment, taking long breaks). Some researchers disregard these distinctions, while others acknowledge them. For example, Skarlicki and Folger's (1997) retaliation measure includes both interpersonal and organizational targets, as does Robinson and O'Leary-Kelly's (1998) antisocial behavior measure. In contrast, both the counterproductive work behavior (Fox and Spector, 2005) and the deviance measures separate interpersonal from organizational targets. Furthermore, some researchers (e.g. Inness et al., 2005; Vigoda, 2002) combine more severe forms of aggression (e.g. violence), and less severe forms such as psychological aggression within the same measure, while others (e.g. Aquino and Douglas, 2003) examine only psychological aggression.

Recent research has demonstrated the importance of separating different targets when examining workplace aggression (e.g. Aquino et al., 1999; Hershcovis et al., 2007). For example, a meta-analysis of the predictors of workplace aggression found that interpersonal and organizational aggression have different predictors (Hershcovis et al., 2007). Interpersonal conflict was related to interpersonal aggression, while job dissatisfaction and situational constraints was related to organizational aggression). Further, this research showed that the interpersonal target should be further refined to explicitly separate different targets of aggression. The meta-analysis found that within the interpersonal dimension, there were different predictors of aggression towards supervisors than of aggression towards co-workers.

The fourth difference in the conceptualization of workplace aggression relates to the perspective taken by the researcher. As noted earlier, workplace aggression research is bifurcated into the predictors of aggression and the outcomes of aggression. Therefore, researchers often take an actor's perspective (i.e. enacted aggression) to investigate the predictors of aggression (e.g. Inness et al., 2005), or a target's perspective (i.e. victims of aggression) to examine the outcomes (e.g. Lim and Cortina, 2005). Research on mobbing, bullying, victimization and incivility all tend to focus on the target (or victim) of aggression. In contrast, deviance, counterproductive work behavior and antisocial behavior tend to focus on enacted aggression. As these streams of research developed largely independent of each other, the labels do not converge. However, the label of workplace aggression encompasses both enacted and experienced aggression.

A final variation related to the conceptualization of aggression is whether intent on the part of the aggressor is considered. There is disagreement among researchers about the use of intention as a defining feature of aggression. Neuman and Baron (2005) argue that intentionality refers to the actual intent of the aggressor, rather than perceived intentionality by the victim. They argue that the exclusion of intent would permit harmful behavior such as pain caused by dentists to be considered aggression. Other researchers (e.g. Andersson and Pearson, 1999) argue that many acts of aggression are ambiguous as to their intent, suggesting that the definition should not include intent as a defining feature. While it is reasonable to argue that those who infer intent from a perpetrator of aggression may experience stronger deleterious consequences, it is still conceivable that aggression without intent will be harmful. For instance, a psychiatric patient who harms a doctor, or an employee who harms a co-worker while under the influence of alcohol may not intend to be aggressive, but the consequences may still be damaging. The question of whether intent is a defining factor of aggression is therefore empirical. We suggest that research should not assume that intent is such a feature. In many cases, perpetrators may not be acting with intent, although the act itself is indeed aggressive. For instance, caregivers in hospitals and psychiatric wards are often victims of aggression from patients who arguably have diminished personal responsibility. Rather, we suggest that *perceived* intent by the victim is a more important consideration for future research, as perceived intent may affect the outcome experienced by the victim. Table 16.1 provides a summary of these five factors in relation to key aggression variables (see also Raver and Barling, in press).

Defining workplace aggression
We have outlined five issues that are the subject of debate and confusion when conceptualizing workplace aggression. We argue that some of these preceding issues are empirical rather than conceptual in nature. For instance, intent to commit harm may or may not have a greater effect on the outcomes of aggression, but it need not be a defining factor. In addition, it is not useful to define workplace aggression in terms of either its target or its actors, because it unnecessarily narrows the aggressive act to contextual factors. These factors are all aspects of the way aggression may operate in organizations, rather than necessary conditions of the workplace aggression definition.

Our definition of workplace aggression is necessarily broad and can be applied to different workplace contexts, actors, and targets. Workplace aggression is 'Any negative act, which may be committed towards an individual within the workplace, or the workplace itself, in ways the target is motivated to avoid.' This definition deviates from existing definitions (e.g. Neuman and Baron, 2005; O'Leary-Kelly et al., 1996; Skarlicki and Folger, 1997) by removing (1) intent, (2) specific targets, (3) harm, and (4) specific actors. Instead of implicitly incorporating these into the definition, future research should examine each of these factors empirically.

It should be noted that although the definitions and labels used to refer to enacted aggression (e.g. retaliation, deviance, counterproductive work behavior) and experienced aggression (e.g. bullying, mobbing, incivility) differ, as do their definitions, the measures used to examine these constructs are remarkably similar (Spector and Fox, 2005). As such, researchers (e.g. Neuman and Baron, 2005; Fox and Spector, 2005) have called for

Table 16.1 Defining features of aggression variables

Aggression variable	Assumption/ conceptualization	Target/victim	Severity	Perspective	Intent
Abusive supervision (Tepper, 2000)	Destructive but not necessarily deviant	Subordinate	Moderate and persistent psychological	Target	No
Anti-social behavior (Robinson and O'Leary-Kelly, 1998)	Destructive counternormative	Combined supervisor, co-worker or organization	Moderate psychological	Actor	No
Bullying (Rayner, 1997)	Destructive and persistent	Co-worker	Moderate to severe psychological and potentially physical	Target	Unstated
Counterproductive work behavior (Fox and Spector, 2005)	Destructive counternormative	Separate interpersonal and organizational targets	Moderate psychological	Actor	Yes
Deviance (Bennett and Robinson, 2000)	Destructive and counternormative	Separate interpersonal and organizational targets	Moderate psychological	Actor	Yes
Emotional abuse (Keashly and Harvey, 2005)	Destructive and counternormative	Subordinate	Moderate to severe psychological	Target	Yes
Mobbing (Zapf and Einarsen, 2005)	Destructive and persistent	Co-worker	Severe psychological and potentially physical	Target	No
Retaliation (Skarlicki and Folger, 1997)	Constructive justice-restoring behaviors	Combined supervisor, co-worker and organization	Moderate psychological and some physical	Actor	Yes
Revenge (Bies and Tripp, 2005)	Constructive justice-restoring behaviors	Combined supervisor, co-worker and organization	Unstated (i.e. I got back at them)	Actor	Yes
Workplace aggression (e.g. Greenberg and Barling, 1999)	Varies	Varies (insiders and outsiders)	Psychological and physical	Actor and target	Varies
Workplace incivility (Andersson and Pearson, 1999; Cortina et al., 2001)	Constructive and destructive	Interpersonal (implied co-workers)	Minor psychological	Target	Ambiguous
Social undermining (Duffy et al., 2002)	Destructive	Interpersonal (implied co-workers)	Minor to severe, persistent, psychological and physical	Target	Yes

integrative work to take stock of the field. To respond to this need for systematic integration, at least five meta-analyses were conducted in 2005 and 2006. The next section provides an overview of the existing research.

Predictors and outcomes of workplace aggression

Predictors of workplace aggression
Four broad categories of predictors have been examined in relation to workplace aggression. First, studies have focused on predictors that have variously been labeled situational, organizational or perceptual. These include predictors that result from conditions within the organization and include, for example, workplace injustice, role stressors and abusive supervision (e.g. Berry et al., in press; Bowling and Beehr, 2006). Second, researchers have examined the individual difference predictors of workplace aggression (e.g. Douglas and Martinko, 2001). These antecedents include factors specific to the individual perpetrator, such as demographic variables, as well as perpetrator dispositional traits such as trait anger, negative affectivity, and the 'big five' personality traits. Third, a few studies have examined characteristics of the victim that might make them more likely to become targets of aggression. These antecedents include the sex, age and organizational status of the victim. Finally, a few studies have examined characteristics of the context, such as societal influences, organizational culture and organizational tolerance for workplace aggression.

Situational factors   Research has generally shown that all three categories are related to workplace aggression, although situational factors seem to be the strongest (in magnitude) predictor. Meta-analytic evidence has shown that distributive, procedural and interpersonal injustice have weak to moderate relationships with workplace aggression when considering main effects only (Berry et al., in press). However, Hershcovis et al. (2007) found that when situational constraints, interpersonal conflict and job satisfaction were included in a path model together with distributive and procedural justice, the justice variables were not significant predictors of workplace aggression. However, this does not rule out the likelihood that these variables interact to predict aggression. Skarlicki and Folger (1997) found that distributive, procedural and interactional injustice interacted to predict workplace aggression. That is, when an individual feels that their rewards are unfair in relation to a comparative other, and when the procedures used to arrive at the rewards are also unfair, individuals were more likely to retaliate. Similarly, when rewards were unfair and were communicated to employees with disrespect, individuals were also more likely to retaliate. Finally, Skarlicki and Folger also found a three-way interaction between all three justice variables and retaliation.

In addition to the aforementioned situational predictors, Bowling and Beehr (2006) conducted a meta-analysis of the relationship between workplace stressors and aggression. They found that role conflict, role overload, role ambiguity and job autonomy were all significantly related to workplace aggression, with role conflict being the strongest predictor.

Individual differences   In terms of individual differences, Berry et al. (in press) found that agreeableness, conscientiousness and emotional stability had the strongest relationship with workplace aggression of the 'big five' personality traits. Hershcovis et al. (2007) also found that trait anger had a strong relationship with workplace aggression, while sex of the perpetrator had a weak but significant relationship, with men being more likely to aggress than women.

In addition to this meta-analytic evidence, a number of individual studies have attempted to determine the relationship between additional individual differences and workplace aggression. Douglas and Martinko (2001) found individual differences explained 62 percent of the variance in workplace aggression. In addition to trait anger, they found that attitude towards revenge, attribution style and previous exposure to aggressive cultures were related to workplace aggression and accounted for significant additional variance after accounting for the effects of demographic variables.

Interactions between situational and individual differences   Folger and Skarlicki's (1998) popcorn model of aggression suggests that while situational predictors may be a necessary condition for workplace aggression, they may not be a sufficient condition. It is therefore critical to also consider the interaction between the person and the situation. Some individuals will choose to exit the organization or to improve workplace conditions, while others will react to the negative environment in such a way that they 'explode' and become aggressive. Inness et al. (2005) conducted a study to examine this interactionist perspective. They studied individuals who worked at two different jobs to determine whether it was the individual, the situation or both that predicted workplace aggression. Their within-person, between-jobs design enabled them to separate the person from the situation, allowing for a unique test of these two different predictors, and they found that individual differences – self-esteem and history of aggression – explained a similar level of variance across jobs, whereas situational factors were job-specific and explained more variance than individual differences. In particular, abusive supervision was a very strong job-specific situational predictor of workplace aggression targeted at the supervisor.

Characteristics of the victim   Few studies have examined the characteristics of the victim of workplace aggression, because doing so suggests a possible 'blame the victim' argument. Nevertheless, certain factors such as victim status, gender and age may help shed light on those individuals most at risk of experiencing workplace aggression. This research can improve an organization's ability to protect higher-risk employees. Using meta-analysis, Bowling and Beehr (2006) examined five victim characteristics that have been studied in the past: victim positive affectivity, victim negative affectivity, victim gender, victim age and victim tenure. They found that only victim negative affectivity was a significant and moderate predictor of workplace aggression. However, it is unclear based on these results whether individuals with high negative affectivity are more likely to be the target of aggression, or whether these individuals are more likely to perceive themselves as victims. Future research needs to tease these plausible explanations apart.

Characteristics of the context   While some researchers (e.g. Aquino and Lamertz, 2004) have suggested that contextual variables such as climate or culture influence the enactment of workplace aggression, very few studies have empirically examined such predictors. One exception is a study by Dietz et al. (2003), which examined the effects of both community-level violent crimes and plant-level procedural justice climate as predictors of workplace aggression. The study showed that wider community violence level predicted workplace aggression, whereas plant-level procedural justice did not predict workplace aggression. This study was surprising given the widely held perception that injustice leads to aggression; however, it supports meta-analytic findings that individual-level perceptions of injustice have a weak relationship with aggression after taking other predictors into account.

Outcomes of workplace aggression

The primary framework used to examine the outcomes of workplace is known variously as the stressor framework or the process model of work stress (e.g. Barling, 1996; Bowling and Beehr, 2006; Schat and Kelloway, 2000; Spector and Fox, 2005; Schat and Kelloway, 2003). This framework suggests that workplace aggression is an organizational stressor (i.e. an aversive environmental stimulus) that leads to stress – a person's immediate affective or cognitive perception of the stimulus, followed by a range of strains – the attitudinal, psychological, physical and behavior consequences (Barling, 1996).

Many existing models of workplace aggression examine some variation of this stressor framework, sometimes drawing on other theories to build on this model. For example, Schat and Kelloway (2000) drew on the stressor framework to posit that fear would mediate the relationship between workplace aggression, and emotional and somatic well-being, and further that emotional well-being would mediate the relationship between fear and somatic health, and neglect of one's work. Similarly, Barling et al. (2001) drew on the stressor framework to test a structural model that posited that fear and negative mood mediate the relationship between workplace aggression and organizational and health-related outcomes.

Two recent meta-analyses found that workplace aggression leads to a wide range of adverse health, attitudinal and behavioral outcomes. We now describe each of these three categories of outcomes in more detail.

Health outcomes   The most widely researched outcome of workplace aggression is the psychological and physical health of the victim. A range of psychological well-being outcomes have been examined, including depression, anxiety, burnout, post-traumatic stress disorder and life satisfaction. Bowling and Beehr (2006) meta-analytically examined each of these outcomes, and found that workplace aggression was moderately related to all these outcomes. Similarly, Hershcovis and Barling (2005) examined a composite of all psychological well-being outcomes, which are highly related (Diener et al., 1999) and found a corrected mean correlation of 0.41 with workplace aggression.

In addition to psychological well-being, researchers have also examined the physical health outcomes of workplace aggression, including doctor's visits and somatic symptoms such as gastrointestinal problems, headaches and sleeping disorders. Bowling and Beehr (2006) found a comparable moderate relationship between workplace aggression and physical symptoms.

Attitudinal outcomes   In addition to the health outcomes for individuals, researchers have examined the attitudinal outcomes of workplace aggression to determine how it impacts employees' attitudes to the organization for which they work. Meta-analytic evidence shows that workplace aggression leads to lower levels of affective commitment, job satisfaction and organizational justice, and higher intentions to leave the organization (Bowling and Beehr, 2006).

Behavioral outcomes   Limited research has examined the behavioral outcomes of workplace aggression. Only five studies have examined the performance outcomes of workplace aggression, and the results are inconclusive. Bowling and Beehr (2006) found no relationship between workplace aggression and job performance or organizational citizenship behaviors across five studies. However, they found a moderate relationship between workplace aggression and counterproductive work behavior, which is consistent with prior research that suggests that aggression begets aggression (Andersson and Pearson, 1999).

Looking ahead: new directions in workplace aggression
The growing literature on the predictors and outcomes of workplace aggression has resulted in at least four recent meta-analyses related to this area (Bowling and Beehr, 2006; Berry et al., in press; Hershcovis et al., 2007; Lapierre et al., 2005). The results of these meta-analyses, summarized in the preceding section, suggest that we now have a good understanding of the predictors and outcomes of workplace aggression. However, previous research has tended to focus on workplace aggression as though the prediction and experience of aggression were the same, regardless of the target or perpetrator of such aggression. The relational aspect of workplace aggression has therefore received limited research or theoretical attention. This perspective is important because individuals are likely to become aggressive towards different people for different reasons, and understanding these specific reasons is important to the prevention of workplace aggression. Similarly, the experience of aggression is likely to differ depending on who perpetrates the aggression, and the victim's resulting responses to aggression are also likely to depend on who perpetrated the aggression.

In the remainder of this chapter, we suggest future research needs to extend the focus of past research on the quality of the relationship between perpetrator and victim, and consider the nature of the relationship between the perpetrator and victim, when examining the predictors and outcomes of workplace aggression.

Target-specific workplace aggression
In the domain of aggression, existing theories lend support to the notion that aggression is target-specific (i.e. perpetrators aggress against a particular target). In particular, cognitive neo-association theory (Berkowitz, 1989) proposes that negative events such as provocations elicit cognitive processes and affective responses that are linked together in memory, and lead to attributions of wrongdoing and ultimately to aggressive responses. This theory suggests that aggression is often *reactive*. That is, it results from a cognitive assessment of a negative event or provocation, and a subsequent attribution about the event.

Along a similar vein, Martinko et al. (2002) argued that attributions of the cause of workplace events motivate the attitudinal and behavioral response to that event. In particular, the experience of negative events leads to an attribution of blame for the event, and such attributions lead to targeted behavioral responses. This is consistent with Aquino et al. (1999), who argued that attributions of blame lead to differential predictions for procedural and distributive justice. They argued that because employees are likely to blame the person responsible for their unfair distributions (i.e. raises, promotions), distributive injustice will be associated with interpersonal-targeted aggression. In contrast,

Aquino et al. (1999) suggest that procedural injustice will lead to organization-targeted aggression because individuals will blame the organization for its irresponsible institutional policies and practices.

Examining these theoretical approaches suggests key consistencies between them. First, each of the theories argues that a trigger, stressor or provocation initiates the subsequent responses. Second, attributions are an underlying mechanism that may lead individuals to aggress against a particular target.

Some research has examined the target-specific nature of workplace aggression. In particular, as mentioned previously, Bennett and Robinson (2000) found that workplace aggression consists of interpersonal- and organizational-targeted aggression. Hershcovis et al. (2007) and Berry et al. (in press) examined these two forms of aggression meta-analytically to determine whether their separation is justified. In both these meta-analyses, the predictors of interpersonal and organizational aggression differed for some variables, supporting the notion of target separation.

While researchers are starting to separate interpersonal and organizational targets, much less research has considered whether the predictors differ for various interpersonal targets (e.g. supervisors, co-workers and subordinates). Attributional arguments described earlier suggest that assailants target aggressive behavior at those individuals who are responsible for transgressions against them (Martinko et al., 2002). That is, if individuals assign blame for perceived injustice, as suggested by several researchers (e.g. Aquino et al., 1999; Berkowitz, 1989; Martinko et al., 2002), then the assignment of blame will be as specific as possible. In particular, if a supervisor treats employees badly, employees are likely to aggress against the supervisor and not their co-workers. Similarly, if a co-worker treats a colleague with disrespect or incivility, the colleague will react against the co-worker and not against their supervisor. In other words, assignment of blame is likely to be directed towards the person perceived to be responsible for the transgression. With one known exception (i.e. Greenberg and Barling, 1999), research has not examined within the same study whether there are different predictors across targets; however, because some research has focused on either supervisor- or co-worker-targeted aggression, and others have used a combined measure, researchers have used meta-analytic techniques to determine whether the predictors differ for each target.

For example, Hershcovis et al. (2007) examined meta-analytically target-specific workplace aggression and found that abusive supervision and interpersonal injustice were strong predictors of supervisor-targeted aggression, while they were much weaker predictors of co-worker-targeted aggression. With the exception of Greenberg and Barling (1999), who found different predictors for supervisor-, co-worker- and subordinate-targeted aggression, no published research has focused explicitly on co-workers as a target; therefore, we have limited knowledge of the predictors of co-worker-targeted aggression. Similarly, virtually no other research has examined subordinate-targeted aggression.

Another related avenue for future research on the predictors of workplace aggression concerns the notion of displaced aggression, which has been examined in social psychology but not in organizational research. Limited findings suggest that aggression is at least partially target-specific; however, recent findings in the social psychology literature suggests that in some instances, workplace aggression may be displaced. Displaced aggression occurs when a perpetrator enacts aggression against an unfortunate third party who happens to be in the wrong place at the wrong time. Dollard et al. (1939) first suggested that displaced aggression is likely to occur when circumstances prevent or deter the enactment of direct aggression. They argued that a given frustration is likely to give rise to the strongest form of direct aggression. That is, when an individual becomes frustrated, they may respond to that frustration by directing aggression towards the source of the frustration. However, in addition to their anger towards the source of their frustration, individuals are also likely to be more irritated with the world in general (Dollard et al., 1939). This may include any person or object that the aggrieved may encounter between the moment the frustration occurs and the time in which the person has a chance to calm down.

Research in experimental social psychology has suggested that sometimes aggression is indeed displaced (e.g. Bushman and Baumeister, 1998; Bushman et al., 2005; Dollard et al., 1939). For example, in a meta-analysis of 49 experimental studies, Marcus-Newhall et al. (2000) found a moderate effect for the presence of displaced aggression under certain conditions. The findings related to target-specificity (Aquino et al., 1999; Bennett and Robinson, 2000; Berry et al., in press; Greenberg and Barling, 1999; Hershcovis et al., 2007), combined with other recent findings in social psychology, could ignite an interesting conversation about the moderators and mediators that may lead to displaced versus target-specific aggression within the workplace. For example, by integrating the notion of blame attributions, one can hypothesize that when an individual is provoked, but cannot identify and blame a particular provoker, displaced aggression may be more likely to occur. Certainly, these seem like fruitful issues for further research.

Outcomes of aggression by different perpetrators
While research on the predictors of aggression has paid limited attention to target-specificity, even less attention has been given to the perpetrators of aggression in research examining the outcomes of workplace aggression. While this is not surprising given the natural compassion and empathy on the part of researchers for victims of aggression, this has resulted in a truncated body of knowledge on workplace aggression. Employees experience workplace aggression from various sources, including insiders to the organization (such as co-workers and supervisors), and outsiders (such as customers and clients). With one published exception (i.e. LeBlanc and Kelloway, 2002), studies that examine these different perpetrators of aggression tend to focus on only one perpetrator, without considering why or whether outcomes might differ depending on who enacted the aggression. In addition, workplace aggression research tends to focus on aggression from within the organization, to the exclusion of aggression from organizational outsiders such as customers and members of the public. Since workplace aggression research is concerned with damaging behaviors towards employees and organizations, aggression from outsiders should not be excluded from the definition. Likewise, since employees in a vast number of organizations have direct interaction with members of the public, a more thorough examination of aggression from outside perpetrators is necessary.

As each relationship differs in such factors as the degree and type of power held by the perpetrator, and the nature of the relationship between the perpetrator and the victim of aggression, it is likely that the experience of aggression from one perpetrator might have a different meaning and subsequently different outcomes than the experience of aggression from another. A greater understanding of how aggression from supervisors, co-workers and outsiders affects employees is needed. The limited evidence that exists suggests that individuals may experience aggression from these sources in different ways (LeBlanc and Kelloway, 2002), leading to attitudinal and behavioral responses that may not be the same for each perpetrator.

LeBlanc and Kelloway (2002) conducted a study that examined the perpetrators of aggression from organizational employees and members of the public. This research found that public- and insider-initiated aggression was differentially related to both organizational and individual outcomes. While LeBlanc and Kelloway (2002) examined two types of aggression, public and 'co-worker' (which combined supervisor and co-worker aggression and therefore would be more appropriately called 'insider'), Schat (2004) extended LeBlanc and Kelloway's (2002) work by separating co-worker and supervisor aggression. Schat (2004) hypothesized and found that fear would mediate both public aggression and supervisor aggression, but not co-worker aggression.

Based on this initial evidence, we propose that future research should consider the perpetrator–victim relationship when trying to understand the outcomes of workplace aggression. Hershcovis and Barling (2005) argued that the nature of this relationship could mitigate or exacerbate the experience of aggression. They suggested that at least three different relational factors are likely to affect the outcomes of experienced workplace aggression. We discuss briefly each of these in turn.

Relational power refers to the level of power held by the perpetrator of aggression relative to the victim. Power – defined as the capacity to produce intended effects and influence the behavior of individuals (Dunbar and Bargoon, 2005) – has received limited consideration in the workplace aggression literature. However, in the related area of sexual harassment, researchers have begun to examine the effects of perpetrator power on the victim. For example, Cortina et al. (2002) found that victims who experienced sexual harassment from individuals who have greater power experienced more negative outcomes of the sexual harassment than victims harassed by those in non-power positions.

This has implications for research on aggression because different types of perpetrators may vary in their degree of power. For example, supervisors generally have greater formal power than employees and customers in that they can control important resources and outcomes for employees. Therefore, one would expect the outcomes of aggression from supervisors to be worse than outcomes of aggression from co-workers and outsiders. In a meta-analysis of the outcomes of workplace aggression by different perpetrators, Hershcovis and Barling (2005) found that victims of aggression from supervisors had significantly lower job satisfaction, affective commitment and psychological well-being, and significantly higher intentions to turnover, than victims of aggression from co-workers and outsiders.

Task interdependence refers to the degree to which the perpetrator and victim influence the performance of each other. Task interdependence is often examined as a moderating factor that may exacerbate or attenuate the relationship between variables (Duffy et al., 2000). However, to date, research in workplace aggression has not considered this factor. The degree to which the perpetrator and victim are task interdependent is likely to affect the outcomes of aggression for the victim, because the meaning of the aggressive act extends beyond the incident of aggression to possible outcomes for the victim's job performance.

There is some empirical evidence to support the moderating role of task interdependence on the outcomes of workplace aggression. For example, research in interpersonal aggression has found that under conditions of low task interdependence, the negative effects of conflict are lower (Jehn, 1995). However, this has not been explicitly tested on victims of workplace aggression.

Relational connectedness consists of two factors: (1) the degree to which the perpetrator and victim work within close physical proximity with one another, and (2) the endurance or length of the working relationship (Hershcovis and Barling, 2005). The greater the physical closeness within the work environment, and the longer the expected endurance of the relationship between the perpetrator and victim, the worse the effects of aggression on the victim are likely to be. The reason for this expected outcome is that victims who are forced to work with perpetrators in close proximity and for an indeterminate length may anticipate continued aggression in the future.

Implications for practice
An examination of the relational factors discussed above is important because it has implications for how workplace aggression is perceived by victims. Such perceptions are likely to affect victim coping responses, and therefore it is important to understand the ways in which victims respond to aggression from different sources to enable organizations to develop strategies to prevent future aggression. For instance, if employees are less likely to report aggression from those with high power, are they more likely to leave the organization? Similarly, if victims work in close proximity to aggressors, are they more likely to call in sick to avoid facing the aggressor? Such responses are costly to the individual in terms of health and well-being implications, and to organizations in terms of turnover and absenteeism costs. Further, if employees are not reporting workplace aggression from certain perpetrators (i.e. those with more power), upper management may be unaware of the problem and therefore unable to prevent its recurrence. Therefore, organizations may need to initiate different organizational policies such as open-door policies that enable employees to anonymously report aggression to a human resources department. The manner in which the perpetrator–victim relationship affects victim responses can guide organizations on what they can do to deal with workplace aggression.

Methodological impediments to the relational model
In the preceding section, we argued that future research should consider the relationship between the perpetrator and the victim when examining the outcomes of workplace aggression. However, conventional research methods in the area of workplace aggression preclude investigations of this type. Most existing workplace aggression research relies on cross-sectional survey methods and asks the participant about their experience of aggression from 'someone at work'. This design cannot easily accommodate the question of whether and how the relationship between the perpetrator and victim might affect the victim's experience of workplace aggression because it would require the victim to identify or refer to a particular perpetrator in some way when filling out the survey. That is, to determine whether task interdependence between a perpetrator and a victim affects a victim's experience of aggression, one would have to match the experience of aggression to a particular perpetrator to assess the task interdependence with that perpetrator.

Most research questions of this type can be examined using an experimental method in which the researcher could directly manipulate or assess the relationship between the perpetrator and victim relationship by using an experimental design. An experimenter would be able to control, for example, the level of task interdependence, power and relational connectedness between the perpetrator and victim. However, experiments examining the outcomes of workplace aggression are difficult for ethical reasons, because they require the participant to experience workplace aggression. This presents obvious ethical concerns that preclude experimental research into the outcomes of workplace aggression; therefore, to assess questions of this type, researchers need to explore different methods from those typically used.

We propose two potential methods for examining this research question. First, a diary study approach would enable researchers to examine: (1) specific incidents of workplace aggression within person; (2) the relationship between the perpetrator and victim; and (3) the participants' behavioral, affective and attitudinal responses. Such methods can use an event study approach to ask participants to answer a series of questions on a pocket computer (or using pen-and-paper surveys) when they experience an act of aggression. For example, when participants experience aggression at work (as defined by the researcher), they are asked to answer a series of short questions related to the severity of the aggression, the power of the perpetrator, the task interdependence and the relational connectedness with the perpetrator. At the end of each day in which an aggression event occurred, participants are asked to answer a short questionnaire to assess the behavioral, attitudinal and/or health outcomes of the aggressive experiences.

The benefits of a diary study are that it enables researchers to conduct a within-person, longitudinal study of how dynamic relationships affect aggression, and the responses to such aggression. This method enables researchers to assess aggression from a particular perpetrator, whereas existing methods ask about their experience of aggression more generally, without identifying a specific perpetrator. In addition, because participants answer questions about aggressive events as they occur, cognitive or affective responses can be examined without the potential biases associated with retroactive recall of an event (Robinson and Clore, 2002). The pitfalls of this approach are that the participants are interrupted during their workday since they are asked to fill out the survey after an event occurs. Therefore the surveys must be very short, to enable the participant to fill out their survey with minimal disruption to their work. In addition, it may be difficult to obtain large samples since organizations may be less inclined to authorize participation in a study that requires repeated disruptions.

A second method for examining this question is to use a critical incident technique by asking participants to recall a time when they experienced aggression at work. Once the participant recalls the incident, they are then asked a series of questions related to the incident, including information about the perpetrator–victim relationship, and the attitudinal, behavioral and health-related responses. While this method allows for lengthier questionnaires, it introduces potential recall biases into the study, particularly if the researcher is attempting to assess any cognitive or affective responses from the experience of workplace aggression.

Summary and conclusion
In this chapter we provided an overview of existing research on the predictors and outcomes of workplace aggression, and we proposed that future research focus on a relational perspective on workplace aggression. We noted the constraints of existing methods that prevent workplace aggression research from taking this relational approach, and

provided some initial suggestions for techniques that can help move us towards a more relational perspective.

Workplace aggression occurs between people, and victim responses to such aggression are at least partially a function of the relationship between the perpetrator and victim. Therefore, understanding how these factors exacerbate or mitigate aggression at work is key to both understanding the phenomenon itself, and to developing strategies to cope with and prevent it.

References

Andersson, L.M. and C.M. Pearson (1999), 'Tit for tat? The spiraling effect of incivility in the workplace', *Academy of Management Review*, **24**, 452–71.

Aquino, K. and S.C. Douglas (2003), 'Identity threat and anti-social behavior in organizations: the moderating effects of individual differences, aggressive modeling, and hierarchical status', *Organizational Behavior and Human Decisions Processes*, **90**, 195–208.

Aquino, K. and K. Lamertz (2004), 'A relational model of workplace victimization: social roles and patterns of victimization in dyadic relationships', *Journal of Applied Psychology*, **89**, 1023–34.

Aquino, K., M.U. Lewis and M. Bradfield (1999), 'Justice constructs, negative affectivity, and employee deviance: a proposed model and empirical test', *Journal of Organizational Behavior*, **20**, 1073–91.

Barling, J. (1996), 'The prediction, experience, and consequences of workplace violence', in G.R. VandenBos and E.Q. Bulatao (eds), *Violence on the Job: Identifying Risks and Developing Solutions*, Washington, DC: American Psychological Association, pp. 29–49.

Barling, J., A.G. Rogers and E.K. Kelloway (2001), 'Behind closed doors: in-home workers' experience of sexual harassment and violence', *Journal of Occupational Health Psychology*, **6**, 255–69.

Bennett, R.J. and S.L. Robinson (2000), 'Development of a measure of workplace deviance', *Journal of Applied Psychology*, **85**, 349–60.

Berkowitz, L. (1989), 'Frustration–aggression hypothesis: examination and reformulation', *Psychological Bulletin*, **106**, 59–73.

Berry, C.M., D.S. Ones and P.R. Sackett (in press), 'Interpersonal deviance, organizational deviance, and their common correlates: a review and meta-analysis', *Journal of Applied Psychology*.

Bies, R.J. and T.M. Tripp (2005), 'The study of revenge in the workplace: conceptual, ideological, and empirical issues', in S. Fox and P.E. Spector (eds), *Counterproductive Work Behavior: Investigations of Actors and Targets*, Washington, DC: American Psychological Association, pp. 65–81.

Bowling, N.A. and T.A. Beehr (2006), 'Workplace harassment from the victim's perspective: a theoretical model and meta-analysis', *Journal of Applied Psychology*, **91**, 998–1012.

Bushman, B.J. and R.F. Baumeister (1998), 'Threatened egotism, narcissism, self-esteem, and direct and displace aggression: does self-love or self-hate lead to violence?', *Journal of Personality and Social Psychology*, **75**, 219–29.

Bushman, B.J., A.M. Bonacci, W.C. Pedersen, E.A. Vasquez and N. Miller (2005), 'Chewing on it can chew you up: effects of rumination on triggered displaced aggression', *Journal of Personality and Social Psychology*, **88**, 969–83.

Cortina, L.M., L.F. Fitzgerald and F. Drasgow, (2002), 'Contextualizing Latino experiences of sexual harassment: preliminary tests of a structural model', *Basic and Applied Social Psychology*, **24**, 295–311.

Cortina, L.M., V.J. Magley, J.H. Williams and R.D. Langhout (2001), 'Incivility in the workplace: incident and impact', *Journal of Occupational Health Psychology*, **6**, 64–80.

Diener, E., E.M. Suh, R.E. Lucas and H.L. Smith (1999), 'Subjective well-being: three decades of progress', *Psychological Bulletin*, **125**, 276–302.

Dietz, J., S.L. Robinson, R. Folger, R.A. Baron and M. Schulz (2003), 'The impact of community violence and organization's procedural justice climate on workplace aggression', *Academy of Management Journal*, **46**, 317–26.

Dollard J., L.W. Doob, N.E. Miller, O.H. Mowrer and R.R. Sears (1939), *Frustration and Aggression*, New Haven, CT: Yale University Press.

Douglas, S.C. and M.J. Martinko (2001), 'Exploring the role of individual differences in the prediction of workplace aggression', *Journal of Applied Psychology*, **4**, 547–59.

Duffy, M.K., J.D. Shaw and E.M. Stark (2000), 'Performance and satisfaction in conflicted interdependent groups: when and how does self-esteem make a difference?', *Academy of Management Journal*, **43**, 772–82.

Duffy, M.K., D. Ganster and M. Pagon (2002), 'Social undermining at work', *Academy of Management Journal*, **45**, 331–51.

Dunbar, N.E. and J.K. Burgoon (2005), 'Perceptions of power and interactional dominance in interpersonal relationships', *Journal of Social and Interpersonal Relationships*, **22**, 207–33.

Folger, R. and D.P. Skarlicki (1998), 'A popcorn metaphor for workplace violence', in R.W. Griffin, A. O'Leary-Kelly and J. Collins (eds), *Dysfunctional Behavior in Organizations: Violent and Deviant Behaviors*, Monographs in organizational behavior and relations, 23, Greenwich, CT: JAI Press, pp. 43–81.

Fox, S. and P.E. Spector (2005), *Counterproductive Work Behavior: Investigations of Actors and Targets*, Washington, DC: American Psychological Association.

Greenberg, L. and J. Barling (1999), 'Predicting employee aggression against co-workers, subordinates and supervisors: the roles of person behaviors and perceived workplace factors', *Journal of Organizational Behavior*, **20**, 897–913.

Hershcovis, M.S. and J. Barling (2005), 'Adding insult to injury: a meta-analysis on the outcomes of workplace aggression', presented at the Annual Academy of Management Conference in Hawaii.

Hershcovis, M.S., N. Turner, J. Barling, K.A. Arnold, K.E. Dupré, M. Inness, M.M. LeBlanc and N. Sivanathan (2007), 'Predicting workplace aggression: a meta-analysis', *Journal of Applied Psychology*, **92**, 228–38.

Inness, M., J. Barling and N. Turner (2005), 'Understanding supervisor-targeted aggression: a within-person, between-jobs design', *Journal of Applied Psychology*, **90**, 731–9.

Jehn, K.A. (1995), 'A multi-method examination of the benefits and detriments of intragroup conflict', *Administrative Science Quarterly*, **40**, 256–82.

Keashly, L. and S. Harvey (2005), 'Emotional abuse in the workplace', in P. Spector and S. Fox (eds), *Counterproductive Work Behavior: Investigations of Actors and Targets*, Washington, DC: American Psychological Association, pp. 201–35.

Lapierre, L.M., P.E. Spector and J.D. Leck (2005), 'Sexual versus nonsexual workplace aggression and victims' overall job satisfaction: a meta-analysis', *Journal of Occupational Health Psychology*, **10**, 155–69.

Latham, L.L. and R. Perlow (1996), 'The relationship of client aggressive and nonclient-directed aggressive work behavior with self-control', *Journal of Applied Social Psychology*, **26**, 1027–41.

LeBlanc, M.L. and E.K. Kelloway (2002), 'Predictors and outcomes of workplace violence and aggression', *Journal of Applied Psychology*, **87**, 444–53.

Lim, S. and L.M. Cortina (2005), 'Interpersonal mistreatment in the workplace: the interface and impact of general incivility and sexual harassment', *Journal of Applied Psychology*, **90**, 483–96.

Marcus-Newhall, A., W.C. Pedersen, M. Carlson and N. Miller (2000), 'Displaced aggression is alive and well: a meta-analytic review', *Journal of Personality and Social Psychology*, **78**, 670–89.

Martinko, M.J., M.J. Gundlach and S.C. Douglas (2002), 'Toward an integrative theory of counterproductive work behavior: a causal reasoning perspective', *International Journal of Selection and Assessment, Special Issue: Counterproductive Behaviors at Work*, **10**, 36–50.

Neuman, J.H. and R.A. Baron (2005), 'Aggression in the workplace: a social-psychological perspective', in S. Fox and P.E. Spector (eds), *Counterproductive Work Behavior: Investigations of Actors and Targets*, Washington, DC: American Psychological Association, pp. 13–40.

O'Leary-Kelly, A.M., R.W. Griffin and D.J. Glew (1996), 'Organization-motivated aggression: a research framework', *Academy of Management Review*, **21**, 225–53.

Raver, J.L. and J. Barling (in press), 'Workplace aggression and conflict: constructs, commonalities and challenges for future inquiry', in C.K.W. De Dreu and M.J. Gelfand (eds), *The Psychology of Conflict and Conflict Management in Organizations*, Mahwah, NJ: Lawrence Erlbaum Associates.

Rayner, C. (1997), 'The incidence of workplace bullying', *Journal of Community and Applied Social Psychology*, **7**, 199–208.

Robinson, S.L. and R.J. Bennett (1995), 'A typology of deviant workplace behaviors: a multi-dimensional scaling study', *Academy of Management Journal*, **38**, 555–72.

Robinson, M.D. and G.L. Clore (2002), 'Belief and feeling: evidence for an accessibility model of emotional self-report', *Psychological Bulletin*, **128**, 934–60.

Robinson, S.L. and A.M. O'Leary-Kelly (1998), 'Monkey see, monkey do: the influence of work groups on the antisocial behavior of employees', *Academy of Management Journal*, **41**, 658–72.

Schat, A.C.H. (2004), 'In praise of tolerance: investigating the effects of organizational tolerance on the incidence and consequences of workplace aggression', Unpublished doctoral dissertation.

Schat, A.C.H. and E.K. Kelloway (2000), 'Effects of perceived control on the outcomes of workplace aggression and violence', *Journal of Occupational Health Psychology*, **5**, 386–402.

Schat, A.C.H. and E.K. Kelloway (2003), 'Reducing the adverse consequences of workplace aggression and violence: the buffering effects of organizations', *Journal of Occupational Health Psychology*, **8**, 110–22.

Schat, A.C.H., M.R. Frone and E.K. Kelloway (2006), 'Prevalence of workplace aggression in the U.S. workforce', in E.K. Kelloway, J. Barling and J.J. Hurrell Jr (eds), *Handbook of Workplace Violence*, Thousand Oaks, CA: Sage, pp. 47–89.

Skarlicki, D.P. and R. Folger (1997), 'Retaliation in the workplace: the roles of distributive, procedural and interactional justice', *Journal of Applied Psychology*, **82**, 434–43.

Spector, P.E. and S. Fox (2005), 'The stressor-emotion model of counterproductive work behavior', in S. Fox and P.E. Spector (eds), *Counterproductive Work Behavior: Investigations of Actors and Targets*, Washington, DC: American Psychological Association, pp. 65–81.

Tepper, B.J. (2000), 'Consequences of abusive supervision', *Academy of Management Journal*, **43**, 178–90.

Vardi, Y. and Y. Weiner (1996), 'Misbehavior in organizations: a motivational framework', *Organizational Science*, **7**, 151–65.

Vigoda, E. (2002), 'Stress-related aftermaths to workplace politics: the relationships among politics, job distress, and aggressive behavior in organizations', *Journal of Organizational Behavior*, **23**, 571–91.

Zapf, D. and S. Einarsen (2005), 'Mobbing at work: escalated conflicts in organizations', in S. Fox and P.E. Spector (eds), *Counterproductive Work Behavior: Investigations of Actors and Targets*, Washington, DC: American Psychological Association, pp. 237–70.

17 Understanding and deterring employee theft with organizational justice

Edward C. Tomlinson and Jerald Greenberg

The unauthorized taking or using of company property for personal use by employees, known as employee theft, is a serious problem in organizations. It has been estimated that 60 percent (Boye and Jones, 1997) to 75 percent (McGurn, 1988) of employees have stolen from their employers at least once, and that some employees engage in such behavior routinely (Sandberg, 2003). Even in the wake of a series of audacious corporate scandals that have stimulated attention to ethical workplace behavior in recent years (Markham, 2005), employee theft has not faded from the scene. Indeed, as many as 11 percent of workers still indicate having witnessed acts of theft by other employees during 2005 (Ethics Resource Center, 2005). Moreover, the impact of employee theft has been considerable. In retail stores alone, for example, employee theft is estimated to have cost over $15 billion in 2001 (Hollinger and Davis, 2002). So profound are these losses that over 30 percent of business failures have been attributed to employee theft (Snyder and Blair, 1989).

Unlike other prevalent and costly forms of dysfunctional organizational behavior (e.g. uncivil and aggressive behavior), theft is a crime (Hollinger and Clark, 1983). As such, it has prompted traditional efforts at criminal mitigation by organizations. This occurs at three different points – before hire, while employed, and upon termination. First, to predict and screen out individuals who are inclined to steal before they are hired, various selection instruments have been used (e.g. Jones, 1990). Second, assuming that screening is not foolproof, organizations also focus on detecting criminal acts among current employees by putting in place sophisticated systems to audit and monitor criminal behavior (e.g. Purpura, 2002). Finally, after an employee has been caught stealing, prohibitions are enforced, often leading to termination and sometimes also turning the matter over to law-enforcement authorities (Gross-Schaefer et al., 2000).

From the layperson's perspective, these traditional approaches might be regarded as ensuring 'justice' in the sense that the organization strives to hire only honest, law-abiding individuals, and actively monitors and enforces legal compliance such that those caught stealing are punished. Although we deny neither the criminality of employee theft nor the relevance of these traditional approaches as responses to it, we argue that relying on them exclusively is overly optimistic and insufficient. Elsewhere (Tomlinson and Greenberg, 2005), we compared these traditional approaches to employee theft with an *organizational justice* approach, which focuses on people's perceptions of fairness in organizations. Specifically, we indicated that each of the traditional approaches is limited in its ability to account for theft completely, and, thus, to manage it effectively. For example, employee theft still occurs even when organizations carefully select prospective employees and remove opportunities for theft. Moreover, simply ascribing employee theft to 'bad apple' employees overlooks key social motives that drive theft behavior (Altheide et al., 1978; Greenberg and Scott, 1996).

In contrast, the organizational justice perspective recognizes that employee theft is a deliberate effort by employees to redress injustices perpetrated by their employers (Greenberg and Tomlinson, 2004; Tomlinson and Greenberg, 2005). This behavior allows employees to 'even the score' by righting a wrong, even if doing so requires reciprocating their employers' deviant ways (Greenberg, 1997b). Hence the key policy implication of this orientation is clear and distinct from those following from traditional, criminal-based approaches: employers who treat their employees fairly discourage those individuals from stealing from them.

Although our earlier writings distinguished between the traditional and organizational justice approaches to employee theft and explicated the value of ensuring fair treatment of employees during their tenure, the literature may leave one with the impression that the organizational justice perspective is fundamentally incompatible with the traditional approaches, and that the former should supplant the latter. For example, Litzky et al. (2006) suggest that monitoring employees may signal that they are not trusted and as a result they will be more likely to retaliate by stealing. Others have reviewed the limitations of integrity tests as a selection tool, noting their limited ability to predict employee theft (Dalton et al., 1994) and the likelihood of generating an unacceptably high degree of false positives (Dalton and Metzger, 1993), clearly suggesting an unfair selection process. Indeed, some have suggested that employees may perceive aggressive implementation of these traditional deterrents as a further source of injustice, thereby inciting further deviance, potentially leading to a dangerously escalating cycle (Bennett and Robinson, 2003).

In contrast, we argue here that a broader justice-based conceptualization of employee theft may supplement the efficacy of more traditional approaches to deterring employee theft. We also assert that organizational justice is relevant not only during the employee's tenure, but also before it begins and after it ends. To make this point, we begin by briefly discussing the traditional approaches to employee theft. We then present three primary types of organizational justice (distributive, interactional and procedural). Following this, we discuss how these types of justice relate to applying traditional efforts to deter employee theft at three distinct junctures: (1) before the employee is hired; (2) during the employee's tenure; and (3) after it is discovered that an employee has stolen from the organization. Beyond simply reviewing the findings from relevant research, we offer managers a framework (summarized in Table 17.1) for conceptualizing what we refer to as broader principles of organizational 'JUSTICE' for use in their own organizations.

Traditional approaches to employee theft

Two traditional approaches to dealing with employee theft involve the steps organizations take before hiring each employee. Specifically, since employee theft is regarded as a crime, employers often carefully screen applicants to avoid hiring individuals with criminal backgrounds or with criminal propensities (e.g. Ash, 1971). The *individual differences orientation* (Tomlinson and Greenberg, 2005) assumes that some applicants are 'bad apples' – that is, individuals with certain personality and/or demographic characteristics that predispose them to steal (Ash, 1991). One popular and frequently used tool to 'weed out' such applicants before they are hired is an integrity (or honesty) test (Miner and Capps, 1996; Sackett, 1994), and there is a body of research that supports the efficacy of this approach (e.g. Ones et al., 1993). In terms of the *psychopathology orientation*

Table 17.1 Comparison of traditional approaches and the organizational JUSTICE approach to employee theft at various times

Time	Traditional approach	Organizational JUSTICE approach
Before employee is hired	Use honesty, integrity, personality tests to screen out potential criminals	**Justify** the job relevance of selection test **Utilize** properly validated tests in an appropriate manner **Select** ethical employees *and* managers
During employee's tenure	Use accountability, monitoring and surveillance to deter/detect theft	**Train** managers and employees **Involve** employees in developing and enforcing fair standards
After employee has been caught stealing	Employee is terminated and turned over to law-enforcement authorities	**Consistent** policy enforcement **Explain** decisions and policies carefully and courteously

(Tomlinson and Greenberg, 2005), organizations also may strive to avoid hiring employees considered likely to steal because of some type of disorder that renders them 'prone to criminal activity because they have developed abnormal, antisocial personalities that lead them to rationalize as appropriate a broader range of activities than the nonpsychopath' (Greenberg, 1997a: 33). A test such as the Minnesota Multiphasic Personality Inventory (MMPI; Graham, 2005) might be used as a selection tool to avoid hiring individuals likely to steal on this basis.

Another traditional approach, the *security orientation* (Tomlinson and Greenberg, 2005), is manifested both during the employee's tenure and after an employee has been caught stealing. This approach conceptualizes employee theft as a crime of opportunity (Sandberg, 2003) that largely can be deterred by removing such opportunities (i.e. promoting accountability and monitoring; Bintliff, 1994; Purpura, 2002). This explains the use of such popular tools as security cameras, periodic loss prevention/accounting audits, and restricted access areas (Sennewald, 1996).

The security orientation also facilitates a response after an employee has been caught stealing. That is, if these preventive measures fail to deter theft by employees, the assumption is that they will at least aid in the detection of theft and apprehension of its perpetrators (Tomlinson and Greenberg, 2005). Many organizations terminate employees for engaging in theft (Hollinger and Clark, 1983; Litzky et al., 2006). Yet still other actions also might be taken, such as 'blacklisting' the culprits within the industry or geographical area (Hollinger and Clark, 1983), and/or reporting the thief to the police for arrest and prosecution.

Dimensions of organizational justice

It is an interesting paradox that employee theft sometimes is motivated by an employee–thief's efforts to restore justice (i.e. perceptions of fairness) following a provocation by an organization and/or its managers. Of course, we recognize that individuals can be quite adept at rationalizing deviant behavior by claiming that they are merely 'righting a wrong' (Anand et al., 2005), and we do not condone employee theft whether or not it is provoked. Nonetheless, the finding that employee theft is promoted by job dissatisfaction or frustration with one's organization (Hollinger and Clark, 1983; Mangione and Quinn, 1975) challenges the widespread, but overly simplistic, assumption that people who steal from their employers are immoral individuals. Instead, we believe that employees who feel treated unfairly at work are likely to be angry and motivated to respond in a manner they believe will restore fairness. This is the case even among individuals who otherwise are disinclined to act immorally and/or to steal. More specifically, when more constructive responses to unfair treatment are not readily available, theft offers a covert way to respond. Illustrating this, Analoui and Kakabadse (1991) interviewed a female bartender whose manager had her work so late that she could not catch a bus home and then denied her request for cab fare even though this was a customary benefit. Although the woman refrained from stealing otherwise, on this occasion she pocketed a customer's payment for a drink claiming, 'I'll get a taxi and he'll pay for it' (p. 52).

Thus unfair treatment by managers may stimulate theft that otherwise would not occur. Viewed in this manner, the occurrence of employee theft may present an opportunity for the organization to become aware of abusive managers or arbitrary and capricious policies that motivate this behavior (Lewicki et al., 1997). Managers who assume simply that stealing is only a result of inadequate security measures or workers who are morally corrupt or psychologically deficient are likely to neglect their own role in contributing to this behavior. As such, they are likely to be ineffective at resolving the root cause of the problem (Litzky et al., 2006). An understanding of how employees form perceptions of fairness enables managers to avoid violating these perceptions, which it is hoped will negate a key motivation to steal in the first place. In this connection, we consider three specific forms of fairness perceptions: (1) distributive justice; (2) interactional justice; and (3) procedural justice.

Distributive justice
Distributive justice is concerned with the outcomes allocated to employees on the basis of what they believe they deserve. Employees expect that the rewards they receive should be proportional to the contributions made to their employers (Homans, 1961) and, according to equity theory (Adams, 1965), that their ratio of rewards to contributions should be equal to the corresponding ratios of others. Employees who perceive that these conditions are not met recognize that a distributive injustice has been done. This leads them to experience negative emotions – such as feeling angry if they are underpaid or guilty if they are overpaid. Such feelings, in turn, motivate employees to neutralize these adverse states by responding behaviorally (e.g. by adjusting outcomes or inputs) and/or psychologically (e.g. by adjusting perceptions of rewards and contributions), thereby seeking to restore justice in their relationships with their employers (Adams, 1965). Therefore, if workers feel that they are underpaid, they may attempt to even the score via theft as a unilateral means of raising their own outcomes (Greenberg, 1990a, 1997b). In other words, employees who believe they are not being given what they deserve are likely to take it anyway by stealing. Illustrating this, a clothing store employee stated in an interview, 'I feel I deserved to get something additional for my work since I was not getting paid enough' (Zeitlin, 1971: 26). In another study, a miner justified theft of a wrench on the grounds that it was a means of creating a wage differential (that otherwise wasn't available) for working in dangerous conditions (Altheide et al., 1978).

Additional insight into how distributive injustice leads to employee theft is offered by Greenberg's (1990a) quasi-experiment conducted in three manufacturing plants operated by the same company. Due to a financial crisis, top management imposed a 15 percent pay cut among all employees at two of the plants for ten weeks. The third plant, in which a similar group of employees performed identical work, experienced no pay change. This control group allowed comparisons of theft in each factory (measured in terms of shrinkage rates) to be made between underpaid and fairly paid employees at three times: before, during, and after the pay cut. The results showed that during the pay cut, theft was significantly higher in the plants experiencing the pay cut than in the control group. This is particularly remarkable considering that theft rates were consistently low among all three plants before and after the pay cut. This supports the argument that employees develop expectations regarding what they deserve in return for their work, and when they are deprived of this reward, they are more likely to raise their outcomes by stealing.

Interactional justice
The term interactional justice refers to employees' perceptions of the quality of interpersonal treatment they receive from their managers (Bies and Moag, 1986). Conceptually,

it has been proposed (Greenberg, 1993b), and empirically, it has been established that interactional justice involves conveying thorough information in a socially sensitive and respectful manner (Colquitt, 2001). The relevance of interactional justice to employee theft is highlighted in an interview with a woman who worked at two record stores (Altheide et al., 1978), one where she felt mistreated by her manager and another where she did not. With respect to the first store, she admitted, 'I stole there all the time, towards the end I did [it] just because I didn't like him [the manager] at all' (p. 105). However, commenting on her experience in the other store, she noted, 'Working for them, you just didn't want to steal, [because] there was no reason to . . . you liked to work there' (pp. 105–6).

Greenberg's (1990a) quasi-experimental study referred to above also examined the impact of interpersonal treatment on employee theft. Specifically, the results of this study indicated that the nature of the explanation managers gave for the pay cut affected the level of theft that resulted from distributive injustice. By design, these explanations varied with respect to the level of interactional justice used in conjunction with describing the pay cut. In one condition, workers were given an elaborate explanation that justified the decision and presented it in a manner that showed considerable social sensitivity. Specifically, the president of the company personally visited this plant to announce the decision and brought extensive supporting materials to document the rationale for the pay cut. He also repeatedly expressed his remorse for having to resort to this decision (e.g. 'it will hurt us all alike . . . it really hurts me to do this, and the decision didn't come easily'). In contrast, workers in another plant were told about the pay cut in a manner reflecting low levels of interactional justice. They received very little information to explain the decision and only the most superficial expressions of remorse. Specifically, at a brief and hastily conducted meeting a junior executive announced the decision without describing the basis on which it was made, doing so in a manner that was far less apologetic in tone.

Among the plants at which pay was cut, the rate of theft during the reduced-pay period was over twice as high in the plant whose employees were exposed to low interactional justice conditions than in the plant whose employees were exposed to high levels of interactional justice. A survey of the employees verified that those in the low interactional justice condition felt more unfairly treated than those in the high interactional justice condition. This evidence supports the argument that low interactional justice exacerbates employees' willingness to steal in response to underpayment inequity. Thus a company that imposed a pay cut in order to survive a financial crisis encountered unexpected financial losses that were dramatically worsened as the insult of a poor explanation was added to the injury inflicted on employees' paychecks (Greenberg and Alge, 1998). These findings were corroborated in a follow-up laboratory experiment (Greenberg, 1993a) that independently manipulated the quality of information and the sensitivity in which it was presented (as these variables were confounded in the field experiment).

Procedural justice

Procedural justice is an assessment of the fairness of the policies and procedures used to allocate outcomes. A sense of procedural justice can be promoted by allowing individuals input, or voice, in decisions that affect them (Thibaut and Walker, 1975). Procedural justice also can be facilitated by making allocation decisions that (1) are based on accurate information that is representative of key constituents, (2) are applied in an ethical, consistent and unbiased fashion, and (3) are capable of being corrected in the event of an error (Leventhal, 1976, 1980). Procedural justice is a particularly salient concern whenever individuals receive undesirable outcomes (Brockner and Wiesenfeld, 1996; Colquitt and Greenberg, 2003).

Shapiro et al. (1995) conducted a field study of employees in 18 fast food restaurants to examine the impact of procedural justice-based interventions on employee theft. Specifically, restaurant managers introduced several theft-reduction interventions designed to enhance procedural justice, such as giving employees a voice in defining theft and drafting a code of ethics that prohibited it, and tracking missing food in an accurate, publicly observable manner. As expected, the researchers found that these techniques of increasing procedural justice were associated with lower theft of food from the restaurant (based on reports of theft by peers).

To summarize, research on organizational justice indicates that managers can reduce employee theft by managing employees' perceptions of fairness during their tenure with the organization. Specifically, employees are more likely to steal from their employers to the extent that they believe they failed to receive rewards commensurate with their work contributions (distributive injustice), that they were denied respectful treatment and adequate reasoning behind an outcome decision (interactional injustice), and that outcome decisions were made with minimal due process (procedural injustice). In the following section, we illustrate a broader application of organizational justice by explicating how key principles of fairness can inform and enhance the efficacy of traditional approaches to addressing employee theft.

How organizational justice explains employee theft

As we have noted, the study of organizational justice has been applied fruitfully to the problem of employee theft, resulting in fresh insights not evident from traditional approaches. Some researchers have extended this argument by suggesting that traditional approaches are ineffective and even counterproductive in eliminating employee theft (Gross-Schaefer et al., 2000; Litzky et al., 2006), and implying they are antithetical to principles of fairness. For example, Gross-Schaefer et al. (2000) have labeled traditional approaches as 'negative [and] reactive' (p. 89), and concluded that they 'fail to deal with the root issues of employee theft' (p. 91). They recommend a more affirmative and proactive approach – such as promoting a more fair and ethical environment – that prevents employees from being disenfranchised. Practically speaking, does this mean that organizations should no longer attempt to screen out dishonest individuals, administer audits or monitoring, or terminate employees caught stealing? We do not believe this is prudent. Indeed, some individuals are more inclined to be dishonest, and the absence of controls can actually invite theft by signaling the organization's lack of interest in controlling it. Instead, we contend that a broader conceptualization of organizational justice can enrich the application of the traditional approach to more effectively combat employee theft at three points – before the employee is hired, during the employee's tenure, and after an employee has been caught stealing. Specifically, we present seven important guidelines for discouraging employee theft, each of which begins with a letter that, when placed in order with the others, spells the word *justice*. We refer to this as the JUSTICE framework, and we now present this conceptualization.

Justice considerations before hire
Although much of the prior research connecting organizational justice to employee theft has concentrated on how to treat the employee during their tenure, we contend that fairness also matters in the fight against theft *before* employees are hired. Specifically, we assert that organizations should be careful: (1) to *justify* the relevance of their selection tests; (2) to *utilize* only properly validated tests; and (3) to *select* ethical employees and managers.

Justify   To promote organizational justice, it is critical for employers to *justify* the job relevance of selection procedures used (e.g. honesty tests, background checks, etc.). Both applicants and current employees react negatively to selection procedures they deem to be unfair (Gilliland, 1994). In fact, although certain tests (such as honesty tests) may screen out dishonest employees (Ones et al., 1993), if those tests are perceived to be unfair they also may result in honest employees not accepting job offers that are extended to them (Singer, 1993). This is in keeping with the tendency for ostensible concerns about fairness to promote positive impressions of organizations (Greenberg, 1990b).

With this in mind, organizational officials should provide thorough explanations for the use of their selection tests, thereby promoting interactional justice. This may entail explaining to applicants the costly impact of employee theft, necessitating use of a tool to screen out potential employee–thieves. It also requires explaining the basis for assuming the validity of these tests, further justifying their use. To the extent that such a case can be made – of course, without insulting candidates by suggesting that they may be perpetrators – the organization faces a good opportunity to present itself as being concerned with fairness.

In keeping with this, the battery of theft-related selection tests clearly should be job-related (Arvey and Sackett, 1993) and calibrated according to the risk of theft in a particular job. For example, invasive personality tests that measure psychological disorders (e.g. the MMPI) may be deemed more appropriate for jobs in which there is a compelling interest in public safety (such as police officer) than those in which this is not the case (such as secretary). Additionally, organizations should make every effort to assure applicants that their selection tests rely on principles of procedural justice, such as by indicating that they are not susceptible to faking, minimize invasion of privacy, and yield accurate information. Officials also should emphasize the distributive justice of the tests by providing assurance that selection decisions are made on the basis of merit (Arvey and Sackett, 1993) and that the tests demonstrate high predictive validity (Gilliland and Hale, 2005).

Utilize   In addition to justifying the use of selection procedures, fairness also is promoted by properly *utilizing* validated tests in an appropriate manner. Specifically, all selection tests used by an organization should meet basic psychometric standards such as reliability and validity (Arvey and Sackett, 1993). This is vital in so far as the accuracy of the test ensures procedural justice. There is a body of research that generally supports the validity of integrity tests (Murphy, 1993; Ones et al., 1993; Sackett, 1994). Nonetheless, integrity testing is very controversial. Some research suggests that these tests have limited validity and generate a high degree of false positives (Dalton and Metzger, 1993; Dalton et al., 1994). Some personality tests (e.g. the MMPI) may be deemed inappropriate for some jobs and/or illegal in some situations. Thus it is vital for managers to evaluate carefully each theft-related selection test they intend to use to ensure its appropriateness.

Occasionally, such tests are criticized on the grounds that they are administered improperly by unqualified personnel (Snyder and Blair, 1989), which would violate principles of procedural justice. Other criticisms stem from rude and disrespectful treatment by potential employers (Bies and Moag, 1986; Gilliland and Hale, 2005), which is clearly a violation of interactional justice. Also, to promote interactional justice, it is useful for officials to go out of their way to explain how these procedures have been followed. Again, it is not merely following fair procedures that promotes justice, but ensuring that others know about this, that promotes impressions of fairness, which in many ways is even more important (Greenberg, 1990b). Thus efforts to *justify* decisions and to use fair procedures go hand in hand.

Select Although our points thus far indicate the need to *justify* the use of theft-related selection tests to applicants and to *utilize* carefully validated tests in a fair manner, these considerations may be rendered moot if the resulting selection decision itself is not considered to be fair. In fact, under such circumstances, justifications may be perceived as manipulative, thereby undermining efforts at promoting justice (Greenberg, 1990b). Thus our final suggestion for promoting justice before hiring requires *selecting* ethical employees and managers. To ensure distributive justice (Gilliland and Hale, 2005), employees and managers should be deserving of the jobs they receive. In the present context, this requires relying on the appropriate, validated tests to select employees who are less predisposed to engage in theft.

In addition, applicants passed over for job openings should be treated with high interactional justice (Gilliland and Hale, 2005). At the very least, this requires treating them in a courteous manner. However, in this case, questions can be raised as to whether applicants rejected on the grounds that they may be inclined to steal are owed, or should be given, explanations to this effect. We hedge here because human resources officials may be unqualified to present this likely upsetting information, potentially doing more harm than good. As such, it seems prudent to guard against venturing into such territory. Ethically, in this connection, omitting theft-proneness as an explanation for not hiring an applicant is akin to the practice of not debriefing research participants fully in instances in which doing so may be expected to do more harm than good (Greenberg and Folger, 1988). Indeed, withholding information for one's own good is considered by many kinder than sharing it (Grover, in press).

It also is worth stressing that when an organization selects an individual to be a manager, procedures should be in place to ensure that he or she is ethical and will refrain from engaging in or condoning employee theft. As we have noted, employees react adversely to managers who are regarded as unfair and arbitrary (Greenberg and Tomlinson, 2004; Tomlinson and Greenberg, 2005). It is important to realize that some managers have particularly insidious effects by promoting or tolerating employee theft. For example, several studies have shown that some managers proactively condone or encourage theft despite their duty to safeguard organizational assets. In a classic study, Gouldner (1954) found an 'indulgency pattern', whereby supervisors openly permitted employees to take tools and other items home for their personal use in his classic interview study of gypsum factory workers. In Ditton's (1977b) ethnographic study of British bakery workers, the theft of bread by employees was so prevalent that managers intentionally raised production levels to avoid shortages. And although managers were aware that bakery delivery drivers frequently shorted customer orders in order to supplement their wages, they did nothing to stop this form of theft. Similarly, interviews of garment workers revealed that supervisors regularly turned a blind eye toward taking small items and scrap materials for personal use (Sieh, 1987).

Some managers go a step further by actively aiding and abetting employee theft. Dalton (1959) discovered that senior officials at one manufacturing plant had items specially produced for employees to take without purchasing. Several studies noted that department store managers intentionally damaged packages so that they could justify selling the merchandise at drastically reduced prices to staff members (Altheide et al., 1978). Finally, managers may send the tacit signal that they condone theft behavior when they engage in theft themselves (Kemper, 1966). Because they are a central source of information regarding employees' role expectations (Wimbush, 1999), managers are salient role models who strongly influence the behavior of their subordinates (Dineen et al., 2006). Therefore it is vital for organizations to ensure that they are carefully selecting ethical managers. For example, although this is not always done, organizations should consider using the same types of theft-related selection tests when hiring managers as they do when hiring lower-level employees. Indeed, given the impact of managers on organizational culture, and as role models, this consideration is especially important.

Justice considerations during employment

During an employee's tenure, fairness principles should also inform the organization's efforts to (1) *train* managers and employees, and (2) *involve* all employees in determining an ethical code and fair workplace standards.

Train   It also is important to *train* managers and employees in ways that recognize and combat employee theft. Because research has shown that employees steal in response to unfair treatment, managerial training should concentrate on how they can promote perceptions of fairness among their employees (Greenberg, 2006; Skarlicki and Latham, 2005). The efficacy of such training in deterring theft was demonstrated in a field study in three discount stores operated by the same company (Greenberg, 1999). Each of these stores was experiencing very high shrinkage from their stock rooms (suggesting employee theft), and a survey of store employees indicated that they felt underpaid and treated disrespectfully by their managers. These perceptions of injustice may have motivated employees to steal.

One of the three stores was selected at random to receive interpersonal justice training (IJT), which involved training managers in techniques of delegation, information sharing, respectful communication and other fairness-related topics. Reducing employee theft was not identified as the motive for the course. After training, shrinkage in this store was compared to the two other stores – one whose managers received training unrelated to organizational justice or to theft, and another whose employees received no training at all. Compared to employees whose managers were not trained in interactional justice, those whose managers were so trained experienced significantly higher levels of interactional justice, and importantly, the rate of theft in this store dropped from about 8 percent to about 4 percent and remained at this level for six months after the study had been completed. However, there was no change in either of the other two stores. It is remarkable that this reduction in theft did *not* occur due to typical forms of training in loss prevention methods (Tilley et al. 1999), but rather by training managers how to treat employees fairly. Importantly, this type of managerial training also can lead to increased fairness perceptions when managers need to resort to disciplinary action (Cole and Latham, 1997), a topic to which we will return when describing how to respond after an employee has been caught stealing. Such training also promotes fairness by enhancing employees' acceptance of unfair conditions and by neutralizing adverse reactions to unfair conditions (Greenberg, 2006).

Training for non-managerial employees also should focus on conveying interactional justice (that is, providing thorough information to support the organization's position against theft). This can be accomplished (1) by communicating the harmful effects of employee theft, (2) by disseminating an ethics program to guide employees' behavior, and (3) by establishing ongoing communication mechanisms to manage employees' perceptions of distributive and procedural fairness. Promoting interactional justice increases fairness perceptions and identifies critical information that employees otherwise are not likely to have. Communicating the harmfulness of employee theft is essential to counter any rationalizations that frame this activity as a benign, victimless and legitimate supplement to wages (Ditton, 1977a). It is vital that employees are informed precisely about how theft is contrary to their own best interests (Hollinger, 1989). Note that using interactional justice to convey the impact of theft need not be contrary to accountability practices such as loss prevention audits. For example, Carter et al. (1988) studied rates of employee theft in a Swedish grocery store in which graphs tracking weekly rates of theft were posted conspicuously for employees. The number of missing items decreased significantly following this intervention and remained below the pre-intervention baseline level throughout the study period.

We also emphasize that training should cover ethical policies specifying acceptable workplace behavior as laid out in ethics codes. Such documents reduce ambiguity regarding what constitutes theft, including items of uncertain ownership (Greenberg, 1997b). Ethics codes also have been effective in creating and maintaining cultures of honesty (Niehoff and Paul, 2000), particularly when these codes are accompanied by a formal program of ethics training and an ethics office that further oversees and promotes ethical standards (Ethics Resource Center, 1994; Treviño and Nelson, 2003). This has been corroborated in a field experiment by Greenberg (2002) comparing theft rates among customer service representatives who either had or did not have an ethics program in place at the time the study was conducted. The ethics program provided employees in one office with training in ethical principles and how those principles were expected to be applied in their jobs, along with practice responding to ethical issues at work, and procedures for seeking additional guidance on ethical matters. The other office did not have an ethics program at the time of the study. Employees in both offices were underpaid for completing a survey, and then were asked to pay themselves the stated amount from a bowl of coins whose exact value was believed to be unknown. Greenberg (2002) found that although workers are prone to steal when underpaid, this effect was attenuated when an ethics program was in place. This was particularly so among individuals who had attained a higher level of cognitive moral development that enabled them to benefit from the training (Treviño and Weaver, 2003; Wells and Schminke, 2001). Despite the contrived nature of this laboratory research, which was required to create clear manipulations and high levels of control, we cannot ignore the two clear implications of this work – that organizations should hire individuals who are least inclined to engage in theft and to train them in precisely what constitutes theft.

In closing this section, we also advise organizations to establish ongoing communication channels to manage fairness perceptions. For example, a 'hotline' or a 'helpline' can be used to help employees get answers to their questions about pay (Taft, 1985). Specifically, such techniques can serve as mechanisms for educating employees about the procedures used to determine their pay (Folger and Greenberg, 1985; Shapiro et al., 1995), to dispel any misperceptions of inequity relative to one's colleagues (Greenberg, 1998), and to correct any inaccurate perceptions of distributive and procedural justice that may be harbored.

Involve   To promote perceptions of justice, it is critically important to *involve* employees in developing and enforcing an ethical code and fair workplace standards, particularly in so far as it incorporates standards and practices regarding theft. It is a fundamental principle of procedural justice that granting employees input in processes affecting them increases perceptions of procedural justice (Greenberg, 2000), and this, in turn, discourages employee theft (Greenberg and Scott, 1996). As Snyder et al. (1991) put it, 'The more involved they [employees] are, the more committed they should be to the decisions made and the more likely they and their fellow employees will not steal from the company' (p. 46). As we noted earlier, Shapiro et al. (1995) reinforced the value of providing employees voice in reducing theft. Specifically, restaurant employees participated in generating a definition of what behaviors constitute theft (which included 'nibbling' on small amounts of food not paid for), a disciplinary policy for employees caught stealing, and a code of ethics for their particular store. Employees also engaged in daily tracking of shrinkage losses, and were given a pre-set budget of 'Buddy Coupons' that allowed them reasonable discretion in selling discounted food to friends and family members. Taken together, these procedures enabled the employees to have input in developing and enforcing their ethics program.

In addition, as mentioned earlier, one frequently used enforcement mechanism is an anonymous corporate hotline, which can also be used to give employees a voice (procedural justice) in enforcing ethical compliance. As Greenberg (1998) noted, 'Clearly, mechanisms that make it easier for employees to "snitch" on thieves will have a deterrent effect insofar as they add significantly to the presence of policing eyes' (p. 180). Nonetheless, some authors (e.g. Litzky et al., 2006) have suggested that enforcement efforts such as monitoring actually incite theft. Specifically, employees may construe monitoring as a sign that management distrusts them, and they are motivated to retaliate by stealing. However, it is not necessarily the case that deterrence methods will be viewed so negatively by employees; this depends on the manner in which these methods are employed. Alge (2001) reported that monitoring job-relevant activities and allowing individuals to have a voice in establishing the monitoring program enhanced perceptions of procedural justice. To the extent that methods of deterrence, such as monitoring, are perceived to be fair, we contend that they will be unlikely to invoke employee theft (for a theoretical analysis of the underlying psychological processes involved, see Alge et al., 2006).

Justice considerations after theft detection

It is hoped that relying on fairness principles before employees are hired and during their tenure will deter employee theft. However, should all else fail and an employee is caught stealing, it is vital for the organization (1) to *consistently* enforce their policy on theft, and (2) to *explain* carefully and courteously the reason for the disciplinary action taken.

Consistent   To ensure both distributive and procedural justice, it is important to be *consistent* when enforcing policies. With respect to distributive justice, those who behave appropriately should be rewarded and those who behave inappropriately should be punished (Mitchell et al., 1996). Furthermore, the degree of punishment should fit the level of the crime to maintain perceptions of fairness (Litzky et al., 2006). Gross-Schaefer et al. (2000: 91) elaborate by arguing, 'Disciplinary procedures should be flexible enough to distinguish between violations that are merely inadvertent, a result of negligence and the more serious intentional violations'. After all, there is no point in having a policy prohibiting theft if it is not enforced. The policy articulates and its enforcement ensures distributive justice with respect to employee theft. Often, a key issue with respect to consistency of punishing employee theft is not matching the degree to which the punishment fits the crime, but more fundamentally, whether the theft goes addressed at all. Turning a blind eye to the problem often occurs both because employers don't know how to respond appropriately and because they don't want to risk sharing with the public (especially competitors) that they are suffering a problem in this regard (Greenberg and Scott, 1996). Understandable though this may be, this practice sends the message that theft may not be unacceptable, thereby tacitly condoning it.

Being consistent in the application of rules is a fundamental tenet of procedural justice (Leventhal, 1980), and this is especially important with respect to the administration of deterrents (Treviño and Weaver, 2003). Specifically, similar infractions must be punished similarly, regardless of the perpetrator (Litzky et al., 2006). This also means that it is imperative for organizations not to allow double standards for executives which grant them impunity for ethical violations (Gross-Schaefer et al., 2000). If enforcement is not consistent, it sends contradictory messages to employees and violates their perceptions of procedural fairness.

Explain   We cannot overstate the importance of *explaining* with the utmost care and courtesy the basis for any disciplinary actions taken. Often, because of its criminal nature, disciplinary responses to employee theft are quite severe, including termination (Hollinger and Clark, 1983) and, possibly, criminal prosecution. Therefore it is essential to provide thorough interactional justice via careful and courteous explanations supporting the disciplinary action taken. The manner in which a terminated employee is treated sends important fairness-related signals to employees who remain (Brockner et al., 1992). In addition, Lind et al., (2000) found that a wrongful termination lawsuit is more likely when a terminated employee is not treated with dignity and respect and given a thorough explanation. Their study further established that managers should deliver the news in person as soon as possible to enhance perceived fairness.

Conclusion

We hope that readers will not dismiss the guidance inherent in our JUSTICE acronym on the grounds of its cuteness. Beneath this mnemonic aid lies a set of principles that can, and should, be used in the ongoing effort to deter employee theft. Importantly, our framework does not challenge existing wisdom in this regard. Rather, the JUSTICE framework complements what we know about traditional approaches (e.g. selection) in ways that allow them to be implemented in a more sophisticated fashion and, it is hoped, yielding more effective results. Our confidence in the JUSTICE framework is based on considerable research, much of which we have identified. However, there clearly is more to be done. We hope that our remarks will have stimulated such efforts.

References

Adams, J.S. (1965), 'Inequity in social exchange', in L. Berkowitz (ed.), *Advances in Experimental Social Psychology*, Vol. 2, New York: Academic Press, pp. 267–79.

Alge, B.J. (2001), 'Effects of computer surveillance on perceptions of privacy and procedural justice', *Journal of Applied Psychology*, **86**(4), 797–804.

Alge, B.J., J. Greenberg and C.T. Brinsfield (2006), 'An identity based model of organizational monitoring: integrating information privacy and organizational justice', in J.J. Martocchio (ed.), *Research in Personnel and Human Resources Management*, Vol. 25, San Diego, CA: Elsevier, pp. 71–135.

Altheide, D.L., P.A. Adler, P. Adler and D.A. Altheide (1978), 'The social meanings of employee theft', in J.M. Johnson and J.D. Douglas (eds), *Crime at the Top*, Philadelphia, PA: Lippincott, pp. 90–124.

Analoui, F. and A. Kakabadse (1991), *Sabotage*, London: Mercury.

Anand, V., B.E. Ashforth and M. Joshi (2005), 'Business as usual: the acceptance and perpetuation of corruption in organizations', *Academy of Management Executive*, **19**(2), 9–23.

Arvey, R.D. and P.R. Sackett (1993), 'Fairness in selection: current developments and perspectives', in N. Schmitt and W. Borman (eds), *Personnel Selection in Organizations*, San Francisco, CA: Jossey-Bass, pp. 171–202.

Ash, P. (1971), 'Screening employment applications for attitudes toward theft', *Journal of Applied Psychology*, **55**(2), 161–4.

Ash, P. (1991), *The Construct of Employee Theft Proneness*, Park Ridge, IL: SRA/London House.

Bennett, R.J. and S.L. Robinson (2003), 'The past, present, and future of workplace deviance research', in J. Greenberg (ed.), *Organizational Behavior: The State of the Science*, Mahwah, NJ: Lawrence Erlbaum Associates, pp. 247–81.

Bies, R.J. and J.S. Moag (1986), 'Interactional justice: communication criteria of fairness' in R.J. Lewicki, B.H. Sheppard and M.H. Bazerman (eds), *Research on Negotiation in Organizations*, Vol. 1, Greenwich, CT: JAI Press, pp. 43–55.

Bintliff, R.L. (1994), *Crime-proofing Your Business*, New York: McGraw-Hill.

Boye, M.W. and J.W. Jones (1997), 'Organizational culture and employee counterproductivity', in R.A. Giacalone and J. Greenberg (eds), *Antisocial Behavior in Organizations*, Thousand Oaks, CA: Sage, pp. 172–84.

Brockner, J. and B.M. Wiesenfeld (1996), 'An integrative framework for explaining reactions to decisions: the interactive effects of outcomes and procedures', *Psychological Bulletin*, **120**(2), 189–208.

Brockner, J., T.R. Tyler and R. Cooper-Schneider (1992), 'The influence of prior commitment to an institution on reactions to perceived unfairness: the higher they are, the harder they fall', *Administrative Science Quarterly*, **37**(2), 241–61.

Carter, N., A. Holström, M. Simpanen and K. Melin (1988), 'Theft reduction in a grocery store through product identification and graphing of losses for employees', *Journal of Applied Behavior Analysis*, **21**(4), 385–9.

Cole, N.D. and G.P. Latham (1997), 'Effects of training in procedural justice on perceptions of disciplinary fairness by unionized employees and disciplinary subject matter experts', *Journal of Applied Psychology*, **82**(5), 699–705.

Colquitt, J.A. (2001), 'On the dimensionality of organizational justice: a construct validation of a measure', *Journal of Applied Psychology*, **86**(3), 386–400.

Colquitt, J.A. and J. Greenberg (2003), 'Organizational justice: a fair assessment of the state of the literature', in J. Greenberg (ed.), *Organizational Behavior: The State of the Science*, 2nd edn, Mahwah, NJ: Lawrence Erlbaum Associates, pp. 165–210.

Dalton, D.R. and M.B. Metzger (1993), ' "Integrity testing" for personnel selection: an unsparing perspective', *Journal of Business Ethics*, **12**(2), 147–56.

Dalton, D.R., M.B. Metzger and J.C. Wimbush (1994), 'Integrity testing for personnel selection: a review and research agenda', in G.R. Ferris (ed.), *Research in Personnel and Human Resources Management*, Vol. 12, Greenwich, CT: JAI Press, pp. 125–60.

Dalton, M. (1959), *Men who Manage*, New York: Wiley.

Dineen, B.R., R.J. Lewicki and E.C. Tomlinson (2006), 'Supervisory guidance and behavioral integrity: relationships with employee citizenship and deviant behavior', *Journal of Applied Psychology*, **91**(3), 622–35.

Ditton, J. (1977a), 'Perks, pilferage, and the fiddle: the historical structure of invisible wages', *Theory and Society*, **4**, 39–71.

Ditton, J. (1977b), *Part-time Crime: An Ethnography of Fiddling and Pilferage*, London: Macmillan.

Ethics Resource Center (1994), *Ethics in American Business: Policies, Programs, and Perceptions*, Washington, DC: Ethics Resource Center.

Ethics Resource Center (2005), *National Business Ethics Survey*, Washington, DC: Ethics Resource Center.

Folger, R. and J. Greenberg (1985), 'Procedural justice: an interpretive analysis of personnel systems', in K. Roland and G. Ferris (eds), *Research in Personnel and Human Resources Management*, Vol. 3, Greenwich, CT: JAI Press, pp. 141–83.

Gilliland, S.W. (1994), 'Effects of procedural and distributive justice on reactions to a selection system', *Journal of Applied Psychology*, **79**(5), 691–701.

Gilliland, S.W. and J.M.S. Hale (2005), 'How can justice be used to improve employee selection practices?', in J. Greenberg and J.A. Colquitt (eds), *Handbook of Organizational Justice*, Mahwah, NJ: Lawrence Erlbaum Associates, pp. 411–38.

Gouldner, A.W. (1954), *Wildcat Strike: A Study in Worker–Management Relationships*, New York: Harper & Row.

Graham, J.R. (2005), *MMPI-2: Assessing Personality and Psychopathology*, New York: Oxford University Press.

Greenberg, J. (1990a), 'Employee theft as a reaction to underpayment inequity: the hidden cost of pay cuts', *Journal of Applied Psychology*, **75**(5), 561–8.

Greenberg, J. (1990b), 'Looking fair vs. being fair: managing impressions of organizational justice', in B.M. Staw and L.L. Cummings (eds), *Research in Organizational Behavior*, Vol. 12, Greenwich, CT: JAI Press, pp. 111–57.

Greenberg, J. (1993a), 'Stealing in the name of justice: informational and interpersonal moderators of theft reactions to underpayment inequity', *Organizational Behavior and Human Decision Processes*, **54**(1), 81–103.

Greenberg, J. (1993b), 'The social side of fairness: interpersonal and informational classes of organizational justice', in R. Cropanzano (ed.), *Justice in the Workplace: Approaching Fairness in Human Resource Management*, Hillsdale, NJ: Lawrence Erlbaum Associates, pp. 79–103.

Greenberg, J. (1997a), 'A social influence model of employee theft: beyond the fraud triangle', in R.J. Lewicki, B.H. Sheppard and R.J. Bies (eds), *Research on Negotiation in Organizations*, Vol. 5, Greenwich, CT: JAI Press, pp. 22–49.

Greenberg, J. (1997b), 'The STEAL motive: managing the social determinants of employee theft', in R. Giacalone and J. Greenberg (eds), *Antisocial Behavior in Organizations*, Thousand Oaks, CA: Sage, pp. 85–108.

Greenberg, J. (1998), 'The cognitive geometry of employee theft: negotiating "the line" between taking and theft', in R.W. Griffin, A. O'Leary-Kelly and J. Collins (eds), *Dysfunctional Behavior in Organizations, Vol. 2: Nonviolent Behaviors in Organizations*, Greenwich, CT: JAI Press, pp. 147–93.

Greenberg, J. (1999), 'Interpersonal justice training (IJT) for reducing employee theft: some preliminary results', unpublished data, The Ohio State University, Columbus, OH.

Greenberg, J. (2000), 'Promote procedural justice to enhance acceptance of work outcomes', in E.A. Locke (ed.), *A Handbook of Principles of Organizational Behavior*, Oxford: Blackwell, pp. 181–95.

Greenberg, J. (2002), 'Who stole the money, and when? Individual and situational determinants of employee theft', *Organizational Behavior and Human Decision Processes*, **89**(1), 985–1003.

Greenberg, J. (2006), 'Losing sleep over organizational injustice: attenuating insomniac reactions to underpayment inequity with supervisory training in interactional justice', *Journal of Applied Psychology*, **91**(1), 58–69.

Greenberg, J. and B. Alge (1998), 'Aggressive reactions to workplace injustice', in R.W. Griffin, A. O'Leary-Kelly and J. Collins (eds), *Dysfunctional Behavior in Organizations, Vol. 1: Violent Behaviors in Organizations*, Greenwich, CT: JAI Press, pp. 119–45.

Greenberg, J. and R. Folger (1988), *Controversial Issues in Social Research Methods*, New York: Springer-Verlag.

Greenberg, J. and K.S. Scott (1996), 'Why do workers bite the hands that feed them? Employee theft as a social exchange process', in B.M. Staw and L.L. Cummings (eds), *Research in Organizational Behavior*, Vol. 18, Greenwich, CT: JAI Press, pp. 111–55.

Greenberg, J. and E.C. Tomlinson (2004), 'The methodological evolution of employee theft research: the DATA cycle', in R.W. Griffin and A. O'Leary-Kelly (eds), *The Dark Side of Organizational Behavior*, San Francisco, CA: Jossey-Bass, pp. 426–61.

Gross-Schaefer, A., J. Trigilio, J. Negus and C. Ro (2000), 'Ethics education in the workplace: an effective tool to combat employee theft', *Journal of Business Ethics*, **26**(2), 89–100.

Grover, S.L. (in press), 'Lying to bosses, subordinates, peers and the outside world: motivations and consequences', in J. Greenberg (ed.), *Insidious Workplace Behavior*, Mahwah, NJ: Lawrence Erlbaum Associates.

Hollinger, R.C. (1989), *Dishonesty in the Workplace: A Manager's Guide to Preventing Employee Theft*, Park Ridge, IL: London House.

Hollinger, R.C. and J.P. Clark (1983), *Theft by Employees*, Lexington, MA: Lexington Books.

Hollinger, R.C. and J.L. Davis (2002), *2001 National Retail Security Survey: Final Report*, Gainesville, FL: Center for Studies in Criminology and Law.

Homans, G.C. (1961), *Social Behavior: Its Elementary Forms*, New York: Harcourt, Brace and World.

Jones, J.W. (1990), 'Megatrends in integrity testing', *Security Management*, **34**(7), 27–30.

Kemper, T.D. (1966), 'Representative roles and the legitimation of deviance', *Social Problems*, **13**, 288–98.

Leventhal, G. (1976), 'The distribution of rewards and resources in groups and organizations', in L. Berkowitz and E. Walster (eds), *Advances in Experimental Social Psychology*, Vol. 9, New York: Academic Press, pp. 91–131.

Leventhal, G. (1980), 'What should be done with equity theory?', in K.J. Gergen, M.S. Greenberg and R.H. Willis (eds), *Social Exchange: Advances in Theory and Research*, New York: Plenum, pp. 27–55.

Lewicki, R.J., T. Poland, J.W. Minton and B.H. Sheppard (1997), 'Dishonesty as deviance: a typology of workplace dishonesty and contributing factors', in R.J. Lewicki, R.J. Bies and B.H. Sheppard (eds), *Research on Negotiation in Organizations*, Vol. 6, Greenwich, CT: JAI Press, pp. 53–86.

Lind, E.A., J. Greenberg, K.S. Scott and T.D. Welchans (2000), 'The winding road from employee to complainant: situational and psychological determinants of wrongful termination claims', *Administrative Science Quarterly*, **45**(3), 557–90.

Litzky, B.E., K.A. Eddleston and D.L. Kidder (2006), 'The good, the bad, and the misguided: how managers inadvertently encourage deviant behaviors', *Academy of Management Perspectives*, **20**(1), 91–103.

Mangione, T.W. and R.P. Quinn (1975), 'Job satisfaction, counterproductive behavior, and drug use at work', *Journal of Applied Psychology*, **60**(1), 114–16.

Markham, J.W. (2005), *A Financial History of Modern U.S. Corporate Scandals: From Enron to Reform*, Armonk, NY: M.E. Sharpe.

McGurn, S. (1988), 'Spotting the thieves who work among us', *The Wall Street Journal*, 7 March, p. A16.

Miner, J.B. and M.H. Capps (1996), *How Honesty Testing Works*, Westport, CT: Quorum.

Mitchell, T.R., D. Daniels, H. Hopper, J. George-Falvy and G.R. Ferris (1996), 'Perceived correlates of illegal behavior in organizations', *Journal of Business Ethics*, **15**, 439–55.

Murphy, K.R. (1993), *Honesty in the Workplace*, Pacific Grove, CA: Brooks/Cole.

Niehoff, B.P. and R.J. Paul (2000), 'Causes of employee theft and strategies that HR managers can use for prevention', *Human Resource Management*, **39**(1), 51–64.

Ones, D.S., C. Viswesvaran and F.L. Schmidt (1993), 'Comprehensive meta-analysis of integrity test validities: findings and implications for personnel selection and theories of job performance', *Journal of Applied Psychology*, **78**(4), 679–703.

Purpura, P.P. (2002), *Security and Loss Prevention*, 4th edn, Boston, MA: Butterworth-Heinemann.

Sackett, P.R. (1994), 'Integrity testing for personnel selection', *Current Directions in Psychological Science*, **3**, 73–6.

Sandberg, J. (2003), 'Office sticky fingers can turn the rest of us into Joe Fridays', *The Wall Street Journal*, 19 November, p. B1.

Sennewald, C. (1996), *Security Consulting*, 2nd edn, Boston, MA: Butterworth-Heinemann.

Shapiro, D.L., L.K. Treviño and B. Victor (1995), 'Correlates of employee theft: a multi-dimensional justice perspective', *The International Journal of Conflict Management*, **6**(4), 404–14.

Sieh, E.W. (1987), 'Garment workers: perceptions of inequity and employee theft', *British Journal of Criminology*, **27**(2), 174–90.

Singer, M.S. (1993), *Fairness in Personnel Selection*, Aldershot, UK: Avebury.

Skarlicki, D.P. and G.P. Latham (2005), 'Can leaders be trained to be fair?', in J. Greenberg and J.A. Colquitt (eds), *Handbook of Organizational Justice*, Mahwah, NJ: Lawrence Erlbaum Associates, pp. 499–522.

Snyder, N.H. and K.E. Blair (1989), 'Dealing with employee theft', *Business Horizons*, May–June, 27–34.

Snyder, N.H., O.W. Broome, Jr, W.J. Kehoe, J.T. McIntyre, Jr, and K.E. Blair (1991), *Reducing Employee Theft: A Guide to Financial and Organizational Controls*, New York: Quorum Books.

Taft, W.F. (1985), 'Bulletin boards, exhibits, hotlines', in C. Reuss and D. Silvis (eds), *Inside Organizational Communication*, 2nd edn, New York: Longman, pp. 183–9.

Thibaut, J. and L. Walker (1975), *Procedural Justice: A Psychological Analysis*, Hillsdale, NJ: Lawrence Erlbaum Associates.

Tilley, B., R. Dafoe and L. Putsey (1999), *Positive Loss Prevention*, Uxbridge, Ontario, Canada: Bob Tilley.

Tomlinson, E.C. and J. Greenberg (2005), 'Discouraging employee theft by managing social norms and promoting organizational justice', in R. Kidwell and C. Martin (eds), *Managing Organizational Deviance*, Thousand Oaks, CA: Sage, pp. 211–32.

Treviño, L.K. and K.A. Nelson (2003), *Managing Business Ethics: Straight Talk About How to Do it Right*, 3rd edn, New York: John Wiley & Sons.

Treviño, L.K. and G.R. Weaver (2003), *Managing Ethics in Business Organizations: Social Scientific Perspectives*, Stanford, CA: Stanford University Press.

Wells, D. and M. Schminke (2001), 'Ethical development and human resources training: an integrative framework', *Human Resource Management Review*, **11**, 135–58.

Wimbush, J.C. (1999), 'The effect of cognitive moral development and supervisory influence on subordinate's ethical behavior', *Journal of Business Ethics*, **18**(4), 383–95.

Zeitlin, L.R. (1971), 'A little larceny can do a lot for employee morale', *Psychology Today*, June, 22, 24, 26, 64.

18 When teams fail in organizations: what creates teamwork breakdowns?
Dana E. Sims and Eduardo Salas

Days before Hurricane Katrina hit the Gulf Coast, the National Hurricane Center issued warnings of the projected devastation of life and property. Ultimately, the warnings did nothing to prevent the ultimate failure to adequately prepare for and respond to the storm by local, state and federal agencies. Hurricane Katrina was not the largest hurricane to strike the USA, nor was it the first time that a hurricane of this magnitude reached the Gulf Coast. Despite this, reports of communication failures, breakdowns in leadership, poor decision making and a lack of situational awareness suggest the response to one of the USA's largest natural disasters was also one of the largest breakdowns of teamwork compounding the devastation of the Gulf Coast (CBS News, 2006; McClatchy Washington Bureau, 2005). The emergency response to Hurricane Katrina is a poignant example of how even expert teams with needed resources and expertise available at the tip of their fingers can fail. The question then arises, what creates teamwork breakdowns? Insights afforded by a century of team theory and empirical research suggest 'chemistry' is undoubtedly a critical building block of successful teams. It is the 'chemistry' that exists between team members, their leaders and their organizational environment that can tip the scales from success to failure.

It has long been understood that when teams gel, they are capable of accomplishments that no individual could hope to achieve. But what does it take to get the 'chemistry' within the team correct? Conversely, what factors can set off a chain reaction that ultimately leads to the derailment of effective team performance? And why are some teams able to rebound from setbacks to ultimately succeed, while other teams cannot? The answers to these important questions can be found in the science of team performance. This chapter uses the science of team performance to identify five broad factors that can derail teams. Team derailment occurs when a highly effective team experiences significant declines in performance (Milanovich et al., 2000). In this chapter, we seek to answer how (1) coordination mechanisms, (2) cooperation mechanisms, (3) communication, (4) team leadership, and (5) organizational characteristics contribute to team derailment. Further, we intend to draw out the critical characteristics of effective teams (see Table 18.1) based on lessons learned from decades of team research to assist practitioners unleash the synergies that teams are capable of. It is argued that failing to proactively manage each of these five elements, stakeholders may inadvertently diminish team performance outcomes, regardless of whether those outcomes are lives saved or organizational profit.

The nature of teams and team performance
Teams are complex entities, comprising two or more individuals, who interact socially, dynamically, episodically and adaptively (e.g. Kozlowski and Bell, 2003; Salas et al., 1992; Salas et al., 2004b). Team members often have distributed roles, share common goals, have

Table 18.1   Characteristics of highly effective teams

Components of team effectiveness	Characteristics of highly effective teams
Coordination	• Self-correct by admitting to and learning from mistakes • Develop and maintain shared mental models • Adapt to change • Manage conflict within the team
Cooperation	• Develop mutual trust and psychological safety within the team • Ensure team members are team-oriented
Communication	• Manage information so there is neither too little nor too much information available to the team • Solicit feedback in order to develop and revise team goals and strategies
Organizational characteristics	• Implement performance management systems that encourage cooperation by discouraging social loafing
Team leadership	• Have a clear and common purpose • Communicate information needed to perform • Effectively span boundaries with outside stakeholders • Ensure teams possess the right mix of competencies

complementary competencies, and are highly interdependent. This interdependence, regardless of its level, creates a sense of responsibility for other team members' behaviors (Kiggundu, 1983) and motivates teammates to engage in teamwork behaviors (e.g. compensatory behavior, performance monitoring; McIntyre and Salas, 1995). Over time, teams become more effective as members become proficient in their individual roles, team tasks and teamwork processes (Morgan et al., 1986). In addition, teams and their successes are shaped by the organizational/environmental context within which they are embedded. Taken together, the transformation of these various inputs and contextual variables into team outcomes (i.e. team performance, team effectiveness) occurs through teamwork.

Teamwork is a set of interrelated thoughts, actions and attitudes that combine to facilitate coordinated, adaptive performance (Salas et al., 2004a) and can have an individual-level (e.g. backup behavior, peer leadership) or team-level referent (e.g. coordination, decision making, dynamic allocation of resources). A number of teamwork models have been proposed over the years (e.g. Campion et al., 1993; Stevens and Campion, 1994; Fleishman and Zaccaro, 1992; Hackman and Morris, 1975; Marks et al., 2000; Roby, 1968; Salas et al., 2005). Regardless of the teamwork model chosen, teamwork is said to lead to both team performance and effectiveness. Although team performance and effectiveness are often discussed interchangeably, we offer some clarification here.

Team effectiveness is an overall assessment of team success or failure in meeting its objectives. Although team effectiveness is important, it is team performance that often leads to consistently effective teams. Team performance describes how the team executes its tasks (e.g. input, processes). Thus, a high-performing team may encounter setbacks but

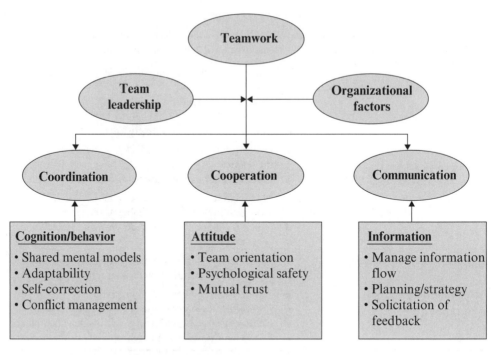

Figure 18.1   Factors influencing teamwork

will typically engage in appropriate attitudes, behaviors and cognitions (i.e. team perform-ance) that will help the team recover from setbacks and reach its goals (i.e. team effect-iveness). However, as most team members will report, teamwork is neither easy nor assured. For the sake of practicality and parsimony, the 'blanket terms' of cooperation, coordination and communication will be used as an organizing framework for discussing a number of factors that contribute to, comprise, flow from, and impinge upon effective team performance.

In this chapter, we sample variables from each of these three broad categories and discuss how they may lead to team derailment (see Figure 18.1). In addition, organiza-tional characteristics and team leadership are discussed as potential failure points for teams. These factors are important to consider in relation to cooperation, coordination and communication because they have the potential to impact the degree to which teams successfully engage in the team processes and drive the success or failure of teams. For each of these five categories, we provide a brief summary and then advance selected exam-ples of issues that can obstruct team success.

What causes teams to derail?

Over the years, many frameworks, checklists and guidelines have been offered to ensure team success. Despite this, many teams continue to fail. It may be that practitioners are unsure about how to apply team research to real-life teams to address real-life challenges. In the following pages, we use the science of team performance to clarify how managers, executives or practitioners can apply this knowledge to their own workplace.

How can poor coordination lead to team derailment?
Coordination is the life-blood of effective teams. Coordination is the compilation of behavioral and cognitive mechanisms, including task strategies, needed to perform a task. Coordination can also be described as team processes that transform team resources (e.g. individual KSAs – knowledge, skills and abilities) into outcomes (Brannick et al., 1995; Gladstein, 1984; Mathieu et al., 2000). Teams must be able to engage in team processes that assist them in maintaining shared awareness and adapting to each other's needs and the changing environment. Unfortunately, many teams are unable to effectively interact and engage in the necessary coordination mechanisms, and as a result do not perform as well as expected.

As described in the introduction of this chapter, the local, state and federal agencies responding to Hurricane Katrina appear to have failed largely due to their inability to coordinate. For instance, many of the delays in providing timely assistance and resources were due to the White House not appointing a clear hierarchy of responsibility or reporting systems to coordinate efforts in the affected areas. This further led local officials to be unable to adapt the initial hurricane response plans or secure the needed assistance when levees broke, flooding portions of New Orleans, and when hurricane victims began arriving at the Superdome. Finally, officials were harshly criticized for not learning from the lessons of the terrorist attacks on September 11th (McClatchy Washington Bureau, 2005). Thus teams are mostly likely to fail when they . . .

. . . *neglect to learn from their mistakes (i.e. self-correct)*. In the execution of any plan or team task, small errors, deviations or mistakes are likely to occur. The difference, however, between teams that succeed from those that fail may lie in their ability to minimize the smaller, unnoticed and preventable errors that often lead to larger team failure (e.g. Perrow, 1984; Reason, 1997; Weick and Sutcliffe, 2001). One way that teams may be able to prevent or minimize these smaller errors in the future is to identify and learn from them (as opposed to hiding or covering up the event) (Carter and West, 1998; Tjosvold et al., 2004; West, 1996). This approach to errors aligns with a learning orientation.

A learning orientation 'reflects the value a firm places not only on adroitly responding to changes in the environment but on constantly challenging the assumptions that frame the organization's relationship with the environment' (Baker and Sinkula, 1999: 412) when a mismatch between expectations and outcomes is observed (Argyris and Schon, 1978). In the team setting, a learning orientation supports members in questioning the norms that exist in the team. In addition, learning-oriented teams try different approaches to task completion to uncover better ways to accomplish the team objectives. While critical to the success of the team, this orientation for learning does not just happen (Baker and Sinkula, 1999). It must be cultivated over time through the attitudes, commitments and processes that are enacted by team members, leaders and management.

. . . *are unable to develop and/or maintain a shared mental model (SMM)*. It can be chaotic when a team of individuals is interdependently engaging in complex tasks in ever-changing environments (e.g. operating rooms, fire rescue teams, SWAT teams). As a result, team members must be able to 'stay on the same page' and have a similar understanding of their environment, team goals, individual team member tasks, and how the team will coordinate to achieve common goals (Cannon-Bowers et al., 1995). Failure to create these shared understandings (i.e. SMM) is likely to lead to team derailment. Thankfully, when teams encounter situations or environments that limit their ability to overtly communicate to coordinate or develop a shared understanding of their environment (i.e. situational awareness), they are not necessarily condemned to failure. Instead, they must rely on other team processes that allow them to work around these communication difficulties, especially in stressful environments where teams rely on SMMs in order to coordinate and adapt (e.g. Campbell and Kuncel, 2001; Cooke et al., 2000; Hinsz et al., 1997; Orasanu, 1990).

An example of the need for SMMs under adverse conditions may be envisioned in the military setting. While team members are on a reconnaissance mission, communication is limited to the bare minimum. A team member may request his 'binos' and the man behind him will instinctively know that he is expected to retrieve binoculars from the requestor's backpack and tap the requestor's back as if to say 'Ready!' once the binoculars have been retrieved. Meanwhile the requestor will maintain watch for the enemy and protect the two of them (Vesterman, 2006). It is only through these types of common understandings of the environment and performance expectations that teams can overcome the hurdles of reduced communication and an ever-changing environment. It is only through communication and continued interaction that teams may create and update their shared understanding to perform the needed teamwork skills (e.g. back-up behavior, mutual performance monitoring) required for effective team performance (e.g. Salas et al., 2005).

. . . *do not adapt to change*. Prior to performing, teams may develop strategies and contingency plans based on prior experiences or expectations to guide the team towards its objectives. However, things do not always go as planned, whether due to the complexity of the task, the environment in which the team is embedded, or the interdependencies which exist between the team members. As a result, the teams must recognize deviations and adjust procedures and predictions as well as individual roles (i.e. one team member's role may become more critical) when new information is presented (Burke et al., 2006; Priest et al., 2002; Smith et al., 1997). In fact, the military teaches its forces to be both leaders and followers in order to adapt to situations as they arise, with the awareness that team success must be put in front of personal egos.

In order to adapt, teams must have a deep understanding of the team, the team task and environment, and what team effectiveness looks like (Salas et al., 2006). If this understanding is lacking, the team may not be able to identify when current strategies are no longer appropriate, develop new strategies, or determine how team mates might need to adjust or the assistance that they might need to perform. Obviously, failing to fully understand the team and its task for the sake of adaptation is a recipe for team failure.

. . . *fail to manage conflict within the team*. Conflict within a team is not always bad (De Dreu and Van de Vliert, 1997; Pondy, 1967). Not only does it depend on the type of conflict (e.g. task versus relationship); it matters how the conflict is managed within the team. Relationship conflict involves interpersonal animosities between individuals and produces tensions that destroy cooperation and communication, and distract from team tasks (Hackman and Morris, 1975; Jehn, 1997). Conversely, task conflicts improve team performance by ensuring that all information and alternatives are considered and reducing groupthink (West and Anderson, 1996). Thus suppressing conflict completely could reduce creativity, innovation, performance, quality of decisions and communication between a group's members (De Dreu and Van de Vliert, 1997). However, because there is a tenuous line between productive and destructive conflict, teams must actively manage how team members communicate with each other and provide constructive feedback to ensure disagreement does not lead to the ultimate derailment of the team.

How can poor cooperation lead to team derailment?
Even when team members have the cognitions and strategies needed to perform as a team, teams that do not have the affective desire or motivation to do so are likely to derail. This affective desire or motivation to perform as a team is often placed under the umbrella term 'cooperation'. Cooperation may be generated by climates, norms and expectations that are formally dictated by the organization or informally developed within the team by its members. Informally developed climates are due to frequent team member interactions and members' shared perceptions of both the organizational environment and team norms (Anderson and West, 1998). The climate within a team is likely to impact the team coordination mechanisms (e.g. adaptability, self-correction) that are expected, rewarded and enacted.

The importance of cooperation becomes most clear when teams must perform in adverse conditions. National Aeronautics and Space Administration (NASA), which has begun to reinforce teamwork behaviors and attitudes that support effective teams, knows all too well that cooperation holds a space exploration crew together. For this reason, NASA now implements activities that not only replicate technical skills (e.g. flight simulators) but also situations for which team members must learn affective teamwork skills (e.g. NASA Extreme Environment Mission Operations). Keeping in mind that different team tasks and events that occur during team performance may require varying levels of coordination, teams may derail if they . . .

. . . *do not trust each other or lose trust in each other.* To ensure important team processes (e.g. communication, information sharing and cooperation) and outcomes (e.g. cycle times, product quality) occur, team members must have a shared perception that team members will perform actions (i.e. tasks, processes) important to the team and protect each others' rights and interests (Bandow, 2001; Webber, 2002). That is, team members must trust each other. In the absence of trust, team members may spend valuable time protecting, checking and inspecting each other to assess their trustworthiness (Cooper and Sawaf, 1996). In addition, team members that do not trust each other are less willing to share accurate information with each other, especially if the information is likely to make the individual more vulnerable (e.g. admitting to errors or lack of experience). When teams are spending time on non-task activities, are uncomfortable with engaging in important team processes (e.g. performance monitoring), and unwilling to share information, they are likely to be derailed. Within-team trust can be cultivated through the actions of the team leader. Research suggests that leaders can facilitate trust through frequent, honest communication (e.g. McAllister, 1995; Roberts and O'Reilly, 1974; Sekhar and Anjaiah, 1995; Treadway et al., 2004) and fairness/consistency of behavior (Clutterbuck and Hirst, 2002).

. . . *do not have a team orientation.* Not everyone wants to or likes to work in teams. For this reason, team members should be chosen who not only have a preference for working with others (i.e. collective orientation) but also seek out opportunities to coordinate, evaluate and utilize the input from other team members to improve team performance (i.e. team orientation; Driskell and Salas, 1992) and share mutual responsibility for team outcomes (Avery et al., 2001). Team orientation serves to improve both individual task performance (Shamir, 1990; Wagner, 1995) and overall team performance (e.g. better decision making) (Driskell and Salas, 1992). For this reason, practitioners should compose teams with team-oriented individuals. However, because it may be difficult to accurately identify those with a team orientation or unfeasible in existing teams, methods to motivate team members (e.g. reward systems, goal setting, performance appraisals) to engage in team-oriented behaviors should be established.

. . . *do not develop a sense of psychological safety.* In order to be effective, team members must feel secure in sharing information and providing feedback even when that means disagreeing with the group, admitting to personal ineptitude, and overcoming any fear of reprisal (Lee, 1997; Michael, 1976). Without this sense of security (i.e. psychological safety), teams are unlikely to be able to respond to, learn from or prevent errors from occurring until the team has already failed or achieved a less-than-stellar outcome (Edmondson, 1999). Teams with psychological safety also tend to value problem solving, focus on mutual responsibility for error resolution, and have an openness to feedback (Argyris and Schon, 1978, 1996; Baer and Frese, 2003; Edmondson, 1999). These teams are also less likely to fall victim to groupthink, which occurs when team members do not question the actions or decisions of team members for the sake of conformity or avoidance of conflict within the team (Janis, 1972). Groupthink has been credited for such team failures as the Bay of Pigs Invasion, the Challenger disaster, and even the decision to go to war in Iraq. For instance, the US Senate Intelligence Committee's Report indicated that when the Intelligence Community (e.g. analysts, collectors, managers) was presented with ambiguous evidence of Iraq's threat (e.g. existence of weapons of mass destruction programs), groupthink lead them to ignore or minimize evidence to the contrary (Select Committee on Intelligence, United States Senate, 2006). Thus, many well-known world crises may have been avoided if psychological safety had been developed within the team.

How can poor communication lead to team derailment?
As work becomes progressively complex and information-based, breakdowns and/or delays in communication can lead to team derailment. Communication is invaluable in teams not only because it transfers needed information to those who must make decisions and perform team tasks, but also because it facilitates teams in maintaining up-to-date SMMs (Salas et al., 2005). For instance, in the medical community communication has been identified as the cause of more than 15 percent of all medical errors (Andrews et al., 1997). In one case, a lack of effective communication between a doctor, an X-ray technician and an attendant in which a shared understanding of the patient's ailments could have been developed meant that poor decisions were made that may have led to the patient's ultimate demise (Howatt, 2003). As the situations that teams encounter become more stressful and the environments more complex, communication becomes even more vital to

maintain the team's SMM and their ability to adapt. Again, in the medical setting in which surgical teams frequently handle trauma patients and other emergencies, stress and complexity are a common factor. Thus, teams are likely to derail when team members . . .

. . . *do not manage information effectively*. A balance of enough information at the right time provided to the right team member is one of the greatest difficulties of communication within a team (Roby, 1968). It is often hard for team members to predict what information is needed, who needs it and when it should be provided (Lanzetta and Roby, 1956). As has been stated throughout this chapter, teams that lack needed information or are unable to access it are likely to fail because they will be unable to make good decisions or know how best to execute their tasks. Conversely, too much communication may also be a derailer because it can overwhelm a team member (i.e. cognitive overload) and reduce his/her ability to manage task responsibilities in stressful situations (Johnston and Briggs, 1968). Thus, not only may team performance suffer when teams do not have access to needed information, but teams may also derail if members are unable to effectively manage the information for their own purposes or provide information to others when it is needed.

A number of solutions have been offered over the years to alleviate communication problems (e.g. providing access to all information to all members at all times; Lanzetta and Roby, 1956). However, the amount of information available to most teams continues to grow exponentially with the advent of more technology, communication modes, and multi-team systems. Organizations must realize that teams need to be provided with the resources (e.g. training, equipment) to manage the information that is used by and generated from their team tasks. Without frequent and effective communication, teams are fated to fall short of their objectives.

. . . *fail to plan/strategize or solicit feedback, ideas and observations from teammates.* A benefit of teams is the access they provide to a wide range of experiences and knowledge. When these are not tapped (i.e. soliciting feedback and ideas), the benefit is lost. These experiences and knowledge can be used to develop more thorough strategies and contingency plans based on the challenges that are likely to occur while performing the team task. Ultimately, strategizing not only leads to better team performance, but also better SMMs and more communication within the team (Stout et al., 1999).

As the team executes its task, team members will observe different aspects of the task execution and may have varying perspectives on how the team performed. Oftentimes, by seeking out this information and soliciting feedback, the team is able to use information about past performance and challenges to strategize for even better performance in the future, thereby potentially inoculating the team from future derailment. The key is that even successful teams hit bumps in the proverbial road; successful teams are those that acknowledged, learned from, and adjusted to the feedback that they received from within (and outside) the team.

The three factors previously discussed (i.e. coordination, cooperation and communication) are internal to the team. However, team derailment is not always due to an internal dysfunction. In fact, a team that does not experience any of the above breakdowns may still fail (or be less effective) if the environment in which it is embedded is faulty or the team is not provided enough direction to manage an ambiguous environment (i.e. poor leadership). The importance of these external factors for the ultimate success of a team, and in the case of Motorola, the ultimate turn-around of the entire organization should not be ignored.

In 2003, Motorola had lost its competitive edge in the telephony marketplace. Through the support of organizational leaders, a renegade team with strong leadership and the necessary players was established. This team was given unlimited resources, isolated to minimize distractions, and allowed the freedom to go against organizational norms to design what was thought to be impossible. It is with this organizational support that the Razr phone emerged to ultimately sell almost as many new phones as Microsoft sold iPods in 2004. In fact, in 2006 Motorola's Razr phone is expected to outsell Microsoft's iPod. The Razr team has since been rewarded with stock options, but more importantly has been given public recognition for its hard work and ingenuity (Lashinsky, 2006). In the following section, we discuss factors external to the team. Specifically, we focus on organizational characteristics and team leadership.

How can organizational characteristics lead to team derailment?
Teams are often implemented as an organizational solution without considering whether the organizational culture is supportive of them. To promote teamwork the organization must encourage common objectives, shared values, mutual trust, frequent and honest communication, empowerment and learning (Castka et al., 2001; Salas et al., 2004a). Unfortunately, organizational policies and procedures are often established that do not promote team-based work but rather focus on individual performance. In addition, teams are hailed as an approach for managing uncertain and ambiguous situations. While we agree teams are typically better at adapting to changing environments, not all teams will succeed in these environments. For this reason, the organizational environment must be considered as a potential cause of team failure (e.g. Gladstein, 1984). Teams are likely to fail when the organization . . .

. . . *uses individual rather than team-based reward systems*. One key to team effectiveness is team members' willingness to put aside personal goals to cooperatively work towards team objectives. Although impacted by personal preferences (e.g. team orientation) and cultural differences (see Hofstede, 2004 regarding individualistic/collectivistic), organizations set the tone for cooperative work environments through their performance management and reward systems (e.g. Hackman, 1983; Lawler, 1981; Pritchard et al., 1988; Steiner, 1972). For this reason, performance management systems that promote individual accountability over team accountability should be replaced with measures of performance that assess team outcomes and provide constructive feedback regarding both team processes and individual performance (Zairi, 1994). By doing this, the organization sends a clear message that it expects teamwork and cooperation from its employees and team members will become more concerned with the success of the team. Failure to measure and reward team performance will result in teams that are less motivated to perform team tasks and team performance will be negatively affected.

. . . *does not manage the environmental uncertainty in which the team is embedded*. Many teams experience environmental uncertainty on a regular basis (e.g. urban combat, fire rescue, cardiac surgery). This environmental uncertainty may be caused by frequent and unexpected changes in the environment, the team not regularly receiving information needed for performance, or the lack of clarity in what is expected of the team (i.e. expectations are not set, needed tasks are uncertain). Regardless of the cause of the environmental uncertainty, these environments are stressful and can hinder team performance (e.g. tradeoffs in the speed and accuracy of task performance or impaired decision making) by impairing a team member's ability to coordinate or engage in other teamwork activities (Salas et al., 2004a).

In general, uncertain environments cannot be altered by the organization but rather are inherent in the task that the team performs. In these cases, organizations should provide teams support by ensuring that the individual/team characteristics, team task and team processes are as effective as possible. Teams will thereby be able to better manage the uncertainty in their environment, reduce their chances of derailment, and increase the probability they will be able to recover from any performance setbacks they may encounter. In cases in which the uncertainty is caused by lack of information and clarity, the organization and team leaders should take steps to rectify the uncertainty.

. . . *if the team task is too complex.* Due to the diversity of KSAs and adaptability that teams offer, teams are often assigned to very complex tasks. The complexity and difficulty of a team task, as well as how the work is structured, can impact the success of the team (Gladstein, 1984; Goodman, 1986; McGrath, 1984; Kabanoff and O'Brien, 1979; Steiner, 1972). This may be because as the team task becomes increasingly complex, the opportunities for errors are likely to increase, become difficult to identify, and ultimately derail the team. Furthermore, as team members become more intertwined or interdependent, the impact of one member's lapse can disrupt the entire team's performance. In these situations, team coordination mechanisms such as communication, performance monitoring, back-up behaviors (i.e. compensatory behaviors), error correction, and development of shared mental models become increasingly important to catch and adjust when errors occur. Obviously, the organization cannot always limit the complexity of team tasks. The organization can, however, allow flexibility in how the task roles are assigned and encourage team members to adjust as needed and provide assistance (or take over teammates' roles) when necessary.

. . . *does not discourage social loafing.* Another advantage of teams is that they can produce more than the sum of their individual parts. Sometimes, however, individuals working in team-based settings actually expend less (or withhold) effort than they would in an individually-based setting (Chapman and Arenson, 1993; Robbins, 2000). This behavior has been referred to as social loafing or the free-riding effect. One outcome of social loafing is that less overall work may be performed. In some cases, teammates will compensate for a team member who is free-riding (Kerr and Bruun, 1983) such that team performance does not decrease. Not surprisingly, when a team member continually underperforms, thereby requiring others to perform extra tasks, the climate within the team may become toxic as team members become suspicious of each others' contributions (Jackson and Harkins, 1985). This climate within the team due to social loafing is another factor that may lead to team derailment.

Social loafing is likely to occur when individual performance is not identifiable within the team output (e.g. Latane et al., 1979; Karau and Williams, 1993). Although we have argued that performance appraisals and reward systems should focus on the team, this does not negate the need to also measure individual performance. Likewise, team members who are personally committed to the team and/or the team task are less likely to free-ride (Ratzburg, 2006). Taken together, the organization must take steps (e.g. implement appropriate performance appraisal systems, select members who are team-oriented, and match employees to tasks and teams that they are personally committed to) to reduce the occurrence of social loafing to provide teams the support needed to succeed.

How can team leadership lead to team derailment?
A significant contributor to the failure of a team is a lack of direction and a clear understanding of purpose and goals (Katzenbach and Smith, 1993; Stewart and Manz, 1995). Team leaders set the tone for team performance by articulating clear and motivating visions, creating supportive climates that promote effective team processes and behaviors (e.g. advanced planning, communication), and engaging in social problem solving that encourages coordination and adaptation (Salas et al., 2004a). Further, team leaders are responsible for ensuring the team has access to the needed resources (e.g. training, equipment) to achieve these goals. In these ways, team leaders impact team performance through many processes (e.g. cognitive, motivational, affective) and may be the most important element in creating a cooperative work environment (Salas et al., 2004a). In some cases leadership is not static but rather shared and transferred to others within the team in order to take advantage of the strengths and expertise of those within it. Regardless of whether team leadership is held by an individual or shared within the team, teams are likely to fail if team leaders . . .

. . . *fail to communicate expectations for individual and team performance.* All too often, teams are expected to know, understand and execute a plan to meet team objectives without ever being informed of their team objectives, what the constraints/parameters are related to achieving those goals, or the expectations for how or when those goals are to be met (Adair, 1986; Scholtes et al., 1996). Without this direction, the team may not have a shared understanding of the goals. The impact of this is that team members may work incongruently or towards goals that are different from the organization's or leader's expectations. As a result, team leaders are critical in 'setting the tone in the organization and determining the kinds of behaviors that are expected and supported' (Baer and Frese, 2003: 52). Team leaders must clearly and regularly discuss (or facilitate the discussion of) team goals, individual member roles and expectations at the outset of the team task as well as throughout the progression of the task.

. . . *do not share information that is important to the team and the team's task.* In addition to setting expectations for team performance, team leaders must share and disseminate knowledge throughout the team to promote effective decision making based on the best available information. Often times, the team leader has sole access to information from each of the team members and other sources both within and outside the organization. In this situation, the team leader is responsible not only for pooling the information to develop plans and evaluate the consequences of team decisions, but also for ensuring the information is distributed to team members as needed. This is a problem with some team leaders, who withhold information to increase their position of power or in organizations that encourage hierarchical patterns in which communication flow is slow and hindered. This failure to communicate or effectively distribute information may have drastic affects on team performance.

. . . *do not span organizational and team boundaries.* The relationships that exist between teams and departments can also influence the adaptability and effectiveness of a team (Brett and Rognes, 1986; Katz and Kahn, 1978; Kotter, 1982; Levinson and Rosenthal, 1984; Likert, 1967; Mintzberg, 1973; Zaccaro, 2001). This is because alignment among all entities within the organization is important for effective organizational functioning (Kur, 1996; Oakland, 1993; Imai, 1986; Senge, 1990). The role of a team leader in maintaining this alignment is referred to as boundary spanning. Boundary spanning is the 'process by which teams manage their interactions with other parts of the organization' (Ancona and Caldwell, 1990: 25). Therefore, the team leader acts as a gatekeeper of information for the team (Katz and Tushman, 1983), which serves as a basis for shared situational awareness (Cannon-Bowers et al., 1995).

An example of the need for boundary spanning might be a team that depends on other teams or departments for information or products. This team may be unable to complete its tasks if it does not receive the needed resources or the products are of low quality. Another example might be if collaborative relations do not exist between teams and departments. In this case, resources may not be shared or expectations and conflicting priorities may not be communicated. In all these situations it becomes clear that when a team is not provided the needed resources (e.g. time, information, materials), its effectiveness will decline (Senge et al., 1999). Thus, it is the responsibility of the team leader to ensure collaborative and cooperative relationships exist between the team and other departments. A suggestion for how to facilitate team leader boundary spanning is creating a network of like-minded contacts and facilitating discussions among team members, suppliers and other stakeholders to ensure communication flows up and down stream.

. . . *do not provide effective feedback or situational updates.* Feedback in the team literature commonly relates to performance monitoring (i.e. advice for avoiding mistakes) or team self-correction (i.e. after-action reviews) (Cannon-Bowers et al., 1995; McIntyre and Salas, 1995). Developmental feedback from team leaders, however, is also important to team functioning because it provides information regarding how well the team is meeting stated objectives. Teams are then able to use this information to adjust their approach to the team task to ensure success. This is related to the goal-setting literature that suggests that without feedback regarding performance, individuals and/or teams will be unsure whether the goals are being met and similarly unable to adjust to meet the team goals.

Situational updates are also important to the team because they provide information regarding the environment in which the team is performing. The team leader as a boundary spanner has greater access to information regarding the environment and how the team strategy may need to adjust in order to maintain high performance. Thus, when team leaders fail to provide teams feedback regarding their performance or regarding changes in the environment, the team is likely to be caught off guard and unable to adjust when needed, thereby leading to team derailment.

. . . *select team members that lack task specific and interpersonal KSAs.* In order to be successful, teams must have an appropriate mix of task-specific (e.g. using a piece of equipment, interpreting reports; statistical skills) (e.g. Gersick, 1988; Morgan et al., 1986; Kozlowski et al., 1996) and interpersonal skills (e.g. Bradley et al., 2003; Druskat and Kayes, 2000; McIntyre and Salas, 1995). However, Colvin (2006) warns that leaders cannot select all-star team members and then sit back and wait for these teams to bring home a win. The members must be the *right* members. Cited in Colvin's article (2006), Mercer Delta's chief, David Nadler, reports that some of the worst teams are those composed entirely of 'potential CEOs'. This seems contrary to conventional wisdom regarding teams but is illustrated not only in the failure of the 2004 US Olympics basketball team composed of NBA stars, but also in the successful design of the first light bulb in 1879 by a machinist, a clockmaker, a glassblower, a mathematician and Thomas Edison (Colvin, 2006).

This potential derailer can be addressed by avoiding skills gaps within a team (e.g. Church, 1993; Katzenback and Smith, 1993; Oakland, 1993). Special attention should be paid when establishing a new team such that each team member should bring a unique set of KSAs and experiences that are needed to meet team objectives. In cases where a team is already formed or membership cannot be changed, it is important to ensure team members are provided training to address the task specific and/or interpersonal skill gaps.

Conclusion

This chapter has reviewed five broad categories of factors (i.e. coordination, cooperation, communication, organizational characteristics and team leadership) that impact the effectiveness and performance of a team. It has been argued in this chapter that by failing to manage any of these five elements, teams may not achieve their proposed levels of performance. For each of the five general factors, we provided some answers as to how they may lead to team derailment and some suggestions that practitioners can use to address these challenges. Further, it is important to emphasize that teams may encounter obstacles that may lead to performance decrements. It is through the proper support of teams within the organization and by their leaders, and engagement in collaboration, cooperation and communication that teams will be able to overcome these challenges and avoid derailment. Although it is not possible to review all of the potential factors that may act as obstacles to team performance, it is hoped that this chapter presents a starting point for practitioners to assess why their teams may not be performing optimally and how to get their teams back on track.

Acknowledgment

This work was supported by funding from the US Army Research Laboratory's Advanced Decision Architecture Collaborative Technology Alliance (Cooperative Agreement DAAD19-01-2-0009). All opinions expressed in this chapter are those of the authors and do not necessarily reflect the official opinion or position of the University of Central Florida, the US Army Research Laboratory or the Department of Defense.

References

Adair, J. (1986), *Effective Team Building*, London: Pan.
Ancona, D.G. and Caldwell, D.F. (1990), 'Beyond boundary spanning: managing external dependence in product development teams', *The Journal of High Technology Management Research*, **1**, 119–35.

Anderson, N. and West, M. (1998), 'Measuring climate for work group innovation: development and validation of the team climate inventory', *Journal of Organizational Behavior*, **19**, 235–58.

Andrews, L.B., Stocking, C., Krizek, T., Gottlieb, L., Krizek, C., Vargish, T. and Siegler, M. (1997), 'An alternative strategy for studying adverse events in medical care', *Lancet*, **349**, 309–13.

Argyris, C. and Schon, D. (1978), *Organizational Learning: A Theory in Action Perspective*, Reading, MA: Addison-Wesley.

Argyris, C. and Schon, D. (1996), *Organizational Learning II: Theory, Method and Practice*, Reading, MA: Addison-Wesley.

Avery, C., Walker, M.A. and Murphy, E.O. (2001), *Teamwork is an Individual Skill: Getting Your Work Done when Sharing Responsibility*, San Francisco, CA: Berrett-Koehler.

Baer, M. and Frese, M. (2003), 'Innovation is not enough: climates for initiative and psychological safety, process innovations, and firm performance', *Journal of Organizational Behavior*, **24**, 45–68.

Baker, W.E. and Sinkula, J.M. (1999), 'The synergistic effect of market orientation and learning orientation on organizational performance', *Journal of the Academy of Marketing Science*, **27**, 411–27.

Bandow, D. (2001), 'Time to create sound teamwork', *The Journal for Quality and Participation*, 41–7.

Bradley, J., White, B.J. and Mennecke, B.F. (2003), 'Teams and tasks: a temporal framework for the effects of interpersonal interventions on team performance', *Small Group Research*, **34**, 353–87.

Brannick, M., Prince, A., Prince, C. and Salas, E. (1995), 'The measurement of team process', *Human Factors*, **37**, 641–51.

Brett, J.M. and Rognes, J.K. (1986), 'Intergroup relations in organizations', in P. Goodman (ed.), *Designing Effective Work Groups* San Francisco, CA: Jossey-Bass, pp. 202–36.

Burke, C.S., Stagl, K.C., Salas, E., Pierce, L. and Kendall, D. (2006), 'Understanding team adaptation: a conceptual analysis and model', *Journal of Applied Psychology*, **91**, 1189–207.

Campbell, J.P. and Kuncel, N.R. (2001), 'Individual and team training', in N. Anderson, D.S. Ones, H.K. Sinangil and C. Viswesvaran (eds), *Handbook of Work and Organizational Psychology*, London: Blackwell, pp. 278–313.

Campion, M.A., Medsker, G. and Higgs, C. (1993), 'Relations between work group characteristics and effectiveness: implications for designing effective work groups', *Personnel Psychology*, **46**, 823–47.

Cannon-Bowers, J.A., Tannenbaum, S.I., Salas, E. and Volpe, C.E. (1995), 'Defining competencies and establishing team training requirements', in R.A. Guzzo and E. Salas (eds), *Team Effectiveness and Decision Making in Organizations*, San Francisco, CA: Jossey-Bass, pp. 333–81.

Carter, S.M. and West, M.A. (1998), 'Reflexivity, effectiveness, and mental health in BBC-TV production teams', *Small Group Research*, **29**, 583–601.

Castka, P., Bamber, C.J., Sharp, J.M. and Belohoubek, P. (2001), 'Factors affecting successful implementation of high performance teams', *Team Performance Management*, **7**, 123–34.

CBS News (2006), 'Katrina: gov't failure, private frauds', 14 February, retrieved on 10 October, 2006 from www.cbsnews.com/stories/2006/02/13/katrina/main1308008.shtml.

Chapman, J.G. and Arenson, S. (1993), 'Motivational loss in small task groups: free-riding on a cognitive task', *Genetic, Social and General Psychological Monographs*, **119**, 57–74.

Church, A. (1993), 'From both sides now: the power of teamwork – fact or fiction?', *Team Performance Management*, **4**, 42–52.

Clutterbuck, D. and Hirst, S. (2002), 'Leadership communication: a status report', *Journal of Communication Management*, **6**, 351–4.

Colvin, G. (2006), 'Why dream teams fail', *Fortune*, **153**, 87–92.

Cooke, N.J., Salas, E., Cannon-Bowers, J.A. and Stout, R.J. (2000), 'Measuring team knowledge', *Human Factors*, **42**, 151–74.

Cooper, R. and Sawaf, A. (1996), *Executive EQ: Emotional Intelligence in Leadership and Organizations*, New York: Grosset/Putnam.

De Dreu, C.K.W. and Van de Vliert, E. (1997), *Using Conflict in Organizations*, London: Sage.

Driskell, J.E. and Salas, E. (1992), 'Collective behavior and team performance', *Human Factors*, **34**, 277–88.

Druskat, V.U. and Kayes, D.C. (2000), 'Learning versus performance in short-term project teams', *Small Group Research*, **31**, 328–53.

Edmondson, A. (1999), 'Psychological safety and learning behavior in work teams', *Administrative Science Quarterly*, **44**, 350–83.

Fleishman, E.A. and Zaccaro, S.J. (1992), 'Toward a taxonomy of team performance functions', in R.W. Swezey and E. Salas (eds), *Teams: Their Training and Performance*, Norwood, NJ: Ablex.

Gersick, C.J.G. (1988), 'Time and transition in work teams: toward a new model of group development', *Academy of Management Journal*, **31**, 9–41.

Gladstein, D.L. (1984), 'Groups in context: a model of task group effectiveness', *Administrative Science Quarterly*, **29**, 499–517.

Goodman, P.S. (1986), 'Impact of task and technology on group performance', in P.S. Goodman (ed.), *Designing Effective Work Groups*, San Francisco, CA: Jossey-Bass, pp. 120–67.

Hackman, J.R. (1983), *A Normative Model of Work Team Effectiveness*, Technical Report No. 2, Research Program on Group Effectiveness, New Haven, CT: Yale School of Organization and Management.

Hackman, J.R. and Morris, C.G. (1975), 'Group tasks, group interaction process, and group performance effectiveness: a review and proposed integration', in L. Berkowitz (ed.), *Advances in Experimental Social Psychology*, Vol 8, New York: Academic Press, pp. 45–99.

Hinsz, V.B., Tindale, R.S. and Vollrath, D.A. (1997), 'The emerging conceptualization of groups as information processors', *Psychological Bulletin*, **121**, 43–64.

Hofstede, G. (2004), *Cultures and Organizations: Software of the Mind*, New York: McGraw-Hill.

Howatt, G. (2003), 'When margin of error is deadly: hospital cases underscore risk of drug mistakes', *Star Tribune*, 8 June, p. A:1.

Imai, M. (1986), *Kaizen: The Key to Japan's Competitive Success*, New York: McGraw-Hill.

Jackson, J.M. and Harkins, S.G. (1985), 'Equity in effort: an explanation of the social loafing effect, *Journal of Personality and Social Psychology*, **49**, 1199–206.

Janis, I. (1972), *Victims of Groupthink*, Boston, MA: Houghton Mifflin.

Jehn, K.A. (1997), 'A qualitative analysis of conflict types and dimensions in organizational groups', *Administrative Science Quarterly*, **42**, 530–57.

Johnston, W.A. and Briggs, G.E. (1968), 'Team performance as a function of task arrangement and work load', *Journal of Applied Psychology*, **52**, 89–94.

Kabanoff, B. and O'Brien, G.E. (1979), 'Cooperation structure and the relationship of leader and member ability to group performance', *Journal of Applied Psychology*, **64**, 526–32.

Karau, S.J. and Williams, K.D. (1993), 'Social loafing: a meta-analytic review and theoretical integration', *Journal of Personality and Social Psychology*, **65**, 681–706.

Katz, D. and Kahn, R.L. (1978), *The Social Psychology of Organizations*, New York: John Wiley & Sons.

Katz, R. and Tushman, M.L. (1983), 'A longitudinal study of the effects of boundary spanning supervision on turnover and promotion in research and development', *Academy of Management Journal*, **26**, 437–56.

Katzenbach, J.R. and Smith, D.K. (1993), *The Wisdom of Teams: Creating the High-Performance Organization*, Boston: Harvard Business School.

Kerr, N.L. and Bruun, S.E. (1983), 'Ringleman revisited: alternative explanations for the social loafing effect', *Personality and Social Psychology Bulletin*, **7**, 224–31.

Kiggundu, M. (1983), 'Task interdependence and job design: test of a theory', *Organizational Behavior and Human Decision Processes*, **31**, 145–72.

Kotter, J. (1982), 'What effective general managers really do', *Harvard Business Review*, **60**, 157–69.

Kozlowski, S.W.J. and Bell, B.S. (2003), 'Work groups and teams in organizations', in W.C. Borman, D.R. Ilgen and R.J. Klimoski (eds), *Handbook of Psychology: Industrial and Organizational Psychology*, vol. 12, Hoboken, NJ: John Wiley & Sons, pp. 333–75.

Kozlowski, S.W.J., Gully, S.M., Salas, E. and Cannon-Bowers, J.A. (1996), 'Team leadership and development: theory, principles, and guidelines for training leaders and teams', in M. Beyerlein, S. Beyerlein and D. Johnson (eds), *Advances in Interdisciplinary Studies of Work Teams: Team Leadership*, Vol. 3, Greenwich, CT: JAI Press, pp. 253–92.

Kur, E. (1996), 'The faces model of high performing team development', *Leadership and Organizational Development Journal*, **17**, 32–41.

Lanzetta, J.T. and Roby, T.B. (1956), 'Effect of work group structure and certain task variables on group performance', *Journal of Abnormal and Social Psychology*, **19**, 94–104.

Lashinsky, A. (2006), 'RAZR's edge', *Fortune*, **153**, 124–32.

Latane, B., Willians, K.D. and Harkins, S.G. (1979), 'Many hands make light the work: the causes and consequences of social loafing', *Journal of Personality and Social Psychology*, **37**, 822–32.

Lawler, E. (1981), *Pay and Organization Development*, Reading, MA: Addison-Wesley.

Lee, F. (1997), 'When the going gets tough, do the tough ask for help? Help seeking and power motivation in organizations', *Organizational Behavior and Human Decision Processes*, **72**, 336–63.

Levinson, L. and Rosenthal, S. (1984), *CEO: Corporate Leadership in Action*, New York: Basic Books.

Likert, R. (1967), *The Human Organization: Its Management and Value*, New York: McGraw-Hill.

Marks, M.A., Mathieu, J.E. and Zaccaro, S.J. (2000), 'A temporally based framework and taxonomy of team processes', *Academy of Management Review*, **26**, 356–76.

McAllister, D.J. (1995), 'Affect and cognition based trust as foundations for interpersonal cooperation in organizations', *Academy of Management Journal*, **38**, 24–59.

McClatchy Washington Bureau (2005), 'Katrina: failure at every turn', 11 September, retrieved 10 October 2006 from http://www.realcities.com/mld/krwashington/12612851.htm.

McGrath, J.E. (1984), *Groups: Interaction and Performance*, Englewood Cliffs, NJ: Prentice-Hall.

McIntyre, R.M. and Salas, E. (1995), 'Measuring and managing for team performance: emerging principles from complex environments', in R.A. Guzzo and E. Salas (eds), *Team Effectiveness and Decision Making in Organizations*, San Francisco, CA: Jossey-Bass, pp. 9–45.

Michael, D.N. (1976), *On Learning to Plan and Planning to Learn*, San Francisco, CA: Jossey-Bass.
Milanovich, D.M., Salas, E., Cannon-Bowers, J.A. and Muniz, E.J. (2000), 'Understanding team derailment: a focus on deficient team skills and attitudes', in M.M. Beyerlein, D.A. Johnson and S.T. Beyerlein (eds), *Advances in Interdisciplinary Studies of Work Teams*, Vol. 7, Greenwich, CT: JAI Press, pp. 187–206.
Mintzberg, H. (1973), *The Nature of Managerial Work*, New York: Harper & Row.
Morgan, B.B., Glickman, A.S., Woodard, E.A., Blaiwes, A.S. and Salas, E. (1986), *Measurement of Team Behavior in a Navy Training Environment*, Technical Report TR-86-014, Orlando, FL: Naval Training Systems Center, Human Factors Division.
Oakland, J. (1993), *Total Quality Management. The Route to Improving Performance*, 2nd edn, New Jersey, NJ: Nichols Publishing.
Orasanu, J. (1990), *Shared Mental Models & Crew Decision Making*, Technical Rep. 46, Princeton, NJ: Princeton University, Cognitive Science.
Perrow, C. (1984), *Normal Accidents: Living with High-Risk Technologies*, New York: Basic Books.
Pondy, L. (1967), 'Organizational conflict: concepts and models', *Administrative Science Quarterly*, **17**, 296–320.
Priest, H.A., Burke, C.S., Munim, D. and Salas, E. (2002), *Understanding Team Adaptability: Initial Theoretical and Practical Considerations*, proceedings of the Human Factors and Ergonomics Society 46th Annual Meeting, USA, pp. 561–5.
Pritchard, R.D., Jones, S.D., Roth, P.L., Stuebing, K.K. and Ekeberg, S.E. (1988), 'The effects of feedback, goal setting, and incentives on organizational productivity', *Journal of Applied Psychology Monograph Series*, **73**, 337–58.
Ratzberg, W.H. (2006), 'Social loafing', retrieved on 31 October from www.geocities.com/athens/forum/1650/htmlgroups16.html.
Reason, J. (1997), *Managing the Risks of Organizational Accidents*, Brookfield, VT: Ashgate.
Roberts, K. and O'Reilly, C. (1974), 'Measuring organizational communication', *Journal of Applied Psychology*, **59**, 321–6.
Robbins, S.P. (2000), *Managing Today!* 2nd edn, Upper Saddle River, NJ: Prentice-Hall.
Roby, T.B. (1968), *Small Group Performance*, Chicago, IL: Rand McNally.
Salas, E., Dickinson, T.L., Converse, S.A. and Tannenbaum, S.I. (1992), 'Toward an understanding of team performance and training', in R.W. Swezey and E. Salas (eds), *Teams: Their Training and Performance*, Norwood, NJ: Ablex, pp. 3–29.
Salas, E., Rosen, M.A., Burke, C.S., Goodwin, G. F. and Fiore, S.M. (2006), 'The making of a dream team: when expert teams do best', in K.A. Ericsson, N. Charness, P.J. Feltovich and R.R. Hoffman (eds), *The Cambridge Handbook of Expertise and Expert Performance*, New York: Cambridge University Press, pp. 439–56.
Salas, E., Sims, D.E. and Burke, C.S. (2005). 'Is there a "Big Five" in teamwork?', *Small Group Research*, **36**, 555–99.
Salas, E., Sims, D.E. and Klein, C. (2004a), 'Cooperation at work', in C.D. Speilberger (ed.), *Encyclopedia of Applied Psychology*, Vol. 1, San Diego, CA: Academic Press, pp. 497–505.
Salas, E., Stagl, K.C. and Burke, C.S. (2004b), '25 years of team effectiveness in organizations: research themes and emerging needs', in C.L. Cooper and I.T. Robertson (eds), *International Review of Industrial and Organizational Psychology*, Vol. 19, Chicester, UK: John Wiley & Sons, pp. 47–91.
Scholtes, P., Joiner, B. and Streibel, B. (1996), *The Team Handbook*, Madison, WI: Oriel Incorporated Publication.
Sekhar, S.F.C. and Anjaiah, P. (1995), 'Organisational communication and interpersonal trust: an evaluation of their relationships', *Psychological Studies*, **40**, 28–32.
Select Committee on Intelligence, United States Senate (2006), 'Report on the U.S. intelligence community's prewar intelligence assessments on Iraq', retrieved on 10 October from www.intelligence.senate.gov/conclusions.pdf.
Senge, P.M. (1990), *The Fifth Directive: The Art & Practice of the Learning Organization*, New York: Doubleday.
Senge, P., Kliener, A., Roberts, C., Ross, R., Roth, G. and Smith, B. (1999), *The Dance of Change: The Challenges of Sustaining Momentum in Learning Organizations*, New York: Doubleday.
Shamir, B. (1990), 'Calculations, values and entities: the sources of collectivistic work motivation', *Human Relations*, **43**, 313–32.
Smith, E.M., Ford, J. and Kozlowski, S.W.J. (1997), 'Building adaptive expertise: implications for training design strategies', in M.A. Quinones and A. Ehrenstein (eds), *Training for a Rapidly Changing Workplace: Applications of Psychological Research*, Washington, DC: American Psychological Association, pp. 89–118.
Steiner, I.D. (1972), *Group Process and Productivity*, New York: Academic Press.
Stevens, M.J. and Campion, M.A. (1994), 'The knowledge, skills and ability requirements for teamwork: implications for human resources management', *Journal of Management*, **20**, 502–28.
Stewart, G.L. and Manz, C.C. (1995), 'Leadership for self-managing work teams: a typology and integrative model', *Human Relations*, **48**, 747–70.

Stout, R.J., Cannon-Bowers, J.A., Salas, E. and Milanovich, D. (1999), 'Planning, shared mental models, and coordinated performance: an empirical link is established', *Human Factors*, **41**, 61–88.

Tjosvold, D., Yu, Z.-Y. and Hui, C. (2004), 'Team learning from mistakes: the contribution of cooperative goals and problem solving', *Journal of Management Studies*, **41**, 1223–45.

Treadway, D.C., Hochwarter, W.A., Ferris, G.R., Kacmar, C.J., Douglas, C., Ammeter, A.P. and Buckley, M.R. (2004), 'Leader political skill and employee reactions', *Leadership Quarterly*, **15**, 493–513.

Vesterman, J. (2006), 'From Warton to War', *Fortune*, **153**, 12 June, 105–8.

Wagner, J.A. (1995), 'Studies of individualism–collectivism: effects on cooperation in groups', *Academy of Management Journal*, **38**, 152–72.

Webber, S.S. (2002), 'Leadership and trust facilitating cross-functional team success', *Journal of Management Development*, **21**, 201–14.

Weick, K.E. and Sutcliffe, K.M. (2001), *Managing the Unexpected: Assuring High Performance in an Age of Complexity*, San Francisco, CA: Jossey-Bass.

West, M.A. (1996), 'Reflexivity and work group effectiveness: a conceptual integration', in M.A. West (ed.), *Handbook of Work Group Psychology*, Chichester, UK: John Wiley & Sons, pp. 555–79.

West, M.A. and Anderson, N.R. (1996), 'Innovation in top management teams', *Journal of Applied Psychology*, **81**, 680–93.

Zaccaro, S.J. (2001), *The Nature of Executive Leadership: A Conceptual and Empirical Analysis of Success*, Washington, DC: American Psychological Association.

Zairi, M. (1994), *Measuring Performance for Business Results*, London: Chapman & Hall.

19 Collective wisdom as an oxymoron: team-based structures as impediments to learning
Michael D. Johnson and John R. Hollenbeck

Interest in team-level information processing and learning has burgeoned in recent years and several theoretical models have been proposed to describe this phenomenon. Although a consensus model of team learning has not yet emerged, the theoretical and empirical treatments of the subject appear to agree that team learning is qualitatively different from individual learning. For example, Argote et al. (2001) suggested that one major shift in thinking about team learning versus individual learning is that team members must coordinate their actions with each other rather than acting alone. The actions of team members affect the team system whether or not they intend to, which can either help or inhibit team learning. Similarly, Hinsz et al. (1997) noted the importance of communication – in terms of sharing information, ideas and cognitive processes – to team-level learning. Larson and Christensen (1993) noted that having multiple conceptualizations of a problem facing the team is a uniquely group-level phenomenon.

Interestingly, in outlining the unique characteristics of team-level learning, all of these conceptualizations draw upon individual-level models as a basis for understanding the similarities and differences between learning at each level (Hinsz et al., 1997). Because team-level learning is qualitatively different from individual-level learning, however, we suggest that these models are inadequate in describing the challenges of learning at the team level. Rather, a true team-level model of learning must incorporate not only the cognitive and affective *intra*personal factors that affect the learning process, but also the social *inter*personal factors that exist at the team level. As noted by Ellis et al. (2003: 822), in their empirical examination of team learning, 'teams can process information not only within, but also between the minds of team members'.

In this chapter, we argue that although teams have greater potential information-processing capacity (Hinsz et al., 1997), they also suffer from certain problems related to motivation and coordination losses (Steiner, 1972) that are unique to contexts characterized by this type of interpersonal, 'between-minds', information processing. As we will demonstrate, these problems make it more difficult for teams to learn from experience – especially failure experiences – relative to individuals. Thus, whereas individuals will often develop wisdom based on experience, there are several reasons why the collective wisdom of teams is much more difficult to develop. We examine eight specific problems confronting teams in learning contexts that are not faced by individuals working alone, and argue that any organization that employs team-based structures needs to address these issues if the goal is to develop team-level learning.

A pyramid model of learning
Drawing upon cognitive models of information processing, we conceptualize learning – whether performed by individuals or teams – as a multiple-stage process (see Figure 19.1).

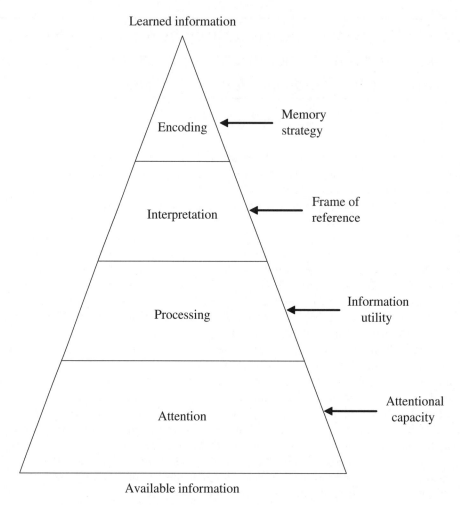

Figure 19.1   A pyramid model of individual learning

Each of these stages is dependent upon the previous stage, in that information must successfully pass through each stage in order to be learned. Because of natural limitations in cognitive processing, however, not all information can pass through each stage. Thus there is information loss at each step of the process, and hence not all of the information that an individual is exposed to is actually available to support learning. Instead, individuals only learn a fraction of what they could potentially learn if they possessed unlimited cognitive resources.

The first stage of learning is *allocating attention* to stimuli. Individuals are exposed to vast amounts of potential information to be learned, but cannot pay attention to all of the stimuli. Instead, we typically allocate our attention to stimuli that are either threatening or offer opportunities to get something we desire, and ignore the rest. This is because individuals have limited *attentional capacity*, and thus must selectively allocate their attention to the most important stimuli. This capacity may vary over time in response to the state of activation an individual is in; that is, when people are highly alert, they may be able to pay attention to more stimuli than when they are more quiescent (Kahneman, 1973). Nevertheless, there is still an upper limit on how many stimuli an individual may attend to, and only information from those stimuli can potentially be learned.

The second stage of learning is *processing* the information to which one has directed one's attention. This 'work space' stage of learning is where individuals manipulate the information they have received in order to make sense of it. As noted by Barrett et al. (2004: 554), individuals may engage in elaborate 'conscious, explicit, or systematic' controlled processing, or may rely on schemas, scripts or concepts and engage in 'nonconscious, implicit, or heuristic' automatic processing. People compare the information to previously learned information to see whether or not the new information is useful. Information that appears to be redundant or irrelevant is discarded, and information that is new and of use is processed. Clearly, this stage is dependent upon the attention stage, as only information that is attended to can be processed.

The third stage of learning is *interpretation*. When information successfully completes this stage, individuals have interpreted the information and integrated it into their overall knowledge structure. Sometimes, however, individuals cannot successfully interpret information. The information may be incomplete or the individual may not have an adequate frame of reference to interpret it successfully. Again, this stage is dependent upon the previous stage – utility determination – because only information that is deemed useful will continue to be processed and interpreted.

The final stage of learning is *encoding and recall*. This stage represents the various memory processes that are used to store and retrieve the information that has been learned. In our usage, encoding refers both to the cognitive strategies used to structure and categorize retained information, and to the physiological and physical structures used to remember and recall that information. For example, information may be encoded cognitively by incorporating it with an existing script or schema, as when a salesperson adds to his knowledge about a particular customer. Information may be encoded physically by adding the information to a computer database or encoded physiologically by committing it to memory. When the information is retrieved, it may be activated cognitively when the schema or script is triggered, and accessed through the physical or physiological mechanism in which it was stored. Memory research and common experience indicate, however, that not all information that has been interpreted is successfully encoded (Symons and Johnson, 1997). As with the other stages of learning, this stage is dependent upon the previous stage, in that only information that was interpreted can be stored and retrieved in the encoding process.

Because each of these four stages builds upon the previous stage, and because each stage represents a progressively smaller amount of information, the model can be conceptualized as a pyramid. At the base of the pyramid is the range of information that could potentially be learned. This total amount of available information is reduced due to the limitations in attentional capacity (Stage 1). This is further reduced by decisions regarding the utility of the information (Stage 2), and is yet further reduced by whether the individual can successfully interpret the information (Stage 3). Finally, the information is yet further reduced by whether the individual can successfully encode and recall the information that has been learned (Stage 4).

The steepness of the sides of pyramid is determined by the amount of information loss at each stage. The steeper the slope, the more information is learned. Although Figure 19.1 displays a consistent slope across the four stages, more information may be lost at one stage than another, creating an uneven slope. For example, an individual presented with a wealth of information may lose more of the information in Stage 1 due to limitations in attentional capacity than in Stage 3 through unsuccessful interpretation.

Dysfunctional team learning
If this model reflects the individual learning process, then learning is a fairly inefficient process, with information being lost at each stage along the way. Only a fraction of the available information that could potentially be learned actually makes it through the four stages and becomes part of the individual's knowledge base. This process is almost certainly affected by various factors that increase or reduce the amount of information loss at each stage. It is not the purpose of this chapter to outline what these might be, but both individual differences and situational factors seem likely to affect the amount of information loss.

Our interest instead is in how the learning process differs for people in team-based structures from those who are working alone. Groups inevitably possess more knowledge together than any one team member does individually, and thus possess an advantage over individuals (Argote et al., 2001). Indeed, in many cognitive activities, research has shown that teams perform better than individuals working alone. Teams tend to recall more information (Hill, 1982; Hinsz, 1990), and tend to be more accurate in the information they recall (Hill, 1982). Teams also tend to perform better than individuals on induction tasks, where the goal is to find general principles or explanations (Laughlin et al., 1991), and on general problem solving (Laughlin et al., 2002).

The news is not all good, however, particularly when one examines criteria that are more obviously based on explicit learning. For example, Chen et al. (2005) found that in a training context, the knowledge and skill of individual team members related much more strongly to learning and adaptive performance over time relative to teams. As noted by Argote et al. (2001: 377), the advantage that teams have over individuals 'is dependent upon the degree to which the knowledge of individuals within the group can be effectively shared, or pooled, during group discussion', and several aspects of group dynamics may interfere with this process.

Similarly, Larson and Christensen (1993: 12) note:

> Groups too must cope with the reality of limited cognitive resources – of the social as well as the individual variety. Consider, for example, the time and effort that group members have to devote to problem solving. These are limited resources that, like attention, can be channeled in one direction or the other for the purpose of acquiring problem-relevant information.

Because teams have these limitations of their *social* cognitive resources in addition to the limitations on each team member's individual cognitive resources, we suggest that teams are much less efficient at learning than individuals working alone. In essence, team-based structures, if not properly managed, can be dysfunctional for the process of learning. Although teams progress through the same four stages of learning that individuals do, we suggest that the shape of the pyramid will be much less steep for teams, indicating that teams lose more information throughout the learning process than individuals do (see Figure 19.2). The base of the pyramid is wider, because teams have access to more

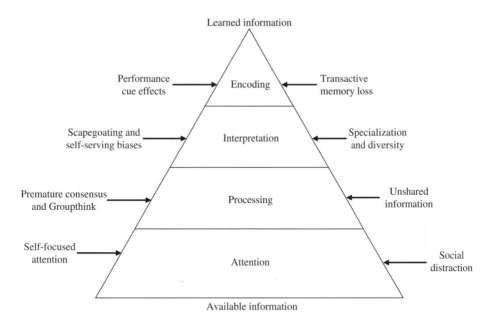

Figure 19.2   Team learning

potential information than individuals due to varied backgrounds of the team members and unshared experiences on their team task.

We note, however, that the amount of available information is not simply the amount of information available to an individual multiplied by the number of team members. This is because team members do not have access to completely unique information, but rather have access to much information that is also available to other team members. This available information is not completely redundant, however, so that teams do have access to more information than any one individual. Below, we outline both general factors that contribute to the additional information loss in teams, as well as factors that may exacerbate the problem in certain types of teams.

Attentional dysfunctions
In terms of attentional allocation, there are two problems confronting teams that are unique to social contexts. That is, individuals working alone and trying to learn from experience do not face either of these issues. The first is cognitive in nature and relates to *social distraction* caused by having other people in the context adding perceptual inputs over and above the task itself. The second, more emotional in tone, is the problem of public self-consciousness, whereby the presence of others becomes a stimulus that promotes higher levels of self-awareness and self-focused (versus task-focused) attention.

Social distraction   As noted above, individuals cannot attend to all of the information available to them, but must focus their attention on information that appears to be the most useful. Team members face all of the attentional demands that individuals working alone face, and more: the attentional demands imposed by the other team members.

In Baron's (Baron et al., 1978) distraction–conflict model, team members generate information that must be attended to by the other team members, which may tax their attentional capacities. Baron and colleagues suggested and found that these additional attentional demands account for worse performance on complex tasks. For example, team members may pay attention to the social cues being generated by other members, and may miss important information that could aid team learning.

The presence of others also creates additional attentional problems in terms of thought regulation. For example, research suggests that competition between two people during a skill acquisition task retards the learning of both individuals due to increased anxiety, threat to self-esteem and perceptual distraction (Thill and Cury, 2000). If teams create a perception of implicit competition and social comparison, then this would trigger the same type of debilitating influences on learning that would not be triggered in an individual working alone. Indeed, even non-competitive and supportive audiences have been found to affect learning complex skill acquisition in a negative manner. For example, Butler and Baumeister (1998) found that in the presence of a supportive audience, individuals were more likely to choose cautious, self-protective, error-minimizing strategies that limited opportunities for learning.

Self-focused attention   In addition to affecting learning strategies, the presence of supportive audiences has also been found to increase the amount of attention directed to the self rather than the task. That is, research has shown that the presence of supportive audiences creates a performance decrement in learning that can be directly attributed to higher levels of self-focused (as opposed to task-focused) attention (Law et al., 2003). The negative impact of self-focused attention on learning has been well documented across a variety of contexts, and even the presence of only one other person has been shown to trigger this effect (Horn et al., 1998).

Self-attention theory (Mullen et al., 1989) describes how individuals become self-conscious in the presence of others and direct attention to evaluating whether they are behaving appropriately in the context of the group. This effect appears to lessen as group size increases, such that individuals direct less attention toward themselves in large groups than they do in small ones. Because work teams are typically relatively small in size, the effect could be quite pronounced, particularly in teams where the members don't know each other well.

Both of these effects – the distraction of attending to other team members and attending to oneself – should severely restrict the amount of information that successfully passes through the attention stage in teams. Considering that these phenomena are unique to group contexts and do not affect individuals learning alone, they should have an effect over and above the loss that occurs due to individual attentional capacity limitations. Thus teams are usually able to attend to less information about their tasks than individuals who are working alone.

Moreover, team composition may exacerbate these effects. In particular, teams that are composed of individuals who are high in neuroticism may be especially susceptible to these effects. Neuroticism is associated with an individual's tendency to experience anxiety and insecurity (Judge et al., 2002). People with high levels of neuroticism feel unsure of themselves and often worry about their behavior in social situations; thus they are likely to direct more attention toward themselves when working in a team than they would when working alone. The degree to which a team is composed of highly neurotic people, then, is likely to cause less information to successfully pass through the attention stage of learning.

Processing dysfunctions
Unshared information: passive and active   Team information processing is fundamentally different from individual information processing. Whereas individuals can only process information within their own minds, teams can process information both within and between the minds of team members (Ellis et al., 2003). Teams have the ability to draw upon unique bits of information that each of the team members hold and piece them together to create a more complete understanding of their tasks than team members may hold individually. On the face of it, then, it would appear that teams are superior in information processing to individuals, and as noted above, teams actually do possess an advantage in certain types of processing.

As noted in Ellis et al.'s (2003: 823) empirical examination of team learning, team information processing involves 'a full and critical discussion of the available ideas and data . . .'. Thus, in order to effectively process information at the team level, team members must communicate their ideas to the rest of the team. MacMillan et al. (2004: 61) call this 'the hidden cost of team cognition', noting that communication between team members has no analogue at the individual level. Unfortunately, intrateam communication is often a less than efficient process, and vital information is often not communicated among team members. Two areas of team research highlight the inherent difficulties in communicating information that can help teams learn.

First, teams often lose important information in the processing stage when it is originally held by only one team member. The work of Stasser and colleagues (Stasser et al., 1989; Stasser and Titus, 1985, 1987; Stasser et al., 2000) has shown that decision-making groups spend much more time discussing information that at least two members had access to prior to the discussion. Information that was held by only one team member was usually not discussed at all. In one experiment, only 18 percent of the information that was held by only one team member was discussed by the team, compared to 58 percent of the information that was shared among more than one member (Stasser et al., 1989).

Moreover, when team members are asked to recall the information that was discussed, they tend to remember only the information that had been shared by more than one team member prior to the discussion, but forgot information they had discussed that had been held by only one team member (Stewart and Stasser, 1995). Thus unshared information is not only far less likely to be discussed by teams; it is also far less likely to be retained for future consideration, even if it was discussed.

It is worth noting that in all of Stasser's experiments, there was no implicit motivation for team members to cover up information. That is, the information being discussed was not related to errors made by the team members and it did not reveal any weakness or deficiency on the part of team members. Instead, the information was neutral and was usually about a third party, such as evaluating candidates for student government. Thus the lack of information sharing in this context could be considered to be passive in the sense that it was unintentional. In contrast, because of scapegoating tendencies in groups (discussed in greater length in a subsequent section), there is often an explicit motivation on the part of some members to actively hide self-incriminating information in the face of a team failure. That is, information that might be highly relevant to team learning is actively covered up by individuals within the group, thus precluding the opportunity or the team to learn from the experience.

A pair of studies conducted by Edmondson and her colleagues demonstrates the critical role of psychological safety in teams and how this impacts the degree to which teams can learn from experience (Edmondson, 1999; Edmondson et al., 2001). Psychological safety is the sense that team members can trust each other enough to risk admitting that they made an error or need help. As noted by Edmondson (1999):

> those in a position to initiate learning behavior may believe they are placing themselves at risk; for example, by admitting an error or asking for help, an individual may appear incompetent and thus suffer a blow to his or her image. In addition, such individuals may incur more tangible costs if their actions create unfavorable impressions on people who influence decisions about promotions, raises, or project assignments . . . Asking for help, admitting errors, and seeking feedback exemplify the kinds of behaviors that pose a threat to face, and thus people in organizations are often reluctant to disclose their errors or are unwilling to ask for help, even when doing so would provide benefits for the team . . .

Clearly, admitting errors and asking for help are risky propositions that can have serious repercussions for team members. It should be no wonder, then, when team members cover up information that could reflect negatively on them, but would be beneficial for team learning if shared with the other team members. Thus it is not surprising that team learning is worse in contexts characterized by low trust relative to high trust (Kirkman et al., 2006).

Both of these phenomena described above appear to be related to the concept of 'truth-supported wins' (Laughlin, 1999), which suggests that groups often do not solve problems correctly when the correct answer is proposed by only one team member (the 'truth wins' model). Instead, correct answers are much more likely to be adopted by groups when at least one other team member supports the solution. The support of an additional team member who has access to the same information can provide both the psychological safety needed for team members to share important information, and the impetus for the team to discuss and retain it. Nevertheless, some important information will inevitably be held by only one team member, and this information is likely to be lost in the processing stage of team learning.

Premature consensus and groupthink   Janis (1972: 9) defined groupthink as

> a mode of thinking that people engage in when they are deeply involved in a cohesive in-group, when the members' strivings for unanimity override their motivation to realistically appraise alternative courses of action . . . Groupthink refers to a deterioration of mental efficiency, reality testing, and moral judgment that results from in-group pressures.

When teams experience groupthink, the drive to achieve quick consensus leads to poor information processing (Isenberg, 1986). Self-managing teams appear to be especially vulnerable to experiencing groupthink, because these sorts of teams are often highly cohesive (Manz and Sims, 1982).

Janis (1972) suggested eight symptoms of groupthink, and although the focus of his discussion was on decision-making accuracy and not learning *per se*, several of these symptoms would be associated with learning difficulties in team contexts. For example, *collective rationalization* occurs when team members discount negative information that threatens their assumptions about their task and decision. If a team does not give proper weight to information that is available to them, this would likely harm their interpretation of that information. The insidious aspect of groupthink is that teams tend to discount *negative* information, leading to overly optimistic projections regarding the outcomes of their decisions.

In addition to collective rationalization, highly cohesive groups also engender higher levels of *pressure on dissenters*. Teams often induce conformity pressures on team members (Barker, 1993; Sewell, 1998) that might restrict a free and open discussion of information that might be critical of the team, but might also be highly relevant for learning. Indeed, individuals may even censor themselves without an explicit pressure from others. That is, even though they have reservations about the inferences or conclusions reached by the group based upon the available evidence, they fail to voice their concerns. Thus, even though one team member may feel the group is discounting important information, he or she may not force the team to confront this evidence, and instead just go along with the majority view. Indeed, Ellis et al. (2003) were able to show directly that teams that were high in agreeableness were least likely to 'connect the dots' in a complex team learning context that required the elimination of multiple hypotheses.

Interpretation dysfunctions

Scapegoating and self-serving biases   When teams finish processing the information that has made it this far in the learning process, they make an interpretation of it. As with the other stages of team learning, there are social factors that limit the successful interpretation of this information, in addition to the cognitive and affective factors that limit individual learning. Second, team interpretation of information may suffer through the process of *scapegoating*. The term arose from the ancient practice of symbolically placing all of the sins of a group of people on a goat and sending it out into the desert in order to make atonement. Scapegoating has not received a great deal of research attention in the organizational literature, but has received some attention in the social psychology literature on the study of prejudice. Allport's (1954) classic text outlined how groups that cannot vanquish a superior opponent transfer their aggression to a weaker opponent, such as when minority groups are blamed for societal problems.

Naquin and Tynan (2003) demonstrated a form of scapegoating in work teams through something they called the 'team halo effect'. Teams, they argued, receive collective credit for successes, but tend to individuate responsibility for their failures. Through the process of counterfactual thinking (imagining alternative outcomes had things gone differently), people often place blame for team failure upon an individual team member. This is a self-serving bias that deflects blame from the focal individual and collective, and instead focuses the blame on one other team member. They cite the example of the failure of the Boston Red Sox to win the 1986 World Series being blamed on first baseman Bill Buckner, who allowed a ground ball to go through his legs. Certainly there were many other factors that contributed to the loss, but it was easy for people to imagine Buckner catching the ball, and thus he was blamed for the loss.

In work teams confronted with failure, members may engage in this same type of counterfactual thinking. If they can imagine avoiding failure had an individual team member performed differently, they are likely to place the blame for the team's failure on that individual. This is unfortunate, because failures often represent the best learning opportunities and are even intentionally incorporated into training procedures (error-based training; Gully et al., 2002). When one team member serves as a scapegoat to take the blame for the team's failure, however, the team makes a misinterpretation of their available information, and their learning suffers as a result.

Functional specialization and demographic diversity   Most work teams are characterized by some degree of functional specialization, such that different members focus on different aspects of the task. This means that these individuals form different mental models of the task situation, and this can create difficulties in interpreting information (Cannon-Bowers et al., 1993; Stout et al., 1999). The construct of shared mental models is relevant to team learning in two ways. First, some research indicates that shared mental models are less complex than individual mental models because only the information that members agree on becomes part of the shared model (Hinsz et al., 1988). Information that was not agreed upon by all of the team members is discarded at this stage, and will not be available to the team when they encounter similar situations in the future. Thus, when the team relies on shared mental models for encoding their learning, they likely encode less information than individuals do alone.

Second, team members may not develop shared mental models due to functional specialization and the lack of compatibility and comparability of information held by different functional specialists. Ellis et al. (2003) showed directly that it was more difficult for teams to learn new contingencies when each member possessed a single functional capacity relative to a context where there was more overlap in skills. Similar results were obtained by Van der Vegt and Bunderson (2005), although this effect was moderated by the degree of collective identification with the team. That is, Van der Vegt and Bunderson found that diversity in expertise was negatively related to learning, but only when teams were low in collective identification.

The demographic make-up of the team can also influence the degree to which team members have shared mental models. Highly diverse teams may struggle to come to agreement on their shared mental models and research by Gibson and Vermeulen (2003) has shown directly that groups marked by moderate levels of diversity learn better relative to highly diverse teams. This seems to be particularly the case in teams with strong faultlines. A team with a strong faultline is not only demographically diverse, but the dimensions of diversity tend to be confounded with another (e.g. all the female members are also young and are part of a minority group whereas all the male members are also older and non-minorities). Lau and Murninghan (2005) showed that teams with strong faultlines evidenced less learning, and this was true even if one controlled for the overall level of diversity in the team.

Encoding, storage and recall dysfunctions
Encoding refers to the way people structure and retain the information they have learned. Storage refers to the memory processes utilized by teams to retain that which they have learned. Finally, recall refers to the process by which people access what they have stored. As we have seen with the other stages of the learning process, there are unique challenges in group contexts that make each of these processes more difficult relative to what one might encounter in individual contexts.

Performance cue effects   Although there are individual-level analogues to the performance cue effect, the research literature suggests that this problem can be exacerbated in team contexts. The performance cue effect simply means that knowledge of how well a group performed will trigger raters' implicit theories about group processes and bias their recall of objective events (Baltes and Parker, 2000; Guzzo et al., 1986). This means that teams that are told they lost a contest or groups that are told they failed to reach their goal will recall their leadership as being less effective and their group dynamics as being less efficient, regardless of the objective behaviors actually exhibited.

Martell et al. (1995) have shown this is a robust effect that is not attributable to demand characteristics, but rather due to systematic memory distortion, whereby performance information directly promotes selective deletion of actual behaviors, as well as false memories of behaviors that were never manifested. This disrupts learning effective processes because teams misattribute failure to behaviors that did not occur and may come to the conclusion that alternative behaviors – which actually occurred – might be more effective.

Transactive memory loss   Although some research has shown that teams retain information better than individuals, this largely depends upon organization of the memory system through the process of transactive memory, where different team members remember different information related to their task (Wegner et al., 1991). The degree to which team members do not develop this transactive memory system, then, will negatively affect their long-term learning. Team members may presume that other members are responsible for recalling certain bits of information; the degree to which this assumption is erroneous will also negatively impact their learning.

The difficulty with transactive memory lies not only with the degree to which teams can effectively develop this type of collective memory system, but also with the fact that teams lose members. A growing stream of research on changes in team membership – referred to as team fluidity (Dineen and Noe, 2003), revolving team membership (Thomas-Hunt and Phillips, 2003), or simply team membership change (Levine and Choi, 2004) – has begun to examine the challenges associated with the addition or loss of team members. The implication for transactive memory systems seems clear: when team members leave the team, the unique bits of knowledge held by those team members leave with them. If this information is not duplicated within the team, the knowledge may be lost to the team for good.

Conclusion

Team-based structures are functional to organizations in many ways, including providing increased effort, better skill usage, and improved problem solving than individuals working in more traditional structures (Morgeson et al., 2006). In terms of learning, however, team-based structures can be dysfunctional due to the difficulties associated with interpersonal information processing. At each stage of the learning process, teams lose more information than individuals do, and thus are inefficient structures for learning. We do not suggest, however, that teams never be assigned learning tasks; at times, the amount of information to be sifted may exceed the capacity of any one individual. Managers should recognize, however, that the team learning process is leaky in terms of information loss and is not likely to be very effective.

References

Allport, G.W. (1954), *The Nature of Prejudice*, Oxford: Addison-Wesley.
Argote, L., Gruenfeld, D. and Naquin, C. (2001), 'Group learning in organizations', in M.E. Turner (ed.), *Groups at Work: Theory and Research*, Mahwah, NJ: Lawrence Erlbaum Associates, pp. 369–411.
Baltes, B.B. and Parker, C.P. (2000), 'Understanding and removing the effects of performance cues on behavioral ratings', *Journal of Business and Psychology*, **15**, 229–46.
Barker, J.R. (1993), 'Tightening the iron cage: concertive control in self-managing teams', *Administrative Science Quarterly*, **38**(3), 408–37.
Baron, R.S., Moore, D. and Sanders, G.S. (1978), 'Distraction as a source of drive in social facilitation research', *Journal of Personality and Social Psychology*, **36**(8), 816–24.
Barrett, L.F., Tugade, M.M. and Engle, R.W. (2004), 'Individual differences in working memory capacity and dual-process theories of the mind', *Psychological Bulletin*, **130**(4), 553–73.
Butler, J.L. and Baumeister, R.F. (1998), 'The trouble with friendly faces: skilled performance with a supportive audience', *Journal of Personality and Social Psychology*, **75**, 1213–30.
Cannon-Bowers, J.A., Salas, E. and Converse, S. (1993), 'Shared mental models in expert team decision making', in N.J. Castellan Jr (ed.), *Individual and Group Decision Making: Current Issues*, Hillsdale, NJ: Lawrence Erlbaum Associates, pp. 221–46.
Chen, G., Thomas, B. and Wallace, J.C. (2005), 'A multilevel examination of the relationships among training outcomes, mediating regulatory processes, and adaptive performance', *Journal of Applied Psychology*, **90**, 827–41.
Dineen, B.R. and Noe, R.A. (2003), 'The impact of team fluidity and its implications for human resource management research and practice', in J.J Martocchio and G.R. Ferris (eds), *Research in Personnel and Human Resources Management*, Vol. 22, Oxford: Elsevier Science, pp. 1–37.
Edmondson, A.C. (1999), 'Psychological safety and learning behavior in work teams', *Administrative Science Quarterly*, **44**(2), 350–83.
Edmondson, A.C., Bohmer, R.M. and Pisano, G.P. (2001), 'Disrupted routines: team learning and new technology implementation in hospitals', *Administrative Science Quarterly*, **46**(4), 685–716.
Ellis, A.P., Hollenbeck, J.R., Ilgen, D.R., Porter, C.O., West, B.J. and Moon, H. (2003), 'Team learning: collectively connecting the dots', *Journal of Applied Psychology*, **88**(5), 821–35.
Gibson, C. and Vermeulen, F. (2003), 'A healthy divide: subgroups as a stimulus for team learning behavior', *Administrative Science Quarterly*, **48**, 202–39.
Gully, S.M., Payne, S.C., Koles, K. and Whiteman, J.-A.K. (2002), 'The impact of error training and individual differences on training outcomes: an attribute–treatment interaction perspective', *Journal of Applied Psychology*, **87**(1), 143–55.
Guzzo, R.A., Wagner, D.B., Maguire, E., Herr, B. and Hawley, C. (1986), 'Implicit theories and the evaluation of group-processes and performance', *Organizational Behavior and Human Decision Processes*, **37**, 279–95.
Hill, G.W. (1982), 'Group versus individual performance: are N+1 heads better than one?', *Psychological Bulletin*, **91**(3), 517–39.
Hinsz, V.B. (1990), 'Cognitive and consensus processes in group recognition memory performance', *Journal of Personality and Social Psychology*, **59**(4), 705–18.
Hinsz, V.B., Tindale, R., Nagao, D.H., Davis, J.H. et al. (1988), 'The influence of the accuracy of individuating information on the use of base rate information in probability judgment', *Journal of Experimental Social Psychology*, **24**(2), 127–45.
Hinsz, V.B., Tindale, R. and Vollrath, D.A. (1997), 'The emerging conceptualization of groups as information processes', *Psychological Bulletin*, **121**(1), 43–64.
Horn, E.M., Collier, W.G., Oxford, J.A., Bond, C.F. and Dansereau, D.F. (1998), 'Individual differences in dyadic cooperative learning', *Journal of Educational Psychology*, **90**, 153–61.
Isenberg, D.J. (1986), 'Group polarization: a critical review and meta-analysis', *Journal of Personality and Social Psychology*, **50**(6), 1141–51.
Janis, I.L. (1972), *Victims of Groupthink: A Psychological Study of Foreign-policy Decisions and Fiascoes*, Oxford: Houghton Mifflin.
Judge, T.A., Heller, D. and Mount, M.K. (2002), 'Five-factor model of personality and job satisfaction: a meta-analysis', *Journal of Applied Psychology*, **87**(3), 530–41.
Kahneman, D. (1973), *Attention and Effort*, Englewood Cliffs, NJ: Prentice-Hall.
Kirkman, B.L., Rosen, B., Tesluk, P.E. and Gibson (2006), 'Enhancing the transfer of computer assisted training proficiency in geographically distributed teams', *Journal of Applied Psychology*, **91**, 706–16.
Larson, J.R. and Christensen, C. (1993), 'Groups as problem-solving units: toward a new meaning of social cognition', *British Journal of Social Psychology*, **32**(1), 5–30.
Lau, D.C. and Murninghan, J.K. (2005), 'Interactions within groups and subgroups: the effects of demographic faultlines', *Academy of Management Journal*, **48**, 645–59.
Laughlin, P.R. (1999), 'Collective induction: twelve postulates', *Organizational Behavior and Human Decision Processes*, **80**(1), 50–69.

Laughlin, P.R., Bonner, B.L. and Miner, A.G. (2002), 'Groups perform better than the best individuals on Letters-to-Numbers problems', *Organizational Behavior and Human Decision Processes*, **88**(2), 605–20.

Laughlin, P.R., VanderStoep, S.W. and Hollingshead, A.B. (1991), 'Collective versus individual induction: recognition of truth, rejection of error, and collective information processing', *Journal of Personality and Social Psychology*, **61**(1), 50–67.

Law, J., Masters, R., Bray, S.R., Eves, F. and Bardswell, I. (2003), 'Motor performance as a function of audience affability and meta-knowledge', *Journal of Sport and Exercise Psychology*, **25**, 484–500.

Levine, J.M. and Choi, H.-S. (2004), 'Impact of personnel turnover on team performance and cognition', in E. Salas and S.M. Fiore (eds), *Team Cognition: Understanding the Factors that Drive Process and Performance*, Washington, DC: American Psychological Association, pp. 153–76.

MacMillan, J., Entin, E.E. and Serfaty, D. (2004), 'Communication overhead: the hidden cost of team cognition', in E. Salas and S.M. Fiore (eds), *Team Cognition: Understanding the Factors that Drive Process and Performance*, Washington, DC: American Psychological Association, pp. 61–82.

Manz, C.C. and Sims, H.P. (1982), 'The potential for "groupthink" in autonomous work groups', *Human Relations*, **35**, 773–84.

Martell, R.F., Guzzo, R.A. and Willis, C.E. (1995), 'A methodological and substantive note on the performance cue effect in ratings of work-group behavior', *Journal of Applied Psychology*, **80**, 191–5.

Morgeson, F.P., Johnson, M.D., Campion, M.A., Medsker, G.J. and Mumford, T.V. (2006), 'Understanding reactions to job redesign: a quasi-experimental investigation of the moderating effects of organizational context on perceptions of performance behavior', *Personnel Psychology*, **59**(2), 333–63.

Mullen, B., Chapman, J.G. and Peaugh, S. (1989), 'Focus of attention in groups: a self-attention perspective', *Journal of Social Psychology*, **129**(6), 807–17.

Naquin, C.E. and Tynan, R.O. (2003), 'The team halo effect: why teams are not blamed for their failures', *Journal of Applied Psychology*, **88**(2), 332–40.

Sewell, G. (1998), 'The discipline of teams: the control of team-based industrial work through electronic and peer surveillance', *Administrative Science Quarterly*, **43**(2), 397–428.

Stasser, G., Taylor, L.A. and Hanna, C. (1989), 'Information sampling in structured and unstructured discussions of three- and six-person groups', *Journal of Personality and Social Psychology*, **57**(1), 67–78.

Stasser, G. and Titus, W. (1985), 'Pooling of unshared information in group decision making: biased information sampling during discussion', *Journal of Personality and Social Psychology*, **48**(6), 1467–78.

Stasser, G. and Titus, W. (1987), 'Effects of information load and percentage of shared information on the dissemination of unshared information during group discussion', *Journal of Personality and Social Psychology*, **53**(1), 81–93.

Stasser, G., Vaughan, S.I. and Stewart, D.D. (2000), 'Pooling unshared information: the benefits of knowing how access to information is distributed among group members', *Organizational Behavior and Human Decision Processes*, **82**(1), 102–16.

Steiner, I.D. (1972), *Group Process and Productivity*, New York: Academic Press.

Stewart, D.D. and Stasser, G. (1995), 'Expert role assignment and information sampling during collective recall and decision making', *Journal of Personality and Social Psychology*, **69**(4), 619–28.

Stout, R.J., Cannon-Bowers, J.A., Salas, E. and Milanovich, D.M. (1999), 'Planning, shared mental models, and coordinated performance: an empirical link is established', *Human Factors*, **41**(1), 61–71.

Symons, C.S. and Johnson, B.T. (1997), 'The self-reference effect in memory: a meta-analysis', *Psychological Bulletin*, **121**(3), 371–94.

Thill, E.E. and Cury, F. (2000), 'Learning to play golf under different goal conditions: their effects on irrelevant thoughts and on subsequent control strategies', *European Journal of Social Psychology*, **30**, 101–22.

Thomas-Hunt, M.C. and Phillips, K.W. (2003), 'Managing teams in the dynamic organization: the effects of revolving membership and changing task demands on expertise and status in groups', in R.S. Peterson and E.A. Mannix (eds), *Leading and Managing People in the Dynamic Organization*, Mahwah, NJ: Lawrence Erlbaum Associates, pp. 115–33.

Van der Vegt, G.S. and Bunderson, J.S. (2005), 'Learning and performance in multi-disciplinary teams: the importance of collective team identification', *Academy of Management Journal*, **48**, 532–47.

Wegner, D.M., Erber, R. and Raymond, P. (1991), 'Transactive memory in close relationships', *Journal of Personality and Social Psychology*, **61**, 923–9.

20 The bright and dark sides of personality: implications for personnel selection in individual and team contexts

Timothy A. Judge and Jeffery A. LePine

That personality has shown itself relevant to individual attitudes and behavior, and to team and organizational functioning, seems an incontrovertible statement. Barrick and Mount (2005: 361) flatly state: 'Personality traits do matter at work' and indeed the data appear to support their conclusion (Hogan, 2005). Barrick et al. (2001) analyzed extant meta-analyses on the relationships between the 'big five' personality traits and job performance, finding a multiple correlation of R = 0.47 when the five traits were used to predict overall job performance. Other large-scale reviews have linked personality to job satisfaction (Judge et al., 2002a), leadership (Judge et al., 2002b), workplace deviance (Salgado, 2002), well-being (DeNeve and Cooper, 1998), and organizational commitment (Erdheim et al., 2006).

However, skeptics remain. One line of criticism argues that whilst personality has non-zero associations with important criteria, the effect sizes are small. In arguing that little has changed since Guion and Gottier's (1965) influential (and pessimistic) review, Schmitt (2004: 348) observed, 'The observed validity of personality measures, then and now, is quite low even though they can account for incrementally useful levels of variance in work-related criteria beyond that afforded by cognitive ability measures because personality and cognitive ability measures are usually minimally correlated'. Hogan (2005) takes issue with this overall assessment, while also arguing that the validity of personality measures is often underestimated by failing to account for poor measures, the source of personality ratings (self versus observer), and the situationally specific nature of performance. He concludes, 'The bottom line is, personality measures work pretty well, especially when compared with all the other measures' (p. 340).

Our own view is that whereas it is true that the validities for personality variables cannot be labeled as strong using the Cohen (1977) effect size conventions, the same is true of virtually any meaningful predictor of broad, complex criteria such as job performance. For example, there is perhaps no theory in organizational behavior more respected for its validity than goal-setting theory. Locke and Latham (2002: 714) concluded, 'Goal-setting theory is among the most valid and practical theories of employee motivation in organizational psychology' and Miner (2003) found that organizational behavior scholars ranked goal-setting theory as the most important of all (73 were rated) management theories. Yet meta-analyses have revealed that the overall validity of goal difficulty in predicting job performance is $d_c = 0.577$ (Wood et al., 1987), which translates into a correlation of $R_c = 0.277$. This differs little from the overall validity of conscientiousness ($R_c = 0.23$) or core self-evaluations ($R_c = 0.23$) in predicting job performance. When one considers the constellation of traits, the validity is much higher ($R_c = 0.47$, as noted above).

Whatever one's position on whether the extant effects are meaningful, one apparent way to reframe this debate is to ask what factors might increase our understanding of the validity of personality variables (however one might characterize their 'main effects'). Although there are many factors that affect the validity of personality traits (Hogan, 2005), one relatively neglected factor is recognition that all traits may have both upsides and downsides. As Nettle (2006: 625) noted, 'Behavioral alternatives can be considered as trade-offs, with a particular trait producing not unalloyed advantage but a mixture of costs and benefits such that the optimal value for fitness may depend on very specific local circumstances'. Thus a more nuanced view of the importance of personality to behavior would recognize that even generally desirable traits (i.e. traits associated with fitness in a general or even evolutionary sense) likely involve trade-offs associated with particular criteria.

As just noted, the likelihood of trade-offs for particular criteria does not mean that some traits are not more generally desirable (whether desirability be defined individually [what is good for one's survival] or collectively [what society deems valuable]) than others. Indeed, the 'big five' traits are socially desirable (Ellingson et al., 2001). Thus, one way to consider the 'fitness' implications of traits is to contrast their social desirability – how the traits are generally viewed – with their actual result in particular contexts. A generally desirable trait (one that is viewed positively by most individuals in society) may lead to poor fitness in a very particular context. For example, the assets in terms of longevity conferred by conscientiousness (Friedman et al., 1995) may be reversed by a catastrophic event (conscientious individuals might be predisposed to make the 'wrong' choices in the wake of a tsunami) or by trait-induced behavior in a particular context (a conscientious bystander may be harmed in seeking to help a victim of crime).

Thus our organizing framework for this section, as shown in Table 20.1, reflects general fitness tendencies as measured by whether the traits are generally seen as socially desirable, and the implications of a trait for fitness in a particular situation or context. We do acknowledge that social desirability is not necessarily isomorphic with generalized fitness. It is possible that society values a particular trait that has no association with fitness. By equating the two, however, we wish to avoid a certain tautological inference whereby generalized fitness is judged by whether traits 'work' since that, we assume, depends on the context.

From Table 20.1 we discuss four possible fitness implications of traits: (a) socially desirable traits that, in certain situations, have positive implications; (b) socially desirable traits that, in certain situations, have negative implications; (c) socially undesirable traits that, in certain situations, have positive implications; and (d) socially undesirable traits that, in certain situations, have negative implications. Below we discuss these categories in more detail. We should note, in keeping with the theme of the book, that our shortest discussion concerns the bright side of bright traits. Our goal here is not to provide an in-depth review of the many positive implications of the 'big five' traits. Such reviews have appeared elsewhere (e.g. Barrick and Mount, 2005; Hogan and Roberts, 2001; Hough and Oswald, 2005). What is often missing from reviews, however, is discussion of the other categories in Table 20.1. Accordingly, that is where we devote the bulk of our attention.

After the first section of the chapter, we shift our focus to a different unit of theory and analysis. Specifically, we discuss research demonstrating that, under certain circumstances, team members' socially desirable traits can have negative implications for team-level criteria. Although there is team-level research analogous to the other categories

Table 20.1 Framework for discussion of implications of personality traits for personnel selection and team composition

Social desirability	Actual effects in specific context or situation	
	Dark	Bright
Dark	Socially undesirable trait that has negative implications for organizations and/or individuals (example: narcissism negatively predicts prosocial behaviors on part of employees toward co-workers)	Socially undesirable trait that has positive implications for organizations and/or individuals (example: neurotic individuals make more accurate/realistic judgments)
Bright	Socially desirable trait that has negative implications for organizations and/or individuals (example: conscientious employees adapt less well to organizational change)	Socially desirable trait that has positive implications for organizations and/or individuals (example: conscientiousness positively predicts individuals' sales performance)

in Table 20.1 – team members' socially desirable traits that, in certain situations, have positive implications for team criteria; team members' socially undesirable traits that, in certain situations, have positive implications for team criteria; team members' socially undesirable traits that, in certain situations, have negative implications for team criteria – the general implications of our discussion for staffing in team contexts remain largely the same.

Before moving on, we wish to disclose that our inspiration for this chapter came from several sources (Hogan, 2005; Moscoso and Salgado, 2004). We are certainly not the only researchers to conceptualize the possible 'downsides' of traits generally deemed positive. Moreover, we are mindful that some 'trait' differences exist because different scales purportedly measuring the same concept in fact measure something quite different (Hogan, 2005). Others argue that broad traits such as those housed within the five-factor model are too 'fat' and obscure offsetting relations among lower-level traits (Hough and Oswald, 2000). We do not consider these issues here, but that should not be construed as a dismissal of them.

Bright and dark effects of bright and dark traits

Bright side of bright traits

Judging from the empirical literature (e.g. Dunn et al., 1995), one would argue that there is a constellation of five-factor model traits that is socially desirable: high emotional stability (or low neuroticism), high extraversion, high openness, high agreeableness and high conscientiousness. Naturally, there are other 'bright' traits, such as high self-esteem or core self-evaluations (Judge and Bono, 2001), and proactive personality (Seibert et al., 2001), but due to space limitations we focus here on the 'big five' traits.

The positive implications of the 'big five' traits are well documented, some more so than others. Of the 'big five' traits, conscientiousness is the best correlate of job performance ($r_c = 0.23$; Barrick and Mount, 1991), followed by emotional stability ($r_c = 0.19$; Judge and Bono, 2001). Extraversion is the strongest correlate of leadership ($r_c = 0.31$; Judge et al., 2002b), followed by conscientiousness ($r_c = 0.28$), openness ($r_c = 0.24$), and emotional stability ($r_c = 0.24$). Openness to experience is related to artistic and scientific creativity (Feist, 1998), as well as to coping with organizational change (Judge et al., 1999), and to adaptability (LePine, 2003). Emotional stability has the highest correlation with subjective well-being ($r = 0.22$; DeNeve and Cooper, 1998), followed by extraversion ($r = 0.17$) and agreeableness ($r = 0.17$). Emotional stability is the best correlate of job satisfaction ($r_c = 0.29$; Judge et al., 2002a), followed by conscientiousness ($r_c = 0.26$) and extraversion ($r_c = 0.25$). Conscientiousness ($r_c = 0.26$) and agreeableness ($r_c = 0.20$) are the strongest correlates of (lack of) workplace deviant behaviors (Salgado, 2002). Emotional stability ($r_c = 0.35$), conscientiousness ($r_c = 0.31$) and agreeableness ($r_c = 0.22$) are the strongest correlates of (lack of) turnover (Salgado, 2002). Agreeableness is related to helping behaviors (e.g. interpersonal facilitation, $r_c = 0.20$; Hurtz and Donovan, 2000) and performance in jobs involving significant interpersonal interactions ($r_c = 0.21$; Mount et al., 1998). Agreeable individuals are motivated to avoid conflict with others, and appear more able to do so (see Graziano and Tobin, 2002).

In sum, the 'big five' traits are 'bright traits' in that each has positive implications for important criteria, and there is direct evidence attesting to the social desirability of these traits (Dunn et al., 1995; Ellingson et al., 2001). Emotionally stable individuals are happier in their jobs, happier in life and are better job performers. Extraverted individuals are more likely to emerge and excel as leaders, and have higher levels of subjective well-being. Open individuals are more creative, adapt better to change and also are more effective leaders. Agreeableness is associated with higher performance in interpersonally oriented jobs. Conscientiousness is linked to job performance, job satisfaction, subjective well-being and leadership. It would appear that an individual who scored highly on all five traits would have enormous advantages at work and in life.

Dark side of bright traits
Having established the bright side of the 'big five' traits, we now turn to their possible dark sides – situations in which or criteria for which high scores on the traits may in fact be harmful.

Extraversion   Judge et al. (1997) found that extraversion was significantly correlated ($r = 0.26$, $p < 0.01$) with absenteeism in a sample of university employees. This is likely heightened by sensation and excitement seeking on the part of extraverted individuals. Other research indicates that extraverts are predisposed to accidents, including one study that linked extraversion to traffic fatalities (Lajunen, 2001). Although extraversion may be an advantage in certain jobs such as sales (Vinchur et al., 1998), it appears to be a disadvantage in others where isolated work is performed, where long attention spans are required, or where the work is routine (Beauducel et al., 2006).

Agreeableness   Despite being a highly socially desirable trait, agreeableness appears to have some drawbacks, too. First, evidence consistently indicates that agreeable individuals fare less well in their careers in terms of extrinsic career success in the form of pay and promotions (Ng et al., 2005). One of the reasons agreeable individuals may be more motivated to avoid conflict is because they find it very distressing (i.e. are less able to cope with conflict; Suls et al., 1998). Finally, Bernardin et al. (2000) found that individuals scoring high on agreeableness are particularly prone to giving lenient performance ratings, which of course could cause organizational performance management problems.

Conscientiousness   Despite the widespread benefits of conscientiousness, there are three dark sides relevant to organizational behavior. First, there is evidence that conscientious individuals may learn less in the early stages of skill acquisition. Martocchio and Judge (1997) hypothesized that this was because conscientious individuals were more prone to self-deception, and a realistic appraisal of one's skills is important in training contexts. Another possible explanation is that conscientious individuals are more likely to have a performance (versus learning) orientation, which detracts from learning, especially during complex skill acquisition (although evidence suggests that conscientiousness is more strongly associated with learning than performance orientation; Colquitt and Simmering, 1998; Yeo and Neal, 2004). Second, perhaps due to greater rigidity, there is evidence that conscientious individuals are less adaptable. Specifically, LePine et al. (2000) found that when conditions of a task were changed, conscientious individuals had difficulty adapting to the change, and their performance declined. Finally, conscientiousness may interact with other traits such that in the presence of other characteristics it has a downside. Witt et al. (2002) found that agreeableness moderated the relationship between conscientiousness and job performance such that highly conscientiousness but disagreeable individuals (those who scored high on conscientiousness but low on agreeableness) were lower performers, perhaps because they were technically competent but interpersonally abrasive.

Emotional stability   Evidence indicates individuals who score low on emotional stability (high on neuroticism) are better at identifying threats in the environment (Tamir et al., 2006). As Nettle (2006) notes, the anxiety aspect of neuroticism may be useful in anticipating (and thereby better avoiding the danger from) threats in the environment. Indeed, individuals who are anxious are able to identify threats and signs of impending danger more quickly (Mathews et al., 1997). Moreover, perhaps due to their vigilance, neurotic individuals may be less likely to take risks that many would see as foolhardy. One study revealed that Mount Everest climbers – the summit of which has been called a 'death zone' (the mortality rate is roughly 1:8) – had extremely high levels of emotional stability (Egan and Stelmack, 2003). (Egan himself died on Mount Everest in 2005.) Finally, individuals low on emotional stability, because they worry about meeting expectations, may actually *exceed* them. For example, one study found that neurotic students were significantly more likely to show up early for a psychological experiment (Back et al., 2006).

Openness   Individuals who score high on openness may be less likely to confirm to organizations' or society's expectations, as evidenced by the somewhat greater tendency of those who score high on openness to engage in counterproductive work behaviors (Hough, 1992; Salgado, 2002). Open individuals are nonconformists and pride themselves on their anti-authoritarian and anti-establishment attitudes (McCrae, 1996), which means they may have difficulty working in hierarchical or traditional work settings. Related, high scores on openness were associated with lower continuance commitment ($r = -0.23$, $p < 0.01$; Erdheim et al., 2006), suggesting that open individuals may have less commitment to remain with their employer. Finally, a meta-analysis (Clarke and Robertson, 2005) of ten studies suggests that individuals who score high on openness to experience are more likely to be involved in accidents ($r_c = 0.32$).

Dark side of dark traits

Interestingly, whereas scholars have argued that organizational behavior researchers have focused more on negative phenomena than positive, in personality research that does not appear to be the case. With the exception of neuroticism – which is often studied from its positive pole, emotional stability – one is hard pressed to identify traits that are socially undesirable. In our consideration of 'dark traits' we focus on four that are prominent in personality psychology: (a) narcissism; (b) impulsivity; (c) trait hostility; and (d) Type A personality.

Narcissism   Judge et al. (2006a) argued that narcissism, reflecting a grandiose sense of self-importance, has been infrequently studied in organizational behavior (OB) research, despite its prominent place in psychological research (e.g. a search of PsycINFO turns up 1245 entries with the word 'narcissism' in the title). Judge et al. (2006a) found that individuals who scored high on neuroticism overestimated their leadership effectiveness, task performance and contextual performance, and underestimated their workplace deviance (overestimation being defined as the discrepancy between self and other ratings). There were cases in which these differences were profound. For example, in one sample in their study, narcissistic managers rated themselves as significantly *higher* on leadership effectiveness, whereas their peers rated them as significantly *lower* on leadership effectiveness.

Impulsivity   Impulsivity – defined as the tendency to act with little prior thought, to be prone to sensation and novelty seeking, and to be behaviorally disinhibited – has been linked to myriad 'negative' outcomes, including drug use, unsafe sexual behaviors, aggressive driving, various psychological disorders, suicide attempts, binge eating and obesity, problem gambling, criminal behavior and violent actions. One of the challenges of this research area is that there are many definitions of impulsivity, numerous measures that may be non-equivalent, and separations of impulsivity into dimensions such as functional versus dysfunctional (e.g. Brunas-Wagstaff et al., 1997). Like narcissism, despite a wealth of research in psychology, there is a dearth of research on impulsivity in OB. However, it is not difficult to speculate on work criteria that impulsivity may predict, such as workplace deviance, job and work withdrawal, and accidents. Moreover, because impulsivity is associated with diminished reasoning ability (Schweizer, 2002), one may find that impulsive employees are less able to use reasoning in work decisions. Finally, research in non-work settings suggests that impulsive individuals have greater performance variability (Lawrence and Stanford, 1999), a finding that might be extended to work situations.

Trait hostility   Ruiz et al. (2001: 540) define trait hostility as 'a set of negative attitudes, beliefs, and appraisal of the worth, intent, and motives of others and often includes a desire to preemptively harm or see harm inflicted on others'. Ruiz et al. (2001) note that trait hostility can be conceptualized broadly to include, as with our definition of state hostility above, trait anger. In addition to the well-documented link between trait hostility and coronary heart disease (Miller et al., 1996), evidence indicates that individuals who score high on trait hostility gauge the reactions of others as less friendly (Smith et al., 1990), experience more conflict in relationships (Newton and Kiecolt-Glaser, 1995), and are more likely to engage in aggressive behaviors toward others (Archer and Webb, 2006). In the workplace, trait-hostile individuals are more likely to engage in workplace deviance ($r = 0.29, p < 0.05$; Judge et al., 2006b; $r = 0.27, p < 0.01$; Lee and Allen, 2002). McCann et al. (1997) found that while individuals scoring high on trait hostility were not significantly more dissatisfied with their jobs, they were significantly less likely to perceive their workplace as collegial ($r = -0.28, p < 0.01$) and to see social support as available in their environment ($r = -0.37, p < 0.01$). Other research has shown similar results – that hostile individuals may not like their job or work less, but have more negative attitudes toward interpersonal relationships at work (e.g. Smith et al., 1988).

Type A personality   Although the trait often has been loosely defined, most consider the Type A personality to be characterized by: (a) a drive to accomplish many things; (b) desire for competition and orientation toward competitiveness; (c) striving for recognition and advancement; (d) habitual time-urgent behavior; (e) acceleration of physical and mental activity; and (f) intense concentration and alertness (Ganster et al., 1991; Rosenman, 1986). The best-known implication of Type A personality is its association with increased risk for coronary disease (Booth-Kewley and Friedman, 1987; Matthews and Haynes, 1986). The likely reason for this is thought to be the result of the heightened sensitivity of Type As to stress (Heilbrun and Friedberg, 1988). Some research also suggests that Type A individuals are more likely to be dissatisfied with their jobs (Jiang et al., 2004), experience higher levels of job burnout (Alotaibi, 2003), and are more likely to suffer from poor mental and physical health (Kirkcaldy et al., 2002).

Bright side of dark traits

Narcissism   Of all the possible combinations of bright and dark traits with positive and negative outcomes, one is perhaps the most pressed to fill in the upsides of narcissism. However, there may be bright aspects to even this dark trait. In competitive situations, such as distributive negotiation or game-theoretic exercises, it appears that narcissists fare better than those who score low on narcissism, though this appears to come at the cost of lower joint outcomes (Campbell et al., 2005). Moreover, evidence indicates that individuals who score high on measures of narcissism report higher levels of life satisfaction, lower levels of stress and anxiety, and are less likely to be depressed (Campbell, 2001). Thus, while it is clear that other individuals suffer from associations with narcissists, and narcissists tend to have negative views toward others (particularly those whom they see themselves in competition with), it is far from clear that narcissists themselves suffer from these processes. Because narcissism is so rarely studied in a work context, whether this (bad for others, good for oneself) view on narcissism extends to workplace criteria is unclear. Paunonen et al. (2006) argued, with some support, for the view that the best leaders are those who have the bright sides of narcissism (high egoism and self-confidence) without the dark sides (manipulativeness). One might argue that this is artificially dividing narcissism, and does not comport with the dimensional structure of most conceptions of narcissism. Still, it may be that for certain criteria, certain aspects of narcissism are 'good' and others are 'bad'.

Impulsivity   Although impulsivity is impressively related to many behaviors organizations and society would deem undesirable, here again there are possible bright spots. Gray (1987) argued that impulsivity reflects individual differences in reward sensitivity whereby individuals who score high on measures of impulsivity are thought to find reward stimuli more pleasurable than those who score low on such measures. Evidence indicates that impulsivity is linked to heightened reward sensitivity (Torrubia et al., 2001). That suggests that impulsive individuals may be relatively more malleable by organizational rewards. Second, there is some evidence that impulsive individuals may perform better at complex tasks, because performing difficult tasks may place impulsive individuals in an optimal range of arousal (Anderson, 1994). Moreover, individuals who score high on impulsivity are inclined toward novelty-seeking behavior (Franken and Muris, 2006), which one might find a desirable trait in certain situations (e.g. a salesperson developing new territories, a marketing manager considering the latest fads in information technology).

Trait hostility   Some research suggests that individuals who score high on trait hostility may have jobs of greater responsibility and wider scope. Dwyer and Fox (2000) found that trait hostility was significantly correlated with nurses' perceived skill utilization and with control on the job (both $r = 0.22$, $p < 0.01$), suggesting that hostile individuals may be more effective at defining and controlling their own work. Although there are few data on the subject, some evidence indicates that hostile individuals exhibit lower levels of service performance (Doucet, 2004), they evince higher levels of task or technical performance (Sarason et al., 1965). Moreover, hostile people are prone to the expression of anger, which has been shown to lead to more favorable settlements in distributive bargaining (Sinaceur and Tiedens, 2006). More generally, Tiedens (2001) showed that individuals confer status on hostile individuals prone to the expression of anger, and these conferrals are made on the perception that hostile or angry individuals are more competent.

Type A personality   There appear to be some salutary effects of Type A. Research has shown that Type A personality is associated with higher performance among management (Taylor et al., 1984) and experimental social psychology (Matthews et al., 1980) faculty, and better grades among college students (Waldron et al., 1980). As Robbins et al. (1991: 756) noted, 'the findings suggest that Type A individuals tend to achieve more than their more laid-back Type B counterparts'. Type A individuals may perform better because they have higher achievement motivation (Matthews et al., 1980), because they set more ambitious goals and are more confident in attaining them (Taylor et al., 1984), because they are more polychromic (able to balance multiple tasks simultaneously; Taylor et al., 1984), or some combination of these factors.

Summary
Table 20.2 provides a summary of our discussion of 'bright' (socially desirable) and 'dark' (socially undesirable) traits, organized by their costs and benefits. In the next section, we extend the line of thought by considering relationships between configurations of team member traits and team-level criteria. As we will discuss below, trying to account for the effects of team-level trait configurations increases the level of complexity of models linking personality to criteria; however, doing so illuminates implications to staffing teams.

Dark side of bright traits for team configuration
In the previous section we discussed how bright and dark traits can have both bright and dark sides, at least in certain situations and for certain criteria. In this section, we consider the dark side of bright traits, but we do so in the context of teams. In contrast to the previous section, which was organized around specific personality traits and their effects, this section is organized around ways in which socially desirable personality traits of team members combine to have dark effects on criteria associated with team functioning and effectiveness. Briefly, we will consider effects, of trait combinations in terms of (a) parallel aggregate effects, (b) similarity and diversity effects and (c) reaction and interaction effects. Before we describe the meaning of these types of traits, we should note that relative to the amount of individual-level research on the dark side of bright personality traits, there has been less research on the dark side of configurations of these bright traits. Accordingly, the following section is much more speculative than the previous sections.

Parallel aggregate effects
One way that personality traits have a dark side in terms of team outcomes is through parallel aggregate effects. These types of effects occur when the team members' traits combine to impact team functioning in a manner that is more or less commensurate with how the

Table 20.2   Possible benefits and costs of 'bright' and 'dark' traits

	Benefits	Costs
Big five ('bright') traits		
Extraversion	Greater leadership emergence and effectiveness; higher job and life satisfaction	More impulsive (deviant) behaviors; more accidents; lower performance in certain jobs
Agreeableness	Higher subjective well-being; more positive interpersonal interactions and helping behavior; lower conflict; lower deviance and turnover	Lower career success; less able to cope with conflict; more lenient in giving ratings
Conscientiousness	Higher job performance; greater leadership effectiveness; higher job satisfaction; lower deviance and turnover	Reduced adaptability; lower learning in initial stages of skill acquisition; more interpersonally abrasive (when also low in agreeableness)
Emotional stability	High job and life satisfaction; better job performance; more effective leadership; lower turnover	Poorer ability to detect risks and danger; more risky behaviors; less likely to exceed expectations
Openness	Higher creativity; greater leadership effectiveness; greater adaptability	More accidents and counterproductive behaviors; greater rebelliousness; lower continuance commitment
Other ('dark') traits		
Narcissism	Better distributive bargainers; higher levels of life satisfaction	Inflated self-views in terms of leadership, performance, etc.; manipulative of others
Impulsivity	Greater reward-sensitivity; better performance at complex tasks	More counterproductive/dangerous behaviors; diminished reasoning; greater performance variability
Hostility	Jobs of greater responsibility and scope; higher levels of task performance; better distributive bargainers	Greater workplace deviance; poorer cardiovascular health; more negative views of others; higher conferral of status
Type A	Higher job performance; greater achievement	Increased cardiovascular disease; higher stress and job burnout; poor mental and physical health

Note: Obviously, if neuroticism is labeled 'Emotional stability', the benefits and costs would be reversed.

traits operate at the individual level. Although Moynihan and Peterson (2001) used 'the universal approach' as a descriptive label for this type of effect, we use an alternative label in recognition that there are dark sides to traits that many scholars assume are universally more socially desirable. Research on parallel aggregate effects has a long history, as is evidenced in reviews of the literature (Heslin, 1964) and is implied in the long standing tradition of research focused on effects of individual personality on individual behavior in group contexts (Mann, 1959). However, research with a focus on the dark side of bright personality traits in the context of teams is somewhat rare. Nevertheless, existing research suggests ways in which these types of effects could occur with conscientiousness and agreeableness.

Conscientiousness   Similar to research indicating that conscientiousness tends to be positively related to individual effectiveness (Barrick and Mount, 1991), there is research indicating that conscientiousness tends to be positively related to individual effectiveness in team contexts (e.g. Hough, 1992; LePine and Van Dyne, 2001b; Mount et al., 1998; Stewart et al., 2005), and in the aggregate, team effectiveness itself (e.g. Barrick et al., 1998). In most circumstances, teams tend to be more effective when they are staffed with people who tend to be achievement-oriented, self-disciplined, perseverant, dutiful and orderly. However, also consistent with research on individual-level relationships, there are indications that at least in certain circumstances, conscientiousness of team members may be negatively related to team effectiveness.

As one example, LePine's (2003) laboratory study of 73 teams examined relationships between aggregate levels of team members' scores on two aspects of conscientiousness and team decision-making performance prior to and after an unforeseen change that necessitated the team members to adapt their roles. Whereas the achievement-striving and dependability components of conscientiousness did not predict team decision-making performance prior to the change, both predicted this criterion after the change. Importantly, whereas members' achievement-striving had a positive effect, dependability had a negative effect. Also, the offsetting effects for these two aspects of conscientiousness appeared to operate, in part, through a process variable reflecting adaptive behavior at the point the unforeseen change occurred. Teams composed of members possessing high dependability appeared to be unwilling and unable to adjust their normal work routine to meet the demands of the new situation.

As another example, Waung and Brice (1998) considered the role of team members' conscientiousness in predicting creative performance in a brainstorming task. They found that although conscientiousness of team members was positively associated with the feasibility of solutions, member conscientiousness was negatively associated with the number of solutions. To the extent that group effectiveness in creative tasks necessitates a large number of potential solutions, the tendency for groups composed of highly conscientiousness members to focus prematurely on the details and positioning of solutions may be deleterious.

In sum, although the dependability aspect of conscientiousness should promote team performance in contexts that depend on an efficient and orderly flow of familiar task activities, this characteristic may be deleterious when the requirements of the task become uncertain, where the members have to work interdependently and coordinate in the context of disorder, and where creativity is a criterion. High-dependability team members may be prone to internalize goals that relate to timeliness and order, and in the context of a change that fundamentally alters the requirements of the team task or when the task itself requires a novel solution, these types of goals may be debilitating.

Agreeableness   Although the evidence is a bit more tenuous, agreeableness may be a second trait where there are dark-side parallel aggregate effects. On the one hand, people who score high on agreeableness would seem to be perfectly suited to team contexts because they tend to be cooperative, helpful and trusting. Indeed, research has demonstrated that agreeableness is linked to cooperative performance in groups, teamwork and other aspects of individual performance that are logically related to effective team functioning (e.g. Hough, 1992; LePine and Van Dyne, 2001b; Mount et al., 1998; Stewart et al., 2005). Following this research, it is not surprising to learn that some research has shown that teams staffed with agreeable members tend to function and perform more effectively than teams staffed with less agreeable members (Barrick et al., 1998).

On other hand, agreeableness may have a dark side in team contexts that parallels the dark side in individual contexts. Because agreeable individuals value and strive for cooperation and harmony, they may avoid engaging in certain functional task-focused behaviors when these behaviors have the potential to upset other individuals with whom they work, and this may explain research that has reported negative relationships between team-level agreeableness and team effectiveness (e.g. McGrath, 1962). In one study, for example, group members' agreeableness was negatively related to voice behavior, which is defined as the extent to which an individual speaks up with constructive suggestions for change (LePine and Van Dyne, 2001b). Because team member voice may be strongly related to team effectiveness in contexts where there is any degree of decision latitude or the need for innovation or adaptability (Erez et al., 2002), staffing a team with highly agreeable members in these types of contexts may be detrimental.

In sum, because teams depend on the cooperativeness and trust of the members, the trait of agreeableness should be highly desirable. However, in many team contexts, there is a need for members to openly challenge the *status quo*, and agreeable individuals may choose not to engage in these sorts of behaviors. Thus, although staffing a team with people who possess high agreeableness may on the surface appear to be appropriate, agreeableness has a dark side that needs to be taken into account. In fact, just as with conscientiousness, the relevance of the dark side of the trait is dependent on the team context.

Diversity

Research aimed at understanding effects of group member diversity has a long tradition in social psychology and organizational behavior, as is evidenced in various reviews of the literature that have appeared over the last several decades (e.g. Haythorn, 1968; Mannix & Neale, 2005; Williams and O'Reilly, 1988). Although much of the research reported in these reviews has focused on member diversity with respect to observable demographic characteristics (e.g. Hoffman and Maier, 1961a; Kent and McGrath, 1969; Riordan and Shore, 1997), there has been research focused on diversity of deeper-level characteristics such as attitudes, interests and, most relevant to this chapter, personality (e.g. Altman and McGinnies, 1960; Fiedler, 1952; Hoffman, 1955, 1959; Hoffman and Maier, 1961a). As we will discuss next, the literature suggests at least two different ways in which diversity with respect to members' personality may have dark side effects.

The majority of scholars who have studied effects of personality diversity in small groups and teams have focused on effects of diversity in and of itself as the focal construct. In this research, diversity has been indicated often by the percentage of members who could be placed in a certain category, or alternatively some metric indicating the degree of variability on that characteristic. In some of this research, diversity in personality resulted in positive effects on group outcomes (e.g. Aamodt and Kimbrough, 1982; Ghiselli and Lodahl, 1958; Hoffman and Maier, 1961b), and as articulated clearly by Hoffman, the mechanism assumed to underlie these effects is that diversity increases the number of ideas and perspectives that can be applied to a problem. This line of thinking has been called the 'information-processing and problem-solving' perspective, and is credited for the belief among laypeople and scholars that diversity enhances team creativity and problem-solving ability (Mannix and Neale, 2005).

Findings from other research, however, have suggested that the degree of diversity among team members in their personality may have deleterious effects on the functioning and effectiveness of teams (e.g. Altman and McGinnies, 1960; Haythorn et al., 1956). Explanations for these negative effects, which are based on theories of social attraction (e.g. Byrne, 1971; Newcomb, 1968), self-categorization (Turner, 1985) and social identity (Tajfel, 1981), are that members of diverse teams tend to be less attracted to each other and the group, less likely to have accurate perceptions of other members and their opinions, and less likely to communicate effectively without dysfunctional conflict (Haythorn, 1968).

What conclusions can we draw from this research? First, consistent with the belief that there is value in diversity (Cox et al., 1991), diversity in team members' personality may have positive effects on team effectiveness. However, these positive effects may be limited to contexts where the team task requires members with diverse perspectives and outlooks. Second, diversity in team members' personality may have negative effects on team effectiveness in team contexts where effective interpersonal processes and social integration are important. Moreover, as research by Harrison and his colleagues suggests (Harrison et al., 2002; Harrison et al., 1998), the negative effects of personality diversity in teams may become more pronounced over time as opportunities to reveal deeply rooted differences accrue. The end result is that although there is a potential bright side of personality diversity, there is a dark side as well, and this dark side may become even darker over time. We should note, however, that the research that generated these conclusions has focused on diversity itself, and thus has ignored the possibility that effects of personality diversity may vary as a function of the personality trait under consideration. Indeed, in his review of the group composition literature almost 40 years ago, Haythorn (1968: 124) noted that 'the effect of homogeneity *per se,* however, cannot be divorced from the individual personality characteristic or value under consideration'.

Perhaps as a consequence of the popularity of the five-factor model beginning in the early 1990s, researchers began to develop and test theories regarding effects of team composition in terms of individual personality characteristics (Barrick et al., 1998; Barry and Stewart, 1997; LePine et al., 1997). Although some of this research may have been focused more on understanding the manner in which member traits should be combined in order to examine team-level relationships (LePine et al., 1997), the research nevertheless paved the way for more fine-grained understanding of effects of personality diversity in teams. In contrast to the research on the general concept of personality diversity, which suggested dark side effects on team functioning and performance in certain situations, this research acknowledges the possibility that the effects of personality diversity vary as a function of the personality characteristic under consideration.

In one example of this research, Barrick and his colleagues (1998) conducted a field study of 51 work teams that considered relationships between the variance among members in their 'big five' characteristics and measures of team functioning (social cohesion, team conflict, flexibility, communication, workload sharing) and team outcomes (team viability and performance). The findings of this study suggested that although diversity in one of the 'big five' characteristics may be beneficial to teams, diversity in two other characteristics may be detrimental. First, variance on members' extraversion was positively related to social cohesion. To some degree this finding is consistent with previous research, which suggested that teams may have reduced cohesion and performance when there are too few or too many extroverted members (Barry and Stewart, 1997). Second, variance in members' agreeableness was positively associated with team conflict, and was negatively associated with social cohesion, communication and workload sharing. Although the mechanisms underlying all these effects were not examined, it seems reasonable that a mix of empathetic, trusting and warm members with unfeeling, distrustful and cold members is a recipe for trouble. Finally, variance in members' conscientiousness was negatively associated with team performance. Although the reasons for this effect were not clear in this particular study, the finding is consistent with research demonstrating that a team member with particularly low conscientiousness may upset other members, especially those with higher levels of achievement striving (e.g. LePine et al., 1997, Jackson and LePine, 2003; LePine and Van Dyne, 2001a).

In summary, the primacy given to specific traits in this stream of research has led to increased understanding of the impact that team members' personality has on important team-level outcomes. Most important, although the amount of research has been fairly limited, the findings reveal that understanding the effects of personality diversity necessitates consideration of specific traits. Specifically, the research suggests that although personality diversity may be beneficial in terms of members' extraversion, it may have a dark side in terms of members' agreeableness and conscientiousness. Clearly more research is needed, not only to assess generalizability of these findings, but also to better understand the mechanisms through which these effects occur.

Reaction and interaction

The third way that bright side personality traits may have a dark side in team contexts is through the reactions of team members to other team members' personality and manifest behavior. Although research on this type of effect has been fairly recent, and is relatively limited, there is a strong possibility that these types of effects may play an important role in determining the effectiveness of groups and teams with respect to both task and social functioning.

In a theoretical paper, LePine and Van Dyne (2001a) used attributional theory (Weiner, 1986, 1995) as a basis for their prediction that the personality of a team's low performer would play an important role in determining how the other team members would react to the low performer. Specifically, when a poor performer has low ability, team members should tend to feel empathetic and should either compensate for the low performer, or help the low performer learn his or her role. When a poor performer has low conscientiousness, team members should tend to feel angry, and should either try to motivate the low performer to work harder, or attempt to remove the low performer from the group. The propositions in the theory are consistent with results of previous empirical research (e.g. LePine et al., 1997; Tagger et al., 1999), and have received direct support in a vignette study where findings suggested that low performer personality may be as important as the group members' own personality in predicting the group members' behavioral intentions (Jackson and LePine, 2003). Tagger and Neubert (2004) reported the results of research conducted in a more naturalistic context which further supported the theory.

As an example of how the theory can be applied to understand dark side personality effects, consider how team members would likely respond to a low-performing peer with high conscientiousness and high agreeableness. According to the theory, the most likely response would be for team members to exert effort focused on helping the low performer do his or her part of the team task effectively. This is because the low performer would be viewed as willing to invest energy in improving. In many team contexts, however, members are specialized along functional lines and are stretched just to accomplish their own tasks. Accordingly, this sort of help may be impossible. The next most likely response would be for team members to exert effort intended to compensate for the low performer – perhaps by taking on some of the low performer's responsibilities. Again, however, because of functional specialization or high work loads, this type of compensating behavior may not be possible. In fact, because team members will be reluctant to do anything that would unduly hurt the high conscientiousness – high agreeableness low performer (e.g. trying to replace this person with someone with higher ability), a very likely response would be for the team to accept the limitation and subsequent performance consequences. In other words, it is quite likely that the team would be willing to trade off some task effectiveness in order to maintain social effectiveness. Of course, as LePine and Van Dyne suggest (2001a), if the team members who are responding to the low performer have high agreeableness, the situation may be exacerbated. High agreeableness team members will be more empathetic and will also believe that the low performer has good intentions and should be especially unlikely to respond with behavior that would be threatening to the low performer.

In summary, although the research from the attribution-based reaction and interaction perspective is somewhat limited, there are some clear implications for how the perspective can be used to understand dark side personality effects. For example, if the team members responding to the low performer in the previous example had high conscientiousness, perhaps the members would attempt to take on low performer tasks for which they were ill equipped to handle. As another example altogether, consider what could happen if the low performer exhibited low conscientiousness but otherwise possessed high ability, and an exaggerated self-concept. In this case, because the team members would likely attribute the cause of the low performance to something under the low performer's control, they would likely respond by trying to motivate this person or by rejecting him or her from the group. These types of behaviors would likely be completely unacceptable to this high self-concept low performer, who would be especially apt to attribute the low performance to external causes. The end result would likely be unproductive emotional conflict and lowered team effectiveness.

Summary
In this section we overviewed various ways in which generally desirable personality traits of team members could have dark side effects on team functioning and effectiveness. This

discussion is summarized in Table 20.3. It is important to note that although the parallel aggregate effects of team members' personality operate in a manner that is mostly consistent with what we know about how individual-level personality functions, diversity and reaction–interaction effects are much more complex. Moreover, because diversity and reaction–interaction effects appear to be at least as powerful as parallel aggregate effects, the additional complexity may need to be considered in staffing models for team-based organizations. In the next section, we discuss specific implications of the two previous sections of this chapter.

Selection system implications of the dark sides of personality

Practical issues in designing selection systems that consider personality
As we described earlier, personality traits have non-trivial relationships with job-related criteria. Evidently, this has not been lost to practitioners given the tremendous popularity of personality-based selection practices. Indeed, personality testing is a $400 million industry, and at least 30 percent of all US organizations use personality tests for hiring or related practices (Daniel, 2005). As we noted, however, there are a number of ways that traits may impact criteria, and this complicates staffing decisions. Organizations are perhaps well advised to select those who score high on bright traits and low on dark traits. However, as we have argued, even bright traits have dark effects in certain circumstances (and dark traits bright effects in certain circumstances). Thus the staffing model becomes more complicated in that the 'side effects' of bright and dark traits need to be taken into account. There are at least three ways in which this more subtle view of personality traits can be implemented.

The first and perhaps most obvious way that a staffing model could address countervailing effects of bright and dark traits would be to exclude some or all personality traits from assessment decisions. Although such an approach would certainly simplify the staffing model and subsequent decisions, it is akin to throwing the baby out with the bath water. If inclusion of a trait significantly improves the predictive power with respect to any important criteria, it should be considered in staffing. Most important decisions carry with them benefits and costs, but it hardly makes sense to use this knowledge by declaring that one will refrain from making decisions. With that said, however, the manner in which it is considered may have to be modified from traditional staffing practice.

One way that a staffing model could address the side effects of bright and dark traits would be to consider scores on narrower traits. Such an approach may be especially appropriate in situations where offsetting effects manifest from different facets of a broader trait. As discussed earlier, for example, whereas the achievement-striving aspects of conscientiousness may be positively related to routine and adaptive performance, the dependability aspect of conscientiousness may be negatively related to adaptive performance. Accordingly, instead of staffing using scores on overall conscientiousness, scores on achievement striving and dependability could be considered – and this might be especially important in contexts when performance occurs in novel or changing contexts. Although this approach would require research that considered relationships among the narrow facets and various performance criteria, current understanding of the structure of broad personality traits and known costs and benefits of the traits such as those listed in Table 20.2 points to several possibilities.

A third approach to address dark side effects would be to use the socially desirable traits in staffing, but also include training to address the issues that pose potential problems.

Table 20.3 Potential bright and dark sides of bright traits in team contexts

Type of effect	Trait	Benefit	Costs
Parallel aggregate effect	Overall level of members' conscientiousness (dependability)	Increased reliability and performance in routine contexts	Reduced performance in changing contexts
	Overall level of members' agreeableness	Higher-quality interpersonal functioning	Reduced effectiveness in contexts requiring constructive debate and conflict
Diversity	Variance in extraversion	Higher-quality team functioning	
	Variance in agreeableness and conscientiousness		Lower-quality team functioning and effectiveness
Interaction and reaction	Low performer with low conscientiousness in a group with other members who are high in conscientiousness and low in agreeableness		Poor-quality team functioning and performance (low conscientiousness member is not helped and may be rejected from the group in terms of both the task and socially)

Such an approach would first require a solid understanding of the specific situations where dark sides manifest, as well as the knowledge, skills, attitudes and behaviors that the employee would need to exhibit in those situations. Although this 'supplemental development' approach to staffing would seem to be somewhat complicated and costly, it is not very different than what is already being done in organizations that use assessment centers and other instruments to identify weaknesses in need of 'development'. The advantage of using this approach in the context of staffing would be that potential weaknesses are identified and addressed earlier rather than later.

Complicating factors based on team composition considerations
As noted earlier, staffing models that account for both bright and dark effects may be quite complicated. In team-based organizations, however, the complexity of staffing model that accounts for these types of effects reaches an even higher level. The primary reason for this added complexity is that staffing models in team-based organizations would need to consider validities of configurations of personality traits, rather than personality traits in isolation – and this would be true regardless of whether the staffing problem focused on the creation of new teams or staffing for existing teams. When staffing new teams using personality information, the issue becomes one of creating effective configurations of members with respect to their personality. When staffing existing teams, the issue becomes one of selecting new members with personalities that 'fit' with the personality of the existing members. Although the traditional staffing model would suggest selecting top down for teams based on traits of the prototypical team player – high in conscientiousness, extraversion and agreeableness – diversity and interaction–reaction effects in regards to dark sides of these bright traits make such an approach problematic. Although much more research needs to be done before specific recommendations can be made, the research discussed in this section of the chapter could provide the foundation for some of this future work.

Expanding the criterion
Much of our discussion regarding the staffing dilemma associated with bright and dark sides of personality centered on how traits have benefits and costs. Although in this discussion the traits were given primacy, benefits and costs are also a function of the criteria that are considered, some of which are not normally considered in staffing contexts. Thus, in order to fully appreciate the fitness consequences of bright and dark traits in staffing models, it may be necessary to explicitly consider an expanded set of criteria.

Stress, or perhaps more precisely the negative physiological and psychological strains that result from the stress process, is one potential criterion that could be included in staffing models that attempt to account more fully for bright and dark side effects. Stress is relevant to organizations today, not only because more and more employees (especially managers and professionals) feel that their jobs are extremely stressful, but also because stress is associated with higher health care costs and lower morale, retention and performance (Johnson and Eldridge, 2004; Sauter et al., 1999).

As an example of a socially desirable trait where stress could be considered as a dark side criterion, consider conscientiousness. Because high conscientiousness is associated with higher achievement striving and dependability, those with higher conscientiousness take on higher workloads and responsibility, and they also feel more pressure to accomplish their work in a timely manner. The problem is that although these tendencies promote job performance (Barrick and Mount, 1991) and may be intrinsically satisfying, coping with these challenges results in strains such as exhaustion and burnout (LePine et al., 2005). In short, the behavioral tendencies of conscientiousness that manifest in contributions to the organization through effective job performance may also detract from the organization through higher costs associated with health care, lost productivity and retention.

Although there are certainly other criteria that we could mention here, the point we are trying to make with this discussion is that in order to fully appreciate the potential range of bright and dark side effects of personality, scholars may need to expand the set of criteria they consider in their research. One approach to identifying new criteria would be to focus on positive and negative contributions of employees that relate to a wider variety of factors that increase or reduce the value of the organization. We mentioned stress in the previous paragraph, but criteria connected to employee commitment, intellectual capital and organizational reputation could also be considered. An alternative approach to identifying new criteria would be to consider relationships with a small set of theoretically derived criteria that are somewhat less distal to the ultimate criterion. Such an approach might make sense given that some traits have offsetting indirect effects with the ultimate criterion through multiple mediating or suppressing processes.

Conclusion

The general purpose of this chapter was to discuss one potential explanation for rather modest validities of personality traits. That is, personality traits have, in certain circumstances, bright sides and dark sides that offset one another. We began by discussing the individual-level research, and in this context, there is plenty of research supporting the premise that, for both bright and dark traits, there are both bright and dark effects. We then turned to overview the research that has examined this issue from a team-level perspective. Although the majority of the research discussed in this section supports the idea that team configuration in terms of traits can have both bright and dark sides, the research has examined the issue only rarely and indirectly. Finally, we discussed selection system implications of bright and dark side effects, in terms of both individual and team contexts. From all of this discussion we conclude that personality traits have both bright and dark effects in both individual and team contexts, and that the ability to predict criteria in both contexts could improve, perhaps dramatically, if our theorizing, research and practice explicitly took these types of effects into account. Unfortunately, however, we regret to say that doing so can only come at the cost of increasing complexity and fragmentation, and thus we will forfeit the beauty of the simplicity of research and practice using a very small set of rather broad personality traits and criteria.

References

Aamodt, M.G. and Kimbrough, W.W. (1982), 'Effect of group heterogeneity on quality of task solutions', *Psychological Reports*, **50**, 171–4.
Alotaibi, A.G. (2003), 'Job burnout among employees in the Kuwaiti civil service and its relationship with Type A personality and intention to leave', *Journal of the Social Sciences*, **31**, 347–85.
Altman, I. and McGinnies, E. (1960), 'Interpersonal perception and communication in discussion groups of varied attitudinal composition', *Journal of Abnormal and Social Psychology*, **12**, 390–95.
Anderson, K.J. (1994), 'Impulsivity, caffeine, and task difficulty: a within-subjects test of the Yerkes–Dodson law', *Personality and Individual Differences*, **16**, 813–29.

Archer, J. and Webb, I.A. (2006), 'The relation between scores on the Buss–Perry Aggression Questionnaire and aggressive acts, impulsiveness, competitiveness, dominance, and sexual jealousy', *Aggressive Behavior*, **32**, 464–73.

Back, M.D., Schmukle, S.C. and Egloff, B. (2006), 'Who is late and who is early? Big Five personality factors and punctuality in attending psychological experiments', *Journal of Research in Personality*, **40**, 841–8.

Barrick, M.R. and Mount, M.K. (1991), 'The Big Five personal dimensions and job performance: a meta-analysis', *Personnel Psychology*, **44**, 1–26.

Barrick, M.R. and Mount, M.K. (2005), 'Yes, personality matters: moving on to more important matters', *Human Performance*, **18**, 359–72.

Barrick, M.R., Mount, M.K. and Judge, T.A. (2001), 'Personality and performance at the beginning of the new millennium: what do we know and where do we go next?', *International Journal of Selection & Assessment*, **9**, 9–30.

Barrick, M.R., Stewart, G.L., Neubert, M.J. and Mount, M.K. (1998), 'Relating member ability and personality to work team processes and team effectiveness', *Journal of Applied Psychology*, **83**, 377–91.

Barry, B. and Stewart, G. (1997), 'Composition, process, and performance in self-managed groups: the role of personality', *Journal of Applied Psychology*, **82**, 62–78.

Beauducel, A., Brocke, B. and Leue, A. (2006), 'Energetical bases of extraversion: effort, arousal, EEG, and performance', *International Journal of Psychophysiology*, **62**, 212–23.

Bernardin, H.J., Cooke, D.K. and Villanova, P. (2000), 'Conscientiousness and agreeableness as predictors of rating leniency', *Journal of Applied Psychology*, **85**, 232–6.

Booth-Kewley, S. and Friedman, H.S. (1987), 'Psychological predictors of heart disease: a quantitative review', *Psychological Bulletin*, **101**, 343–62.

Brunas-Wagstaff, J., Tilley, A., Verity, M. and Ford, S. (1997), 'Functional and dysfunctional impulsivity in children and their relationship to Eysenck's impulsiveness and venturesomeness dimensions', *Personality and Individual Differences*, **22**, 19–25.

Byrne, D. (1971), *The Attraction Paradigm*, New York: Academic Press.

Campbell, W.K. (2001), 'Is narcissism really so bad?', *Psychological Inquiry*, **12**, 214–16.

Campbell, W.K., Bush, C.P., Brunell, A.B. and Shelton, J. (2005), 'Understanding the social costs of narcissism: the case of the tragedy of the commons', *Personality and Social Psychology Bulletin*, **31**, 1358–68.

Clarke, S. and Robertson, I.T. (2005), 'A meta-analytic review of the Big Five personality factors and accident involvement in occupational and non-occupational settings', *Journal of Occupational and Organizational Psychology*, **78**, 355–76.

Cohen, J. (1977), *Statistical Power Analysis for the Behavioral Sciences*, New York: Academic Press.

Colquitt, J.A. and Simmering, M.J. (1998), 'Conscientiousness, goal orientation, and motivation to learn during the learning process: a longitudinal study', *Journal of Applied Psychology*, **83**, 654–65.

Cox, T., Lobel, S. and McLeod, P. (1991), 'Effects of ethnic group cultural differences on cooperation and competitive behavior on a group task', *Academy of Management Journal*, **34**, 827–47.

Daniel, L. (2005), 'Use personality tests legally and effectively', Society of Human Resources Management, online (www.srrm.org/ema/sm/articles/2005/apriljune05cover.asp). Retrieved 8 November.

DeNeve, K.M. and Cooper, H. (1998), 'The happy personality: a meta-analysis of 137 personality traits and subjective well-being', *Psychological Bulletin*, **124**, 197–229.

Doucet, L. (2004), 'Service provider hostility and service quality', *Academy of Management Journal*, **47**, 761–71.

Dunn, W.S., Mount, M.K. and Barrick, M.R. (1995), 'Relative importance of personality and general mental ability in managers' judgments of applicant qualifications', *Journal of Applied Psychology*, **80**, 500–509.

Dwyer, D.J. and Fox, M.L. (2000), 'The moderating role of hostility in the relationship between enriched jobs and health', *Academy of Management Journal*, **43**, 1086–96.

Egan, S. and Stelmack, R.M. (2003), 'A personality profile of Mount Everest climbers', *Personality and Individual Differences*, **34**, 1491–4.

Ellingson, J.E., Smith, D.B. and Sackett, P.R. (2001), 'Investigating the influence of social desirability on personality factor structure', *Journal of Applied Psychology*, **86**, 122–33.

Erdheim, J., Wang, M. and Zickar, M.J. (2006), 'Linking the Big Five personality constructs to organizational commitment', *Personality and Individual Differences*, **41**, 959–70.

Erez, A., LePine, J.A. and Elms, H. (2002), 'Effects of rotated leadership and peer evaluation on the functioning and effectiveness of self-managed teams: a quasi-experiment', *Personnel Psychology*, **55**, 929–48.

Feist, G.J. (1998), 'A meta-analysis of personality in scientific and artistic creativity', *Personality and Social Psychology Bulletin*, **2**, 290–309.

Fiedler, F. (1952), 'Unconscious attitudes as correlates of sociometric choice in a social group', *Journal of Abnormal and Social Psychology*, **47**, 790–96.

Franken, I.H.A. and Muris, P. (2006), 'Gray's impulsivity dimension: a distinction between reward sensitivity versus rash impulsiveness', *Personality and Individual Differences*, **40**, 1337–47.

Friedman, H.S., Tucker, J., Schwartz, J.E., Martin, L.R., Tomlinson-Keasey, C., Wingard, D. and Criqui, M. (1995), 'Childhood conscientiousness and longevity: health behaviors and cause of death', *Journal of Personality and Social Psychology*, **68**, 696–703.

Ganster, D.C., Schaubroeck, J., Sime, W.E. and Mayes, B.T. (1991), 'The nomological validity of the Type A personality among employed adults', *Journal of Applied Psychology*, **76**, 143–68.

Ghiselli, E.E. and Lodahl, T.M. (1958), 'Patterns of managerial traits and group effectiveness', *Journal of Abnormal and Social Psychology*, **57**, 61–6.

Gray, J.A. (1987), 'Perspectives on anxiety and impulsivity: a commentary', *Journal of Research in Personality*, **21**, 493–509.

Graziano, W.G. and Tobin, R.M. (2002), 'Agreeableness: dimension of personality or social desirability artifact?', *Journal of Personality*, **70**, 695–727.

Guion, R.M. and Gottier, R.F. (1965), 'Validity of personality measures in personnel selection', *Personnel Psychology*, **18**, 135–64.

Harrison, D.A., Price, K.H. and Bell, M.P. (1998), 'Beyond relational demography: time and the effects of surface- and deep-level diversity on work group cohesion', *Academy of Management Journal*, **41**, 96–107.

Harrison, D.A., Price, K.H., Gavin, J.H. and Florey, A.T. (2002), 'Time, teams, and task performance: changing effects of surface- and deep-level diversity on group functioning', *Academy of Management Journal*, **45**, 1029–45.

Haythorn, W.W. (1968), 'The composition of groups: a review of the literature', *Acta Psychologica*, **28**, 97–128.

Haythorn, W.C., Couch, A., Haefner, D., Langham, P. and Carter, L. (1956), 'The effects of varying combinations of authoritarian and equalitarian leaders and followers', *Journal of Abnormal Social Psychology*, **53**, 210–19.

Heilbrun, A.B. and Friedberg, E.B. (1988), 'Type A personality, self-control, and vulnerability to stress', *Journal of Personality Assessment*, **52**, 420–33.

Heslin, R. (1964), 'Predicting group task effectiveness from member characteristics', *Psychological Bulletin*, **62**, 248–56.

Hoffman, L.R. (1955), 'Similarity of personality: a basis for interpersonal attraction?', *Sociometry*, **21**, 300–308.

Hoffman, L.R. (1959), 'Homogeneity of member personality and its effect on group problem solving', *Journal of Abnormal and Social Psychology*, **58**, 27–32.

Hoffman, L. and Maier, N. (1961a), 'Sex differences, sex composition, and group problem solving', *Journal of Abnormal and Social Psychology*, **63**, 453–56.

Hoffman, L. and Maier, N. (1961b), 'Quality and acceptance of problem solutions by members of homogeneous and heterogeneous groups', *Journal of Abnormal and Social Psychology*, **62**, 401–7.

Hogan, R. (2005), 'In defense of personality measurement: new wine for old whiners', *Human Performance*, **18**, 331–41.

Hogan, R.T. and Roberts, B.W. (2001), 'Introduction: personality and industrial and organizational psychology', in B.W. Roberts and R.T. Hogan (eds), *Personality Psychology in the Workplace*, Washington, DC: American Psychological Association, pp. 3–16.

Hough, L.M. (1992), 'The "Big Five" personality variables–construct confusion: description versus prediction', *Human Performance*, **5**, 139–55.

Hough, L.M. and Oswald, F.L. (2000), 'Personnel selection: looking toward the future – Remembering the past', *Annual Review of Psychology*, **51**, 631–64.

Hough, L.M. and Oswald, F.L. (2005), 'They're right, well . . . mostly right: research evidence and an agenda to rescue personality testing from 1960s insights', *Human Performance*, **18**, 373–87.

Hurtz, G.M. and Donovan, J.J. (2000), 'Personality and job performance: the Big Five revisited', *Journal of Applied Psychology*, **85**, 869–79.

Jackson, C.L. and LePine, J.A. (2003), 'Peer responses to a team's weakest link: a test and extension of LePine and Van Dyne's Model', *Journal of Applied Psychology*, **88**, 459–75.

Jiang, J., Yan, X. and Li, Z. (2004), 'The influence of Type A personality and locus of control upon job satisfaction and mental health among medical staff', *Chinese Journal of Clinical Psychology*, **12**, 359–61.

Johnson, S.R. and Eldridge, L.D. (2004), 'Employee-related stress on the job: sources, consequences, and what's next', Technical Report no. 003. Rochester, NY: Genesee Survey Services, Inc.

Judge, T.A. and Bono, J.E. (2001), 'Relationship of core self-evaluations traits – self-esteem, generalized self-efficacy, locus of control, and emotional stability – with job satisfaction and job performance: a meta-analysis', *Journal of Applied Psychology*, **86**, 80–92.

Judge, T.A., Martocchio, J.J. and Thoresen, C.J. (1997), 'Five-factor model of personality and employee absence', *Journal of Applied Psychology*, **82**, 745–55.

Judge, T.A., Thoresen, C.J., Pucik, V. and Welbourne, T.M. (1999), 'Managerial coping with organizational change: a dispositional perspective', *Journal of Applied Psychology*, **84**, 107–22.

Judge, T.A., Heller, D. and Mount, M.K. (2002a), 'Five-factor model of personality and job satisfaction: a meta-analysis', *Journal of Applied Psychology*, **87**, 530–41.

Judge, T.A., Bono, J.E., Ilies, R. and Gerhardt, M.W. (2002b), 'Personality and leadership: a qualitative and quantitative review', *Journal of Applied Psychology*, **87**, 765–80.

Judge, T.A., LePine, J.A. and Rich, B.L. (2006a), 'The narcissistic personality: relationship with inflated self-ratings of leadership and with task and contextual performance', *Journal of Applied Psychology*, **91**, 762–76.

Judge, T.A., Scott, B.A. and Ilies, R. (2006b), 'Hostility, job attitudes, and workplace deviance: test of a multilevel model', *Journal of Applied Psychology*, **91**, 126–38.

Kent, R. and McGrath, J. (1969), 'Task and group characteristics as factors affecting group performance', *Journal of Experimental Social Psychology*, **5**, 429–40.

Kirkcaldy, B.D., Shephard, R.J. and Furnham, A.F. (2002), 'The influence of Type A behavior and locus of control upon job satisfaction and occupational health', *Personality and Individual Differences*, **33**, 1361–71.

Lajunen, T. (2001), 'Personality and accident liability: are extraversion, neuroticism and psychoticism related to traffic and occupational fatalities?', *Personality and Individual Differences*, **31**, 1365–73.

Lawrence, J.B. and Stanford, M.S. (1999), 'Impulsivity and time of day: effects on performance and cognitive tempo', *Personality and Individual Differences*, **26**, 199–207.

Lee, K. and Allen, N.J. (2002), 'Organizational citizenship behavior and workplace deviance: the role of affect and cognitions', *Journal of Applied Psychology*, **87**, 131–42.

LePine, J.A. (2003), 'Team adaptation and postchange performance: effects of team composition in terms of members' cognitive ability and personality', *Journal of Applied Psychology*, **88**, 27–39.

LePine, J.A. and Van Dyne, L. (2001a), 'Peer responses to low performers: an attributional model of helping in the context of groups', *Academy of Management Review*, **28**, 67–84.

LePine, J.A. and Van Dyne, L. (2001b), 'Voice and cooperative behavior as contrasting forms of contextual performance: evidence of differential effects of Big-Five personality characteristics and general cognitive ability', *Journal of Applied Psychology*, **86**, 326–36.

LePine, J.A., Colquitt, J.A. and Erez, A. (2000), 'Adaptability to changing task contexts: effects of general cognitive ability, conscientiousness, and openness to experience', *Personnel Psychology*, **53**, 563–93.

LePine, J.A., Hollenbeck, J.R., Ilgen, D.R. and Hedlund, J. (1997), 'Effects of individual differences on the performance of hierarchical decision making teams: much more than *g*', *Journal of Applied Psychology*, **82**, 803–11.

LePine, J.A., Podsakoff, N.P. and LePine, M.A. (2005), 'A meta-analytic test of the challenge stressor–hindrance stressor framework: an explanation for inconsistent relationships among stressors and performance', *Academy of Management Journal*, **48**, 767–75.

Locke, E.A. and Latham, G.P. (2002), 'Building a practically useful theory of goal setting and task motivation: a 35-year odyssey', *American Psychologist*, **57**, 705–17.

Mann, R.D. (1959), 'A review of the relationship between personality and performance in small groups', *Psychological Bulletin*, **56**, 241–70.

Mannix, E. and Neale, M.A. (2005), 'What differences make a difference? The promise and reality of diverse teams in organizations', *Psychological Science in the Public Interest*, **6**, 31–55.

Martocchio, J.J. and Judge, T.A. (1997), 'Relationship between conscientiousness and learning in employee training: mediating influences of self-deception and self-efficacy', *Journal of Applied Psychology*, **82**, 764–73.

Mathews, A., Mackintosh, B. and Fulcher, E.P. (1997), 'Cognitive biases in anxiety and attention to threat', *Trends in Cognitive Sciences*, **1**, 340–45.

Matthews, K. and Haynes, S. (1986), 'Type A behavior pattern and coronary disease risk: update and critical evaluation', *American Journal of Epidemiology*, **123**, 923–59.

Matthews, K.A., Helmreich, R.L., Beane, W.E. and Lucker, G.W. (1980), 'Pattern A, achievement striving, and scientific merit: does pattern A help or hinder?', *Journal of Personality and Social Psychology*, **39**, 962–7.

McCann, B.S., Russo, J. and Benjamin, G.A.H. (1997), 'Hostility, social support, and perceptions of work', *Journal of Occupational Health Psychology*, **2**, 175–85.

McCrae, R.R. (1996), 'Social consequences of experiential openness', *Psychological Bulletin*, **120**, 323–37.

McGrath, J.E. (1962), 'The influence of positive interpersonal relations on adjustment and interpersonal relations in rifle teams', *Journal of Abnormal and Social Psychology*, **65**, 365–75.

Miller, T.Q., Smith, T.W., Turner, C.W., Guijarro, M.L. and Hallet, A.J. (1996), 'A meta-analytic review of research on hostility and physical health', *Psychological Bulletin*, **119**, 322–48.

Miner, J.B. (2003), 'The rated importance, scientific validity, and practical usefulness of organizational behavior theories: a quantitative review', *AOM Learning and Education*, **2**, 250–68.

Moscoso, S. and Salgado, J.F. (2004), ' "Dark side" personality styles as predictors of task, contextual, and job performance', *International Journal of Selection and Assessment*, **12**, 356–62.

Mount, M.K., Barrick, M.R. and Stewart, G.L. (1998), 'Five factor model of personality and performance in jobs involving interpersonal interactions', *Human Performance*, **11**, 145–65.

Moynihan, L.M. and Peterson, R.S. (2001), 'A contingent configuration approach to understanding the role of personality in organizational groups', *Research in Organizational Behavior*, **23**, 327–78.

Nettle, D. (2006), 'The evolution of personality variation in humans and other animals', *American Psychologist*, **61**, 622–31.

Newcomb, T.M. (1968). *The Acquaintance Process*, New York: Holt, Rinehart and Winston.
Newton, T.L. and Kiecolt-Glaser, J.K. (1995), 'Hostility and erosion of marital quality during early marriage', *Journal of Behavioral Medicine*, **18**, 601–19.
Ng, T.W.H., Eby, L.T., Sorensen, K.L. and Feldman, D.C. (2005), 'Predictors of objective and subjective career success. A meta-analysis', *Personnel Psychology*, **58**, 367–408.
Paunonen, S.V., Lönnqvist, J., Verkasalo, M., Leikas, S. and Nissinen, V. (2006), 'Narcissism and emergent leadership in military cadets', *Leadership Quarterly*, **17**, 475–86.
Riordan, C.M. and Shore, L. (1997), 'Demographic diversity and employee attitudes: examination of relational demography within work units', *Journal of Applied Psychology*, **82**, 342–58.
Robbins, A.S., Spence, J.T. and Clark, H. (1991), 'Psychological determinants of health and performance: the tangled web of desirable and undesirable characteristics', *Journal of Personality and Social Psychology*, **61**, 755–65.
Rosenman, R.H. (1986), 'Current and past history of Type A behavior pattern', in T. Schmidt, T.M. Dembroski and G. Blumchen (eds), *Biological and Psychological Factors in Cardiovascular Disease*, New York: Springer-Verlag, pp. 15–40.
Ruiz, J.M., Smith, T.W. and Rhodewalt, F. (2001), 'Distinguishing narcissism and hostility: similarities and differences in interpersonal circumplex and five-factor correlates', *Journal of Personality Assessment*, **76**, 537–55.
Salgado, J. (2002), 'The Big Five personality dimensions and counterproductive behaviors', *International Journal of Selection and Assessment*, **10**, 117–25.
Sarason, I.G., Ganzer, V.J. and Granger, J.W. (1965), 'Self-description of hostility and its correlates', *Journal of Personality and Social Psychology*, **1**, 361–5.
Sauter, S., Murphy, L., Colligan, M., Swanson, N., Hurrell, J., Jr, Scharf, F. Jr, Sinclair, R., Grubb, P., Goldenhar, L., Alterman, T., Johnston, J., Hamilton, A. and Tisdale, J. (1999), *Stress at Work, DHHS (NIOSH) Publication No. 99-101*, Cincinnati, OH: National Institute for Occupational Safety and Health.
Schmitt, N. (2004), 'Beyond the Big Five: increases in understanding and practical utility', *Human Performance*, **17**, 347–57.
Schweizer, K. (2002), 'Does impulsivity influence performance in reasoning?', *Personality and Individual Differences*, **33**, 1031–43.
Seibert, S.E., Kraimer, M.L. and Crant, J.M. (2001), 'What do proactive people do? A longitudinal model linking proactive personality and career success', *Personnel Psychology*, **54**, 845–74.
Sinaceur, M. and Tiedens, L.Z. (2006), 'Get mad and get more than even: when and why anger expression is effective in negotiations', *Journal of Experimental Social Psychology*, **42**, 314–22.
Smith, T.W., Sanders, J.D. and Alexander, J.F. (1990), 'What does the Cook and Medley Hostility scale measure? Affect, behavior, and attributions in the marital context', *Journal of Personality and Social Psychology*, **58**, 699–708.
Smith, T.W., Pope, M.K., Sanders, J.D., Allred, K.D. and O'Keeffe, J.L. (1988), 'Cynical hostility at home and work: psychosocial vulnerability across domains', *Journal of Research in Personality*, **22**, 525–48.
Stewart, G.L., Fulmer, I.S. and Barrick, M.R. (2005), 'An exploration of member roles as a multilevel linking mechanism for individual traits and team outcomes', *Personnel Psychology*, **58**, 343–65.
Suls, J., Martin, R. and David, J.P. (1998), 'Person–environment fit and its limits: agreeableness, neuroticism, and emotional reactivity to interpersonal conflict', *Personality and Social Psychology Bulletin*, **24**, 88–98.
Tagger, S. and Neubert, M. (2004), 'The impact of poor performers on team outcomes: an empirical examination of attribution theory', *Personnel Psychology*, **57**, 935–68.
Tagger, S., Hackett, R. and Saha, S. (1999), 'Leadership emergence in autonomous work teams: antecedents and outcomes', *Personnel Psychology*, **52**, 899–26.
Tajfel, H. (1981), *Human Groups and Social Categories: Studies in Social Psychology*, Cambridge, UK: Cambridge University Press.
Tamir, M., Robinson, M.D. and Solberg, E.C. (2006), 'You may worry, but can you recognize threats when you see them?: Neuroticism, threat identifications, and negative affect', *Journal of Personality*, **74**, 1481–506.
Taylor, M.S., Locke, E.A., Lee, C. and Gist, M. (1984), 'Type A behavior and faculty research productivity: what are the mechanisms?', *Organizational Behavior and Human Performance*, **34**, 402–18.
Tiedens, L.Z. (2001), 'Anger and advancement versus sadness and subjugation: the effect of negative emotion expressions on social status conferral', *Journal of Personality and Social Psychology*, **80**, 86–94.
Torrubia, R., Ávila, C. and Moltó, J. (2001), 'The Sensitivity to Punishment and Sensitivity to Reward Questionnaire (SPSRQ) as a measure of Gray's anxiety and impulsivity dimensions', *Personality and Individual Differences*, **31**, 837–62.
Turner, J. (1985), 'Social categorization and the self-concept: a social cognitive theory of group behavior', *Advances in Group Processes*, Vol. 2, Greenwich, CT: JAI Press, pp. 77–121.
Vinchur, A.J., Schippmann, J.S., Switzer, F.S. III and Roth, P.L. (1998), 'A meta-analytic review of predictors of job performance for salespeople', *Journal of Applied Psychology*, **83**, 586–97.

Waldron, I., Hickey, A., McPherson, C., Butensky, A., Gruss, L., Overall, K., Schmader, A. and Wohlmuth, D. (1980), 'Type A behavior pattern: relationship to variation in blood pressure, parental characteristics, and academic and social activities of students', *Journal of Human Stress*, **6**, 16–27.

Waung, M. and Brice, T.S. (1998), 'The effects of conscientiousness and opportunity to caucus on group performance', *Small Group Research*, **29**, 624–34.

Weiner, B. (1986), *An Attributional Theory of Achievement Motivation and Emotion*, New York: Springer-Verlag.

Weiner, B. (1995), *Judgments of Responsibility: A Foundation for a Theory of Social Conduct*, New York: Guilford Press.

Williams, K.Y. and O'Reilly, C.A., III (1998), 'Demography and diversity in organizations: a review of 40 years of research', *Research in Organizational Behavior*, **20**, 77–140.

Witt, L.A., Burke, L.A., Barrick, M.A. and Mount, M.K. (2002), 'The interactive effects of conscientiousness and agreeableness on job performance', *Journal of Applied Psychology*, **87**(1), 164–9.

Wood, R.E., Mento, A.J. and Locke, E.A. (1987), 'Task complexity as a moderator of goal effects: a meta-analysis', *Journal of Applied Psychology*, **72**, 416–25.

Yeo, G.B. and Neal, A. (2004), 'A multilevel analysis of effort, practice, and performance: effects of ability, conscientiousness, and goal orientation', *Journal of Applied Psychology*, **89**, 231–47.

21 Motives and traits as a driver of adaptive and maladaptive managerial styles
Sharon L. Grant

Occupational stress and the inherently stressful nature of managerial work

Managerial work is disorderly, fragmented and hectic (Antonioni, 1996; Fogarty et al., 1999; Hooijberg et al., 1997; Mintzberg, 1973; Yukl, 1989). According to Mintzberg (1973), the typical manager is simultaneously a (a) figurehead, leader and liaison (interpersonal role), (b) disseminator, monitor and spokesman (informational role); and entrepreneur, disturbance handler, negotiator and resource allocator (decisional role). Given the multifaceted nature of their work, managers are expected to be goal-oriented, motivated and, most importantly, 'stress-tolerant' (Lusch and Serpkenci, 1990).

While there is some research to suggest that occupational stress is more prevalent at shopfloor level than at management level (see, e.g., Karasek and Theorell, 1990), a recent survey found that the incidence of occupational stress in managers was as high as 70 per cent (Wheatley, 2000). Managers encounter a high pressure environment on a day-to-day basis (Ducharme, 2004), with the constant need for 'fire fighting' contributing to a cumulative effect on stress.

Other work has indicated that 80% of managers believe that their work is more stressful than it used to be (Webster, 1998). Over the past decade, managers have had to cope with significant organizational change, aimed at realigning organizational structure with advancing globalization and technology (Callan, 1993; Mishra and Spreitzer, 1998; Rosen, 1997; Terry and Callan, 1997). 'Surviving' managers are faced with the task of leading staff through cultural and structural change, are required to do more work with fewer staff, and are often met with considerable resistance from employees who are anxious about the impact of change (Antonioni, 1996; Callan, 1993; Callan et al.,1994; Hooijberg et al., 1997). In short, today's manager must innovate but avoid (t)error, consider the 'big picture' but increase productivity and efficiency now, downsize but improve teamwork, be receptive and responsive and, at the same time, tackle his or her own uncertainty (Rosen, 1997; Stöber and Seidenstücker, 1997). While compliance, effort and loyalty used to be the key to managerial success, it is innovativeness and initiative that are rewarded under the 'managerial leadership' contract (Rosen, 1997). And, while some managers have made a smooth transition, for many the shift to managerial leadership has led to career derailing, citing inability to cope (McGill and Slocum, 1998; Wheatley, 2000).

Are managers themselves part of the problem? Wheatley (2000) argued that many managers make their jobs more stressful by doing them badly: they not only *feel* unable to cope, but *are* unable to cope. Hogan and Kaiser (2005) argued that managers who rise to the top of the corporate ladder are distinguished by ambition, hard work, intelligence, luck and political skill but not necessarily by 'leadership talent'; many fail because they are simply unable to make the transition. The base rate for managerial incompetence is in the range of 30 per cent to 75 per cent (Hogan and Kaiser, 2005). Hogan and Warrenfeltz

(2003) argued that managerial competence can be captured in terms of four broad types of skills: (1) intrapersonal skills (e.g. self-awareness and self-regulation); (2), interpersonal skills (e.g. cooperating, communicating, conflict resolution, empathizing, listening, providing encouragement and support, sensitivity and tact); (3) business/management skills (e.g. budgeting, coordinating, following up, decision making, monitoring, organizing, planning, problem solving, scheduling); and (4) leadership skills (building teamwork, developing people, driving accountability and performance, securing commitment not just compliance, strategic planning and visioning).

Reducing distress and dysfunction in managers is vital to the health and performance of the organization as a whole (Quick et al., 1996; Schreurs et al., 1996). Distressed and dysfunctional managers may affect company image, morale, organizational climate and productivity, as well as the rate of sick leave and medical consumption (Schreurs et al., 1996). For instance, supervisor satisfaction is a major determinant of overall job satisfaction, with up to 75 per cent of employees rating their immediate supervisor as the worst aspect of their jobs (Hogan and Kaiser, 2005). Furthermore, managers may directly affect the development of other people within the organization, such as their direct reports (Ducharme, 2004).

The starting point for intervention is diagnosing the relationship of the manager to his or her work environment (Elo et al., 1998). The role of human resources (HR) professionals and organizational researchers is to identify the characteristics that influence managerial functioning and to evaluate the 'fit' between the needs of the manager and the needs of the job (Conrad, 1997). The focus for this chapter is the relationship between personality characteristics and managerial styles. It is argued that personality characteristics give rise to managerial styles that are more or less adaptive due to the presence or absence of various competencies ('behaviorally specific skills'). 'Adaptive' managerial styles are styles that have a positive outcome for the manager, other employees and/or the organization. In contrast, 'maladaptive' managerial styles are styles that have a negative outcome for the manager, other employees and/or the organization. Adaptive and maladaptive managerial styles are explained as a function of the interaction between two major levels of personality: unconscious needs (or implicit motives) and traits. In addition, Winter and colleagues' (Winter et al., 1998) channelling hypothesis (the expression of motives is channelled by traits) is extended by integrating it with a person–environment fit approach to occupational stress. It is argued that the extent to which unconflicted motive expression is adaptive versus maladaptive for managers is likely to vary depending on the degree of fit between the motive and the job environment. This chapter should assist HR professionals, consultants and senior managers in implementing personnel selection, job assignment, training and professional development for middle- to upper-level managers whose jobs entail staff management. Key terms used throughout the chapter (stress, stressor, strain, occupational stress, fit) are defined below. Limitations of past research on personality and occupational stress are then considered, focusing on the neglect of an idiographic approach examining the interaction between different levels of personality (i.e. motives and traits). Next, the relationship between motives and managerial styles is examined. The expression of motives through goals and traits is discussed before presenting a motive–trait taxonomy of adaptive and maladaptive managerial styles. Finally, strategies for managing maladaptive managerial styles through intervention (e.g. stress education, stress management training) and prevention (e.g. personnel selection, job assignment) are presented.

The stressor–strain relationship: a stimulus–response process

Defining stress and strain

Stress has been defined as a 'stimulus' ('engineering approach': e.g. a demand in the internal or external environment), a 'response' ('medico-physiological approach': e.g. a generalized physiological response to a demand) and, more recently, a stimulus–response process ('psychological approach') (see Brantley and Garrett, 1993; Cox and Ferguson, 1991; Dewe et al., 1993; Fleming et al., 1984; Jex, 1998). When the last definition is used, the term *stressor* is used to indicate a demand that is psychologically meaningful, and the term *strain* is used to describe the negative outcome of the individual's response to the stressor (Jex, 1998). According to this view, then, a stressor is the agent of stress (Shinn et al., 1984).

A stressor may be physical (e.g. noise) or psychosocial (e.g. interpersonal conflict), and its source may be academic, family-oriented, maturational, personal or occupational (Endler, 1997). Stress is typically associated with an alteration in the intensity of affect or mood, which is in turn thought to trigger a cycle of change in the person's psychological and physiological functioning, i.e. a deviation from normal functioning (Cox and Ferguson, 1991). Accordingly, strain may be psychological (e.g. anxiety) and/or physical (e.g. high blood pressure) (Jex, 1998). At a general level, stress is hypothesized to contribute to illness and disease through deregulation of (a) the autonomic nervous system and (b) the immune system, although it may also affect illness and disease indirectly, via maladaptive coping or risky health behaviour (Brantley and Garrett, 1993; Brown, 1993; Siegrist, 1995; Wiebe and Smith, 1997). However, it should be noted that the precise psychological and physiological meaning of stress is still under debate (Brantley and Garrett, 1993; Friedman, 1990). Genetic predisposition to a specific illness or disease, or psychological make-up, may intensify the impact of stress (Endler, 1997). Indeed, Brantley and Garrett (1993) described the effect of stress on illness and disease as 'complex' and 'multiply-determined'.

Occupational stress

From a stimulus–response perspective (psychological approach), *occupational stress* is defined as a situation in which the interaction between the employee and the work environment is associated with an alteration in the employee's psychological and/or physical functioning (Beehr and Newman, 1978). Specifically, there is a perception, on the part of the employee, of a need to adapt to a stressor in the work environment (Adkins, 1997). In an occupational sense, strain is used to denote the negative outcome of the interaction between the employee and the work environment (Adkins, 1997). At the employee level, occupational stress is associated with a range of physical and psychological symptomatology as well as chronic illness such as cardiovascular disease and depression (National Institute for Occupational Safety and Health, 2002). In addition, there is increasing consensus that occupational stress is related to short-term and long-term quality of life (Langan-Fox and Poole, 1995). For example, occupational stress may have a collateral effect on health behaviour (e.g. substance use), relationship quality and self-esteem (Murphy, 1996). At the organizational level, it has been linked with absenteeism, counterproductivity, job dissatisfaction and turnover (Hepburn et al., 1997; Jex, 1998).

Occupational stress among managers may stem from the following stressors: (a) *the job itself* (decision making, financial responsibility, planning, problem solving, leading/supervising), leading to fatigue and tension; (b) *quantitative workload* (e.g. email, deadlines, interruptions, meetings, paperwork), leading to 'burnout'; (c) *lack of support* (e.g. getting information, internal communication, understaffing), leading to frustration and irritability; (d) *the corporate ladder* (e.g. career advancement, income, job security, organizational politics, power, underutilization), leading to anxiety and insecurity; (e) *work–life balance* (long hours, overtime, work–family conflict), leading to isolation, relationship breakdown and family discord; and, as mentioned above, (g) *organizational change*, such as downsizing, reorganization and restructuring (Antonioni, 1996; Callan, 1993; Long, 1993; Stöber and Seidenstücker, 1997; Terry and Callan, 1997; Webster, 1998; Wheatley, 2000). The high interpersonal demand associated with the job is a further source of stress, and the manager is often a 'scapegoat' (and target) for angry clients/customers and staff. Occupational stress is particularly prevalent among middle managers, with those lower down in the hierarchy feeling the pressure from above and below (Webster, 1998).

The types of coping skills required of managers are also unique. Given their onus of problem solving and decision making, managers are expected to use problem-focused coping (e.g. active coping, instrumental support seeking, planning) as opposed to dysfunctional or avoidance coping (e.g. behavioural disengagement, denial, self-distraction, substance use, venting), thus restricting the number of coping strategies available to them for dealing with stress (Long, 1993).

The person–environment fit model of occupational stress
The engineering approach and medico-physiological approach to stress fail to account for individual differences in the experience and outcome of stress (Cox and Ferguson, 1991). In contrast, a defining characteristic of the psychological approach to stress is its focus on the role of individual differences in the stimulus–response process. Accordingly, contemporary research has focused on how people respond to stress in a cognitive and behavioural sense rather than a biological or physiological one. According to the current, prevailing framework, stress is interactional or 'transactional' in nature, and can be conceptualized as a product of the perceptual interface between person and environment (Dewe et al., 1993; Monroe and Kelley, 1997). This approach can be dated to Lewin's interactional psychology, specifically the notion that behaviour is a function of the interaction between person and environment (Jex, 1998; Revenson, 1990).

In the person–environment (P–E) fit model, occupational stress is thought to arise from a lack of *fit* or congruence between the employee and the work environment (Chemers et al., 1985). Fit is defined as the match between employee characteristics and job or organizational characteristics (see Wilk et al., 1995). Some measured aspect of the person is tested for its degree of fit with some measured aspect of the job or organization (Schneider et al., 1995). For example, P–E fit has been operationalized as the fit between employee ability and job demand, employee values and organizational values, and personality characteristics and job characteristics (Cox and Ferguson, 1991; Edwards, 1996; Hobfoll, 1988; Semmer, 1996). The better the fit, the better the outcome for health, wellbeing and performance (Van Harrison, 1985). The current work is concerned with the fit between personality characteristics and managerial work. Edwards (1996) argued that the P–E fit model has a conceptual advantage over the alternative approach in which stress is seen as a stimulus or response in isolation, in that stress (poor P–E fit) and strain (a negative condition resulting from poor fit) are cast as distinct, causally related phenomena.

Furthermore, there is evidence to suggest that 'goodness of fit' is a stronger predictor of strain than person or environment *per se* (Hobfoll, 1988).

Personality and occupational stress
There is a wealth of research on the role of personality in the stressor–strain relationship that has focused almost exclusively on nomothetic trait personality, in particular individual differences in traits such as Type A behaviour pattern, locus of control, negative affectivity and dispositional optimism (Code and Langan-Fox, 2001). By comparison, research on the role of other 'levels' (e.g. motives, cognitions) and 'domains' (e.g. idiographic as opposed to nomothetic) of personality in the stressor–strain relationship is scarce, particularly in the occupational stress literature. This is problematic for two reasons. First, traits only represent one level of personality – that of readily observable, consistent behaviour (Winter and Stewart, 1995). Within the current, prevailing view of personality, there are at least *three* levels: motives, cognitions and traits (McAdams, 2000; Winter, 1996). This 'integrative view' is consistent with McClelland's (1951) longstanding argument that at least three types of variables are necessary to explain personality: motives, schemas *and* traits. McClelland and colleagues' (McClelland et al., 1989; Weinberger and McClelland, 1990) referred to the first two levels as emotion-driven 'implicit motives' and cognition-driven 'explicit motives' respectively. McClelland's (1985) influential theory of human motivation identified three implicit motives: need for achievement (*n*Ach), need for affiliation (*n*Aff), and need for power (*n*Pow). Implicit motives are relatively *unconscious*, while explicit motives (e.g. personal goals) and traits (e.g. extraversion, neuroticism, conscientiousness, agreeableness, openness) are relatively *conscious*. As Emmons (1991) argued, trying to predict health and well-being on the basis of one level of personality (e.g. traits) alone may create an unnecessary 'handicap' for the practitioner or researcher and, consequently, lead to a serious underestimation of the role of personality in the stressor–strain relationship. Indeed, a review of the literature on personality and health (Wiebe and Smith, 1997) called for a more 'comprehensive' use of the field of personality psychology in future research.

The second problem is that there are two domains that together define personality psychology as a discipline: (1) the nomothetic or 'dispositional' approach (i.e. individual differences in global personality dimensions), and (2) the idiographic approach (i.e. the organization and interaction of personality elements – e.g. motives and traits – within the person) (Winter, 1996). Epstein (1994) argued that the nomothetic approach is of limited use for understanding how people function and that it is necessary to examine the patterning and interaction of personality at the individual level (idiographic approach) for this purpose.

The focus of this chapter is the interplay of *implicit* motives (*n*Ach, *n*Aff, *n*Pow) with traits, given that such motives (1) are more enduring and stable than explicit motives, (2) have proven utility in the long-term prediction of behaviour outside the laboratory in both the health domain and the organizational domain (McClelland, 1979; McClelland and Boyatzis, 1982), and (3) are based on an affective, biologically based system, suggesting an underlying relationship to physiological functioning and affective experience, thus making them directly relevant to stress. Implicit motives are assessed using the projective, Thematic Apperception Test (TAT) or 'picture-story exercise' (see Smith, 1992).

While past research has considered the combined/interactive effect of various implicit motives (see, e.g. Jemmott et al., 1990; Jemmott and McClelland, 1989; McClelland, 1979, 1992; McClelland et al., 1982; McClelland, Floor et al., 1980, 1985; McClelland and

Jemmott, 1980; McClelland et al., 1985), the combined/interactive effect of implicit motives *with* traits in the stressor–strain relationship has not been considered. Thorne (1995) argued that the dynamic interplay among multiple levels of personality has been neglected in past research due to over-attention to between-person differences in traits. Elliot and Sheldon (1997) similarly noted that much of the research on personality and health has been conducted within constructs, with little effort to forge a link between them. Neglect of the idiographic domain of personality psychology in the occupational stress literature may essentially mean that we only have 'half the picture' (or perhaps even an inaccurate one) of the role of personality in occupational stress and strain. If this is the case, then current thinking in regard to intervention and prevention may be flawed and our ability to reduce occupational stress and strain severely limited. Implicit motives are briefly described below, before considering how motives and traits might combine or interact to produce adaptive and maladaptive managerial styles.

The 'big three' motives

The achievement motive (nAch)
People who score high on *n*Ach are concerned with doing better than other people, doing better themselves, i.e. improving personal performance, or doing things in a better way, e.g. more efficiently (McClelland, 1993, 1985). They favour moderate task difficulty, prefer to assume personal responsibility for performance, and only derive satisfaction from doing better if they feel personally responsible for the performance outcome (Koestner et al., 1991; McClelland, 1993; McClelland and Koestner, 1992). They eagerly seek quantitative feedback (Koestner et al., 1991; McClelland, 1993; Stahl, 1986) and generally perform better when such feedback is readily available (McClelland, 1993; McClelland and Koestner, 1992). McClelland (1993) noted that high *n*Ach does not adequately prepare the person for leading or managing other people. For instance, a focus on personal performance is likely to be maladaptive in a managerial leadership environment where it is important to delegate in order to manage workload and instil a sense of ownership of organizational goals. In a large organization, the achievement-motivated person is more likely to succeed as an 'individual contributor' than as a leader (McClelland and Boyatzis, 1982). Those who score high on *n*Ach are perhaps better suited to entrepreneurship, which is typically characterized by innovation (i.e. doing things in a better way), moderate risk, personal responsibility for performance, and quantitative feedback (McClelland, 1987; McClelland and Koestner, 1992; Winter and Carlson, 1988). Indeed, there is evidence to suggest that achievement-motivated people are more likely to enter and succeed in small business (McClelland, 1987; McClelland and Koestner, 1992). They also perform well as salespeople, presumably because sales is similar to small business in that the key people do most of the work themselves (McClelland, 1987).

The affiliation motive (nAff)
People who score high on *n*Aff are concerned with establishing, maintaining or restoring a positive affective relationship with other people (McClelland, 1985). They are cooperative and caring, and interact with other people more frequently, although their relationship quality is not necessarily superior (Koestner and McClelland, 1992). That is, *n*Aff does not necessarily translate into popularity or social confidence; those who score high

on *n*Aff are only sociable in the presence of 'safe' people who are similar to themselves and/or reciprocate their friendliness (Winter and Carlson, 1988). In the presence of people who are dissimilar and do not reciprocate, they feel ill at ease and present as defensive and prickly (Winter and Carlson, 1988). As such, *n*Aff may be better described as a measure of affiliative anxiety or 'fear of rejection' (Koestner and McClelland, 1992).

Managers who score high on *n*Aff may be uncomfortable with the need to be authoritative and 'take charge', dictated by their role. For instance, they are likely to avoid conflict or decision making that could impinge on their likeability and, as such, may be reluctant to give negative feedback or reprimand staff for inappropriate behaviour (McClelland, 1985). To the extent that they are eager to please those around them, they may be unable to deal with staff objectively, and may manage on the basis of subjective criteria, e.g. favouritism (Stahl, 1986).

The power motive (nPow)

People who score high on *n*Pow are concerned with establishing, maintaining or restoring control and influence (Winter, 1992b). Although not especially popular, they raise morale among those around them and are skilled at drawing out and influencing other people in a group setting (Winter, 1992a). They strive to enhance their visibility wherever possible, and typically befriend people of lower status who are not in a position to compete with them for power (McClelland, 1975; Winter, 1992a). People who score high on *n*Pow are attracted to jobs such as management that provide legitimate scope for control and influence (Winter, 1992a). For instance, a longitudinal study (Jenkins, 1994) found that high *n*Pow, assessed in women during their final year of college, was associated with a greater tendency to seek, enter and remain in power-related jobs. In addition, high *n*Pow predicted greater career progression among those in power-related jobs at 14-year follow-up.

Activity inhibition, or self-restraint, is thought to moderate the expression of *n*Pow in behaviour (Jemmott, 1987) and is measured by counting the frequency of the word 'not' in the picture-story exercise (McClelland and Boyatzis, 1982). People who score high on *n*Pow and low on activity inhibition are impulsive and selfish and use power for the purpose of self-gain, e.g. dominance or superiority ('personalized' power), whereas people who score high on *n*Pow and high on activity inhibition are assertive and hard driving but less self-indulgent and use power for the purpose of group or organizational gain ('socialized' power) (Jemmott, 1987; Stahl, 1986; Winter and Carlson, 1988).

McClelland (1975) hypothesized that a Leadership Motive Syndrome (LMS) consisting of high *n*Pow, high activity inhibition and low *n*Aff should predict managerial effectiveness because: (a) high *n*Pow should predict control and influence behaviour, which is necessary to secure follower commitment, respect and trust; (b) high *n*Pow should predict satisfaction from control and influence, which is necessary to sustain leadership behaviour over time; (c) the combination of high *n*Pow and high activity inhibition should predict socialized rather than personalized power; and (d) low *n*Aff should predict assertiveness and independence, enabling tough decision making without undue concern about its impact on staff. However, the relationship between LMS and managerial effectiveness would appear to apply to upper-level, non-technical management only. For example, McClelland and Boyatzis (1982) found that LMS was related to upper-level, non-technical managerial success at 8- and 16-year follow-up, whereas *n*Ach was related lower-level, non-technical managerial success, presumably because the ability to lead and manage other people was less important at this level than the manager's individual contribution. Furthermore, LMS was unrelated to technical managerial success, most likely because leadership ability was less important than technical ability (e.g. engineering) for this group. When considering the relationship between *n*Pow and managerial effectiveness, it is important to distinguish between those who score high on *n*Pow but low on *n*Aff (dominant *n*Pow) versus those who score high on *n*Pow but higher on *n*Aff (ambivalent *n*Pow); only dominant *n*Pow has been linked with managerial effectiveness (McClelland, 1992).

It is noteworthy that outside the organizational behaviour literature LMS, in this context referred to as 'Inhibited Power Motive Syndrome' (IPMS), has been linked with high blood pressure, hypertension and self-reported illness (e.g. McClelland and Jemmott, 1980). Thus an important question is whether the relationship between IPMS and strain is context-specific. That is, to the extent that IPMS is a 'good fit' for the managerial environment, as per the P–E fit theory of occupational stress, it should predict lower stress and, correspondingly, a positive outcome for health and well-being. McClelland (1979) himself conceded that power motivation that is successfully expressed and rewarded may lead to better adjustment. Indeed, Stahl et al. (1986) found that *n*Pow was negatively correlated with occupational stress and strain among managers. Notably, however, this study focused on *n*Pow rather than IPMS.

The expression of motives through goals and traits
While there is considerable research on the independent role of individual differences in traits and, to a lesser extent, motives in the stressor–strain relationship (nomothetic approach), their combined or interactive effect within the person (idiographic approach) has not been considered. Thus it is possible that the role of personality in stress and strain has been seriously underestimated in past research.

Historically, optimal health and well-being were thought to arise from a personality system that was brought together or 'integrated' into a harmonious whole via the service of a common goal or purpose (see Sheldon and Kasser, 1995). Personality was represented as a top–down hierarchical control structure, ranging from a 'broad and abstract level' (e.g. unconscious needs) to a 'narrow and concrete level' (e.g. goals, traits) (Emmons et al., Sheldon, 1993; Sheldon and Kasser, 1995). The importance of 'personality integration' is evident in behavioural, cognitive and psychodynamic theory, all of which emphasize the need to maintain consistency within the self to avoid inner conflict and promote inner strength (Emmons, 1986; Emmons and King, 1988; Emmons et al., 1993). Emmons (1986) described conflict in the personality system as a 'chronic stressful event'. Indeed, inner conflict has been linked with a range of symptomatology including anxiety, confusion, depression, fatigue, hostility, social dysfunction, tension and uncertainty, as well as a host of physical symptoms (see Emmons and King, 1988; Emmons et al., 1993). In addition to the direct effect of personality integration on emotional stress and health, the 'inner strength' of integrated people may mean that they are better able to manage external stress in the environment (Sheldon and Kasser, 1995). Thus personality integration may also act as a buffer in the stressor–strain relationship. However, despite its significance for health and well-being, personality integration has received only modest attention in the modern empirical literature (Sheldon and Kasser, 1995).

Winter and Stewart (1995) highlighted the need to examine within- and between-level personality conflict in order to better explain and understand the relationship between personality and health. In the context of contemporary personality theory, personality integration can be defined with reference to the congruence of motives, cognitions (personal goals) and traits. Indeed, recent evidence from the personal goals literature (Brunstein et al., 1998; Hofer and Chasiotis, 2003; Kehr, 2004; Schultheiss and Brunstein, 1999; Sheldon and Elliot, 1998, 1999; Sheldon and Kasser, 1995) has suggested that personality integration (e.g. motive–goal congruence) is positively related to adjustment: 'That the symptoms of psychopathology may be explained, at a motivational level, as the consequences of disordered self-regulation and goal guidance is a vaguely articulated view that is slowly gaining popularity' (Karoly, 1999: 278).

Motive–trait congruence has received less attention in the literature, although preliminary research has suggested that the combined/interactive effect of motives and traits is an important predictor of behaviour. For example, Winter (1996) argued that traits represent the 'stylistic context' for the expression of motives and identified introversion–extraversion as a potential moderator of the expression of *n*Aff and *n*Pow in behaviour. Winter (1996) distinguished between *n*Aff, friendship as a goal, and extraversion, friendliness as an interpersonal style, and argued that the combination of high *n*Aff with low extraversion (strong desire for friendship; apprehensive and uncomfortable around people) would give rise to conflicted motive expression, while the combination of high *n*Aff with high extraversion (strong desire for friendship; socially confident and at ease around people) would give rise to unconflicted motive expression. Winter (1996) similarly distinguished between high *n*Pow–low extraversion (strong desire for control/influence; passive, quiet, reserved and shy) as a predictor of conflicted motive expression, and high *n*Pow–high extraversion (strong desire for control/influence; active, assertive, lively and sociable) as a predictor of unconflicted motive expression. In short, he argued that extraversion – as a general dimension of sociability – should facilitate the expression of the affiliation and power motives.

In an elaboration of this hypothesis, Winter et al. (1998) proposed that traits represent individual differences in 'psychophysiological mechanisms' (e.g. reactivity, thresholds and preferred levels of arousal, variability, tolerance of stimuli, perseveration and oscillation) that channel the expression of motives and goal-directed behaviour throughout the life course. Based on a longitudinal study of women, Winter and colleagues found that high *n*Aff–high extraversion was positively related to volunteer work and work–family role combination, while high *n*Aff–low extraversion demonstrated the opposite pattern of association. In addition, high *n*Aff–low extraversion was positively related to relationship difficulty/dissatisfaction and divorce, while high *n*Aff–high extraversion was associated with relationship longevity. In relation to *n*Pow and extraversion, Winter and colleagues found that high *n*Pow–high extraversion and high *n*Pow–low extraversion were positively and negatively related to impact career involvement respectively. Furthermore, those characterized by high *n*Pow with high extraversion emphasized the importance of other people at work, while those characterized by high *n*Pow with low extraversion did not. Winter and colleagues concluded that extraversion facilitated unconflicted expression of *n*Aff and *n*Pow in the career and relationship domain over time, while introversion deflected *n*Aff and *n*Pow away from motive-congruent goals and/or thwarted the attainment of such goals.

While a personality integration perspective would argue that unconflicted motive expression should lead to a generally adaptive outcome, in the current work it is argued that unconflicted motive expression may give rise to a negative or positive outcome, depending on the degree of fit between the motive and the managerial environment. For example, based on the description of high *n*Aff managers provided above, unconflicted expression of this motive (high *n*Aff–high extraversion) might be expected to give rise to a maladaptive managerial style and, as a result, higher occupational stress and strain. In this way, Winter and colleagues' channelling hypothesis (the expression of motives is channelled by traits) is extended by integrating it with a P–E fit approach to occupational stress and strain.

Although Winter and colleagues did not consider *n*Ach in their work, the trait of conscientiousness (achievement striving, competence, deliberation, dutifulness, order, self-discipline) should facilitate the expression of this motive (strong desire to 'do better'); thus the combined effect of *n*Ach and conscientiousness on managerial style is also considered in the current work. Neuroticism could arguably moderate the expression of all three motives, and agreeableness could perhaps moderate the expression of *n*Aff and *n*Pow; however, the link between these traits and unconflicted versus conflicted motive expression is less clear cut. Thus the focus of the current work is the combined/interactive effect of the 'big three' motives with conscientiousness (*n*Ach) and extraversion (*n*Aff, *n*Pow), rather than with all 'big five' traits (i.e. extraversion, neuroticism, conscientiousness, agreeableness, openness).

A motive–trait taxonomy for predicting adaptive and maladaptive managerial styles is presented below. Managerial styles resulting from various 'high–low' motive–trait combinations are described in terms of their impact on the skills identified in Hogan and Warrenfeltz's (2003) model of managerial competencies, i.e. intrapersonal skills, interpersonal skills, business skills, leadership skills. While all maladaptive styles are likely to be associated with a deficit in intrapersonal skills to some extent, these skills are particularly relevant to high *n*Ach and high *n*Aff types, as these styles are associated with unrealistic goals that need to be recognized and regulated (see the section on rational emotive behaviour therapy, below, for more detail).

A motive–trait taxonomy of adaptive and maladaptive managerial styles

The combined/interactive effect of *n*Ach and conscientiousness on managerial style is considered in Table 21.1. Unconflicted expression of the achievement motive (high *n*Ach–high conscientiousness) is expected to give rise to a maladaptive managerial style and hence a negative outcome for health and well-being. On the positive side, high *n*Ach–high conscientiousness managers are ambitious, focused, project-driven and results-oriented. On the negative side, they have a strong need to outperform other people or 'win', and are thus concerned with individual (as opposed to team or organizational) performance. The high *n*Ach–high conscientiousness manager is a 'perfectionist' and may be reluctant to give up control, preferring to micro-manage rather than to delegate. This inability to let go is likely to alienate staff (who may feel that the manager does not have any confidence in them) and limit their professional development. Furthermore, the high *n*Ach–high conscientiousness manager's 'all work and no play attitude' may prevent people from seeing his or her 'human side', leading to isolation and a strained relationship with staff. Due to their self-imposed drive for perfection and self-sufficiency, high

Table 21.1   Managerial styles as a function of nAch *and conscientiousness*

	High conscientiousness	Low conscientiousness
	Unconflicted motive expression	*Conflicted motive expression*
High nAch	• Ambitious and production-minded but concerned with individual (as opposed to team) performance • Reluctant to give up control (prefer to 'micro-manage' rather than to delegate) • Tendency to get 'bogged down' in detail and workload • Find it difficult to deliver work on time • Stress-prone and ineffective due to a self-imposed drive for perfection and self-sufficiency	• Would like to do everything personally, but may lack the capacity (e.g. focus, organization) to give tasks the attention they need or see them through to completion • Prone to procrastination • Unreliable and ineffective
Low nAch	• Willing to delegate authority and responsibility and share workload • Organized • Hardworking • Dependable and effective	• Willing to delegate authority and responsibility and share workload • Tendency to rely on other people to take charge and follow through • Prone to 'social loafing'

nAch–high conscientiousness managers may get 'bogged down' in detail and excessive workload and, as a result, may find it difficult to deliver work on time. As a consequence, high nAch–high conscientiousness managers are likely to be stress-prone and ineffective. In terms of Hogan and Warrenfeltz's (2003) managerial competencies, high nAch–high conscientiousness managers are likely to be high on business skills but low on intrapersonal and leadership skills and some interpersonal skills (e.g. cooperating, listening, providing encouragement and support). Conflicted expression of the achievement motive (high nAch–low conscientiousness) is also expected to lead to a poor outcome in a managerial leadership context. For example, as with the previous combination, high nAch–low conscientiousness managers are characterized by a reluctance to delegate. However, in this case, low conscientiousness may mean that although they would like to do everything themselves, they may lack the capability (e.g. focus, organization) to give tasks the attention they need and/or see them through to completion, amounting to an unreliable and ineffective managerial style. Such managers may be prone to procrastination. High nAch–low conscientiousness managers lack intrapersonal and leadership skills, as well as some business/management skills (e.g. following up, organizing, planning and scheduling) and interpersonal skills (see high nAch–high conscientiousness). In contrast, the combination of low nAch with high conscientiousness should predict a willingness to delegate and share workload as necessary, coupled with a hardworking and reliable managerial style. Finally, the combination of low nAch with low conscientiousness

Table 21.2   Managerial styles as a function of n*Aff and extraversion*

	High extraversion	Low extraversion
	Unconflicted motive expression	*Conflicted motive expression*
High *n*Aff	• Strong desire to be accepted/liked • Eager to please • Interpersonally adept and well regarded, but may struggle to act independently • Unable to deal with staff objectively; may award precedence to friendship over duty as manager (e.g. reluctant to give negative feedback and/or reprimand inappropriate behaviour) • Likely to manage on the basis of subjective criteria, e.g. favouritism • Seen as 'soft' and easily exploited • On good terms with staff but ineffective as a leader	• Strong desire to be accepted/ liked • Eager to please • Ill at ease around staff; may feel isolated and rejected • Unable to secure the respect and trust of staff • Likely to avoid conflict or decision making that could impinge on popularity; may lack conviction and struggle with assertiveness • Reluctant to monitor and discipline staff • Submissive and timid • Passive and ineffective as a leader
Low *n*Aff	• Interpersonally adept and well regarded, but not overly dependent • Able to carry out difficult decision making without undue concern about its impact on staff • Willing to monitor and discipline staff and should execute this task effectively • Approachable and personable, but fair and objective at the same time	• Comfortable and effective working alone, but may be ill at ease in a team-based environment • Willing to monitor and discipline staff but may lack the social sensitivity and tact needed to execute this task effectively • Could alienate staff or engender resentment

is characterized by a willingness to delegate and share workload, but a tendency to rely on other people to take charge and follow through. Such managers are low in business/management skills.

As shown in Table 21.2, high extraversion should see high *n*Aff managers successfully attain their goal of establishing a positive affective relationship with their staff (unconflicted motive expression). As a result, however, high *n*Aff–high extraversion managers may be unable to act decisively or independently, becoming too close to their subordinates to manage and lead them objectively. High *n*Aff–high extraversion managers are likely to sacrifice their authority for their need to please, awarding precedence to friendship over their duty as managers. For instance, such managers may be reluctant to provide negative feedback or reprimand inappropriate behaviour, preferring to manage on the basis of subjective criteria (e.g. favouritism). Subordinates may see such managers as 'soft' and easily exploited, a reputation that is likely to be disastrous in the managerial leadership environment where the ability to control and influence other people is essential for effectiveness. In terms of Hogan and Warrenfeltz's (2003) model, high *n*Aff–high extraversion managers lack intrapersonal skills and leadership skills. In Table 21.2, conflicted motive expression is represented by the combination of high *n*Aff with low extraversion. Like high *n*Aff–high extraversion managers, high *n*Aff–low extraversion managers are characterized by a strong desire to be accepted/liked and are eager to please. However, the high *n*Aff–low extraversion manager may be ill at ease with staff, making it difficult to secure their respect and trust. Compounded by a sense of isolation and rejection, he or she is likely to struggle with assertiveness and may avoid confrontation or decision making that could impinge on his or her popularity. In addition, the high *n*Aff–low extraversion manager may be reluctant to monitor and discipline staff, translating into a passive and ineffective managerial style. Like high *n*Aff–high extraversion managers, these managers are low in intrapersonal and leadership skills. In addition, these managers also lack the interpersonal skills needed to carry out their role. In contrast, the combination of low *n*Aff with high extraversion should see the manager execute his or her role effectively (this combination is similar to high *n*Pow–high extraversion; see below). Low *n*Aff–high extraversion managers are likely to be interpersonally adept and well regarded, but not overly dependent and should therefore be able to carry out difficult decision making without undue concern about its impact on staff. Such managers should have no problem with the need to monitor and discipline staff, presenting as approachable and personable, but fair and objective at the same time. Finally, the low *n*Aff–low extraversion manager is predominantly characterized by poor interpersonal skills. He or she is likely to be a 'loner' and may be more comfortable working independently than in a team-based environment. While low *n*Aff–low extraversion managers are unlikely to feel conflicted about monitoring and disciplining staff, they may lack the social sensitivity and tact needed to execute this task effectively, and their impersonal approach may alienate staff or engender resentment. Without the confidence of their subordinates, they are unlikely to lead successfully.

In contrast to unconflicted expression of the achievement and affiliation motives, unconflicted expression of the power motive should give rise to an adaptive managerial style (see Table 21.3). For example, high extraversion should see high *n*Pow managers realize their desire to control and influence, through the expression of a confident and charismatic interpersonal style. High *n*Pow–high extraversion managers are likely to be interpersonally adept and well regarded, and skilled at acquiring status and building teamwork. They should easily motivate those around them, but should utilize team morale as a vehicle for leadership rather than for friendship. In Table 21.3, conflicted motive expression is represented by the combination of high *n*Pow with low extraversion. This combination is likely to lead to stress and strain, in that the manager has a strong desire to lead but does not have the social confidence and/or competence to realize this goal. These managers are low in interpersonal skills. Conversely, the low *n*Pow–high extraversion manager may be reluctant to lead, even though he or she has the communication and social skills to execute this role effectively. These managers lack the leadership skills needed to complement their strong interpersonal skills. Finally, the low *n*Pow–low extraversion manager (similar to the high *n*Aff–low extraversion manager described above) is characterized by a lack of influence ability. Such managers lack both the interpersonal skills and the leadership skills needed to lead successfully. They are likely to be as hesitant and submissive, amounting to a passive and ineffective managerial style.

Table 21.3   Managerial styles as a function of nPow *and extraversion*

	High extraversion	Low extraversion
	Unconflicted motive expression	*Conflicted motive expression*
High nPow	• Strong desire to lead • Confident and charismatic interpersonal style; ability to inspire • Interpersonally adept and well regarded • Should utilize staff morale as a vehicle for leadership rather than for friendship • Dynamic and effective leader	• Strong desire to lead • May lack the social confidence and competence to be effective as a leader
Low nPow	• Reluctant to lead but has the interpersonal skills to do so effectively	• No desire to lead • Ill at ease around staff; may struggle with assertiveness • Hesitant and submissive • Passive and ineffective as a leader

Note: In considering the unconflicted expression of the power motive, it will also be important to consider activity inhibition and *n*Aff (see section on Leadership Motive Syndrome above).

The 12 managerial styles identified above are likely to vary in their prevalence and some styles may be more problematic for the organization than others. For instance, to the extent that people who score high on *n*Pow are attracted to managerial jobs (Jenkins, 1994; Winter, 1992a), high *n*Pow types may be more prevalent than low *n*Pow types. However, the low *n*Pow–low extraversion manager may be more difficult to deal with than the high *n*Pow–low extraversion manager. While the high *n*Pow–low extraversion manager is likely to benefit from assertiveness and social skills training, the low *n*Pow–low extraversion manager may struggle to stay motivated, even with appropriate behavioural therapy. The managerial styles associated with low *n*Ach–high conscientiousness, low *n*Aff–high extraversion and high *n*Pow–high extraversion are relatively adaptive, while the styles associated with the remaining 9 motive–trait combinations are more or less maladaptive. A general strategy for addressing maladaptive managerial styles through intervention (e.g. stress education, stress management training) and prevention (e.g. personnel selection, job assignment) is outlined below, along with more specific strategies tailored to particular managerial styles.

Intervention: managing maladaptive managerial styles
Often, the organization simply does not know what to do with dysfunctional managers: a 'problem' individual may be transferred around the organization or gradually 'phased out' through a dismissal settlement, with a single case potentially dragging on for several years (Schreurs et al., 1996). Furthermore, maladaptive managerial styles are usually evident to the manager's peers and subordinates, adding to the pressure of the situation (Wheatley, 2000). The 12 managerial styles identified above are helpful in the sense of enabling risk assessment and identifying distressed managers who can then be provided with appropriate assistance and support. Within this 'employee-centred' approach to stress management, the aim is to develop managers who can meet the needs of their job

by helping them to understand and manage their 'maladaptive' styles. Stress intervention should include stress education coupled with specific stress management training, with the aim of helping managers learn about their problem behaviour, its source, and strategies for dealing with it (Murphy, 1996; Vrugt, 1996).

Stress education
The first step is promoting awareness and recognition of maladaptive managerial styles. Managers should be provided with interactive feedback about their strengths and weaknesses (e.g. preferences, skills), based on a detailed personality evaluation (e.g. picture-story exercise, NEO-Personality Inventory (Costa and McCrae, 1985)) and an in-depth interview (e.g. work history), from a trained counsellor or consultant (Quick et al., 1996). Multi-source or 360-degree feedback, which can be used to assess the impact of the manager's behaviour on other people in the organization (Diedrich, 1996), may also be a useful tool for this purpose. In 360-degree feedback, ratings of the manager's behaviour (in terms of key competencies, managerial style and organizational climate) are collected from the manager's supervisors, peers and direct reports, thus providing a complete and representative assessment of different aspects of the manager's performance (Day, 2000; Diedrich, 1996). Ratings are usually aggregated and may be collected from up to as many as 15 people (Orenstein, 2006). Dominant themes are identified, and the 360-degree feedback ratings may be compared with the manager's self-ratings to determine whether the results are more positive from the perspective of the manager (Diedrich, 1996). Orenstein (2006) noted that 360-degree feedback can be 'revelatory' to managers, who may be completely oblivious to their maladaptive behaviour. Putting the feedback 'out there' can help legitimize the fact that the problem behaviour is occurring, thus raising the manager's awareness and accountability (Day, 2000). In addition, 360-degree feedback may serve as a tool for 'validating' the manager's 'style', as conveyed in the results of the personality evaluation. For instance, the phrase 'low *n*Pow–low extraversion style' is likely to sound abstract to most managers, but helping managers to see how their motives and traits interact to affect what they do (and what they don't do) by drawing on concrete behaviour(s) reflected in 360-degree assessment should improve their understanding of their managerial style.

Stress management training
After conducting a detailed personality evaluation, in-depth interviewing and the 360-degree feedback process, the next step is to use the information gleaned from the problem analysis to develop an action plan for behavioural change. This may include setting short-term goals of increasing difficulty to target maladaptive behaviour(s) and a schedule for addressing these goals through stress management training (Vrugt, 1996).

Rational emotive behaviour therapy (REBT)   In the past, stress management intervention has tended to be generic (Murphy, 1996), rather than personality-oriented. A personality-oriented approach for modifying maladaptive behaviour in high *n*Ach and high *n*Aff managers might be to modify irrational thinking (e.g. 'I must do everything myself, otherwise it won't be done properly') or unrealistic goals (e.g. 'I must be liked by all my subordinates') through rational emotive behavior therapy (REBT); (Murphy, 1996; Semmer, 1996). In terms of Hogan and Warrenfeltz's (2003) model of managerial competencies, REBT should increase self-awareness and self-regulation or 'intrapersonal skills'. The goal of REBT is to increase the person's ability to engage in critical and psychologically sophisticated reasoning, thus enabling them to identify, challenge and replace unreasonable, performance-inhibiting goals/thinking (Ellis, 1994 cited in Sherin and Caiger, 2004). For instance, during this process, absolute thinking (e.g. 'I must . . .') may be converted to preferential thinking ('I prefer . . .') (Sherin and Caiger, 2004). The focus for change is the person's implicit and explicit belief system and this is altered by working through the 'ABCDE' model: A = Activating event, B = Belief, C = Consequence, D = Dispute, and E = Effective outlook (Sherin and Caiger, 2004). REBT has had some success in the organizational arena, including executive and managerial training (see Sherin and Caiger, 2004 for a review).

Skills training   REBT may be useful in helping high *n*Ach managers to let go of their need to be 'in control'. In addition, such managers should be encouraged to handle their workload more effectively by prioritizing tasks, delegating less difficult or less important tasks to their subordinates, and reaching out to peers and subordinates for advice and support rather than 'going it alone'. In this regard, they are likely to benefit from training in group and team management or 'person-orientated management', for instance getting the most out of their staff, developing goals for the team rather than for themselves, and developing and rewarding staff. Low-conscientiousness managers (high *n*Ach–low conscientiousness, low *n*Ach–low conscientiousness) should benefit from general management training, including organization, planning and time management skills. High *n*Aff and low *n*Pow managers need to focus on their personal impact, and should benefit from training in assertiveness (e.g. conveying what is expected, giving direct feedback, handling subordinates who have a discipline or performance problem), and high *n*Ach, high *n*Aff and low *n*Pow managers are likely to benefit from leadership training. In addition, low extraversion types (high *n*Aff–low extraversion, low *n*Aff–low extraversion, high *n*Pow–low extraversion, low *n*Pow–low extraversion) may benefit from communication and social skills training (e.g. active listening, building consensus, conflict resolution, relating to people effectively). Notably, however, interpersonal skills may be more difficult to train than leadership skills (Hogan and Kaiser, 2005).

The results of a 'problem analysis' might be confronting for the dysfunctional manager to say the least, and some managers may prefer the one-to-one, personalized nature of executive coaching to management and leadership training. An executive coach might be beneficial in assisting the manager to digest the feedback and navigate the behaviour change process (Hall et al., 1999). As such, executive coaching, described in more detail below, may increase the likelihood of sustained behaviour change (Ducharme, 2004).

Executive coaching   Executive coaching (EC) can be defined as a formal, ongoing, relationship between a manager who has a performance problem requiring behaviour change and a coach (or consultant) who has expertise in personal behaviour change and management/leadership effectiveness (Anderson, 2002; Kampa and White, 2002; Orenstein, 2006; Quick and Macik-Frey, 2004). The coaching process is structured, and may involve data gathering, needs analysis, goal setting, coaching, measuring and reporting results, and the transition to long-term development planning (Berman and Bradt, 2006). Several clinical models of behaviour change have been adapted for the purpose of executive coaching including cognitive–behavioural models (Ducharme, 2004; Sherin and Caiger,

2004) and psychodynamic models (Kilburg, 2004). A review of the literature on different types of executive coaching is beyond the scope of this chapter; thus the focus here is on general (rather than specialized) developmental coaching.

Developmental coaching is typically recommended when the manager has self-limiting personality characteristics (i.e. a maladaptive style) but none the less has the potential to offer substantial benefit to the organization (Berman and Bradt, 2006). For instance, the high *n*Ach–high conscientiousness manager is highly effective as an individual contributor but is ineffective as a leader. Berman and Bradt (2006) noted that highly successful people often advance in an organization based on their business savvy or technical competence only to discover that they lack the 'soft side' (e.g. interpersonal) skills needed to succeed at a more senior level.

As a one-to-one intervention, developmental coaching may include personal counselling and/or practical advice (Anderson, 2002). The aim is to 'turn around' dysfunctional managers by identifying and modifying the impact of their style on individual, team and organizational performance (Diedrich, 1996). Adaptive managerial behaviour is strategically developed by using targeted behavioural coaching to (a) modify specific behaviour(s) (e.g. non-assertiveness) and (b) develop new behaviour(s) (e.g. delegation) that enhance or improve the person's managerial and leadership skills (Kampa and White, 2002; Orenstein, 2006; Sherin and Caiger, 2004; Stern, 2004). Part of this process may involve helping the manager to 'internalize' personal insight into his or her maladaptive behaviour (Brotman et al., 1998). The learning and development process is incremental, and the expected outcome is sustained change in the targeted behaviour(s) that is maintained under stress (Berman and Bradt, 2006; Brotman et al., 1998; Ducharme, 2004; Wasylyshyn, 2003). The ultimate end point is increased individual and organizational performance (Kampa and White, 2002).

EC may involve a fixed-term relationship focused on a few, relatively narrow goals or a longer-term relationship focused on multiple, complex goals (Smither et al., 2003). In addition to behaviour change, common goals of EC include increasing or improving flexibility (e.g. behavioural and emotional range), psychological and social awareness, self-reflection, stress management skills and tolerance (Berman and Bradt, 2006; Kilburg, 1996). Although EC is likely to require psychological insight on the part of the coach, it can be distinguished from psychotherapy on the basis that (a) it is usually short-term and issue-focused, and therefore does not allow for the development of a therapeutic alliance, and (b) the coach may offer advice, information and guidance that is consistent with his or her understanding of the manager within the organizational setting (Levinson, 1996).

Feldman and Lankau (2005) noted that despite a dramatic increase in the use of EC as an intervention and a growing practitioner literature on the topic, the empirical and theoretical literature has lagged behind. Research to date is generally supportive of EC. For instance, one survey (Wasylyshyn, 2003) found that over 75 per cent of managers who had received EC rated the experience favourably. In addition, more than 50 per cent of those surveyed rated their 'sustainability level' at between 6 and 8 on a 1–10 scale (where 10 = higher sustainability). Smither et al. (2003) found that managers who worked with an executive coach were more likely to set specific (versus vague) goals than other managers and improved more in their 360-degree feedback ratings than other managers. Bush (2005) found that the following variables contributed to the perceived effectiveness of EC: commitment and motivation, good client–coach rapport, inclusion of other people (e.g. supervisor) in the coaching process, structure/development focus, working with a 'seasoned coach' who can provide a practical contribution, and results that benefit the client. Effectiveness was found to be the shared responsibility of the client (commitment, motivation, openness, willingness), the coach (credibility, expertise, support) and the organization (development and learning culture, sponsorship) (Bush, 2005). Luebbe (2005) found that trust was rated as the most important coach attribute among managers and coaching and HR professionals alike. Other important attributes included the coach's ability to (1) extract and relay valuable themes from assessment data, (2) give candid, direct feedback, (3) foster client independence through self-awareness and sustained behaviour change, and (4) achieve buy-in from HR professionals within the organization. Coaching was perceived as a useful intervention when (a) the client and coach were appropriately matched (e.g. compatibility) and (b) the organization communicated the intent, philosophy and purpose of the coaching intervention.

In addition to its potential to achieve sustained behaviour change, EC may be more effective than other types of intervention (e.g. training) in ensuring that managers do not regress back to their old pattern or 'style' of behaviour (Ducharme, 2004). Olivero et al., (1997) argued that EC should facilitate the transfer of training. In support of this hypothesis, they found that EC increased productivity by 88 per cent, a significantly greater gain than training alone. The major advantage of EC is its integrative, developmental approach (assessment, challenge, support); the major disadvantage is its hefty price tag, e.g. from $1500 per day to $100 000+ for a multi-year programme for a single manager (Day, 2000). The return on financial investment in EC has not been addressed in the literature to date. A further issue is the need to establish a universal code of practice and set of coaching competencies within the coaching community (Luebbe, 2005).

Evaluating the behaviour change process
Managers should monitor and record their behaviour (e.g. in a diary) over the course of the behaviour change process, including the factors that trigger stress and unwanted behaviour, and evaluate their progress against set goals (Vrugt, 1996). In addition, they should be given appropriate feedback and reinforcement to ensure that maladaptive behaviour is effectively regulated, modified and maintained over time (Vrugt, 1996). The final step is to identify the factors that cause 'setbacks' and develop strategies for tackling these factors (Vrugt, 1996). Objective behavioural data are often used as an index of behaviour change (Ducharme, 2004) and ongoing 360-degree feedback ratings could be used to track behaviour change and quantify performance improvement over time (Smither et al., 2003).

Quick et al. (1996) described management development as an ongoing process of learning, growth and self-improvement. While traditional management development has focused on the acquisition and mastery of various technical skills, a critical element of development in today's managerial environment may be accepting long-term responsibility for self-change and development (Quick et al., 1996).

What do we do when intervention fails?
For any intervention initiative to be effective, the manager must be (a) willing to accept feedback as relevant and useful, (b) open to change, and (c) realistic and resilient in the change process (Day, 2000). As Day (2000) pointed out, the path to behaviour change is

rarely an easy one, and a considerable amount of energy and time is needed if the change is to be permanently embedded in the manager's behavioural repertoire. Some managers may resist (or even resent) intervention, thus preventing them from learning from past 'mistakes' and adapting their behaviour (Goldberg, 2005; Stevens, 2005). Hogan and Kaiser (2005: 178) noted that '[e]very organization has its share of bad managers' but when is it futile to continue to employ them? One answer to this question is to introduce a programme for managing underperformance with a set timeline (e.g. six month 'reappraisal') for performance improvement. The manager is effectively counselled and put 'on notice'. The aforementioned intervention strategies would be implemented during this period and, at the conclusion of the intervention period, the manager's performance would be assessed for improvement against key performance indicators (KPIs), including competencies and 360-degree feedback ratings. If the manager was unable to meet the benchmark for performance after this period, then his or her position would be re-evaluated, with the strong possibility of dismissal. As Wasylyshyn (2003) cautioned, it is futile for an organization to waste energy and time on a 'rescue fantasy' when there are serious performance issues that can only be remedied by the manager's exit from the organization. Honesty combined with one-on-one outplacement support to help the person identify an appropriate career move may be the best solution in this situation (Wasylyshyn, 2003).

An alternative to intervention is prevention: employing the 'right people' and/or matching managers to suitable job assignments at the outset. Prevention strategies are discussed in more detail below.

Prevention: personnel selection
Although some might argue that applicant screening is associated with an ethical risk of 'blaming the victim' (Elo et al., 1998), the role of personality in the occupational stressor–strain relationship is favourable to a personality-driven approach to personnel selection. Furthermore, Attraction–Selection–Attrition (ASA) Theory (see Schneider et al., 1995) and Wilk and colleagues' (1995) Gravitational Hypothesis imply that a proactive selection strategy would simply 'speed up' the inevitable, since people leave jobs for which there is a poor person–environment fit. Indeed, Schneider et al. (1995) found direct and indirect support for within-organization homogeneity in employee characteristics over time. Similarly, Wilk et al. (1995) found that cognitive ability predicted movement in a job complexity hierarchy over a five-year period. In addition (using job as the unit of analysis), less experienced employees were less homogeneous with respect to cognitive ability than were more experienced employees.

Even if people who do not fit the job or organization eventually leave, this may be a slow process. Furthermore, achieving or moving increasingly closer to 'best fit' may take several years. Ensuring that there is optimal job placement initially, by selecting for person–job fit, should prevent the need for a 'correction mechanism' at a later date, saving the individual and the organization a lot of unnecessary discomfort, energy and time (Schneider et al., 1995; Wilk et al., 1995). Schneider et al. (1995: 768) identified the need to incorporate personality characteristics in personnel selection 'in addition to the traditional knowledge, skills and abilities (KSAs) on which so much attention has been focused related to the job'. They argued that assessing personality characteristics that are a good fit for the job, in combination with KSAs needed for job performance, should enhance the validity of personnel selection. For instance, personnel selection based on the motive–trait taxonomy presented in the current work could be used to diagnose a candidate's potential for adaptive versus maladaptive managerial behaviour. Alternatively, one might adopt a 'placement model'. Thus, at the outset, managers would not be screened out by virtue of their personality characteristics but instead directed towards or promoted into a job assignment that is a good fit for their personality characteristics.

Another potential application of the taxonomy is in career guidance and vocational counselling. Managers may be 'stuck in neutral, lacking personal drive as a result of not being sure why they are working and what they care about most' (Stern, 2004: 159). Using the taxonomy as a tool for vocational counselling may help the manager to plan for a new and different role that is more suitable and gratifying.

Conclusion

In summary, the current work adopted by Winter and colleagues' view that traits facilitate the behavioural expression of motives, but extended their channelling hypothesis by proposing that the extent to which unconflicted motive expression is adaptive versus maladaptive will vary depending on the degree of fit between the motive and the job environment. This proposal was illustrated through the introduction of a motive–trait taxonomy encompassing 12 managerial styles. As Winter et al. (1998) acknowledged, there are several personality elements that could potentially interact in the prediction of behaviour. While certainly not exhaustive, the current work examined the combined/interactive effect of two major *levels* of personality – implicit motives and traits – in an attempt to highlight the importance of considering the structure and organization of personality within the person (idiographic approach) in predicting occupational stress and strain in a managerial context.

References

Adkins, Joyce A. (1997), 'Base closure: a case study in occupational stress and organizational decline', in Marilyn K. Gowing, John D. Kraft and James C. Quick (eds), *The New Organizational Reality: Downsizing, Restructuring and Revitalization*, Washington, DC: American Psychological Association, pp. 111–41.

Anderson, J.P. (2002), 'Executive coaching and REBT: some comments from the field', *Journal of Rational-Emotive and Cognitive Behavior Therapy*, **20**(3), 223–33.

Antonioni, D. (1996), 'Two strategies for responding to stressors: managing conflict and clarifying work expectations', *Journal of Business and Psychology*, **11**(2), 287–95.

Beehr, T.A. and J.E. Newman (1978), 'Job stress, employee health, and organizational effectiveness: a facet analysis, model, and literature review', *Personnel Psychology*, **31**(4), 665–99.

Berman, W.H. and G. Bradt (2006), 'Executive coaching and consulting: "Different strokes for different folks"', *Professional Psychology: Research and Practice*, **37**(3), 244–53.

Brantley, Phillip J. and V. Diane Garrett (1993), 'Psychobiological approaches to health and disease', in Patricia B. Sutker and Henry E. Adams (eds), *Comprehensive Handbook of Psychopathology*, 2nd edn, New York: Plenum Press, pp. 647–70.

Brotman, L.E., W.P. Liberi and K.M. Wasylyshyn (1998), 'Executive coaching: the need for standards of competence', *Consulting Psychology Journal: Practice and Research*, **50**(1), 40–46.

Brown, Daniel (1993), 'Stress and emotion: implications for illness development and wellness', in Steven L. Ablon, Daniel Brown, Edward J. Khantzian and John E. Mack (eds), *Human Feelings: Explorations in Affect Development and Meaning*, Hillside, NJ: Analytic Press, pp. 281–301.

Brunstein, J.C., O.C. Schultheiss and R. Grässmann (1998), 'Personal goals and emotional well-being: the moderating role of motive dispositions', *Journal of Personality and Social Psychology*, **75**(2), 494–508.

Bush, M.W. (2005), 'Client perceptions of effectiveness in executive coaching', *Dissertation Abstracts International Section A: Humanities and Social Sciences*, **66**(4-A), 1417.

Callan, V.J. (1993), 'Individual and organizational strategies for coping with organizational change', *Work and Stress*, **7**(1), 63–75.

Callan, V.J., D.J. Terry and R. Schweitzer (1994), 'Coping resources, coping strategies and adjustment to organizational change: direct or buffering effects?', *Work and Stress*, **8**(4), 372–83.

Chemers, M.M., R.B. Hays, F. Rhodewalt and J. Wysocki (1985), 'A person–environment analysis of job stress: a contingency model explanation', *Journal of Personality and Social Psychology*, **49**(3), 628–35.

Code, S.L. and J. Langan-Fox (2001), 'Motivation, cognitions and traits: predicting occupational health, well-being and performance', *Stress and Health*, **17**(3), 159–74.

Conrad, Kelley A. (1997), 'The psychological assessment of middle managers', in Curtiss P. Hansen and Kelley A. Conrad (eds), *A Handbook of Psychological Assessment*, New York: Quorum Books, pp. 112–30.

Costa, P.T. and R.R. McCrae (1985), *The NEO Personality Inventory Manual*, Odessa, FL: Psychological Assessment Resources.

Cox, Tom and Eamonn Ferguson (1991), 'Individual differences, stress and coping', in Cary L. Cooper and Roy Payne (eds), *Personality and Stress: Individual Differences in the Stress Process*, New York: John Wiley & Sons, pp. 7–30.

Day, D.V. (2000), 'Leadership development: a review in context', *Leadership Quarterly*, **11**(4), 581–613.

Dewe, P., T. Cox and E. Ferguson (1993), 'Individual strategies for coping with stress at work: a review', *Work and Stress*, **7**(1), 5–15.

Diedrich, R.C. (1996), 'An iterative approach to executive coaching', *Consulting Psychology Journal: Practice and Research*, **48**(2), 61–6.

Ducharme, M.J. (2004), 'The cognitive-behavioral approach to executive coaching', *Consulting Psychology Journal: Practice and Research*, **56**(4), 214–24.

Edwards, J.R. (1996), 'An examination of competing versions of the person–environment fit approach to stress', *Academy of Management Journal*, **39**(2), 292–339.

Elliot, A.J. and K.M. Sheldon (1997), 'Avoidance achievement motivation: a personal goals analysis', *Journal of Personality and Social Psychology*, **73**(1), 171–85.

Elo, A.L., A. Leppänen and P. Sillänpää (1998), 'Applicability of survey feedback for an occupational health method in stress management', *Occupational Medicine*, **48**(3), 181–8.

Emmons, R.A. (1986), 'Personal strivings: an approach to personality and subjective well-being', *Journal of Personality and Social Psychology*, **51**(5), 1058–68.

Emmons, R.A. (1991), 'Personal strivings, daily life events, and psychological and physical well-being', *Journal of Personality*, **59**(3), 453–72.

Emmons, R.A. and L.A. King (1988), 'Conflict among personal strivings: immediate and long-term implications for psychological and physical well-being', *Journal of Personality and Social Psychology*, **54**(6), 1040–48.

Emmons, Robert A., Laura A. King and Ken Sheldon (1993), 'Goal conflict and the self-regulation of action', in Daniel M. Wegner and James W. Pennebaker (eds), *Handbook of Mental Control*, Englewood Cliffs, NJ: Prentice-Hall, pp. 528–51.

Endler, N.S. (1997), 'Stress, anxiety and coping: the multidimensional interaction model', *Canadian Psychology*, **38**(3), 136–53.

Epstein, S. (1994), 'Trait theory as personality theory: can a part be as great as the whole?', *Psychological Inquiry*, **5**(2), 120–22.

Feldman, D.C. and M.J. Lankau (2005), 'Executive coaching: a review and agenda for future research', *Journal of Management*, **31**(6), 829–48.

Fleming, R., A. Baum and J.E. Singer (1984), 'Toward an integrative approach to the study of stress', *Journal of Personality and Social Psychology*, **46**(4), 939–49.

Fogarty, G.J., M.A. Machin, M.J. Albion, L.F. Sutherland, G.I. Lalor and S. Revitt (1999), 'Predicting occupational strain and job satisfaction: the role of stress, coping, personality, and affectivity variables', *Journal of Vocational Behavior*, **54**(3), 429–52.

Friedman, Howard S. (1990), 'Personality and disease: overview, review and preview', in Howard S. Friedman (ed.), *Personality and Disease*, New York: John Wiley & Sons, pp. 3–13.

Goldberg, R.A. (2005), 'Resistance to coaching', *Organization Development Journal*, **23**(1), 9–16.

Hall, D.T., K.L. Otazo and G.P. Hollenbeck (1999), 'Behind closed doors: what really happens in executive coaching', *Organizational Dynamics*, **27**(3), 39–53.

Hepburn, C. Gail, Catherine A. Loughlin and Julian Barling (1997), 'Coping with chronic work stress', in Benjamin H. Gottlieb (ed.), *Coping with Chronic Stress*, New York: Plenum Press, pp. 343–66.

Hobfoll, Stevan E. (1988), *The Ecology of Stress*, New York: Hemisphere.

Hofer, J. and A. Chasiotis (2003), 'Congruence of life goals and implicit motives as predictors of life satisfaction: cross-cultural implications of a study of Zambian male adolescents', *Motivation and Emotion*, **27**(3), 251–72.

Hogan, R. and R.B. Kaiser (2005), 'What we know about leadership', *Review of General Psychology*, **9**(2), 169–80.

Hogan, R. and R. Warrenfeltz (2003), 'Educating the modern manager', *Academy of Management Learning and Education*, **2**(1), 74–84.

Hooijberg, R., J.G. Hunt and G.E. Dodge (1997), 'Leadership complexity and development of the Leaderplex Model', *Journal of Management*, **23**(3), 375–408.

Jemmott, J.B. (1987), 'Social motives and susceptibility to disease: stalking individual differences in health risks', *Journal of Personality*, **55**(2), 267–98.

Jemmott, J.B., C. Hellman, D.C. McClelland and S.E. Locke (1990), 'Motivational syndromes associated with natural killer cell activity', *Journal of Behavioral Medicine*, **13**(1), 53–73.

Jemmott, J.B. and D.C. McClelland (1989), 'Secretory IgA as a measure of resistance to infectious disease: comments on Stone, Cox, Valdimarsdottir, and Neale', *Behavioral Medicine*, **15**(2), 63–71.

Jenkins, S.R. (1994), 'Need for power and women's careers over 14 years: structural power, job satisfaction, and motive change', *Journal of Personality and Social Psychology*, **66**(1), 155–65.

Jex, Steve M. (1998), *Stress and Job Performance: Theory, Research, and Implications for Managerial Practice*, Thousand Oaks, CA: Sage.

Kampa, Sheila and Randall P. White (2002), 'The effectiveness of executive coaching: what we know and what we still need to know', in Rodney L. Lowman (eds), *Handbook of Organizational Consulting Psychology: A Comprehensive Guide to Theory, Skills, and Techniques*, San Francisco, CA: Jossey-Bass, pp. 139–58.

Karasek, Robert A. and Töres Theorell (1990), *Healthy Work: Stress, Productivity and the Reconstruction of Working Life*, New York: Basic Books.

Karoly, P. (1999), 'A goal systems-self-regulatory perspective on personality, psychopathology, and change', *Review of General Psychology*, **3**(4), 264–91.

Kehr, H.M. (2004), 'Implicit/explicit motive discrepancies and volitional depletion among managers', *Personality and Social Psychology Bulletin*, **30**(3), 315–27.

Kilburg, R.R. (1996), 'Toward a conceptual understanding and definition of executive coaching', *Consulting Psychology Journal: Practice and Research*, **48**(2), 134–44.

Kilburg, R.R. (2004), 'When shadows fall: using psychodynamic approaches in executive coaching', *Consulting Psychology Journal: Practice and Research*, **56**(4), 246–68.

Koestner, R., J. Weinberger and D.C. McClelland (1991), 'Task-intrinsic and social-extrinsic sources of arousal for motives assessed in fantasy and self-report', *Journal of Personality*, **59**(1), 57–82.

Koestner, Richard and David C. McClelland (1992), 'The affiliation motive', in Charles P. Smith (ed.), *Motivation and Personality: Handbook of Thematic Content Analysis*, New York: Cambridge University Press, pp. 205–10.

Langan-Fox, J. and M.E. Poole (1995), 'Occupational stress in Australian business and professional women', *Stress Medicine*, **11**(2), 113–22.

Levinson, H. (1996), 'Executive coaching', *Consulting Psychology Journal: Practice and Research*, **48**(2), 115–23.

Long, B.C. (1993), 'Coping strategies of male managers: a prospective analysis of predictors of psychosomatic symptoms and job satisfaction', *Journal of Vocational Behavior*, **42**(2), 184–99.

Luebbe, D.M. (2005), 'The three-way mirror of executive coaching', *Dissertation Abstracts International: Section B: The Sciences and Engineering*, **66**(3-B), 1771.

Lusch, R.F. and R.R. Serpkenci (1990), 'Personal differences, job tension, job outcomes, and store performance: a study of retail store managers', *Journal of Marketing*, **54**(1), 85–101.

McAdams, Dan P. (2000), *The Person: An Integrative Introduction to Personality Psychology*, Fort Worth, TX: Harcourt College.

McClelland, D.C. (1951), *Personality*, New York: Sloane.

McClelland, D.C. (1975), *Power: The Inner Experience*, New York: Irvington.

McClelland, D.C. (1979), 'Inhibited power motivation and high blood pressure in men', *Journal of Abnormal Psychology*, **88**(2), 182–90.

McClelland, D.C. (1985), *Human Motivation*, Glenview, IL: Scott, Foresman.

McClelland, D.C. (1987), 'Characteristics of successful entrepreneurs', *Journal of Creative Behavior*, **21**(3), 219–33.

McClelland, D.C. (1992), 'Motivational configurations', in Charles P. Smith (ed.), *Motivation and Personality: Handbook of Thematic Content Analysis*, New York: Cambridge University Press, pp. 87–99.

McClelland, D.C. (1993), 'Motives and health', in Gary G. Brannigan and Matthew R. Merrens (eds), *The Undaunted Psychologist: Adventures in Research*, New York: McGraw-Hill, pp. 129–141.

McClelland, D.C. and R.E. Boyatzis (1982), 'Leadership motive pattern and long-term success in management', *Journal of Applied Psychology*, **67**(6), 737–43.

McClelland, D.C. and J.B. Jemmott (1980), 'Power motivation, stress and physical illness', *Journal of Human Stress*, **6**(4), 6–15.

McClelland, D.C. and R. Koestner (1992), 'The achievement motive', in Charles P. Smith (eds), *Motivation and Personality: Handbook of Thematic Content Analysis*, New York: Cambridge University Press, pp. 143–152.

McClelland, D.C., R. Koestner and J. Weinberger (1989), 'How do self-attributed and implicit motives differ?', *Psychological Review*, **96**(4), 690–702.

McClelland, D.C., G. Ross and V. Patel (1985), 'The effect of an academic examination on salivary norepinephrine and immunoglobulin levels', *Journal of Human Stress*, **11**(2), 52–9.

McClelland, D.C., E. Floor, R.J. Davidson and C. Saron (1980), 'Stressed power motivation, sympathetic activation, immune function, and illness', *Journal of Human Stress*, **6**(2), 11–19.

McClelland, D.C., E. Floor, R.J. Davidson and C. Saron (1985), 'Stressed power motivation, sympathetic activation, immune function and illness', *Advances*, **2**, 43–51.

McClelland, D.C., C. Alexander and E. Marks (1982), 'The need for power, stress, immune function, and illness among male prisoners', *Journal of Abnormal Psychology*, **91**(1), 61–70.

McGill, M.E. and J.W. Slocum, Jr (1998), 'A little leadership, please?', *Organizational Dynamics*, **26**(3), 39–49.

Mintzberg, Henry (1973), *The Nature of Managerial Work*, New York: Harper & Row.

Mishra, A.K. and G.M. Spreitzer (1998), 'Explaining how survivors respond to downsizing: the roles of trust, empowerment, justice, and work redesign', *Academy of Management Review*, **23**(3), 567–88.

Monroe, Scott M. and John M. Kelley (1997), 'Measurement of stress appraisal', in Sheldon Cohen, Ronald C. Kessler and Lynn Underwood Gordon (eds), *Measuring Stress: A Guide for Health and Social Scientists*, New York: Oxford University Press, pp. 122–47.

Murphy, Lawrence R. (1996), 'Stress management techniques: secondary prevention of stress', in Marc J. Schabracq, Jacques A.M. Winnubst and Cary L. Cooper (eds), *Handbook of Work and Health Psychology*, New York: John Wiley & Sons, pp. 427–41.

National Institute for Occupational Safety and Health (2002), *Stress at Work (Publication No. 99–101)*, Washington, DC: Department of Health and Human Services.

Olivero, G., K.D. Bane and R.E. Kopelman (1997), 'Executive coaching as a transfer of training tool: effects on productivity in a public agency', *Public Personnel Management*, **26**(4), 461–9.

Orenstein, R.L. (2006), 'Measuring executive coaching efficacy? The answer was right here all the time', *Consulting Psychology Journal: Practice and Research*, **58**(2), 106–16.

Quick, J.C. and M. Macik-Frey (2004), 'Behind the mask coaching through deep interpersonal communication', *Consulting Psychology Journal: Practice and Research*, **56**(2), 67–74.

Quick, James C., Paul B. Paulus, James L. Whittington, Timothy S. Larey and Debra L. Nelson (1996), 'Management development, well-being and health', in Marc J. Schabracq, Jacques A.M. Winnubst and Cary L. Cooper (eds), *Handbook of Work and Health Psychology*, New York: John Wiley & Sons, pp. 369–87.

Revenson, Tracey A. (1990), 'All other things are not equal: an ecological approach to personality and disease', in Howard S. Friedman (ed.), *Personality and Disease*, New York: John Wiley & Sons, pp. 65–94.

Rosen, Robert (1997), 'Leadership in the new organization', in Marilyn K. Gowing, John D. Kraft and James C. Quick (eds), *The New Organizational Reality: Downsizing, Restructuring and Revitalization*, Washington, DC: American Psychological Association, pp. 221–38.

Schneider, B., H.W. Goldstein and D.B. Smith (1995), 'The ASA framework: an update', *Personnel Psychology*, **48**(4), 747–73.

Schreurs, Paul J.G., Jacques A.M. Winnubst and Cary L. Cooper (1996), 'Workplace health programmes', in Marc J. Schabracq, Jacques A.M. Winnubst and Cary L. Cooper (eds), *Handbook of Work and Health Psychology*, New York: John Wiley & Sons, pp. 463–81.

Schultheiss, O.C. and J.C. Brunstein (1999), 'Goal imagery: bridging the gap between implicit motives and explicit goals', *Journal of Personality*, **67**(1), 1–38.

Semmer, Norbert (1996), 'Individual differences, work stress and health', in Marc J. Schabracq, Jacques A.M. Winnubst and Cary L. Cooper (eds), *Handbook of Work and Health Psychology*, New York: John Wiley & Sons, pp. 51–85.

Sheldon, K.M. and A.J. Elliot (1998), 'Not all personal goals are personal: comparing autonomous and controlled reasons for goals as predictors of effort and attainment', *Personality and Social Psychology Bulletin*, **24**(5), 546–57.

Sheldon, K.M. and A.J. Elliot (1999), 'Goal striving, need satisfaction, and longitudinal well-being: the self-concordance model', *Journal of Personality and Social Psychology*, **76**(3), 482–97.

Sheldon, K.M. and T. Kasser (1995), 'Coherence and congruence: two aspects of personality integration', *Journal of Personality and Social Psychology*, **68**(3), 531–43.

Sherin, J. and L. Caiger (2004), 'Rational-emotive behavior therapy: a behavioral change model for executive coaching?', *Consulting Psychology Journal: Practice and Research*, **56**(4), 225–33.

Shinn, M., M. Rosario, H. Morch and D.E. Chestnut (1984), 'Coping with job stress and burnout in the human services', *Journal of Personality and Social Psychology*, **46**(4), 864–76.

Siegrist, J. (1995), 'Emotions and health in occupational life: new scientific findings and policy implications', *Patient Education and Counseling*, **25**(3), 227–36.

Smith, Charles P. (1992), *Motivation and Personality: Handbook of Thematic Content Analysis*, New York: Cambridge University Press.

Smither, J.W., M. London, R. Flautt, Y. Vargas and I. Kucine (2003), 'Can working with an executive coach improve multisource feedback ratings over time? A quasi-experimental field study', *Personnel Psychology*, **56**(1), 23–44.

Stahl, M.J., W.H. Hendrix and J. Coleman (1986), 'The positive effects of need for power on job stress and job related symptoms for managers', in Michael J. Stahl (ed.), *Managerial and Technical Motivation: Assessing Needs for Achievement, Power and Affiliation*, New York: Praeger, pp. 83–7.

Stahl, Michael J. (1986), *Managerial and Technical Motivation: Assessing Needs for Achievement, Power and Affiliation*, New York: Praeger.

Stern, L.R. (2004), 'Executive coaching: a working definition', *Consulting Psychology Journal: Practice and Research*, **56**(3), 154–62.

Stevens, J.H. (2005), 'Executive coaching from the executive's perspective', *Consulting Psychology Journal: Practice and Research*, **57**(4), 274–85.

Stöber, J. and B. Seidenstücker (1997), 'A new inventory for assessing worry in managers: correlates with job involvement and self-reliance', *Personality and Individual Differences*, **23**(6), 1085–7.

Terry, D.J. and V.J. Callan (1997), 'Employee adjustment to large-scale organizational change', *Australian Psychologist*, **32**(3), 203–10.

Thorne, A. (1995), 'Juxtaposed scripts, traits, and the dynamics of personality', *Journal of Personality*, **63**(3), 593–616.

Van Harrison, Richard (1985), 'The person–environment fit model and the study of job stress', in Terry A. Beehr and Rabi S. Bhagat (eds), *Human Stress and Cognition in Organizations: An Integrated Perspective*, New York: John Wiley & Sons, pp. 23–55.

Vrugt, Anneke (1996), 'Perceived self-efficacy, work motivation and well being', in Marc J. Schabracq, Jacques A.M. Winnubst and Cary L. Cooper (eds), *Handbook of Work and Health Psychology*, New York: John Wiley & Sons, pp. 389–403.

Wasylyshyn, K.M. (2003), 'Executive coaching: an outcome study', *Consulting Psychology Journal: Practice and Research*, **55**(2), 94–106.

Webster, Simon (1998), 'Stress affecting 70% of managers', *Corporate Sector Review*, **26** (October–December).

Weinberger, Joel and David C. McClelland (1990), 'Cognitive versus traditional motivational models: irreconcilable or complementary?', in Edward T. Higgins and Richard M. Sorrentino (eds), *Handbook of Motivation and Cognition: Foundations of Social Behavior*, Vol. 2, New York: Guilford Press, pp. 562–97.

Wheatley, R. (2000), *Taking the Strain: A Survey of Managers and Workplace Stress*, London: Institute of Management.

Wiebe, Deborah J. and Timothy W. Smith (1997), 'Personality and health: progress and problems in psychosomatics', in Robert Hogan, John A. Johnson and Stephen R. Briggs (eds), *Handbook of Personality Psychology*, San Diego, CA: Academic Press, pp. 891–918.

Wilk, S.L., L.B. Desmarais and P.R. Sackett (1995), 'Gravitation to jobs commensurate with ability: longitudinal and cross-sectional tests', *Journal of Applied Psychology*, **80**(1), 79–85.

Winter, D.G. and L.A. Carlson (1988), 'Using motive scores in the psychobiographical study of an individual: the case of Richard Nixon', *Journal of Personality*, **56**(1), 75–103.

Winter, D.G., O.P. John, A.J. Stewart, E.C. Klohnen and L.E. Duncan (1998), 'Traits and motives: toward an integration of two traditions in personality research', *Psychological Review*, **105**(2), 230–50.

Winter, D.G. and A.J. Stewart (1995), 'Commentary: tending the garden of personality', *Journal of Personality*, **63**(3), 711–27.

Winter, David G. (1992a), 'Power motivation revisited', in C.P. Smith (ed.), *Motivation and Personality: Handbook of Thematic Content Analysis*, New York: Cambridge University Press, pp. 301–10.

Winter, David G. (1992b), 'A revised scoring system for the power motive', in C.P. Smith (ed.), *Motivation and Personality: Handbook of Thematic Content Analysis*, New York: Cambridge University Press, pp. 311–24.

Winter, David G. (1996), *Personality: Analysis and Interpretation of Lives*, New York: McGraw-Hill.

Yukl, G. (1989), 'Managerial leadership: a review of theory and research', *Journal of Management*, **15**(2), 251–89.

22 Avoiding entrepreneurial frustration: building a management team
Robert D. Hisrich and Julie Lutz

Introduction

In order to successfully launch and grow a new venture, the entrepreneur must build a strong management team with the necessary talent. Such a management team establishes, through its abilities and connections, the much-needed credibility that allows the venture to obtain the necessary resources (particularly financial support).

While the decision to hire a new employee is an important one for every business, its impact is even more significant for an entrepreneurial company. Every new addition to the management team helps determine the ability of the venture to launch and grow. Bad hires are expensive, and no organization, especially a small entrepreneurial one, can afford too many of them. It is thought that an employee hired in a typical entry-level position who quits after three months costs a company about $9,000 in salary, benefits, and training. In addition, the intangible costs – time invested in hiring and developing the new employee, lost opportunities, reduced morale among co-workers, and business setbacks – are seven times this cost, making the total cost for this bad hire about $72,000.

For many companies, attracting and retaining qualified employees remains a challenge, but the problem is especially acute among rapidly growing small businesses. A comprehensive study of companies' hiring practices conducted by Staffing.org indicates that:

- Staffing costs are rising overall, despite increased use of the Internet.
- New-hire quality is the top staffing priority for 70 percent of the companies surveyed.
- Most companies have not differentiated between employees desired and those not desired.
- The workforce shortage will get worse. Between 2000 and 2020, an estimated 76 million baby boomers will retire from the workforce with only 45 million Generation Xers in the pipeline to replace them (Datz, 2000).

Building a strong management team is not easy. Of every three employees a business hires, frequently one makes a solid contribution, one is a marginal worker, and one is a hiring mistake. Because employees' roles in a small company's success are significant, due to the company's size, entrepreneurs can *least* afford to make hiring mistakes. Often those hiring mistakes occur because entrepreneurs rush into a hiring decision or neglect to investigate thoroughly a candidate's qualifications and suitability for a job, particularly checking the candidate's references. One small entrepreneurial company in the telecommunications industry failed to check the references of one candidate who was hired as a sales manager. The individual was let go after just 11 months on the job, having achieved very disappointing results.

Hiring process approach

Although the importance of hiring decisions is significant in small companies, small businesses are most likely to make hiring mistakes because they lack the human resource expertise and the disciplined hiring procedures which are usually a part of a large company. In this regard it is particularly important for the entrepreneur to avoid the frustration in hiring by both understanding the attributes of his/her venture that will appeal to individuals and taking a planned approach to the hiring process. The hiring process is a continuum that can be addressed in five steps: define, post, date, negotiate and bind.

- Define – describe the job position, the need for the employee, the necessary skills and attributes of the employee, and a logical path for advancement.
- Post – advertise the job opening through databases, agencies, online services and word of mouth.
- Date – conduct background checks, call on references, interview, take the possible candidate out for lunch, evaluate samples of work, and consider a grace period of work.
- Negotiate – know what the industry pays for a similar position, know how much you can afford, and know what the employee values; then develop a benefit package that complements the individual's greatest motivators.
- Bind – develop a contract that allows the termination of the employee in the same manner as the hire.

Define

The first step is critical as it lays the framework for the entire hiring process. This is where the entrepreneur determines exactly what the position involves, why a new employee is needed, and how much salary can be paid. Often the employee is needed to help grow the company when there is just not enough time for the entrepreneur to do everything. Or the new employee may be needed to provide advanced skills that the entrepreneur does not have. In either case, it is important to know why the employee is needed. Hetherington (2006) feels that the need for additional new employees is indicated when:

- you struggle to balance work with family life;
- you find it difficult to meet deadlines;
- your health is suffering as a result of high stress levels and long hours;
- personal relationships are adversely affected;
- you find yourself increasingly reliant on independent contractors to help you with particular projects;
- you waste valuable time on non-core business activities such as typing or filing;
- you find yourself turning away clients because you just don't have the time to take on any new customers.

Once it is determined what the position involves, a detailed job description with all needed skills should be written. Once this is done, a value proposition can be developed as well as a structure for output expectations and salary and fringe benefits. The entrepreneur must know how important this employee is to determine the compensation level.

Comparable salaries of competitors are needed. Beyond defining the immediate need for the employee, think ahead to future growth opportunities. Having growth potential for the employee will make the appeal of the company more attractive and help in the hiring process.

Post

Finding suitable candidates is half the battle in the hiring process; this is sometimes the most frustrating part for entrepreneurs. According to a survey of the National Federation of Independent Businesses (NFIB) 19 percent of small businesses have a job opening they can't fill and 77 percent of the companies felt that a shortage of qualified applicants was their greatest challenge. These job openings may be available for various reasons, but the majority are directly tied to financing the openings and finding the right people to fill them (Weisul, 2003).

The challenge arises for the small business owner in a couple of ways. Derek Sankey, a leading author on human resource issues, wrote that 'many of the casualties in the intensifying war for talent are small business owners who lack the resources to compete with large corporations, causing many entrepreneurs to fight the problem on several new fronts' (Sankey, 2006: 65). However, one solution to this dilemma can be developed by 'positioning the company, by putting its strengths forward, and displaying security to potential employees that there is a solid ground and future', says Michael Schell, president of Vancouver-based The Approved Group.

Research done by workopolis.com shows that in the last five years, people's top priority has shifted from career to work–life balance. 'Money is not the No. 1 attracting force for most applicants', Schell says. This can be a real advantage to small firms that can offer more flexibility in the job, faster career advancements, and a greater focus on the employee. Once the entrepreneur understands some of the shifts in the job market it will be easier to conduct a more effective search process (Sankey, 2006).

The next challenge comes in locating potential employees. Sankey suggests that the traditional newspaper advertisements are still very effective for entry-level positions. More small businesses are also starting to advertise outside of their region and may do so to target a segment of people with specific skill sets. Career fairs as well as online job databases such as DirectHire Plus are great outlets for possible candidates. Other sources for prospective employees include vendors, professional associations and customers. Spread the word among your social contacts as well – you never know who might know of the right candidate for you business. Schell also emphasizes that singing bonuses may also be considered in the job description to lure individuals to the company; entrepreneurs need to move quickly with little bureaucracy, a competitive advantage over the large corporations.

Date

The interviewing process is the time to learn more about the candidate and the key success factor here is to listen. Ask plenty of questions and understand how a person's work experiences relate to the open position. Perform a second interview and spend more than an hour or two with the person before bringing him/her into your organization. Run a background check on the individual and follow your intuition. Often your first instinct about a candidate is correct. However, Malcolm Gladwell cautions employers in his book,

Blink, how rapid analysis or what he calls 'thin-slicing' can be dangerous in hiring situations. He writes about the 'dark side of rapid cognition' which is often the origin of prejudice and discrimination. In his example, he writes about the history of past president Warren Harding, who was perceived as a 'Roman' figure, with a strong build and endearing features. Harding rose through the political ranks primarily because he looked like a great president, not because he was a brilliant politician. He is known as one of the worst presidents in US history (Gladwell, 2005: 72–6).

Because the hire of a new employee is critical and intuition cannot be taken lightly, always conduct a second interview and possibly even a third. Have the top candidates meet with someone else in your organization or outside, if needed, to get another perspective. The candidate may seem completely different to you the second or third time around. Don't hire someone simply because you like them in the interview without checking their qualifications. If you're not 100 percent sure about someone, interview some more people, says Wesman. 'When you look at them, you should be able to say, I want this person in my office tomorrow' (Sankey, 2006).

Negotiate

Don't hire the least expensive person because you feel you can't afford better talent. Instead, invest in someone who has the skills and abilities you need and who can help expand the business. It may be tempting to cut financial corners with payroll, but the consequences of losing talented employees to competitors could be the result. Offer the best financial package the business can provide at the present time, and then focus on offering fringe benefits, stock ownership and other perks.

Consider a trial period or other mutual evaluation method; one technique frequently used is to give a prospective employee an actual assignment. Ask them to complete a project similar to the actual work they'd be doing and pay them for it. The process provides an insight to both the employee and entrepreneur of what each can expect.

Be prepared to make an offer on the spot. This is an advantage over the large corporations that need to take a series of steps to put an offer letter together and get approval from various departments. This is not to say that a formal process is not necessary, with legal paperwork and contracts, but be ready, have your homework done, know what you can offer, and you will be able to make an offer when you come across the best candidate.

Bind

The process of hiring new employees is a legal one, and all paperwork and documentation need to be arranged. A human resources (HR) department is a critical interface for employee satisfaction and includes the responsibilities for payroll, benefits, hiring/firing, and keeping up to date on all state and federal laws. In a small business the entrepreneur may very well be the HR department, and may not have much expertise in this area. However, HR plays a critical role in keeping an employee satisfied, and if this is incorrectly managed it could cause significant legal issues.

The US Small Business Association (SBA) is a great source for HR standards and laws, and can be accessed through local chapters or online at sba.gov. Another option for maintaining proper HR processes is to outsource a portion or entire department to a third-party vendor. According to an article on Entrepreneur.com, the HR outsourcing industry grew from $13.9 billion in 1999 to $37.7 billion in 2003 (Lee, 2002).

The hiring process doesn't end with making the selection. Be prepared for the employee by having a place set up for him/her to work, and making the individual comfortable with a warm welcome into the company. Success of a new hire may depend significantly on how much up-front knowledge is provided. Avoid unnecessary mistakes, confusion and financial losses through a structured training program.

A solid and detailed hiring process can avoid future headaches for the entrepreneur and serves as the foundation for acquiring new employees. This process is easily neglected by entrepreneurs without prior experience in hiring and a formal HR department; however, while it is one attribute that affects successful hiring, there are four more critical ones in developing a credible management team. These include: develop and maintain core values; develop a culture and competent organization; develop appropriate compensation packages; and develop appropriate employee benefits.

Develop and maintain core values
In an era of hypercompetition and economic turbulence, amid skepticism about the value and integrity of businesses, in order to build a strong credible management team the entrepreneur must establish a well-articulated company mission and a consistently practiced set of core values. Employees today more than ever before are seeking meaning in their jobs and want their work to be purposeful. While compensation is important, the real motivation of most potential members of the management team goes far beyond monetary reward; a higher-order motivation arises out of believing that your work has a purpose and is a part of something larger in the company context that will achieve something truly worthwhile. The mission of the company that delivers a clear sense of direction and purpose is a good way to give value and meaning to your employees. Table 22.1 presents the central concepts distilled from the mission statements of such selected US companies as 3M, General Electric, Marriott and Wal-Mart. When these mission statements are analyzed, several underlying themes emerge. First, successful companies feel that their most valuable asset is their people, and will go to great lengths to make sure it is fun to go to work. Given enough time and resources, any innovative product or service can be replicated and often bettered. However, it is extremely hard to replicate, even in the long run, a company with highly motivated loyal employees who are having fun.

Second, successful entrepreneurial companies focus on customer satisfaction. The purpose of any company is serving its customers (as well as all of its stakeholders). Superior service and satisfied customers produce greater market share and the ability to sustain profitable margins. This results in a greater growth rate and profitability, which maximizes shareholder wealth. A company's ability to survive and prosper is directly related to how well it serves and satisfies its customers.

Third, successful companies continually innovate, constantly improving not only the quality of their own products and services but also the quality of life of their stakeholders. This focus on creativity and continuous innovation ensures that the company is always at the cutting edge of technology, producing high-quality, reliable products and services. Finally, successful companies operate with honesty and integrity. The scandals at Tyco, Worldcom, Enron and Adelphia show the importance of this aspect of a good mission statement and maintaining high core values. There is never a concern about the way any stakeholder will be treated in a successful company. When the mission statement embodies

Table 22.1   Central concepts of the mission statements of selected US companies

Company	Concepts
3M	• Innovation: 'thou shalt not kill a new product idea' • Absolute integrity • Respect for individual initiative and personal growth • Tolerance for honest mistakes • Product quality and reliability
American Express	• Heroic customer service • Worldwide reliability of services • Encouragement of individual initiative
Ford	• People as the source of our strength • Products as the 'end result of our efforts' (we are *about* cars) • Profits as a necessary means and measure for our success • Basic honesty and integrity
General Electric	• Improving the quality of life through technology and innovation • Interdependent balance between responsibility to customers, employees, society and shareholders (no clear hierarchy) • Individual responsibility and opportunity • Honesty and integrity
Marriott	• Friendly service and excellent value (customers are guests): 'Make people away from home feel that they're among friends and really wanted' • People are number one – treat them well, expect a lot, and the rest will follow • Work hard, yet keep it fun • Continual self-improvement • Overcoming adversity to build character
Procter & Gamble	• Product excellence • Continuous self-improvement • Honesty and fairness • Respect and concern for the individual
Wal-Mart	• 'We exist to provide to our customers' – to make their lives better via lower prices and greater selection; all else is secondary • Swim upstream buck conventional wisdom • Be in partnership with employees • Work with passion, commitment and enthusiasm • Run lean • Pursue ever higher goals

Source: Adapted from James C. Collins and Jerry I. Porras, *Built to Last*, New York: HarperCollins, 2002.

these four concepts consistently over time, employees will take ownership and make the commitment necessary to ensure the company is successful regardless of the hours of work needed.

This mission statement sets the stage for the development of a set of core company values that need to be practiced daily by everyone in the organization. Core values of good companies are very similar and center around such things as servicing customers, high-quality products and services, integrity in all activities, respect for employees, focusing on all the stakeholders, continually being innovative, and contributing to society. The entrepreneur and his or her management team need to make sure that the core values of the company are known and followed. This means that the values are continuously reinforced and reflected in the actions of the company at all levels.

Unless the entrepreneur establishes a clearly articulated set of values, it is unlikely that there will be employees' trust and support of the company and its mission. It takes a long time to establish this trust and commitment, which can be lost in just one single act.

The set of core values underpins the purpose of the company – the ultimate reason for its existence. Every company has a core purpose of which every employee must clearly and fully be aware. Example core purposes for selected companies follow:

- Hewlett-Packard: to make technical contributions for the advancement and welfare of humanity
- Mary Kay: to give unlimited opportunity to women
- McKinsey: to help leading corporations and governments be more successful
- Merck: to preserve and improve human life
- Wal-Mart: to give ordinary people the chance to buy the same things as anyone else
- Walt Disney: to make people happy

The mission, core values and purpose are the foundations of every company. Every policy, strategy practice and tactic should be governed by and support them.

Care needs to be taken to separate the established core values and purpose from best practices and strategies. For example, IBM at one point believed its strategy of developing, selling and servicing mainframe computers was its core value. This idea, for a period of time, brought havoc on IBM's market position as it delayed its response to the smaller personal computers coming into the market. Once the core values and strategies were separated and IBM went back to its basic core values, the company responded to this competitive threat with its own version of the small personal computer and reversed its downward trend.

In 1967 Truett Cathy started his company, Chick-fil-A, a fast-food chicken restaurant, now a chain, juggling profit and prayer. This private, family-owned business has used these principles to become the number two fast-food chain in the world in 2002, with over 1055 restaurants and revenues of over $1.2 billion. The fast-food chain is closed on Sundays and spends millions each year on college scholarships, foster homes, and summer camps. *QSR Magazine* recently ranked its drive-through service as number one in the industry. Except for a few hundred licensed stores in airports and on college campuses, the company owns most of its restaurants, each of which is run by a manager who shares in the profits but not the ownership of the company. Typically, when the company is expanding to a new location, the selected manager puts up between $5000 and $10 000 and is guaranteed a minimum income. Each manager pays the company 15 percent of the gross revenue and 50 percent of the profits of his or her particular restaurant(s). The company has grown by carefully selecting capable, hungry entrepreneurs for each of its stores. The company prefers this private family ownership rather than franchising or being a publicly traded company. Managers of large stand-alone Chick-fil-A restaurants can earn upward of $140 000 per year.

The company, now under Truett's son, Dan, has some aggressive growth plans. Chick-fil-A added about 80 stores in 2003, mostly in the Southeast, and plans to add an additional 420 stores by 2006. Plans are also in the works for adding such new menu items as fresh-squeezed lemonade smoothies and a spicy salad. Prayer is welcome at the company's headquarters or stores, as Chick-fil-A's religious base and inspiration has served the company well, especially during these times of corporate scandals.

What a contrast there is between Truett and Dan Cathy of Chick-fil-A and Dennis Kozlowski, the former CEO of Tyco. Dennis allegedly has taken over $600 million from Tyco through theft, misuse of loans, and selling shares of company stock while concealing what was really happening. While honing a reputation for frugality and stating that he did not believe in perks, Dennis Kozlowski allegedly siphoned millions from Tyco to buy yachts, paintings and luxury apartments. His $30 million Fifth Avenue apartment supposedly has a $6000 shower curtain and a $15000 poodle-shaped umbrella stand. Perhaps his greatest exploitation was having Tyco pay for half of the $2.1 million birthday party for his wife, Karen. This price tag included flying 75 people to the Italian island of Sardinia and showcasing a big ice sculpture of David at the party.

For more information on core values and writing an effective mission statement see American Marketing Association (2002) and Kattenmaker (2002).

Develop a culture and competence

The company culture is the unwritten code of conduct that governs the behavior, attitudes, relationships and style of an organization. It embodies the way the company does things. In many entrepreneurial companies, culture plays an equally important role in gaining a competitive advantage as strategy does. A company's culture has a powerful impact on the way people work together, how they do their jobs, and how they treat their customers. The culture is reflected in how workers dress and act, and in the language used. The dress code varies greatly by company. At some companies, the dress code is suits and ties, while at others it is more relaxed, even to jeans and T-shirts.

The culture of the organization reflects the deep-seated philosophy of the founder or executives on how the people in the organization should behave toward the customers as well as toward each other. A company's culture arises from an entrepreneur's consistent and relentless pursuit of a set of core values that everyone in the company can believe in.

The culture of the company along with the core values and competencies need to align with the employees of the company to maximize their level of motivation. If misalignment occurs between these three factors and the employee or if there is any ambiguity, it will be difficult to keep employees at peak performance or even keep them at all, regardless of the type and level of compensation.

Building a company with a strong management team that is credible to the external environment, particularly financial supporters, requires that the entrepreneur develop competence within the organization. Overall company competence provides the company the ability to build, combine and integrate resources into the products and/or services it offers. Some of the company's competencies are distinctive enough to be labeled core competencies; these provide it with significant sustainable competitive advantages over competition, and offer real benefits to customers and are difficult to imitate.

Competence of the company can be classified along three dimensions: attitudes, knowledge and know-how. *Attitudes* in terms of behavior, identity and determination are sometimes overlooked as part of the competence of a company. Yet they are essential for any individual or company to achieve anything significant. *Knowledge* is the assimilated information and data of the company, enabling it to successfully build the quality products and services from the resources obtained. Finally, *know-how* reflects the skills and capabilities that define the company's ability to act and produce output according to the developed objectives and processes.

Besides these three competencies, which collectively make up what is sometimes called cognitive capabilities, the company must also have competence in terms of tangible and intangible assets (equipment, buildings, products and services, brand equity, software and customer loyalty); organizational structure (the structural design of the company and its coordinating mechanisms and processes); and company identity (the beliefs, values and overall culture of the company). The development of these competencies allows the company to continue to operate and survive for a long period of time despite the presence of hypercompetition and economic and governmental instability.

For more information on company culture see Vargo (2006) and Collins (2006).

Develop an appropriate compensation plan

Given the hypercompetition, the need for shareholder value, and economic turbulence in today's business climate, it is important that each entrepreneur construct the appropriate compensation package in order to build a strong, credible management team. Compensation is more than just money, whether it is paid in wages, salaries, commissions or bonuses. Other forms of extrinsic compensation include equity; stock options; perquisites, such as a company car; child care; expense account; membership privileges; health care; personal insurance; and pension contribution. Extending the term compensation to the fullest would include such intrinsic compensation as status; independence; power; office; company parking place; type of office furnishings and computer; vacations and holidays; and family, personal and sick leave. Compensation options are listed in Figure 22.1. Using these items, the entrepreneur can develop a compensation package consisting of economic and non-economic aspects for each potential member of the management team and then, most importantly, review this with the employee(s) on an annual basis.

While there is nothing new about using incentives to motivate workers, shareholder mistrust and economic turbulence have caused the shift in motivational leadership to a variety of incentive/pay-for-performance plans. In the extreme case, this makes every employee's compensation a variable cost dependent on his or her productivity and the successful performance of the company. This type of compensation system tends to keep fixed costs low and motivates employees to achieve greater productivity.

There are many types of incentive plans that can be classified in several ways. They can be classified by level, with the individual compensation plans providing income to individual employees over and above their base salary when specific individual performance goals are met. If the level is not individual, then it is a group incentive plan, which pays all members in the group or team when the performance goals/standards established for the group are met. Profit-sharing plans provide all or almost all employees with a share of the company's profits in a specific period of time. There are also employee group plans such as those for sales employees, operating employees and distribution employees.

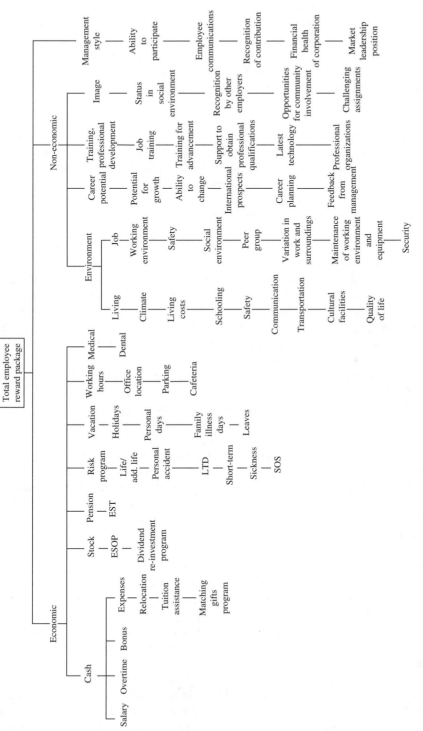

Source: Adapted from material by Gerard Torma, Director of Compensation and International Human Resources, Nordson Corporation, in Robert D. Hisrich, *Small Business Solutions*, New York: McGraw-Hill, 2004, pp. 55–6.

Figure 22.1 Economic and non-economic compensation options

Incentives for non-managerial employees
Almost all entrepreneurs employ some individuals who are non-managerial and actually perform the operational work of the company. These can include the janitor who cleans the offices, the production worker who makes the product, the receptionist who handles a variety of company tasks, to the data processing clerk who inputs the orders. There are several types of incentive plans that can be used for this type of employment.

Salaried hour plan
The salaried hour plan is the most common plan used for non-managerial employees. Under this plan an employee is paid a basic hourly rate and an extra percentage of his or her rate for output exceeding the standard. If Sally, a sales lead specialist, is paid $80 per day for getting 40 new leads and she obtains 60 new leads one day, her pay would be $80 + (50 % × $80) or $120 that day. Care must be taken by the entrepreneur using this plan that the quality is not sacrificed for the quantity that results in increased pay.

Piecework plan
In the widely used piecework plan, an employee is paid an amount, called a piece rate, for each unit produced. If Sam receives $1.25 for each email sales lead found, he will receive $100 for obtaining 80 leads in one day. The problem for the entrepreneur in implementing a piecework plan is determining the correct rate to pay per piece. In the case of Sam in the above example, the entrepreneur felt that Sam was worth $10/hour and that eight good leads per hour was a good standard product rate; therefore a piece rate of $1.25 (10/hour divided by 8) was established.

The piecework can be either straight or shared depending on the desire of the entrepreneur. The previous case was an example of straight piecework as there is a strict relationship between results and rewards. If shared piecework is used and Sam continually obtains 100 leads per day instead of 80, which was the initial standard, then his piece rate for leads above 90 might be $1.35.

A piecework compensation plan is very understandable and equitable, and it provides good incentives for the employees, as rewards are proportionate to performance. However, this compensation plan can lead to some employee rigidity in terms of resisting improving or even meeting quality standards and not being interested in switching to another job, which may reduce output. The plan also increases resistance to any other change, including using new technology.

Team (group) incentive plans
Team (group) incentive plans reward the team for its performance, from which each team member's pay is derived. The members of the team are paid based on each team member receiving pay equal to the average pay earned by the group or each member receiving the same pay earned by either the highest-paid or the lowest-paid member of the team. Instead of being based on pay, another individual compensation method is to set an engineered production standard: each member of the team then receives the same pay based on the piece rate of the output of the team. If it is wished to avoid using an engineered standard, then the entrepreneur should tie the rewards of the team, and hence the individual, to goals reached based on some overall standard, such as the number of defective products and/or number of labor hours per product. This latter plan usually produces

good results as the team members are motivated to achieve greater and greater efficiencies determined by management without the use of an engineered standard, which team members usually disagree with.

Generally, team incentives work very well for motivating non-management employees when the work is organized around teams. This type of incentive reinforces team planning and problem solving while helping build *esprit de corps* and collaboration among team members. The entrepreneur should make sure, when using a team incentive plan, that no individual(s) becomes disgruntled because he or she is 'carrying' the team, resulting in rewards and pay not proportionate to his or her efforts.

Incentives for salespeople

Incentives for salespeople are some of the most important incentives to establish, as salespeople drive the top line of the company. As the age-old adage states: 'Nothing happens until a sale is made.' Sales compensation plans tend to be of three types: straight commission, straight salary plan, or a combination of salary and commission.

Straight commission The straight commission compensation plan maximizes incentives, minimizes security, and frequently results in very high productivity and earning levels for salespeople. This plan is usually employed in direct marketing, some industrial sales, retail furniture sales, automotive sales, international sales of the company's local salespeople selling in their country's market; real-estate transactions; and group sales. Under this plan, unproductive salespeople eventually resign because their salaries are derived from paid commissions based only on performance, as measured in terms of sales and sometimes profits.

When establishing a straight commission plan, the company first must determine the base or unit. This becomes the basis for paying commissions, and is usually stated in units of sale, dollar sales, gross profits, or some sales/profit combination. Second, the company must determine the rate that will be paid per unit, which is often expressed as a percentage of gross profit or sales. Third, the company must establish a starting point for commissions. This point can be the first unit sold, the first unit sold after obtaining a specific level of sales, or an established quota. Finally, the company must decide on the time period for payment of commissions, as well as the method for handling sales returns, canceled orders and non-payments.

Commissions are usually paid when the order is received, goods are shipped, or payment is received. Commissions often are adjusted in the next payment period for any non-payments, canceled orders or returned merchandise in the previous period. To help ensure prompt delivery and build customer relations, most companies usually pay commissions once the order is shipped. Under this system, salespeople work with production and shipping to ensure that the order is sent on a timely basis, and is not canceled due to delay.

To help offset fluctuations in salary, and to help salespeople on straight commissions, some companies provide a draw, in addition to the established commission plan. A draw is a sum of money paid to salespeople against future commissions. The 'drawn' money is deducted from commissions earned in the next payment period.

With or without a guaranteed draw, straight commission plans are used in many industries, particularly when the company wants a strong incentive to sell. Some industries, such as consumer packaged goods, tend not to use a straight commission plan because of the difficulty in relating sales volume to the efforts of a particular salesperson. For example, the sale of a 96-ounce box of Ultra Tide at a Giant Eagle store in Cleveland, Ohio, might have been the result of a manufacturer's coupon from Procter and Gamble, not the work of the salesperson calling on the account. It also may have resulted from a call by the sales manager at Giant Eagle's headquarters, a display allowance given by Procter and Gamble to the Giant Eagle store for displaying the product, a product advertisement in the Cleveland *Plain Dealer*, or the salesperson's call on the manager of another Giant Eagle store in the area. In all likelihood, a combination of several of these activities affected the sale.

Straight salary plan   Even though individuals with good selling ability are better rewarded (if they can perform) under a straight commission plan, many people do not like to work under conditions of uncertainty and potential for wide fluctuations in income. These more security-minded salespeople prefer a dependable, regular income rather than making a larger amount of money under the uncertain straight commission plan. Security with a straight salary plan is particularly important in widely fluctuating company and market situations and when the company's sales are periodic or seasonal.

A company should definitely consider a straight salary plan in the following circumstances, even though the incentive for higher sales volume may be reduced:

1. When a long learning period is needed for salespeople to perform effectively. A straight salary is needed, at least in the beginning, to cover the training period until commissions are large enough to provide an adequate standard of living. Initially, without a straight salary plan, it would be very difficult to recruit good salespeople.
2. When a major capital expenditure is involved with an extended negotiation period in the selling process. A company may take more than a year to make such a big decision. A salesperson might be calling on and working with a company during this entire period in order to make the final sale, and yet would not earn any commission during this time.
3. When sales, usually more technical in nature, require team selling among such people as a salesperson, a marketing support person, a technical engineer and an upper-level manager. Because each individual plays a role in the final sale, it is difficult to assign total credit to the salesperson.
4. When advertising, sales promotion, and/or a direct-mail piece have a significant effect on the final sale, and when the extent of that effect with respect to the efforts of the salesperson is difficult to evaluate. A straight salary plan in this case also rewards non-selling activities, commonly called missionary selling. These include providing customer assistance, setting up in-store displays, redesigning an entire area of a store for introducing a new line of products, or calling on potential new customers.

Because a salesperson's compensation in a straight salary plan is not based on productivity, which is usually measured by sales and/or profits, this compensation plan provides salespeople with the most security and allows the company to direct all the sales activities. This helps to ensure that the company will reach its established objectives. In industries such as heavy machinery, aerospace, chemical, petroleum, and consumer non-durable goods, a straight salary compensation plan is widely used. Sometimes salespeople are even called consultants or engineers, and 'sales' is not even a part of their title.

Combination compensation plans   A combination compensation plan integrates characteristics of both the straight salary and straight commission plans. The salary part of the compensation package provides security and a base reward for minimal level of sales performance. The commission and/or bonus part of the compensation package is reward for achieving or exceeding volume and/or profit goals. The critical factor in developing an effective combination compensation plan is the proportion of salary to commission incentive. The ideal combination is a salary large enough to attract talented salespeople coupled with an incentive plan large enough to strongly motivate them. Although the salary incentive mix varies depending on the industry, the competition, and the nature of the selling task, a compensation package that is 70 to 80 percent salary and 20 to 30 percent incentive is usually considered balanced and attractive.

Incentives for managers and executives

Probably no other area is more important for the success of the entrepreneur and the business than attracting and retaining key managers and executives. Since these individuals influence directly the overall performance in terms of sales and profits for the company, the entrepreneur needs to put considerable thought into how to reward them. Most managers receive both short-term bonuses and long-term incentives in addition to their salary.

Short-term incentives   Most firms have annual bonus plans designed to motivate the short-term performance of managers and executives; these bonuses are tied to the profitability of the company. Short-term bonuses can significantly adjust pay, sometimes up to 30 percent or more of the total pay received. In establishing the annual bonus or any other short-term incentive plan, the entrepreneur needs to keep in mind three things: eligibility, total size of the reward, and individual rewards. In terms of eligibility, it is usually better to have as much eligibility as makes sense, including both upper- and lower-level managers. This eligibility can be decided in a number of ways, but it is usually best to determine it based either on job level (title) or a combination of factors such as job level (title), base salary level, and discretionary considerations such as jobs that are key to the company's performance. The size of the bonus received usually varies by job level (title), with top-level executives receiving a higher percentage bonus than lower-level managers.

The entrepreneur also must decide the total amount of bonus money available – the size of the bonus pool. Entrepreneurs make this decision in several different ways. Some entrepreneurs use a straight percentage (usually of the company's net income) to create the bonus pool. This is called a *non-deductible formula approach*. Other entrepreneurs feel that the bonus pool should be based on amounts achieved only after specified levels of earnings are reached. This is called a *deductible formula approach*. Still other entrepreneurs do not use a formula but determine the size of the bonus pool on some discretionary basis. While there are no hard-and-fast rules for determining the proportion of the profits to pay out through the bonus pool, the entrepreneur should make this determination carefully so that both managers and shareholders are rewarded and the company can continue to perform and grow.

The third task in developing a good annual bonus plan is deciding the individual rewards. Usually an entrepreneur establishes a larger bonus and a maximum bonus (usually twice the size of the target bonus) for each eligible position, and the actual individual bonus received reflects the individual's performance. To implement this, the entrepreneur must establish a process for computing the performance ratings of each manager; the preliminary total bonus estimates; the total amount of money required with the total bonus fund available; and then, if applicable, any necessary adjustments to each individual's bonus. While there are not hard-and-fast rules, usually top-level executives' bonuses are tied to overall company results rather than individual performance, while at the lower levels of management, individual performance affects the bonus paid.

Long-term incentives   Long term incentives are used to make sure decisions are made that will impact the long-term (not just the short-term) results of the company and will encourage managers and executives to stay with the company by letting these individuals accumulate capital that can only be cashed in after a specified number of years of employment, the vesting period. In terms of long-term incentives, the entrepreneur can use cash, stock, stock appreciation rights and stock options. Since long-term incentives are so important and are now being scrutinized and reviewed by the legislature in the USA, various stock option plans will be discussed in the next section of this chapter, 'Equity-based compensation'.

The long-term incentives have such a profound impact on the strategic success of the company that the entrepreneur should use them over a long period of time to reward managers and executives for contributing to the success of the business. This requires that the entrepreneur first define the company's strategy and then creates the compensation package that will reward managers for carrying out this strategy.

Equity-based compensation

Some entrepreneurs recognize that talented people are indispensable to the success of their business and design compensation packages that will attract and retain key employees without overextending the company's resources. Since oftentimes the salary levels needed are beyond the capacity of the firm, equity in the company has become the currency, allowing the entrepreneur to compete for the key individual needed. In addition to attracting and retaining key employees, equity-based compensation serves other purposes. It reduces cash flow and book expenses; it minimizes and postpones certain tax liabilities of the company; and, most importantly, it helps employees be concerned about and focus on improving the value of the company.

Stock options

By far the most popular equity incentive used by entrepreneurs is stock options. A stock option gives the employee the right to buy stock in the company at a stated price (the exercise price) for a specified period of time (option term). When granting a stock option, the company presently does not take any charge to earnings (although this law may change due to increasing legislative interest following several scandalous company situations such as Enron, WorldCom, and Adelphia Cable). The company also realizes positive cash flow when the option is exercised (turned in for stock) while obtaining loyalty to the company from individuals critical to its success. Stock options are of two types: incentive stock options (ISOs) and non-qualified stock options (NQSOs).

Incentive stock options can only be used upon shareholder approval. They enjoy a special tax treatment, as the employee realizes no taxable income when receiving the option or exercising it. The employee is only taxed when the acquired stock is sold, and then the applicable tax rate is the capital-gain tax rate, which is lower than the employee's personal income tax rate. The employee must hold the options and the stock for the required time period. The entrepreneur needs to follow the rules governing incentive stock options carefully, and employees need to observe the rules regarding their exercise.

Non-qualified stock options are different in that there are no restrictions on option price, term number of options granted or vested in a given year, or the disposition of the stock acquired through exercising an option. There are three different categories of non-qualified stock options. Market value options have an exercise price equal to the fair market value of the company's stock on the date of issuing the option. Discounted stock options have an exercise price below the fair market value of the company's stock on the issuance of options. Finally, premium-priced options have an exercise price above the fair market value of the stock when the option was received. When exercised, the company is entitled to a tax deduction on the amount of tax to the employee. All things being equal from the company's standpoint, non-qualified stock option plans are preferred over incentive stock option plans.

Restricted stock
An entrepreneur also can award key employees additional shares of restricted stock – stock not vested until the employee achieves his or her performance objectives or completes a prescribed number of years of employment. The employee is taxed on the value of these shares when they are no longer restricted (are freely transferable) or subject to a substantial use of forfeiture. The company has a tax deduction equal to the amount of income the employee recognized as a tax liability.

Regardless of controversy and the fact that many stock plans, mainly options, are under water (having no value with the option price being higher than the present stock price); stock-based compensation is still a good idea for entrepreneurs to use in attracting and retaining key employees, even if stock options are required to be charged against earnings when issued. Companies such as Nanoventions, a micro-options manufacturer, continue to use them, believing that employees of the company still like them, particularly those that really believe in the product and its future potential. For more information on employee compensation see McGarvey and Harrison (2006), Frye (2004), Johnson and Tian (2000) and 'Compensation Guide' (2006).

Motivation and compensation
A survey conducted from 2001 to 2004 by Sirota Survey Intelligence questioned 1.2 million employees from 52 Fortune 1000 companies and found that 85 percent of them felt that their employees' motivations had decreased significantly after six months of employment. The survey also found that management was a direct cause for this demotivation. Recommended to counteract a decline in motivation, management must understand three sets of goals that the majority of workers desire from their work – and then satisfy those goals.

1. Equity: to be respected and be treated fairly in pay, benefits, and job security.
2. Achievement: to be proud of one's job, accomplishments and employer.
3. Camaraderie: to have good, productive relationships with fellow employees.

The survey found that all three sets of goals must be maintained to keep an employee motivated. It does not help to offer more incentives in one category in place of the other categories; all three must be fulfilled. For example, 'improved recognition cannot replace better pay, money cannot substitute for taking pride in a job well done, and pride alone will not pay the mortgage' (*Hindustan Times*, 2006).

A lack of balance between these three factors may be leading to the exodus of employees from big pharmaceutical companies. Scott Hull writes about the major draws away from big pharmaceutical companies to smaller biotech companies. Some people, he says, are leaving for the opportunities of bigger money in the upcoming biotech industry while others are simply seeking more satisfying jobs. Some of the points of satisfaction come from: being closer to innovation; doing research that focuses on patients rather than diseases; being more entrepreneurial; having the freedom to explore and experiment; and the possibility a quicker advancing career (Hull, 2006).

One help in addressing the motivation issue is to have appropriate economic and non-economic compensation options. The numerous economic compensation options that can motivate are indicated in Figure 22.2 and some non-economic compensation options are indicated in Table 22.2.

If employees have migrated to smaller business, such as in the case of biotech companies, it is then the manager's task to keep employees motivated. Eight tips to improve employee motivation provided by the article 'Stop demotivating your employees!' (*Hindustan Times*, January 2006) are as follows:

● Instill an inspiring purpose
● Provide recognition
● Be an expediter for your employees
● Coach your employees for improvement
● Communicate fully
● Face up to poor performance
● Promote teamwork
● Listen and involve

Employee motivation can be understood even more granularly by looking at the core motivators of individual employees, which can further aid in determining what mix of

Table 22.2   Non-economic compensation

Fun/exciting	=	stock ownership driven by new innovations
Making a difference	=	doing research that focuses on patients
Speed of decision making	=	more entrepreneurial and less bureaucratic
Autonomy	=	freedom to explore, experiment, take risks and make decisions
Career advancement	=	quicker in smaller companies

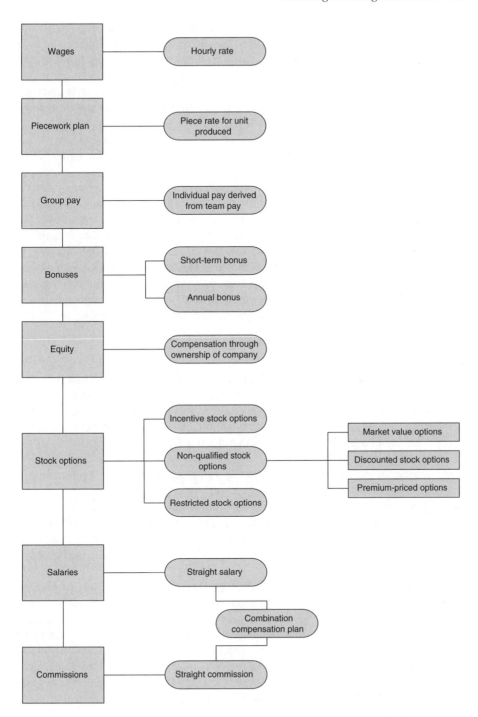

Figure 22.2   Economic compensation options

economic and non-economic incentives to offer an employee. The core motivators are described through a longstanding concept of career anchors by Edgar Schein. Schein indicated that there are eight main motivators for employees that define how they perceive themselves and their work. The key to using his framework is to first identify which anchors your employees most relate to. This will allow managers to communicate better with employees and bundle incentive packages that target their needs and ultimately drive them to be more productive (Schein, 1990).

If you are good at assessing people you can determine the career anchor for each of your employees, or for more assistance Schein offers an evaluation that can identify each employee's strongest tendencies (Field, 2003).

The eight career anchors represent overall categories for an employee's main characteristics and are described through key attributes (see Table 22.3). The greatest advantage in Schein's model comes from identifying how to communicate with an employee dependent on the career anchor and how to offer appropriate recognition. For example, if you hire a new employee who clearly holds the greatest tendencies in the Lifestyle Career Anchor, recognize that the employee places the greatest importance on maintaining a work–life balance, is best communicated to in a direct and concise manner, and is motivated through rewards of a flexible schedule and time for more activities outside of work.

For more information on employee motivation see Daniels (2001) and 'Motivating employees guide' (2006).

Develop appropriate employee benefits

Smaller entrepreneurial firms generally provide fewer and different benefits than larger firms. While this reflects the size of the business, it also is a result of the fact that smaller firms are less likely to be unionized. One cause of this difference is the substantial overhead cost of benefit administration, which could include having a benefits administrator or a human resource manager on the company's payroll. Since these personnel costs can be amortized over the entire employee base, it takes a certain organizational size in terms of the number of employees to make having a human resource manager and/or benefit administrator cost-effective.

In today's environment, it is particularly important to accommodate the increased interest in a greater work–life balance. Entrepreneurs particularly can use flexible scheduling as a low-cost but extremely attractive incentive to attract and retain top-level talent at all levels of the organization. Some feel that flexibility is the number one benefit sought by all employees.

A survey of the employee benefits of the top 100 companies according to *Entrepreneur Magazine* is indicted in Table 22.4. As indicted, flextime and telecommuting are on the increase over the last three years, with most other benefit categories (health insurance 401(k) plans, stock options, tuition reimbursement and job salary) remaining relatively stable.

Some companies have had greater success in attracting and retaining employees by hiring local people. Jameson Inns, a regional hotel chain, has had great success in hiring local managers and other employees for each of its 121 hotels. These managers know the area and the competition, and have proven to be very successful at building a strong clientele.

Similarly, New Ravenia, a company that creates custom mosaics, hired all its 105 employees, even the CEO, from Virginia's eastern shore. Even though each of the

Table 22.3   Edgar Schein's eight career anchors

Career anchors	Key attributes	How to communicate	Best type of recognition
1 Technical/functional	• Desire to excel in chosen line of work • Opportunity to refine skills is bigger driver than money and promotions	• Appeal to them as experts and try to have others do the same • Don't pretend to have knowledge in a field when you don't; you'll quickly lose their respect	• Allow them to continually refine their skills • Help 'keep their edge' by sending them on conferences or seminars
2 General/managerial	• Looks for upward movement in a company • Wants to learn many functions • Enjoys compiling information, supervising groups, and applying interpersonal skills	• Converse with them over performance and results • Include them in administration matters and ask their input	• Money • Promotions • Leadership in key projects • Prestigious title • Training through workshops or seminars
3 Autonomy/ independence	• Goal is freedom to work	• Avoid having group meetings and calls • Set a timetable to meet for work updates	• Try not to interfere in their work • Motivate by allowing them to 'take the ball and run with it'
4 Security/stability	• Value predictable environment the most	• Communicate with them frequently • Urge them to take action and pursue continuous learning	• Show appreciation for their loyalty • Take them to lunch • Provide organized activities
5 Entrepreneurial creativity	• Want to create something of their own or desire to lead	• Challenge with goals rather than assignments • Criticize in private	• Money • Public recognition • Opportunities to create new ventures
6 Sense of service	• Desire to focus on a certain	• Focus on their values of interest	• Provide opportunities to

Table 22.3   (continued)

Career anchors	Key attributes	How to communicate	Best type of recognition
	cause and set of values	• Match projects with these values • Communicate how their job will contribute to a greater cause	work for their causes
7 Pure challenge	• Driven by conquering big goals	• Be prepared to negotiate with employee's thoughts • Ask for more information regarding actions • Confirm employee is driving towards correct goals	• Provide many challenges • Assign new projects before others end • Praise is less necessary; keep them going on the next project
8 Lifestyle	• Want work to provide freedom in private life	• Be direct and concise • Clearly communicate all needs • Organize schedules to accommodate their requests	• Allow them to have a flexible schedule • Reward with time away from work

Source: Edgar H. Schein, *Career Anchors, Discovering your real values*, San Francisco, CA: Jossey-Bass/Pfeiffer, 1990.

Table 22.4   Employee benefits

	2006	2005	2004
Health insurance	96	97	91
401(k) plans	79	76	59
Car allowances/company cars	45	43	45
Flextime	43	34	34
Stock options	29	28	16
Telecommuting	33	28	24
Tuition reimbursement	27	28	26
Job sharing	8	8	6

Source: *Entrepreneur*'s Hot 100 2006, 2005, 2004, *Entrepreneur*, June 2006, p. 28.

employees had no previous experience with mosaics and needed training, Sam Baldwin, founder, reports a near 100 percent retention rate. According to Baldwin, the company 'has lots of opportunities for growth. I have supervisors who started on the production floor' (*Entrepreneur*, June 2006).

Conclusions

In order for small entrepreneurial firms to have a better probability of success and be able to address the opportunities available, hiring additional staff must be done on a timely basis. To avoid the frustration that often occurs, and particularly to avoid bad hires, each entrepreneur should establish his/her process for hiring and have in place the appropriate environment for motivating and compensating each new hire. This will allow hiring mistakes to be avoided, and the appropriate personnel to be brought on board in a timely manner.

References

American Marketing Association (2002), 'Ethics and integrity are listed as core values by 76% of companies', www.amanet.org/press/amanews/corporate_values.htm.

Collins, James C. and Jerry I. Porras (2002), *Built to Last*, New York: HarperCollins.

Collins, Michelle (2006), '5 steps to a strong company culture', www.microsoft.com/smallbusiness/resources/management/pay_benefits/5_steps_to_a_strong_company_culture.mspx.

'Compensation guide' (2006), www.inc.com/guides/hr/20678.html.

Daniels, Aubry (2001), 'Rewarding your employees: you don't have to spend a bundle to reinforce good behavior', www.entrepreneur.com.

Datz, Todd (2000), 'Measuring employee quality – not', *Darwin*, October, www.darwinmag.com/read/100100/buzz_hr.html.

Entrepreneur Magazine (2006), June, p. 103.

Field, Anne (2003), 'Speak to what drives them: identifying the motivations that anchor employees' careers can help managers spur and reward achievement in a high-demand economy', *Harvard Management Communication Letter*, **6**(9).

Forster, Julie (2002), 'Early retirement may create worker shortage', *Greenville News*, 7 December, p. F1.

Frye, Melissa (2004), 'Equity-based compensation for employees: firm performance and determinants', *CFA Digest*, **34**(3).

Gladwell, Malcolm (2005), *Blink, the Power of Thinking Without Thinking*, New York and Boston, MA: Little, Brown and Company.

Hetherington, Sally (2006), 'Know when it's time to get help', www.bizland.co.za/articles/employ/timetohire.htm, 10 June.

Hull, Scott (2006), 'The war for talent', www.pharmexec.com, April.

Johnson, Shane A. and Yisong S. Tian (2000), 'The value and incentive effects of nontraditional executive stock option plans', *Journal of Financial Economics*, **57**(1), 3–34.

Kattenmaker, Tom (2002), 'Write a mission statement that your company is willing to live', *Harvard Management Communication Letter*, **5**(3).

Lee, Mie-Yun (2002), 'Outsource your HR', BuyerZone.com, www.entrepreneur.com/article/0.4621.305528.00.html, 23 December.

McGarvey, Robert J. and Barb S. Harrison (2006), 'Money talks: resources that offer guidance on the how-tos of paying your employees', www.entrepreneur.com.

'Motivating employees guide' (2006), www.inc.com/guides/hr/20776.html.

Sankey, Derek (2006), 'Hiring the best tough for small firms: facing a worker shortage, businesses forced to really sell themselves', *The Calgary Herald*; CanWest News Service, 12 April.

Schein, Edgar H. (1990), *Career Anchors: Discovering Your Real Values*, San Francisco, CA: Jossey-Bass/Pfeiffer.

'Stop demotivating your employees!' (2006), *Hindustan Times*, New Delhi, India, 30 January.

Vargo, Angela (2006), 'Chatting to customers at Southwest', *Strategic Communication Mangement*, **10**(4).

Weisul, Kimberly (2003), 'Few big axes at small businesses', *Business Week Online*, 6 January.

23 Organizational change and its dysfunctional effect on managers in large organizations
Les Worrall, Cary L. Cooper and Kim Mather

Introduction

One of the best-known opening lines in English literature comes from Charles Dickens's book, *A Tale of Two Cities* (1859). The opening of the book reads:

> It was the best of times, it was the worst of times, it was the age of wisdom, it was the age of foolishness, it was the epoch of belief, it was the epoch of incredulity, it was the season of Light, it was the season of Darkness, it was the spring of hope, it was the winter of despair, we had everything before us, we had nothing before us, we were all going direct to heaven, we were all going direct the other way . . .

A Tale of Two Cities is set in the French Revolution, a period of tumultuous change. The opening quotation demonstrates how, in an era of overt class conflict, intense and persistent change can generate paradox and contradiction. This 'best of times–worst of times' dichotomy is a useful device for looking at contemporary change in large UK business organizations. The 'best of times' adherents, marching under the banner of the 'high performance work organisation' (Guest et al., 2000) and the rhetoric of strategic human resource management (HRM), would see employees marching towards the heavenly light of empowerment, autonomy and self-management. The 'worst of times' adherents would emphasize that the rhetoric of strategic HRM bears no resemblance to the reality of everyday organizational life as work both intensifies and extensifies, employees labour under increased surveillance through ever more intrusive performance management systems and increasingly lose control over their workloads as terms and conditions of work deteriorate (Legge, 2005; Noon and Blyton, 2002; Burchell et al., 2002). An important question we seek to answer here is what proportion of UK managers are living in the 'spring of hope' and what proportion in the 'winter of despair'.

While much of the analysis of stress and organizational dysfunction has been conducted from the perspective of organizational behaviourists or organizational psychologists, the purpose of this chapter is to explore the political economy of workplace stress and organizational dysfunction. While organizational psychologists tend to focus on the individual and their workplace setting, the purpose of this chapter is to explore the factors that affect these workplace settings and environments, that drive change in organizations, and then to assess the effects of these changes on the managers of those organizations. Our prime argument is that we must develop a more multidisciplinary and multi-level understanding of workplace stress and organizational dysfunction if we are to provide more informed and effective responses, and more sensitive policy. Our key aim in this chapter is to develop such an understanding by looking at how organizational contexts are changing in response to the change at the whole economy and sectoral levels, and how these changes filter through to affect workers' perceptions and experiences. Clearly, different business sectors are affected differently by changes in macroeconomic conditions and factors influencing the nature of competition, and this is a point we shall examine later. We are also concerned that many of the changes that take place in organizations happen in an uncoordinated way, and that this has been exacerbated by the trend towards more complex and multifaceted change that now confronts many organizations.

The purpose of this chapter is to use a large time-series data set to explore the 'best of times–worst of times' theme. The data set has been developed out of the Quality of Working Life project that the authors, working in conjunction with the Chartered Management Institute in the UK, have been involved with since 1997. The survey will not be described in detail here as its aims, objectives and methodology are described in detail elsewhere (Worrall and Cooper, 1997, 1998, 1999, 2001, 2006). The analysis presented here will focus mainly on the most recent data set (collected in late 2005) and explore the changes that are occurring primarily in large organizations that are either public limited companies (plcs) or public sector bodies (such as local and central government, the health and education sectors). However, reference will be made throughout to conditions in private limited companies for comparative purposes.

The chapter will consist of four main sections. In the first, the task will be to identify the economic and political contexts in which large plcs and public sector organizations (psos) operate and how these external pressures on organizations are manifest within organizations in the form of changed structures, cultures, business processes and behavioural settings. In the second section, the aim is to discuss the theoretical framework in the context of which research and analysis have taken place. The theoretical framework that underpins our thinking here is labour process theory, as we see this as a useful device for explaining how the macro-level changes outside the organization are translated into micro-level effects on managers both individually and collectively (Braverman, 1974; Knights and Willmott, 1986). We have argued elsewhere (Mather et al., 2007, forthcoming) that while the rhetoric of management has focused on concepts such as inspirational leadership and empowerment, the reality of management has often focused on increased central control, cost reduction and strategies designed to improve productivity by intensifying the utilization of assets – particularly labour. The work intensification thesis inherent in labour process theory implies that increased competition will lead to reduced worker discretion, workers becoming increasingly overloaded, having less influence over their pace of work and reduced influence over how they do their job. A central theme of the Quality of Working Life (QoWL) research project – which provides the empirical foundation of our research – has been to quantify the scale and persistence of organizational change and to explore the effects of these changes on managers' working and non-working lives using items that are directly redolent of the central tenets of labour process theory. Consequently, the third section of this chapter will discuss the scale and extent of organizational change and how different forms of change have differentially affected managers' perceptions of their organization, their sense of psychological well-being, their absence levels and propensity to report symptoms of ill-health. In the fourth and final section, the aim will be to develop some contemporary, empirically grounded insights into what it is that differentiates well-functioning organizations from dysfunctional organizations.

The prevailing business climate in the UK, 'financialization' and its effect on large organizations

All business organizations are embedded within complex economic, social and institutional settings to which they have to adapt if they are to survive. Institutional theorists and organizational ecology theorists would argue that an organization adapts and survives by managing the complex relationship between the organization and its environment. Structural contingency theorists would argue that the internal configuration and morphology of an organization is largely defined by the nature and exigencies of the environment in which that firm operates. Resource-base theorists would argue that a firm has to define and then develop its distinctive competencies if it is to survive in its current product market, if it is to develop new product markets and if it is to outperform its competitors. Developing the 'core competencies' organizations need to deliver competitive advantage, which became the fad of the 1990s (Prahalad and Hamel, 1990). Increasingly, the human resource base of a business and its capacity to develop new knowledge is being seen as an effective way for organizations to develop products and services that are non-imitable and will lead to sustainable competitive edge. There is a welter of theories in the business strategy literature that can be invoked to explore how firms interact with their operational environments, how this interaction impacts on the morphology and internal configuration of the firm, and how a firm will develop its resources, competencies and skills sets to achieve high levels of productivity that will translate into competitive advantage.

As Porter and Ketels (2003: 7) argued in their DTI-sponsored study of competitiveness in the UK, 'True competitiveness then, is measured by productivity'. If we are to take Porter and Ketels's dictum at face value, which the UK government certainly seems to have done, then the competitiveness of the UK economy and its ability to survive the global threat of low-wage economies such as China and India will depend on the generation of increased productivity – particularly labour productivity. The concept of productivity clearly implies an equation where outputs are divided by inputs – the higher the number, the better. Productivity can be improved by increasing output and either holding inputs constant or ensuring that inputs increase at a slower rate than outputs. Productivity can also be improved by cutting inputs, using them more intensively or substituting a less expensive input (technology) for a more expensive input (labour). A central thesis of this chapter is that a continuing trend over the last decade – at least – has been for employers to develop labour-handling strategies that have culminated in the more intensive use of managerial labour by modifying the managerial labour process, increasing control and surveillance through performance management regimes or, in the form of delayering and redundancy, eliminating some managers from the productivity equation altogether. These have all had differential impacts on managers' behaviours in the workplace and on their sense of physical and psychological well-being, as they have reacted to and internalized these changes.

We also see it as essential to understand what it is that drives business if we are to understand and explain what is going on within organizations. One of the prime tenets of the modern corporation is the separation of ownership from control. In this regime, the directors of an organization become the agents of the owners with the responsibility of maximizing returns to investment. Given the presence of an active stock market in the UK and the growth of the institutional investor, often in the form of pension funds, the period from the 1980s has been marked by an increased emphasis on the generation of shareholder value. Institutional investors are very influential in driving firms to achieve high levels of return using metrics such as 'return on capital employed' (ROCE) or 'economic value added' (EVA). But the path of causality here is not unidirectional. The development of techniques such as the balanced scorecard (Kaplan and Norton, 1996), for example, emphasizes the development of metrics such as EVA as a prime driver of business growth that firms must achieve if they are to secure investment by 'looking good' in the capital market. Additionally, directors' remuneration often comprises a mix of salary and share option preferences: consequently, it is in directors' own interest to maximize shareholder value as they will invariably have a binary interest in the firm. Indeed, some might see the 'financialization' of the modern corporation (Fround et al., 2000a,b) as the capital market's way of overcoming 'the agency problem' of keeping the directors of a company in line with the needs of the shareholders. Our concern with financialization is that it has become a very monochromatic way of managing organizations as wider sets of aims and objectives, particularly those related to improving the quality of working life, have been made subservient to achieving rates of return or other 'bottom-line' metrics. Indeed, the core aims of the QoWL project (Worrall and Cooper, 1997) have been to produce a more 'socially complete' and holistic view of the impact of recent business and economic trends and developments on the quality of working life; to develop a better understanding of the processes and factors that influence the quality of working life; and to develop softer measures of business performance to parallel the 'hard' measures regularly published in corporate annual reports.

Researchers in the shareholder value field argue that financialization has changed business 'priorities and behaviours'; it has been used as a 'management justification' for corporate restructuring and downsizing, particularly in the USA and the UK; and it has delivered 'a different and more carnivorous type of capitalism' (Williams, 2000: 1). The carnivorous form of capital seems to be particularly dangerous to labour as it involves 'downsizing the corporate labour-force' (ibid.: 4) and an increased desire to 'sweat out labour' (ibid.: 6). Froud et al. (2000a: 771) argue that 'labour is usually the first casualty' of shareholder value maximization driven restructuring; that there is a prevailing logic of 'the more redundancies, the better for shareholders' (ibid.: 776); and that 'restructuring works directly for capital and against labour' as attempts to increase returns to capital are often 'at the expense of the internal workforce'. Jones (2002) argues that corporate restructuring, often in the form of headcount culls, are in effect often little more than cynical signalling mechanisms to the market designed to improve share prices.

These authors have also identified a degree of cultural specificity in the way that restructuring is enacted. Froud et al. (2000b: 776) see business organizations as embedded in national, institutional structures, and they cited the research of Usui and Cilignon, 1996: 551), which contrasts the Anglo-American model, characterized by 'widespread lay-offs and worker terminations as a prevailing strategy', with behavioural models in Germany and Japan where firms 'use alternative employment adjustment measures with worker termination as a last resort'. Clearly, the Anglo-American form of shareholder value maximization is a more 'carnivorous form of capitalism' than those in Germany or Japan. While some neoclassical economists might see 'restructuring' as a means of reallocating workers from less to more productive parts of the economy, the objective in this chapter is to take a wider view, and this is reinforced by Cascio (1993, 2005), who found that organizations that had downsized did not outperform those that had not culled the workforce on an array of financial and business performance measures. This finding echoes Froud et al. (2000b: 795), who predicted that 'late capitalist restructuring is likely to be a negative process for labour with transitory gains for capital'. If the assertion that gains to capital will be 'transitory' is true, this raises significant questions about the logic of the more carnivorous forms of restructuring that many firms in the UK, operating in the Anglo-American culture of restructuring, have adopted. However, more recent research has called into question Cascio's findings. De Meuse et al. (2004: 174) suggested that 'when a company implements downsizing it will take several years before its financial health will re-emerge' and add that Cascio 'simply may not have investigated the down-sizing process long enough'. While firms may eventually recover from downsizing, there is a considerable literature to suggest that the effects can be profound in the short term (Worrall et al., 2000a,b) and that recovery periods can be protracted (De Meuse et al., 2004). Clearly, downsizing and redundancy cannot be considered as short-term fixes or as a means of cynically manipulating share prices.

It is also interesting that Usui and Cilignon published their paper in 1996 based on even earlier research: in September 1999 Michelin announced that it intended to make 7500 workers across Europe redundant, affecting production at its plants in France, Germany, Italy, Spain and the UK. The announcement coincided with a 17 per cent increase in company profits for the first half of 1999 and was accompanied by a 12.5 per cent increase in Michelin's share price on the Paris stock exchange.[1] Perhaps the Anglo-American, car-nivorous model has become more pervasive since the publication of Usui and Cilignon's research. Interestingly, Froud et al. (2000b) argue that the obsession with the generation of shareholder value and the growing trend towards 'financialization' as a means of man-aging organizations has degraded management as emphasis has moved away from 'improving the numerator' in the productivity equation through creativity and innovative product and market development strategies towards management actions geared to reducing the denominator in the productivity equation by obsessively driving down costs and 'making the assets sweat'. They argue that 'even in blue-chip companies . . . operat-ing management becomes an endless series of cheap financial dodges: this year's target is met by ending the defined benefit pension scheme, which saves labour costs, and next year's dodge is leasing the trucks so that the capital appears on someone else's balance sheet' (Froud et al., 2000a: 109). They see this degraded work as being punctuated and interrupted by major restructurings – 'where it is the financial engineering that is crucial' – and mergers, where the key question is 'how many workers can be sacked?'. There is compelling evidence from Froud et al. (2000a,b) and Williams (2000) that shareholder value maximization, for the workforce especially, leads to working environments at the 'worst of times' end of our continuum.

So far, our discussion of the drivers of organizational change has focused on the private sector and the primacy of shareholder value logic. Yet our objective in this chapter is to explore organizational change and its effects on managers' perceptions of their organiza-tion and their behaviours within it in both the private and public sectors. While the public sector clearly does not have shareholders, it does have other forms of stakeholder that are keen to see change, but change in the public sector is usually articulated in terms of efficiency savings and legitimized through the language of 'modernization'. The main stakeholder in the public sector is the ruling political party and, while shareholders are keen to maximize their return on investment, the ruling political party is keen to maximize its probability of being re-elected by delivering an agenda for the public sector based on, for example, 'marketization' (Conservative government, 1979 to 1997) or, more recently, 'modernization' (Labour governments, 1997 to present), though both variants of change have been delivered through the medium of an increased 'managerialization' of the public sector (Clarke and Newman, 1997). Since the late 1970s, the public sector has been the focus of a barrage of change designed to expose that sector to market forces through initiatives such as compulsory competitive tendering, 'market testing', 'best value' and, in more extreme cases, the wholesale privatization of, for example, the former public utilities. In the early 1980s, some saw the need to 'reinvent government' (Osborne and Gaebler, 1992) through the adoption of a more 'entrepreneurial spirit'. The transformation of the public sector since the early 1980s has been considerable, and the transformation process has led to a complete revision of the nature of managing in the public sector and the creation of a 'new public management' (Ferlie et al., 1996). The rise of the new public management has been associated with the introduction of performance management systems which, some would argue, have been put in place to 'name and shame' poor performers. Regimes such as comprehensive performance assessment (CPA) have been developed to categorize local authorities on a scale from poor to excellent, with the threat that poorly performing local authorities that do not improve may be removed from local control. Some have argued (Mather et al., 2007, forthcoming) that the managerialization of the public sector has been designed to ship power from 'the professionals' to 'the managers' and to 'whip the professionals into shape' (Pollitt, 1993; Walsh, 1995) so that the public sector can be run on 'sound business principles' (Boyne, 2002; Martin, 2002; Clarke and Newman, 1997).

The 'modernization agenda' in the public sector, designed to deliver both cost savings and service quality improvements, has resulted in reduced staffing, work intensification, the growth of performance-monitoring regimes and control architectures (Richardson et al., 2005), a shift in power from professionals to managers (Mather et al., 2007, forthcoming) and reduced 'worker discretion' (Grugulis et al., 2003; Rainbird et al., 2004: 94). Felstead et al. (2004) provide evidence of significant changes in job complexity and task discretion since the mid-1980s. For example, a much lower proportion of workers in the public sector now report that they have choice over the way that they do their job; less influence over how hard they work; less influence over what tasks get done; less influence over how they do their job; and less influence over quality standards. Others argue that change in the public sector has resulted in increased efficiency, lower costs and higher levels of customer satisfaction. It has certainly resulted in the degradation of work, work overload and less job involvement for many public sector workers.

Public sector organizations have been 'the test-bed' for ministerial 'experimentation with free market principles' (Legge, 2005: 267). Indeed, in the National Health Service (NHS), managerial instruments redolent of the 'financialization' metrics used in the private sector (such as EVA or ROCE) have been adopted in the sector: hospitals, for example, were required to generate a 'surplus' equal to 6 per cent capital employed after meeting all operating costs (Shaoul, 1999: 48–9). For hospital managers this meant tinkering with the productivity equation by either increasing income or reducing costs (mainly labour costs) or mothballing assets (closing wards). Given the public opprobrium generated by closing wards and the difficulty in raising additional revenue, 'efficiency savings' were invariably focused on labour cost reduction, achieved either by lowering the overall pay bill through initiatives such as 'casualization', by deskilling and by intensifying the work effort of existing employees (Hewison, 1999). Our own research has identified that the key stressors for public sector managers included the unmanageability of work overload, persistent organizational change, having little control over key aspects of their job, over-zealous performance monitoring and low levels of job involvement (Worrall and Cooper, 2006). Similar issues have been reported by Ball (1993); Barry et al. (2001); Bryson (2004); Harris (1998); Kirkpatrick and Ackroyd (2003a,b). The broad thrust of these studies reveals a pattern of senior management behaviour and organizational change in the public sector that is directly analogous to that found in most private sector organizations. To Boyne's question in his 2002 paper, 'Public and private management; what's the difference?', our response would be – very little.

If the shareholder value maximization agenda in the private sector and the modernization agenda in the public sector are to be delivered, organizational strategies, tactics and actions have to be created to bring about their delivery. The key means of delivering these agendas have been cost reduction programmes and the intensification of the use of assets (primarily labour), the redefinition of organizational labour-handling strategies and the redesign of the employment relationship by creating more flexible forms of employment where more of the costs associated with employing workers are transferred from the employer to the worker. Downsizing, delayering and redundancy programmes have been used to reduce headcounts. Organizational boundaries have been redefined through the use of outsourcing and by the development of networks, partnerships and shared service agreements. Other tactics have involved shifting production to lower-wage economies (offshoring); deploying new technology and substituting technology for labour; downscoping (i.e. focusing in on a narrower set of functions/products); and merger and acquisition. In addition to these more substantive, tangible changes, many organizations have also put in place culture change programmes that can, cynically, be interpreted as attitudinal and behaviour modification programmes to educate workers to expect less from the employing organization, particularly in terms of their own conditions of employment (e.g. zero hours contracts and worse pension entitlements) and job security (Burchell et al., 2002; Worrall et al., 2000c). While we have identified that there are many possible forms of change, it is important not to see these as unrelated single change initiatives. It has become increasingly common for several change projects to run simultaneously within organizations. Indeed, Ichniowski et al. (1997) and MacDuffie (1995) have suggested that organizational change is normally multidimensional and multistrand, and we argue that these complex patterns of change will have a substantially greater impact on employees as organizational structures, processes, boundaries, cultures, roles and performance expectations change simultaneously and occasionally in contradictory ways.

Here, the objective has been to develop a framework that will allow us to understand the logics that drive organizational change. We argue that the increased 'financialization' and 'metricization' in the way that businesses are managed tends to drive the directors of organizations to manage more by manipulating the bottom line of the productivity equation (i.e. by first looking to reduce costs or export them outside the boundary of the business) than to engage with innovation, new business development and techniques designed to affect the numerator in the productivity equation. To invoke our 'best of times–worst of times' metaphor, we would argue that in organizations where denominator management

prevails, workers are more likely to be in 'the winter of despair' while in those organizations where numerator management takes place, workers are more likely to be in 'the spring
of hope'.

The emphasis on shareholder-driven metrics in the private sector and the emphasis on
modernization and marketization in the public sector have both had huge impacts on how
organizations are designed, how their borders are defined and what it is like to work within
them. Having developed a framework for understanding why and how organizations
change, we now turn to examining what effects these changes have had on managers' perceptions of organizational life, their sense of well-being, their behaviours in the workplace
and in the way that they too manage the boundary between their working lives and their
non-working lives. Our tasks in the following sections will be to quantify the scale and
dimensionality of organizational change, before going on to assess the effects of change
on managers.

The scale and dimensionality of change affecting UK business organizations
The analysis reported here is derived from the Quality of Working Life project that the
authors have conducted in conjunction with Chartered Management Institute since 1997.
The latest study was conducted in late 2005[2] in order to assess the scale and complexity
of organizational change in UK business organizations and to assess the impact of
change on managers' perception of their organization, their views about the impact of
change on their organization and, using the ASSET instrument,[3] to assess the effect
of change on their physical and psychological well-being. The questionnaire was structured to allow analysis to be conducted by respondent's seniority in the organization
(director, senior, middle and junior manager) and by business sector. Given that the literature review above has focused explicitly on plcs and the public sector, the analysis presented below is confined largely to these two types of organization, but reference is made
to private limited companies for comparative purposes.

Our review of the literature on organizational change provided us with a series of
themes that can be explored in the 2005 data set and a comparison of change against
earlier data sets in the QoWL series. The themes explored below are:

- The scale, nature, intensity and complexity of organizational change since
  1999/2000 – is this consistent with the expectations derived from the literature
  review?
- The effects of managers' experiences of organizational change on their perceptions
  of their organization as a place to work – what are they and do different forms of
  change have different impacts?
- Do the views of directors and other managers about the effects of organizational
  change differ significantly?
- The effects of organizational factors and organizational climate on managers' sense
  of well-being.

The scale, nature, intensity and complexity of organizational change
Our review of the literature suggests that as the environment becomes more competitive, the scale, intensity and complexity of organizational change should increase, and
this was borne out by our data. In 2005, more managers (89 per cent) had experienced

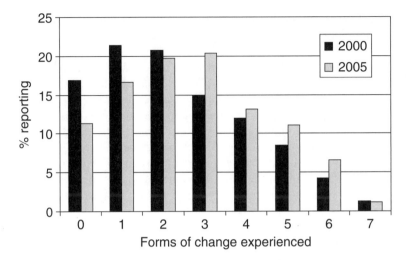

Figure 23.1   The distribution of forms of change experienced – 2000 and 2005 compared

organizational change than in 2000 (83 per cent). The pace and scale of change had been most intense in the public sector and in plcs (where 97 per cent and 94 per cent of respondents respectively had experienced change in the last year) but it was somewhat lower (82 per cent) in private limited companies. While a higher proportion of public sector managers than plc managers had experienced change, managers in plcs had experienced more forms of change concurrently (3.5 on average) than managers in the public sector (3.2) and in private limited companies (2.3).

Figure 23.1 reveals how the distribution of the number of forms of change managers had experienced (full data set) had changed since 2000. In 2000, 38 per cent of managers had experienced no or one form of change, but by 2000 this had declined to 26 per cent. Between 2000 and 2005, the mode of the distribution moved from one form of change to three. The proportion of managers affected by five or more forms of change increased from 14 per cent to 18 per cent.

While the average number of changes experienced by managers in plcs increased marginally (from 3.14 to 3.27), the average number experienced by public sector managers increased from 2.65 to 3.18, revealing that change in the public sector had become more multidimensional over time. Since 2000, a higher proportion of managers had been affected by change and a higher proportion experienced more forms of change concurrently. Managers in private limited companies were less likely to be confronted by change and had also experienced fewer forms of concurrent change.

The expectation from our review of the literature suggests that cost reduction should be the prime driver of change: cost reduction was cited most often in both the 2005 and the 1999[4] studies (64 per cent in both surveys). In 1999, 53 per cent had cited culture change programmes, but this increased marginally to 56 per cent in 2005. While there was a degree of stability in the proportions citing cost reduction and culture change, there was a major increase in the proportion of managers reporting the use of contract staff. This increased from 33 per cent in 1999 to 57 per cent by 2005. This increase is significant and indicative of a structural change in both the managerial labour market and the nature of

Table 23.1   The form of organizational change and its incidence by type of organization

% of managers reporting each type of change	Private limited company	Plc	Public sector	All 2005
Cost reduction programme	54	69	79	64
Use of short-term contract staff	44	64	67	57
Culture change programme	40	59	72	56
Redundancies	34	49	34	36
Outsourcing	22	38	26	25
Delayering	17	32	24	22
Merger	10	18	16	14
Offshoring	9	21	0	8
Expansion into new markets	52	46	N/A	N/A

the employment relationship as employers seek to create a more flexible labour market and to minimize employment overheads. The increased use of managers with a lower level of attachment to an organization yields increased flexibility and, more important, reduces some of the long-term costs of employment to the firm, particularly pension liabilities, as the employee is increasingly expected to invest in their own pension, thus absolving employers of this liability. The increased use of contract workers also has implications for the nature of the internal labour market and career structures within the firm as managers previously employed within the organization are replaced by self-employed workers or managers recruited from the large network of agencies that now exists to supply interim managers.

The mix of change instruments used varies by type of organization (Table 23.1). The public sector was most affected by cost reduction and culture change programmes with levels substantially above plcs but it experienced levels of redundancy, outsourcing and delayering substantially below those in plcs. Some might interpret this as evidence that, while in the public sector there is a great deal of apparent emphasis on cost reduction and culture change, this is much less likely to result in people actually losing their jobs than in plcs, where the reported levels of cost reduction and culture change are lower but the actual outcomes (i.e. people losing their jobs through redundancy, delaying or outsourcing) are much more prevalent.

The differences between plcs and private limited companies are profound. Managers in private limited companies were much less likely than those in plcs to experience cost reduction programmes, the use of contract staff, culture change, redundancies, outsourcing and delayering. Managers in private limited companies were, however, more likely to report that their companies had expanded into new markets. This provides some evidence that senior managers in private limited companies may be more minded to manage the productivity equation by working on the numerator while the emphasis in plcs seems to be much more denominator-focused. The extent, dimensionality and pattern of organizational change are more benign in private limited companies than in either the public sector or plcs. In the public sector, there is some justification for arguing that while they are more likely to talk about reducing costs, unlike plcs, they are less likely to do it.

Table 23.2   Patterns of organizational change in growing, static and declining businesses

% of managers reporting	Declining	Static	Growing	All
Cost reduction programme	89	69	50	63
Use of short-term contract staff	63	54	56	57
Culture change programme	64	54	53	56
Redundancies	64	34	27	36
Outsourcing	33	23	23	25
Delayering	42	22	14	22
Merger	14	9	17	14
Offshoring	8	8	8	8

While we have identified significant differences in the scale and pattern of change in different types of organization, there were significant differences in the scale and nature of change in business that were perceived to be declining, static and growing.[5] While 85 per cent and 89 per cent of managers in growing and static businesses respectively had experienced some form of change, this increased to 98 per cent in declining businesses. Managers in growing businesses experienced (on average) 2.5 forms of change, but this increased to 2.7 in static businesses and to 3.8 in declining businesses. In declining businesses, more managers experienced organizational change and did so on more fronts simultaneously. In addition to the greater incidence of change in declining businesses compared to static and growing businesses, the pattern of change in these three types of business varied considerably. Managers in declining businesses (see Table 23.2) were much more likely to experience cost reduction programmes, redundancies, delayering and outsourcing than managers in both static and growing businesses. Elsewhere (Worrall et al., 2000b), we have argued that these forms of change have a particularly injurious effect on the perceptions and behaviours of surviving managers.

Since 2000, an increased proportion of UK managers have been subject to organizational change. The percentage of managers reporting change increased by six percentage points between 2000 and 2005, to stand at 89 per cent. The intensity of change increased as the average manager experienced more forms – and thus a greater complexity – of organizational change. While cost reduction remained the prime instrument of organizational change, there were significant changes in the pattern of change. Redundancies and delayering became less prevalent (but are still key change instruments in certain sectors) but the use of short-term contract staff increased markedly, indicating a change in the structure of the managerial labour market. This we see as evidence of organizations redefining their labour-handling strategies to increase flexibility and to reduce costs.

Since our last survey, change had become more prevalent and more multifaceted, particularly in the public sector and among managers in plcs. This we ascribe partly to the fact that these organizations tend to be larger, but also to the power of shareholder value logic in plcs and to the government's modernization agenda that is driving large-scale, complex change throughout the sector. Having identified that the extent and complexity have both increased, we now turn to examining how these organizational changes have affected managers' perceptions of the organizations within which they work.

Table 23.3   Managers' perceptions of the effect of organizational change

% of managers responding . . .	Strongly disagree	Disagree	No change	Agree	Strongly agree	Net agree[a]
Accountability has increased	3	13	32	43	10	36
Key skills and experience have been lost	5	20	27	35	13	23
Profitability has increased	3	17	42	33	4	17
Productivity has increased	3	20	38	36	3	17
Flexibility has increased	6	22	35	34	3	10
Employee participation has increased	6	23	34	35	3	9
Decision making is faster	8	29	38	22	3	−12
Motivation has increased	9	42	31	17	1	−33
Employee well-being has increased	8	40	39	11	1	−37
Loyalty has increased	8	39	44	9	0	−38
Morale has increased	15	46	24	14	1	−45
Perceptions of job security have increased	15	41	33	10	1	−46

Note: [a] A 'net score' is calculated by adding the percentage who strongly agree or agree with a statement together and subtracting from this the percentage that strongly disagree or disagree. Consequently, a positive net agree score indicates the strength of opinion in favour of a given statement.

The effects of managers' experiences of organizational change on their perceptions of their organization as a place to work

Managers who had undergone organizational change were asked to indicate what effect change had had on their perceptions of their organization. While the effects of organizational change had been considerable, they were often not seen positively by managers and more likely to be seen positively by directors – an issue to which we will return later. Table 23.3 contains a summary of managers' views about the effects of organizational change.

While there is a relatively strong agreement that change has increased managers' sense of accountability, managers were much less of the opinion that profitability and productivity had increased as a result of change: this echoes Cascio's (1993, 2005) findings and, because of the recency of change, the necessary 'healing period' identified by De Meuse et al. (2004) had clearly not elapsed. There was a relatively strong view that organizational change had led to the loss of key knowledge and skills, indicating one of the main damaging effects of redundancy, delayering and the increased use of contract staff. Despite the flattening of hierarchies and the increased level of accountability, the speed of decision making was not felt to have increased: 37 per cent of managers did not agree that organizational change had increased the speed of decision making and a further 38 per cent felt there had been no change. In the public sector, where change had been most intense, 47 per cent felt that change had actually slowed down decision making, with a further 34 per cent feeling that change had had no effect on the speed at which decisions were made. There is little evidence here to support the view that change induces improved performance, productivity, efficiency or profitability, particularly in the public sector.

More worryingly, change was felt to have had a particularly negative effect on perceptions of job security, morale, loyalty, employee well-being and motivation: 51 per cent of

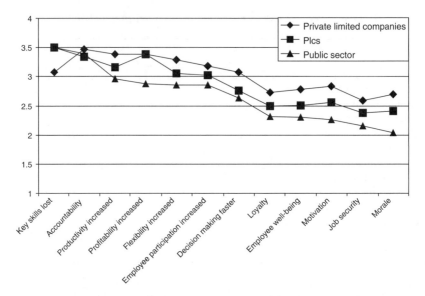

Figure 23.2   The effect of organizational change on managers' perceptions of their organization (mean scores on items) by type of organization

managers felt that change had reduced motivation, 48 per cent felt it had reduced their sense of well-being and 61 per cent felt it had reduced morale. In the clear majority of cases, and particularly among managers in the public sector and plcs, change had led to lower motivation, morale and loyalty, a reduced sense of job security and heightened concerns among employees about their own well-being. Managers in the public sector (Figure 23.2) were substantially more negative about the effects of change than managers in plcs, who were, in turn, substantially more negative than managers in private limited companies. The differences between managers in plcs and the public sector were most marked on the morale and motivation items, while the widest differences between managers in plcs and those in private limited companies were on the 'key skills being lost' and the 'decision making is faster' items. Clearly, change in private limited companies is seen to be much less likely to lead to the loss of knowledge and skills and more likely to increase the speed of decision making.

Managers were asked if they felt that organizational change had had any effects on the organization in terms of levels of staff turnover, sickness, absence and industrial action (see Table 23.4). In the public sector a relatively high proportion of managers thought that staff turnover, the sickness rate, the level of absence and the level of industrial action had increased as a result of change. The perceived effects of change in private limited companies were, again, the most benign, with managers here least likely to think that turnover, absence and industrial relations had been adversely affected by change.

While we accept that these are perceptual measures, we are concerned about the logic of organizational change, particularly in the public sector and in plcs: while the scale of change is immense in these sectors, there is a strong perception that the main effects of change are to reduce employees' sense of well-being, to increase staff turnover,

Table 23.4   Changes in organizational measures by type of organization

% saying that . . .	Private limited company	Plcs	Public sector	All
Staff turnover increased	61	71	80	69
Sickness rate increased	51	64	68	60
Absence increased	49	63	68	58
Strikes increased	19	21	64	40

to increase the sickness rate and to increase absence levels. We are led to question whether the gains in productivity – which are far from clear – are really worth the effort and cost of implementing change. The clear message from the public sector is that change is generating a great deal of perceived pain but relatively little perceived gain. Our findings also call into question just how well change is being managed in many organizations.

Not surprisingly, managers in organizations that were declining had significantly worse views of the effects of organizational change than managers in stable and growing businesses. In declining organizations, managers were much less likely to be of the view that productivity or profitability had improved, and their scores on the loyalty, morale, motivation, job security and employee well-being measures were considerably lower than those of managers in static businesses, let alone those in growing businesses. Unfortunately, the change programmes that had been put in place in declining firms were seen far more negatively than change programmes in static or growing firms. In declining organizations the pace of change is more intense, more multifaceted and, clearly, more 'carnivorous', given the more pronounced use of outsourcing, contract staff, redundancy and delayering. Not surprisingly, managers in declining businesses were particularly negative about the effect of organizational change on the loyalty, morale, motivation, sense of job security and employee well-being items (see Figure 23.3).

Do the views of directors and other managers about the effects of organizational change differ significantly?
Elsewhere (Worrall and Cooper, 2004; Worrall et al., 2004), we concluded that directors' views about change and its impact differed markedly from those of other levels of management. Table 23.5 compares the mean scores of directors with other levels of manager on each of 12 measures used to assess the perceived effect of organizational change. It is evident that directors recorded more positive scores than each other level of manager on each measure. Some of the differences between directors and junior and middle managers, for example, were considerable. In all cases, the views of directors were significantly different[6] from those of middle and junior managers. In all but three instances (i.e. on the accountability, profitability and productivity measures) the views of directors were also significantly different from the views of even senior managers.

Just as we have identified that directors and other managers had radically different perceptions of some of our 'softer' measures of change, they were also much less likely to be of the view that staff turnover, sickness rates, absence levels and industrial action had increased over the last year in response to organizational change (Table 23.6).

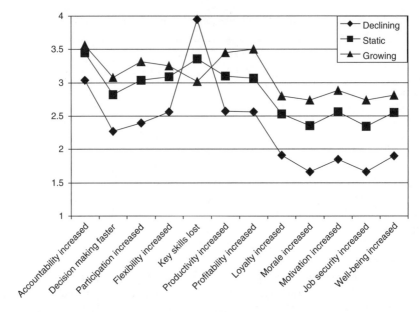

Figure 23.3   Perceptions of the effect of organization change by organizational growth – mean scores per measure

Table 23.5   Perceptions of the effect of organizational change by level in the organization

Level in the organization	Director	Senior manager	Middle manager	Junior manager	All
Accountability has increased	3.59	3.44	**3.38**	**3.31**	3.43
Key skills and experience have been lost	2.79	**3.28**	**3.56**	**3.48**	3.31
Profitability has increased	3.36	3.19	**3.12**	**3.09**	3.18
Productivity has increased	3.38	3.23	**3.05**	**3.04**	3.17
Flexibility has increased	3.35	**3.10**	**2.95**	**2.96**	3.08
Employee participation has increased	3.37	**3.09**	**2.92**	**2.86**	3.05
Decision making is faster	3.27	**2.82**	**2.70**	**2.66**	2.84
Motivation has increased	3.06	**2.60**	**2.42**	**2.28**	2.58
Employee well-being has increased	2.99	**2.55**	**2.38**	**2.40**	2.56
Loyalty has increased	2.95	**2.53**	**2.41**	**2.36**	2.54
Morale has increased	2.95	**2.41**	**2.23**	**2.11**	2.41
Sense of job security has increased	2.78	**2.40**	**2.24**	**2.27**	2.40

Note: The figures in bold identify where the views of directors and other levels of manager are significantly different.

We see this dissonance in the views of directors and other managers as a significant finding and we argue that this is entirely consistent with the arguments developed in our review of the literature. Our analysis implies that directors are living in a parallel universe to other levels of manager, where the reality of organizational life as experienced by the

Table 23.6   Changes in key organizational measures over the last year by managers' level

Percentage of managers agreeing that	Director	Senior manager	Middle manager	Junior manager	All
Staff turnover increased	47	68	78	78	69
Sickness rate increased	37	58	71	69	60
Absence increased	32	57	69	70	58
Strikes increased	12	38	54	31	39

majority of managers is radically different from the rhetoric-laden – and far more rosy – world of directors. While only 22 per cent of directors think that organizational change has reduced loyalty in their organization, 60 per cent of junior managers felt that change had done so. The world-view of directors is significantly different from that of all other levels of manager. Our concern is that there is a clear hiatus in many organizations at the boardroom door that needs to be overcome if directors are to develop a better understanding of the lived realities of the organizations that they are attempting to lead and if they are to learn from the effects that organizational change is having on their workforce.

Conclusions
Over the last decade, there have been massive changes in the large firms that dominate the economic landscape of the UK. Organizations have see headcount culls, layers removed, functions outsourced, functions offshored, processes re-engineered, and cultures redefined. Career structures have been flattened, pension entitlements reduced, jobs have become less secure, and workers have been put under considerable pressure from performance management regimes to work harder and longer and to deliver more with less. Our research has clearly shown that work overload, increasing surveillance and control, lack of job involvement, persistent organizational change 'for change's sake' and managers being set unrealistic targets over which they have little or no influence have a huge effect on managers' physical and psychological well-being. More disturbingly, our analysis indicates that since our survey in 2000 a higher percentage of managers have been affected by more forms of concurrent change, more intensively. The pace, variety and impact of change all seem to be increasing, particularly in public sector organizations and in plcs, but with managers in private limited companies being less affected and less likely to be exposed to redundancy, delayering and outsourcing.

Large proportions of managers have not seen organizational change positively. Generally, it has been seen to reduce loyalty, motivation, morale; to increase managers' sense of job security and to undermine their sense of physical and psychological well-being. There was also a strength of opinion, especially in plcs and public sector organizations, that change had led to increased levels of workplace ill-health, absence and staff turnover. While these views were commonly held by senior, middle and junior managers, the view of directors were quite different. Directors were much less likely to see organizational change as having negative effects and more likely to think that it had led to increased productivity and output. We see this radical difference of views within and without the boardroom to be very problematic and perhaps at the root of some of the issues of organizational dysfunction and workplace stress that managers in many UK business organizations are clearly experiencing.

While organizational psychologists might see stress and the effects of organizational dysfunction as situated in the individual or the workgroup, our perspective leads us to a much wider frame of reference as we see many of the problems in the workplace to be a consequence of an Anglo-American form of late capitalism that has become increasingly 'carnivorous'. The prevailing psychology in many large organizations seems to favour managing by cost reduction and intensifying the use of assets – particularly labour – rather than focusing on growing the numerator in the productivity equation by using directors' own creativity and imagination, and the creativity and imagination of a workforce that feels a sense of loyalty and commitment to the organization and is motivated by working within it. We consider Froud et al.'s (2000a: 109) assertion that management has become 'an endless series of cheap financial dodges' to be disconcerting, saddening but probably accurate. We see management as being about much more than managing by metrics or managing by a few key financial ratios, yet some influential business leaders have argued that the 'first requirement' of strategy is 'to set out the financial objectives that the company should be seeking to achieve' and that 'specific financial objectives' should provide the 'framework within which strategy should be developed' (Lees, 1997: 254–5).

Within the public sector, we are very concerned about the plethora of change programmes and initiatives that are taking place in the face of increasing employee resistance. Even the Local Government Employers' Organisation (undated: 1) was led to conclude that

> Many change initiatives are limited in their strategic impact because organisations try to implement a number of loosely connected activities too fast without proper co-ordination and follow through. People management and development implications are often not fully appreciated or addressed as part of the change process. The result is *'initiative fatigue'* where staff become disillusioned and more resistant when managers try to implement the next major change.

We believe that our analysis has found exactly that, but that these issues have been exacerbated by the substantial increase in the complexity and scope of change we have found in the public sector and in plcs since 2000.

Our comments about the management and effect of change have focused on the negative aspects of change when change has become a commonplace organizational reality for many managers. Organizations often have to change but there seems to be little consensus about how this can be done without creating major problems and dysfunctions within organizations, although authors such as Cascio (2005) have identified strategies for the less disruptive implementation of change. However, we feel that there are many paradoxes to be faced here in an era when employees are seen primarily as a cost to be cut rather than an asset to be developed. We are concerned about the pace of change and the legitimacy of the need for so much change: clearly, many of those affected by change see it as being for change's sake and not something that affects the bottom line as effectively as the drivers of change think it will. We are concerned that change is often used as a signalling mechanism to markets and we feel that the directors of organizations should spend more time working through the likely impacts of change on their workforce on several dimensions, not just the financial dimension to the blinkered exclusion of all others. Indeed, one of the prime aims of our Quality of Working Life research has been to encourage more organizations to evaluate their performance on a wider set of measures than just financial measures. Perhaps our success has been limited here.

We are certainly not against change *per se*, but we are against change that is badly thought through, which is geared to the cynical manipulation of a few key ratios to improve shareholder value in the short term or to achieve short-term political objectives. Change is a long-term issue: it needs to be planned as a long-term project and coordinated so that employees buy into it rather than switch off from it. As Dickens might have said, we need to move from the 'age of foolishness' to the 'age of wisdom' and from 'the winter of despair' to 'the spring of hope'.

Acknowledgements

The authors would like to acknowledge the Chartered Management Institute in the conduct of the 2005 Quality of Working Life project, particularly Petra Cook and Nicky Jackson. They would also like to acknowledge the support of Workplace Health Connect working in partnership with the Health and Safety Executive (HSE) who part-funded the research.

Notes

1. See www.eiro.eurofound.eu.int/1999/11/inbrief/eu9911210n.html.
2. The fieldwork for the study was conducted in the period October to November 2005. The Chartered Management Institute's (CMI) membership database was used as a sampling frame for the exercise. A self-completion questionnaire was designed and e-mailed to 10 000 members of the Institute. In 2005, the exercise generated 1541 valid responses, giving a response rate of 15 per cent. It is important to emphasize that the sample reflects the structure of the membership of the CMI. The 2005 survey, like the previous QoWL surveys, tends to overrepresent managers at more senior levels.
3. See www.robertsoncooper.com/Wellbeing/ASSETProgram.aspx
4. 1999 data are used here because the 2000 data are not directly comparable with the 2005 data set.
5. Managers were asked to identify if it was their perception that they were working in a growing, a static or a declining business – 49 per cent thought they were working in a growing business, 32 per cent thought their organization was static and 19 per cent thought their organization was declining.
6. Analysis of variance (ANOVA) supplemented by a Bonferroni *post-hoc* test procedure.

References

Ball, S. (1993), 'Education policy, power relations and teachers' work', *British Journal of Educational Studies*, **41**(2), 106–21.

Barry, J., Chandler, J. and Clark, H. (2001), 'Between the ivory tower and the academic assembly line', *Journal of Management Studies*, **38**(1), 87–101.

Boyne, G. (2002), 'Public and private management: what's the difference?', *Journal of Management Studies*, **39**(1), 97–122.

Braverman, H. (1974), *Labour and Monopoly Capital*, New York: Monthly Review Press.

Bryson, C. (2004), 'What about the workers? The expansion of higher education and the transformation of academic work', *Industrial Relations Journal*, **35**(1), 38–57.

Burchell, B., Lapido, D. and Wilkinson, F. (2002), *Job Insecurity and Work Intensification*, London: Routledge.

Cascio, W.F. (1993), 'Downsizing: what do we know? What have we learned?', *Academy of Management Executive*, **7**(1), 95–104.

Cascio, W.F. (2005), 'Strategies for responsible restructuring', *Academy of Management Executive*, **19**(4), 39–50.

Clarke, J. and Newman, J. (1997), *The Managerial State: Power, Politics and Ideology in the Remaking of Social Welfare*, London: Sage.

De Meuse, K.P., Bergmann, T.J., Vanderheiden, P.A. and Roraff, C.E. (2004), 'New evidence regarding organisational downsizing and a firm's financial performance: a long term analysis', *Journal of Management Issues*, **XVI**(2), 155–77.

Felstead, A., Gallie, D. and Green, F. (2004), 'Job complexity and task discretion: tracking the direction of skills at work in Britain', in C. Warhurst, I. Grugulis and E. Keep (eds), *The Skills that Matter*, London: Palgrave. pp. 148–69.

Ferlie, F., Ashburner, L., Fitzgerald, L. and Pettigrew, A. (1996), *The New Public Management in Action*, Oxford: Oxford University Press.

Froud, J., Haslam, C., Johal, S. and Williams, K. (2000a), 'Shareholder value and financialization: consultancy promises, management moves', *Economy and Society*, **29**(1), 80–110.

Froud, J., Haslam, C., Johal, S. and Williams, K. (2000b), 'Restructuring for shareholder value and its implications for labour', *Cambridge Journal of Economics*, **24**(6), 771–97.

Grugulis, I., Vincent, S. and Hebson, G. (2003), 'The future of professional work? The rise of the "Network Form" and the decline of discretion', *Human Resource Management Journal*, **13**(2), 30–44.

Guest, D., Michie, J., Sheehan, M., Conway, N. and Metochi, M. (2000), *Effective People Management*, London: Chartered Institute of Personnel and Development.

Harris, J. (1998), 'Scientific management, bureau professionalism, new managerialism: the labour process of state social work', *British Journal of Social Work*, **28**(2), 839–62.

Hewison, A. (1999), 'The new public management and the new nursing: related by rhetoric?', *Journal of Advanced Nursing*, **29**(6), 1377–84.

Ichniowski, C., Shaw, K. and Prenushi, G. (1997), 'The effects of human resource management practices on productivity: a study of steel finishing lines', *American Economic Review*, **87**(3), 291–313.

Jones, M.T. (2002), 'Globalization and organizational restructuring: a strategic perspective', *Thunderbird International Business Review*, **44**(3), 325–51.

Kaplan, R.S. and Norton, D.P. (1996), *The Balanced Scorecard: Translating Strategy into Action*, Boston, MA: Harvard Business School Press.

Kirkpatrick, I. and Ackroyd, S. (2003a), 'Transforming the professional archetype? The new managerialism in UK social services', *Public Management Review*, **5**(4), 511–31.

Kirkpatrick, I. and Ackroyd, S. (2003b), 'Archetype theory and the changing professional organisation: a critique and alternative', *Organization*, **10**(4), 731–50.

Knights, D. and Willmott, H. (eds) (1986), *Managing the Labour Process*, Aldershot, UK: Gower.

Lees, D. (1997), 'The management of strategy', *Journal of Applied Management Studies*, **6**(2), 253–60.

Legge, K. (2005), *Human Resource Management: Rhetorics and Realities*, 2nd edn, Basingstoke, UK: Palgrave Macmillan.

Local Government Employers' Organisation (undated), 'Making sense of change: saying goodbye to initiative fatigue', London: I&DeA, www.idea-knowledge.gov.uk/idk/aio/4450597.

MacDuffie, J.P. (1995), 'Human resource bundles and manufacturing performance: organizational logic and flexible production systems in the world auto industry', *Industrial and Labor Relations Review*, **48**(2), 197–221.

Martin, S. (2002), 'The modernization of local government: markets, managers and mixed fortunes', *Public Management Review*, **4**(3), 291–307.

Mather, K., Worrall, L. and Seifert, R. (2007, forthcoming), 'Reforming further education: the changing labour process for college lecturers', *Personnel Review*.

Noon, M. and Blyton, P. (1997), *The Realities of Work*, Basingstoke, UK: Palgrave Macmillan.

Osborne, D. and Gaebler, T. (1992), *Reinventing Government: How the Entrepreneurial Spirit is Transforming the Public Sector*, Boston, MA: Addison-Wesley.

Pollitt, C. (1993), *Managerialism and the Public Services: Cuts or Cultural Change in the 1990s?*, Oxford: Blackwell.

Porter, M.E. and Ketels, C.H.M. (2003), 'UK competitiveness: moving to the next stage', DTI Economics Paper No. 3, ESRC,www.dti.gov.uk/files/file14771.pdf.

Prahalad, C.K. and Hamel, G. (1990), 'The core competence of the corporation', *Harvard Business Review*, **68**(3), 79–91.

Rainbird, H., Munro, A. and Holly, L. (2004), 'Exploring the concept of employer demand for skills and qualifications: case studies from the public sector', in C. Warhurst, I. Grugulis and E. Keep (eds) (2004), *The Skills that Matter*, London: Palgrave, pp. 91–108.

Richardson, M., Tailby, S., Danford, A., Stewart, P. and Upchurch, M. (2005), 'Best value and workplace partnership in local government', *Personnel Review*, **34**(6), 713–27.

Shaoul, J. (1999), 'The shrinking state?', in S. Corby and G. White (eds), *Employee Relations in the Public Services: Themes and Issues*, London: Routledge.

Usui, C. and Cilignon, R.A. (1996), 'Corporate restructuring: converging world pattern of societally specific embeddedness', *Sociological Quarterly*, **37**(4), 551–78.

Walsh, K. (1995), *Public Services and the Market Mechanism: Competition, Contracting and the New Public Management*, London: Macmillan.

Williams, K. (2000), 'From shareholder value to present day capitalism', *Economy and Society*, **29**(1), 1–12.

Worrall, L. and Cooper, C.L. (1997), *The Quality of Working Life: The 1997 Survey of Managers' Experiences*, Chartered Management Institute Research Report, London: Chartered Management Institute.

Worrall, L. and Cooper, C.L. (1998), *The Quality of Working Life: The 1998 Survey of Managers' Experiences*, Chartered Management Institute Research Report, London: Chartered Management Institute.

Worrall, L. and Cooper, C.L. (1999), *The Quality of Working Life: The 1999 Survey of Managers' Experiences*, Chartered Management Institute Research Report, London: Chartered Management Institute.

Worrall, L. and Cooper, C.L. (2001), *The Quality of Working Life: The 2000 Survey of Managers' Experiences*, Chartered Management Institute Research Report, London: Chartered Management Institute.

Worrall, L. and Cooper, C.L. (2004), 'Managers, hierarchies and attitudes: a study of UK managers', *Journal of Managerial Psychology*, **19**(1), 41–68.

Worrall, L. and Cooper, C.L. (2006), *The Quality of Working Life: A Survey of Managers' Health*, Chartered Management Institute, Research Report, London: Chartered Management Institute.

Worrall, L., Cooper, C.L. and Campbell-Jamison, F.K. (2000a), 'The impact of organizational change on the work experiences and attitudes of public sector managers', *Personnel Review*, **29**(5), 613–36.

Worrall, L., Cooper, C.L. and Campbell, F.K. (2000b), 'The impact of redundancy: perceptions of UK managers', *Journal of Managerial Psychology*, **15**(5), 460–76.

Worrall, L., Cooper, C.L. and Campbell, F.K. (2000c), 'Perpetual change and employment instability: the new reality for UK managers', *Work, Employment and Society*, **14**(4), 647–68.

Worrall, L., Cooper, C.L. and Parkes, C. (2004), 'The impact of organisational change on the experiences and perceptions of UK managers from 1997–2000', *European Journal of Work and Organizational Psychology*, **13**(2), 139–63.

24 Helping creativity and innovation thrive in organizations: functional and dysfunctional perspectives
Neil Anderson and Rosina M. Gasteiger

The processes, antecedents and outcomes of creativity and innovation in organizations have held the interests of both organizational researchers and change management practitioners for several decades now. Research into innovation has continued to shed light upon the factors that help and hinder innovation at several levels of analysis in organizational settings. Indeed, factors at the individual, group and organizational level have now been repeatedly identified across such a number of separate research studies that there is a reliable body of evidence to underscore pragmatic intervention attempts to enhance and improve innovation processes in organizations. Yet despite this continued growth in research and practical innovation change management programs, there remains a 'dark side' to innovation procedures and outcomes that has been far less attended to by researchers and practitioners alike. The purpose of this chapter is to explore some of these more dysfunctional, conflictual and counterproductive aspects of innovation in work organizations.

Innovation research has grown apace, especially over the last 20 years, as organizations have needed to respond to changing environments by becoming more flexible and adaptive, by becoming more dependent upon team-based structures, and by downsizing and flattening their structures to facilitate more responsive and flexible decision making (Axtell et al., 2000; Howard, 1995). These environmental and business drivers toward increasing innovation in organizations have had the positive effect of stimulating research and improvements in professional practices of change management intervention, but on the downside have obscured the inherently problematic and disruptive effects that individual creativity and work group innovation attempts can exert upon various aspects of organizational functioning and performance. Truly, there is a *dysfunctional* aspect to innovation, less visible or managerially appealing, but an aspect nevertheless that has surfaced repeatedly across empirical studies and narrative reviews as being unavoidably present and, if not correctly managed, then potentially seriously harmful to individuals, work teams, or the wider organization as a whole (Anderson et al., 2004). This chapter draws attention to these rather overlooked aspects of innovation at different levels of analysis by providing a summary of existing studies and theoretical models that have direct bearing upon this 'dark side' of innovation processes, largely portrayed in some areas of the literature as entirely positive and unproblematic.

Defining creativity and innovation at work
For any review chapter in this area, one of the initial tasks is to overview established definitions of creativity and innovation, largely on the grounds that debate continues to rumble on over their precise meanings and clarifying distinctions between the two terms.

Although there remains no general consensus over precise definitions, the most widely accepted definition of workplace innovation was proposed by West and Farr (1990: 9):

> the intentional introduction and application within a role, group or organization of ideas, processes, products or procedures, new to the relevant unit of adoption, designed to significantly benefit the individual, the group, the organization or wider society.

Their definition distinguishes between creativity and innovation in the crucial regard that the latter involves 'intentional introduction and application' of new and improved ways of doing things, whereas creativity can simply refer to idea generation alone (King, 1992, further extends this distinction to refer to the 'ideation–implementation dilemma'). Second, West and Farr (1990) point out that innovation must confer intended benefits at one or more levels of analysis: the work role, group or organization. Again, this is not necessarily the case for creativity, where benefits can be impossible to quantify or assign. Third, and finally, innovation implies relative novelty as opposed to absolute novelty (Zaltman et al., 1973). That is, any change need only be new to the relevant unit of adoption, not absolutely new, allowing for innovations to be adopted and adapted from other organizations or work teams (West and Anderson, 1996). This definition accepted, it is apparent at this early stage that even widely applied definitions of innovation fail to highlight its negative aspects in precedence, process or outcome. Thus an innovation attempt designed to improve individual job performance might have deleterious effects at the level of the work group; a team-level innovation in one area might generate intergroup tensions and even conflicts over time; or, for a final example, a newly launched product line at the organizational level of analysis may throw up difficulties in response for work groups responsible for its implementation or for individuals who need to adjust their present ways of working. Recognizing that facilitating and inhibiting factors may vary regarding the different types of innovation, various ways in which innovation can be categorized have been proposed by researchers (see, e.g., Anderson and King, 1993). Table 24.1 illustrates five useful typologies of innovation focusing on different aspects of innovation.

One useful distinction of innovation displayed in Figure 24.1, the 'socio-technical systems approach' proposed by Damanpour and Evans (1984; Damanpour, 1987), distinguishes between *technical* and *administrative changes*, and, subsequently, *ancillary innovation*. Technical innovations lead to organizational change through the introduction of new tools, technologies (e.g. computer systems) and so on, whereas administrative innovations cause changes as regards the organizational structure or administrative workflows. Ancillary innovations involve changes at the organizational–environment boundary and go beyond the primary objectives of an innovation (e.g. career development programs offered by a library). Technological innovations are often implemented more quickly and are generally perceived to be more effective in comparison to administrative or ancillary innovations. Nevertheless, administrative innovations were shown to have a bigger impact on organizational performance for the most part (Damanpour, 1990). The overestimation of the effectiveness of technological innovations can be explained by the visibility and status associated with their adoption, which tends to be much higher than that for administrative or ancillary innovations (Anderson and King, 1993). The 'innovation characteristics' approach by Zaltman et al. (1973) represents another main theme evident as regards innovation typology. Instead of categorizing innovations according to the system within

Table 24.1 Summary of innovation typologies

Author(s)	Damanpour (1987) Damanpour and Evans (1984)	Zaltman, et al. (1973)	Peters and Waterman (1982) Kanter (1983)	Anderson (1990)	West and Anderson (1992)
Description of typology	Sociotechnical systems typology of innovation	Interaction typology of innovation characteristics	Radicalness of innovation typology	Sources of innovation typology	Innovation characteristics and outcome effects of typology (health care organizations)
Innovation types proposed	*Technical* Changes in production methods or products manufactured *Administrative* Changes in social relationships at work *Ancillary* Innovations which cross organization–environment boundaries	*Programmed–non programmed* Innovations vary in the extent of pre-planning, scheduling and organizational programming undertaken *Instrumental–ultimate* Instrumental innovations facilitate larger-scale ultimate innovations which can be self-contained change processes *Radicalness* (a) Novelty – degree of newness of the innovation (b) Risk – degree of risk involved in implementation	*Evolutionary–revolutionary continuum* Evolutionary innovations as minor improvements on existing designs/systems. Revolutionary innovations as paradigm-breaking redesigns of existing designs/systems *See also* Kirton (1976, 1978) at the individual level of analysis who proposes an adaption–innovation continuum of creativity styles	*Emergent innovations* Novel, unproven ideas and proposals developed and implemented unique to a particular organization or organizational sub-unit *Adopted innovations* Systems/procedures already in use within comparator organizations which are replicated and adopted by other organizations *Imposed innovations* Where changes in environmental contingencies force the organization to develop innovative responses	*Magnitude* Size of innovation and the extent of likely consequences *Novelty* Relative newness of the innovation *Radicalness* Extent of likely change to the *status quo* *Effectiveness–patient care* Likely benefit to patient care *Effectiveness–staff well-being* Likely benefit to staff well-being *Effectiveness–hospital administration* Likely benefit to hospital administrative efficiency

Source: Reproduced with permission from John Wiley & Sons Ltd, Anderson and King (1993).

which they occur, Zaltman et al. (1973) focus on characteristics of the innovations themselves that can be classified into the following three dimensions: *programmed* versus *non-programmed*, *instrumental* versus *ultimate innovations*, and *radicalness*. Programmed innovations are scheduled in advance and represent further development of extant products or services. Non-programmed innovations are not planned ahead and are triggered either by the detection of slack resources or an imminent crisis. However, other non-programmed innovations may derive from attempts by individuals or groups to draw the organization's attention to areas where possibilities for improvement had not been recognized. These so-called *proactive innovations* are often impeded or stifled and rather depend on the power and influence of their initiator(s) to get implemented. As regards the second dimension by Zaltman et al. (1973), instrumental innovations are introduced to facilitate subsequent, more radical, innovations, while ultimate innovations may be considered as ends in themselves. The third dimension, *radicalness*, refers to whether an innovation represents a major or minor departure from the past and the degree of risk involved with its implementation. Radicalness has received much attention from researchers (e.g. Peters and Waterman, 1982; Kanter, 1983; West and Anderson, 1992). There is a consensus in the literature that more radical innovations will meet greater resistance by employees and executives because they challenge the *status quo* more fundamentally and are likely to involve higher costs than less radical ones (Anderson and King, 1993). A third approach taken by Anderson (1990) to categorize innovation is by its source. The author distinguishes between three different *sources of innovation – emergent, adopted* and *imposed innovations*. Emergent innovations are generated within the organization and represent unique, unproven responses to challenges and problems particular to the organization (e.g. the creation of a staff rota system to meet the needs of the employees). Adopted innovations are imported from outside the organization, for example, from other organizations in the same sector, from other sectors, research institutions and so on (e.g. adopting ISO 9000 standards). Finally, imposed innovations are forced on the organization by external agencies (e.g. newly enacted health and safety legislation).

In a British hospital ward study, Sauer and Anderson (1992) compared the development of imposed and emergent innovations. The research revealed that imposed innovations showed a much more complex pattern in their development, including a proliferation of secondary innovations stemming from the emergent innovation. On the other hand, employees indicated higher emotional involvement and agreement on the key steps in the process concerning fully emergent innovations. Employees' commitment or resistance to change (see Herscovitch and Meyer, 2002), thus, may depend highly on the precise source of an innovation.

Not only the source of an innovation but also the way it is instigated, the prestige of the champion steering its implementation, its rationale, and its pace of change are likely to impact its subsequent success or failure. Innovations aimed at enhancing the productivity or service procedures and processes of a firm, for instance, business process reengineering (BPR), total quality management (TQM), or just-in-time production (JIT), are often bought in 'off the shelf' while too often neglecting the human side of the sociotechnical system (see, e.g., Harmon, 1992). In order to minimize potential costs for the firm as well as for the individual employee, innovations with relevance to the whole organization may be established step by step, starting in one unit first while allowing for adjustment and familiarization.

Pro-innovation bias: reinventing managerial fads

Kimberly (1981) first coined the term 'pro-innovation bias' to describe the uncritical acceptance that all innovation is good, and that more innovation is without exception better. Beyond initial definitions, this bias appears still to be deeply rooted in many empirical studies if key recent reviews of this area are consulted, but even more so in popular texts on 'how to' stimulate and introduce innovation into organizations. Even a cursory glance at the most recent major reviews of the innovation literature confirms that pro-innovation bias is alive and unwell in its influence and limited perspective (recent major reviews include Frese et al., 1999; West, 2001; Patterson, 2002; Anderson et al., 2004). Yet it is the continuing deluge of popular management texts where this bias finds its most extreme and vocal expression. In this espoused view innovation is to be garnered at all costs by any organization, its antecedents and consequences are universally positive, and the ramping-up of potential for innovation is to be pursued unabated as the holy grail of medium- to longer-term managerial objectives. This torrent of books can be traced back now several decades, although perhaps the most impactful (i.e. best-selling) example is the book by Peters and Waterman (1982), and yet only more recently have several empirical studies emerged that seriously challenge this bias as being unjustifiable, unwise and potentially harmful to organizations and individuals within them.

A more balanced and critical view of the benefits, costs and disruptive aspects of any innovation attempt has in fact come into sight only quite recently across the research literature. Intuitively, and with some common-sense reflection, it becomes rather obvious that innovation processes are likely to be inherently disruptive, that all innovations may not be universally beneficial, and that maximizing organizational innovativeness as a managerial objective is most likely to result in unmanageable structures and clashing goals being sought by teams and individuals within organizations to the detriment of common performance or even survival (Daft, 1978). In fact, the prospect of achieving constant innovativeness, continuous change, and a deluge of new products and procedures within any organization is a chimera and as nonsensical as it would be commercial suicide; any organization would eventually implode into a vacuum of routinized procedures for essential tasks, internal conflicts of interests, and borderline anarchy, with senior managers struggling to keep any semblance of control over production methods or provision of services to its clients (see also King and Anderson, 2002). In support of this more balanced view also stand an increasing number of studies and proposed models of innovation processes that have either found evidence of, or propose likely effects of, negative aspects of creativity and innovation in the workplace (e.g. Janssen, 2003; Janssen et al., 2004; Miron et al., 2004; Townsend et al., 2004; Shalley et al., 2000). Summarizing these recent findings of both positive and negative outcomes, Table 24.2 overviews these effects at three main levels of analysis – within the individual, work team and organizational.

As can be seen from this table, whilst any single innovation attempt can have hugely positive outcomes, it can also simultaneously confer a potential series of problematic and dysfunctional outcomes. However, Table 24.2 considers only some possible types of innovation at each of the three levels of analysis. Other dysfunctional effects may be present in addition, as might cross-level effects mentioned above, whereby an innovation at one level has unavoidable causal effects at other levels of analysis (for a further discussion see Anderson et al., 2004). In summary, innovation is likely to lead to a variety of potential benefits and costs. With Table 24.2 we have not attempted to list these

Table 24.2   Functional and dysfunctional aspects of workplace creativity and innovation at different levels of analysis

Author(s)	Research object	Dimensions	Level of analysis			Key findings or proposed outcomes of innovation	
			Individual	Work team	Organization	Positive outcomes	Negative outcomes
Livingstone et al. (1997)	Creativity and person–environment fit; examining supply value and demand ability versions of fit	Creativity, person–environment fit, strain, job satisfaction, performance	x		x	A fit between demands and abilities for creativity was related to lower strain and higher job satisfaction	Discontentment, and low performance as consequence of a lack of fit between creativity demands, individual skills and organizational conditions
James et al. (1999)	Antecedents and outcomes of positive and negative creativity in organizations	Positive and negative creativity	x			Positive creativity may result in, e.g., job improvement, reduced health costs, adaptability to change in environment, product creation and marketing ideas	Negative creativity may result in, e.g., theft, sabotage, harmful behavior to other employees, and undermining of organizational goals, and policies
Shalley et al. (2000)	Work environment characteristics facilitating or inhibiting creativity at work; effects on employee satisfaction and intentions to leave	Creativity, work environment, satisfaction, intention to leave	x			Individuals were more satisfied and reported lower intentions to leave when their work environments complemented the creativity requirements of their jobs Job-required creativity, job–environment (J–E) fit or complementarity had a significant effect on employee's affective outcomes	

Table 24.2 (continued)

| Author(s) | Research object | Dimensions | Level of analysis | | | Key findings or proposed outcomes of innovation | |
			Individual	Work team	Organization	Positive outcomes	Negative outcomes
Zhou and George (2001)	Creativity as consequence of job dissatisfaction depending on conditions conducive to the expression of voice	Creativity, job dissatisfaction, continuance, commitment	x			If new ideas proposed by the employees are accepted and subsequently implemented by the organization, it is likely that employees' job dissatisfaction decreases	If new ideas proposed by the employees are not accepted and implemented by the organization, employees' may become even more dissatisfied with their job
Janssen (2003)	Conflict and less satisfactory relations with co-workers as consequence of innovative behavior and job involvement	Conflict, job involvement satisfaction with co-worker relations	x	x		A worker's innovative initiatives may contribute to organizational effectiveness	A worker's innovative behavior interacts with job involvement in providing conflict and less satisfactory relations with co-workers
Janssen et al. (2004)	The bright and the dark sides of individual and group innovation	Conflict, performance, success/failure, job attitudes, well-being	x			Constructive conflict, innovation success, performance improvement, positive job attitudes, well-being	Destructive conflict, innovation failure, lowered performance, negative job attitudes, stress
		Success/failure, group cohesion and potency, clearity of objectives and leadership		x		Successful innovation, group cohesion, group potency, clear objectives, clear leadership, group effectiveness, receptivity to future innovation	Failure, lowered group cohesion and potency, unclear objectives, lack of clarity over leadership, group ineffectiveness resistance to future innovation
Miron et al. (2004)	Personal and organizational	Cognitive styles, initiative,	x		x	Creativity positively affected innovation at	Creativity was found to have a significant

Author (year)	Focus	Key concepts				Contribution	Findings
	factors that enhance or hinder innovation; factors that contribute to quality and efficiency	innovative culture				the implementation stage given high initiative and an organizational culture that supports innovation	negative effect on performance quality when the task required accuracy and adherence to rules
Townsend et al. (2004)	Implementation of virtual team work	Stress, trust, and cohesion issues, and structural resistance	x	x	x	Synergy of teamwork and use of information and communication technology	Employees' being assigned to more teams, working in a more complex environment may experience more stress and are more likely to suffer from burnout

Free flow of team members' communication may be inhibited by concerns about privacy and system security

Organizational restructuring may cause resistance by employees |
| De Dreu (2006) | Relationship between task conflict and innovation in teams; effect of innovation on team performance | Task conflict, team innovation | x | | | Task conflict in teams can be positively related to innovation; potential positive impact on performance parameters, e.g., learning, innovativeness | Too much or too little conflict was detrimental to team innovation, i.e. teams were more innovative when the level of task conflict was moderate.

While teams may benefit from innovations in the long run, immediate goal attainment may be reduced due to lowered efficiency of work processes |

dysfunctional and functional effects of creativity and innovation comprehensively. Instead we gathered examples in the literature that contribute to heighten the awareness of a more balanced and realistic understanding of the benefits and detriments of innovation at the workplace. Considering each of our three levels of analysis, the processes of creativity and innovation will be subject to a closer examination in the following section. Moreover, current research findings indicative of functional and dysfunctional aspects are outlined and some of the likely deleterious consequences of innovation for individuals, groups and organizations are highlighted.

The processes of creativity and innovation in organizations
The term 'innovation' comprises result- as well as process-related aspects (Anderson and King, 1993; West, 2001). The outcome of an improvement process is referred to as innovation, just as is the process that leads to an innovation itself. Depending on the approach taken, this two-sidedness implies that 'innovation' can be considered either as dependent (result-oriented) or independent (process-oriented) variable. With regard to the promotion of innovation in organizations, the complex process of innovation is of particular importance. As Kanter (1988) pointed out, the process of innovation is highly uncertain, knowledge-intensive, controversial and boundary-crossing. It involves uncertainty because the actual outcome and the success of this process are often unpredictable. The innovation process is subject to knowledge creation as a certain degree of expertise and short-term acquisition of additional knowledge by the employees involved is indispensable for the initiation of innovation. Furthermore, the innovation process is controversial because innovation often provokes resistance to change within the organization, e.g. because of the reallocation of resources and the challenge of established procedures, and crosses boundaries as the introduction of an innovation may affect other divisions or break existing and establish new interdependencies. Keeping these attributes of innovation in mind, it is plausible to assume that the process of innovation is marked by detrimental 'processual side effects' for the innovator as well as for other individuals affected, and ultimately the wider organization. Stated simply, innovation processes are inherently problematic and quite easily tip over into becoming more or less dysfunctional for those individuals, groups or organizations involved.

Innovative behavior in organizations is often delineated by models on the sequence of events in the innovation process (for a critical overview on the plethora of models on the innovation process see King and Anderson, 2002; Anderson and King, 1993). These models are mostly based on theoretical considerations, in contrast to empirical research examining their validity with regard to innovation processes in real life. In spite of the criticism of stage-based models (King and Anderson, 2002), differentiating the innovation process into discrete phases or stages is especially of heuristic value for the description of sub-processes and constituent parts – also with regard to potential dysfunctional effects for individuals, teams and the organization at the respective stages.

Following a generic model outlined by Anderson and King (1993), any innovation process begins with the *recognition of a problem*. In this initial stage it is crucial that individuals identify a need for change, accompanied by the confidence that deficits can be rectified through modification which justifies that an innovative action is undertaken (Gebert et al., 2003). Against conventional wisdom, the majority of innovation is not the result of a brilliant flash of inspiration but of a well-aimed, intentional search for improvement (Drucker, 1985). Ideas and suggestions for improvement made not only by employees but also, for instance, by product users are crucial sources of innovation. Attempts for improvement made by users have led to inventions such as kite-surf equipment (von Hippel, 1988, 2005). Customer demands may instigate innovation also with regard to organizational practices that often require further development in order to satisfy customer needs (e.g. establishing a just-in-time supply chain to meet the requirements for fresh food or the latest goods).

According to the 'investment theory of creativity' put forward by Sternberg and Lubart (1991), creative individuals are characterized by taking up ideas with high development potential at a time when these ideas are still largely unknown, relatively unpopular or even disrespected by others (see our argument in the following section that such behavior is actually tantamount to 'counterproductive work behaviors'). Creative individuals stick to their idea and make an effort to convince others of the usefulness of their idea in order to put it into practice eventually. Thus creative behavior requires specific personality traits, intelligence, knowledge, specific thinking, and working styles as well as motivation on the part of the ideator (Amabile, 1988; Sternberg and Lubart, 1996; for a comprehensive overview on individual predictors of innovation see Patterson, 2002). In terms of the capacities for innovation within organizations, good ideas and proposals for improved work practices or products may come from workers having jobs at the shopfloor lowest levels in the hierarchy. However, looking at bottom–up and top–down processes of innovation, inventions at the senior managerial level may get implemented more often simply due to high power, influence and, thus, better access to resources in the hands of senior managers.

Whereas the *idea identification* may be unrelated to detrimental effects on the personal level, negative effects for the individual already become likely at the subsequent *initiation phase*. For instance, the ideator may be required to break given routines and rules in order to act according to the new idea. Extra-role behavior such as task revision (Staw and Boettger, 1990), personal initiative (Frese and Fay, 2001) or self-responsible behavior (Kaschube, 2006) may possibly lead to innovation in the long run. At the outset, however, it is also likely that voice behavior, i.e. speaking up with suggestions for change (see Rank et al., 2004), causes a field of tension. For instance, conflicts between the ideator and his or her supervisor may occur when the latter is reluctant to change and rather sticks to the tried and tested instead of taking the risk to engage in uncertain, unapproved activities. In fact, a considerable portion of inventions goes back to senior managers. Executives often initiate innovation and change with regard to organizational processes and procedures (e.g. setting up 'shared services' or adopting ISO 9000 standards) that may be conducive to the effectiveness and competitiveness and, thus, the long-term survival of the organization, but also to personal goals such as an increase in power and influence.

Individuals can certainly recognize problems and generate ideas for improvement as an end in itself; producing ideas per se does not involve negative effects. However, as soon as access to resources is required for further development and implementation of ideas, the support of a second party becomes indispensable (Axtell et al., 2000). Eventually, the prestige of a champion becomes a deciding factor when it comes to the implementation of an idea. Therefore, from a psychological point of view, it is crucial to take individual as well as interpersonal, job-related, organizational and other contextual factors into account when examining how innovation in organizations can be fostered or impeded (Axtell et al., 2000; Maier et al., 2001).

During the *initiation phase* of an innovation, the organization becomes aware of the existence of a novelty that could be utilized. After decision makers have formed and expressed their attitudes towards a specific idea, a decision whether the innovation should be pursued or not is made. At this stage conflicts between the ideator or champions, i.e. promotors of an idea (see Howell and Higgins, 1990), and the organization may arise, e.g. when the idea is not recognized but abandoned by the top management. On condition that the organization makes an *adoption decision*, i.e. the organization wants to proceed with the implementation of an idea, the subsequent *implementation phase* usually includes initial attempts to make use of the innovation which may require further modifications and redefinitions. Introducing an organizational innovation is often a venture that encounters a number of challenges and obstacles. For instance, the introduction of virtual teams necessitates both organizational restructuring and the use of new work technologies. Therefore start-up problems and intentional opposition by the employees are likely to occur (Townsend et al., 2004). Hereby the source of an innovation (see Table 24.1; King and Anderson, 2002) may be a deciding factor for whether employees accept an innovation and therefore commit themselves to a change process (Herscovitch and Meyer, 2002) or rather thwart the plans of the organization ('not-invented-here syndrome').

According to conventional stage models, it can be assumed that the innovation becomes more and more routinized during the sustained implementation phase (see King and Anderson, 2002; Zaltman et al., 1973). Van de Ven et al. (1999), however, pointed out that innovation processes in reality are often terminated before an innovation is implemented, e.g. due to deficient resources, and before *routinization* starts off. Criticizing the widely held assumption that the innovation process unfolds in a linear sequence of distinct stages, the authors proposed an alternative approach based on longitudinal data from the Minnesota Innovation Research Program (MIRP). This model acknowledges the non-linear character of the innovation process that usually involves a great extent of cycling back and forward, and overlap between the different stages. Furthermore, the process of innovation is not settled with its routinization but is rather likely to influence the initiation of future innovations – that is, past innovation begets future innovativeness (King, 1992). This approach is compatible with the much more fluid depiction of innovation as a series of processes which constitute the 'innovation life-cycle' by Kimberly (1981).

Using longitudinal data, Van de Ven et al. (1999) also identified some common features of innovation, such as the fact that success and failure are often not attributed correctly. As pointed out by King and Anderson (2002), most models of innovation ignore that an innovation process may be perceived from different angles within the organization. Whereas the top management, for instance, might assume that the innovation has been successfully implemented and routinized, the innovation may have been rejected and abandoned by certain work groups or individual employees. The rejection of the innovation on the part of the employees may have its roots in negative effects, such as heavy workloads and, as consequence, mental strain and stress symptoms, accompanying the innovation (Bunce and West, 1996).

Negative outcomes from innovation: three levels of analysis

Individual level

Several studies cited in Table 24.2 suggest that creativity and innovation processes can have negative outcomes for those involved, interestingly either as a cause underlying innovation as an attempt to change and improve the situation, or as a consequence whereby innovation at work can lead to useful as well as less than positive consequences. Janssen et al. (2004), for instance, pointed out that on the one hand engaging in innovative activities can be conducive for employees to adapt effectively to the job, to increase job satisfaction and subjective well-being. On the other hand modifying oneself or the work environment through innovation may bring unintended costs, such as increased stress levels, for innovators and other individuals affected in its wake. Stress can be caused by numerous different kinds of stressors, such as aspects of the employee's work role, specific job characteristics and demands, and the physical work environment (Hart and Cooper, 2001) or stressors that are of a more interpersonal nature (Spector and Jex, 1998). Janssen (2003) demonstrated that innovative employees are indeed more susceptible to involvement in interpersonal conflicts with co-workers, e.g. when facing resistance to the innovative idea. Again this can have a negative impact on the innovator's state of health, at least when the organizational environment is perceived as to be unfair (Janssen, 2004). Furthermore, a lack of fit between job demands, e.g. to be creative, and individual abilities may result in job dissatisfaction, intentions to leave, and lower job performance (Livingstone et al., 1997; Shalley et al., 2000). In their model, James et al. (1999) distinguish between positive and negative creativity and organizations. Whereas the former is expressed in ideas and innovations that are useful for the organization, the latter is revealed as theft, sabotage, social attacks, and exploitation, and the undermining of organizational goals and policies. Perceived injustice or lack of control (Gebert et al., 2003) stimulate negative emotions and individual goals and are thus conducive to negative creativity.

As intriguing to note is that definitions of, and research into, counterproductivity at work overlap quite notably with creativity and innovation studies and definitions. Sackett and DeVore (2001: 145) define counterproductivity as follows:

> Counterproductive workplace behavior at the most general level refers to any intentional behavior on the part of an organization member viewed by the organization as contrary to its legitimate interests.

Thus, behavior by individuals that challenges established practices, that violate existing rule structures, or that involve the misuse of organizational resources for non-sanctioned activities is potentially understood as being counterproductive. Ironically, as noted earlier, all of these elements are often present in the early phases of innovation attempts (e.g. West, 2001), and the elements of this definition, including the intentionality of behavior, present a striking, inverted mirror-image of their positive connotations put forward in the innovation literature. For instance, Sackett and DeVore (2001: 146) in their review of the various categories of counterproductive behavior proposed over the years include the 'misuse of time and resources' as a polemic opposite. Kanter (1983) identified 'skunk works' activities where employees engage in non-sanctioned tasks using organizational time or resources as being a significant means through which innovation can be stimulated and encouraged. The dilemma here, of course, is that innovation by its very nature is often 'non-sanctioned' behavior which flourishes best under such covert conditions, and which may well be seen by some in the organization as rather more counterproductive than innovative. Innovation, it seems, is truly in the eye of the beholder (Amabile, 1988).

Work group level

Given the nature of innovation as being highly unpredictable, controversial, and in competition with alternative courses of actions (Kanter, 1988), it is not surprising that conflict is a common feature of innovation (King and Anderson, 2002). Other research hints at the negative effects sometimes involved in team-level innovation attempts. De Dreu, for instance, in a series of papers, has highlighted the effects that conflict can have upon stimulating creative ideas within group innovation, but also that innovation itself can provoke further conflict within work teams (De Dreu, 2006; De Dreu and Weingart, 2003).

Conflicts in teams are either relationship- or task-related. Examples of relationship conflicts are divergences with regard to personal taste and political preferences, whereas disputes about the distribution of resources and the interpretation of facts are examples of task conflicts (De Dreu, 2006). Relationship conflicts were shown to have a negative impact on task performance (e.g. Jehn, 1995). Pelled (1996), for instance, demonstrated that relationship conflicts between team members are bound up with lower productivity due to high claims of time and energy used up by the conflict. By contrast, task conflicts spur on team members to examine subject matters more thoroughly and to engage in deliberate processing of task-related information. Groups who encounter task conflicts where found to make better decisions due to a higher cognitive understanding of the issue under consideration (see Simons and Peterson, 2000). Thus task conflicts can contribute to the recognition of inefficiencies, foster learning, and lead to the development of novel ideas. Whereas initial research findings have prompted many to argue that task conflict has a positive impact on team effectiveness, a meta-analysis of relevant work resulted in a moderately negative correlation between task conflict and overall team effectiveness (De Dreu and Weingart, 2003).

In an attempt to resolve the contradiction of previous findings, De Dreu (2006) points out that the line of argument underlying the prediction that task conflict is conducive to team performance relates mainly to the ability to learn, to develop new insights and understanding, and to solve complex problems. However, learning and complex problem solving take up time, effort and energy. Therefore task conflicts may be detrimental to goal attainment and efficiency of work processes, at least in the short term. At the same time, task conflict can be conducive to those subcomponents of overall team performance that are subject to team members' learning ability and innovativeness. Furthermore, it has been demonstrated that task conflict is actually related to innovation in work teams in a curvilinear fashion, i.e. too much or to too little task conflict was detrimental to team innovation. Accordingly, teams were more innovative when the level of task conflict was moderate. The challenge here, of course, is to maintain a certain level of task conflict that leads to functional in contrast to dysfunctional outcomes. Whereas individual creativity and work team innovation can be the outcome of conflicts, innovation itself may be a source of dissent among team members, e.g. due to heavy workload, or uncertainties about the distribution of resources and power, and a lack of clear guidelines. Although work groups may profit from innovation in the long term, the immediate chances of goal attainment and effectiveness are rather restricted (De Dreu, 2006).

Organizational level

Looking at the more problematical aspects of innovation in the workplace, far less research has been published on the organizational level of analysis. However, on the assumption that an innovation is successful in terms of profit, a number of 'collateral damages' are still likely to occur, e.g. increased employee turnover due to changed working conditions through organizational restructuring or the introduction of new work technologies. Furthermore, concentrating on one innovation ties up resources (e.g. material, financial or managerial resources) that are usually reserved for other areas such as specific functions and product groups and therefore may cause inefficiencies elsewhere (see Van de Ven et al., 1989).

Distress-related innovation: a multi-level model

Anderson et al. (2004) propose a so-called 'distress-related' model of innovation at work. Their model is reproduced in Figure 24.1.

Essentially, the phrase 'necessity is the mother of all invention' partly explains the orientation of this model, but not fully. The model in essence proposes a series of distress–innovation response–outcome relationships in a multi-level framework. Here, innovation is provoked not by slack resources, positive work group climates, or individual propensity to innovate altruistically, but by distress events such as organizational decline, and work group and role conflict. The necessity to be more innovative at the organizational level of analysis often results from changing business environmental circumstances that are beyond immediate control, such as the changing nature of work (West, 2002; Howard, 1995). At the group level, minority dissent and moderate task conflict can stimulate teams to be more innovative (De Dreu, 2006). Regarding the individual level, job dissatisfaction and negative mood states can provoke creativity and innovation (George and Zhou, 2002; Zhou and George, 2001). In effect, the distress-related model by Anderson et al. (2004) depicts innovation as a process with distress-related variables acting as triggers for innovation. At the same time the innovation itself or its consequences may be the determining factor of any distress experienced by individual employees, work teams or the wider organization. Furthermore, the model illustrates that innovative attempts might potentially cause cross-level effects. For instance, group innovation such as the development of a new product may not only impact the work group but also result in undesirable consequences for the individual or organizational level of analysis.

Whereas antecedents of creative and innovative behavior have been widely studied, the critical factors and process mechanisms that regulate positive and negative consequences of innovation remain neglected to a large extent (Janssen et al., 2004). Although Anderson and King (1993) have pointed to the fact that the outcomes of innovations in terms of their effects on the entire organization, its constituent units and individual employees should be included in research on innovation processes, hardly any research has tried to fill this research gap so far (for exceptions see Table 24.2). Thus, while assumptions about the beneficial effects of innovation at all these levels of analysis are commonly made in research and practice alike, the more problematical, but ever-present, aspects of initiating new and improved ways of doing things in the workplace have remained widely ignored. Taking this shortcoming into account, the distress-related model illustrated above considers negative consequences of innovations as regards three different levels of

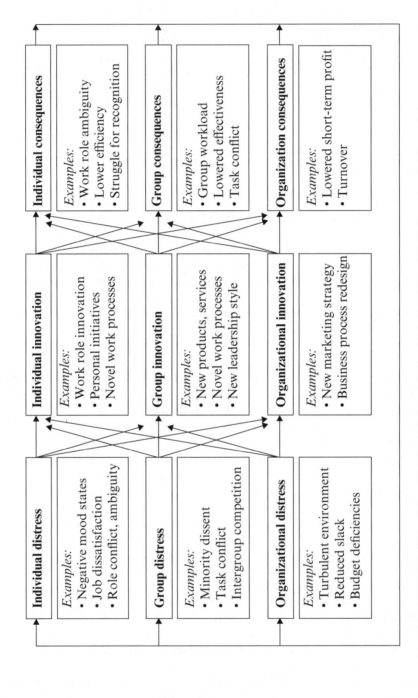

Source: Copyright © 2004, John Wiley & Sons, Ltd, *Journal of Organizational Behavior*, **25**, pp. 147–73. Reproduced with permission.

Figure 24.1   Distress-related innovation at three levels of analysis

analysis. Subsequent to the implementation of an innovation, individuals may, for instance, experience higher levels of stress due to increased workload caused by the change, e.g. new technologies and work processes. Where employees perceive their changed work situation as highly stressful over a longer period of time, for instance, health problems and burnout as well as reduced work motivation become likely to emerge. Examples of potential detrimental outcomes of innovations as regards the work group are conflicts with co-workers or supervisors due to task-related disagreements and increased workloads. The implementation of virtual teamwork, for instance, may affect the cohesion and trust of team members and thus be detrimental to the effectiveness of the work group in the medium and long term (see Townsend et al., 2004). With regard to the organization as a whole, the introduction of innovations may not only result in reduced short-term profit, but also higher employee turnover due to less attractive working conditions. Whereas the former is more or less 'part of the business', the latter potentially implies a loss of valuable human resources which again may cause lowered efficiencies, output losses and follow-up costs. Furthermore, real cases such as Enron in the past have shown that innovation can also be associated to unethical practices and, thus, eventually cause the organization to start floundering.

In general, the distress-related model contributes to a more balanced view of innovation, which may in fact involve beneficial as well as detrimental effects. However, it is crucial to note that the cycle depicted in the model may not necessarily start with distress but with the introduction of an innovation – whether invented or discovered in the organization or adopted from outside. However, distress may also take on other developments and, for example, spill over from one level of analysis to the others and eventually cause more damage than can be compensated for by secondary innovations arising from it. Similarly, because a certain degree of task conflict has been shown to be conducive to innovation (De Dreu, 2006), a moderate level of distress may instigate innovative at the workplace. However, the crucial question here again is: what represents a 'moderate' level of distress and how can this be balanced in order to prevent far-reaching damage way beyond the scope of the present innovation attempt? For instance, induced task conflict can all too easily lead to irreparable interpersonal conflicts, an endemic loss of leadership credibility, and longer-term declines in work group climate or even wider declines in organizational culture that may undermine other aspects of organizational performance. Referring to the last, various innovation researchers have argued directly against the 'benefits' of conflict-induced innovation (e.g. West, 2001; Baer and Frese, 2003). Indeed, they have argued for the establishment of a climate conducive to innovation in work teams that is not characterized by conflict and distress but by (a) a shared vision, (b) participative safety, (c) task orientation and (d) support of innovation (West and Anderson, 1996). Thereby individuals are encouraged to propose new ideas and discuss them openly without fear of negative consequences such as rejection or interpersonal conflicts.

Concluding comments

The starting point of this chapter was that the more dysfunctional, conflictual and counterproductive aspects of innovation have been largely ignored in the literature so far. Currently, the majority of applied studies deal with creativity and innovation as if the antecedents, processes and outcomes involved are unswervingly positive throughout. In this chapter we have highlighted the 'darker' sides of workplace innovation, whether at the individual, work group or organization-wide level of analysis. After years of extensive research into innovation, these dysfunctional elements of the innovation process are only just coming to light. Such elements – nonconformist behavior, rule breaking by work groups, deviant norms, counterproductivity, to name but a few – are in fact part and parcel of the early phases of the innovation cycle (West, 2001). Innovation, it seems, is not only in the eye of the beholder but is also a disruptive process often born of disruptive ingredients, which may lead eventually to other unforeseen innovation attempts.

Considering the far-reaching consequences innovations can have on individuals, work groups and organizations, the question arises as to what kind of research into the more problematical outcomes of innovation would advance theory and practice alike. In the previous section, we presented a model of distress-related innovation at multiple levels of analysis. This model may guide future research into the 'darker sides' of innovation; in this connection promising avenues include looking at the causes and consequences of innovation in longitudinal studies and, ideally, using multi-level research designs (see Anderson et al., 2004).

In many ways, however, this more balanced portrayal of the benefits and disbenefits of innovation antecedent factors, processes and outcomes is to be welcomed. It provides a clear antidote to the excessively positive accounts generated by some authors falling foul of so-called 'pro-innovation bias' and who have fallen into the trap of presenting a managerially enhanced fictitious account of the true processes involved in stimulating and implementing innovativeness in workplace settings. One manager's radical innovation is truly another's counterproductive behavior; the challenge for researchers is to unravel these widely divergent perceptions and for managers in organizations it is to balance the value of such nonconformist behavior against its likely costs and benefits to the organization in the longer term.

Acknowledgments

We are grateful to the editors, Janice Langan-Fox and Cary L. Cooper, and especially to Richard J. Klimoski for his insightful comments on an earlier version of this chapter. This work was supported by a fellowship within the Postdoc-Program of the German Academic Exchange Service (DAAD) to Rosina M. Gasteiger and by the University of Amsterdam Business School.

References

Amabile, T.M. (1988), 'A model of creativity and innovation in organizations', in B.M. Staw and L.L. Cummings (eds), *Research in Organizational Behavior*, Vol. 10, Greenwich, CT: JAI Press, pp. 123–67.
Anderson, N.R. (1990), 'Innovation in work groups: current research concerns and future directions', paper presented to the British Psychological Society Annual Conference, Bowness-on-Windermere, Cumbria, January.
Anderson, N. and King, N. (1993), 'Innovation in organizations', in C.L. Cooper and I.T. Robertson (eds), *International Review of Industrial and Organizational Psychology*, Vol. 8, Chichester, UK: John Wiley & Sons, pp. 1–34.
Anderson, N., De Dreu, C.K.W. and Nijstad, B.A. (2004), 'The routinization of innovation research: a constructively critical review of the state-of-the-science', *Journal of Organizational Behavior*, 25, 147–73.
Axtell, C.M., Holman, D.J., Unsworth, K.L., Wall, T.D. and Waterson, P.E. (2000), 'Shopfloor innovation: facilitating the suggestion and implementation of ideas', *Journal of Occupational and Organizational Psychology*, 73, 265–85.
Baer, M. and Frese, M. (2003), 'Innovation is not enough: climates for initiative and psychological safety, process innovations, and firm performance', *Journal of Organizational Behavior*, 24, 45–68.
Bunce, D. and West, M.A. (1996), 'Stress management and innovation interventions at work', *Human Relations*, 49, 209–32.

Daft, R.L. (1978), 'A dual-core model of organizational innovation', *Academy of Management Journal*, **21**, 193–210.

Damanpour, F. (1990), 'Innovation effectiveness, adoption and organizational performance', in M.A. West and J.L. Farr (eds), *Innovation and Creativity at Work. Psychological and organizational strategies*, Chichester, UK: John Wiley & Sons, pp. 125–41.

Damanpour, F. (1987), 'The adoption of technological, administrative, and ancillary innovations: impacts of organizational factors', *Journal of Management*, **13**(4), 675–88.

Damanpour, F. and Evans, W.M. (1984), 'Organizational innovation and performance: the problem of "organizational lag"', *Administrative Science Quarterly*, **29**, 392–409.

De Dreu, C.K.W. (2006), 'When too little or too much hurts: evidence for a curvilinear relationship between task conflict and innovation in teams', *Journal of Management*, **32**, 83–107.

De Dreu, C.K.W. and Weingart, L.R. (2003), 'Task versus relationship conflict, team performance, and team member satisfaction: a meta-analysis', *Journal of Applied Psychology*, **88**, 741–49.

Drucker, P.F. (1985), 'The discipline of innovation', *Harvard Business Review*, **85**, 67–72.

Frese, M. and Fay, D. (2001), 'Personal initiative: an active performance concept for work in the 21st century', in B.M. Staw and R.M. Sutton (eds), *Research in Organisational Behavior*, Vol. 23, Amsterdam: Elsevier Science, pp. 133–87.

Frese, M., Teng, E. and Wijnen, C.J.D. (1999), 'Helping to improve suggestion systems: predictors of making suggestions in companies', *Journal of Organizational Behavior*, **20**, 1139–155.

Gebert, D., Boerner, S. and Lanwehr, R. (2003), 'The risks of autonomy: empirical evidence for the necessity of a balance management in promoting organizational innovativeness', *Creativity and Innovation Management*, **12**, 41–9.

George, J.M. and Zhou, J. (2002), 'Understanding when bad moods foster creativity and good ones don't: the role of context and clarity of feelings', *Journal of Applied Psychology*, **87**, 687–97.

Harmon, R.L. (1992), *Reinventing the Factory*, New York: Macmillan.

Hart, P.M. and Cooper, C.L. (2001), 'Occupational stress: toward a more integrated framework', in N. Anderson, D.S. Ones, H.K. Sinangil and C. Viswesvaran (eds), *Handbook of Industrial, Work, and Organizational Psychology*, Vol. 2, Thousand Oaks, CA: Sage, pp. 93–114.

Herscovitch, L. and Meyer, J.P. (2002), 'Commitment to organizational change: extension of a three-component model', *Journal of Applied Psychology*, **87**, 474–87.

Hippel, E. von (1988), *The Sources of Innovation*, Oxford: Oxford University Press.

Hippel, E. von (2005), *Democratizing Innovation*, Cambridge, MA: MIT Press.

Howard, A. (ed.) (1995), *The Changing Nature of Work*, San Francisco, CA: Jossey-Bass.

Howell, J.M. and Higgins, C.A. (1990), 'Champions of change: identifying, understanding, and supporting champions of technological innovations', *Organizational Dynamics*, **19**, 40–54.

James, K., Clark, K. and Cropanzano, R. (1999), 'Positive and negative creativity in groups, institutions, and organizations: a model and theoretical extension', *Creativity Research Journal*, **12**, 211–26.

Janssen, O. (2003), 'Innovative behaviour and job involvement at the price of conflict and less satisfactory relations with co-workers', *Journal of Occupational and Organizational Psychology*, **76**, 347–64.

Janssen, O. (2004), 'How fairness perceptions make innovative behavior more or less stressful', *Journal of Organizational Behavior*, **25**, 201–15.

Janssen, O., van de Vliert, E. and West, M. (2004), 'The bright and dark sides of individual and group innovation: a special issue introduction', *Journal of Organizational Behavior*, **25**, 129–45.

Jehn, K.A. (1995), 'A multimethod examination of the benefit and detriments of intragroup conflict', *Administrative Science Quarterly*, **40**, 256–82.

Kanter, R.M. (1983), *The Change Master: Corporate Entrepreneurs at Work*, New York: Simon & Schuster.

Kanter, R.M. (1988), 'When a thousand flowers bloom: structural, collective, and social conditions for innovation in organization', *Research in Organizational Behavior*, **10**, 169–211.

Kaschube, J. (2006), *Eigenverantwortung – Eine neue berufliche Leistung. Chance oder Bedrohung für Organisationen? [Self-responsibility – A New Occupational Performance. Opportunity or Risk for Organizations?]*, Göttingen: Vandenhoeck & Ruprecht.

Kimberly, J.R. (1981), 'Managerial innovation', in P.C. Nystrom and W.H. Starbuck (eds), *Handbook of Organizational Design*, Oxford: Oxford University Press, pp. 84–104.

King, N. (1992), 'Modeling the innovation process: an empirical comparison of approaches', *Journal of Occupational and Organizational Psychology*, **65**, 89–100.

King, N. and Anderson, N. (2002), *Managing Innovation and Change: A Critical Guide for Organizations*, London: Thompson.

Kirton, M.J. (1976), 'Adaptors and innovators: a description and measure', *Journal of Applied Psychology*, **61**(5), 622–9.

Kirton, M.J. (1978), 'Have adaptors and innovators equal levels of creativity?', *Psychological Reports*, **42**, 695–8.

Livingstone, L.P., Nelson, D.L. and Barr, S.H. (1997), 'Person–environment fit and creativity: an examination of supply-value and demand-ability versions of fit', *Journal of Management*, **23**, 119–46.

Maier, G.W., Frey, D., Schulz-Hardt, S. and Brodbeck, F.C. (2001), 'Innovation', in G. Wenninger (eds), *Lexikon der Psychologie [Encyclopedia of Psychology]*, Heidelberg: Spektrum, pp. 264–7.

Miron, E., Erez, M. and Naveh, E. (2004), 'Do personal characteristics and cultural values that promote innovation, quality, and efficiency compete or complement each other?', *Journal of Organizational Behavior*, **25**, 175–99.

Patterson, F. (2002), 'Great minds don't think alike? Person-level predictors of innovations at work', in C.L. Cooper and I.T. Robertson (eds), *International Review of Industrial and Organizational Psychology*, Vol. 17, Chichester, UK: John Wiley & Sons, pp. 115–44.

Pelled, L.H. (1996), 'Demographic diversity, conflict, and work group outcomes: an intervening process theory', *Organization Science*, **7**, 615–31.

Peters, T.J. and Waterman, R.H. (1982), *In Search of Excellence: Lessons from America's Best Run Companies*, New York: Harper & Row.

Rank, J., Pace, V.L. and Frese, M. (2004), 'Three avenues for future research on creativity, innovation, and initiative', *Applied Psychology: An International Review*, **53**, 518–28.

Sackett, P.R. and DeVore, C.J. (2001), 'Counterproductive behaviors at work', in N. Anderson, D.S. Ones, H.K. Sinangil and C. Viswesvaran (eds), *Handbook of Industrial, Work, and Organizational Psychology*, Vol. 2, London/New York: Sage, pp. 145–99.

Sauer, J. and Anderson, N. (1992), 'Have we misread the psychology of innovation? A case study from two NHS hospitals', *Leadership and Organizational Development Journal*, **13**, 17–21.

Shalley, C.E., Gilson, L.L. and Blum, T.C. (2000), 'Matching creativity requirements and the work environment: effects on satisfaction and intentions to leave', *Academy of Management Journal*, **43**, 215–23.

Simons, T. and Peterson, R. (2000), 'Task conflict and relationship conflict in top management teams: the pivotal role of intragroup trust', *Journal of Applied Psychology*, **68**, 102–11.

Spector, P.E. and Jex, S.M. (1998), 'Development of four self-report measures of job stressors and strain: interpersonal conflict at work scale, organizational constraints scale, quantitative workload inventory, and physical symptoms inventory, *Journal of Occupational Health Psychology*, **3**, 356–67.

Staw, B.M. and Boettger, R.D. (1990), 'Task revision: a neglected form of work performance', *Academy of Management Journal*, **33**, 534–59.

Sternberg, R.J. and Lubart, T.I. (1991), 'An investment theory of creativity and its development', *Human Development*, **34**(1), 1–32.

Sternberg, R.J. and Lubart, T.I. (1996), 'Investing in creativity', *American Psychologist*, **51**, 677–88.

Townsend, A., DeMarie, S. and Hendrickson, A.R. (2004), 'Virtual teams: technology and the workplace of the future', in R. Katz (eds), *The Human Side of Managing Technological Innovation. A Collection of Readings*, New York: Oxford University Press, pp. 269–82.

Van de Ven, A., Angle, H.L. and Poole, M. (eds) (1989), *Research on the Management of Innovation: The Minnesota Studies*, New York: Harper & Row.

Van de Ven, A.H., Polley, D.E., Garud, R. and Venkataraman, S. (1999), *The Innovation Journey*, New York: Oxford University Press.

West, M.A. (2001), 'The human team: basic motivations and innovations', in N. Anderson, D.S. Ones, H.K. Sinangil and C. Viswesvaran (eds), *Handbook of Industrial, Work, and Organizational Psychology*, Vol. 2, London/New York: Sage, pp. 270–88.

West, M.A. (2002), 'Sparkling fountains or stagnant ponds: an integrative model of creativity and innovation implementation in work groups', *Applied Psychology: An International Review*, **51**(3), 355–424.

West, M.A. and Anderson, N.R. (1992), 'Innovation, cultural values and the management of change in British hospital management', *Work and Stress*, **16**, 293–310.

West, M.A. and Anderson, N.R. (1996), 'Innovation in top management teams', *Journal of Applied Psychology*, **81**, 680–93.

West, M.A. and Farr, J.L. (1990), 'Innovation at work', in M.A. West and J.L. Farr (eds), *Innovation and Creativity at Work*, Chichester, UK: John Wiley & Sons, pp. 3–13.

Zaltman, G., Duncan, R. and Holbek, J. (1973), *Innovations and Organizations*, New York: Wiley.

Zhou, J. and George, J.M. (2001), 'When job dissatisfaction leads to creativity: encouraging the expression of voice', *Academy of Management Journal*, **44**, 682–96.

25 'Dysfunctional' subcultures in organizations: threat or a key to enhancing change?
Roy J. Lewicki, David Greenberger and Erin Coyne

Children are taught to recognize right versus wrong and good versus evil at the earliest age (Stillwell et al., 2000). Not only do they learn these dichotomies and their importance, but they are also trained to recognize the most obvious cues associated with them. Even the smallest delay in identifying evil, they are told, has the potential to lead one in the wrong direction. So, it is not sufficient for everyone just to know right versus wrong; everyone must be on guard for the first signs or cues of evil – so that we can keep our distance from it. Because this is so ingrained in us as children, it is not surprising that most individuals, as adults, similarly are primed to identify cues that are associated with evil, to generalize from these cues, and then look either to eliminate or to put distance between themselves and this evil. With the risks associated with evil, only a few cues are required to initiate a set of responses; real evil is not necessary. In other words, as individuals mature, it is often the proxies of evil to which individuals react. However, the cues themselves that serve as these proxies are, at least in hindsight, often not sinister or actually harmful. For example, having others disagree and appear to be different can lead to labeling and stereotyping. Whether it is the Salem Witch Trials in the late 1600s or McCarthyism in 1950s, the majority quickly move to deal with even the slightest signs of inappropriateness.

When one sees subcultures develop within an organization, it is not surprising that most see them as potentially harmful. While only a few might be disagreeing with the majority, it is common for the majority to engage in this type of categorization – seeing that minority as something sinister, 'evil' or potentially harmful to the organization. The subcultures that emerge among those individuals who disagree with the core culture are necessarily seen as bad, a threat to the majority's status and power, and something must be done to eliminate them. Having stated this, however, most adults understand, from experience, two things that children are not taught by their parents or teachers. First, while it is easy to label things in a dichotomous manner, like good or evil, in actuality, these terms anchor ends of a broader continuum. In many circumstances the 'truth' is not at either end of the continuum. Second, the definition of what is 'good' or 'evil' is a matter of perspective: what is seemingly wrong for one may, in fact, be right for another.

We believe these same categorization and perception processes commonly occur within organizations. And while the 'majority' would see the purpose of identifying 'destructive' subgroups as one of rooting out and eliminating dysfunction, these very efforts may actually be creating the dysfunction. This chapter first will explore the issue of why subcultures develop and how these subcultures fit into the context of the larger organization. In so doing, we pose three important questions: first, are some cultures particularly fertile to cultivate subcultures? Is this a 'natural' process, ubiquitous in all organizations, and does it occur more frequently in some organizational cultures than in others? Second, why do many of these subcultures come to be labeled as dysfunctional? What are the threats that subcultures pose to the established organization? Finally, is it possible that successful organizations may use subcultures to enhance themselves and increase their ability to adapt to change? Moreover, if subcultures were not labeled negatively, is it possible that they could actually enhance engagement and trust among members?

To understand the zeitgeist of subcultures, we begin by looking at how seemingly dysfunctional subcultures are showcased in business school pedagogies. In the cases we highlight, different subgroups have grown up within a larger organization culture, and embrace one or more practices which students quickly intuitively see as 'problems'. Even productive groups can be labeled as 'dysfunctional' if important norms or practices diverge from the core culture, and despite their effectiveness at achieving organizational goals. We then move on to explore how this labeling occurs. Subgroups naturally form in organizations, and from these subgroups, cultures (i.e. subcultures) unique to these subgroups form. These subcultures can be simple variations of the broader organizational culture, or they may contain significant alterations. Rather than being anomalous, their development should be viewed as normative for organizations. With the formation of these subcultures coming out of various subgroups, however, the social categorization literature (e.g. Brewer, 1991) is quite clear in illuminating how ingroups and outgroups are labeled and begin to perceive and interact with one another. It is a simple extension to suggest that some of the subcultures are labeled as 'dysfunctional'. In turn, this has an impact both upon the treatment of these subcultures but also upon the ways the individuals within the subculture view themselves. In the final section of the chapter, we discuss the implications of this labeling and stereotyping for organizations in terms of enhancing the organization's capability to change and to embrace change, as well as the degree to which individuals are engaged and trust others.

Exploring subculture dynamics in early management education cases

The role of formal and informal subgroups in organizations has long been recognized as important. It would be expected that educators as well as those in industry would design pedagogies to enhance individuals' competencies in working with and managing these informal groups. Some of the classic case studies in the management disciplines were written to help students understand the systems that operate within work groups and organizations, particularly insofar as the dynamics of these formal and informal groups affect individual and group productivity. Several of the cases focused on the development of informal subgroups within productive work groups, and challenge students to consider how to understand their dynamics and 'operate' on these subgroups without impacting overall group productivity. It is not clear where the impetus for this kind of case developed, although two aspects of the development of management theory had some impact. First, the prescribed development of the theory of organizations specified the broader framework of bureaucratic organization structures and processes, and specified how workers should be arranged, organized and controlled for maximum organizational efficiency (Drucker, 1954). Examples of these 'informal subgroups' appeared to create interesting challenges for this theory, since they offered examples of productivity that seemed to be outside the boundaries of bureaucratic theory. Second, the focus on groups, productivity and the impact of norms was clearly strengthened by the Western Electric studies (Roethlisberger and Dickson, 1939), where informal subjects were first identified as being an independent force operating within the organization and as impacting individual, group, and organizational performance.

Three classic management cases focus on the important role played by subgroups in organizations: Claremont Instruments Company, 'Work Group Ownership of an Improved Tool', and the Slade Company. Let us offer a quick review of each of these cases, and illustrate how formal and informal groups operate within the context of the larger organization.

Claremont Instruments Company (Hower and Lawrence, 1948) was a company that produced a varied line of high-quality glass pieces for laboratory equipment and supplies. A group of highly skilled workers produced many of the glass pieces by hand, while other pieces were machine-blown into a variety of molds. Four shifts worked in the department on a 24-hour, seven-day-a-week basis. Working conditions were hot, smoky and noisy. In one department, the glass department, a 'problem' developed: occasional outbursts of horseplay among the workers. The horseplay involved workers throwing wet waste paper at each other, occasionally squirting each other with fire hoses, or extensive banter among key workers in the department. Generally, the horseplay was short-lived and workers quickly returned to their assigned duties. However, one night a worker slipped in a puddle of water after a fight, dropped a box of glass, and burned herself on some hot glass. Management's challenge was to decide whether to 'tighten up' on discipline and punish the horseplay, but without disrupting the overall productivity of the department.

In 'Work Group Ownership of an Improved Tool' (1956), a group of skilled craftsmen machine-lathed highly sophisticated component parts for aircraft engines. Eight skilled machinists were of the same nationality and worked in four shifts of two workers each on a 24/7 production schedule. They were paid hourly plus a modest piece rate, and usually completed 22 units per shift. Their productivity rate was hampered by the lathe equipment, which frequently had to be shut down and cleaned to maintain quality production. One day, one of the informal leaders of the group created a new lathe tool bit which reduced the amount of time the lathes had to be stopped for cleaning (which led to increasing productivity). The worker eventually shared the tool with his seven other comrades so that workers on all four shifts had the tool. However, the workers refused to share the discovery of the tool with the company. They believed that the amount of a one-time bonus they would receive as a reward for discovering the tool was significantly less valuable than the continuing bonuses they could accrue by increasing their productivity with the tool, but not letting management know about it. They feared that once management was told about the tool, the piece rate quota would be adjusted and/or some workers might be laid off, and thus there would be little if any long-term benefit from their invention. The workers decided to use the tool to increase productivity modestly, and continually tricked the 'methods supervisor' who tried to investigate the new tool. The ongoing tension between the workers and methods supervisor eventually led to a major confrontation with the unit supervisor. The student challenge is to act as this unit supervisor, carefully unravel the problem, and determine an optimal solution.

Finally, the Slade Company (Lawrence and Seiler, 1960) is probably the best known of the three cases.[1] The case described the complex social structure of the plating department under the oversight of its foreman, Ralph Porter. The department contains several well-organized and complex work groups who work together to accomplish a variety of metal-plating tasks. The groups appear to operate with very strong norms for quality and productivity, and little supervisory oversight. However, a significant problem occurs in the abuse of the department's time clock. Workers were scheduled for 12-hour shifts (7–7), and often voluntarily came in to work to perform overtime and on weekends. However, supervisors only worked until 5 pm and were seldom present on weekends. So the workers often completed work by 5:30 pm, a half hour after the supervisor departed, and left one of their colleagues behind to punch others' time cards out at 7 pm. Workers also punched each other in or out to cover up lateness or absence, but no workers ever punched out early when important productivity deadlines had to be met. When asked whether they would prefer to work shorter hours for a higher hourly wage rate, one of the key group leaders laughs and says, 'it wouldn't even be an even trade'. Again, the student challenge is to determine whether the 'time clock' problem is a serious problem, and how to 'fix' it without undermining the morale or productivity of the plating department.

When these cases were used in classrooms, the challenge for students was to understand both the 'analytical' and 'action' perspectives on the case. To understand the analytical perspective, students were often introduced to a framework to assist them in understanding some of the most important forces that impact work group dynamics (see McCaskey, 1979). This framework gave students the tools to understand how components of context, people, task, and the formal organizational structure itself – often called the 'formal system' – worked together to create an *emergent system*, or the group's *culture*. As groups work together within the required system (defined by the nature of the people, the nature of their collective task, the nature of the formal organization structure, and the nature of the physical, social and economic context of the work), patterns of behavior emerge, some of which are related to completing the task, whereas others are more ritualistic. A related pattern might be the degree to which members pitch in to help others when work is backlogged; a ritualistic pattern might be deciding to collectively take a break at 3 pm every day, or meet in a local bar after work. Neither of these patterns is specified by the components of the required system, but both may be instrumentally important to the group's work output and member retention. Components of an emergent system include the norms of the group; roles taken on by particular group members, rituals, stories and unique language; and shared cognitions (Klimoski and Mohammed, 1994). Thus, in each of the cases described above (Claremont Instruments, Work Group Ownership and Slade Company), students needed to understand the factors that contribute to the group's culture and that lead to the group being perceived as functional and dysfunctional.

From an action perspective, students had to determine whether, and how, to operate or take actions on the emergent system so as to fix the 'deviant' emergent behavior without disturbing dynamics that kept these work groups productive. Thus, in Claremont Instruments, the challenge is to determine whether the worker injury is sufficiently critical to justify managerial intervention in the glass-blowing area in order to curtail the horseplay. In Work Group Ownership of an Improved Tool, the challenge is to find a way for management to encourage the group to share the tool with those outside the immediate group, so as to improve overall company productivity, without negatively impacting the compensation or morale of the work group that invented it. Finally, in the Slade Company, the challenge is to examine the legal and ethical implications of the 'punch out' system, propose effective changes, and help the workers accept and endorse those changes without negatively impacting the group's effectiveness and productivity. In most cases, instructors helped students develop remedies that focused on recognizing the positive aspects of the group's functioning and performance, not acting precipitously or heavy-handedly as a manager, and participatively involving the group in developing solutions.

Although these cases were used to teach some basic management and human resources theories, they also focused attention on why and how subcultures develop, and, more specifically, on how what seems to be a 'dysfunctional' set of norms and practices can emerge within a highly 'functional' work group environment. There are two particularly interesting implications from these classic cases. First, changing one's perspective – from management's view to the workers' view and back again – quickly results in different perceptions of the unfolding events. That is, if the manager mentally shifts from the organizational perspective to the work group's perspective – as one would in looking at the classic Gestalt figure-ground pictures – one would potentially view who is right versus who is wrong (and the resulting actions) very differently. As one shifts perspectives and imagines oneself a member of each work group, seemingly dysfunctional actions and subcultures can be seen as functional both to the group and even to the organization. Thus, although one might at first view them as dysfunctional, these groups and their culture may actually have a positive impact on the organization as a whole. In Claremont Instruments, the water-throwing was a functional way to cool workers off in a hot, poorly ventilated environment, as well as a means to combat the monotony and mental tediousness of the work. In Work Group Ownership, the group's secrecy about the new tool was a way to improve the equipment used on the job, to increase their direct rewards, and to 'beat' a supervisory group whom they did not trust to reward them appropriately for their efforts. Finally, in the Slade Company, the punch out system was a way to occasionally cover for a sick or tardy co-worker, increase compensation (avoiding management's wrath and punishment), and demonstrate to management that they, too, had power and control over the work environment.

Understanding cultures and subcultures
What is culture? The dictionary suggests that a culture is

> the integrated pattern of human behavior that includes thought, speech, action and artifacts and depends on man's capacity for learning and transmitting knowledge to succeeding generations. (*Merriam-Webster's Collegiate Dictionary*, 2001)

As applied to organizations (rather than societies), culture can be defined in many ways, and scholars have proposed many definitions. Researchers have suggested that a culture is the norms that evolve as groups of people work together; the rules that guide how people can (and should) get along with each other inside the organization; the core values that are endorsed by a group or organization; the 'climate' or 'atmosphere' within an organization; and the overall 'philosophy' that guides an organization's policies and practices toward people (i.e. its human resources policies and practices, both formal and informal) (Schein, 1988). Schein argues that while all of these things may be diagnostic of a culture, they are not definitions. Instead, Schein (1988: 9) argues that culture is:

> a pattern of basic assumptions – invented, discovered or developed by a given group as it learns to cope with its problems of external adaptation and internal integration – that has worked well enough to be considered valid, and, therefore to be taught to new members as the correct way to perceive think and feel in relation to those problems.

Implicit and explicit in this definition are some important elements that will shape our discussion in this chapter.

First, a culture is a property of a social unit. Social units develop a 'culture' as groups within that unit interact with each other. Culture 'is a learned property of group experience' (Schein: 7).

Second, culture develops as those within that social unit solve internal and external problems, and develop common experiences around solving those problems. These common experiences created a 'shared view' of the world, which, if it persists long enough, comes to be taken for granted by the members of that social unit.

Third, in larger social units, stable subgroups are likely to develop their own cultures. These groups might mobilize around a particular level in the hierarchy (such as managers, supervisors and workers), around different physical locations (plants, offices, retail outlets, etc.), different occupational groups (sales, research and development), etc.

Fourth, viewed more broadly, culture can be applied to any size social unit. Cultures can be found at the level of entire civilizations (Eastern versus Western), countries (Great Britain versus China), ethnic groups, occupations and professions, organizations, families, or various kinds of groups and teams.

Schein (1988, 1999) also stresses that cultures are more than just 'the way we do things around here'. His research shows that cultures are composed of three major levels. These levels move from the most visible and easy to see, to the most implicit and difficult to see.

Level 1: artifacts
Artifacts are what you see, feel and hear as you move around the physical space of culture. Culture is reflected in the architecture, the décor, the decorations, or the way you are treated as you enter the space. Artifacts are easy to discern as one views faculty offices. Some are messy, crammed with books, journals and papers; others are spotlessly clean. Some have plaques, trophies and awards, others have attractive paintings and photos, others are completely stark and bare. In some offices, you are greeted pleasantly, while in others, people stare at you coldly. Clothing stores that appear to particular age groups (e.g. teenagers versus mature adults) intentionally use furniture, decoration, lighting and sound to create an emotional experience for the intended customer. In offices, one can look at pace of action (how people are moving around), formal versus informal dress, or the number of open versus closed office doors. People behave the way they do because that's the way they do it in this organization, although it may never be clear why they do it this way.

Level 2: espoused values
At a second, deeper level, culture is reflected in what matters to the organization, and why they do what they do. Why is the teenage clothing store filled with glitzy décor and loud contemporary music, while the mature adult clothing store is filled with expensive formal chairs and lounges, oriental rugs and classical music? These choices presumably reflect the strategies, goals and philosophies (espoused justifications) of those who are appealing to a particular type of customer and want to draw them into the store. Similarly, in the office setting, the amount of formality, activity and/or privacy reflects the organization's strategies and goals with regard to the organizational value of employee interaction, teamwork, easy communication, open debate and discussion, etc. These dynamics may be explicitly

espoused by current management, or may be the legacy of the informal rules created by the long-since-departed founder of the organization.

Level 3: shared tacit assumptions
Finally, at the third (deepest) level, a culture reflects the unconscious, shared, taken-for-granted beliefs, perceptions, thoughts, feelings and assumptions about 'how things ought to be done'. These assumptions probably go all the way back to the founder of the group or organization, who had some very strong assumptions about 'the way the world worked'. These assumptions and values were imparted to others, who engaged in a joint learning process to follow these assumptions and found that they created group or organizational success. They are then imparted to newcomers to the group, who often persist in using those processes and procedures, even if they no longer are important or relevant for producing success in a changed environment. Thus, even those in the current culture cannot reconstruct why it is that this is the way we do things around here, without standing outside themselves (and the context) to gain perspective or see it differently.

The formation of subcultures in organizations
While each of the subgroups identified in the previous three cases adopted the rules, norms, rituals and practices of the organization in which they were located, each also had evolved a set of unique practices that had meaning, significance and value for them, but not necessarily for the broader organization. Before delving into the issue of whether these different subcultures are functional or dysfunctional, it is important to understand why and how these subcultures develop.

In any large organization, the maintenance of consistency across the organization is very difficult. Divisions, departments, regions and facilities simply don't experience the same organizational reality the same way. Because of this, subgroup formation is usually ubiquitous. Research on group size (Brewer and Kramer, 1986; Wagner, 1995) suggests that this decrease in consistency is manifested in a variety of ways, including: increasing numbers of subgroups; lack of consensus about the organization's strategic objectives and priorities; a decrease in cooperation across organizational units and an increased effort to protect and defend one's own local unit; and a diminished sense of identity for the organization as a whole. In other words, given their size, we would expect that the larger the organization, the more likely subgroups will be to form, and that each subgroup would develop its own set of norms and cultural values.

This decrease in consistency across subgroups can occur for a number of reasons (but are not limited to these). First, the larger the group, the less possible it is to have consensus in terms of common goals (and often, any consensus that does exist is implied), and, thus, its members are unlikely to feel as though their needs are being met (Brewer and Kramer, 1986). Second, with increasing size, the available rewards frequently have to be split among more individuals, meaning that each individual's action will be less likely to be directly contributing to the desired outcome. Third, the larger the group, the more likely clear communication will be problematic. That is, it is harder for the senior executives (top) of the organization to communicate with every single member of the organization. Similarly, the larger the organizational context, the more difficult it will be for group members to be heard by those senior executives. In either case, with increasingly little voice and direct communication with the larger organization, the less able individuals will be to standardize their actions and beliefs, or even know and understand the meanings and intents of senior leadership. Fourth, because of the deindividuation dynamics in larger organizations (Wagner, 1995), as the size of the organization grows, there is less pressure on any individual to conform to the explicit and implicit rules and routines of the organization.

Taking these circumstances together, we see two consequences. Individuals tend to look for smaller units within which to work and interact with others. As social beings, particularly in times of uncertainty, we look to others for support. When it is feasible, we form *ad hoc* groups when formal ones do not fulfill our needs. Moreover, individuals' identities are tied to the groups with which they associate – either because they choose those groups, or come to identify with that group after membership. Although it is rarely thought of in this context, one need look no further than an obituary to understand the role of groups in establishing a person's identity. Invariably the person is described briefly, and then there is a listing of the groups of which the individual was a member. These include civic, religious, work groups and military; collectively they serve to capture who the person was. Thus within organizations we find subgroup formation to be a natural occurrence within large organizations, and we also see individuals increasingly identifying with these groups.

As more individuals attempt to identify with these groups, it is also reasonable to expect that the same differing goals, perceptions and attitudes (that is the ones that lead people to associate with others) are communicated more directly within this smaller group. In this way, new subcultures develop out of these groups and, not surprisingly, these differ in varying degrees from those defined by the larger organization. In fact, the development of a different subculture may even be critical to the enhancement of the subgroups' identities. The greater the cultural distance between the subgroups and the organization, the greater the sense of individuality and, hence, identity with the subgroups. Let us explain how this occurs.

Much of the work on culture within organizations focuses on culture at the broad level of the organization (and, to some degree, as embedded within the broader global and national context of that organization). However, as we noted in our introductory case examples, this broad view of culture often fails to take into account the multiple cultures contained within an organization. Given the size and complexities of most organizations, one should expect that they contain multiple subcultures (Brown, 1995; Trice and Morand, 1991; Gregory, 1983).

Organizational subcultures are composed of distinctive subsets of individuals who operate within broader cultures. These individuals are seen as sharing unique values, behaviors, artifacts and practices (Lok et al., 2005). They depart from the broader organizational culture in which they work either by intensifying the culture's understandings and practices or deviating from them (Trice and Morand, 1991). Martin (1992) differentiates various types of subcultures into three categories: enhancing, orthogonal and countercultural. Each type differentiates the degree to which members adhere to norms and the dominant culture, and the degree to which they view themselves as independent: the norms in enhancing groups support the primary culture, the norms in orthogonal groups differentiate by pursuing an independent direction, and the norms in the countercultural groups differentiate by explicitly challenging the primary cultural norms. Taking all of these together, subcultures usually develop either as caricatures (intensified) or antitheses of the dominant culture, and there usually is some awareness on the part of the members of the subculture as to how they relate to the prevailing culture.

This is not to say that all organizations, even large ones, necessarily will develop subcultures. However, there are some significant causal elements or precipitating incidents that will increase the likelihood that such subcultures will develop. We will describe these in two major categories: environmental characteristics and individual characteristics.

Environmental characteristics
One of the most obvious environmental characteristics that can lead to the development of a subculture is the physical geography of a group relative to the main organization. The greater spatial distance a group has from the rest of the organization, the greater tendency it has to create a subgroup (Friedkin, 1999). The boundary formed by the geographic location separates the group from the larger organization, which can lead to stronger identification with the subgroup. This is true in the three cases discussed, where each group was physically separated from the rest of the organization. This geographic isolation caused these individuals to identify one another, which led to the development of a subculture within the organization.

External forces such as *mergers and acquisitions* create uncertainty and ambiguous circumstances that can impact the culture of an organization (Nahavandi and Malekzadeh, 1988). In particular, members of the acquired organization are likely to be acting under the culture of their previous organization (Berry, 1983). Moreover, the acquired would be expected to resist adaptation to the dominant cultural norms and remain separate for as long as possible. Since they would, at least at first, be separated geographically, they would tend to stick together, and might act in defiance of the organization that has taken over.

As indicated, the *size of the organization* may also influence subculture development. Larger organizations have more departments and functions, and therefore have more opportunities to develop subcultures within their smaller groups (Van Maanen and Barley, 1985). In addition, research has shown that people often strive for a balance between conflicting motives of being included and being unique (Hogg and Terry, 2000). In large organizations, individuals tend to feel over-included and seek distinctiveness by identifying with subgroups or creating subcultures.

Organizations with less *power centrality* (more decentralization) are more susceptible to subculture development since employees have greater autonomy and resources to support their own subculture (Boisnier and Chatman, 2003). Large organizations with many separate product lines, divisions, geographic regions or manufacturing facilities should expect to see some subcultural variation across these units. Similarly, an organization that basically acts as a holding company for other organizations would be expected to have different subcultures within each. Investor Warren Buffett is quite explicit in encouraging each of his holdings (e.g. See's Candies; Geico; Kirby Vacuum; Dairy Queen) to maintain strong organizational identity and autonomy, and it would be expected that each, despite being owned by Berkshire Hathaway, would have its own unique culture.

Job task is still another environmental characteristic that can influence subculture development. Organizations with employees who perform differentiated tasks may be more likely to have subcultures develop since these individuals would be expected to be generally more dependent on others than would those performing the same task (Koene et al., 1997). Differentiated tasks are common in large organizations that perform a wide variety of tasks. Groups of individuals who perform a task that is distinct from other groups in the organization often develop into a subculture. The cases we cited earlier provide excellent examples: each group performed a set of tasks that were relatively difficult and unpleasant, requiring both highly developed skill and teamwork.

Certain *national cultural* dimensions, such as collectivism and high power distance (Hofstede, 1980), may influence the development of subcultures. In collectivistic cultures, individuals value harmony and the well-being of the larger group, which in this case would be the dominant culture (Goncalo and Staw, 2006). Members of individualistic cultures value uniqueness, in contrast, and would strive to develop individualistic subcultures. Similarly, countries high in power distance, where power is distributed unequally, may have organizational members who are less likely to deviate from organizational norms (Muijen and Koopman, 1994). This is comparable to centralized power structures of the organization itself, just extended to a national level.

When a critical event occurs challenging the *organizational values*, individuals are forced to consider (and take a stand on) whether they agree or disagree with the prescribed course of action. Based upon their level of agreement or disagreement, they could form subgroups with those others who share in their beliefs against or in favor of the dominant organizational culture (Boisnier and Chatman, 2003; Rose, 1988). When they oppose the culture, they can be labeled as countercultures, or pockets of dissent. Nonconformity with the organization can often be a very powerful tool used by subgroups in directing attention to it (Griskevicius et al., 2006). Those in the dominant culture are forced to attend and deal with those proponents of the subculture. Martin (1992) sees these groups as having the potential to be a direct challenge to the core values of the dominant culture. One example is the counterculture created by John DeLorean at General Motors. DeLorean openly displayed his opposition to the organizational values of respecting authority, fitting in, and being loyal by refusing to partake in impractical rituals such as picking up supervisors from the airport with a limo and entourage, using subjective performance criteria, keeping all offices a faded beige color, and remaining blindly loyal to all products, no matter how unworthy they might be (Martin and Siehl, 1983). He painted his division of the company a bright color and challenged any decision or product that seemed questionable.

Individual characteristics

Many of the same *demographic* characteristics that cause subgroups and subcultures to form outside of organizations have the same impact within them. Within the organization, cross-cutting memberships and affiliations based on gender, ethnicity, religion and age can lead to the formation of informal groups which, in turn, lead to subcultures within the organization (Boisnier and Chatman, 2003; Jermier et al., 1991). Likewise, social demographics such as education and family background may also play a role in the formation of subcultures. In some cases, the groups may bond together simply based on a common demographic identity, while in other cases the bonding may be encouraged as a response to a specific organizational event. Thus, in the former case, a women's organization may form to organize social events of interest, while in the latter case, a women's group may organize to combat what it perceives to be some form of systematic discrimination in hiring, compensation, etc.

In addition, subcultures can be created based on *occupations* within or across organizations. Trice (1993) describes occupational subcultures as dynamic, responding to changes in technology, the demands of the job, and the relationship to other occupations. As career patterns change and individuals become less tied to a single organization (Hall and Miller, 1975) – and more tied a profession – we can expect that these occupational subcultures will become even more important. Many occupations have stories, rituals and traditions that are passed down through new employees. For example, new pipeline welders often go through something similar to hazing, where they are teased and harassed before becoming a member in the group (Trice, 1993).

Some individuals have *personality dispositions* that make them psychologically reactive, argumentative, deviant and uncooperative (Dowd et al., 1991). These individuals are predisposed to disagree for the sake of disagreement and thus would be more likely to join a subculture simply to go against the values of the organization (Boisnier and Chatman, 2003). For example, Cohen (1955) described troubled youth in society that are likely to join countercultures of gangs due to their desire to rebel against a culture in which they do not fit.

Finally, a lack of *employment alternatives* may lead an individual to join a subculture. Because of perceived unsatisfactory employment conditions, some employees may band together to share their unhappiness. Over the longer term, this subgroup may move toward some form of collective action, grievance or unionization process. Boisnier and Chatman (2003) suggest that when dissatisfied individuals have alternatives, they may choose to leave a firm rather than join or form a subculture. However, when options are more constrained, or a lack of alternatives exists due to poor labor market conditions, individuals may be more likely to join or form a subculture.

The impact of social identity on stereotyping
Given the right set of environmental and individual characteristics, whether they derive from mergers, decentralized power, concern about values or personality, it is natural (and expected) that subgroups will form in an organization. The degree to which a culture will develop within subgroups – that is, a subculture – is a function, however, of the degree to which members share some social identity, something that typically emerges when groups form.

Brewer and Brown (1998: 559) state that decades worth of research (begun by Tajfel's 1970 paradigm) have demonstrated that 'any salient and situationally meaningful ingroup–outgroup . . . distinction is sufficient to activate differential responses to others'. Research has shown that individuals consistently discriminate in favor of their ingroup and reject the outgroup, and this disposition has impact on a variety of measures. For example, ingroups are more positively valued, generate more positive affect and trust, and obtain more cooperation than do outgroups (Brewer and Brown, 1998). In contrast, stereotyping and prejudicial behaviors are consistently directed to the outgroup.

As indicated, the larger and more diverse the organization, the greater the probability that individuals will have a range of attitudes and values, many of which are quite different from those of the dominant culture. When individuals note this discrepancy, they are likely to feel some uncertainty. When individuals see themselves as 'outliers' relative to the dominant attitudes and dispositions of a majority of those in the organization, they experience distress and seek to make sense of the cause of this distress. The attributions and evaluations they make are a function of the dominant and relevant comparison group, and it is most common that they seek out others who share their beliefs.

Associating with others who hold beliefs similar to their own points to the rationality of these beliefs and thus serves to enhance their self-concept and reduce uncertainty (Hogg and Terry, 2000). As individuals with similar beliefs interact, informal groups with shared perceptions, attitudes, feelings and behaviors form. Individuals within each of these groups develop shared identity to this group, and because of the immediacy and salience of these groups, allegiance and loyalty to this subgroup may surpass that toward the organization. As identification with this group grows, referent informational influence occurs in which social categorization predicts and determines actions and behaviors of the group (Straub et al., 2002). This signals and distinguishes the thoughts and actions of the ingroup from those of the outgroup.

An essential component of a subculture's social identity is to establish positive distinctiveness from the rest of the organization (Hornsey and Hogg, 2000). The optimal distinctiveness theory (Brewer, 1991) suggests that the balance between a unique identity and a group identity occurs when people are satisfied with the group they belong to and are differentiated from outgroups. Some subcultures seek differentiation in non-threatening ways such as healthy competition or establishing symbols and behaviors specific to their culture, while others use aggressive means to differentiate themselves (Hornsey and Hogg, 2000). For example, subcultures may partake in negative stereotyping, criticisms or attacks on other groups in order to protect the subculture's positive identity. Aggressive behaviors may be pursued by a subculture when members feel their identity threatened by a potential loss of status or social uncertainty. According to social identity theory, this self-definition in a social context provides an ingroup perspective that opposes those of the outgroup. Therefore, another fundamental component of social identity theory is having another group for contrast (Fiske, 2004). In this case, the group in contrast to the subculture is the dominant culture of the organization.

In sum, rather than being anomalous, subgroups and their resulting subcultures exist naturally in almost all types of organizations. They are inevitable, insofar as everyone will not agree with every component of the dominant culture, and employees tend to seek out and identify with those others whom they find to be most similar to themselves. That being said, if all organizations have them, why are some more 'extreme' than others?

We believe that one need look no farther than the classic work on group polarization (Myers and Lamm, 1976). That is, building on the 1960s research on the so-called risky shift in group decision making, researchers found that groups tend to shift to extreme solutions – either risky or conservative. The degree to which the group attitude moved was found to be a function of the average initial set of attitudes of the group. Once the group collectively came together around a decision, it became polarized. Recall that we indicated earlier that subcultures develop within subgroups either by strongly embracing the norms of the larger culture or by going against them. Polarization research describes how this occurs (i.e. based upon the individuals' initial tendency to agree or disagree with the cultural norms).

How subcultures become 'dysfunctional'
When the mix of these increasingly extreme positions held by individuals is combined with a strong sense of internal identity in the subgroup, it is not surprising that subcultures develop that are often labeled as 'countercultures'. These groups are seen by those in the dominant culture (and sometimes by the subgroup members themselves) as

representing pockets of resistance whose values directly conflict with the core values of the organization. In fact, there are times when the values and behaviors of the subculture appear to go against the dominant culture. Because of this, there appears to be a popular misconception, stemming from literature in sociology and anthropology, that subcultures are *always* composed of deviant individuals, or have embraced a collective ideology which is in strong opposition to the dominant culture (Cohen, 1955; Coleman and Ramos, 1998; Wolfgang and Ferracuti, 1970; Yinger, 1970). As Martin (1992) and other organizational researchers have demonstrated, several types of subcultures can exist; while some are opposed to the main culture, others may actually be strongly aligned with it (Brown, 1995; Jermier et al., 1991).

There are two issue-related dynamics that deserve mention here. First, the labeling of a group as 'dysfunctional' is not only common, but expected. Labeling is a cyclical process that has a tendency to reinforce perceptions of a particular group or subculture – usually the dominant group, or the group holding power. First, because of social identity theory, social categories are used as a basis of relating and comparing to other groups (Tajfel and Turner, 1979). In defining other groups with these categories, individuals simultaneously define themselves and create intergroup conflict (Ashforth and Humphrey, 1997). Perceivers such as upper management may unconsciously label the subculture to further differentiate themselves from the others. Schaller (1991) discusses how individuals are more inclined to ascribe socially undesirable attributes to groups in which they are not categorized. Since managers categorize subcultures as different than themselves, they may develop negative perceptions and attitudes to the subculture. Therefore the subculture and its members may be labeled as dysfunctional. This negative categorization can impact members of the subculture, creating what some refer to as 'secondary deviation' (Lemert, 1967). Secondary deviation is the response an actor makes to the dysfunctional label, reconstituting their own self-concept to fit the label ascribed to them by others. In other words, members of the subculture react to their label by confirming its existence and redefining themselves to embody this deviant identity. A common example is members of gangs who are perceived and labeled as 'thieves' and 'punks', and modify their actions to fit those stereotypes and to rebel against the dominant group that is stigmatizing them (Cohen, 1955). Members of a subculture in an organization may act in a similar manner, such as the horseplay mentioned in the Claremont Instruments Company case study, which only further serves to stereotype the group and affirm their identity as being dysfunctional. This reaffirmation of the label leads the subgroup to enact its own self-fulfilling prophecy, which confirms the stereotypic perceptions of the dominant group.

A second issue is that even when a subgroup actually has a culture different from the core culture of an organization, rather than necessarily being dysfunctional, the subculture may in fact be functional. That is, the mere fact that a subculture has different norms, beliefs and values compared to those of the core culture does not make the subgroup dysfunctional. It is critical that organizational scholars not fall into the same trap as do those in organizations who tend to both label and often marginalize those different from themselves.

Despite the fact that some subcultures may be aligned with the main culture, stereotypes of the subculture itself, as well as its members, are common. Not only is misperception common, but it should be expected. Two most significant consequences of this identity are enhancements of the ingroup and the denigration of the outgroup.

Substantial research on stereotyping points to the negative ways in which outgroups are characterized (Fiske, 2004). The outgroup itself is perceived negatively, as are its members. In fact, research points to the fact that the ingroup members will attend specifically to those cues that support their beliefs about the outgroup, often ignoring other information such as that group members may be working in the best interest of the organization (Hogg and Terry, 2001). Studies illustrate that members of a group who deviate from the norms and traditions of the overall group are frequently viewed as 'black sheep' (Marques et al., 2001). These deviants can differ positively or negatively from the group, but are considered dysfunctional because they create less consensus and more uncertainty about accepted norms, beliefs and behaviors. It is again important to emphasize this because some significant members of the dominant culture may perceive the subculture as a threat to their own identity, power and status within the norms of the organization. Subcultures disrupt the existing norms and social patterns in the organization, creating perceived instability, uncertainty and a challenge to the power and status of the dominant majority.

Taking this together, it is indeed a paradox of the seemingly dysfunctional subculture that these cultures may, in fact, not really be dysfunctional at all. Subcultures are often perceived as dysfunctional simply because they are different on some norms, beliefs or value premises, but actually may have other norms, beliefs and value premises that are quite consistent with those of the majority. However, subcultures may also have very significant differences from the main culture. In fact, these same values, rituals and behaviors may be intentionally designed to challenge the dominant organization. In some situations, these could be potentially harmful to the organization, but in other situations, rather than being dysfunctional, these may be helpful and critical to the organization's success. In the DeLorean example discussed above, his direct challenges caused the company to look at its product line and eliminate products (like the Corvair) that cast a shadow on the entire organization (Martin and Siehl, 1983). What remains constant across all the subcultures is the fact that members of the dominant culture must either attend and deal with the subculture or remove them – physically or psychologically.

Enhancing a culture of change

In order to survive in an increasingly complex and fast-paced world, organizations must be able to rapidly innovate and adapt. This means that they must be able to discern the need for change, develop the necessary innovations to address those needs, and then implement them. Organizations that have a single, uniform culture are likely, almost by definition, to suppress innovation and change (Boisnier and Chatman, 2003). In organizations that have a dominant culture and several subcultures, those in the dominant culture usually label diverse subcultures as 'deviant', 'problematic' or 'dysfunctional'. However, while protecting the dominant culture, labeling a subculture as dysfunctional can have negative effects over the longer term, since then it is unlikely to take advantage of the two main benefits of diverse subcultures – enhancing change and fostering innovation.

First, subcultures that deviate from the norms break the uniformity of tasks and thinking. Behavior that is inconsistent with or outside the norms of what is typically done indeed captures immediate attention and analysis (Fiske, 2004). This forces individuals in the dominant culture to re-evaluate and rethink the way they see and do things, which is often time-consuming, distracting and seen as a challenge to legitimate power and authority. The disruption caused by a subculture that goes against the norms of the organization induces divergent thinking, focuses attention on differences, and provokes consideration and thought on the environment and events happening in the organization (Nemeth, 1986). Research on schemas suggests that people attend to and process inconsistent information longer than consistent information (Fiske, 2004). However, subcultures make people aware of issues in the organization that may need to be better understood or changed. The stir raised by subcultures in an organization can challenge norms of the organizational culture that are out of date, conservative, restrictive or inappropriate. Therefore subcultures can also help create a culture of change in an organization, where questioning practices and evaluating all information and options becomes a norm.

The second benefit of having a subculture develop in an organization is the fostering of innovative practices. Subcultures provide a safe haven for the development of innovative ideas in that members are willing to challenge the *status quo* because they feel protected by their identity with the subgroup (Martin and Siehl, 1983). Identity can facilitate innovation in that it provides a sense of security. Members who identify with the subculture feel more comfortable expressing ideas that may deviate from those in the dominant culture or within the subculture itself since social identity gives them a feeling of belonging and acceptance (Fiske, 2004). Also, due to minority influence, subcultures may cause members of the organizational culture to re-evaluate their surroundings and values to determine where they stand. The exposure to minority group ideas leads individuals to consider a wider range of alternatives, which has been shown to result in improved judgments and performance, and greater creativity (Hogg and Terry, 2001; Nemeth, 1986). Boisnier and Chatman (2003) propose that strong-culture firms that allow subcultures to emerge will be more innovative than cultures that do not allow subcultures to form. This may be true because the debate of new ideas, generated by subcultures, introduces functional conflict into the system that is likely to enhance the quality of ideas and group solutions. A good example of this dynamic is provided by Kidder (1981), who described an experiment in the Digital Equipment Corporation where the company delegated two separate groups to design a new computer architecture. Subcultures provide flexibility by allowing subunits to innovate in their own way, while still having the support and resources from the dominant organizational culture.

Enhancing identity to the organization

If organizations and players in the dominant culture continue the practice of labeling subcultures as 'deviant', and treating them in a cavalier manner, these actions (rather than anything members of the subculture might do) represent a very serious threat to the organization. The threat arises for a number of reasons, *all* of which underlie identification with the organization. First, it is critical that organizations have their members engaged in the organization. The more group members see themselves as different from, or dissociated from, the core culture, the greater the likelihood that they will not be engaged. Second, research on groupthink (Fuller and Aldag, 1998) points to the important role of stimulating group conflict by having a devil's advocate in a group, and the same holds true at the organizational level. For organizations to succeed in the ever-challenging business environment, the dominant culture needs subgroups and subcultures that challenge and question assumptions, norms, plans and processes that may be stagnating it or leading it astray. Third, allowing a subculture to exist in an organization may enhance subgroup identity by signaling that it trusts and values independent thinking and expression of opinion. Finally, organizations can be harmed if they do not allow subcultures to exist in the organization through stereotype threat, or the lower performance that can occur from groups that are labeled negatively. We will look at each of these.

According to the group engagement model (Tyler and Blader, 2003), organizations benefit when employees engage themselves in subgroups, especially when that engagement is based on internal motivation. People are more likely to become internally motivated to engage themselves in a group when they use the group to shape and sustain their identity. This intrinsic motivation creates more self-initiated cooperation with the norms of the organization and less need for extrinsic incentives or punishments to motivate behavior. Identification with the subculture is beneficial to the organization not only by influencing employee engagement, but also by creating less need to use extrinsic rewards to sustain cooperative behavior. Organizational engagement is enhanced by subcultures that, by definition, enable individual social identity to align with the organization.

Moreover, subcultures can play the role of devil's advocate in an organization in a similar manner to the way this technique is used in groups. Research on the prevention of groupthink suggests that having a devil's advocate in a group can be beneficial for group decision making by stimulating cognitive activity and creative thinking, and allowing the group to reconsider all options in the decision (Schwenk, 1990; Schweiger et al., 1986). The role of the devil's advocate is to critique the plan or position, surfacing assumptions, inferences or logic that may be wrong or debatable. Similarly, a technique referred to as 'authentic dissent' has been used to generate original thought and improve group decision making (Nemeth et al., 2001). Authentic dissent is allowing those diverse and contradictory opinions that occur naturally in a group to surface, whereas 'devil's advocate' roles are typically artificially enlisted to critique the group decision in the absence of naturally occurring dissent. Nemeth et al. (2001) discovered that those individuals who used authentic dissent in a group generated both higher-quantity and better-quality alternatives to the group solution. Since subcultures are most likely to exist in any organization, and they are likely to share different perspectives on the group's strategies and plans, they are most like the 'authentic dissent' alternative. In particular, the more individuals identify with the subculture, the more likely they are to use 'natural dissent' to publicly announce differences from the dominant culture and challenge the dominant norms and values, assuming that such challenges are not likely to be punished by the leadership of the dominant culture.

Because subcultures may form due to a shared identity among the group members, employees may have a greater amount of trust for others in the subgroup and act trustfully (Hogg and Terry, 2001). The shared collective identity and cooperative practices of a subculture can help members decide what to do in trust-dilemma situations. The psychological security offered to those who are members of a subculture leads to higher levels of trust. Clegg et al. (2002) even suggest that an innovation trust exists in which an expectancy of reasonable and positive reactions by others makes people more likely to try innovative ideas. They propose that the more people believe they are being listened to and that they will share benefits from the implementation of ideas, the more likely they are to engage in innovative processes. Subcultures allow a trusting environment for employees to test out innovative ideas before introducing them to the organization. Finally, when people are under threat of confirming a negative stereotype, they actually perform lower and verify the stereotype due to the interference and worry about proving the stereotype to be true (Steele et al., 2002). The actual level of stereotype threat experienced depends upon the identification with the stereotyped/labeled group. Since subcultures are based on identity with the dissenting group, members may experience stereotype threat and lower their performance in response to the negative labels bestowed upon them by the organization. Without acknowledging the benefits of a subculture and by labeling them as dysfunctional, organizations may be unintentionally stimulating poor performance.

Conclusion

Whereas it is rather easy for those located in a dominant culture to identify immediately and label particular groups' actions as dysfunctional, the truth is that dysfunctional is often confused with different. The fact that individuals and the organizations often fail to understand that differences in groups' cultures naturally occur and that they may actually be critical for the organizations' success can, in itself, be a warning sign for the organization. While we did not discuss issues of when a culture crosses the line, in reality, sometimes even the most seemingly egregious examples may, in hindsight, not be so clear-cut. Not only may different cultures within organizations act to shake up the norms and force individuals to assess the ways they do things, but, as significantly, the explicit inclusion of those who behave differently can send messages of inclusion or trust. While we are not the first to point to the importance of including different cultures, it is too easy to accept the prevailing cultures – whether in the organization or in the academic research – as normative. Rather than focusing on the alignment of cultures and conformity of behaviors as we have done so frequently in the management literature, perhaps it would be valuable to focus on the functionality of dysfunction.

Note

1.   For years, the Slade Company was one of the bestselling cases on the human aspects of administration at the Intercollegiate Case Clearing House (now Harvard Business School Publishing).

References

Ashforth, B.E. and Humphrey, J. (1997), 'The ubiquity and potency of labeling in organizations', *Organization Science*, **8**(1), 43.

Berry, J.W. (1983), 'Acculturation: a comparative analysis of alternative forms', in R.J. Samucks and S.L. Woods (eds), *Perspectives in Immigrant and Minority Education*, Orlando, FL: Academic Press, pp. 11–27.

Boisnier, A.D. and Chatman, J. (2003), 'The role of subcultures in agile organizations', in R. Petersen and E. Mannix (eds), *Leading and Managing People in Dynamic Organizations*, London: Lawrence Erlbaum Associates, pp. 87–112.

Brewer, M. (1991), 'The social self: on being the same and different at the same time', *Personality and Social Psychology Bulletin*, **17**, 475–82.

Brewer, M. and Brown, R.J. (1998), 'Intergroup relations', in D.T. Gilbert, S.T. Fiske and G.Lindzey (eds), *The Handbook of Social Psychology*, 4th edn, Vol. 2, New York: McGraw-Hill, pp. 554–94.

Brewer, M. and Kramer, R. (1986), 'Choice behavior in social dilemmas: effects of social identity, group size, and decision framing', *Journal of Personality and Social Psychology*, **50**, 543–7.

Brown, A. (1995), *Organizational Culture*, London: Pitman.

Clegg, C., Unsworth, K., Epitropaki, O. and Parker, G. (2002), 'Implicating trust in the innovation process', *Journal of Occupational and Organizational Psychology*, **75**(4), 409.

Cohen, A.K. (1955), *A General Theory of Subcultures. Delinquent Boys: The Culture of the Gang*, New York: The Free Press, pp. 49–72.

Coleman, J.W. and Ramos, L.L. (1998), 'Subcultures and deviant behavior in the organizational context', in S.B. Bacharach, P.A. Bamberger and W.J. Sonnenstuhl (eds), *Research in the Sociology of Organizations*, London: JAI Press, pp. 3–35.

Dowd, T.E., Milne, C.R. and Wise, S.L. (1991), 'The therapeutic reactance scale: a measure of psychological reactance', *Journal of Counseling and Development*, **69**, 541–5.

Drucker, P.F. (1954), *The Practice of Management*, New York: Harper and Row.

Fiske, S.T. (2004), *Social Beings: A Core Motives Approach to Social Psychology*, New Jersey: John Wiley & Sons.

Friedkin, N. (1999), 'Choice shift and group polarization', *American Sociological Review*, **64**, 856–75.

Fuller, S.R. and Aldag, R.J. (1998), 'Organizational tonypandy: lessons from a quarter century of the group-think fiasco', *Organizational Behavior and Human Decision Processes*, **73**, 163–84.

Goncalo, J.A. and Staw, B.M. (2006), 'Individualism–collectivism and group creativity', *Organizational Behavior and Human Decision Processes*, **100**(1), 96.

Gregory, K.L. (1983), 'Native-view paradigms: multiple cultures and culture conflicts in organizations', *Administrative Science Quarterly*, **28**(3), 359.

Griskevicius, V., Goldstein, N., Mortensen, C., Cialdini, R. and Kenrick, D. (2006), 'Going along versus going alone: when fundamental motives facilitate strategic (non)conformity', *Journal of Personality and Social Psychology*, **91**(2), 281–94.

Hall, K. and Miller, I. (1975), *Retraining and Tradition: The Skilled Worker in an Era of Change*, London: Allen & Unwin.

Hofstede, G. (1980), *Culture's Consequences: International Differences in Work-related Values*, Beverly Hills, CA: Sage.

Hogg, M.A. and Terry, D.J. (2000), 'Social identity and self-categorization processes in organizational contexts', *Academy of Management Review*, **25**(1), 121.

Hogg, M.A. and Terry, D.J. (2001), *Social Identity Processes in Organizational Contexts*, Ann Arbor, MI: Psychology Press.

Hornsey, M.J. and Hogg, M.A. (2000), 'Assimilation and diversity: an integrative model of subgroup relations', *Personality and Social Psychology Review*, **4**(2), 143.

Hower, Ralph M. and Lawrence, Paul R. (1948), *Claremont Instruments Co.*, Cambridge, MA: Harvard Business School Publishing.

Jermier, J.M., Slocum Jr, J.W., Fry, L.W. and Gaines, J. (1991), 'Organizational subcultures in a soft bureaucracy: resistance behind the myth and facade of an official culture', *Organization Science*, **2**(2), 170.

Kidder, J.T. (1981), *Soul of a New Machine*, New York: Atlantic–Little, Brown.

Klimoski, R. and Mohammed, S. (1994), 'Team mental model: construct or metaphor?', *Journal of Management*, **20**(2): 403–37.

Koene, B., Boone, C. and Soeters, J. (1997), 'Organizational factors influencing homogeneity and heterogeneity of organizational cultures', in S. Sackmann (ed.), *Cultural Complexity in Organizations*, Thousand Oaks, CA: Sage, pp. 273–94.

Lawrence, P. and Seiler, J. (1960), *The Slade Company*, Cambridge, MA: Harvard Business School Publishing.

Lemert, E.M. (1967), *Human Deviance, Social Problems and Social Control*, Englewood Cliffs, NJ: Prentice-Hall.

Lok, P., Westwood, R. and Crawford, J. (2005), 'Perceptions of organizational subculture and their significance for organizational commitment', *Applied Psychology: An International Review*, **54**, 490–514.

Marques, J.M., Abrams, D., Paez, D. and Martinez-Taboada, C. (2001), 'The role of categorization and in-group norms in judgments of groups and their members', *Journal of Personality and Social Psychology*, **75**, 976–88.

Martin, J. (1992), *Cultures in Organizations: Three Perspectives*, New York: Oxford University Press.

Martin, J. and Siehl, C. (1983), 'Organizational culture and counterculture: an uneasy symbiosis', *Organizational Dynamics*, **12**(2), 52.

McCaskey, M. (1979), *Framework for Analyzing Work Groups*, Boston, MA: Harvard Business School Press.

Merriam-Webster (2001), *Collegiate Dictionary*, Springfield, MA: Merriam-Webster.

Muijen, J.J. and Koopman, P.L. (1994), 'The influence of national culture on organizational culture: a comparative study between 10 countries', *European Work and Organizational Psychologist*, **4**(4), 367.

Myers, D.G. and Lamm, H. (1976), 'The group polarization phenomenon', *Psychological Bulletin*, **83**(4), 602.

Nahavandi, A. and Malekzadeh, A.R. (1988), 'Acculturation in mergers and acquisitions', *Academy of Management Review*, **13**, 79–90.

Nemeth, C.J. (1986), 'Differential contributions of majority and minority influence', *Psychological Review*, **93**, 23–32.

Nemeth, C., Brown, K. and Rogers, J. (2001), 'Devil's advocate versus authentic dissent: stimulating quantity and quality', *European Journal of Social Psychology*, **31**(6), 707.

Roethlisberger, F.J. and Dickson, W.J. (1939), *Management and the Worker: An Account of a Research Program Conducted by the Western Electric Company*, Chicago, IL: Hawthorne Works.

Rose, Randall A. (1988), 'Organizations as multiple cultures: a rules theory analysis', *Human Relations*, **41**(2), 139.

Schaller, M. (1991), 'Social categorization and the formation of group stereotypes: further evidence for biased information processing in the perception of group–behavior correlations', *European Journal of Social Psychology*, **21**(1), 25.

Schein, E. (1988), *Organizational Culture and Leadership*, San Francisco, CA: Jossey-Bass.

Schein, E. (1999), *The Corporate Culture Survival Guide*, San Francisco, CA: Jossey-Bass.

Schweiger, D.M., Sandberg, W.R. and Rechner, P.L. (1986), 'Experiential effects of dialectical inquiry, devil's advocacy, and consensus approaches to strategic decision making', *Academy of Management Journal*, **32**, 745–72.

Schwenk, C.R. (1990), 'Effects of devil's advocacy and dialectical inquiry on decision making: a meta-analysis', *Organizational Behavior and Human Decision Processes*, **47**(1), 161.

Steele, C.M., Spencer, S.J. and Aronson, J. (2002), 'Contending with group image: the psychology of stereotype and social identity threat', in M.P. Zanna (ed.), *Advances in Experimental Social Psychology*, San Diego, CA: Academic Press, pp. 379–440.

Stillwell, B.M., Galvin, M.R. and Kopta, S.M. (2000), *Right vs. Wrong – Raising a Child with a Conscience*, Indianapolis, IN: Indiana University Press.

Straub, D., Loch, K., Evaristo, R., Karahanna, E. and Strite, M. (2002), 'Toward a theory-based measurement of culture', *Journal of Global Information Management*, **10**(1), 13.

Tajfel, H. (1970), 'Experiments in intergroup discrimination', *Scientific American*, **223**(5), 96–102.

Tajfel, H. and Turner, J.C. (1979), 'An integrative theory of intergroup conflict', in W.G. Austin and S. Worchel (eds), *The Social Psychology of Intergroup Relations*, Monterey, CA: Brooks-Cole, pp. 33–47.

Trice, H. (1993), *Occupational Subcultures in the Workplace*, Ithaca, NY: ILR Press.

Trice, H. and Morand, D. (1991), 'Organizational subculture and countercultures', in G. Miller (ed.), *Studies in Organizational Sociology*, Greenwich, CT: JAI Press, pp. 45–69.

Tyler, T.R. and Blader, S.L. (2003), 'The group engagement model: procedural justice, social identity, and cooperative behavior', *Personality and Social Psychology Review*, **7**(4), 349.

Van Maanen, J. and Barley, S.R. (1985), 'Cultural organization: fragments of a theory', in P. Frost et al. (eds), *Organizational Culture*, Beverly Hills, CA: Sage, pp. 31–53.

Wagner, J.A. (1995), 'Studies of individualism–collectivism: effects on cooperation in groups', *Academy of Management Review*, **38**, 152–72.

Wolfgang, M.E. and Ferracuti, F. (1970), 'Subculture of violence: an integrated conceptualization', in D.O. Arnold (ed.), *The Sociology of Subcultures*, Berkeley, CA: The Glendessary Press, pp. 135–49.

'Work Group Ownership of an Improved Tool' (1956) From P. Pigors, C.A. Myers, *Personnel Administration: A Point of View*, New York: McGraw-Hill.

Yinger, J.M. (1970), 'Contraculture and subculture', in D.O. Arnold (ed.), *The Sociology of Subcultures*, Berkeley, CA: The Glendessary Press, pp. 121–34.

Index